BEFORE WRITING

VOLUME I

FROM COUNTING TO CUNEIFORM

BEFORE WRITING

Volume I

FROM COUNTING TO CUNEIFORM

BY DENISE SCHMANDT-BESSERAT

FOREWORD BY WILLIAM W. HALLO

UNIVERSITY OF TEXAS PRESS, AUSTIN

First Edition, 1992

∞ The paper used in this publication meets the minimum requirements of American National Standard for Information Sciences—Permanence of Paper for Printed Library Materials, ANSI Z39.48-1984.

This book has been supported by a grant from the National Endowment for the Humanities, an independent federal agency.

LIBRARY OF CONGRESS CATALOGING-IN-PUBLICATION DATA

Schmandt-Besserat, Denise.
Before writing / by Denise Schmandt-Besserat ; foreword by William W. Hallo. — 1st ed.
p. cm.
Includes bibliographical references and index.
Contents: v. 1. From counting to cuneiform.
ISBN 0-292-70783-5 (v. 1 : alk. paper)
1. Tokens—Middle East. 2. Middle East—Antiquities. I. Title.
CJ4867.S36 1992
737'.3'0956—dc20 90-23615
CIP

TO MY FAMILY,
as a token of love:

JÜRGEN

ALEXANDER AND MOLLY

CHRISTOPHER

PHILLIP AND JEANINE

NICOLAUS

DANIELLE

CONTENTS

FOREWORD

EVERY SO OFTEN, a field of study is revolutionized by a single discovery or a unique hypothesis. *Before Writing* promises to play such a role in our understanding of the emergence of civilization. Writing itself is a crucial component of civilization, together with the formation of capital and the emergence of cities. All three of these innovations occurred together in lower Mesopotamia—the ancient land of Sumer—toward the end of the fourth millennium B.C. Most notably they can be traced at Uruk (the Biblical Erech), where German excavations have profited from a 100-year concession to unearth the transition to civilization in annual seasons of excavations since 1928—interrupted only by the exigencies of war.

The first epigrapher of the Uruk expedition was the noted German Sumerologist Adam Falkenstein. As early as 1936, he published his pioneering study of the "archaic texts from Uruk" (*Archaische Texte aus Uruk*), which identified the basic character of the new invention. The tradition has been carried forward by subsequent expeditions and epigraphers, notably Hans Nissen and his team of specialists in Berlin. But their researches have left open the question of how a fully formed system of writing could have emerged at Uruk and elsewhere without any visible prehistory. This is the question to which Denise Schmandt-Besserat has devoted her research for the last fifteen years.

As long ago as 1974, she published the first of several articles on the earliest uses of clay in the Near East, which occurred at or just before the beginning of the neolithic or New Stone Age. From this preoccupation with the purely artifactual remains of preliterate cultures, she was led inexorably to a closer study of small clay objects recovered in large numbers from neolithic age sites all over the Near East, but often enough dealt with in the excavation reports cursorily—if at all—because of their inexplicable or even seemingly trivial character.

A first breakthrough occurred when these objects were linked with the stone pebbles of mid-second-millennium date long known from a chance find at Nuzi as "an operational device in Mesopotamian bureaucracy." Pierre Amiet, excavator of Susa and the author's teacher, had made the link in an oblique allusion as early as 1972 (*Glyptique Susienne* 1:69 n.3), but they became a cornerstone of the new theory as historic survivals of a prehistoric counting technique as well as the likeliest key to its explanation. Though the pebbles themselves had meantime been lost, they were described, on the round clay envelope in which they had been found, and on a related tablet, as "stones" (Akkadian *abnāti*). Her earliest papers in which this relationship was explored actually proposed to use the Akkadian term to designate the comparable prehistoric phenomenon. Happily, she soon replaced it with the more serviceable (and less anachronistic) term "token." Recent collation of the texts by Tzvi Abusch has permitted further precision in the matter (E. R. Lacheman Volume, 1981).

In subsequent research, the author has tirelessly reviewed the evidence of numerous museum collections, identifying, dating, and comparing the clay tokens recovered in excavations all over the Near East. She has attempted to develop a coherent hypothesis accounting for the evolution of the original tokens into a full writing system. In brief, it may be outlined thus: Writing was preceded by counting, and counting was done with clay tokens such as occur as early as the ninth millennium B.C. throughout the Near East, i.e., shortly after the neolithic revolution or "agricultural revolution" and probably as a consequence of it. After some millennia of simple token assemblages, it was found convenient, before the end of the fourth millennium, to string the tokens together and enclose the end of the string in a ball of clay ("bulla") or to deposit them inside round and hollow clay envelopes. Before drying, these bullae and envelopes were impressed with stamp seals characteristic of the prehistoric period or, more often, with the cylinder seals which replaced them as the glyptic form most characteristic of Mesopotamia. Originally devised for impressing the wet clay which covered the neck of a clay vessel, that form proved equally serviceable for the rounded bullae and envelopes. On the evidence of later periods, the seals already performed their historic functions of signaling ownership, obligation, or authority.

Some envelopes, in addition, were impressed with tokens like those enclosed in them to indicate what they contained. But their format itself was not ideal for record-keeping. To verify the contents and to reuse the tokens required breaking the envelope open. It was simpler to rely on the impression of the tokens on the outside of the envelope, and simpler still to dispense with the making and enclosing of ever new tokens and to rely exclusively on their impressions on the outside. That given, it was a short logical step to abandoning the envelope shape entirely in favor of a simple rectangular tablet whose shape was only slightly rounded on the writing surfaces. In short order the rounding of the obverse (front) writing surface was replaced by a flat obverse, probably to minimize contact between writing surface and palm of the hand when the tablet was turned over to impress the reverse while the clay of the tablet was still wet. The cylinder seal continued to be used for impressing the newly devised clay tablet, usually before the tokens were impressed on it. The final transformation occurred when a reed stylus was employed to impress the clay tablet with designs resembling in two-dimensional format the three-dimensional tokens that had preceded. With this step, full writing had been achieved. The subsequent history of the invention involves refinements that belong to the history of writing rather than to its prehistory.

The new thesis thus reviewed here in its barest outlines first appeared in 1978–1979 in major refereed publications such as *Scientific American, Archaeology,* and *The American Journal of Archaeology*. It was in the last-named journal that, a year later, it faced its severest challenge when Stephen J. Lieberman faulted it from the vantage-point of rigorous attention to the evidence of the subsequent history of cuneiform writing. The meanings attested for word-signs (logograms) in their fully developed cuneiform shapes could reasonably be argued to apply already to their linear and pictographic forerunners, but in no case was he prepared to see conclusive proof that the same meanings attached to their alleged three-dimensional prototypes (*AJA* 84 [1980]: 351–358). He raised a second major objection as well. While number tokens had turned up inside bullae which were either opened or X-rayed in modern times to reveal their contents, such investigations had turned up not one example of tokens regarded in the hypothesis as prototypes of logograms *other* than numbers. He was therefore prepared to grant the possibility of a token system for counting, but dismissed as purely speculative the idea of a token system for representing and recording any other concepts. Additional reservations were expressed by I. J. Gelb (in *Processing of Visible Language* 2, 1980), by Mark Brandes (in *Akkadica* 18 [1980]), by M. J. Shendge (in *Journal of the Social and Economic History of the Orient* 26 [1983]), and by others.

In her gradual refinement and development of the hypothesis, the author has confronted all of these challenges. She has identified envelopes, notably from Susa and Habuba Kabira, impressed with non-numerical tokens, indeed with the very tokens enclosed inside. Not trained as an Assyriologist in her own right, she has wisely sought the collaboration of specialists in cuneiform writing and the Sumerian language, including Margaret Green, a former member of the Berlin team dealing with the archaic texts from Uruk. These texts may be said to stand midway between the tokens of the neolithic period and the fully evolved cuneiform script of the Early Dynastic and subsequent periods in Mesopotamia. The case for linking the tokens via the archaic Uruk texts to the clearly intelligible logograms of the third and second millennia is today substantially stronger than when the first tentative suggestions were advanced in this regard in the 1970's. In a special issue of *Visible Language* devoted to "aspects of cuneiform writing" in 1981, this point was already recognized by Green and by Marvin Powell. Powell's defense of the thesis (its *ad hominem* arguments apart) is particularly important for its numerical aspects, given his long involvement with the evolution of cuneiform numeration systems in the historic period.

But what about the rest of the hypothesis? Here its latest refinement as first elaborated in the pages of this book is crucial. In effect, we are offered a credible hypothesis that provides a possible, even a plausible evolutionary model, not only for the emergence of literacy but of "numeracy." According to this working hypothesis, the earliest tokens represented given quantities of given commodities. It required another quantum leap to conceptualize or at any rate to represent the idea of quantity *apart* from any specific commodity. But once taken, this leap implied at the same time the ability to represent any specific commodity *apart from its quantity*. If so, then the prehistoric token system may be said to have bequeathed three-dimensional representations of *both* numbers *and* commodities to the writing system that emerged at the beginning of history.

The new refinement of the thesis will no doubt face its own challenges, not only from Assyriologists but also from archaeologists, historians, linguists, and even psychologists. The search for complex tokens contained in envelopes will continue; so far the efforts to this end have turned up some three dozen, or 10 percent of the entire assemblage, at three different sites. Other early scripts may well have to be brought into the discussion, both as to their implications for the new thesis and vice versa. And if the conceptualization of pure number is indeed, as often averred, so early an attainment of human speech, it may need to be asked why its representation in token form should lag so far behind.

Whatever challenges have been or are yet to be encountered by the thesis, however, these would have to offer an equally systematic alternative to be convincing. The sudden appearance of the sophisticated script of the archaic texts from Uruk *ex nihilo* and *de novo* is an argument sustained neither by reason nor by the evidence. *Before Writing* furnishes to date the most coherent working hypothesis to account for the prehistory of the historic invention known as writing.

October 1990

WILLIAM W. HALLO
The William M. Laffan Professor of Assyriology and Babylonian Literature and Curator of the Babylonian Collection, Yale University

ACKNOWLEDGMENTS

IT IS A GREAT PLEASURE to express my gratitude to the many individuals who have made my work on ancient Near Eastern tokens possible. William W. Hallo has contributed in many ways to the realization of the book. On multiple occasions through the years, I have turned to him for information, advice, and support. It is a great honor and pleasure to me that he accepted to write the foreword to the volume. I deeply thank him.

I am most indebted to the publication committee: Robert H. Dyson, Jr; David Stronach, and William M. Sumner. I wholeheartedly thank them for their invaluable help and advice.

I owe special thanks to Marvin A. Powell, who generously shared with me his experience as an Assyriologist. His help and critique have allowed me to develop and amend the original manuscript presented to the University of Texas Press. The collaboration of Margaret W. Green at the beginning of the study has had a great impact on my work. I am very thankful to her for her careful guidance.

Marjorie Irwin has read and edited all the various drafts of the manuscript and helped in library research. I cannot thank her enough for her time, interest, and friendship. I am most thankful also to Agnès Spycket, who was a tremendous help in proofreading.

I am greatly indebted to W. D. Kingery at the Massachusetts Institute of Technology and Bernard François in Grenoble, who conducted clay analyses of great importance for the study, and to Pierre Amiet and Robert J. Braidwood, who provided the samples.

It is not possible to express adequate appreciation to the friends and colleagues who showed interest in my work, gave me encouragement, and facilitated my study of token collections in museums. Not all can be mentioned here, but I wish to thank personally, in Aleppo: Mahmoud M. Heretani and Antoine Suleiman; in Amman: Musa Zayyat; in Ankara: Enver Y. Bostanci, David H. French, and Raci Temizer; in Ann Arbor, Michigan: Henry T. Wright; in Austin: Winfred P. Lehmann; in Baghdad: Muayad S. Demerji and Bahija Khalil Ismail; in Beersheba: Joseph Dubbi; in Berkeley: Guitty Azarpay, Anne Draffkorn Kilmer, and Wolfgang Heimpel; in Berlin: Liane Jacob-Rost, Evelyn Klengel-Brandt, Rainer M. Boehmer, Ricardo Eichmann, Kay Kohlmeyer, Ursula Moortgat-Correns, and Eva Strommenger; in Cairo: Dia Abu el-Ghazy and James Allen; in Cambridge, Massachusetts: C. C. Lamberg-Karlowsly and Cyril S. Smith; in Chicago: Robert D. Biggs, Robert J. Braidwood, John Carswell, Judith A. Franke, Bruce Howe, Carol Meyer, and Donald Whitcomb; in Copenhagen: Marie-Louise Buhl, Soran Dietz, and Peder Mortensen; in Damascus: Adnan Bounni, Abdul Faraj, André Raymond, and Nassib Saliby; in Heidelberg: K. Deller and Nadja Wrede; in Istanbul: Halet Çambel and Edibe Uzunoglu; in Jaffa: Jacob Kaplan; in Jerusalem: Ruth Amiran, Ruth Hestrin, Marcel Sigrist, Miriam Tadmor, and Joe Zias; in Khartoum: El-Saddig Satti Hamad; in Leningrad: Vadim A. Alekshin and Vladimir Masson; in London: Edmond Sollberger; in Madison: Emmett L. Bennett; in Milwaukee: Rudolf H. Dornemann;

in Montreal: Philip E. L. Smith; in Moscow: O. N. Bader, Nicolai I. Merpert, and Rauf M. Munchajev; in Mosul: Behnam Abu Es-Soof and Najat Younis Altotonchi; in New Haven: Frank Hole; in Palmyra: Khaleb Assad and Khaled Kanbar; in Paris: Pierre Amiet, Béatrice André-Salvini, Dominique Beyer, Annie Caubet, Agnès Spycket, Geneviève Teissier; in Philadelphia: Robert H. Dyson, Jr., Samuel N. Kramer, and Maude de Schauensee; in Rochester: Judith K. Brown; in Rome: Alessandra Lazzari and Giovanna Lombardo; in San Jose: Carol Justus; in Shaar Hagolan: Roth Jehudah; in Sidney: Louis Goldberg; in Teheran: Ali Hakemi, Ezat O. Negahban, Gholam Ali Shamloo, and David Stronach; in Tel Aviv: Uzza Zevulun; in Toronto: T. Cuyler Young, Jr.; in University Park, Pennsylvania: Frederick Matson; in Waco, Texas: Bruce C. Cresson; in Warsaw: Krystyna Szarzynska.

At the University of Texas, I thank for their continuous support Paul W. English, Gerhard J. Fonken, Robert D. King, William S. Livingston, Ian R. Manners, and Maurice J. Sevigny.

I am thankful to the following individuals who made available to me artifacts held in their private collections: Thomas C. Barger, La Jolla, California; Teresa Barger, Washington, D.C., and Shucri Sahuri, Amman, Jordan.

I have benefited from the generosity of many colleagues who made available to me unpublished archaeological information. I want to express my gratitude specially to Pierre Amiet, for data concerning Susa; O. N. Bader: Maghzaliyah; Rainer M. Boehmer: Uruk; Sabah Abboud Jasim: Tell Abada; Ghazi Bisheh: Ktar Tell Kazarei; Enver Y. Bostanci: Beldibi; R. J. Braidwood: Çayönü Tepesi, Tepe Asiab, and Tell Sarab; Bennet Bronson: Jemdet Nasr and Kish; Halet Çambel: Çayönü Tepesi; Annie Caubet: Tello, Moussian, Sialk, Susa, and Tepe Giyan; Henri de Contenson: Ghoraife, Tell Aswad, and Tell Ramad; John E. Curtis: Arpachiyah, Chagar Bazar, Geoy Tepe, Eridu, Jericho, Nineveh, Tell Brak, Tell Halaf, and Ur; Moshe Kochavi: Tell Aphek; Rudolf H. Dorneman: Tell Hadidi; G. van Driel: Jebel Aruda; Robert H. Dyson, Jr.: Dalma Tepe, Tal-e Malyan, Sippar, Tell Billa, Tepe Gawra, Tepe Hissar, and Ur; Richard S. Ellis: Gritille; André Finet: Tell Kannas; David French: Can Hasan; Carney Gavin: Nuzi; McGuire Gibson: Nippur; Elizabeth F. Hendrickson: Seh Gabi; Frank Hole: Ali Kosh and Chagha Sefid; Bruce Howe: Tepe Asiab; Jean-Louis Huot: Tell Oueili and Larsa; Liane Jacob-Rost: Uruk; Gregory A. Johnson: KS 34, KS 54, and KS 76; Helene J. Kantor: Chogha Mish; Kay Kohlmeyer: Habuba Kabira; Stefan K. Kozlowski: Nemrik; Ernest R. Lacheman: Nuzi; C. C. Lamberg-Karlowsky: Tepe Yahya, Anau, and Tall-i-Bakun; Louis D. Levine: Seh Gabi; Vladimir Masson: Jeitun; Fred Matson: Tepe Siahbid; Ken Matsumoto: Tell Songor; Andrew M. T. Moore: Abu Hureira; Peder Mortensen: Tepe Guran; Rauf Munchaev: Yarim Tepe; Ezat O. Negahban: Zagheh; Joan Oates: Choga Mami; Martha Prickett: Tepe Gaz Tavila and Tepe Muradabad; Judith Pullar: Tepe Abdul Hosein; Gary O. Rollefson: Ain Ghazal; Eva Strommenger: Habuba Kabira; David Stronach: Ras al Amiyah; William M. Sumner: Tal-e Malyan; Maurizio Tosi: Shahr-i-Sokhta; Mary M. Voigt: Gritille and Hajji Firuz; Marguerite Yon: Ras Shamra; T. Cuyler Young, Jr.: Godin Tepe. I specially express my appreciation to William W. Hallo, who is currently engaged in a full study of the tablets of Godin Tepe, for his permission to use the material.

Sanjiiv Bajaj, Donald Blais, Debra Katz, and Solveig A. Turpin performed the enormous task of computer coding and data manipulation. I thank each of them for their expertise and for the long hours they have devoted to the project, even in times of scarcity.

At the University of Texas Press, I am grateful to Theresa May and Barbara N. Spielman for their attention to the editing and production of the volume. I also offer my appreciation to George Lenox, Ellen McKie, and David Cavazos for the talent and patience they have expressed in designing and producing the book. Ellen Simmons, Corinna Maschin, and Petra Müller deserve credit for the illustrations, charts, and maps.

I wish to acknowledge the following institutions who have supported the project: the American Council of Learned Societies; the Bunting Institute (formerly Radcliffe Institute); the German Academic Exchange Service; the German Archaeological Institute, Berlin, West Germany; the Institute for Research in the Humanities, University of Wisconsin at Madison; the National Endowment for the Humanities; the University of Texas Research Institute; and the Wenner Gren Foundation for Anthropological Research.

The publication of *Before Writing* was sponsored in part by Una's Lectures in the Humanities, University of California at Berkeley. It was a great honor for me to be invited to deliver the 1989 Una's lectures. In that lecture series, four in all, entitled "Writing and Counting: The Near Eastern Legacy," I presented the materials of chapters 7, 8, and 9. I am grateful for the generous grant extended in support of publishing the volume by the Una's Lecture Committee and thank Thomas G. Barnes, Chair 1989, and Anne Draffkorn Kilmer, Chair 1990.

Finally, I am indebted for the authorization to reproduce in the volume, in more or less modified form, the following publications:

"Symbols in the Prehistoric Middle East," in Richard Leo Enos, ed., *Oral and Written Composition: Historical Approaches*, Written Communication Annual, Vol. 4 (Newbury Park: Sage Publications, 1990), pp. 16–31.

"Tokens as Funerary Offerings," *Vicino Oriente* 7 (1988): 3–9.

"Tokens at Uruk," *Baghdader Mitteilungen* 19 (1988): 1–175.

"Tokens at Susa," *Oriens Antiquus* 25, nos. 1–2 (1986): 93–125.

"The Origins of Writing—An Archaeologist's Perspective," *Written Communication* 3, no. 1 (1986): 31–45.

"Before Numerals," *Visible Language* 18, no. 1 (1984): 48–60.

"Tablets and Tokens: A Re-Evaluation of the So-Called Numerical Tablets," *Visible Language* 15, no. 3 (1981): 321–344.

"The Envelopes That Bear the First Writing," *Technology and Culture* 21, no. 3 (1980): 357–385.

BEFORE WRITING

VOLUME I

FROM COUNTING TO CUNEIFORM

INTRODUCTION:
TOKENS, A NEW THEORY

Man's development and the growth of civilizations have depended, in the main, on progress in a few activities—the discovery of fire, domestication of animals, the division of labor; but, above all, in the evolution of means to receive, to communicate, and to record his knowledge, and especially in the development of phonetic writing.
—Colin Cherry[1]

SPEECH, THE UNIVERSAL WAY by which humans communicate and transmit experience, fades instantly: Before a word is fully pronounced it has already vanished forever. Writing, the first technology to make the spoken word permanent, changed the human condition.

It was a revolution in communication when a script, providing a way to encode data, allowed individuals to share information without meeting face to face. Writing also made it possible to store information, creating a pool of knowledge well beyond the ability of any single human to master yet, at the same time, available to all. Writing is regarded as the threshold of history, because it ended the former reliance upon oral tradition, with all the inaccuracies it had entailed. Business and administration are now inconceivable without bookkeeping to balance income and expenditures. Among other innumerable benefits, writing allows us to capture our ideas when they arise and, in time, sort and scrutinize them, revise, add, subtract, and rectify them to arrive at a rigor of logic and a depth of thought otherwise impossible.

How did writing come about? It is now generally agreed that writing was invented in Mesopotamia, present-day Iraq, in the late fourth millennium B.C. and spread from there to Egypt, Elam, and the Indus Valley.[2] It is also generally agreed that other scripts developed later, independently, in China and Mesoamerica.[3] The origin of Chinese and Mesoamerican writing is still enigmatic. New archaeological evidence, presented fully in this volume, reveals that the Mesopotamian script derived from an archaic counting device. This immediate precursor of the cuneiform script was a system of tokens, small clay counters of many shapes, which served for counting and the accounting of goods in the prehistoric cultures of the Near East.

The idea that Mesopotamian writing emerged from a counting device is new. It was a common belief until the 1700s that the alphabet was of divine origin. Then, in the Enlightenment, the theory that scripts started with picture writing was put forward. This view endured until the present.[4]

The Myths

Until the eighteenth century, the origin of writing was the subject of myths crediting gods, fabulous creatures, or heroes for its invention. In the ancient Near Eastern tradition, writing was also conceived as an eternal principle of civilized life held by a divinity such as Enki or Nabu. In the earlier Sumerian myths the scribal art is listed with crafts such as metal, wood, and leather working, while in Babylon it was promoted to the arts and sciences.

The oldest and most casual account of the invention of writing is perhaps that of the Sumerian epic *Enmerkar and the Lord of Aratta*.[5] The poem relates how Enmerkar, the lord of Uruk-Kulaba, solicited timber, gold, silver, lapis lazuli, and precious stones from the lord of Aratta to rebuild the Gipar, the residence of the goddess Inanna. A speedy emissary was sent back and forth over the seven mountains that separate Uruk from Aratta delivering pleas, threats, and challenges between the two lords. The emissary faithfully transmitted the messages word for word until the day Enmerkar's instructions were too difficult for him to memorize. The lord of Kulaba promptly invented writing, tracing his message on a clay tablet:

—The emissary, his mouth [being] heavy, was not able to repeat (it).
—Because the emissary, his mouth (being) heavy, was not able to repeat (it).
—The lord of Kulaba patted clay and wrote the message like (on a present-day) tablet—
—Formerly, the writing of messages on clay was not established—
—Now, with Utu's bringing forth the day, verily this was so,
—The lord of Kulaba inscribed the message like (on a present-day) tablet, this, verily, was so.[6]

In a second Sumerian poem, *Inanna and Enki, the Transfer of the Arts of Civilization from Eridu to Erech,* writing is conceived as one of a hundred basic elements of civilization held by Enki, the lord of wisdom.[7] Inanna coveted the divine decrees for her city, Uruk, and set her mind to getting them. This was done when Enki, drunk, donated to her each and every one of the crafts. In Samuel Noah Kramer's words:

After their hearts had become happy with drinks, Enki exclaims: . . .
"... O name of my power, O name of my power,
To the bright Inanna, my daughter, I shall present . . .
The arts of woodworking, metalworking, writing, toolmaking,
leatherworking, . . . building, basketweaving."
Pure Inanna took them.[8]

Inanna loaded writing and the other divine decrees on the Boat of Heaven and started an eventful journey back to Uruk. After overcoming tempests and sea monsters sent by Enki to recapture his possessions, she finally reached the city, where she unloaded her precious booty to the delight of her people.

According to Berossus' *Babyloniaca,* Oannes, a divine messenger, taught the Babylonians the basic principles of civilization. He was a sea creature with the body of a fish and the head, feet, and voice of a man who appeared from the Erythraean Sea, close to Babylon, and gave to humans the knowledge of language, writing, science, and crafts of all types before plunging back into the abyss.[9] His revelation included all the arts necessary for civilized life, such as planting seeds, measuring land, building cities and temples, and creating laws. In other early Babylonian texts, the god Ea, the Lord of wisdom, was the source of all secret magical knowledge, writing in particular.[10] In Assyria, Nabu, son of Marduk, was revered as the instructor of mankind in all arts and crafts including building, agriculture, and writing.[11]

The classical world inherited from Egypt the myth that Thoth, the baboon, the god of wisdom, knowledge, language, arithmetic, medicine, and magic, had presented writing to the world.[12] The belief apparently passed on with little change to Greece, where an Egyptian god named Teuth was deemed to be the inventor of arithmetic, calculation, geometry, and, foremost, letters.[13] But in Aeschylus' tragedy, Prometheus plays the role of the inventor of writing, while Palamedes was granted that honor by other authors.[14] During the

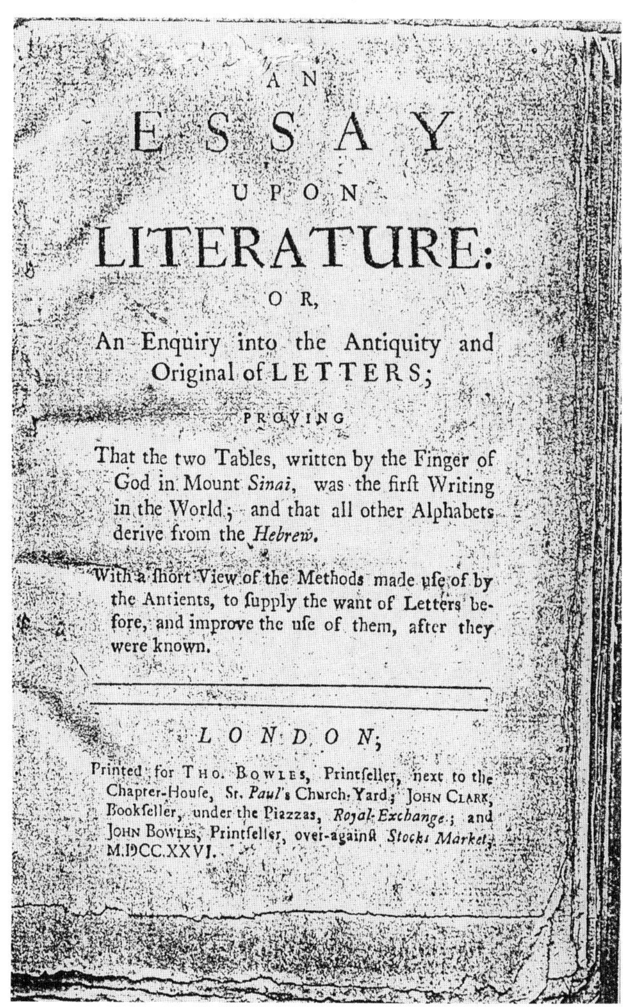
AN
ESSAY
UPON
LITERATURE:
OR,
An Enquiry into the Antiquity and Original of LETTERS;
PROVING
That the two Tables, written by the Finger of God in Mount *Sinai*, was the firſt Writing in the World; and that all other Alphabets derive from the *Hebrew*.
With a ſhort View of the Methods made uſe of by the Antients, to ſupply the want of Letters before, and improve the uſe of them, after they were known.

LONDON;
Printed for THO. BOWLES, Printſeller, next to the Chapter-Houſe, St. *Paul's* Church-Yard; JOHN CLARK, Bookſeller, under the Piazzas, *Royal-Exchange*; and JOHN BOWLES, Printſeller, over-againſt *Stocks Market*. M.DCC.XXVI.

Roman period, the merit of teaching writing and astronomy to humankind was attributed to Mercury, the god of trade and messenger of the pantheon.[15] These combined myths were to reappear in the Renaissance, when Theuth-Hermes, counselor and scribe to the Egyptian king Thamus of Thebes, was identified as having invented writing nine hundred years after the deluge.[16]

Writing inspired powerful poetic narratives in the early Jewish, Christian, and Muslim traditions, which allude to writing as having existed forever, before the creation of the world. Scripture was God's way of communicating his will to humans and recording humanity's fate.

Jewish myths describe the Torah as one of the seven things first created, "two thousand years before the heaven and earth, . . . written with black fire on white fire, and lying in the lap of God."[17] Elsewhere the letters of the alphabet are personified, addressing God:

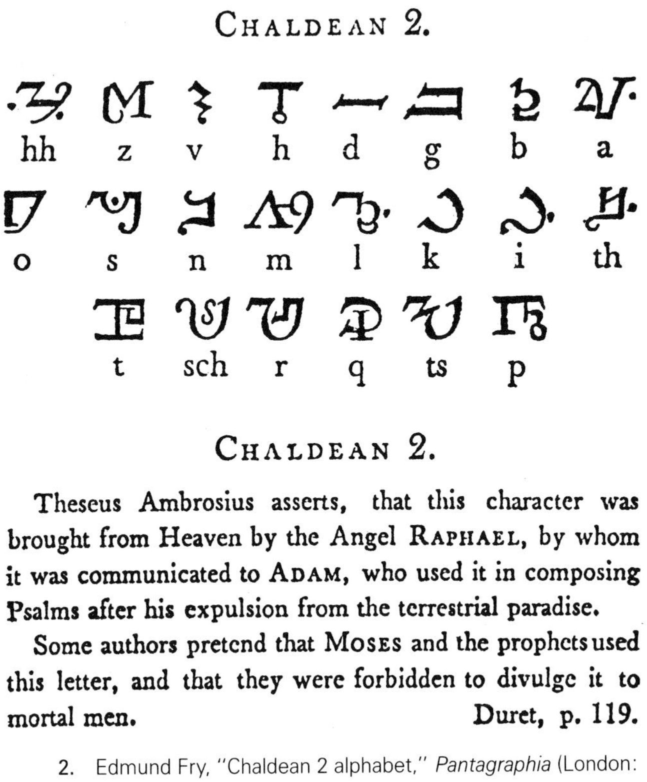

CHALDEAN 2.

hh z v h d g b a

o s n m l k i th

t sch r q ts p

CHALDEAN 2.

Theseus Ambrosius asserts, that this character was brought from Heaven by the Angel RAPHAEL, by whom it was communicated to ADAM, who used it in composing Psalms after his expulsion from the terrestrial paradise.

Some authors pretend that MOSES and the prophets used this letter, and that they were forbidden to divulge it to mortal men. Duret, p. 119.

2. Edmund Fry, "Chaldean 2 alphabet," *Pantagraphia* (London: Cooper & Wilson, 1799). Courtesy Harry Ransom Humanities Research Center, University of Texas at Austin.

1. Cover of Daniel Defoe's *An Essay upon Literature* (London: Thomas Bowles, 1726). Courtesy Harry Ransom Humanities Research Center, University of Texas at Austin.

"When God was about to create the world by His word, the twenty-two letters of the alphabet descended from the terrible and august crown of God whereupon they were engraved with a pen of flaming fire. They stood round about God, and one after the other spake and entreated."[18]

In the Muslim literature, according to Ibn Abbas, Allah's first creation was a tablet made of white pearl that was to record "all that ever shall be." Then, Allah created a Pen "the length of which would take five hundred years to traverse . . . and from it light flows as ink flows from the pens of the people of this world . . . The Pen was told, 'Write!' And, as the Pen trembled because of the awesomeness of the proclamation, it began to reverberate in exaltation, as thunder reverberates. Moved by God, it flowed across the Tablet, writing what is to be until the Last Day."[19]

In the Bible, God revealed his will to mankind with the Tables of the Law "written by the finger of God."[20] These words, which became the source of great debates, were interpreted by Daniel Defoe as meaning that "the two Tables, written by the Finger of God in Mount *Sinai,* was the first Writing in the World; and that all other Alphabets derive from the *Hebrew*" (fig. 1).[21] For others, however, writing preceded Moses. In his alphabetology *The Olive Leaf,* published in 1603, Alexander Top was of the opinion that God created the alphabet by acrophony. He named the twenty-two labors of the Creation by words starting with each of the letters of the Hebrew alphabet: "Seeing that all thinges which the Lord wrought or commaunded in the first weeke, exceeded not the number of two and twentie . . . Wherefore I may conclude, that euery of these seueral Hebrew letters, should signifie or import some speciall workmanshyp of the Lordes Creation."[22]

According to other authorities, Adam was the inventor of writing. It is barely conceivable to us that John Wilkins, bishop of Chester, was serious when he wrote in 1668 that Adam had invented the Hebrew alphabet: "though not immediately after his creation, yet in process of time, upon his experience of their great necessity and usefulness."[23] Wilkins was one of the founders of the Royal Society and one of the most influential and respected English scholars.[24] In fact, as late as 1799, Edmund Fry, a typefounder of London, published and documented not one but two "Chaldean" alphabets used by Adam.[25] According to him and a certain Theseus Ambrosius, one of these two scripts had been brought from heaven by the Angel

Raphael and was used by Adam for composing psalms after his expulsion from paradise (fig. 2). Moses and the prophets were also regarded as having used these letters, but they had been forbidden to communicate them to mortal men.

The myths of all ages on the origin of writing shared one common characteristic: They presented writing as emerging, on one day, as a full-fledged script. None of them convey the notion of an evolution from a simple to a more complex system of communication. The concept of a ready-made alphabet handed down from heaven persisted until the eighteenth century.

The Pictographic Theory

In the eighteenth century, William Warburton, future bishop of Gloucester, introduced the first evolutionary theory of writing. He argued that all scripts originally developed from narrative drawings that in time became more and more simplified and developed into abstract characters. The theory was presented in Warburton's book *Divine Legation of Moses,* published in London in 1738, and made its way into the article entitled "Ecriture" in Diderot and d'Alembert's *Encyclopédie,* giving it a wide diffusion.[26] Warburton's pictographic theory remained practically unchallenged for over two hundred years. For example, in the revised edition of *A Study of Writing* (1974), the presently best-known scholarly publication on writing, I. J. Gelb still stated, "It became clear that the Mesopotamian cuneiform writing has developed from a pictographic stage."[27]

Warburton based his theory on three scripts: "Mexican paintings" (Aztec codices), Egyptian hieroglyphs, and Chinese characters, which he viewed as representing three stages in the evolution of writing. According to him, the Mexican paintings illustrated the first stage. They were "a rude picture writing" that traced images of things, as is universally done in primitive societies. At the second stage, exemplified by the Egyptian script, hieroglyphs conveyed more abstract ideas by analogy or metaphor: The sunrise was signified by "two eyes of the crocodile, because they seemed to emerge from its head . . . an Eye eminently placed was designed to represent God's Omniscience." Furthermore, the hieroglyphs became abbreviated into marks to satisfy the requirements of a popular script. Finally, the Chinese "refined Hieroglyphs" marked the third stage. In Warburton's words, "The Chinese writing went still further, threw out the images and retained only the contracted marks, which they increased to a prodigious number: in this writing every distinct idea has its distinct mark . . . The shapes and figures of these marks, however, now disguised, do yet betray their original from picture and images."[28] Madeleine V.-David explains the success of Warburton's idea of a continuous development as being "rassurante pour l'esprit et favorable à la vulgarisation."[29]

Ancient Near Eastern scripts did not play a role in the elaboration of the pictographic theory because they were little known in 1738. Although the existence of cuneiform had been noticed by Western travelers as early as the fifteenth century and the first copies of cuneiform signs were sent back to Europe as early as 1621 by Pietro della Valle, the decisive breakthrough came only in the nineteenth century, when Georg Friedrich Grotefend published his partial decipherment of Persian cuneiform. Definitive decipherment of both Persian and cuneiform Babylonian-Assyrian was not achieved until the middle of the nineteenth century. Many scholars participated in the decipherment process, but the key contribution was made by H. C. Rawlinson a century after Warburton's *Divine Legation of Moses,* when, between 1835 and 1851, he succeeded in acquiring and publishing a more or less accurate text of the trilingual inscription of Darius the Great at Bisutun as well as making a convincing decipherment. Archaeological expeditions started to take place in the Near East late in the nineteenth century, resulting in the first great harvests of cuneiform texts. The cuneiform tablets came from the excavations of Nineveh in 1845, Girsu in 1877, Nippur between 1889 and 1900, and Shuruppak in 1902–1903. These sites produced texts by the tens of thousands spanning three millennia, from the Parthian to the Early Dynastic period or from the early third millennium B.C. to the first millennium A.D.

In the nineteenth century, the cuneiform script was regarded as conforming to Warburton's paradigm. Assyriologists such as Jules Oppert and A. H. Sayce noted that some of the first millennium cuneiform characters became increasingly pictorial when traced back to more archaic forms in the Babylonian and Sumerian periods of the second and third millennia B.C.[30] The only challenge to the pictographic theory came in 1897 from Friedrich Delitzsch. In his volume *Die Entstehung des ältesten Schriftsystems,* Delitzsch proposed that the cuneiform script derived from twenty-one primary signs and that the repertory was enlarged by multiplying these basic signs or by modifying or combining them together.[31] For example, the *gunû,* which uses striation (the addition of parallel lines on a Sumerian sign or part thereof) to reinforce or intensify the meaning of a sign (such as house/residence; fill/become enormous), played a major role in his scheme.[32]

Delitzsch convinced some of his colleagues, one of whom, the well-known epigrapher S. Langdon, published the tablets from Kish.[33] According to George A. Barton of Bryn Mawr College, even the great François Thureau-Dangin followed Delitzsch's theory.[34] However, in 1902 Barton noted that Delitzsch's explanation for the beginning of writing was too abstract to correspond to reality.[35] A thesis by his student Ellen S. Ogden in 1910 further put Delitzsch's theory in question, thus resulting in reviving the pictographic theory.[36] Barton, who based his opinion on picture writing mostly on American Indian, Chinese, and ancient Egyptian, came to the same conclusions as Warburton. "The investigator must proceed upon the hypothesis that Babylonian writing, like other primitive writing, originated in pictographs." The pictographic theory scheme was modified, however, to include a three-step progression from ideographic to phonetic writing. "Indeed, wherever the beginnings of writing could be traced, it took the form of picture writing, so that it seems safe to regard it as a working hypothesis, if not as a law, that all early systems of writing began in a series of pictographic ideographs, that syllabic values were developed from these and in some cases alphabetic values."[37]

In fact, the idea that the cuneiform script started with picture writing was by no means a perfect fit. In 1928, a year before the discovery of the Uruk tablets, William A. Mason noted, "We must admit, that even in the earliest and most archaic inscriptions discovered, it is not always easy to recognize the original objects." The pictographic theory, however, was never questioned. Instead, the Babylonian scribes were blamed for the discrepancy between preconceived ideas and facts: "Owing to the limitations of primitive culture, the inexperience of the scribes and the lack of artistic ability, each scribe drew the characters in his own crude, faulty way, often incorrectly; so that it is quite impossible always definitely to distinguish the character and identify it with the object intended."[38] In 1927, Georges Contenau had another explanation. He argued that with some ingenuity one could reconstruct the original pictographs, but unfortunately "la mentalité des Sumériens et des Sémites du quatrième millénaire était évidemment très différente de la nôtre"; therefore, there was little chance of figuring out the metaphors they used to translate abstract ideas.[39]

The excavation season of 1929–30 at Uruk revealed considerable new information on the beginning of writing. Hundreds of archaic tablets were unearthed that pushed writing back to the fourth millennium B.C. The signs traced or impressed with a stylus in a technique different from the cuneiform script had been termed *pictographic*. The archaic tablets, however, contradicted the pictographic theory. Adam Falkenstein, the German scholar who studied the texts, noted that when writing began in Mesopotamia, truly pictorial signs were rare exceptions. The signs for "plow," "chariot," "sledge," or "wild boar" were not only few but of uncommon use, represented by a single occurrence on one tablet alone.[40] The common signs were abstract: The sign for "metal" was a crescent with five lines; the "pictograph" for "sheep" was a circle with a cross. The Uruk tablets seriously strained the pictograph theory by showing that when writing began in Mesopotamia pictographic signs were rarely used.

Edward Chiera and others tried to reconcile Falkenstein's observations with the pictographic theory. They argued that the Uruk texts represented an already evolved script and that a previous stage, consisting of true pictographs, probably had been written on a perishable material such as wood, bark, papyrus, or parchment which had disintegrated in time and could never be recovered.[41] What Chiera had done was to invent a *deus ex machina*.

The excavation campaign at Uruk in 1930–31 produced impressed tablets that further weakened the pictographic theory. These texts, like others found previously at Susa and later at Khafaje, Godin Tepe, Mari, Tell Brak, Habuba Kabira, and Jebel Aruda, were more ancient than the "pictographic" Uruk tablets studied by Falkenstein. They were, however, not made of wood, bark, papyrus, or parchment, as Chiera had hypothesized. This earliest form of writing consisted of wedges, circles, ovals, and triangles impressed on clay tablets that were anything but pictographic. The gulf between the neat charts of pictographs illustrated in books and reality became even wider.

By the second half of the twentieth century, enough data had accumulated to make a serious breach in the pictographic theory. From Champollion in 1822 to Ventris in 1953, each great decipherment eroded the premise upon which the pictographic theory was built and determined that the early scripts all had phonetic features. Anthropologists like André Leroi-Gourhan entered the debate, warning against preconceptions about primitive picture writings. In his volume *Le Geste et la parole,* he contends that "the linguists who have studied the origin of writing have often conferred to pictographic systems a value which derives from literacy."[42] Leroi-Gourhan noted that the only true pictographic scripts were recent phenomena; that most had emerged in groups that did not have writing prior to contacts with travelers or colonists from literate countries. He concluded, "Therefore it seems impossible to use Eskimo or Indian pictography in order to understand the ideography of preliterate societies."[43]

In recent years, scholars have become weary of schemes that present the emergence of writing as the rational decision of a group of enlightened individuals, such as that put forward by V. Gordon Childe in *What Happened in History*: "The priests . . . have agreed upon a conventional method of recording receipts and expenditures in written signs that shall be intelligible to all their colleagues and successors; they have invented *writing*."[44] It is now accepted that, like other human inventions, writing did not come *ex nihilo.* According to Chiera, "There never was a first man who could sit down and say, 'Now I am going to write.' That supreme achievement of mankind, the one which makes possible the very existence of civilization by transferring to later generations the acquisitions of the earlier ones, was the result of a slow and natural development."[45]

Above all, the pictographic theory does not agree with current archaeological research. In recent years, Near Eastern excavations have focused on the beginning of agriculture and cities and have tried to determine how these developments have affected society. Viewed in the perspective of the urban phenomenon, the first "pictographic" tablets of Uruk and for that matter the earlier impressed tablets are out of step with other socioeconomic developments. As will be discussed in detail later, these first documents occur in level IVa of Uruk, lagging far behind the rise of cities and the emergence of the temple institution, which was already well under way some two hundred years earlier (in levels X–IV). If writing emerged so late, it could not play a role in state formation. How then did the Mesopotamian city-states function without record keeping?

Whereas popular books have continued to present the traditional pictographic theory,[46] as early as three decades ago scholars began to anticipate the discovery of an antecedent of the Mesopotamian script. Some, like V. Gordon Childe, looked for it in seals, others in potters' marks.[47] Most, like Seton Lloyd, foresaw an even earlier script: "The degree of competence . . . [attained by script of the Uruk IV tablets] suggests that earlier stages in its development may eventually be recognized elsewhere, perhaps in levels corresponding to Uruk V and VI."[48] David Diringer simply referred to "another more primitive writing" or "an at present unknown, early script, which may have been the common ancestor of [the Indus Valley Script and] also of the cuneiform and early Elamite writings."[49] I propose that the antecedent of writing proves not to be an earlier script but a counting device.

The pictographic theory will remain a landmark in the history of ideas because it was the first evolutionary explanation of writing, departing from the former belief that a full-fledged script had been communicated to humans by divine revelation. It was based, however, on a set of supporting facts that proved erroneous. During the twentieth century, archaeology has steadily generated new evidence that contradicts the paradigm. Since the beginning of the twentieth century, excavations have steadily produced small tokens that, as I will attempt to show, were the antecedent of writing.

Tokens

Archaeological work to date suggests that a prehistoric counting device led ultimately to writing following interrelated economic, social, and conceptual changes. In this volume I intend to demonstrate that the immediate precursor of cuneiform writing was a system of tokens, small clay counters of many shapes such as cones, spheres, disks, and cylinders, which served for accounting in prehistory. I will also propose that the tokens reflected an archaic mode of "concrete" counting prior to the invention of abstract numbers. This is supported by the fact that there are no tokens to express abstractly numbers such as "1" or "10." Instead, a particular counter was needed to account for each type of goods: Jars of oil were counted with ovoids, small measures of grain with cones, and large measures of grain with spheres. This is also why tokens were used in one-to-one correspondence: One jar of oil was shown by one ovoid, two jars of oil by two ovoids, and so on.

Tokens can be traced to the Neolithic period, starting about 8000 B.C. They evolved following the needs of the economy, at first keeping track of the products of farming and expanding in the urban age to keep track of products manufactured in workshops. The development of tokens was tied to the rise of social structures, emerging with rank leadership and flourishing during state formation. Also, corresponding to the increase in bureaucracy, methods of storing tokens in archives were devised. One method that had a prominent future was clay envelopes, simple hollow clay balls in which the tokens were placed and sealed. A drawback of the envelopes was that they hid the enclosed tokens. Accountants resolved the problem by imprinting the shapes of the tokens on the surface of the envelopes prior to enclosing them. The number of units of goods was still expressed by a corresponding number of markings. An envelope containing seven ovoids bore, for example, seven oval markings.

The substitution of signs for tokens was a first step toward writing. At Susa, the envelopes with tokens inside and their impressions outside clearly preceded the first clay tablets. This suggests that the fourth Millennium accountants soon realized that the tokens within the envelopes were made unnecessary by the presence of markings on the outer surface. As a result, tablets—solid clay balls bearing markings—replaced the hollow envelopes filled with tokens. These markings became a system of their own that developed to include not only impressed markings but more legible signs traced with a pointed stylus. Both these types of symbols, which derived from tokens, were picture signs or "pictographs." They were not, however, pictographs of the kind anticipated by Warburton. The signs were not pictures of the items they represented but rather the pictures of tokens used as counters in the previous accounting system. When pictography was achieved, the token system reverted to a few shapes, mostly spheres and disks, probably used as an abacus.

Writing not only resulted from new bureaucratic demands but from the invention of abstract counting. Once the item counted and the number indicating pure quantity were finally separated from each other, two kinds of signs were necessary, explaining the differentiation between the incised signs, which represented commodities, and the impressed signs, which expressed abstract numbers. Incised signs were never repeated in one-to-one correspondence, but impressed signs were. For example, five jars of oil were indicated by one incised oval (= jar of oil) and five impressed wedges (= 5). In sum, in the notation system used to record units of commodities, the abstract numerals, shown by impressed wedges, were, in fact, nothing else but the former units of grain (a cone in the token system) endowed with a new abstract meaning, "1."

The archeaological data alter in major ways the previous conception of the origin of writing in Mesopotamia. According to this new source of evidence, the Mesopotamian script did not develop from pictures but from three-dimensional tokens; the need for record keeping did not first arise in cities but five thousand years before that, with the beginning of agriculture; the script was not an invention *ex nihilo* but was the final outcome of a long chain of inventions responding to socioeconomic and conceptual changes. The most important evidence uncovered is that counting was not, as formerly assumed, subservient to writing but, on the contrary, writing emerged from counting.

STUDIES ON TOKENS

This is the first systematic study of tokens, based on the analysis and interpretation of a selection of eight thousand specimens from 116 sites in Iran, Iraq, the Levant, and Turkey. It took a great deal of work and time to find out what the small clay artifacts were all about, but I was able to discover that the tokens were no less than the fountainhead of abstract counting and writing.

I must say that the tokens came my way by chance. It all started in 1969–71, when I was awarded a fellowship from the Radcliffe Institute, Cambridge, Massachusetts (now the Bunting Institute), to study the use of clay before pottery in the Near East. This led me to visit systematically Near Eastern archaeological clay collections dating from 8000 to 6000 B.C. stored in museums of the Near East, North Africa, Europe, and North America. I was looking for bits of Neolithic clay floors, hearth lining, and granaries, for bricks, beads, and figurines, and I found these aplenty. I also came across a category of artifacts that I did not expect—miniature cones, spheres, disks, tetrahedrons, cylinders, and other geometric shapes. The artifacts were made of clay and belonged, therefore, to my study. I noted their shape, color, manufacture, and all possible characteristics, counted them, measured them, sketched them, and they entered my files under the heading "geometric objects." Later, the term *token* was substituted when it became obvious that all the artifacts were not in geometric form; some were in the shape of animals, vessels, tools, and other commodities.

I became increasingly puzzled by the tokens because, wherever I would go, be it Iraq, Iran, Syria, Turkey, or Israel, they were always present among the early clay assemblages. If they were so widely used, I reasoned, they must have had a useful function. I noted that the tokens were often manufactured with care and that they were the first clay objects to have been hardened by fire. The fact that people went to such efforts for their preparation further suggested to me that they were of importance. I sensed that the tokens were part of a system because I repeatedly found small and large cones, thin and thick disks, small and large spheres, and even fractions of spheres, such as half and three-quarter spheres. But what were they for?

I asked archaeologists about the tokens and learned that all those who had excavated early sites had encountered them in their trenches. No one, however, knew what they were. I looked in site reports and noted that tokens were usually omitted or relegated to such headings as "enigmatic objects" or "objects of uncertain purpose." The authors who risked an interpretation identified the tokens as amulets or game pieces. Carleton S. Coon is among those that simply wondered. He jovially reported about the five cones he found at Belt Cave, Iran, as follows: "From levels 11 and 12 come five mysterious conical clay objects, looking like nothing in the world but suppositories. What they were used for is anyone's guess."[50]

I feel very fortunate that the data I collected on tokens that first seemed of little significance made it possible to identify the artifacts and realize their importance. The information on the Neolithic counters turned out to be like the piece of a puzzle that finally gives a clue to the entire picture. I am greatly indebted to the many scholars who, since the beginning of the century, have provided pieces to the puzzle.

Archaeologists

Many archaeologists, starting with Jacques de Morgan in 1905, Roland de Mecquenem in 1924, Julius Jordan in 1929, Henri de Genouillac in 1934, Arthur J. Tobler in 1950, Louis le Breton in 1957, and Robert J. Braidwood in 1960, should be recognized for excavating, preserving, and publishing pictures of tokens when they seemed insignificant. Vivian L. Broman should be credited for her study of the hundreds of tokens from Jarmo as part of her thesis on the clay artifacts of the site.[51] Her thorough and careful work remains unmatched. When Broman completed her thesis in 1958, like all those who had preceded her, she had no alternative but to guess from the shape of the objects what they might have been. Consequently, she attributed a different function to each particular type. She viewed the cones as being perhaps schematic figurines and the spheres as sling stones or marbles. She also earmarked cones, spheres, and hemispheres as possible counters, arguing that some Iraqi shepherds today keep track of their flocks with pebbles.[52] At that time her insight could not be supported by archaeological evidence. Only a year later, however, the use of counters in the ancient Near East was documented.

A. Leo Oppenheim

In 1959, A. Leo Oppenheim of the University of Chicago wrote a perceptive article on counters of the second millennium B.C. which proved to be the key to understanding what the tokens were.[53] The paper was about a peculiar hollow tablet recovered in the late 1920s at the site of Nuzi, north of Babylon in northern Iraq (fig. 3).[54] This egg-shaped tablet belonged, together with a normal tablet bearing the account of the same transaction, in the family archive of the sheep owner Puhisenni, son of Musapu.[55] The cuneiform inscription on the hollow tablet read as follows:

Counters representing small cattle:
21 ewes that lamb
6 female lambs
8 full grown male sheep
4 male lambs
6 she-goats that kid
1 he-goat
3 female kids
The seal of Ziqarru, the shepherd.[56]

3. "Hollow tablet," Nuzi, Iraq. Courtesy Ernest Lacheman.

When opening the hollow tablet, the excavators found it to hold forty-nine counters which, as stipulated in the text, corresponded to the number of animals listed.[57] This hollow tablet constitutes the Rosetta stone of the token system. The counters (Akkadian *abnu,* pl. *abnati,* translated "stone" by Oppenheim), the list of animals, and the explanatory cuneiform text leave no possible doubt that at Nuzi counters were used for bookkeeping. Although no other example of a cuneiform tablet holding counters has ever been encountered in Nuzi or, for that matter, in Mesopotamia or the Near East, Oppenheim made a case that *abnati* were commonly used in the bureaucracy. He suggested that each animal of a flock was represented by a stone held in an office in a container. The tokens were transferred to various receptacles to keep track of change of shepherds or pasture, when animals were shorn, and so on. He based his argument on short cuneiform notes found in archives that referred to *abnati* "deposited," "transferred," and "removed" as follows:

—These sheep are with PN; the [pertinent] stones have not been yet deposited.
—Three lambs, two young he-goats, the share of PN, they are charged to his account [but] not deposited among the stones.
—One ewe belonging to PN, its stone has not been removed.
—Altogether 23 sheep of Silwatesup, PN brought . . . their stones have not been transferred.
—x ewes that have lambed, without [pertaining] stones, belonging to PN.[58]

Since then, Marcel Sigrist has pointed out further texts that probably also allude to counters in the Third Dynasty of Ur, ca. 2000 B.C. For instance, a tablet dealing with oxen reads: "The remaining part of the account is held in the leather pouch" (Sumerian: **kuš du$_{10}$-gan**).[59]

When Oppenheim wrote his article, no one knew what the counters looked like. Of course, the *abnati* mentioned in the texts were not described and those held in the Nuzi hollow tablet were lost. They were simply referred to as "pebbles" in the site report, with no information as to their shapes or the material of which they were made.[60] The next important piece of the puzzle was to be provided by Pierre Amiet in Paris.

Pierre Amiet

For his work on glyptics, Pierre Amiet, Conservateur en Chef, Département des Antiquités Orientales at the Louvre, studied well-preserved seal impressions on globular clay objects from Susa. The artifacts were hollow and contained small clay objects.

Following Oppenheim's lead, Amiet interpreted the small clay objects enclosed in the clay envelopes as calculi that stood for commodities.[61] The proposition was daring, since the Susa envelopes were two thousand years earlier than the Nuzi egg-shaped tablet, with no known example in the interval. It was a leap of great importance for three reasons. First, the counters were revealed: They were miniature clay artifacts modeled in various, mostly geometric, shapes. Second, the Susa envelopes showed that counters held in envelopes were not restricted to the historical period but extended into the protoliterate period. Third, Amiet foresaw the possibility that the calculi were an antecedent of writing. In his own words: "On peut ainsi se demander si [le scribe] ne s'inspirait pas des petits objets de terre enfermés dans les bulles, et qui symboliseraient très conventionnellement certaines denrées."[62]

The major pieces added to the puzzle by Amiet were still not sufficient, however, to reveal the entire picture. It should be kept in mind that in 1966, prehistoric tokens were not known and the only published parallels to the Susa envelopes were those recently excavated in Uruk.[63] Six years later, in 1972, when Amiet published the Susa envelopes in his *Glyptique susienne,* he still described the markings on envelopes as follows: "Une série d'encoches rondes ou allongées, semblable aux chiffres que l'on observe sur les tablettes, et qui correspondent au nombre que donne l'addition des calculi serrés à l'intérieur, à cela près que leurs formes ne sont pas aussi diversifiées que celles des derniers."[64] Amiet recently summarized his position as follows: "Je me demandais donc si cette écriture ne s'inspirait pas de certains des calculi enfermés dans les bulles."[65]

Maurice Lambert, also at the Louvre, took Amiet's insight two steps farther. He clearly identified that the first impressed signs of writing were reproducing the shape of the former calculi. "L'écriture a copié, ici comme ailleurs, ce qui existait en vrai."[66] Consequently, he assigned the values 1, 10, 60, 600, and 3,600 to, respectively, the tetrahedron, sphere, large tetrahedron, punched tetrahedron, and large sphere, a route that proves now to have been, partly, a false one.

To recognize that the tokens constituted an accounting system that existed for five thousand years in prehistory and was widely used in the entire Near East was to be my own contribution. I was also able to draw parallels between the shapes of the tokens and those of the first incised signs of writing and establish the continuity between the two recording systems. Finally, much later, I realized the mathematical importance of the tokens as an archaic reckoning device, preceding the invention of abstract counting. I recall vividly when, in 1970, two pieces of the puzzle snapped together for me. In order to prepare a class lecture, I pulled from my files Amiet's 1966 article, which I had not seen since I began collecting tokens. I could not believe my eyes when I saw the small clay cones, spheres, and tetrahedrons illustrating the paper. I instinctively dismissed the idea that the Susa artifacts could have anything to do with the tokens found in Neolithic villages. After all, the calculi from Susa were held in envelopes and the Neolithic tokens were loose and, foremost, the objects were separated by thousands of years. The next day, however, I was intrigued enough to check several excavation reports of sites of the fourth, fifth, and sixth millennia and saw the possibility that tokens might have been used, with no discontinuity, between 8000 and 3000 B.C. The rest was hard work. My first publications on tokens and their relation to writing date from 1974 to 1978 and on tokens and concrete counting from 1983 to 1986.[67]

THE PRESENT STUDY

This volume constitutes the first comprehensive study of the Near Eastern tokens used as counters in prehistory. The work is based on a data bank of some ten thousand tokens, representing an almost complete documentation of the artifacts excavated and preserved to date. The material, mostly previously unpublished, was collected and studied firsthand in thirty museums in fifteen countries. The volume also includes the first systematic study of the 200 envelopes, used to keep tokens in archives, and the 240 impressed tablets presently known. These two types of objects illustrate the major steps of the transition from tokens to writing. The tokens from early excavations often lack a precise stratigraphy. Even so, the large assemblage presented here gives a reliable picture of the types and subtypes of the counters, their geographic and chronological distribution, their evolution over time, and the transition from tokens to writing. The work is organized into three parts.

The Evidence

The first four chapters of the book are devoted to the analysis of the token assemblage and Chapters 5 and 6 to that of envelopes and impressed tablets.

Chapter 1 describes the counters, their shapes, markings, and manufacture, and their evolution from "plain" to "complex" tokens. The chapter also introduces the token assemblage used in the study.

Chapter 2 presents the geographic and chronological distribution of plain tokens in the Near East. This is followed by the analysis of the Iranian and Iraqi material from 8000 to 3500 B.C. These collections illus-

4. Tokens, Uruk, Iraq. Courtesy Vorderasiatisches Museum, Staatliche Museen zu Berlin.

trate the homogeneity of the token system in the two countries during its first 4,500 years.

Chapter 3 is devoted to complex tokens, the hallmark of the urban period. The discussion focuses on the token collections from three major fourth-millennium cities: Uruk in southern Mesopotamia, Susa in Elam, and Habuba Kabira in Syria.

Chapter 4 identifies the context in which the tokens were used: the type of settlements to which they belonged; their spacial distribution within those settlements; the structures and assemblages with which they were associated. Special attention is given to tokens found in tombs.

Chapter 5 describes methods for holding tokens in archives devised in the fourth millennium and, in particular, envelopes. The following topics are covered: discovery of the envelopes, their number, geographic distribution, chronology, context, the assemblages of tokens they held, the markings they bore, and their role in the transmutation of tokens into writing.

Chapter 6 deals with impressed tablets. After a review of the history of their discovery, their number, geographic distribution, chronology, and context, the documents and the signs they bear are described and their contribution to writing is assessed.

Interpretation

The last three chapters evaluate the role of tokens in the evolution of communication, social structures, and cognitive skills. The interpretations are tentative. There is no doubt that some of the conclusions will have to be revised in the future, when more and better data will be available.

In Chapter 7, tokens are interpreted as the second step in the development of record keeping, following Paleolithic tallies. The token was the first code to record economic data, providing the immediate background for the invention of writing.

Chapter 8 shows how both plain and complex tokens were determined in their form, content, and function by the life-style and economy of the cultures that used them and how, in turn, the counters had an impact on society.

Chapter 9 discusses the evolution of counting and its role in the invention of writing. Tokens are shown to reflect an archaic mode of "concrete counting" while writing derived from abstract counting.

5. Plain tokens, Jarmo, Iraq. Courtesy Prehistoric Project, Oriental Institute, University of Chicago.

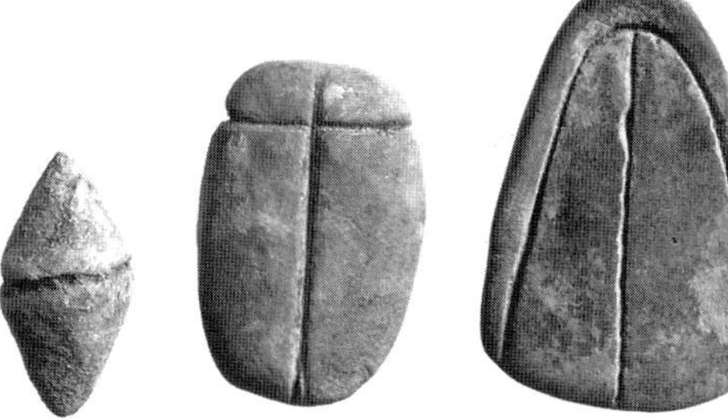

6. Complex tokens, Susa, Iran. Courtesy Musée du Louvre, Département des Antiquités Orientales.

7. Envelope and token contents, Uruk (W 20987.8), Iraq. Courtesy Deutsches Archaeologisches Institut, Abteilung Baghdad.

8. Bulla, Susa (Sb 1948 bis), Iran. Courtesy Musée du Louvre, Département des Antiquités Orientales.

9. Impressed tablet, Susa (Sb 6289), Iran. Courtesy Musée du Louvre, Département des Antiquités Orientales.

In the Conclusions, I summarize the wealth of information provided by tokens on communication, mathematics, economy, social structures, and cognitive skills in prehistoric Near Eastern cultures.

Documentation

A separate catalog (*Before Writing, Volume II*) presents detailed information on seven thousand tokens from Iran, Iraq, Turkey, Syria, Jordan, and Israel (referenced in this text as "Cat. no."). The material is organized by country and sites. The tokens are classified into sixteen types, according to shapes, and about five hundred subtypes, according to variations of size or addition of markings. To the extent available, the following information is given for each artifact: size, stratigraphic level, date, museum or excavation number, and publication reference.

DEFINITIONS

Because the topic is new, I found the existing vocabulary often inadequate. I note here the meaning I give to some of the key words used in the text:

Token: Small artifact, generally modeled in clay according to one of the following sixteen types: cones, spheres, disks, cylinders, tetrahedrons, ovoids, rectangles, triangles, biconoids, paraboloids, bent coils, ovals, vessels, tools, animals, and miscellaneous. I propose that these objects were used as counters to keep records of goods (fig. 4).

Plain token: Token typical of the periods between 8000 and 4300 B.C. and after 3100 B.C. The shapes are mostly restricted to cones, spheres, disks, cylinders, and tetrahedrons. The surface is usually plain (fig. 5).

Complex token: Token typical of the fourth millennium B.C. temple administration. This category includes all sixteen types of tokens described above. The artifacts are characterized by an extensive use of markings, either linear, punctuated, or appliqué (fig. 6).

Envelope: Hollow clay ball of spherical, ovoid, or oblong shape holding tokens and usually bearing seal impressions (fig. 7).

Bulla: Oblong or biconoid clay tag bearing seals. I propose that some of these artifacts secured strings of tokens (fig. 8).

Impressed tablet: Tablet bearing notations impressed with tokens or the blunt end of a stylus. These tablets were referred to in the literature as "numerical tablets." I argue that the signs do not refer to numbers but to units of goods (fig. 9).

Incised tablet: Tablet bearing notations traced with the sharp end of a stylus (fig. 10).

Pictographic tablet: Tablet bearing notations traced with the sharp end of a stylus. These tablets were held to bear signs in the shape of the things they represented. Here "pictographic" also refers to the signs perpetuating the shape of tokens (fig. 10).

Marking: Notations on tokens and envelopes (fig. 11).

Near East: The term is synonymous to Middle East. It includes the following countries: Iran, Iraq, Turkey, Syria, Lebanon, Jordan, and Israel or the ancient provinces of Persia, Mesopotamia, Anatolia, Syria, and Palestine. (I have used the name of the Roman province to refer to the material of Israel and Jordan because the amount of material in each country was small).

10. Incised, or "pictographic," tablet, Uruk, Iraq. Courtesy Vorderasiatisches Museum, Staatliche Museen zu Berlin.

11. Markings on envelope, Susa (Sb 6350), Iran. Courtesy Musée du Louvre, Département des Antiquités Orientales.

PART ONE: THE EVIDENCE

12. Plain tokens, Seh Gabi, Iran. Courtesy Louis D. Levine.

I
WHAT ARE TOKENS?

Une activité particulièrement importante à Tell Aswad, surtout dans le niveau II au cours de la première moitié du 7e millénaire, était la fabrication de petits objets en argile modelée et durcie au feu . . . Il s'agit . . . d'objets de formes géometriques, telles que boules, disques et coupelles.

—Henri de Contenson[1]

WHEN TOKENS WERE INVENTED, they were great novelties. They were the first clay objects of the Near East and the first to be fired into ceramic. Their shapes also were revolutionary since, as Cyril Smith has pointed out, they first exploited, systematically, all the basic geometric forms (fig. 12).[2] In this first chapter, I deal with the physical aspect of the tokens. I describe the types and subtypes; the evolution from "plain" to "complex" tokens; the materials of which the artifacts were made; and the technique used for their manufacture. I introduce the token collection available for this study.

Types and Subtypes

Tokens are small clay objects modeled into the following sixteen main forms or types: (1) cones, (2) spheres, (3) disks, (4) cylinders, (5) tetrahedrons, (6) ovoids, (7) rectangles, (8) triangles, (9) biconoids, (10) paraboloids, (11) bent coils, (12) ovals, (13) vessels, (14) tools, (15) animals, and (16) miscellaneous, including hyperboloids (fig. 13). The counters are further classified into subtypes according to intentional variations in shape, size, or the addition of markings. Cones (figs. 14 and 15), spheres (fig. 16), disks, and tetrahedrons (fig. 17), for example, are consistently represented in two sizes, "small" and "large." Spheres also occur in fractions such as hemispheres and three-quarter spheres (fig. 18.1). The markings consist of incised lines, notches, punches, pinched appendices, or appliqué pellets. There are about five hundred token subtypes divided among the sixteen types as follows: cones 49, spheres 33, disks 87, cylinders 32, tetrahedrons 16, ovoids 28, rectangles 32, triangles 45, biconoids 15, paraboloids 26, bent coils 12, ovals 14, vessels 46, tools 11, animals 28, miscellaneous 16.

Because they were handmade the size of the counters varies from artifact to artifact and from site to site. The usual dimension of tokens ranges between 1–3 cm across. The "large" subtypes of cones, spheres, disks, and tetrahedrons measure about 3–5 cm. There are also slight discrepancies noticeable between sites. Tepe Asiab, for example, has a number of spheres that are smaller than usual, measuring less than 1 cm. On the other hand, Tepe Yahya and Tell Hadidi produced tokens larger than the norm.

Evolution

The system started with a basic repertory of "plain tokens" in geometric and naturalistic shapes that remained in use during the entire five thousand years of its existence. After four millennia, the system reached a second stage when the plain tokens were supplemented by new types and subtypes. These "complex tokens" were characterized by a great variety of markings, as well as featuring some additional geometric and naturalistic shapes.

PLAIN TOKENS

At the beginning of the token system, about 8000 B.C. and until 4400 B.C., tokens were "plain."

13. Token assemblage illustrating the major types of tokens, Uruk, Iraq. Courtesy Deutsches Archaeologisches Institut, Abteilung Baghdad.

14. Cone assemblage (from left to right, type 1: 4, 4, 1, 5, 2, 19), Tepe Hissar, Iran. Courtesy University Museum, University of Pennsylvania.

15. "Small" and "large" cones (type 1: 1, 2), Tepe Hissar, Iran. Courtesy University Museum, University of Pennsylvania.

16. "Small" and "large" spheres (type 2: 1, 2), Seh Gabi, Iran. Courtesy Louis D. Levine.

17. "Small" and "large" tetrahedrons enclosed in an envelope, Susa (Sb 1967), Iran. Courtesy Musée du Louvre, Département des Antiquités Orientales.

18.1. Hemispheres and three-quarter spheres, Susa, Iran. Courtesy Musée du Louvre, Département des Antiquités Orientales.

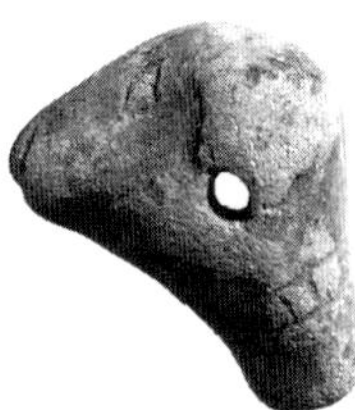
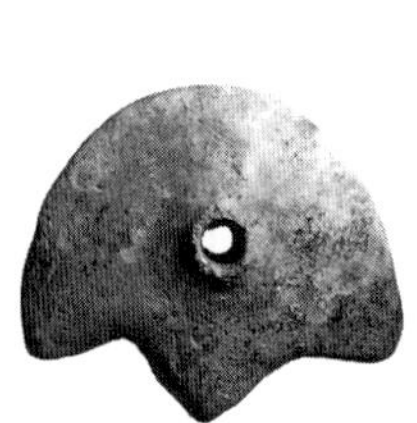

18.2. Tokens in the shape of a miniature vase, animals, and pomegranate, Susa, Iran. Courtesy Musée du Louvre, Département des Antiquités Orientales.

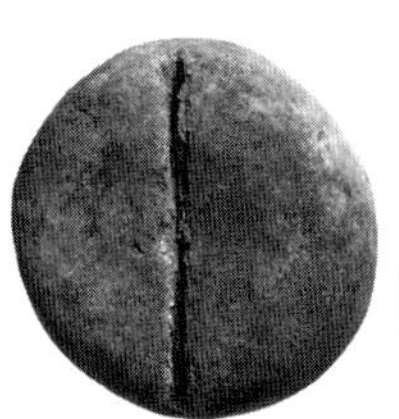

18.3. Tokens with linear markings, Susa, Iran. Courtesy Musée du Louvre, Département des Antiquités Orientales.

18.4. Tokens with one line, Tello, Iraq. Courtesy Musée du Louvre, Département des Antiquités Orientales.

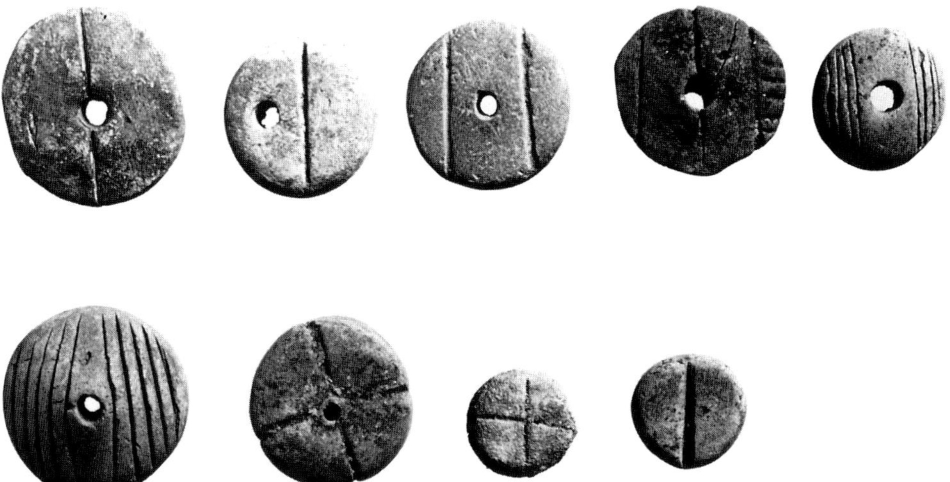

18.5. Disks with sets of equal number of markings, Susa, Iran. Courtesy Musée du Louvre, Département des Antiquités Orientales.

18.6. Tokens with punctated markings, Susa, Iran. Courtesy Musée du Louvre, Département des Antiquités Orientales.

18.7. Labels, Susa, Iran. Courtesy Musée du Louvre, Département des Antiquités Orientales.

The forms consisted mainly of geometric shapes such as cones, spheres, flat and lenticular disks, cylinders, and tetrahedrons (types 1, 2, 3, 4, 5; fig. 12) and only occasionally ovoids, rectangles, triangles, biconoids, and hyperboloids (types 6, 7, 8, 9, 16). The naturalistic shapes such as vessels and animals were also limited (types 13 and 15). The animal heads consisted of a cone pinched at the top into a beak or a muzzle with details such as eyes, ears, or a mustache (type 15: 1–2).

Although the earliest assemblages of the eighth millennium B.C., like Tepe Asiab and Ganj Dareh, produced a few tokens with an occasional incised line or a punctation, markings remained rare. Plain tokens usually have a smooth face.

COMPLEX TOKENS

New Types

Complex tokens can be traced as early as about 4400 B.C. Their full development belongs to the fourth millennium B.C. when, about 3500 B.C., the token types become far more diversified, consisting of a larger repertory of geometric as well as naturalistic forms (fig. 18.2). First, they include three additional geometric types: paraboloids, bent coils, and ovals/rhomboids (types 10, 11, and 12). Second, triangles, ovoids, rectangles, and biconoids become more widely used and acquire multiple subtypes (types 6, 7, 8, and 9). Third, new naturalistic forms appear in the shape of miniature tools (type 14), furniture (type 14: 10), fruit, and humans (type 16: 8, 1–3). Fourth, vessels and animals also diversify into many subtypes (types 13 and 15). The animal representations are less schematic, showing either a reclining beast, a head, or a protome (type 15: 3–13). On the other hand, hyperboloids become rarer (type 16: 13–15).

Markings

The profusion of markings is another distinctive feature of the complex counters. They occur on all types of tokens, geometric or naturalistic. The markings are displayed on the most conspicuous part of the object and only rarely along the sides.[3] In the case of flat tokens, they are shown on a single face, except in rare instances when both sides are involved.[4]

Linear Markings. Among the markings, lines and short strokes are most frequently used (fig. 18.3). Sets of parallel lines are displayed with a concern for symmetry. For instance, when the strokes are uneven in number, the median is placed at the center (fig. 18.4). Again, when the number is even, the lines are often divided into two equal sets (fig. 18.5). Other linear patterns include perpendicular lines, crosses, stars, St. Andrew's crosses, ladders, herringbones, checkers, and crisscrossing. Only a few of the various designs give the impression of being decorative. They include two cones inscribed with dotted triangles or circles (type 1: 22, 45) and a cylinder with sets of lines and zigzags (type 4: 22).

Punctated Markings. Punctations occur as early as linear patterns. The assemblage of Tepe Asiab about 7500 B.C., for example, yields two punched tokens. This mode becomes more common among fourth-millennium complex token assemblages, remaining, however, at all times far less frequent than linear patterns.

There is a great variety of punctations. Some are deep circular markings made with a more or less blunt stylus; others consist of small circles, probably applied with a straw. Finally, particular tokens are covered, either all over or partially, with a fine pitting produced by a needle.

Circular impressions occur on most types, except biconoids, ovals, vessels, tools, and miscellaneous (types 9, 12, 13, 14, and 16). They feature, in particular, on cones (type 1: 18–21); spheres (type 2: 3–5, 13, 21, 28); disks (type 3: 8–12); cylinders (types 4A, 22A); tetrahedrons (type 5: 5–6); ovoids (type 6: 3–4, 21–22); quadrangles (type 7: 2–4); triangles (type 8: 4, 31–35); paraboloids (type 10: 2A–3, 8); bent coils (type 11: 3, 10–12); animals (type 15: 5, 18).

Punctations (fig. 18.6) appear singly (types 1: 18–19) 23; 2: 3, 13; 3: 8; 5: 5–6; 6: 3–4; 7: 2) or in sets of six, either arranged in one (type 8: 4, 34) or two lines (types 3: 10; 4: 4A, 22A; 6: 22; 11: 3, 10–11; 15: 5, 18). They are rarely in groups of two (type 1: 21), three (type 2: 4), seven (type 3: 11), or ten (type 7: 3). Small circles are usually shown in an overall pattern covering the entire counter. This is the case with an occasional disk, cylinder, or rhomboid (types 3: 12–13; 4: 5; 12: 9).[5]

There are examples of tokens entirely covered with fine pitting among spheres (type 2: 6); disks (type 3: 15); tetrahedrons (type 4: 13); ovoids (type 6: 6A); cubes (type 7: 30); biconoids (type 9: 5); and animals (type 15: 10). In other instances, spheres (type 2: 6A–6B) and ovoids (type 6: 5–6) may show pitting only in a restricted area. In the case of disks and paraboloids, the area treated is clearly delineated by lines (types 3: 58–59; 10: 24–26). In some cases the design may be indicative of the commodity represented; for

19. Disks with a painted cross, Susa, Iran. Courtesy Musée du Louvre, Département des Antiquités Orientales.

example, pitting shown at the mouth of some vessels may suggest the foam of beer or the cream of milk (type 13: 6, 8).

Circular markings may be combined with linear patterns. This happens on cones (type 1: 43); spheres (type 2: 13, 21); disks (type 3: 52A, 68–69); cylinders (type 4: 20A, 22A); triangles (type 8: 31–35); biconoids (type 9: 9); paraboloids (type 10: 8); and bent coils (type 11: 10–12).

Notched, Pinched, and Appliqué Markings. The other types of markings such as notches, nail incisions, painting, pinching, and appliqué pellets and coils are rarely used. Deep notches occur only on spheres (type 2: 7–8); all-over nail incisions turn up on an occasional disk, quadrangle, or triangle (types 3: 16; 7: 9; 8: 45).

There are pinched specimens among cones (type 1: 15–16), spheres (type 2: 14–15, 29), disks (type 3: 73–74), ovoids (type 6: 26), rectangles (type 7: 27), triangles (type 8: 40), and paraboloids (type 10: 2). The tokens provided with appliqué pellets or with pinched appendices may be, in fact, naturalistic representations. For example, the cubes topped by a pellet depict a box secured by sealings. In other words, the tokens are the facsimile of shipments illustrating the position of strings and sealings (type 7: 25, 26, and 30). The pinched appendix attached to spheres is a humorous device since, according to a Sumerian pictograph, it suggests a sheep's tail (type 2: 15).[6]

Painted Tokens. Painted tokens are rare. The list of counters covered all over with either black or red paint includes a lenticular disk at Tello and a cone at Arpachiyah.[7] In other equally unusual cases tokens bear painted markings or patterns; for example, at Arpachiyah and Jaffarabad.[8] Painted crosses are known only in Susa (type 3: 80; fig. 19).[9]

Pictographs. Some of the markings inscribed on tokens also feature in the list of Sumerian pictographic signs. Among them, for example, is the sign for cereal, shown as a stylized ear of wheat (types 7: 31–32; 6: 11, 20).[10] Two perpendicular strokes occur on spheres and tetrahedrons (types 2: 11; 5:11; 6: 23; 13: 27); the star pattern appears on spheres, cylinders, and/or vessels (types 2: 12A; 4: 22B; 13: 5); finally, a cross matches the sign KIB (types 4: 22B; 6: 24).[11]

A last group of objects, referred to as "labels" in the literature, is tentatively included among the complex tokens (fig. 18.7).[12] They consist of seven rectangles, perforated through their length or width and inscribed with Sumerian pictographs (type 7: 20–23A). These signs are read respectively as follows: DIN "wine" (type 7: 22), a name, title, or profession (?) (type 7: 21A),[13] and SUKKAL(?) (type 7: 23A).[14] Lastly, one of the labels bears the representation of a procession standard (type 7: 22A).[15] According to Krystyna Szarzynska, the pictograph represents the title of the standard bearer or identifies a god (probably Nanna) or an institution.[16]

Token Series

There are, among complex tokens, intriguing series of counters of identical shape that bear a different number of lines arranged in a similar pattern. For example, there are disks which display 1, 3, 4, 5, 6, 8, or 10 lines (type 3: 19–25). Other disks show sets of lines symmetrically arranged as follows: 1-1, 2-1, 2-2, 3-3, 4-4, and 5-5 (type 3: 28–35). The largest series of disks shows the following combination of lines and strokes: 1-7, 2-1, 2-5, 2-6, 2-7, 2-8, 3-5, 5-6, 5-7, 5-13, 10-6, 10-9, and 12-7 (type 3: 36–48; fig. 20.1).

There are token series among all types except cones, spheres, tetrahedrons, tools, and animals. There are, for instance, cylinders with 4, 6, 7, or 8 lines (type 4: 15–17; fig. 20.1), ovoids with 2 and 4 vertical lines (type 6: 8–9), or with 1 horizontal line and 4, 5, 6, or 10 vertical lines (type 6: 14–18; fig. 20.1). Rectangles occur with sets of 6 and 7 horizontal lines (type 7: 10–11) or various numbers of strokes: 3-5, 4-5, 5-5 (type 7: 5–7; fig. 20.2).

Triangles occur almost exclusively in series. A first group has instances of 1, 2, 3, 5, 7, or 10 strokes along

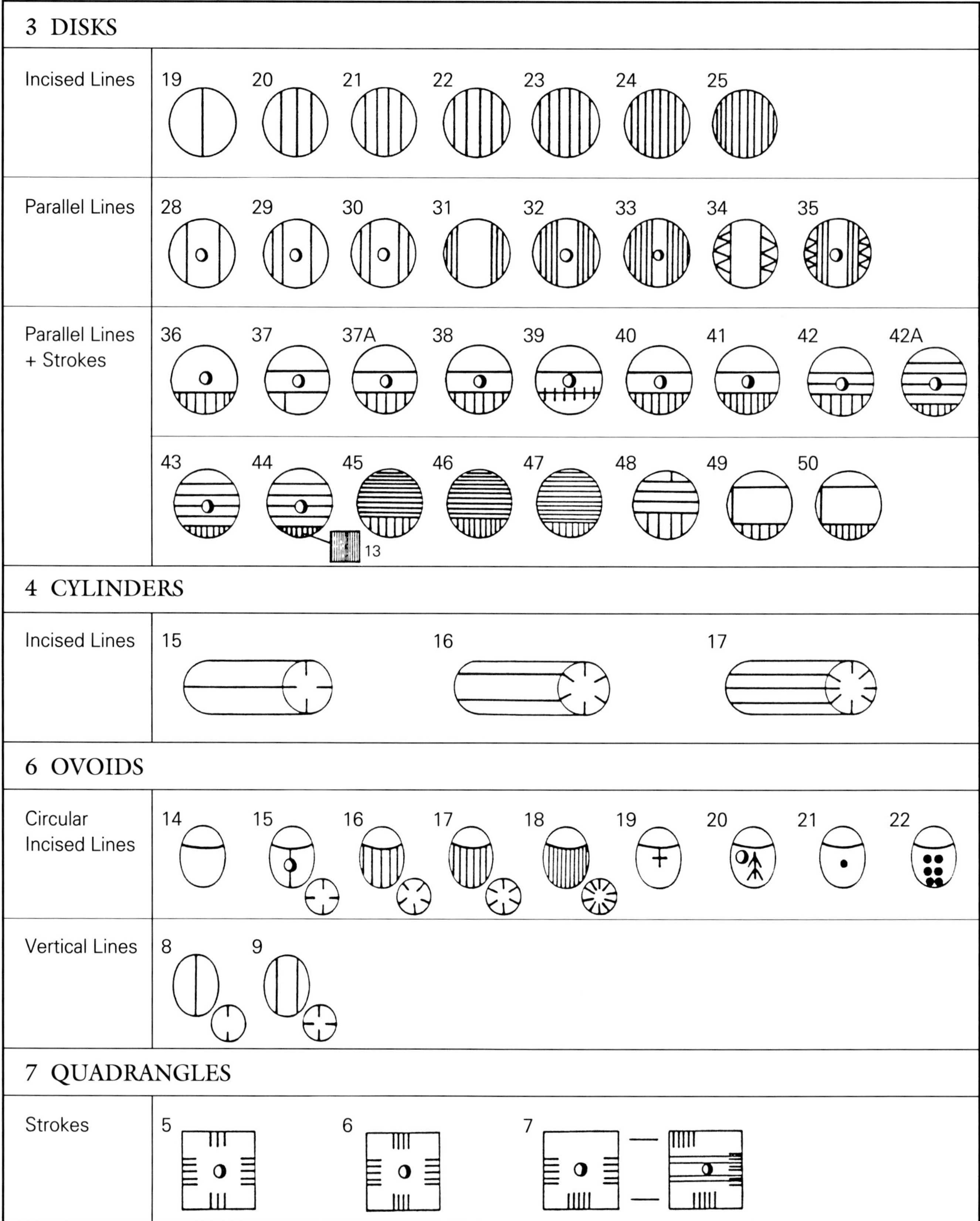

20.1 Token Series

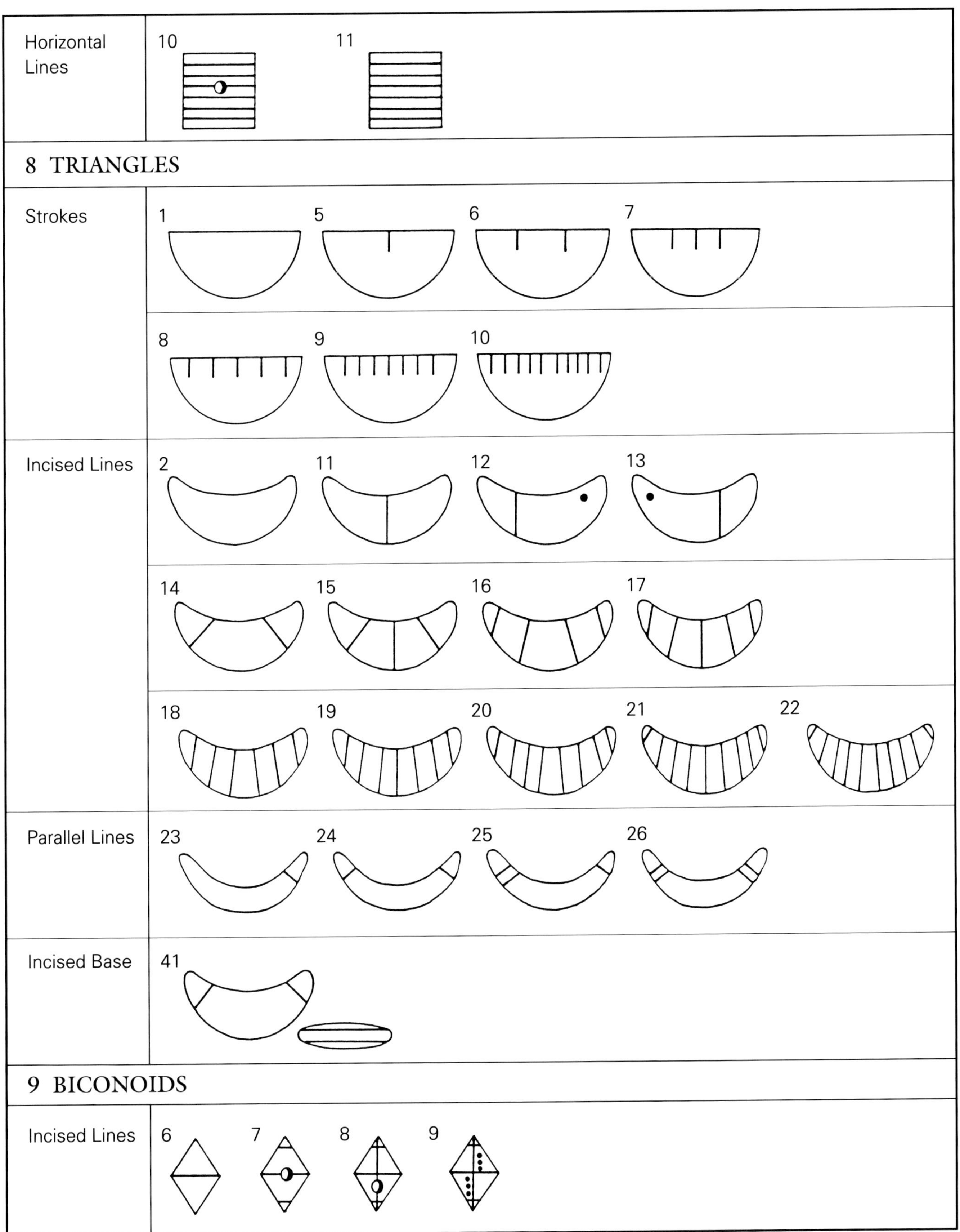

20.2 Token Series

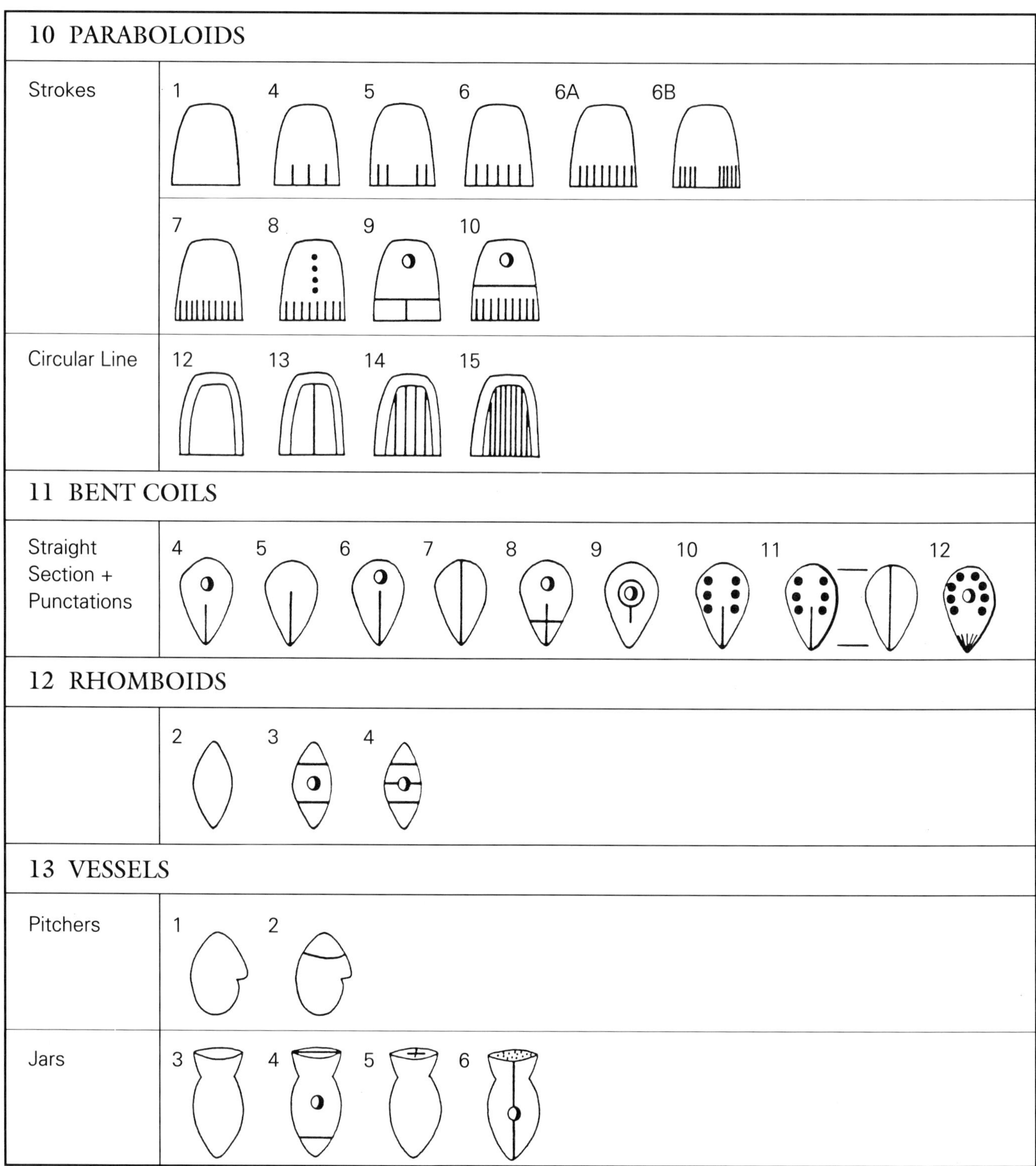

20.3 Token Series

20.1–20.3 Token series. Courtesy Deutsches Archaeologisches Institut, Abteilung Baghdad.

the longest side (type 8: 5–10). A second displays either 1, 2, 3, 4, 5, 6, 7, 8, 9, or 10 lines (type 8: 11–22). Still another group has distinctive sets of parallels: 1, 1-1, 1-2, 2-2 (type 8: 23–26; figs. 20.2 and 20.3).

Paraboloids, like triangles, mostly belong to series. Some bear 3, 4, 5, 8, 9, or 10 strokes (type 10: 4–7) and others 1, 3, or 8 (type 10: 12–15; fig. 20.3).

Among the series, all subtypes are not represented equally. Instead, some tokens bearing a particular set of lines seem to be particularly popular. For instance, the triangles showing five lines are more frequent than those with any other set (type 8: 17).

REVERTING TO PLAIN TOKENS

When sites like Tell Hadidi, Larsa, or Malyan of the second and third millennia B.C. yield tokens, they are plain. The late token assemblages are restricted to very few shapes, including mostly spheres, disks, and, occasionally, cones and cylinders. Plain and complex tokens represent steps in the evolution of the ancient Near Eastern reckoning device. The complex counters developed from plain tokens, adopting their size, material, and method of manufacture. They also continued the same basic shapes; namely, cones, spheres, disks, cylinders, tetrahedrons, ovoids, quadrangles, triangles, vessels, and animal heads. The complex tokens only expanded the repertory of shapes of counters and of markings on their face. When the token system started dwindling, it reverted to a few plain shapes.

The fact that plain and complex tokens were part of the same reckoning system, used by the same people for the same function, is obvious for several reasons. First, as will be discussed later in the volume, both categories of counters were found together in the same sites and the same hoards and were enclosed in the same envelopes. Second, they started being perforated at the same time, showing that they were strung together. Third and finally, both plain and complex tokens are the prototypes of pictographs representing basic commodities in the Sumerian script.

Materials

The material most commonly used for the manufacture of the counters was a variety of clay common in Southwest Asia called montmorillonite. In fact, tokens, together with figurines, were the earliest uses of clay of the Neolithic farmers of the Near East before it served for pottery and architecture.[17] During the Neolithic and Chalcolithic periods, the clay selected for modeling the counters seems unprepared and sometimes includes impurities such as gravel or even small pebbles. In the fourth millennium B.C. tokens were made of a usually very fine paste, suggesting that it was refined. As a rule, tokens show no indication of any tempering, either mineral or vegetable, which is not surprising since the objects were not subjected to tensile strength. The clay appears to have been worked while very wet, because the artifacts are often covered by a self-slip. Also, traces of fingerprints are frequently visible on the surface. Otherwise, there is no particular treatment, although an occasional painted or burnished specimen may occur.

There are few examples of plain tokens, and even fewer complex tokens, made of stone (fig. 21), bitumen, or plaster. Stone tokens are often colorful. They are made of pink, green, or black marble, white alabaster, grey slate, brown sandstone, or reddish ocher.

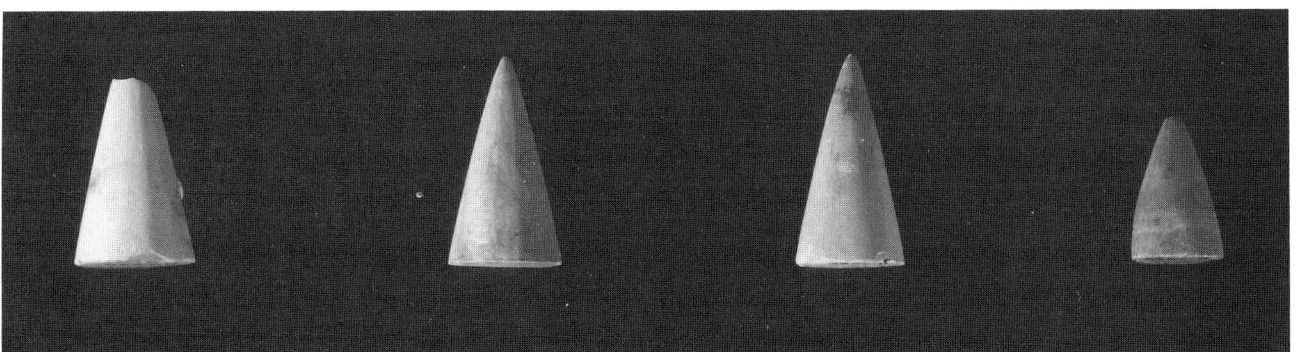

21. Stone tokens, Tepe Hissar, Iran. Courtesy University Museum, University of Pennsylvania.

The stone tokens originate most frequently from northern Mesopotamia.[18] Beldibi in Turkey also produced a few specimens made of ocher.[19] The bitumen examples seem confined to southern Mesopotamia and the Susiana Plain of western Iran.[20] There are occasional tokens made of plaster; for example, at Suberde in Turkey.[21]

Manufacture

The manufacture of the plain clay tokens was simple. It required neither skill in craftsmanship nor a complex technology. In fact, tokens could be shaped by anyone without the help of any tool. The spheres, ovoids, and cylinders were rolled between the palms of the hands. The three-quarter and half spheres were flattened by applying pressure to a sphere against a flat surface. The disks, cones, biconoids, and tetrahedrons were fashioned by pinching a small lump of clay between the fingertips. All these shapes are very easy to achieve; they are in fact the shapes which emerge spontaneously when doodling with clay. Only the tokens of naturalistic shapes representing miniature vessels, tools, and animals required additional skill for their execution.

All the various types of complex tokens were also made by simply pinching a small lump of clay between the fingers, except, perhaps, in the case of some flat tokens, which may have been molded. There is among complex tokens a curious series of disks with strongly tapering sides, crisp edges, and a convex upper face resembling the shape of a muffin. The form, which would be difficult to make by hand, could possibly result from the use of an open mold. The tapering sides would be particularly functional for removing tokens from the mold, and a round top typically results from overfilling a form. However, no evidence exists for any mold other than one stone object found by Steve and Gasche.[22] According to them, the artifact could have been used to produce small terracotta objects, but if so, they would be the tokens in zigzag shapes (type 14: 9) rather than disks. If there is a slight possibility that an open mold was used to make certain flat tokens in fourth-millennium sites, there is none for making globular tokens in bipart molds. There are no instances of tokens exhibiting the characteristic lines left where the two parts of a mold join. Furthermore, visibly, tokens do not exhibit a standard size as would be expected from mass-produced, molded artifacts. Instead, as was discussed above, each token shows slight variations in size, shape, and finish that reflect individual treatment.

There are great differences in the care given to the manufacture of tokens from site to site and even among specimens from the same assemblage. Most clay counters are modeled into a well-defined shape with precise and crisp edges, but some are sloppily done, exhibiting an uneven contour. The stone tokens, which required far greater skill to manufacture and a time-consuming polishing process, usually show excellent craftsmanship.

Markings were performed either with the fingernail or, more commonly, by tracing strokes and lines with a stylus or pointed instrument. The type of tool used to trace the markings has not yet been identified. One possibility worth considering is the bone points held in a bitumen handle recovered by Mecquenem at Susa.[23] Punctations were made by impressing the clay with the blunt end of a stylus. As a rule the markings were applied when the clay was still moist. There are five instances at Habuba Kabira, however, when lines were scratched after firing either on a previously plain specimen[24] or supplementing a first set of markings applied before firing.[25] These examples provide a glimpse at how the fourth-millennium accountants resorted to bricolage to meet their needs. The markings are displayed with clarity on the face of the counters but with no particular concern for aesthetics. For example, lines are not perfectly parallel or punctations regularly aligned. The lines and punctations are shown on a single face of disks, triangles, paraboloids, and other flat tokens but cover the entire surface of cones, spheres, ovoids, and other globular forms.

Several tests of token samples prove that there was no such thing as an aceramic Neolithic. There is no evidence for a stage when clay was just modeled, but instead, the earliest clay objects of the Near East show traces of firing.[26] Differential thermal analysis (DTA) and electron microscopy of samples from Tepe Asiab, ca. 7800 B.C. (fig. 22), Tepe Sarab, ca. 6500 B.C., and Susa, ca. 3300 B.C. have determined that tokens were consistently baked at a low temperature never exceeding 700° C.[27] DTA is based on the fact that exothermic and endothermic effects are produced by physical and chemical transformation of material (dehydration, oxidation, fusion, vaporization, crystal transitions, etc.). The analysis involved placing individually the powdered samples from each of the three sites in a source of heat at constant rate (10° C) per minute and measuring their reactions in comparison with a sample of in-

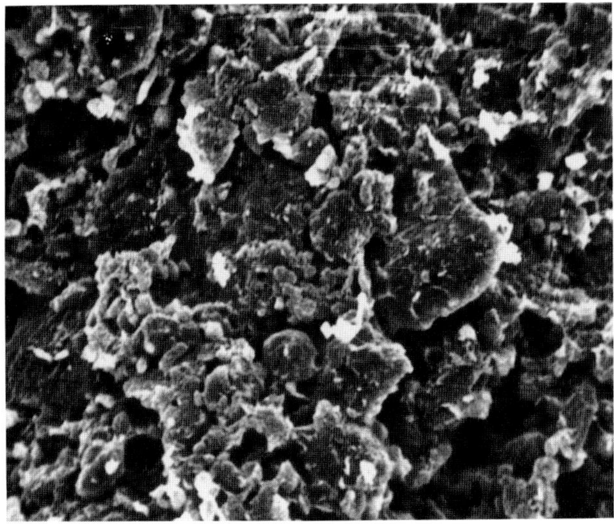

22. Tepe Asiab, Iran, scanning electron magnification 1,000×. Courtesy W. David Kingery, Massachusetts Institute of Technology.

ert material (aluminum oxide). The resulting graphs exhibited a substantial endothermic peak at a temperature of about 200° C, which corresponds to the elimination of water in unfired clay and seemingly indicates that the tokens were not baked. The same reaction was noted, however, in well-fired pottery sherds from Sialk, ca. 4500 to 4000 B.C., demonstrating that, after a period of several millennia in the ground, the material could rehydrate, thus making the results of this first part of the test inconclusive.[28] The graphs showed a second peak between 800° and 900° C, characteristic of the crystallization process in montmorillonite. This revealed that crystallization temperature had never been reached previously. In conclusion, DTA only indicated that if the tokens had been fired the temperature never reached 800° C.

The second test, scanning electron microscopy, magnifies between 20 and 100,000 times, allowing the examination of the crystal structure of the material. In the case of the sample from Tepe Asiab, the ordinarily hexagonal shapes of the individual crystals of montmorillonite have lost their sharp edges and become rounded. Furthermore, the mass appears fused in an aggregate with noticeable continuity, suggesting that the artifacts were subjected to a temperature above 500° C. The combined results of both tests set, therefore, the firing temperature of the prehistoric tokens between 500 and 800° C.

Tokens of the Neolithic period were not thoroughly baked and often exhibit a black core, whereas those of the fourth millennium B.C. are usually buff-pink throughout their thickness, showing a perfect control of the firing process. It is likely that, at least at the time when Tepe Asiab was occupied, the objects were heated in an open fire, since ovens had not yet been invented at the time. This explains why the counters vary in color from buff to black with grey, red, pink, and greenish specimens. The oxidizing combustion at the periphery of the hearth produced buff and red artifacts, while the greenish, gray, and black examples resulted from the reducing atmosphere at the center. It is interesting to note that scanning electron microscopy of the samples of Tepe Sarab indicated a firing temperature not exceeding 300° C. This suggests that in the seventh millennium B.C. tokens may have been baked in domestic ovens.

The Token Collection

The catalog of seven thousand tokens has been compiled by studying the collections in the museums where they were stored or from site reports and, ideally, by combining the two sources.

NUMBER OF TOKENS PER SITE

The number of tokens recorded for each of the sites featured in the catalog is as follows (fig. 23):

In Iran: Anau 56, Bampur 2, Belt Cave 6, Chagha Sefid 34, Chogha Bonut 3, Chogha Mish (?), Dalma Tepe 3, Deh Luran 24, Geoy Tepe 1, Hajji Firuz 13, Jaffarabad 70, Jeitun 81, KS 34. 23, KS 54. 7, KS 76. 2, Malyan 17, Moussian 19, Sharafabad 8, Seh Gabi 61, Shahr-i Sokhta 53, Sialk 8, Sorkh-i-Dom 1, Susa 783, Tall-i-Bakun 56, Tal-i-Iblis 39, Tepe Abdul Hosein 26, Tepe Asiab 193, Tepe Bouhallan 4, Tepe Farukhabad 5, Tepe Gaz Tavila 93, Tepe Giyan 15, Tepe Guran 34, Tepe

Hissar 92, Tepe Muradabad 1, Tepe Sarab 114, Tepe Siahbid 3, Tepe Yahya 142, Tula'i 7, and Zagheh 29.[29]

In Iraq: Arpachiyah 93, Billa 18, Choga Mami 18, Eridu 12, Fara 15, Gird Ali Agha 3, Gird Banahilk 1, Hassuna 3, Ischali 3, Jarmo 2022, Jemdet Nasr 27, Khafaje 10, Kish 60, Larsa 3, Maghzaliyah 8, Matarrah 1, M'lefaat 2, Nemrik 69, Nineveh 12, Nippur 26, Nuzi 27, Ras al Amiya 30, Sippar 1, Tell Abada 50, Tell Agrab 1, Tell Asmar 7, Tell es-Sawwan 77, Tell Oueili 4, Tell Raschid 4, Tell Songor 1, Tello 92, Tell Yelkhi 5, Telul eth Thalathat 11, Tepe Gawra 485, Ubaid 1, Umm Dabaghiyah 11, Umm Hafriyat 26, Uqair 5, Ur 107, Uruk 812, and Yarim Tepe 59.[30]

In Syria: Abu Hureira 5, Amuq 17, Chagar Bazar 9, Cheikh Hassan 2, Ghoraife 11, Habuba Kabira 141, Hadidi 147, Jebel Aruda 11, Mureybet 2, Ras Shamra 16, Tell Aswad 320, Tell Brak 3, Tell Halaf 5, Tell Kannas 58, and Tell Ramad 380.

In Palestine: Ain Ghazal 12, Beidha 20, Beisamoun 4, Jericho 3, Ktar Tell Kazarei 1, Megiddo 9, Munhata 1, and Tell Aphek 1.

In Turkey: Beldibi 11, Can Hasan 41, Çayönü Tepesi 31, Gritille 33, and Suberde 66.

The catalog suggests two observations. First, the number of tokens differs greatly from site to site. Compare, for example, the largest assemblages—Jarmo 2,022, Uruk 812, Susa 783, Tepe Gawra 485, Tell Ramad 380, and Tell Aswad 320—with some of the smallest collections—Matarrah 1, Tell Songor 1, Ubaid 1, and Tell Hassuna 3. Second, small token assemblages are more frequent than large ones—as many as thirty collections have fewer than ten tokens.

Unfortunately, the number of counters per site does not seem to reflect particular socioeconomic factors but, rather, the technical difficulties first in excavating the material and second in compiling the catalog. There is no indication, for example, that life at Jarmo, which produced two thousand tokens, was much different from that of other Neolithic sites such as Hassuna, which yielded three counters.

NUMBER OF TOKENS EXCAVATED

First, the large discrepancy between the number of tokens at each site has to do with the type of expedition involved. It should be kept in mind that excavations depend greatly upon luck: One trench may produce numerous artifacts whereas the next remains sterile. Consequently, short-term salvage projects limited to soundings, carried out at Tell Songor, Tell Abada, Tell Rashid, Tell Oueili, or Tell Yelkhi, should be expected to produce uneven assemblages. This probably explains why Tell Abada, for example, produced an assemblage of fifty tokens,[31] whereas the other tells yielded fewer than five tokens each. In particular, short-term excavations are more vulnerable to chance than extensive expeditions, like at Jarmo.

Methods of excavation are also responsible for the uneven number of counters. Tokens pose a challenge to the best excavators because of their size and color. Being small and blending in with the fill, they are particularly difficult to spot. Expeditions such as Jarmo and Ganj Dareh, where the dirt was systematically sifted, had a better chance of salvaging tokens from the excavation dumps than those where this did not occur.

NUMBER OF TOKENS REPORTED

In fact, the lack of documentation was the major problem in compiling the token catalog. Often, the counters are not yet published and thus the collections available represent only a fraction of the actual assemblages. This is the case, for instance, for Chogha Mish, Chogha Bonut, Ganj Dareh Tepe, Umm Dabaghiyah, and Jebel Aruda.

Moreover, in earlier excavations, such as Khafaje, Nippur, Ischali, Nineveh, or Sippar, tokens are glossed over in the site reports. At other times they are alluded to in ways difficult to translate into concrete information. For example, the mention that "odd disks" were recovered at Matarrah[32] becomes in the token catalog "1 unspecified disk," which certainly misrepresents the findings. The same applies to Cheikh Hassan or Mureybet.

In some cases, the lack of publication could be compensated for by studying the material stored in museums, but more often this could not be done. For example, the following statement in the Hassuna report—"pellets . . . were found in considerable quantities in every level of the main sounding at Hassuna"[33]—suggests that, in fact, many tokens were collected at the site. However, there is no trace of any such artifact at the Iraq Museum, where the Hassuna material is stored, except for one clay cone and two stone spheres. The remainder of the "considerable quantities" of pellets can no longer be accurately documented. The three tokens reported for Hassuna in the catalog are not a representative sample of the original collection.

Unfortunately, Hassuna is not the only example where the number of tokens excavated does not correspond to the collections at hand. In fact, this state of

23. Distribution of tokens.

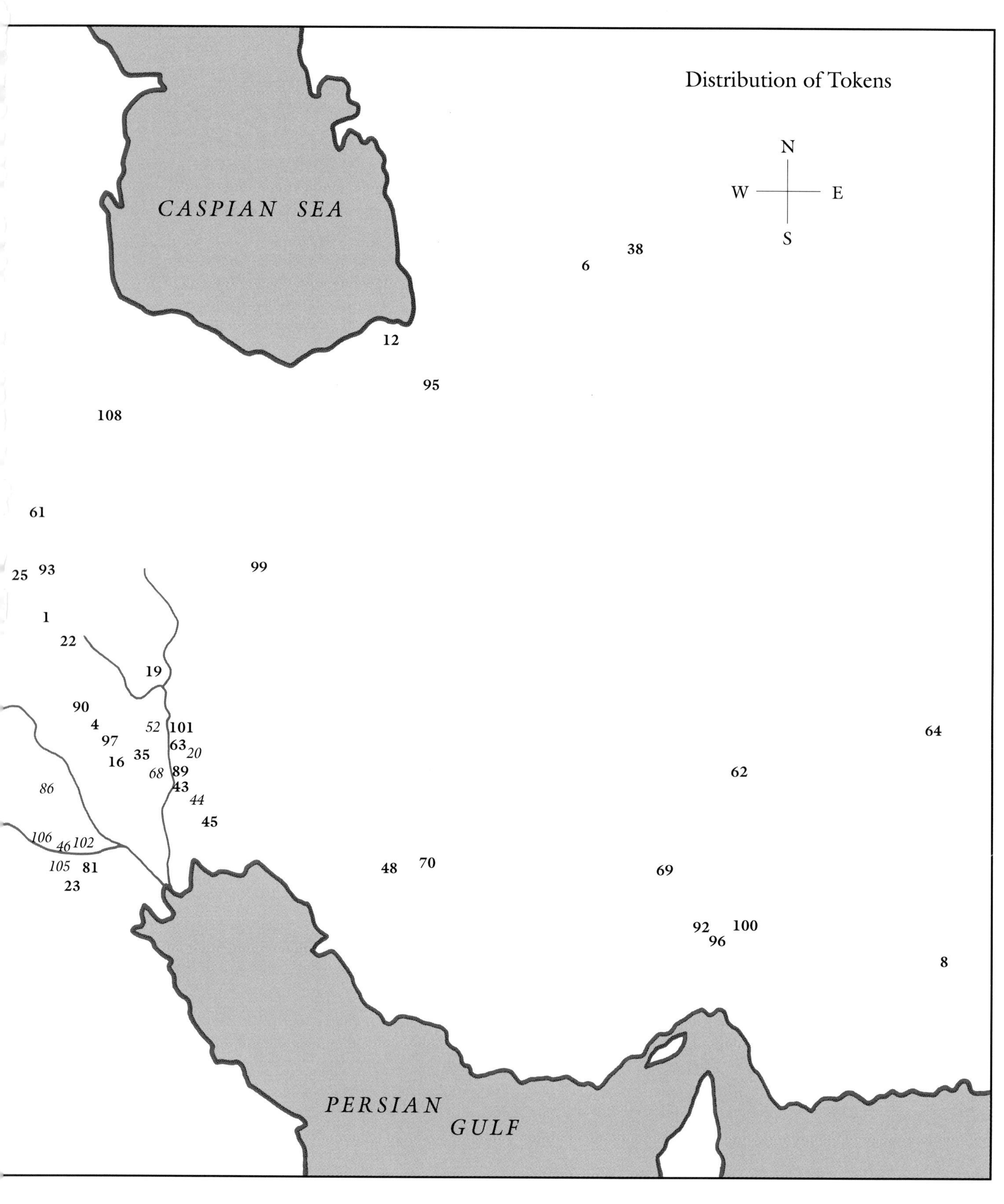

Nemrik
Nineveh
Nippur
Nuzi
Ras al Amiya
Ras Shamra
Seh Gabi
Shahdad
Sharafabad

64 Shahr-i Sokhta
65 Siahbid
66 Sippar
67 Suberde
68 Susa
69 Tal-i-Iblis
70 Tall-i-Bakun
71 Tell Agrab
72 Tell Aphek

73 Tell Arpachiyah
74 Tell Asmar
75 Tell Aswad
76 Tell Billa
77 Tell Brak
78 Tell es-Sawwan
79 Tell Halaf
80 Tell Kannas
81 Tell Oueili

82 Tell Ramad
83 Tell Raschid
84 Tell Songor
85 Tell Yelkhi
86 Tello
87 Telul eth Thalathat
88 Tepe Asiab
89 Tepe Bouhallan
90 Tepe Farukhabad

91 Tepe Gawra
92 Tepe Gaz Tavila
93 Tepe Giyan
94 Tepe Guran
95 Tepe Hissar
96 Tepe Muradabad
97 Tepe Sabz
98 Tepe Sarab
99 Tepe Sialk

100 Tepe Yahya
101 Tula'i
102 Ubaid
103 Umm Dabaghiyah
104 Uqair
105 Ur
106 Uruk
107 Yarim Tepe
108 Zagheh

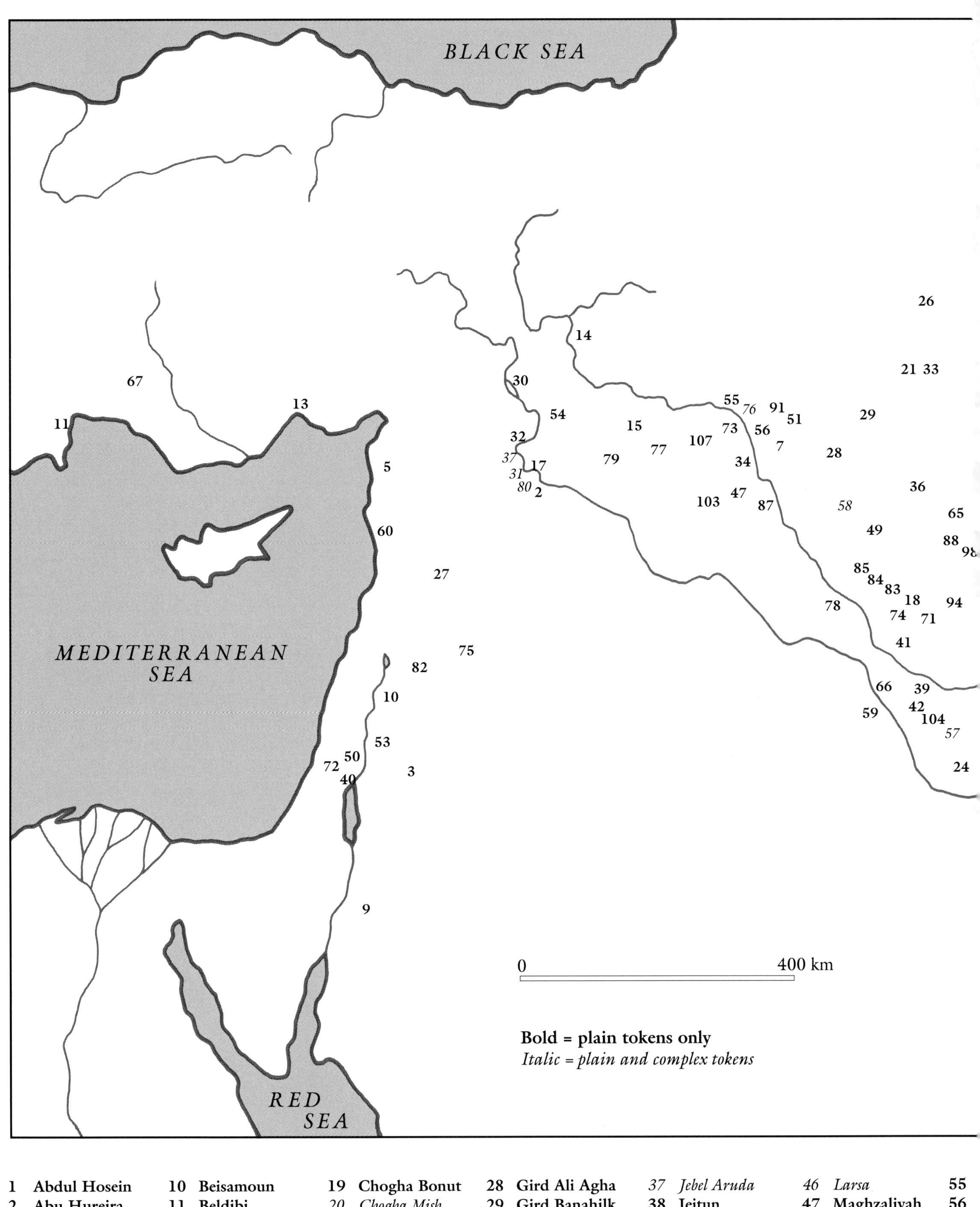

1 **Abdul Hosein**
2 **Abu Hureira**
3 **Ain Ghazal**
4 **Ali Kosh**
5 **Amuq**
6 **Anau**
7 **Arpachiyah**
8 **Bampur**
9 **Beidha**
10 **Beisamoun**
11 **Beldibi**
12 **Belt Cave**
13 **Can Hasan**
14 **Çayönü Tepesi**
15 **Chagar Bazar**
16 **Chagha Sefid**
17 **Cheikh Hassan**
18 **Choga Mami**
19 **Chogha Bonut**
20 Chogha Mish
21 **Dalma Tepe**
22 **Deh Luran**
23 **Eridu**
24 **Fara**
25 **Ganj Dareh**
26 **Geoy Tepe**
27 **Ghoraife**
28 **Gird Ali Agha**
29 **Gird Banahilk**
30 **Gritille**
31 Habuba Kabira
32 **Hadidi**
33 **Hajji Firuz**
34 **Hassuna**
35 **Jaffarabad**
36 **Jarmo**
37 Jebel Aruda
38 **Jeitun**
39 **Jemdet Nasr**
40 **Jericho**
41 **Khafaje**
42 **Kish**
43 **KS 34**
44 KS 54
45 **KS 76**
46 Larsa
47 **Maghzaliyah**
48 **Malyan**
49 **Matarrah**
50 **Megiddo**
51 **M'lefaat**
52 Moussian
53 **Munhata**
54 **Mureybet**

55
56
57
58
59
60
61
62
63

affairs is prevalent. Jemdet Nasr, for instance, is another site where, according to the report, cones were found "in great number," but seven specimens only are documented.[34] According to Mallowan, cones "were common" at Arpachiyah, but only twenty-four can be traced in the reserves of the British Museum and the Iraq Museum in Baghdad.[35]

The reports often communicate incorrect perceptions. For example, because the stone counters had more aesthetic appeal than their more modest clay counterparts, they were often given more attention in the publications, sometimes suggesting that stone specimens were more numerous than the clay ones when the reverse was true. At Hassuna, for instance, the only specimens illustrated in the report are two stone spheres.[36] The same happens at the site of Amuq and at Tepe Gawra, where the stone counters were published but three hundred clay specimens were dismissed.[37]

The Ubaid report includes information on a single token, a paraboloid, described as "the tongue of an animal sculpture."[38] In this case, presumably, the paraboloid was deemed important enough to be published because its form seemed unusual and interesting, while the more inconspicuous types were ignored. As a result, Ubaid appears, probably erroneously, as a unique assemblage yielding a complex token but no plain ones.

ACTUAL NUMBER OF TOKENS

On the other hand, the outstanding number of tokens collected at Jarmo can be explained in several ways. First, Jarmo was a long-term, extensive excavation where the dirt was sytematically sifted. Perhaps more importantly, a member of the team, Vivian L. Broman, was studying clay artifacts. It is likely that her interest generated among the workers the necessary vigilance for finding the objects and keeping them. Furthermore, Broman included her results in her thesis, making the material available.[39] Her study remains unique to this day in presenting a detailed report of a token assemblage. It is obvious that, without Broman's work, we would know today as much—or rather as little—about the Jarmo tokens as we do about other Neolithic token assemblages such as that of Hassuna. In this perspective, the fact that no tokens were reported at Bouqras, Koum Shemshara, or Yanik Tepe provides no proof that none were used at those sites.

The two thousand tokens excavated at Jarmo give us a tantalizing idea of the number of tokens that could be expected at each site. Jarmo was no more and no less than an average farming community in the seventh and sixth millennia B.C. Its token collection should be considered, therefore, as an average token Neolithic assemblage. By contrast, the 3 tokens from Hassuna and even the 812 tokens of Uruk, 783 from Susa, and 485 from Tepe Gawra are only a pale reflection of the collections that could have been recovered.

NUMBER OF TOKENS PER TYPE

The total assemblage of 8,162 tokens considered in this study consists of 3,354 spheres, 1,457 cones, 1,095 disks, 806 cylinders, 278 rectangles, 233 triangles, 220 tetrahedrons, 204 ovoids, 129 animals, 85 paraboloids, 81 vessels, 60 bent coils, 51 biconoids, 45 ovals, 33 miscellaneous, and 31 tools.

It is to be expected that the poor conditions of recovery and the inaccuracy of reporting affect these results to a considerable extent. It is likely that the plain cylinders, which are not much bigger than a grain of wheat, are among those which were most missed. It is very possible that spheres were indeed the most popular token shape; on the other hand, they were often taken for marbles and therefore had the best chance of being entered in site reports under the rubric "games." The token assemblages presently available give at best precarious and at worst unreliable information on the number of tokens at each site and the frequency of token types. On the other hand, the same data plotted on a map of the Near East create an awesome picture of the vast geographic expanse where the system of reckoning was used.

2
PLAIN TOKENS

In these gamesmen we see a very human side of the inhabitants of Jemdet Nasr. That the games played with these pieces were extremely popular is proved from the great number found.
—Ernest Mackay[1]

THE FOLLOWING three chapters are devoted to the documentation of the token system. After an introduction on the geographic distribution of the counters in the Near East, I present in this chapter, chronologically, the evidence I have collected on prehistoric or plain tokens of Iran from 8000 to 3500 B.C. and, subsequently, those from Iraq in the same time period.

The Geographic Distribution

The some 115 sites where tokens have been recovered illustrate that whenever modern excavations were carried out in a Near Eastern site of the eighth to the fourth millennium B.C., they usually generated a crop, large or small, of counters. There are, however, exceptions to the rule. The region of Central Anatolia is devoid of tokens and some sites, like Bouqras and Koum in Syria, Yanik Tepe in northwestern Iran, or Shemshara in Iraq, have conspicuously produced none.

Proceeding from west to east, tokens have been reported in sixteen Syrian sites from the eighth to the fourth millennium B.C. Among them, Tell Aswad, Tell Ramad, Habuba Kabira, and Tell Kannas have the most representative assemblages.[2] The distribution of the counters extends to Israel, to the western end of the Fertile Crescent. There are eight Palestinian sites that produced clay counters, including Ain Ghazal, Beidha, Beisamoun, Jericho, and Megiddo.[3] There are indications that some tokens were part of archaeological assemblages as far south as Khartoum in the Sudan.[4]

In Turkey, tokens are limited to five sites located in the Taurus Mountains, like Gritille and Çayönü Tepesi, or along the Mediterranean coast, like Can Hasan, Suberde, and Beldibi. There is no evidence for the use of clay counters, however, at Çatal Hüyük or Hacilar, suggesting that the token system never reached Central Anatolia.

Iraq has forty-three sites yielding tokens.[5] Among them, the earlier settlements are located in the uplands along the Zagros Mountains, such as, for example, Maghzaliyah, Nemrik, Jarmo, M'lefaat, Yarim Tepe, Tell es-Sawwan, Arpachiyah, and Tepe Gawra.[6] The more recent sites, like Uruk, Ur, Tello, Fara, and Nippur, are spread in the alluvial plain of southern Mesopotamia, which was not settled prior to the sixth millennium B.C.

The majority of the forty Iranian sites which produced tokens are clustered in the western part of the country; for example, Ganj Dareh Tepe, Tepe Asiab, Ali Kosh, Tepe Sarab, Hajji Firuz, Zagheh, Chagha Sefid, Seh Gabi, Susa, Chogha Mish, Tepe Farukhabad, and KS 54. The others are distributed on all sides of the Persian Deserts, with Tepe Sialk, Tall-i-Bakun, and Tall-i-Mushki to the west,[7] Tepe Yahya, Shahdad, Tal-Iblis, and Bampur to the south, Shahr-i Sokhta to the east,[8] and Tepe Hissar, Anau, and Jeitun to the north.[9]

Dharan is the only site yielding tokens presently identified in Saudi Arabia.[10] There is evidence for the use of plain tokens as far east as Pakistan; for example,

24.1. Cones, Tell Aswad II, Syria. Courtesy Henri de Contenson.

24.2. Cones, Tell Aswad II, Syria. Courtesy Henri de Contenson.

24.3. Pinched cones, Tell Aswad II, Syria. Courtesy Henri de Contenson.

24.4. Spheres, Tell Aswad II, Syria. Courtesy Henri de Contenson.

24.5. Disk, Tell Aswad II, Syria. Courtesy Henri de Contenson.

tokens are reported in the pre-Harappan site of Mehrgahr.[11] These latter specimens are beyond the scope of this volume.

Tokens pervaded, therefore, most inhabitable regions of the Near East from Israel to Syria, Turkey, Iraq, and Iran, with the exception of Central Anatolia. Mesopotamia and western Iran have produced, however, the greatest concentration of sites yielding tokens and the largest number of counters. These two regions are discussed in detail below.

Chronology

Stratigraphic excavation and carbon datings provide a chronological framework for the token system, in particular, its three major landmarks: The first appearance of the clay counters, the beginning of complex types, and the terminal phase of the reckoning device can be dated with reasonable certainty.[12]

THE FIRST TOKENS

The first clay counters appear between 8000 and 7500 B.C. in five sites of Syria and Iran. At Tell Mureybet in Syria, the first tokens occur in level III, about 8000 B.C. (P. 1220: 8000 ± 100 B.C.; Mc735: 7800 ± 150 B.C.) but there are none in the two preceding levels, I and II, dated to 8500 to 8200 B.C.[13] A sounding at Cheikh Hassan, located in close proximity of Mureybet, also produced clay counters of the early eighth millennium B.C.[14] Finally, Tell Aswad, level I (GIF-2633: 7790 ± 120 B.C.; GIF-2372: 7690 ± 120 B.C.) is the third of the earliest Syrian sites yielding tokens.[15]

In Iran, the oldest tokens come from the deepest layer of Ganj Dareh, level E, formerly dated to 8500 B.C. but now estimated to about 8000 B.C. (GAK-807: 8450 ± 150 B.C.).[16] Finally, the tokens recovered in the single prehistoric layer of Tepe Asiab are also from the same time period (UCLA B and C: 7900–7700 B.C.).

Tokens start occurring in the same time range in the Levant and in Iran, making it unclear where the counting device was first invented in the Fertile Crescent. Even northern Mesopotamia cannot be dismissed as a possible cradle for the token system since the absence of early eighth-millennium tokens in the region probably reflects only a lack of excavations. Wherever they originated, the tokens spread in a matter of centuries to other regions of the Near East. By the late eighth millennium B.C. the clay counters can be traced to Maghzaliyah in Iraq and as far as Beldibi in Anatolia.

THE TIME EXTENSION OF THE TOKEN SYSTEM

Once the token system was established in the early eighth millennium B.C. it was to remain a common feature in Near Eastern settlements for several millennia.

In the seventh millennium the clay counters are represented in sites such as Ali Kosh (Shell 1246: 6450 ± 200 B.C.), Ganj Dareh A and B (GAK-994: 6960 ± 170 B.C.), Tepe Abdul Hosein (GX 6353: 6715 B.C.), and Belt Cave in Iran; Jarmo (H-551/491: 6575 ± 175 B.C.), M'lefaat, and Maghzaliyah in Iraq; Tell Aswad II (GrN-6678: 6935 ± 55 B.C.; GrN-6679: 6915 ± 60 B.C.; figs. 24.1–24.5),[17] Tell Ramad I (GrN-4426: 6260 ± 50 B.C.; GrN-4428: 6250 ± 80 B.C.),[18] as well as Ghoraife I in Syria; Ain Ghazal and Munhata in Palestine; and Can Hasan level 3 (BM-1667: 6410 B.C.), Suberde levels 2–3 (P-1388: 6226 ± 79 B.C.), Gritille, and Çayönü Tepesi (Michigan 1609: 6840 ± 250 B.C.) in Turkey.

In the sixth millennium B.C. tokens continued to be used in Iran at Tula'i levels 3–6, Zagheh (TUNC-12: 5500 ± 100 B.C.; figs. 25.1 and 25.2), Tepe Sarab (P-465: 5655 ± 96 B.C.; figs. 26.1 and 26.2), Deh Luran, Tepe Guran levels D–E, Hajji Firuz levels A–D (P-455: 5537 ± 89 B.C.; figs. 27.1 and 27.2), Tepe Gaz Tavila levels 3–6, Yarim Tepe, Anau (fig. 28), and Jeitun; in Iraq at Choga Mami, Gird Ali Agha, Hassuna, Matarrah (W-623: 5620 ± 250 B.C.), M'lefaat, Tell es-Sawwan levels 1–3 (P-855: 5506 ± 73 B.C.), Yarim Tepe, and Umm Dabaghiyah; in Syria at Amuq level B and Tell Ramad levels 2 (GrN-4427: 5970 ± 50 B.C.: GrN-4822: 5950 ± 55 B.C.)[19] and 3 (GrN-4822: 5950 ± 50 B.C.); and in Turkey at Can Hasan level 10.

The list of sites yielding tokens in the fifth millennium B.C. in Iran includes Chagha Sefid, Chogha Bonut, Dalma Tepe (P-503: 4036 ± 87 B.C.), Deh Luran, Jaffarabad levels 1–5, Seh Gabi levels 9–10 (figs. 29.1 and 29.2), Sialk levels 1 and 3–5 (GX 949: cal

25.1. Cones, spheres, lenticular disks, Zagheh, Iran. Courtesy Ezat O. Negahban.

25.2. Flat disk, cubes, rectangles, ovoids, Zagheh, Iran. Courtesy Ezat O. Negahban.

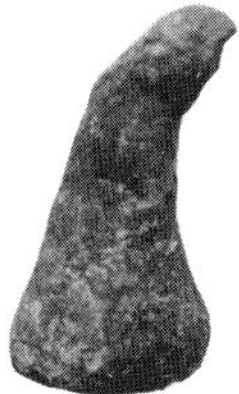

26.1. Cones, tetrahedron, Tepe Sarab, Iran. Courtesy Prehistoric Project, University of Chicago.

26.2. Spheres, tetrahedron, Tepe Sarab, Iran. Courtesy Prehistoric Project, University of Chicago.

4885–4405 B.C.), Tall-i-Bakun (P-438: 4220 ± 83 B.C.), Tal-i-Iblis levels 1–4, Tepe Giyan level 5, and Siahbid (P-442: 4039 ± 85 B.C.). In Iraq tokens occur in the fifth millennium at Choga Mami (BM-483: 4896 ± 182 B.C.), Nineveh level 1, Arpachiyah (P-548: 5077 ± 83 B.C.), Tepe Gawra levels 18–19 (P-1495: 4470 B.C.), Gird Banahilk, Uruk XVIII–XV (H-138/123: 4120 ± 160 B.C.), and Ras al Amiya. In Syria, the tokens of Tell Halaf may also be attributed, tentatively, to the fifth millennium; in Palestine, Ktar Tell Kasarei; and in Turkey, at Can Hasan level 12.

The first well-documented complex tokens are those of the deep sounding of the sanctuary of Eanna at Uruk. The 169 counters recovered in the so-called *Tiefschnitt,* dug below the Limestone Temple, provide a reliable sequence from level V, in the late Uruk period, ca. 3500 B.C. to level XVIII, in the late Ubaid period, about 4400 B.C.[20] The chronology of the complex tokens is discussed in detail in Chapter 4.

In the fourth millennium tokens were recovered in Iran at Susa (SPr1: 3143 ± 104 B.C.), Chogha Mish, KS 34., KS 54., KS 76., Moussian, Sharafabad, Seh Gabi level 7, Tepe Bouhallan, Farukhabad (M-2152: 3310–3210 B.C.), Hissar levels 1A–2 (P-2699: cal 3290–2920 B.C.),[21] and Tepe Muradabad; in Iraq at Uruk levels XVIII–IV, Tello, Ur, Telul eth Thalathat, Khafaje levels 3–7, Tepe Gawra levels 10–16 (fig. 30), Nineveh levels 3–4, and Tell Abada (BM-1823: 3820 B.C.); in Syria at Amuq level E, Chagar Bazar, Tell Brak, Habuba Kabira, Tell Kannas, and Jebel Aruda.

There is still evidence for the use of tokens in Iran in the third millennium at Malyan, Geoy Tepe, Hissar level 3, Tepe Yahya, and Bampur. The Iraqi tokens from Fara, Ischali, Kish, Larsa, Nuzi, Sippar, Tell Agrab, and Tell Asmar are perhaps dated to the fourth to third millennium B.C. Those of Tepe Gawra levels 8–6 can be securely dated to the third millennium. In Syria tokens are encountered at Amuq levels G–H and Tell Kannas. Tokens still occurred at Gritille in Turkey in the third millennium.

Tell Hadidi in Syria still produced a large token assemblage (147 tokens) in the second millennium B.C. and the counters from Megiddo, Palestine, may tentatively be estimated as of the same period. Finally, the last tokens to be traced in Iran belong to Hissar IIIc (TUNC-20: cal 1890–1740 B.C.) and Sorkh-i-Dom in the second millennium. No clay tokens are reported in Iraq in the second and first millennia B.C. The *abnati* of Nuzi attest to the use of counters in Mesopotamia about 1500 B.C., but it is not certain whether they were pebbles or tokens.

The use of tokens can be documented, therefore, from about 8000 to 1500 B.C. According to the available data, the system started tapering off in Mesopotamia in the third millennium B.C. while lingering longer in Syria and Iran.

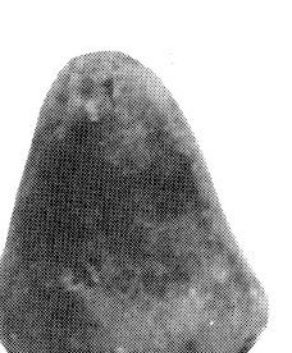

27.1. Cones, Hajji Firuz, Iran. Courtesy Mary M. Voigt.

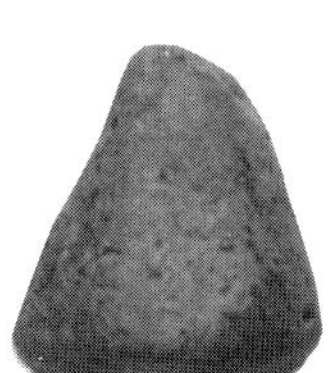
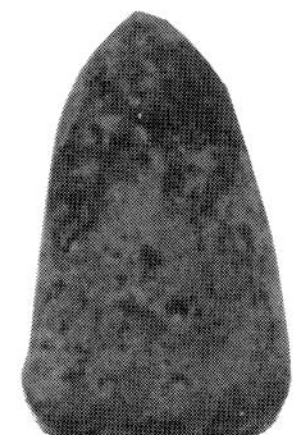

27.2. Cones, Hajji Firuz, Iran. Courtesy Mary M. Voigt.

28. Spheres, Anau, Iran. Courtesy Peabody Museum, Harvard University.

29.1. Tetrahedron and cones, Seh Gabi, Iran. Courtesy Louis D. Levine.

29.2. Disk and spheres, Seh Gabi, Iran. Courtesy Louis D. Levine.

Tokens in Iran

Forty sites of Iran have produced a total of 2,612 tokens. I chose to start with the presentation of this material because it was recovered in relatively recent excavations and provides, therefore, more reliable information.

THE EIGHTH MILLENNIUM B.C.

The earliest tokens of Iran occur at Ganj Dareh Tepe and Tepe Asiab.[22] The two sites are located in the Zagros Mountains in the Kermanshah area and both belong to the early eighth millennium B.C. or Neolithic I.[23] Tokens are present in the earliest level of occupation of Ganj Dareh level E, which is dated to about 8000 B.C. (GAK-807: 8450 ± 150 B.C.).[24] The single archaeological level of Tepe Asiab is either contemporaneous or follows closely thereafter (UCLA B and C: 7900 and 7700 B.C.).[25]

The settlement pattern at Ganj Dareh E[26] and Tepe Asiab was a complete departure from the Paleolithic and Mesolithic traditions. Instead of the previous habitats in caves and rock shelters, the two sites were open-air encampments, probably consisting of huts of perishable material.

Although domestication of plants and animals was already under way in other regions of the Near East, the economy of both Ganj Dareh and Tepe Asiab still relied, allegedly, upon hunting and gathering. Neither botanical nor osteological analyses have brought any clear evidence for agriculture at Ganj Dareh, and the proof for animal husbandry at Tepe Asiab is being disputed.[27] The early Zagros settlers are credited, however, for increasing reliance upon cereals for their subsistence, thus laying the foundation for an economy based on grain consumption. People also devised more successful techniques of gathering cereals by using sickles and, at Tepe Asiab, more efficient ways of processing grains with grinding mortars and pestles.[28]

Technological changes of the times involved working a greater variety of materials, including soft stones and clay. Pottery, the hallmark of Neolithic craftsmanship, started to be manufactured in Ganj Dareh E,[29] whereas limestone was ground and polished at Tepe Asiab. Obsidian was traded at Tepe Asiab, as had been done in the region since Mesolithic times.[30] No trace of the volcanic glass, however, was recovered at Ganj Dareh.[31] Lastly, the Neolithic symbolic paraphernalia was already in place at Tepe Asiab and Ganj Dareh. First, clay figurines of humans and animals were modeled at both sites.[32] Second, tokens, which are a familiar feature of Near Eastern Neolithic assemblages, were introduced.

The eighth millennium token assemblage of Tepe Asiab is particularly interesting because it demonstrates best how elaborate the system had been since its beginning. The collection is unique in size and variety among all the Near Eastern contemporaneous sites. It consists of 193 tokens including 6 cones, 101 spheres, 5 disks, 73 cylinders, 1 tetrahedron, 4 ovoids, 1 rectangle, 1 triangle, and 1 animal head. The number of tokens in Ganj Dareh E is yet unpublished.

At Tepe Asiab, several token types can be further divided into different subtypes on the basis of size, frac-

30. Spheres, disk, cones, tetrahedron, Tepe Gawra, Iraq. Courtesy University Museum, University of Pennsylvania.

tions, and the addition of markings. For example, there are 43 spheres measuring about 1.5–3 cm in diameter; 55 small spheres measuring less than 1 cm; 3 hemispheres; 2 flat disks; 2 lenticular disks; and 1 high disk. Lastly, 6 tokens at Tepe Asiab bear markings, a technique also used at Ganj Dareh E. At Tepe Asiab 1 sphere and 3 cones bear punctations; 1 disk is incised; lastly, 1 ovoid has both incised lines and 1 punctation.

Tokens thus appear in Iran at the transition between the Middle and New Stone Ages. Ganj Dareh and Tepe Asiab, while still preserving features typical of the Mesolithic period, exhibit new traits in settlement pattern, economy, technology, and the use of symbols, indicating the beginnings of the Neolithic era. The first tokens of Iran clearly illustrate that the clay counters were an invention of the people who initiated a new way of life in the Fertile Crescent. They were not a legacy of the past but were part and parcel of the Neolithic phenomenon; that is, the so-called agricultural revolution.

7500–6500 B.C.

Between 7500 and 6500 B.C. the evolution, or rather the stability and consistency, of the token system is exemplified at the three Iranian sites known for the period: Ganj Dareh Tepe levels D–A; Ali Kosh, Bus Mordeh phase; and Belt Cave levels 11–12. Only twelve spheres are reported from the Bus Mordeh period at Ali Kosh.[33] Ganj Dareh, on the other hand, produced a large collection of several hundred tokens, including spheres, disks, cones, and tetrahedrons, some of them bearing pinched, punched, or incised markings.[34] The artifacts were recovered among the maze of storage cubicles occupying the ground floor of buildings.[35] Groups of two to three dozen tokens clustered together suggest that the artifacts were kept in perishable containers such as leather pouches.

The so-called Gazelle Mesolithic of Belt Cave, near the Caspian Sea, produced one cylinder and five cones dating about 6600 B.C. The artifacts puzzled the excavator, Carleton S. Coon, as was mentioned above.[36] Besides illustrating the kind of reactions the tokens used to trigger not so long ago, the Belt Cave artifacts are interesting in showing an increased geographic extension of the system toward the east. They also document the pervasiveness of counting at the time, showing that reckoning took place not only in sedentary villages but also in the caves of herders.

6500–5500 B.C.

Four developments are worth attention in the late seventh and early sixth millennia B.C.: (1) an increase in the geographical extension toward the east, reaching as far as Russian Turkmenia; (2) new, unusual shapes in the token repertory of Tepe Sarab, Zagheh, and Jeitun, perhaps indicating regional developments; (3) tokens used as funerary offerings; and (4) the introduction of stone tokens.

Between 6500 and 5500 B.C., tokens are reported in two separate areas of Iran. In the west, they occur at Tepe Abdul Hosein, Ali Kosh, Chagha Sefid, Tula'i, Tepe Guran, and Tepe Sarab. In the northeast, Jeitun appears presently as an isolated outpost of the token system in Russian Turkmenia. The gap between Jeitun and Deh Luran can be explained easily, however, by the lack of excavation.

As in the previous period, reckoning took place in settled villages of mud-brick houses and in nomadic encampments. Tula'i is an example of a herders' campsite around 6200 to 5900 B.C. that yielded a few spheres and cones.[37]

Among the collections of the period, Tepe Sarab with 114 tokens offers the largest and most diverse assemblage.[38] The group consists of isosceles and equilateral cones, spheres of various sizes, flat and lenticular disks, cylinders, tetrahedrons and pyramids (with four sides, type 5: 14), rectangles, and finally one unique triangle with an all-over nail-incised pattern (type 8: 45; figs. 26.1 and 26.2). Zagheh (fig. 25.1) and Jeitun also produced innovative shapes in their assemblages of, respectively, 29 and 81 tokens.[39] Plain cubes (type 7: 29) are a shape unique to Zagheh (fig. 25.2), which is surprising since it is a form easy to model and identify and it could be expected to feature among the most popular geometric forms.[40] Jeitun, on the other hand, offers a peculiar series of carinated cones (type 1: 11) that suggest the form of a small metal vessel with a pointed base and angular shoulder.[41] The cubes of Zagheh, the carinated cones from Jeitun, and the triangle from Tepe Sarab can be considered, perhaps, as local variations. It is possible that each of these forms stood for goods typical of a particular ecological area but unavailable elsewhere. It is also possible that these tokens represented the products of different economies. Tepe Sarab, which is considered to have been the seasonal encampment of goat herders, could have dealt with commodities other than those of agricultural communities.[42] Lastly, the same product could be expressed by different symbols in different sites with little chance for us to find out about it.

Tokens trickle through the various strata of Ali Kosh, Chagha Sefid, Tepe Abdul Hosein, and Tepe Guran.[43] These are small, traditional assemblages, including mostly cones, spheres, disks, and cylinders with a few punched or incised specimens. These tokens are usually carefully modeled except in the case of Chagha Sefid, where a group was apparently accidentally squeezed while the clay was still soft. As a result it is difficult to decide whether the shape meant was a sphere or an ovoid, a hemisphere or a disk.

Ali Kosh and Tepe Guran provide information on various contexts in which tokens occurred. At Ali Kosh, some of the counters were recovered inside buildings among flint tools and ground stone implements such as mortars and grinding stones. Others were found outside buildings mixed with animal bones and other debris in what appear to be piles of refuse.[44] In both instances, within and without structures, the tokens never give the impression of being *in situ* but rather of having been among other trash discarded in antiquity either in dumps or in a house after it was abandoned.

Although it is frustrating not to recover the counters in the context in which they were used, the fact that tokens were thrown out after use is interesting. This constitutes the first instance of an all too familiar pattern of the recovery of archival material in the ancient Near East. The Uruk and Susa protoliterate tablets were never found *in situ* but in dumps with sealings and other trash,[45] indicating that tokens had a short life expectancy. They recorded one particular transaction until its completion, after which they were neither saved nor reused but were discarded. The systematic elimination of economic documents dealing with individual accounts continued to be customary in later times. The small tablets were seemingly not kept after the information was compiled on large ledgers.

Tepe Guran provides the first evidence of tokens used as funerary offerings in Iran. Namely, two tombs at the site were respectively provided with one clay sphere and one clay cone.[46] The custom of depositing tokens as grave furniture also begins in the same time range in Mesopotamia, as will be discussed in the next section. This tradition suggests that the tokens served as status symbols to those who used them. In fact, they probably constitute the first identifiable status symbol in Iran, prior to the appearance of seals, maceheads, or the offerings of precious metal in burials. The presence of status symbols in the form of counters in turn would suggest the emergence of a group of specialists whose expertise was to count, account, and register with tokens, deriving power and prestige from such activities.

The last major development in the token system between 6500 and 5500 B.C. consists of the appearance of a few spheres made of stone, rather than clay, at Tepe Guran and Tula'i.[47] It is difficult to imagine why anyone would opt for the time-consuming and arduous task of grinding stone into tokens when they are so easily made of clay. It is possible that the choice of stone for manufacturing tokens indicates a new usage, such as, for example, the deposits of counters as funerary offerings. This cannot be verified, however, since the precise context of the stone sphere from Tepe

Guran is not known. On the other hand, the two tokens excavated in graves were made of clay.

The period 6500 to 5500 B.C. in Iran represents a first climax of the token system, marking its full establishment in the agricultural communities. More important, the reckoning device was more than a mere counting device. It brought prestige to selected individuals versed in the art of counting.

5500–4500 B.C.

For the period between 5500 and 4500 B.C. tokens have been located in several parts of Iran, including Azerbaijan at Hajji Firuz, Khuzistan at Chagha Sefid and Ali Kosh, Susiana at Chogha Bonut and Jaffarabad, and Turkmenia at Anau. Anau and Hajji Firuz, dated ca. 5500 to 5000 B.C., are among the earliest of these sites. Little is known about the original context of the collection of fifty-six tokens of Anau excavated by Raphael Pumpelly in 1904 (fig. 28).[48] The careful work of Mary M. Voigt, however, provides good information on the small assemblage of eleven cones (figs. 27.1 and 27.2), one sphere, and one incised hemisphere at Hajji Firuz.[49] Three of these counters were scattered among trash deposits in open spaces. The association of a cone with clumps of clay bearing reed impressions may be significant since the objects may represent an early form of sealings.[50] Two further tokens can be traced to a domestic setting, with one cone belonging to the storage area of the house.[51] The case of a cluster of six cones in a building merits particular scrutiny. The structure was anomalous in many ways. First, it was considerably smaller than any of the other buildings of Hajji Firuz; second, it consisted of a single room instead of two; third, a low platform and two posts were built inside; fourth and most significantly, the house did not yield any trace of domestic activity, such as the debris of flint chipping or cooking. The six cones which belonged to the building lay in a corner, in an area defined by a low curb.[52] It is possible that the cones were associated with human bones found in proximity. If not, the location of tokens in a unique structure, clearly nondomestic, has great implications for explaining their function. It implies that the tokens were used in a communal building of specialized function. In fact, both contexts—public architecture or a special funerary setting—support the hypothesis that accounting served administrative goals and were operated by individuals of the elite.

The Deh Luran region, which never yielded a large variety of tokens, produced an even smaller or no assemblage in the Choga Mami and Sabz periods.[53] This coincided with a change in the local economy with the introduction of the cultivation of six-row hulled barley, free-threshing hexaploid wheat, large seeded lentil, and flax as well as cattle and dog domestication.[54] This in turn is perhaps related to the first use of irrigation for farming, which Frank Hole hypothesized on the basis of the increased size of private landholdings and more intensive agriculture.[55] Reckoning would undoubtedly play a lesser role in a society dominated by large, self-sufficient family units. In such a situation the public control is lessened and exchanges between members of a family take place in face-to-face situations requiring no record keeping.

There is no breakdown per level, unfortunately, for the seventy tokens excavated at Jaffarabad, and, therefore, it is not possible to know whether the development of a pottery workshop had any impact on record keeping.[56] Little is known, also, of the tokens of Chogha Bonut, except that the strata involving industrial installations and kilns included plain spheres and incised cones.[57]

In sum, the Iranian token assemblages of 5500 to 4500 B.C. show the consistent use of the system through the fourth millennium following the advent of agriculture. It is possible that the important economic changes of the time, namely, irrigation and the development of workshops, created regional differences in the need for accounting. For example, tokens perhaps continued to be used for administration at Hajji Firuz and Anau, where subsistence still relied upon dry farming, but decreased in importance with the irrigation and creation of large family landholdings in Deh Luran. Finally, it is logical to assume that specialized workshops could bring new pressures on accounting.

4500–3500 B.C.

Well-documented material from Seh Gabi, Farukhabad, Tal-i-Iblis, and Tepe Yahya indicate that counters continued to exist, with little or no change, during the period immediately preceding state formation. In particular, neither the development of towns nor the introduction of stamp seals in Iran seems to have had any noticeable impact on accounting. The only visible changes in the early fourth millennium B.C. feature the introduction of a new type, biconoids, and the use of paint on counters.

Seh Gabi in the central Zagros produced a good collection of sixty-two tokens from the levels corresponding to the Godin strata VII to X, ca. 4600 to

3500 B.C. (figs. 29.1 and 29.2).[58] The assemblage includes 8 cones, 22 spheres, 19 disks, 2 tetrahedrons, 3 cylinders, 7 ovoids, and 1 hyperboloid, none of which is in any way different from the counters of previous periods.

There is also no apparent difference from that time between tokens from various geographical regions of Iran. For example, Tepe Yahya VI–V,[59] Tal-i-Iblis I,[60] and Tall-i-Bakun[61] in the south produced collections similar to those of Tepe Hissar in the north;[62] Jaffarabad[63] and Susa A in Susiana;[64] and Seh Gabi, Siahbid,[65] Dalma Tepe,[66] and Tepe Giyan in the northwest.[67]

The creation of preurban centers which, according to Henry T. Wright, immediately preceded state formation, did not entail any changes in the token system. For example, Farukhabad, described as the seat of a ranking group, produced only a small collection of plain tokens in the Farukh period.[68] Tokens also are unchanged at Tall-i-Bakun A, where buildings with door sealings suggest a hierarchy in the control of the movement of goods.[69] The same is true in Susiana, where there is no notable difference between the tokens from Susa, an administrative center, and those from subsidiary villages such as Jaffarabad and Tepe Bouhallan.

Presumably, the tokens and seals were closely connected since both were used for controlling goods. This relationship remains elusive, however. There is no apparent distinction, for example, between the token assemblages of sites which produced stamp seals like Tepe Giyan, Tepe Hissar, Tepe Yahya, and Farukhabad[70] and those that did not, such as Seh Gabi, Dalma Tepe, and Siahbid.

The appearance of biconoids at Jaffarabad, Tepe Bouhallan, and Tepe Sabz suggests that the type might be a local development restricted to Susiana.[71] On the other hand, the custom of painting tokens does not seem to be geographically bound since colored tokens occur at Dalma Tepe in the northwest as well as Susa A and Jaffarabad in the southwest.[72]

The context of tokens at the turn of the fourth millennium B.C. remains enigmatic. The cache of thirty-four cones and a sphere at Tepe Gaz Tavila, southern Iran, was located in a storage room.[73] On the other hand, some of the counters of Seh Gabi were, in some cases, scattered among structures, next to a jar, or mixed with the ashes of a hearth, at other times in open areas, and, finally, next to children's funerary urns.[74] In each of these circumstances, however, it cannot be established whether the association was intentional or fortuitous. It is not possible to know, for example, whether the counters were placed in the fire in order to be baked, or, rather, were swept with other trash into the ashes in order to be disposed of. It is also not possible to know whether or not the counter recovered next to the funerary urns was meant as an offering.

It seems significant that the token system remained the same when preurban centers and seals herald socioeconomic changes. Instead, the counters of the late fifth millennium B.C. exhibit a remarkable stability. It is also noteworthy that the slight modifications initiated during the period 4500 to 3500 B.C. proved of no consequence. Painted tokens continued to remain oddities in later times, and while biconoids survived, they never developed into a particularly popular type in the late fourth millennium B.C.

The tokens of Iran present the following evidence. First, once tokens were established in the early eighth millennium B.C. they continued to be used in the region during five millennia, without discontinuity and with no major change. Second, all the Iranian sites of the eighth to fourth millennia B.C. produced tokens, except at Yanik Tepe.[75] Finally, in all instances the counters shared the same types, size, and method of manufacture. It can be concluded, therefore, that the token system in Iran in the eighth to fourth millennia B.C. was independent of geographical area, size of settlement, and technological level of the societies that used them.

Tokens in Iraq

The documentation on tokens from Iraq is sporadic and ranges from excellent to very poor or nonexistent. Most of the excavations took place in times when archaeologists were not aware of the importance of tokens. They appeared as odd, inconspicuous artifacts which, compared to pottery, bore no chronological significance and compared to flint, bone, and organic material brought no information on trade, technology, or socioeconomic developments. Consequently, no one paid special attention to finding them. Furthermore, the counters also lacked the aesthetic appeal of figurines and so were particularly neglected in site reports.

PALEOLITHIC AND MESOLITHIC

None of the Upper Paleolithic sites excavated in Iraq, such as Shanidar, Palegawra, and Zarzi, ca. 10,000

B.C., have produced any clay artifacts and, in particular, any clay tokens. The subsequent Mesolithic period is, unfortunately, poorly known in Iraq. No excavations have been carried out, in particular, in sites of the critical period between 8000 and 7500 B.C., when tokens began to be used for record keeping elsewhere in the Fertile Crescent. The two Iraqi Mesolithic sites excavated, Zawi Chemi Shanidar and Karim Shahir, are dated, respectively, to 8500 and 7500 to 7000 B.C. In other words, either they precede or follow, by some five hundred years, the sites of Ganj Dareh Tepe, Tepe Asiab, Tell Mureybet, and Tell Aswad, which yielded the earliest token assemblages in neighboring Iran and Syria. Zawi Chemi, still following the Upper Paleolithic tradition, had neither tokens nor clay artifacts in its assemblage. Karim Shahir produced two clay figures but, seemingly, no tokens.

Despite the evidence presently available, it is unlikely that Iraq was out of step with its eastern and western neighbors in using tokens for counting goods. It is to be expected that further investigations in sites of the early eighth millennium B.C. will prove instead that tokens were also part of Iraqi assemblages of the late Mesolithic/early Neolithic period.

EARLY NEOLITHIC

The earliest tokens presently recovered in Iraq come from Maghzaliyah and M'lefaat, the latter a site in Kurdistan excavated in 1954 by the University of Chicago Oriental Institute Prehistoric Project, directed by Robert J. Braidwood.[76] The small token assemblage, consisting of a few spheres and cylinders, is unfortunately not well dated as no carbon 14 results are available for the site. According to Braidwood, the site was occupied as early as 7500 to 7000 B.C., but, according to James Mellaart, it was as late as 6700 to 6300 B.C.[77] The Polish excavations at the site of Nemrik near Eskimosul have produced 11 cones, 6 spheres, 48 disks, 1 cylinder, 1 tetrahedron, and 2 ovoids in layers K and KM dating from the eighth and early seventh millennia B.C.[78] Data on the material and its context have not yet been published. Tokens also are part of the assemblage of Tell Maghzaliyah in the Sinjar Hills, an excavation of the Moscow Soviet Academy. The site is dated to the late eighth and early seventh millennia B.C.[79] Consequently, the earliest tokens of Iraq have a time discrepancy with those of Iran and Syria presently estimated to between 500 to 1,300 years. Whatever the situation may be, it is noteworthy that the setting of M'lefaat replicates exactly that in which tokens appeared elsewhere. Like its counterparts in Iran (Ganj Dareh Tepe and Tepe Asiab) and in Syria (Mureybet and Tell Aswad), M'lefaat was a small compound of round/ovoid pit dwellings exhibiting some degree of permanence in occupation. M'lefaat also shared with Ganj Dareh Tepe, Tepe Asiab, Mureybet, and Tell Aswad an economy based upon grain consumption (agriculture?) while providing no evidence for herding or animal domestication. Maghzaliyah, on the other hand, was a fortified settlement showing considerably more importance and sophistication.

JARMO

With its impressive collection of some two thousand tokens, Jarmo is presently the token capital of the world. The assemblage includes 1,246 spheres, 86 hemispheres, 28 three-quarter spheres, 206 disks, 140 cones, 20 tetrahedrons, 5 ovoids, 250 cylinders, and 1 hyperboloid (fig. 5). Forty spheres and 16 hemispheres bear incised lines, including short strokes and spirals.[80]

According to Braidwood, tokens were present throughout the occupation of Jarmo,[81] which he estimates between 7000 and 6300 B.C. (compared to Mellaar's date of 6400 to 5400 B.C.).[82] A precise chronological distribution of the tokens is not available since the grid excavation technique experimented with at Jarmo made it difficult to deal with relative stratigraphy. Vivian L. Broman noted only that cones seemed more frequent in the lower levels while tetrahedrons belonged mostly to the upper levels.[83] Accordingly, she suggested a possible relationship between the decline of the former and the appearance of the latter. In the light of our present knowledge of the evolution of the token system, the rarity of cones in the upper levels of Jarmo appears accidental. Cones and tetrahedrons are present without discontinuity in archaeological assemblages of Iran and Syria from the beginning of the eighth millennium to the end of the fourth millennium B.C. The cones and tetrahedrons cannot be interpreted, therefore, as representing two stages of the evolution of a single artifact. Instead, they were two distinct counters, the cone, which probably stood for a small unit of grain, and the tetrahedron, which may have represented a unit of work.

Jarmo was no more and no less than an average farming community of the northern Mesopotamian uplands in the seventh to sixth millennia B.C. As discussed above, its token collection should be considered, therefore, as an average token Neolithic assemblage. The gross disproportion between the Jarmo collection and that of contemporary sites suggests only the considerable quantities of tokens which passed unnoticed elsewhere and at best remained unreported or at worst ended up on excavation dumps. It is puzzling, however, that Umm Dabaghiyah, a site overlapping with Jarmo about 5900 to 5600 B.C. that has been carefully excavated, seemingly did not produce a comparable token assemblage. We know that it yielded "pierced disks" and "sling missiles" but are yet unaware whether or not these included tokens.[84]

HASSUNA

During the Hassuna culture, which developed about 5700 to 5000 B.C., some tokens started being manufactured in stone. It is difficult to understand why people would switch to stone, which required a time-consuming process as well as special craftsmanship skills, when the objects could be modeled in clay so easily. Perhaps it was an aesthetic concern, since the stones usually selected to make the counters were colorful and could receive an attractive polish (marble, for example) or perhaps it was a preoccupation with hardness and durability. It could also be postulated that the stone tokens had an altogether different function. They could presage, for instance, the distinction between the clay and stone tablets of the Uruk–Jemdet Nasr period, the former being used for economic records and the latter for land deeds. Accordingly, it could be postulated that the stone counters represented land units, whereas the clay counters stood for grain measures. This in turn could have been prompted by the fact that units of area were calculated in terms of the quantity of seeds necessary for planting and therefore may have been expressed with signs similar to those standing for grain measures, thus necessitating a distinction. This explanation could be supported by the fact that stone tokens are mostly restricted to cones, spheres, and disks, although there are also instances of stone ovoids. Whatever the function of the Hassuna stone tokens may be, they started a new tradition which was to coexist with the usual clay tokens from this time forth to the third millennium B.C. Because of their usual careful craftsmanship and their aesthetic quality, archaeologists have given attention to the stone tokens more readily than to their more modest clay counterparts. As a result we often have more information on the probably rarer and more unusual stone specimens than on the more common and more numerous clay tokens. This is the case for the type site of Tell Hassuna, where the report gives no information on the "pellets . . . found in considerable quantities in every level of the main sounding at Hasuna" but provides illustrations on two stone spheres.[85] What is even more distressing is that the Iraq Museum in Baghdad contains the two stone spheres in its collections (cat. nos. 2 and 3) but only one clay cone (cat. no. 1) from Tell Hassuna, suggesting that the "pellets" were discarded during or after the excavations.

Most reports dealing with sites of the Hassuna period suggest a wealth of unpublished clay artifacts that, with little doubt, included tokens. For example, there are such tantalizing statements concerning, alternatively, the assemblages of Yarim Tepe and Telul eth Thalathat: "There was a considerable quantity of . . . clay implements" and "sling balls are found in quantity."[86] Twenty-one cones, 10 spheres, 5 disks, 2 cylinders, and 1 token in the shape of a vessel were located at Yarim Tepe, among which 1 cone and 1 sphere are made of stone (cat. nos. 18 and 40). These artifacts constitute the presently available evidence for the continuation of the use of clay tokens into the Hassuna period with the addition of one cone cited by Mallowan in Nineveh I and some additional material from the excavations of the Oriental Institute Prehistoric Project.[87] For example, the test trench excavated by Braidwood and Broman at Gird Ali Agha produced one sphere, one cone, and several fragments of cylinders, and finally, "odd disks" were recovered at the site of Matarrah.[88]

SAMARRA

There is evidence for tokens being included among burial goods in the Samarra culture, located to the south of the Hassuna culture and partly overlapping with it in time. This occurs, for example, in 3 of the 130 graves of Tell es-Sawwan level I, ca. 5600 to 5500 B.C. In these instances, individuals, including infants, were furnished with spheres and cones of black, white, and grey stone.[89] These tokens might be interpreted as symbolic offerings of quantities of goods to the dead and may provide yet another plausible explanation for the choice of stone for the manufacture of certain tokens. They could suggest, for example, that these tokens needed to be made of a hard material since the symbolic foods were meant to last for eternity. However, on the one hand, clay tokens were also used as funerary deposits,[90] and on the other hand, stone tokens equally occurred in living quarters. For example, a stone sphere was reported in a storage area, and a group of tokens, including alabaster ovoids, cones of white and grey stone, and clay cylinders, lay on a house floor.[91]

No tokens are reported at Tell Shemshara, but there are some thirteen from Choga Mami stored at the Oriental Institute of the University of Chicago. These objects, attributed to the Samarra period, probably correspond to the following description in the report: "number of extremely attractive stone objects . . . including carefully polished 'gaming pieces,' one 'marble,'" "cone-like figures," and "unusual clay objects of unknown function."[92]

HALAF AND UBAID

Mallowan commented that cones and spheres were common at Arpachiyah in both the Halaf and Ubaid levels.[93] Only ninety-three of these tokens have made their way to either the Iraq Museum in Baghdad or the British Museum in London, representing presumably only a fraction of the actual finds. In the light of new excavations at the site, the Halaf assemblage, formerly dated by Mellaart to 5600 to 4500 B.C., is now estimated to start as late as 5200 B.C., whereas the Ubaid occupation was a short interval about 4200 to 4100 B.C.[94] What seems important about the Arpachiyah collection of clay counters is a sizable increase in types and subtypes which presages the assemblages of complex tokens of the late fourth millennium B.C. There are as many as ten types of tokens at Arpachiyah, including cones, spheres, disks, cylinders, tetrahedrons, ovoids, rectangles, vessels, tools, animals, and miscellaneous. Subtypes also proliferate either by slight variations in the shapes or by the addition of markings. For example, there are nine different subtypes of cones, including isosceles, large, long, equilateral, and truncated examples, whereas others are punched, painted, or bear appliqué coils and pellets. Cylinders, quadrangles, vessels, animals, and a sphere also bear various incised or punched markings. The multiplication of types and subtypes at Arpachiyah is significant in three ways. First, it is a unique phenomenon in the Halaf and Ubaid periods. There is apparently nothing equivalent at contemporaneous Halafian sites such as Yarim Tepe II and Tell Songor, where few or no tokens at all have been reported, and at Tell Banahilk, where only disks seem to occur.[95] Second, Arpachiyah has also produced an unusual collection of stamp seals and sealings. In particular, the sealings of Arpachiyah provide the first evidence for the presence of two different seals on one sealing. Consequently, the multiplication of token shapes coincides with other signs of an escalation in bureaucracy at the site.[96] Third, most of the new shapes such as the pronged tool, the vessels, and the animal legs do not seem to be kept in later times. Truncated cones (type 1: 12) and the animal shapes (type 15: 19 and 20) constitute, however, interesting prototypes for fourth millennium tokens.

The varied token assemblage of Arpachiyah is also unmatched at the neighboring sites such as Tepe Gawra, where only plain cones, tetrahedrons, disks, and ovoids occur in levels XIX–XIII, ca. 4300 to 3500 B.C.[97] Plain tokens also constitute the bulk of the Ubaid assemblages of the sites of the Hamrin Basin such as Tell Abada[98] or Tell Oueili.[99] Only the transition layer between the Ubaid and Uruk periods of Telul eth Thalathat yields cylinders and rectangles bearing incised markings, which will be discussed later.

Tokens continue to be used in burials both at Arpachiyah and at Tepe Gawra, but the practice is not known in the south.[100] Of course, little is known of the Persian Gulf area, where the water table makes prehistoric strata inaccessible. Ras al Amiya is one of the few prehistoric southern settlements providing a good assemblage of disks and cones dated to about 4300 B.C.[101] Eridu, which offers the earliest sequence of shrines, could be expected to have produced particularly interesting administrative material, but it is apparently not so. The site report does not indicate any finds of seals, sealings, or tokens,[102] and neither the British Museum nor the Iraq National Museum offer more than a banal collection of a few spheres, disks, and a tetrahedron which cannot be dated.

THE GAWRA PERIOD

The token assemblages of northern Mesopotamia are different from those of the south in the fourth millennium B.C. The dichotomy consists of the appearance of new shapes and markings in the southern Sumerian cities, whereas the northern collections remain primarily unchanged (fig. 30).

Some 120 tokens originating from levels XII–IX of Tepe Gawra are discussed by Arthur J. Tobler in the site report. On the one hand, the collection is characteristic of the northern Mesopotamian Gawra period of 3500 to 3100 B.C. in consisting of only the most common token types, including cones, spheres, disks, tetrahedrons, cylinders, and rectangles, usually plain-faced.[103] On the other hand, it is singular in yielding mostly stone artifacts. The report itemizes about one hundred stone tokens against seventeen made of clay.[104] The assemblage of Tepe Gawra in northern Mesopotamia is therefore different from that of Uruk in the south, which produced only fifteen stone specimens in a collection of about eight hundred tokens. The large proportion of stone tokens at Tepe Gawra can be explained in two different ways. First, the custom of including stone counters in burials, which accounts for fifty-seven of the stone tokens, may have been more frequent in the north.[105] Second, the stone specimens were included in the report while those made of clay were not. This second alternative seems the most plausible, since 250 unpublished clay tokens from Tepe Gawra are stored at the Iraq National Museum in Baghdad and 80 at the University Museum, University of Pennsylvania.

The assemblages of other northern sites such as Telul eth Thalathat, Tell Billa, Nineveh, and Nuzi are generally small and, like that of Tepe Gawra, are mostly composed of plain specimens. Telul eth Thalathat, for example, has only two tokens bearing incised markings out of a collection of eleven specimens.[106] It is noteworthy that the north has not produced any triangles, paraboloids, animal heads, or bent coils characteristic of late fourth-millennium sites in the south, such as Uruk and Tello. In particular, the northern sites did not produce any token series. Furthermore, only a few of the tokens bearing markings have direct parallels with complex tokens of the south.[107] Otherwise, the incised disks and cylinders at these different sites have seemingly no tie to the southern assemblages and can perhaps be considered, therefore, as regional developments.

Two important facts emerge from the Iraqi data. First, the use of tokens in northern Mesopotamia is continuous from the late eighth to the Gawra period in the late fourth millennium B.C. Second, the material is fully homogeneous with that of Iran. In both regions, tokens are made in the same way, of the same material, in the same types and subtypes. They occur in similar settings, either domestic or funerary. The evolution of the system is also synchronic; for example, stone tokens occur in the same time range in the two regions and the use of the counters as funerary offerings appears in comparable periods. The token system of southern Mesopotamia, however, becomes differentiated in the fourth millennium B.C., when it started producing complex tokens.

3
COMPLEX TOKENS

Schliesslich mögen zur Belebung unserer IV. Schicht noch sonderbare kleine Gegenstände aus Ton erwähnt . . . werden, die ich für Nachbildungen verschiedenster Gegenstände des täglichen Lebens halte . . . Sie mögen im Tempelkult verwandt worden sein, von dem wir ja noch keine rechte Vorstellung haben.
—Julius Jordan[1]

AFTER 4000 YEARS characterized by a remarkable continuity, a major change occurred in the token system in the fourth millennium B.C. "Complex tokens" in new shapes and bearing typical markings were introduced in several administrative centers. The Uruk, Susa, and Habuba Kabira complex token assemblages are the largest fourth-millennium collections and document best the diversity, size, chronology, context, and geographic distribution of the complex tokens.

Uruk

The site of Uruk has produced eight hundred tokens. The study of the collection is important for several reasons. First, Uruk was the first and foremost Sumerian city and is, therefore, one of the most significant southern Mesopotamian sites in the fourth millennium B.C. Second, Uruk yields the largest and most varied collection of complex tokens ever recovered in a fourth-millennium site. Third, one of the deep soundings in Eanna, the sanctuary of the goddess Inanna at Uruk, offers a reliable stratigraphy for a period of one thousand years, from the late Ubaid period, ca. 4500 B.C., to the late Uruk period, ca. 3500 B.C. This unique sequence provides a chronological framework for the phenomenon of complex tokens. Fourth, the parallelism between the development of complex tokens and that of Eanna is a key to understanding the changes in a method of reckoning.

SOURCES

The discussion on the Uruk tokens in this chapter is based on a collection of 778 specimens. In fact, after the completion of the study, I was still able to identify 34 more specimens, bringing the present final count to 812. The tokens from Uruk were recovered in the course of thirty-six out of the thirty-eight campaigns carried out at the site between 1928 and 1985. The collection is divided between the Vorderasiatischen Museum in Berlin, the Iraq National Museum in Baghdad, and the Seminar für Kulturen und Sprachen des Vorderen Orients at the University of Heidelberg. The excavations at Uruk have been performed with high scientific standards, which explains why the artifacts are reported with consistency throughout the field registers. The excavation field records constitute the main source of information on the collection, although, as presented below, excavators such as Jordan, Lenzen, and Boehmer have systematically included them in the published reports.

When W. K. Loftus laid the first trenches in Eanna in the middle of the nineteenth century, he could well have encountered some of the counters when he excavated the spectacular cone mosaic court, but at the time archaeology was not concerned with such inconspicuous artifacts. It is not surprising, therefore, that there is no mention of tokens in the accounts of his findings in his *Travels and Researches in Chaldea and Susiana*.[2]

Julius Jordan collected the first harvest of tokens during the first scientific expedition conducted at Warka, the campaign of November 1928 to March 1929. The fifty-six specimens, which are not mentioned in the report, can be identified by their field numbers.[3] He first reported tokens in the second preliminary report after a large number of the artifacts were found in the deep sounding (*Tiefschnitt*) below the Limestone Temple.[4] The diary of the second campaign at Warka, which took place from October 1929 to March 1930, describes the events as follows: December 4, 1930, "In Tiefschnitt befindet sich etwa 1,95m unter Oberkante Steinsockel V ein Stiftlager"; December 5, "In diesem Stiftlager stecken viele kleine Ton-Nachbildungen. z.b. Dattelkerne, Bröte, Tetraeder, Kegel, Kügelchen"; December 6, "Im Tiefschnitt die Stiftschicht ist sehr ausgebreitet. Dicke und dünne kleine Tonkegel . . . darin weitere Tonnachbildungen."[5] Jordan, who referred to the artifacts in the report as "curious little objects" ("sonderbare kleine Gegenstände"), outlined in this report, with extraordinary insight, all the important features concerning tokens: The objects are of small size and are made of clay; some are perforated and could be threaded; they represented commodities of daily life and probably belonged to a cult practice; they were used in a wide area of the Near East, including Mesopotamia and Elam; similar objects were enclosed in clay envelopes.

The largest number of tokens was collected by Jordan in the third campaign of November 1930 to March 1931, most of them also originating in the deep sounding below the Limestone Temple. The field register entries concerning the artifacts are not as precise as one would wish them to be. They read, for example, "Tonabbildungen (Kugeln, Pyramiden, Kegel, Dattelkerne, u.a.)," with no indication of the exact number of artifacts in each category.[6] Nevertheless, 235 counters can be securely attributed to this season of excavation, with some 160 from the deep sounding.

It is puzzling that, when Arnold Nöldeke succeeded Jordan in the leadership of the Uruk expeditions, tokens became rare. Very few bear field numbers corresponding to the campaigns he directed. Nine specimens can be identified as belonging to the fourth expedition of 1931–32.[7] For the remaining seasons, the count is as follows: fifth, 14; sixth, 1; seventh, 16; eighth, 17; ninth, 6; tenth, 4; eleventh, 2; twelfth, 2; thirteenth, 3; and fourteenth, 12.[8] None of these artifacts are ever mentioned in the excavation reports.

Tokens reappeared in the literature as soon as Heinrich J. Lenzen assumed the directorship of the excavations starting in the fall of 1956. From there on, tokens trickle into the yearly reports under headings such as "amulets" ("amulettartige Gegenstände") or "small clay objects" ("kleine Tongegenstände"). The number of tokens which can be identified for each season is as follows: fifteenth, 8;[9] sixteenth, 12;[10] seventeenth, 26;[11] eighteenth, 2; nineteenth, 7; twentieth, 2;[12] twenty-first, 77 as well as 25 envelopes holding tokens:[13] twenty-second, 6;[14] twenty-third, 9;[15] twenty-fourth, 3;[16] twenty-fifth, 87.[17] This was the last campaign conducted by Lenzen, after which, once again, tokens vanished for a decade from the reports.

Only a few tokens came to light between 1968 to 1977, when the Uruk excavations were directed by Jürgen Schmidt. Only one counter can be attributed to the twenty-sixth season; eight to the twenty-seventh; none to the twenth-eighth and twenty-ninth; one to the thirtieth; three to the thirty-first; five to the thirty-second; nine to the thirty-third; and three to the thirty-fourth.[18]

When, after a five-year interruption, work resumed at Warka in 1982 under the leadership of Rainer M. Boehmer, the extensive three-year survey of the ancient city of Uruk included two tokens from the thirty-fifth campaign,[19] eight from the thirty-sixth; and ten from the thirty-seventh. The objects are reported in *Baghdader Mitteilungen,* when, for the first time, they are identified as *Symbolsteinen.*[20] None were recovered in the thirty-eighth season.

ASSEMBLAGE

The Uruk collection, which yields sixteen types of tokens, is more diversified than those of earlier Iraqi sites. It includes, in particular, new "complex types"—geometric and naturalistic shapes such as paraboloids, bent coils, rhomboids (types 10–12), miniature tools (type 14), and humans (type 16: 2) that never occurred in prehistoric sites such as Jarmo, Ras al Amiya, or Tell Abada. The assemblage also consists of a record number of 241 subtypes that illustrate new patterns of linear, punched, pinched, notched, and appliqué markings. It should be well understood, however, that plain tokens continued to exist unchanged at Uruk throughout the fourth millennium B.C. The complex tokens were thus in no way supplanting the plain ones but rather complementing them.

31.1. Cones, Uruk, Iraq. Courtesy Deutsches Archaeologisches Institut, Abteilung Baghdad.

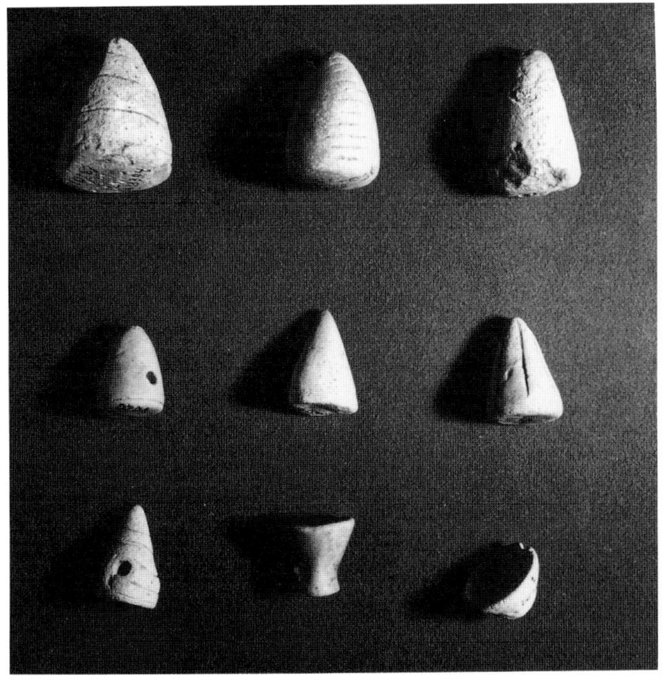

31.2. Cones, Uruk, Iraq. Courtesy Vorderasiatisches Museum, Staatliche Museen zu Berlin.

31.3. Spheres, Uruk, Iraq. Courtesy Deutsches Archaeologisches Institut, Abteilung Baghdad.

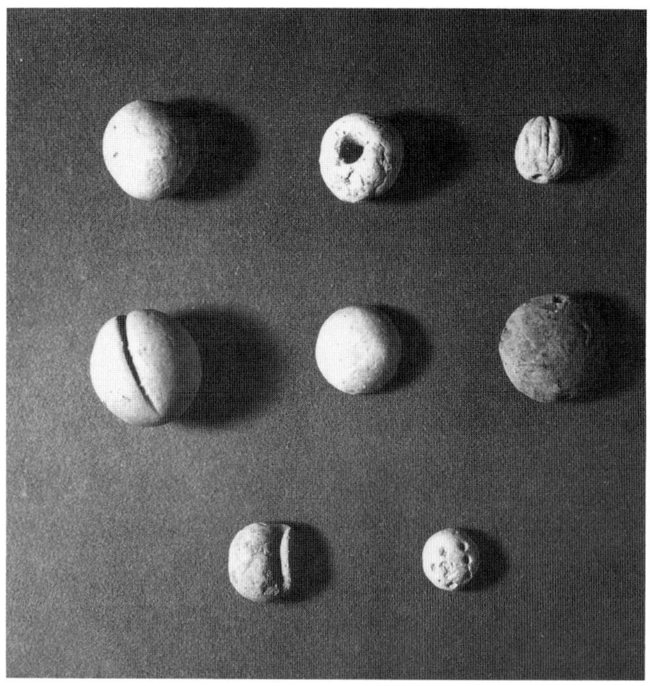

31.4. Spheres, Uruk, Iraq. Courtesy Vorderasiatisches Museum, Staatliche Museen zu Berlin.

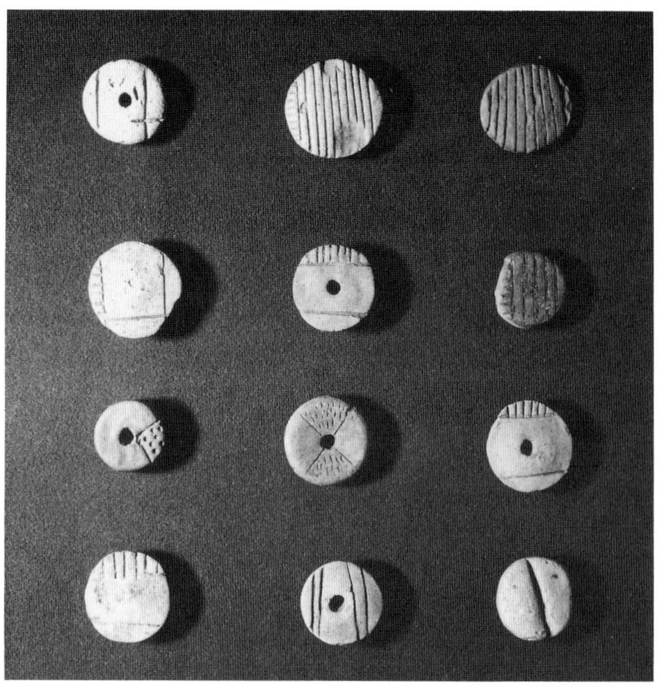

31.6. Disks, Uruk, Iraq. Courtesy Vorderasiatisches Museum, Staatliche Museen zu Berlin.

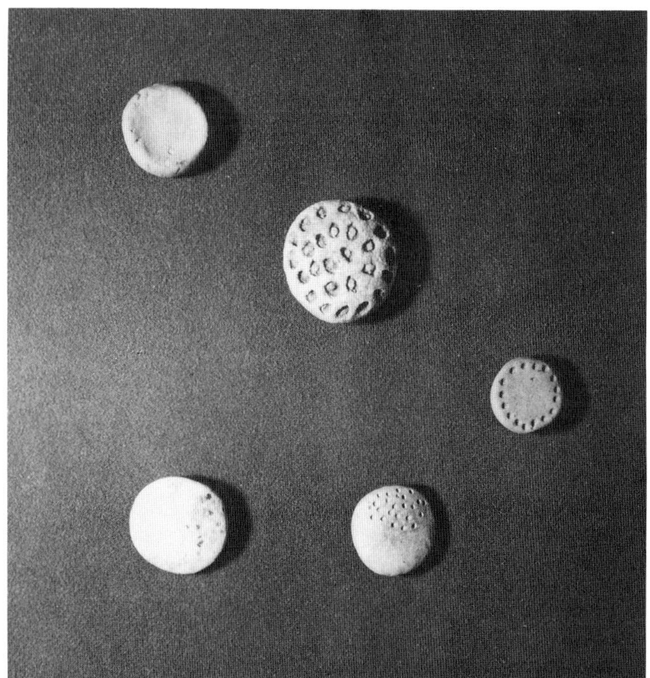

31.5. Disks, Uruk, Iraq. Courtesy Vorderasiatisches Museum, Staatliche Museen zu Berlin.

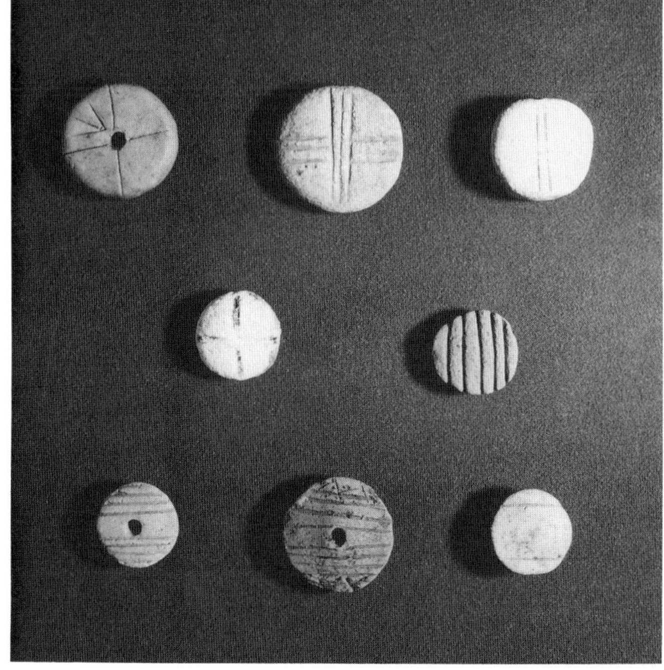

31.7. Disks, Uruk, Iraq. Courtesy Vorderasiatisches Museum, Staatliche Museen zu Berlin.

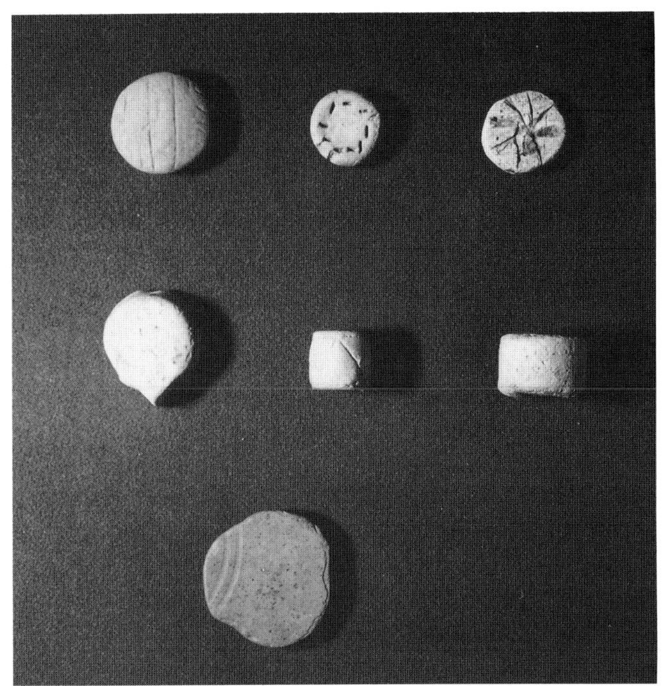

31.8. Disks, Uruk, Iraq. Courtesy Vorderasiatisches Museum, Staatliche Museen zu Berlin.

31.10. Tetrahedrons, Uruk, Iraq. Courtesy Vorderasiatisches Museum, Staatliche Museen zu Berlin.

31.9. Cylinders, Uruk, Iraq. Courtesy Vorderasiatisches Museum, Staatliche Museen zu Berlin.

31.11. Ovoids, Uruk, Iraq. Courtesy Deutsches Archaeologisches Institut, Abteilung Baghdad.

31.12. Ovoids, Uruk, Iraq. Courtesy Vorderasiatisches Museum, Staatliche Museen zu Berlin.

31.15. Rectangles, Uruk, Iraq. Courtesy Vorderasiatisches Museum, Staatliche Museen zu Berlin.

31.13. Rectangles, Uruk, Iraq. Courtesy Vorderasiatisches Museum, Staatliche Museen zu Berlin.

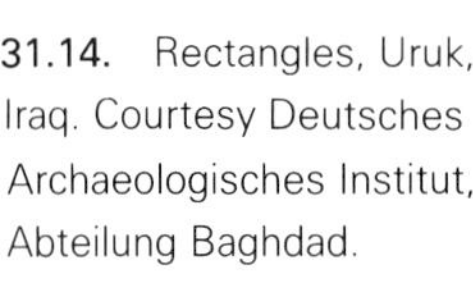

31.14. Rectangles, Uruk, Iraq. Courtesy Deutsches Archaeologisches Institut, Abteilung Baghdad.

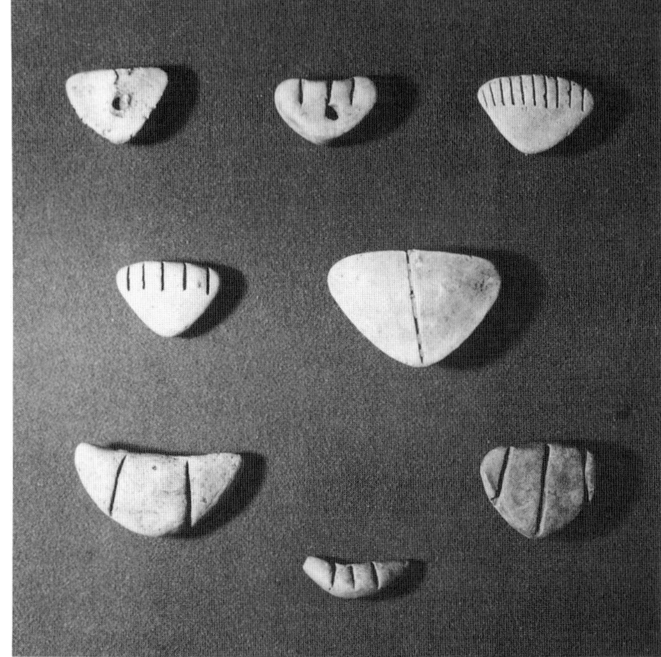

31.16. Triangles, Uruk, Iraq. Courtesy Vorderasiatisches Museum, Staatliche Museen zu Berlin.

31.17. Triangles, Uruk, Iraq. Courtesy Deutsches Archaeologisches Institut, Abteilung Baghdad.

31.18. Triangles, Uruk, Iraq. Courtesy Vorderasiatisches Museum, Staatliche Museen zu Berlin.

31.19. Triangles, Uruk, Iraq. Courtesy Vorderasiatisches Museum, Staatliche, Museen zu Berlin.

31.20. Biconoids, Uruk, Iraq. Courtesy Vorderasiatisches Museum, Staatliche Museen zu Berlin.

31.21. Paraboloids, Uruk, Iraq. Courtesy Vorderasiatisches Museum, Staatliche Museen zu Berlin.

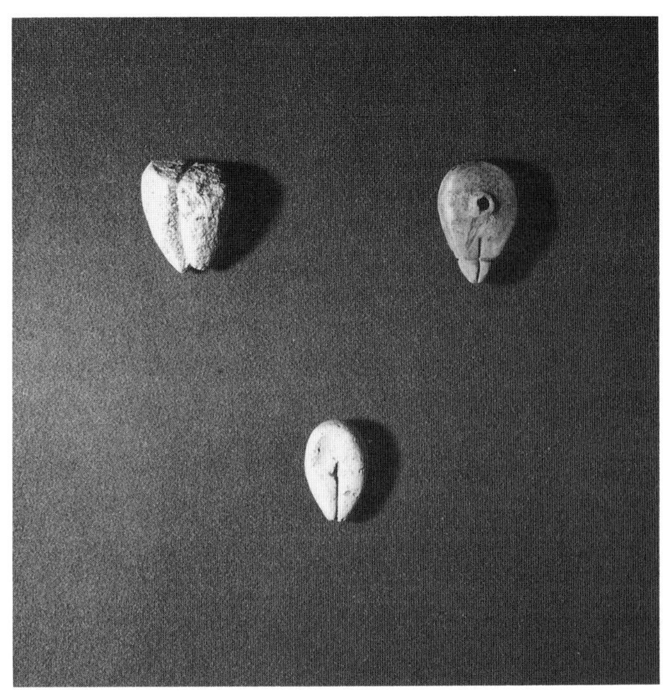

31.23. Bent coils, Uruk, Iraq. Courtesy Vorderasiatisches Museum, Staatliche Museen zu Berlin.

31.22. Paraboloids, Uruk, Iraq. Courtesy Deutsches Archaeologisches Institut, Abteilung Baghdad.

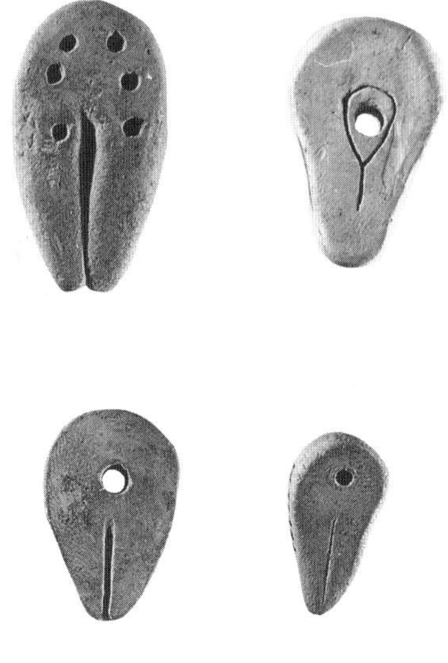

31.24. Bent coils, Uruk, Iraq. Courtesy Deutsches Archaeologisches Institut, Abteilung Baghdad.

31.25. Ovals, rhomboids, tools, and miscellaneous shapes, Uruk, Iraq. Courtesy Vorderasiatisches Museum, Staatliche Museen zu Berlin.

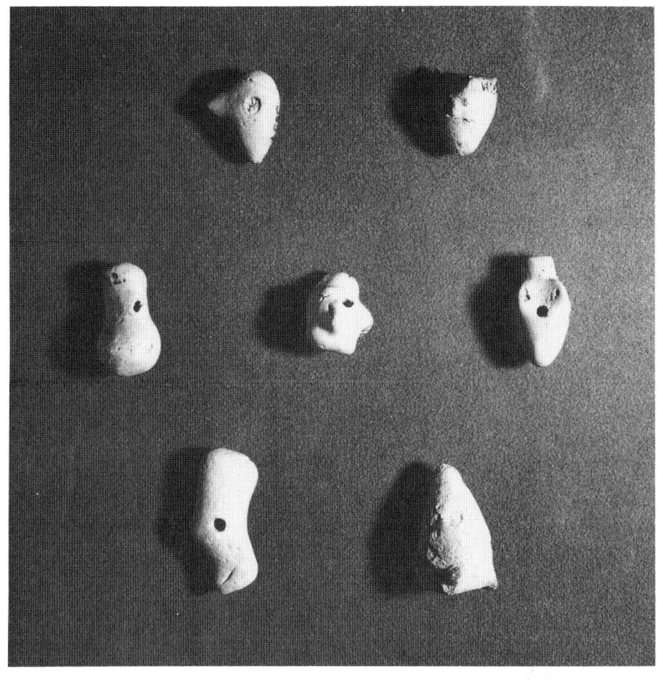

31.27. Vessels and animals, Uruk, Iraq. Courtesy Vorderasiatisches Museum, Staatliche Museen zu Berlin.

31.26. Vessels, Uruk, Iraq. Courtesy Deutsches Archaeologisches Institut, Abteilung Baghdad.

31.28. Animals, Uruk, Iraq. Courtesy Vorderasiatisches Museum, Staatliche Museen zu Berlin.

31.29. Cylinder, tetrahedron, rectangle, biconoid, tools, and ring, Uruk, Iraq. Courtesy Deutsches Archaeologisches Institut, Abteilung Baghdad.

The composition of the Uruk token assemblage is as follows: type 1 (cones; figs. 31.1 and 31.2): 43 specimens representing 5.5 percent of the total number of tokens at the site; type 2 (spheres; figs. 31.3 and 31.4): 206, 26.6 percent; type 3 (disks; figs. 31.5–31.8): 132, 17 percent; type 4 (cylinders; figs. 31.9 and 31.29): 68, 8.7 percent; type 5 (tetrahedrons; figs. 31.10 and 31.29): 39, 5 percent; type 6 (ovoids; figs. 31.11 and 31.12): 56, 7.2 percent; type 7 (quadrangles; figs. 31.13–31.15 and 31.29): 18, 2.3 percent; type 8 (triangles; figs. 31.16–31.19): 72, 9.1 percent; type 9 (biconoids; figs. 31.20 and 31.29): 16, 2 percent; type 10 (paraboloids; figs. 31.21 and 31.22): 42, 5.5 percent; type 11 (bent coils; figs. 31.23 and 31.24): 24, 3 percent; type 12 (ovals/rhomboids; fig. 31.25): 15, 1.5 percent; type 13 (vessels; figs. 31.26 and 31.27): 18, 2.3 percent; type 14 (tools; fig. 31.29): 13, 1.6 percent; type 15 (animals; figs. 31.27 and 31.28): 14, 1.8 percent; type 16 (miscellaneous; fig. 31.29): 4, 0.5 percent. Among the Uruk tokens, 344 are plain, including 25 cones, 185 spheres, 50 disks, 53 cylinders, and 31 tetrahedrons.[21] The remaining 434 tokens are complex.

The collection of tokens from Uruk shows an unprecedented use of markings such as lines and short strokes or punctations made either with a needle, a blunt stylus, or a straw. It yields as many as 241 subtypes, divided among the main types as follows: type 1 (cones): 15; type 2 (spheres): 13; type 3 (disks): 53; type 4 (cylinders): 15; type 5 (tetrahedrons): 8; type 6 (ovoids): 18; type 7 (rectangles): 14; type 8 (triangles): 22; type 9 (biconoids): 11; type 10 (paraboloids): 20; type 11 (bent coils): 5; type 12 (ovals/rhomboids): 4; type 13 (vessels): 14; type 14 (tools): 5; type 15 (animals): 13; and type 16 (miscellaneous): 4.

The complex tokens from Uruk form interesting series, especially among disks. There are, for example, disks showing 1, 5, 8, or 10 lines[22] or parallel groups of lines such as 1-1, 2-1, 2-2, and 4-4 (figs. 31.6–31.8).[23] The most striking series of disks involves lines and strokes in the following composition: 2-1, 2-5, 2-6, 2-7, 2-8, 3-7, 5-6, 5-7, 10-9, and 1-4-4 (fig. 31.6).[24] The disks with an incised cross, common in several sites, have also several unique variations in Uruk.[25] These consist of the addition of dots or a herringbone pattern (figs. 31.6 and 31.7), the doubling and tripling of the lines (fig. 31.7), or the filling of one or two quarters with fine pitting (fig. 31.6).[26]

Uruk has further series among ovoids, triangles, biconoids, and paraboloids. There are ovoids with 2 and 4 vertical lines (fig. 31.12)[27] and others with a horizontal line plus 4 vertical lines, a cross, or a dot (fig. 31.11).[28] Uruk has produced one of the largest series of triangles, with specimens showing either strokes along the long side (fig. 31.16)[29] or lines across the face (figs. 31.16–31.18). Triangular tokens appear in various sites bearing 1, 2, 3, 5, 8, or 10 lines, but at Uruk alone there are also examples with 6 and 7 lines.[30] Among the biconoids, some have a circular line at the thickest diameter and others have additional patterns of lines and punctations (fig. 31.20).[31] Examples of paraboloids with 3, 5, and 8 to 10 strokes also occur at Uruk[32] as well as some involving a circular line and 1, 3, or 8 lines (figs. 31.21 and 31.22).[33] Uruk, however, does not have any tokens belonging to series of rectangles with various numbers of strokes represented elsewhere.

One hundred nineteen tokens from Uruk are perforated, representing 14.7 percent of the collection. All types of tokens have perforated examples but in different proportions; for example, only 3 percent of the cylinders have a suspension hole compared to 61 percent of the tools.[34]

The 812 tokens from Uruk are made of clay except for 11 specimens made of stone[35] and 4 of bitumen.[36] The color of the clay counters is predominantly reddish-buff, with some greenish and blackish examples. The clay used for their manufacture was fine and usually did not include impurities. The objects were carefully crafted and fired.

As will be discussed at length in the next chapter devoted to the storage of tokens, a number of tokens were recovered enclosed in envelopes.[37] The total number and the types and subtypes of these specimens are not known because some of the envelopes are still intact and perfectly sealed and the counters included are, therefore, not visible. Eighty-three counters, however, were associated with envelopes found damaged. The list of these artifacts and their token contents: W 20987.3, which held 1 sphere, 1 flat disk, and 1 rectangle; 20987.7, 7 incised ovoids; 20987.8, 2 flat disks and 5 tetrahedrons; 20987.15, 4 spheres, 1 flat disk; 20987.17, 3 spheres, 1 flat disk, 2 lenticular disks, 1 cylinder, 1 small tetrahedron, and 1 large tetrahedron.[38] Finally, a group of 52 tokens was connected with the remains of crushed cases.[39] The assemblage of 83 tokens held in envelopes at Uruk features both plain and complex counters, including spheres and tetrahedrons in two distinct sizes, disks, cylinders, a rectangle, plain and incised ovoids, triangles, paraboloids, and, finally, trussed ducks, one of which bears incised markings. As the artifacts were meant to be held together in a case rather than strung, none is provided with a perforation.

With its 812 tokens, Uruk has the largest fourth-millennium collection. Susa follows closely with 783 counters and Habuba Kabira–Tell Kannas with 199. More importantly, the assemblage of Uruk has the most diversified complex token collection. There are 241 subtypes at Uruk compared to 190 at Susa and 62 at Habuba Kabira–Tell Kannas. The tokens from Uruk are similar in material, shape, size, and manufacture to those of other contemporaneous sites such as Tello, Susa, and Habuba Kabira and to earlier Iraqi sites such as Jarmo and Tell Abada. The collection is different, however, from the earlier assemblages; namely, it yields a far greater diversity of shapes and markings and includes token series and perforated counters.

EANNA

There are several landmarks in the evolution of Eanna during pre- and protohistory which are important to keep in mind in the course of this study. Founded in the late Ubaid period, about 4500 to 4200 B.C. (levels XVIII–XVI),[40] Eanna remained, probably, a modest shrine during the Proto and Early Uruk periods (levels XVI–X). The first signs of its transformation into a prestigious temple occurred in the Middle Uruk period, in levels IX–VI, ca. 3800 to 3500 B.C., with the appearance of monumental architecture decorated with clay cone mosaics. The intense artistic activity and unprecedented prosperity which characterize the Middle Uruk period continued in the Late Uruk period, represented by levels V–IV, ca. 3500 to 3100 B.C. This creativity is expressed, in particular, by the extensive architectural program which produced the Stone Cone Temple in level VI; the Limestone Temple in level V; the complex of Buildings F, G, H in level IVb; and, finally, Temples C and D and the Hallenbau in level IVb–a, to name only a few of the most splendid buildings.[41] These monuments formed a homogeneous architectural ensemble sharing the same orientation, similar plans consisting mostly of a large central hall surrounded by smaller rooms, identical building techniques involving *Riemchen* mud bricks with a characteristic square section, and a similar style of decoration, including cone mosaics and buttressed facades.[42]

The period of floruit of Eanna in levels VI–IV is not only characterized by monumental architecture decorated with cone mosaics and niches but also by a typical pottery assemblage, glyptics, and writing. Among the vessels, four lugged jars with incised motifs are most characteristic as well as beveled-rim bowls, the latter being recovered by the hundreds. Cylinder seals are one of the most outstanding contributions of Eanna during this period. The glyptic motifs sometimes feature the most important individual at the sanctuary, the priest king or En, wearing a recognizable headdress and a unique type of garment in a netlike textile. Finally, in level IV of Eanna begins the technique of keeping records by writing with a reed stylus on clay tablets.

Apparently, the growth of Eanna did not proceed without upheavals. There is evidence, in fact, for two far-reaching reorganization phases. The first occurred at the end of period IVb, when the central part of Eanna, with the exception of Temple C, was completely remodeled. At that time Building E, referred to as the "Palace," and Temples B and F were dismantled in an orderly manner to be replaced by a bathhouse, the Hallenbau, Temple D, and the Great Court.[43] The process of dismantling consisted of tearing down the walls of each structure to the height of two or three layers of bricks and using the debris to level the space for new foundations to be laid. The new buildings were still made of *Riemchen*, and the Pillar Hall, the Great Court, and, probably, the Hallenbau were still decorated with cone mosaics. Throughout this period, the assemblage of pottery remained unchanged, and glyptics, among many patterns, continued to portray the En.

The second reorganization phase, perhaps prompted by an internal struggle for power, took place at the end of period IVa.[44] It resulted in the complete destruction of Eanna, this time using violence.[45] When order was reestablished in level III, ca. 3000 B.C., possibly under a new political faction, the previous style of building with a central hall was discontinued. Instead, work started on a ziggurat, or temple on a monumental terrace.[46] At that time, the beveled-rim bowls were supplanted by a new type called *Blumentopf,* and the En disappeared forever from glyptics. Level IVa of Eanna marks, therefore, the end of a brilliant era at Eanna and level III is the beginning of another.

DISTRIBUTION

Tokens were spotted all over the mound of Warka and even beyond the city walls.[47] The bulk of the artifacts, however, comes from the precinct of Eanna. On the one hand, it should be kept in mind that the temple of Inanna was where most excavations were conducted and therefore the information at hand may present a distorted picture. On the other hand, it is

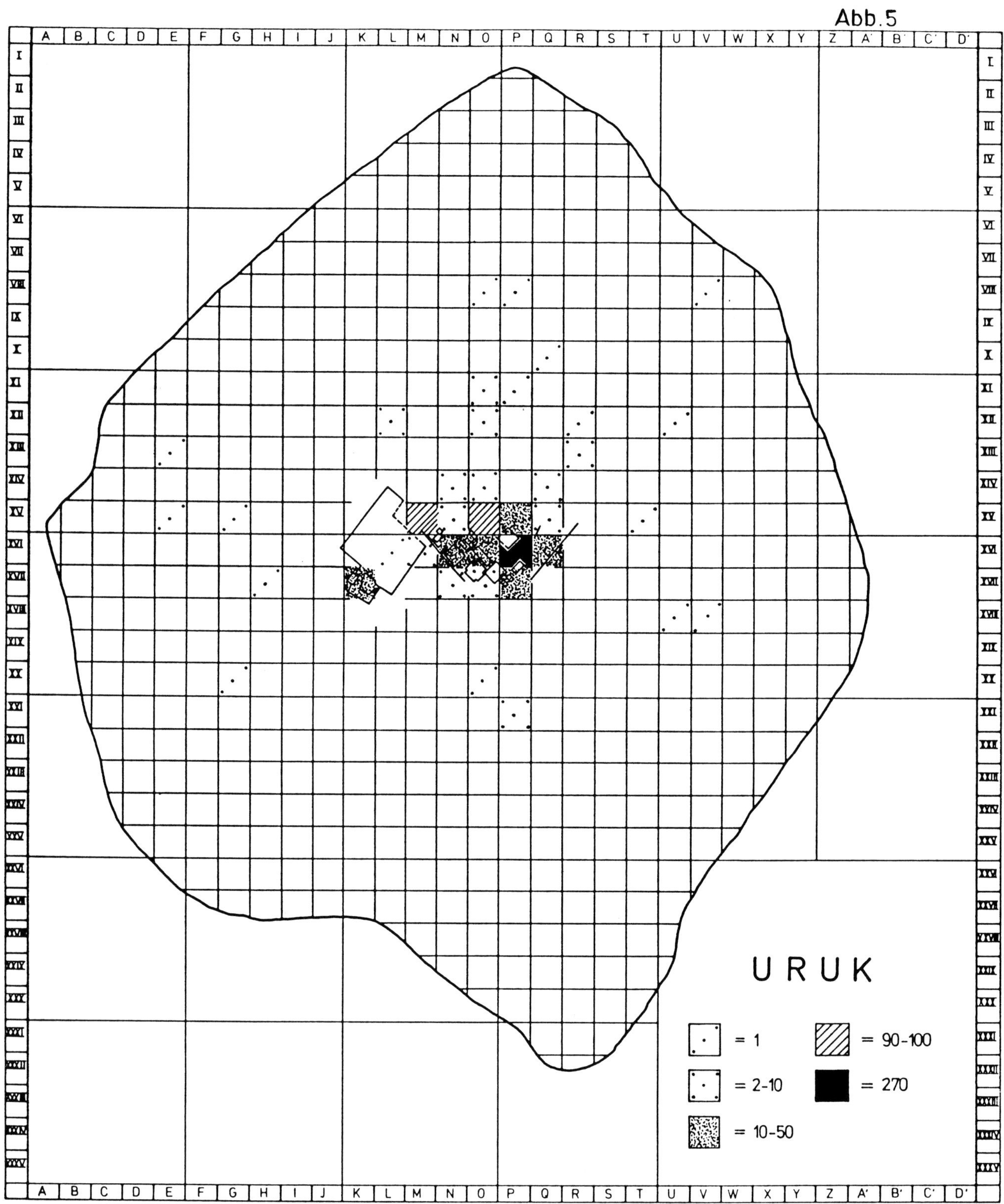

32.1. Location of tokens at Uruk, Iraq. Courtesy Deutsches Archaeologisches Institut, Abteilung Baghdad.

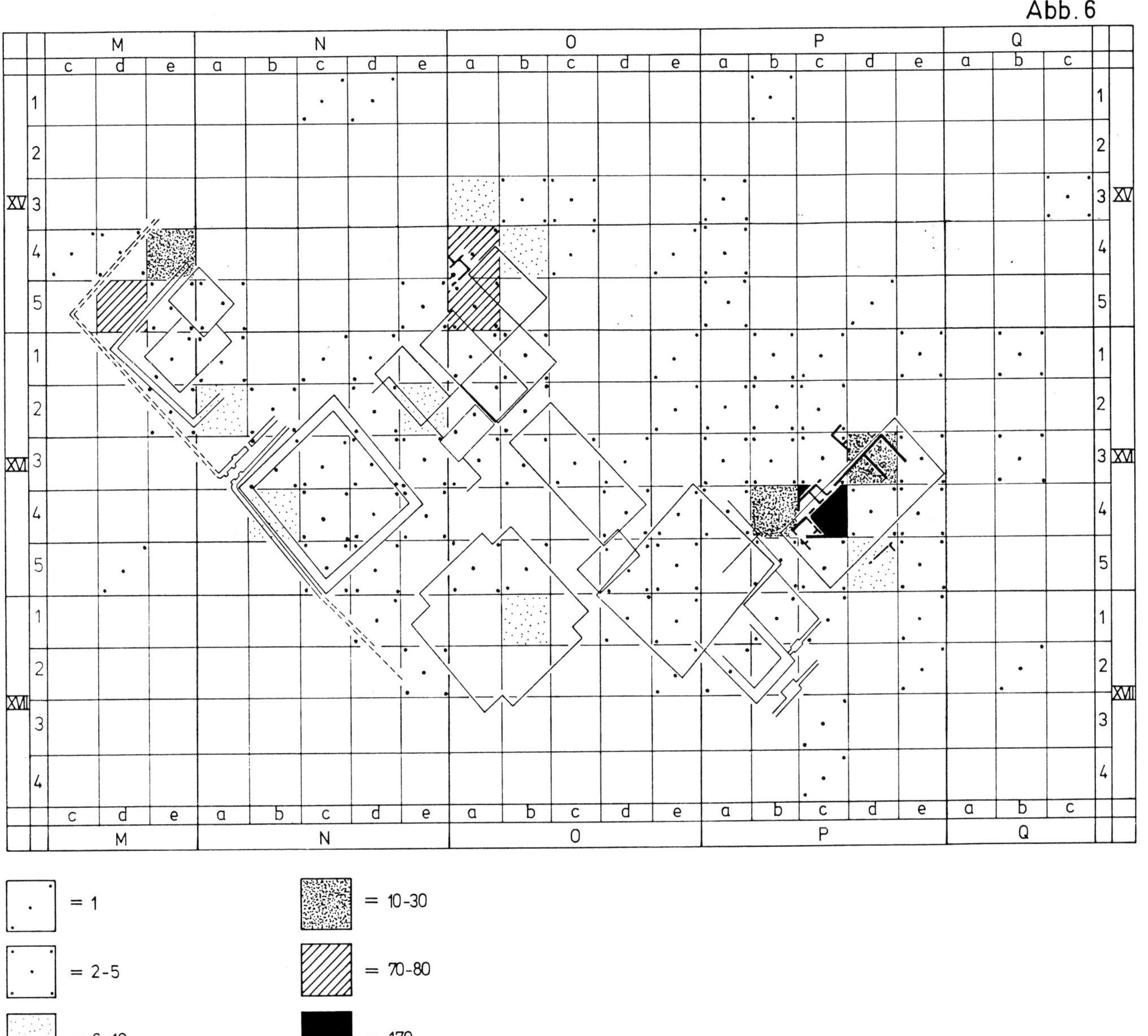

32.2. Location of tokens at Eanna, Uruk, Iraq. Courtesy Deutsches Archaeologisches Institut, Abteilung Baghdad.

logical to assume that much of the accounting in Uruk must have taken place in the administration buildings of the Sumerian temple (fig. 32.1).

Because of the constant remodeling of the sanctuary, the artifacts of the protoliterate period at Eanna are found consistently in a disturbed context and usually cannot be related to particular buildings. The matter is further complicated when dealing with tokens, tablets, and sealings, which were customarily eliminated as soon as their function was fulfilled. For these various reasons, the counters from Uruk, like the impressed and pictographic tablets,[48] were recovered among refuse discarded in antiquity. Only in one instance, perhaps, were tokens recovered *in situ*. The analysis of the context in which tokens were recovered can nonetheless provide some important information. For instance, it seems revealing that among the 812 tokens from Uruk, 719 or 88.5 percent were excavated in the sacred precinct of Eanna. From the remaining 93 examples, 50 or 6.2 percent originated in the city's private quarters and 43 or 5.3 percent from the Anu Ziggurat. The tokens from Uruk, therefore, can be said to belong primarily to the sanctuary of Inanna. Furthermore, it seems significant that tokens are not distributed evenly within Eanna but are most heavily represented in the northern section, in squares P XVI, O XV, and M XV (fig. 32.2).

About one-third of the Uruk tokens originated in the northeastern section of the precinct in square P XVI.[49] In turn, most of this collection, some 170 specimens, was recovered in Pc XVI 4, in a trench laid in the central hall of the Limestone Temple. Started in the second season,[50] the *Tiefschnitt* was extended in the third to a maximum exposure of 14.65 × 10.30 m, reaching virgin soil in the fourth season at a depth of 17 m below the floor of the Limestone Temple.[51] The deep sounding cut through thirteen consecutive building layers, which define levels XVIII–VI of Uruk.[52] Tokens are present from the deepest layers of the trench, level XVII, to the highest, level V, with a large concentration in level VI B2.

Little can be said concerning the context of the earliest plain tokens of levels XVIII–VII, except for the style of Ubaid and early Uruk pottery prevalent at the time. It is a different matter for the large number of tokens of level VI, located about 1–2.2 m below the foundation of the Limestone Temple, which form the bulk of the counters from the deep sounding. The some 150 tokens, among which were a number of complex specimens, were immediately associated with two superimposed layers of clay cone mosaics (fig. 42.1).[53] This is very significant since these mosaics represent the earliest securely dated evidence for monumental architecture at Eanna.[54] Furthermore, the tokens of level VI were also connected to fragments of beveled-rim bowls (fig. 43).[55] These vessels, which have been discussed above among the hallmarks of Eanna, occur in great quantities during the period of splendor of Eanna.[56] The large group of tokens of level VI, in other words, was related to two major indicators of the economic takeoff of the Sumerian temple institution: the beveled-rim bowls and clay cone mosaics. The conclusions to be drawn from this fact will be discussed later in the book.

The remaining tokens of P XVI came from disturbed contexts.[57] For example, six are related to the wadi of Pa–c XVI 3–5 and its accumulated debris.[58] Others belonged to the fill around monuments of various periods such as the Ur Nammu Ziggurat. It is probable that the counters were small enough to be included with other rubbish in the clay mix used to manufacture bricks and mortar of the various phases of reconstruction.[59] Other tokens were located in the proximity of the Mosaic Building in Pa XVI 4[60] or the Limestone Temple but cannot in any way be precisely related to these monuments.[61]

It seems also that the tokens scattered in the area of the Red Temple, in squares Pb–e XVI 2–4, cannot be convincingly connected to that building. The Red Temple was a mud brick structure of level IVa, built upon a terrace and painted red. It fails to conform to the expected configuration of a temple and, despite its name, it is now believed to have served as an administration office.[62] Cone mosaics and fragments of a clay frieze with rosettes, rearing animals, and bundles of reeds were among the most characteristic findings in the vicinity of the Red Temple. It is also in the same area that 120 archaic pictographic tablets and a number of broken jar sealings were recovered.[63] These sealings featured glyptic motifs, such as temple facades, felines attacking peaceful animals, and fabulous monsters with intertwined necks, typical of the level IVa period.[64] A single token is earmarked as originating from the vicinity of the important cache of archaic tablets found along a wall of the Red Temple.[65] Otherwise, there is some indication that some of these 32 tokens of Pd–e XVI 3 belonged either to the fill of periods earlier or later than level IVa. For example, a cylinder is identified as coming from a niche of the Red Temple but in a level earlier than the Red Temple (levels V–IV?),[66] whereas others may have belonged to the layer of the dismantlement of the Limestone Temple[67] or were intrusive among debris of later periods.[68]

Despite the poor conditions of recovery, the tokens at Uruk may provide some important information. Although the artifacts were stirred up through all the various layers of the mound of Warka, their spatial distribution does not seem to be random. Instead, they cluster in particular places. Apparently the perpetual terracing activity at Eanna brought to the surface ancient material without moving it much from its original location. In other words, the disturbances created may have displaced the material more vertically than horizontally. It must not be by chance, for instance, that 170 tokens of P XVI were concentrated in the area of the *Tiefschnitt* whereas only three appeared in the *Sägegraben,* a second deep sounding excavated close by in Pa XVI 5/Pa XVII 1.[69] It is also worth noting that P VI, the square which yields the most tokens of Uruk, was surrounded by squares that produced only exceedingly few of the artifacts. For example, there were 11 tokens in P XVII, 13 in P XV, 22 in O XVI, and 17 in Q XVI.[70]

The 25 envelopes holding counters,[71] the 83 tokens originating from envelopes which are presently known, and 35 found loose were recovered at the opposite northwestern end of Eanna in squares M–N XV–XVI.[72] From levels VI–IV, this area was occupied by the Stone Cone Temple, a small structure built on a terrace and faced with pink, white, and blue stone cone mosaics.[73] The temple formed a self-contained compound within Eanna, being enclosed by a wall also richly decorated with blue and green cone mosaics. The hoard of 25 envelopes was tucked in a depression in a *Riemchen* wall in Md XV 5.[74] Seventeen further tokens came from the northern part of the courtyard[75] with a concentration of thirteen in Me XV 4 and fifteen more from the southern part of the courtyard, with, in particular, seven in Na XVI 2.[76] The loose tokens were mixed with fragments of pottery typical of Uruk VI–IV, including shallow bowls, the ever-recurring beveled-rim bowls, goblets, and tall-spouted jars. The area also produced interesting sealings depicting prisoners.[77] It is likely that the tokens and envelopes, beveled-rim bowls, and sealings were originally part of the Stone Cone Temple administration. They were scattered on its grounds, probably after its destruction, once the site became a quarry and dumping area.

Six further tokens can be attributed to the Stone Cone Temple area.[78] They were recovered next to[79] or in the *Riemchen* building interpreted by Lenzen as a *favissa,* or ritual burial of the Stone Cone Temple possessions when it was condemned, possibly as early as level IVc or b.[80] The tokens lay in Me/Na XV 5, two in the corridor[81] and two in the central room of the *Riemchen* building.[82] Apparently they were not among the enclosed goods, which consisted of lapis lazuli inlaid furniture, bronze and stone weapons, boxes, and textiles, but instead were part of the fill of mixed debris that covered the material.[83]

As in the eastern part of Eanna, the tokens of M XV/XVI and N XVI form a cluster with the heaviest density in Mc–e XV 4–5, Md–e XVI 1–2, and Na–b XVI 1–2. On the other hand, no counter came to light in the remainder of M XV and M XVI and only four specimens at the opposite ends of N XV.

The third largest concentration of tokens came from square O XV, which was occupied in period IVb by a complex of three buildings, F, G, and H, built at right angles around a courtyard.[84] The three monuments conformed to the usual Uruk plan, with a central hall flanked by subsidiary rooms on three sides. They also had the familiar facades decorated with a vigorous pattern of recesses and indentations.[85] We know only parts of this impressive ensemble, which, apparently, extended to the northwest of Building H in yet unexcavated areas. This is particularly unfortunate because it is in Room I,[86] adjacent to Building H, which is not yet fully disengaged, that a group of 75 tokens was found together *in situ* (fig. 33). The cache of tokens consisting of 61 spheres, 7 large spheres, 3 tetrahedrons, 2 cones, and 2 cylinders lay on the floor of a room in Oa XV 4/5, in a large circular hearth with a long appendix of the *Pfannenstiel* (frying pan) type.[87] The location of the tokens within the hearth is enigmatic. The group can hardly have come together by chance and it is likely that they were placed there intentionally. It might be hypothesized that it was in order to bake them but, more likely, the tokens were swept into the hearth with other refuse such as fragments of beveled-rim bowls in order to be discarded.[88] Either way, the only tokens "*in situ*" at Uruk say little about how accounting was practiced in the Sumerian city.

Twenty-two further tokens were clustered in the area of the three buildings F, G, and H in Oa–c XV

33. Cache of tokens found in a hearth, Uruk (Oa XV 4/5), Iraq. Courtesy Deutsches Archaeologisches Institut, Abteilung Baghdad.

3–5, whereas the remainder of the square produced a single specimen.[89] Six of these tokens appeared in the excavations of the superimposed *Stampflehm* building—the building of beaten earth. The gigantic structure, first thought to have served as stables but now regarded as an administration building, is dated to the late Early Dynastic period. In this instance, the tokens appeared among refuse discarded in a courtyard in Ne XV 5, Oa XVI 1, and Ob XVI 1.[90] Other debris included pieces of inlays identical to those buried in the *Riemchen* building. Lenzen proposed, therefore, that the counters probably belonged originally to the underlying layer of level IV.[91] They could have been part, for instance, of a building such as the Hallenbau, a curious structure perhaps covered with small domes upon whose ruins the *Stampflehm* building had been built. Even more likely, the tokens could have originated from the complex F, G, and H still below the Hallenbau. It is possible that the artifacts were brought to the surface as a result of the incessant remodeling of the *Stampflehm* building.

The adjacent area to the east (Pa XV 3–5) held ten tokens, all from layers of later times.[92] Two of these are identified as originating in a trench laid on the north side of the ziggurat.[93] Others surfaced, even more out of context, in the area of the Northwest Temple of the Babylonian period.[94]

Tokens were also present in the central part of Eanna but in lesser quantities. Thirty-two turned up in and about the Great Courtyard in square N XVI, with a concentration of thirteen in Nb XVI 3–4.[95] The courtyard consisted of a quadrangular space with two concentric rows of benches surrounded by a wall decorated with cone mosaics. It was built and destroyed within period IVa, when it became a dumping ground. The tokens discarded in the northwestern part of the Great Courtyard were associated with torn jar sealings and, perhaps, with a number of archaic tablets reported in Nb XVI 4.[96]

Two tokens were located in the area of Building E, whose function as a "palace" or reception hall is still conjectured.[97] This striking building, with large porticoes opening onto an inner courtyard, perhaps represents best the splendor of early Sumerian architecture.[98] The token came from Oa XVI 5 but cannot be associated with the large basin, which produced a quantity of broken jar sealings with motifs typical of period IV.[99]

The ruins of Temple C, which has been termed the foremost model of a Sumerian temple, yielded two tokens, one of them in the central hall, but both were part of the fill and not *in situ*.[100] Finally, eleven tokens were scattered in the area of Temple D, the largest and most imposing temple ever built in Eanna.[101]

Some tokens have been recovered in later buildings where they were also part of the fill and totally out of context. For example, one turned up near a bench in room 5 of Irigal, also named the South Building, of the Seleucid period in the first millennium B.C.[102] A group of four lenticular disks, two of them with incised perpendicular lines, was associated with a double grave of the New Babylonian period.[103] Another sphere lay in the fill of a plano-convex building of the Early Dynastic period.[104]

Finally, a few more tokens can be traced to Eanna but with no precise place of origin. Some of them are surface finds.[105] Still others had escaped the scrutiny of excavators and were located in the excavation dumps.[106]

The information concerning the forty-six tokens from the Anu Ziggurat, the other main religious center of Uruk, is scanty. Some were discovered in or about the terrace of large bricks (*Patzen*) situated on the southeastern side of the temple.[107] Others occur to the northwest[108] or the west side.[109] The tokens recovered in the various trenches I, II, IV, V, and VIII also provide no particular information.[110] Finally, one bent coil was located at the top of a wall of the Stone Building,[111] also called the Cenotaph.[112] In the case of the Anu Ziggurat, as in Eanna, none of the tokens were *in situ*. Their position in particular layers provides at best a *terminus ante quem* for their manufacture. For example, two ovoids sealed in level C can only belong to that or previous periods.[113]

The study of tokens from the city's private quarters is blurred by the fact that little excavation has taken place outside the temple areas. Some fifty counters have been recovered in the city, the majority of which are surface finds. For example, the extensive survey of seasons thirty-six through thirty-seven brought about the discovery of as many as eighteen tokens.[114] These artifacts are important in showing that tokens were sparsely scattered about the entire mound[115] with one specimen located, for example, as far south as the so-called Gareus Temple in Q XXIV.[116] There is, however, no visible pattern for their distribution and, in particular, none originated from the squares identified as having large quantities of late Uruk potteries.[117]

The excavations carried out in the private quarters in O XI–XII and in K–L XII[118] have produced a small number of tokens. These specimens are significant since they attest that tokens were handled outside the temple precincts. On the other hand, it may also be significant that the counters found in these trenches were exceedingly few, amounting to no more than a total of seven for the four squares involved.[119] No tokens were recovered in the archaic settlement of level III, located north of the mound of Warka, which was investigated during the winter of 1960–61.[120]

The distribution of tokens at Uruk does not indicate, as one would wish, the precise areas in which accounting took place at Uruk. Two major pieces of information can be gleaned, however, from the data at hand: First, tokens were substantially more numerous in the district of Eanna than in the Anu Ziggurat and the city's private quarters. In other words, tokens like the later pictographic tablets belonged mostly to the economic center of the metropolis, where, no doubt, most of the accounting in Uruk took place. The relationship between accounting and public offices is particularly well illustrated in the instance of the deep sounding, where the bulk of the counters of level VI b2 was immediately connected with monumental architecture decorated with cone mosaics.

Second, the counters of Eanna tend to cluster in particular areas which might be diagnostic. For example, tokens are most numerous in the northeastern, northern, and northwestern parts of the district, with close to 300 specimens in P XVI, 100 in M/N XV, and 100 in O XV, compared, for example, to 22 specimens in O XVI at the center of the site.

Third, tokens occur repeatedly in conjunction with other artifacts which have to do with administration, such as monumental public buildings decorated with clay cone mosaics, sealings, and beveled-rim bowls.

There are several ways to interpret the distribution of tokens within Eanna. The concentration in the northern part of the precinct of counters, envelopes, and sealings can suggest that the administrative offices were situated at the periphery of the sanctuary in locations easily accessible from particular gates.

It seems even more significant that the areas where tokens are concentrated played a major role in periods prior to level IVa. In particular, the counters were mostly associated with the Stone Cone Temple of level VI, the Limestone Temple of level V, and the complex of Temples F, G, and H of period IVb. On the other hand, the counters were in far smaller quantities in the southern sectors of the precinct where the predominant architecture is of period IVb and IVa and exceedingly few seem to be associated with tablets. Excavations, as well as surveys, have not revealed the same density of material in the Late Uruk period and, in particular, in level IVa. Tokens were not encountered in the archaic settlement of level III.

In sum, tokens were recovered in greatest quantities at Uruk when levels VI–IVb were exposed, suggesting a period of floruit of the token system at that time. Of course, these conclusions have to remain tentative until more is known of the earliest levels of Warka.

CHRONOLOGY

Unlike pictographic tablets, seals, and even the most famous sculptures of Sumerian art excavated at Uruk, which are dated according to style because their level of origin is unknown,[121] as many as 249 or 32 percent of the tokens of Eanna were recovered in a stratigraphic context. First, a cache of 78 counters was found *in situ*. Second, and far more important, 169 tokens were excavated in two deep soundings; 168 came from the *Tiefschnitt*, below the Limestone Temple, and 1 from the *Sägegraben*. The *Tiefschnitt* provides a reliable stratigraphy from level XVIII, in the late Ubaid period, to level V, in the late Uruk period, since the artifacts were sealed between a series of superimposed building foundations (fig. 34).[122] Unfortunately, however, the *Tiefschnitt* was confined to a restricted area, starting with a trench of 14.65 × 10.30 m in level V and decreasing progressively through the following layers, to be finally reduced to a surface of 6.3 × 1.2 m in level XVIII.[123] As a consequence, the assemblage recovered depends to a considerable extent on excavator's luck. For this reason, the various tokens from the *Tiefschnitt* at Eanna can serve only to mark a *terminus ante quem* in the development of the counting device.

The earliest tokens of the *Tiefschnitt* occur in the late Ubaid period at a depth of 4.5–5.5 m in level XVII. These tokens, recovered below the first building level identified at Uruk, consist of two spheres (type 2: 1), one of them perforated; one flat disk (type 3: 1); and a perforated cylinder with incised markings (type 4: 8).[124] As small as it is, the collection is typical of an Ubaid token assemblage in including some of the most basic prehistoric types, such as plain spheres and disks. The assemblage, however, also yields a cylinder which can be considered a complex token. First, the cylindrical shape with flat ends is familiar from later assemblages. Second, the pattern of strokes is more elaborate than is usual in early specimens. The token, however, does not belong to one of the token series that are characteristic of complex assemblages but, instead, is unique. Third, the cylinder is perforated, showing that the custom of stringing tokens was already practiced in the late Ubaid period. Consequently, the earliest group of tokens at Uruk already yields one complex and two perforated specimens.

The Early Uruk period is represented by yet another restricted number of counters recovered in levels XIVa, XIIa–b, and X. These consist of two cones (type 1: 1), one sphere (type 2: 1), and one triangle (type 8: 3), none with markings.[125] The triangle is particularly significant because it is of a subtype otherwise unknown in the Ubaid period but familiar in complex token assemblages. Such triangles are known to occur in the last phase of the token system in levels VI–IV in series showing many different numbers of strokes or lines (type 8: 7–36). Although the evidence is scanty, level X may be considered, therefore, as the *terminus ante quem* for the point of departure for token series.

Tokens continue to trickle through the Middle Uruk period in the deep sounding of Eanna. Level IX produced a single plain triangle,[126] and level VIII one plain sphere,[127] but in the late Uruk period the number of counters becomes substantial, suggesting a florescence of the system.

The assemblage of 155 counters recovered in level VI of Uruk constitutes the largest cluster of tokens identified at the site. The collection includes specimens of the following thirteen types: type 1 (cones): 4; type 2 (spheres): 51; type 3 (disks): 16; type 4 (cylinders): 45; type 5 (tetrahedrons): 10; type 6 (ovoids): 3; type 8 (triangles): 11; type 9 (biconoids): 1; type 10 (paraboloids): 4; type 12 (ovals): 9; type 13 (vessels): 1; type 15 (animals): 1. Only types 7 (rectangles), 11 (bent coils), and 16 (miscellaneous) are not represented. Although

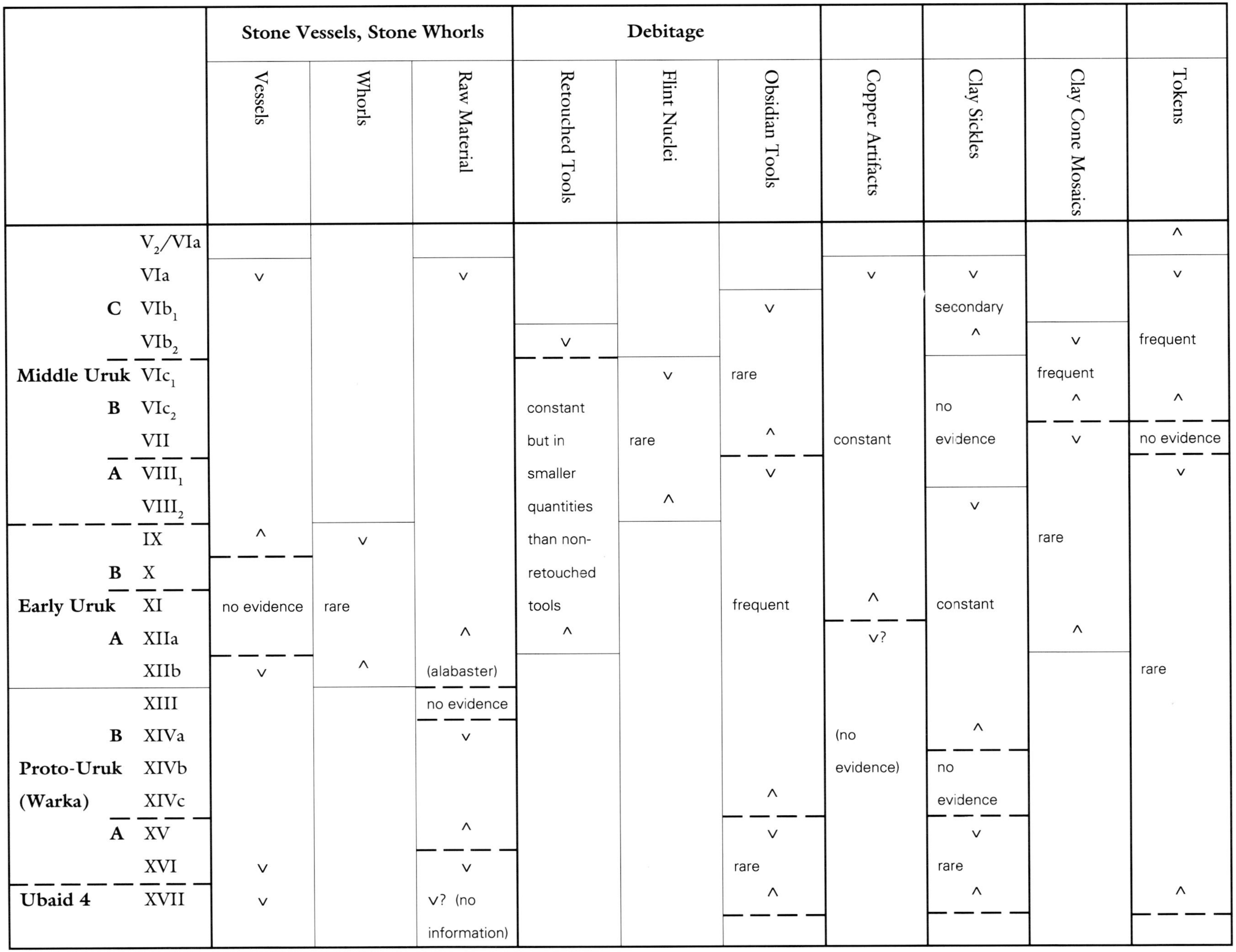

Period	Phase	Level	Stone Vessels, Stone Whorls: Vessels	Whorls	Raw Material	Debitage: Retouched Tools	Flint Nuclei	Obsidian Tools	Copper Artifacts	Clay Sickles	Clay Cone Mosaics	Tokens
		V_2/VIa										^
		VIa	v		v				v	v		v
	C	VIb_1						v		secondary		
		VIb_2				v				^	v	frequent
Middle Uruk		VIc_1					v	rare			frequent	
	B	VIc_2				constant				no	^	^
		VII				but in	rare	^	constant	evidence	v	no evidence
	A	VIII_1				smaller		v				v
		VIII_2				quantities	^			v		
		IX	^	v		than non-					rare	
	B	X				retouched						
Early Uruk		XI	no evidence	rare		tools		frequent	^	constant		
	A	XIIa			^	^			v?		^	
		XIIb	v	^	(alabaster)							rare
		XIII			no evidence							
	B	XIVa			v				(no	^		
Proto-Uruk		XIVb							evidence)	no		
(Warka)		XIVc						^		evidence		
	A	XV			^			v		v		
		XVI	v		v			rare		rare		
Ubaid 4		XVII	v		v? (no			^		^		^
					information)							

Distribution of artifacts (excluding ceramic vessels) in the "Tiefschmitt"

34. Occurrence of tokens in the deep sounding of Uruk, Iraq. Courtesy D. Sürenhagen and Deutsches Archaeologisches Institut, Abteilung Baghdad.

Jordan commented in his report that these specimens were smaller than those he had recovered in the previous year,[128] the assemblage is fully homogeneous with the remaining collection of Uruk tokens. In particular, they share the same size, measuring about 1–3 cm across.

Among the 26 subtypes represented in the assemblage of Eanna VI, 6 are plain and 18 complex.[129] Accordingly, the 155 tokens from level VI of the *Tiefschnitt* can be divided into 124 plain and 31 complex tokens. Furthermore, the complex tokens include 15 specimens bearing markings and 5 perforated to allow stringing.[130]

Among the thirty-one complex tokens from level VI of the *Tiefschnitt,* the triangles and ovoids are of particular interest. There are 12 triangles which constitute the first documented token series including plain counters;[131] examples showing 3, 5, 7, or 9 lines;[132] or a combination of lines and punctations.[133] Two of the ovoids also belong to series.[134] Whereas the deepest layers of the *Tiefschnitt* (levels XVII–XIV) hold spheres, cones, and flat disks, which are the antecedents of the Sumerian *impressed signs,* indicating measures of cereals or numerals, it is to level VI that can be traced the first precursors of the Sumerian *incised signs,* traced with a stylus.[135] Among them, the incised ovoid, for example, is the prototype of the sign i3 (ATU 733), meaning "oil."[136] The triangle with five lines can also be matched to Ku3 (ATU 703), "metal,"[137] and the notched sphere is the precursor of the sign for a particular measure of grain (ATU 898).[138] A significant outcome of the *Tiefschnitt* is, therefore, to clarify the relationship between tokens and the Sumerian pictographic script. Although a number of authors have argued that the complex tokens followed, rather than predated, pictographic writing,[139] the deep sounding shows clearly that the complex token antecedents of some of the most frequently used Sumerian pictographs can be traced to level VI of Uruk and, therefore, preceded writing by at least two hundred years.

The second deep sounding, the *Sägegraben,* was far less productive. Among the three tokens recovered in the trench, only one can be attributed with certainty to level V-1 corresponding to VIa–b1.[140] The remaining two are from a disturbed context.

Beyond level VI/Va, the artifacts recovered in the Limestone Temple area are part of the fill and can no longer with certainty be assigned to particular levels. A number of tokens recovered on the floor or in close proximity to the Limestone Temple can be considered good candidates for the counters of level V but with no certainty, since they were not *in situ.*[141] Whatever the level of origin of these artifacts, be it V or IV, they are all complex specimens.

The group of tokens enclosed in the twenty-five clay envelopes comes, probably, next in the chronology of Eanna.[142] An unknown number of these specimens is still included in several envelopes which are intact. Others were recovered while still associated with partly crushed cases. Finally, a group of fifty-two separated tokens[143] brings the total number of tokens originating from envelopes to eighty-three. This assemblage features both plain and complex counters, including spheres and tetrahedrons in two distinct sizes, disks, cylinders, a rectangle, plain and incised ovoids, triangles, paraboloids, and, finally, trussed ducks, one of which bears incised markings.

Because the envelopes were not found *in situ,* their date is problematic. Four kinds of evidence can be used in order to identify the period to which they belong: architecture, pottery, glyptics, and parallels in other sites. The information concerning the architecture is at best vague and contradictory. The cache of tokens and envelopes was found in a hole in a *Riemchen* wall within the complex of the Stone Cone Temple. This part of Eanna is estimated by Heinrich to be as early as level VI.[144] According to Jürgen Schmidt, however, the Stone Cone Temple was erected in levels V–IVc and dismantled in IVa.[145] On the one hand, the *Riemchen* wall, in which the cache of envelopes was lodged, may have belonged to an earlier phase of the temple and could be of level VI or earlier. On the other hand, the artifacts need not be of the time of occupation or of dismantlement of the Stone Cone Temple but could have been dumped at any time thereafter when the building was abandoned. The pottery recovered in the area adds little precision since it consists of fragments of shallow bowls, beveled-rim bowls, goblets, and tall-spouted jars which were used consistently during periods VI–IV.[146] Consequently, the range of time suggested by architecture and pottery is as vague as levels VI–IVa.

The third criterion available for dating is glyptics. The twenty-five envelopes are covered by imprints of cylinder and stamp seals.[147] The style of the impressions is homogeneous and the fact that three of the envelopes bear the mark of the same seal[148] supports the probability that all belonged to the same period, which remains to be defined. The motifs represented on the cylinders, which feature lines of quadrupeds, rearing caprids, felines attacking cattle, and humans in procession, are familiar from the repertory generally assigned to level IV[149] with the exception of a hero astride a lion, which has no known parallel.[150] The unusually vigorous rendering of the designs points to a definite archaism, suggesting an early period. The hero is massive and heavy and could be considered, for lack of parallels, as belonging to level V.[151] According to the present knowledge of Uruk glyptics, the fact that both cylinder and stamp seals were used on the envelopes dates the artifacts between levels V–IVb since level V is the earliest limit set for the use of cylinder seals and IVb is when stamp seals fell into disuse. These landmarks for the chronology of the Uruk glyptics are, however, more assumptions than evidence, since no seals and no sealings were recovered in the stratigraphed context of the *Tiefschnitt*.

Envelopes like those of Uruk, holding identical tokens and also bearing similar seal impressions, have been recovered in several sites and, in particular, Habuba Kabira, Susa, and Farukhabad. Habuba Kabira produced two envelopes including the same incised ovoids as W 20987.7 of Uruk. The envelopes from Habuba Kabira can be considered as more evolved than those of Uruk since they bore signs depicting the tokens held inside. Since Habuba Kabira was occupied only during a brief period corresponding to levels VI–V of Eanna, the envelopes belong with certainty to that time.[152] The same is true for the envelopes of Susa, among which are some with markings. These artifacts were recovered in level 18 of Susa, which corresponds to Eanna VI–V.[153] Finally, the envelope from Farukhabad dates from the Middle Uruk period.[154] It is likely that the Uruk envelopes were contemporaneous with those from Habuba Kabira, Susa, and Farukhabad. It is even logical to assume that the Uruk specimens, which bear no markings and show particularly archaic seal impressions, were among the earliest of the kind. Consequently, whereas the contextual architecture, pottery, and glyptics of Uruk offer a choice of levels as broad as VI–IV, the material from stratigraphed sites permits a narrowing down of the dating of the tokens and envelopes from the Stone Cone Temple to the earlier part of this time range, namely, levels VI–V.

The cache of seventy-eight artifacts located in a hearth in Oa XV 4–5 forms the second substantial group of tokens which, like those of the *Tiefschnitt*, can be satisfactorily dated. Building H and the adjacent Room I, in which the counters were recovered, were dated by Heinrich to IVc.[155] On the other hand, Jürgen Schmidt estimates that the structures were built and dismantled during IVb.[156] According to him, therefore, the tokens can be assigned to IVb, whether they were *in situ* or had been brushed into the hearth when the temple was evacuated in order to be dismantled. The group consisted of four types of plain tokens—cones, spheres, cylinders, and tetrahedrons—which were either meant to stay that way or were blanks intended to be incised and perforated into complex specimens. In any case, it is not surprising to find a group of plain tokens in level IVb, since all plain forms remained in use until the invention of writing. In fact, they consistently make up a large number of tokens in protoliterate assemblages, which is to be expected, since they represented units of the major staples.

A last group of complex tokens recovered among the refuse accumulated about the Great Courtyard can be attributed to level IVa,[157] since it was built in that level and destroyed immediately after.[158] Among these counters are two small rectangles which bear pictographs on one face.[159] The objects, usually referred to as "labels" in the literature,[160] are tentatively included here among tokens since they closely resemble the usual rectangular type of counters and, unlike tablets, are perforated. The first of these artifacts features a pictograph which reads "ADAB," either referring to the name of the city or, perhaps, a personal name.[161] The second probably shows a title.[162] In fact, a total of five of these artifacts has been located at Uruk. Two were sealed in the fill of Temple C, below the construction layer of level III.[163] One of these specimens bears two pictograhs listed by Falkenstein as ATU 372 and 465.[164] The first sign is a title, ATU 372 = UMUN 2 and ATU 465 = DIN, "wine."[165] Finally, the last specimen, of unknown provenience, shows two signs which read SUKKAL, indicating, perhaps, a profession.[166] If the artifacts are tokens, or perhaps labels to identify strings of tokens, they would show that borrowing took place between the two methods of record keeping, the pictographs adding, possibly, specific information either on the quality of merchandise dealt with or, more probably, on the identity of a donor or recipient.

A single token originated from the thin layer between levels IVa and III.[167] The stratum represented a short interval between the destruction of level IVa and the construction of the monumental terrace of level III. Only a few artifacts were recovered in this context, including several pictographic tablets.[168]

This last token recovered in the intermediate layer between levels IVa and III represents the last example which can be traced with reasonable certainty to a particular level. No tokens were found in an undisturbed level III context; for example, the cone no. 29, labeled to that level, was in an area where burials had been dug.[169] No tokens appeared, either, in the archaic settlement. The tokens found in an Early Dynastic context, such as that of the *Stampflehm* building, were mixed with other displaced remains of layer IV.

In sum, the most important chronological landmarks in the evolution of tokens illustrated in the *Tiefschnitt* or in Eanna at large can be summarized as follows:

1. Level XVII: First complex and perforated token.
2. Level X: Beginning of token series.
3. Level VI: Large assemblage of plain and complex tokens associated with a public building decorated with clay cone mosaics.
4. Levels VI–V: Appearance of envelopes holding plain and complex tokens. Complex tokens also continue to be used without envelopes, either loose or strung.
5. Tokens, including plain and complex specimens, can be traced through level IVa, after which there is no longer any evidence for their use.

This chronology gives new information on four important aspects of the final phase of development of the token system prior to the invention of writing. First, the *Tiefschnitt* sheds new light on the transition from plain to complex tokens. The process can no longer be considered as a sudden development, as previously assumed. Instead, the assemblage of level XVII attests that complex tokens have their roots in prehistory, as early as the late Ubaid period. The point of departure of the complex counters remains problematic since levels XVII and X of Uruk can only be considered as a *terminus ante quem* for the appearance of single complex specimens or series.

Second, the Uruk assemblage shows that plain and complex tokens can be traced through levels IVb and IVa and the layer between IVa and III, demonstrating that plain and complex tokens coexisted with pictographic writing in its early phase. This overlap of the token system and writing, during half a century in level IVa, was to be expected since the new technology could hardly have eradicated instantly the age-old counters.

Third, the tokens of Eanna also provide new insights into how tokens were kept in archives, which is important for this study, since I will propose that the storage of counters played a significant role in the invention of writing. According to the material from the *Tiefschnitt,* counters were strung together by means of perforations as early as level XVII. The hoard of tokens and envelopes from the Stone Cone Temple suggests that tokens, both plain and complex, began to be enclosed in sealed cases in levels VI to V. From then on, the two systems of securing counters by stringing or in envelopes coexisted. This is suggested by the perforated tokens located in the Great Courtyard, attributed to level IVa.[170] It is conceivable that the five "labels," bearing pictographs from the Great Courtyard, served to identify strings of tokens with the name/title of a person involved.

Fourth, and finally, level VI appears as a turning point in the counting device. From then on, types and subtypes start proliferating, with the creation of tokens which are the direct ancestors of Sumerian incised pictographs. The large collection of counters in level VI of the deep sounding reinforces the notion of a floruit of the counting device in the Middle Uruk period, as first suggested by the distribution of counters in Eanna. Furthermore, it does not seem fortuitous that the same level VI also features the first ruins of a major public building decorated with clay cone mosaics. The idea of a correlation between the development of accounting and monumental architecture seems worth further investigation.

PARALLELS

The tokens from Uruk have parallels elsewhere in northern and southern Mesopotamia, Syria, and Iran. It is noteworthy, however, that contemporaneous Near Eastern sites share the Uruk types and subtypes in different ways.

A first group of assemblages has only plain tokens such as cones, spheres, disks, cylinders, or tetrahedrons in common with Uruk. Among them are, in Iraq: Tell Agrab, Fara, Tepe Gawra, Jemdet Nasr, Khafaje, Kish, Nineveh, and Telul eth Thalathat; in Syria: Amuq, Chagar Bazar, and Jebel Aruda; in Iran: Tepe Bouhallan, Farukhabad, Tepe Giyan, Hissar, KS 34, KS 76, Tepe Sialk, Seh Gabi, and Tepe Yahya.

A second group shares with Uruk not only plain but also complex tokens. These sites include, in Iraq: Tell Billa, Nippur, Nuzi, Tello, and Ur; in Syria:

Habuba Kabira and Tell Kannas; in Iran: Chogha Mish, KS 54, Moussian, and Susa. Among them, Tell Billa,[171] Nippur,[172] Nuzi,[173] and Moussian[174] have, in fact, only a single complex counter in common with Uruk. KS 54 yields two[175] and Ur three complex tokens identical to those of Uruk.[176]

Among the assemblages with complex counters, Susa[177] and Chogha Mish in Iran,[178] Tello in southern Mesopotamia,[179] and Habuba Kabira in Syria[180] should be considered as a special group, not only because they have numerous parallels but they also share token series with Uruk. The four sites have substantial collections of complex tokens with, respectively, 66, 20, 28, and 29 subtypes parallel to those of Uruk. It is important to note that "parallel" means tokens of the same shape and bearing identical sets of markings. It is also noteworthy that the 66 parallel subtypes of Susa represent a total of 472 tokens, which means that 67.4 percent of the tokens from Susa are identical to those from Uruk; 100 counters or 78.8 percent of the counters from Habuba Kabira have identical counterparts in Uruk. Finally, Tello has 75 tokens, or 81.5 percent of its assemblage, which could just as well have belonged to Eanna (figs. 35.1–35.7).[181]

Tello, Susa, and Habuba Kabira have numerous token series in common; that is, counters of the same type with a distinctive pattern of markings but with a variable number of elements. There are, for example, particularly intriguing series of disks which occur in the four sites. Some of the disks display various numbers of lines, with examples of either 1, 3, 4, 5, 6, 8, or 10 lines (type 3: 19–25) distributed among Uruk (figs. 31.6–31.8), Susa (fig. 36.3), Habuba Kabira, and Tello (fig. 35.1).[182] Another group shows sets of lines symmetrically arranged as follows: 1-1, 2-1, 2-2, 4-4, and 5-5 (subtypes 28–33), which has examples in the four sites (figs. 31.6, 31.7, 36.3, and 37.2).[183] In both instances Uruk yields the most variations. The largest disk series represented in Uruk, Susa, and Habuba Kabira involves a combination of lines and strokes as follows: 1-7, 2-1, 2-5, 2-6, 2-7, 2-8, 3-5, 5-6, 5-7, 5-13, 10-6, 10-9, and 12-7 (subtypes 36–48; figs. 31.5 and 31.6).[184]

Such series occur among all types of counters, except cones, spheres, tetrahedrons, tools, and animals. There are, for example, cylinders with 4 lines at Uruk (type 4: 15) and the same token with 8 lines at Tello (subtype 17). Ovoids with 1 horizontal line and 4 vertical lines are represented at both Uruk and Susa, where there are also examples with 5, 6, and 10 vertical lines (type 6: 14–18). Rectangles occur with sets of 6 horizontal lines at Susa and Uruk, which also yields a further example with 7 lines (type 7: 10–11).

Triangles as well as paraboloids occur almost exclusively in series. A first group of triangles with a flat section has instances of 1, 2, 3, 5, 7, and 10 strokes incised along the large side (type 8: 5–10). A second group with an oval section displays either 1, 2, 3, 4, 5, 6, 7, 8, 9, or 10 lines (subtypes 11–22). Still another group has distinctive sets of parallel lines: 1, 1-1, 1-2, 2-2 (subtypes 23–26).[185] Some among these tokens reoccur more frequently than others. Triangles with 3 and 5 lines seem the most popular with, for example, 11 of the former at Uruk and 12 at Susa (subtype 15), and 12 of the latter at Susa and 5 at Uruk (subtype 17). Finally, there are two main series of paraboloids represented in the four sites. The first shows 3, 4, 5, 8, 9, or 10 short strokes along the straight edge (type 10: 4–7) and the second a pattern of 1, 3, or 8 lines (subtypes 12–15).[186] In these various series, the pattern of markings is clearly the same and it cannot be by chance that such tokens, partly identical and partly different, are distributed among assemblages of major sites in Mesopotamia, Syria, and Iran.

It would be erroneous to believe that the composition of fourth-millennium token assemblages is entirely due to excavation luck. The assemblage of 120 plain tokens recovered throughout levels XII–IX of Tepe Gawra, with no example of any complex specimens, seems to demonstrate that some sites had no use for complex counters.[187] The presence of complex tokens in particular sites and their absence in others provides significant information concerning the development of accounting and bureaucracy in the fourth millennium B.C.

The difference between plain versus complex token assemblages may first reflect a chronological discrepancy. The collections of sites such as Fara, Kish, Jemdet Nasr, Tell Agrab, Khafaje, Nippur, Nuzi, Jebel Aruda, and Tepe Yahya are likely to come from layers corresponding to Eanna level III, when complex tokens were discontinued. Second, the sites which shared complex tokens with Uruk may have had special socioeconomic ties with the southern Mesopotamian metropolis. This question is investigated in the following sections concerning the complex assemblages of Susa and Habuba Kabira.

The fact that Uruk has the largest fourth-millennium token collection may be unimportant since the num-

35.1. Tokens, Tello, Iraq. Courtesy Musée du Louvre, Département des Antiquités Orientales.

35.2. Cones, Tello, Iraq. Courtesy Musée du Louvre, Département des Antiquités Orientales.

35.3. Disk, Tello, Iraq. Courtesy Musée du Louvre, Département des Antiquités Orientales.

35.4. Ovoids, Tello, Iraq. Courtesy Musée du Louvre, Département des Antiquités Orientales.

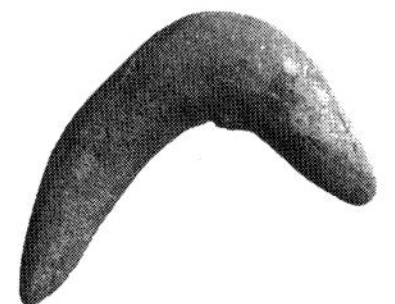

35.5. Triangles, Tello, Iraq. Courtesy Musée du Louvre, Département des Antiquités Orientales.

35.6. Paraboloid, Tello, Iraq. Courtesy Musée du Louvre, Département des Antiquités Orientales.

35.7. Assemblage, Tello, Iraq. Courtesy Musée du Louvre, Département des Antiquités Orientales.

ber of artifacts recovered is largely due to excavator's luck. The unique diversity of complex counters at the site, which illustrates a new stage of evolution in the system, should be considered, however, as a significant event in the evolution of the reckoning device.

The deep sounding excavated in the sanctuary of Eanna reveals that complex tokens started at Uruk in level XVII, in the late Ubaid period. The chronology and distribution of the counters at Uruk show that the development of complex tokens is remarkably in tune with the evolution of archaic Eanna. For example, the first complex specimens follow immediately the establishment of the sanctuary; the florescence of the system takes place when Eanna is at the peak of its glory in levels VI–IV, and the disappearance of complex counters coincides with the temple collapse in level IVa. This indicates that the complex tokens were closely related to the vicissitudes of archaic Eanna in levels XVII–IV. The fact that Uruk shares the same complex tokens with particular sites but not with others demands an explanation. This problem is addressed in the following sections devoted to the analysis of the Susa and Habuba Kabira collections.

Susa

Susa, the greatest metropolis of Elam, has produced the second largest collection of tokens in the fourth millennium B.C. The assemblage is also the largest and most diversified in Iran. The most interesting feature of the tokens from Susa is their similarity to those from Uruk. Unfortunately, the bulk of the 783 tokens from Susa was recovered when archaeology was still in its infancy and when tokens were not yet identified as counters. The information available is, therefore, often inadequate. This section attempts to bring together what is presently known on the Susa tokens and compare the data to those of Uruk. The purpose of comparing the two assemblages is twofold. First, the Uruk collection, being better documented, might help in filling in gaps in the information. Second, the analysis of the similarities and differences between the tokens from Susa and those of Uruk may bring a new understanding of the development of complex tokens in cities of the fourth millennium B.C.

SOURCES

The French Mission Archéologique has faithfully led annual campaigns to Susa since 1897, except for interruptions caused by political upheavals.[188] The findings are reported in numerous volumes and articles which are not always easy to decipher. This is why it seems pertinent to summarize here the information on tokens, or the lack thereof, provided by the various teams who have worked at the site.

Mémoires, vol. 7 (1905)

Considering that, at first, the goals of archaeology were mainly to unearth spectacular museum pieces, it is quite unexpected to find tokens mentioned in reports as early as 1905. Five examples, apparently chosen from a large collection of complex tokens, are illustrated in *Mémoires,* vol. 7, with a caption reading "clay beads of an undetermined period".[189] The objects were recovered, probably, from La Grande Tranchée opened by Jacques de Morgan in the southern part of the Acropolis. The discussion in the report about "quantities of small clay objects" suggests that the artifacts attracted Morgan's attention neither by their lavishness, as they are made of mere clay, nor by their dimension, which is barely 3 cm, but by their sheer number.

Mémoires, vols. 12–13 (1911, 1912)

The reports on the famous *vase à la cachette* excavated by Morgan in the Tell of the Acropolis in 1907 do not mention that the vessel held a group of tokens.[190] As a result, the collection of eleven cylinders and one triangle, which is now on display at the Louvre, has been generally overlooked. These tokens are unusual in many ways. First, they were part of a hoard of alabaster vessels, seals, gold beads, and copper artifacts such as weapons, tools, and vessels found enclosed in two large pottery containers. Second, they were not made of clay but rather were manufactured with great care and skill in fine colorful stones such as grey and pink marble. The most puzzling feature, however, is to find tokens in an assemblage unmistakably dated to the Early Dynastic period at a time when tokens had long been supplanted by writing. For the sake of completeness, it should be noted that Paul Toscanne included a token with a zigzag shape in his study of the snake symbol in *Mémoires,* vol. 12.[191]

Mémoires, vols. 16–17 (1921, 1923)

Envelopes excavated perhaps by Jacques de Morgan in 1901 or, more likely, by Roland Mecquenem in 1907 in trench 7 south of the Acropolis entered the literature in *Mémoires,* vols. 16[192] and 17[193] with only short and vague comments. No one at the time seemed to have noticed that they held tokens. As a result, they were associated, wrongly, with the many types of sealings used to secure bags and bundles of goods. This unfortunate identification as "bullae" contributed, certainly, in blurring for a long time their role as accounting devices and a precursor of writing.

Revue d'Assyriologie et d'Archéologie Orientale 21, no. 3 (1924)

Mecquenem became aware that the envelopes held tokens when, during the campaigns of 1923 and 1924, in the course of excavations at the Acropolis, specimens were found broken and exhibiting their contents.[194] He hypothesized that the enclosed tokens, "grains, cones, pyramids and pills," were used as identification marks for individuals delivering or handling merchandise in magazines.

Mémoires, vol. 25 (1934)

After a period of silence lasting ten years and eighteen site reports, tokens reemerge at various depths of Roland de Mecquenem's Sondage 2 at the southern end of the Acropolis. It may be noteworthy that complex and perforated tokens ("small bits of clay of various shapes and often perforated") were present between the depth of 0 to 3.8 m[195] whereas only plain tokens ("marbles, stone and bitumen disks") are described in deeper levels, between 3.8 and 5.6 m.[196] There is an intriguing comment concerning a clay box made of two oval parts tightly fitting together holding three of these disks. This container may represent a yet unknown means of holding tokens.

The word *jeton,* "token," is used in *Mémoires,* vol. 25 for the first time to refer to the artifacts. Mecquenem attributed the objects, however, to funerary deposits in children's graves and interpreted them, therefore, as toys such as "gaming pieces or knuckle bones."

Mémoires, vol. 29 (1943)

Mecquenem seemed to be quite at a loss with the large harvest of "small terra cotta objects" recovered in the seasons of 1933 to 1939. He attributed a different function to each new shape encountered. For instance, he interpreted cones as game pieces, weights, or pestles;[197] tetrahedrons as dice;[198] ovoids as spinning tops;[199] complex tokens as pearls[200] or teaching aids for children to learn vocabulary;[201] and, finally, tokens enclosed in envelopes as identification marks for warehouse men.[202]

Not only were tokens found in great number during the campaigns of 1933 to 1939 but in a larger area of the site. Whereas until then the artifacts seemed to belong exclusively to the Acropolis, incised ovoids were reported in Sondage 1 at the southeastern end of the Tell of the Ville Royale, which, in Proto-Elamite times, was separated from the Acropolis, according to Mecquenem, only by the width of a road.[203]

The bulk of the collection excavated in those years was produced, however, by the Acropolis. This group constitutes probably most of the assemblage of some three hundred tokens and fifty envelopes presently stored at the Louvre. The objects are reported to occur in several parts and at several depths of the Sondage 2 at the southern end of the Acropolis as follows: At 17.3 m, impressed tablets were found in a context of collapsed magazines, one still filled with long spouted jars holding an unidentified black powdery substance.[204] Below, at 17.5 m, numerous envelopes and tablets were collected in what appears to have been a shallow pit about thirty cm deep which may represent a dump of archival material.[205] Numerous complex tokens, often perforated, are reported on two occasions between 17.5 and 21 m.[206] In these levels the prevalent architecture was pisé buildings, which involved large cones in their construction. The structures were divided into small compartments about 2 m in size, suggesting a complex of warehouses.[207] Rightly or wrongly, Mecquenem did not see any relationship between the tokens and the architectural features he uncovered but instead associated them with funerary deposits from children's graves of an intrusive necropolis.[208] Finally, only rare cones, plain and painted, are reported in the earliest levels of Susa, contemporary with the painted pottery of the first style.[209] The architectural features of these strata, such as ovens, suggest workshop activities.[210]

This unique assemblage of plain and complex tokens, envelopes, and tablets, if excavated with scientific methods, probably could have answered many questions concerning the chronology, context, and function of the tokens at Susa. Unfortunately, the chronological sequence suggested by the reports—few plain tokens in the earliest levels, followed in time by numerous complex tokens, envelopes, and tablets—remains unprecise and undated. The relationship between the objects and their context is only sketchy.

R. H. Dyson, Jr. (1966)

The sondage made by Robert H. Dyson, Jr., in 1954, during Ghirshman's directorship, on the eastern edge of Morgan's Grande Tranchée can be considered the first modern scientific excavation in the archaic layers of the Acropolis. The trench, which provided the first controlled stratigraphy of the prehistoric and protohistoric levels of Susa, produced a trickle of thirteen tokens throughout the forty strata.[211] It is noteworthy that complex tokens occur only in the upper levels and that the lower levels yield only plain tokens. Unfortunately, none of the artifacts were found *in situ* but rather belonged to trash deposits accumulated outside of buildings.

Mémoires vol. 46 (1971)

The campaigns of 1965 to 1968, under the direction of Roman Ghirshman, constitute a turning point in understanding the importance of the Acropolis at Susa during the protoliterate period. M. J. Steve and Hermann Gasche discovered that the center of the mound was occupied by a shrine built upon a monumental terrace similar to those of Mesopotamia.[212] Although Mecquenem had suspected for some time the existence of a temple precinct on the Acropolis,[213] this discovery fully explained, for the first time, after three-quarters of a century of excavations, the concentration of archival material, including the large collections of tokens, envelopes, and impressed tablets as well as the context of workshops, warehouses, and magazines in which they were uncovered.

Only four tokens were found in the immediate vicinity of the monumental terrace.[214] Among them two perforated specimens with zigzag edges attributed to level A1 constitute the earliest occurrence of complex tokens at Susa.[215] Because, however, the artifacts were found in areas carrying a great deal of traffic and where sacrifices may have been performed,[216] the stratigraphy may well not be entirely reliable.

Cahiers de la Délégation Archéologique Française en Iran, vol. 1 (1971)

Operations to the south of the Acropolis were resumed under the leadership of Jean Perrot in the so-called Chantier de l'Acropole I. After the seasons of 1969 to 1971, the following chronological sequence was established for the preliterate period of Susa:[217] Period I (levels 27–23), in which only two plain rectangles may be identified as tokens,[218] was partly contemporary with the initial building of the monumental terrace. These earliest strata are characterized by structures with small rooms probably unfit for habitation. Period II (levels 22–17) shows a succession of floors provided with hearths and basins. One complex token only is reported in level 17[219] with an assemblage consisting of a scattering of impressed tablets, seals and seal impressions, crude pottery such as beveled-rim bowls, and clay cone mosaics.[220]

Mémoires vol. 43 (1972)

La Glyptique susienne by Pierre Amiet represents the only systematic publication of the seals and seal impressions on artifacts, including envelopes, recovered at Susa between 1897 and 1967. The volume provides, for the first time, a complete description of the form, size, content, seal impressions, and markings of the envelopes stored at the Louvre. Furthermore, one page of discussion devoted to these artifacts outlines, with great insight, most of their important features.[221] Amiet presents the envelopes as accounting devices holding tokens which, according to him, represented quantities of goods or numbers. He notes the presence of markings on some envelopes corresponding to the number of tokens they held inside. He fails, however, to see a relationship between the shape of the tokens and that of the markings, arguing that there were many more shapes of tokens than there were shapes of markings. In other publications, Amiet hypothesized that the envelopes were bills of lading accompanying shipments of goods from centers of production in the country to administrative centers in cities.[222] This interpretation is now disputed.[223]

Cahiers de la Délégation Archéologique Française en Iran, vols. 8–9 (1978)

The campaign of 1972 in Chantier Acropole I explored level 17B. The archival material recovered in the season consists of six impressed tablets, one envelope with no visible markings,[224] and eleven plain[225] and two complex tokens found loose.[226] The material was scattered in and about structures where stone working may have taken place.

The results of the last campaign of 1977 are not yet fully published, and in particular the report on small clay finds is not available. The excavations of level 18 produced a significant assemblage of eleven impressed tablets, seventeen envelopes with eight specimens bearing markings showing the continuation of the use of the same archival material as in the structures of the previous level.[227] Furthermore, among the numerous

36.1. Cones, Susa, Iran. Courtesy Musée du Louvre, Département des Antiquités Orientales.

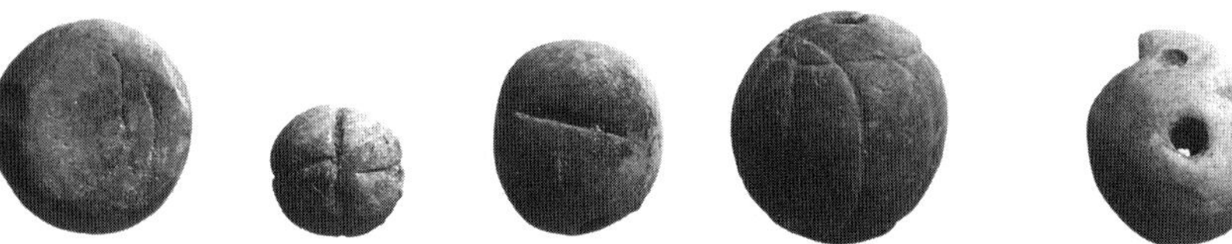

36.2. Spheres, Susa, Iran. Courtesy Musée du Louvre, Département des Antiquités Orientales.

sealings recovered, one solid clay ball bears the impression of a complex token.[228]

ASSEMBLAGE

The token assemblage from Susa broke away from the traditional Iranian collections of the early fourth millennium B.C. In particular, it was larger and included a far greater variety of types and subtypes than any other earlier sites (figs. 36.1–36.15).

It is difficult, of course, to compare the number of tokens of different sites because the amount of artifacts recovered depends on many variables such as the number of cubic meters of dirt examined, the methods of excavation, and luck. It may be significant, however, that Susa produced the largest collection of tokens in Iran. There are 783 tokens at Susa, compared, for instance, to 62 at Seh Gab, an Iranian site typical of the late fifth and the early fourth millennia B.C.[229] It may be equally significant that the early phases of Susa produced only a dozen counters, whereas the bulk of the collection belongs to the middle of the fourth millennium B.C.

The most important feature of the Susa collection consists, however, of a large increase of types and subtypes. The Seh Gabi assemblage, for example, includes only the seven following shapes: spheres, disks, cones, tetrahedrons, ovoids, cylinders, and hyperboloids. That of Susa, on the other hand, lacks hyperboloids but yields nine additional forms: biconoids, bent coils, triangles, parabolas, rectangles, rhomboids, vessels, tools, and animals. Of these types, only the disks, cones, and rectangles can be documented in the early layers of Susa.

The most striking feature of the Susa token assem-

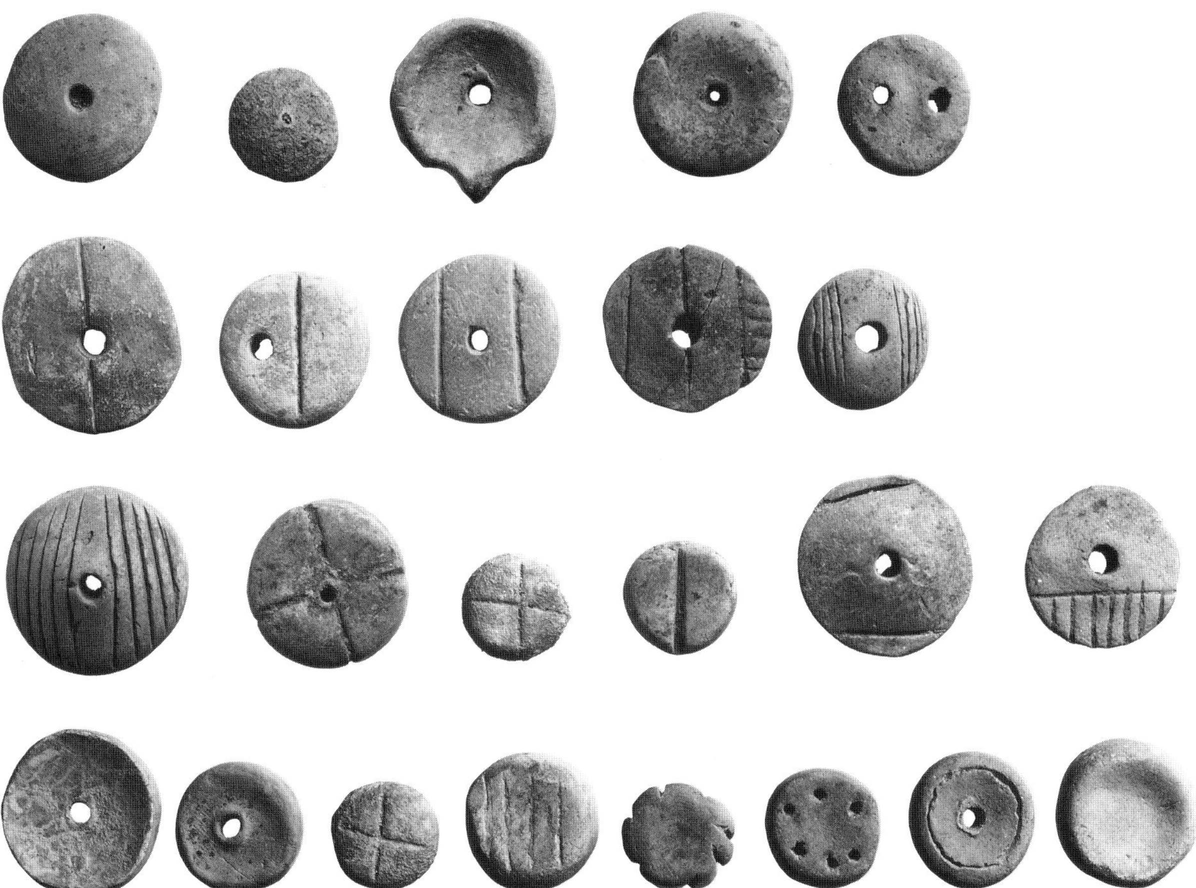

36.3. Disks, Susa, Iran. Courtesy Musée du Louvre, Département des Antiquités Orientales.

blage of the middle fourth millennium B.C. consists of a quantum jump in the number of subtypes. As discussed above, subtypes entail a voluntary modification of the basic types of tokens either by a variation in the size, a division into fractions, an alteration of the shape by pinching, and, mostly, the addition of features such as punched and linear markings or appliqué coils and pellets. Seh Gabi, for instance, has altogether 12 subtypes of tokens compared to 190 at Susa. Seh Gabi and the early levels of Susa have only plain-faced tokens (figs. 29.1 and 29.2), but 50.1 percent of the late fourth-millennium tokens bear markings. Seh Gabi has only one type of plain, medium-sized sphere, but there are ten varieties at Susa, including two different sizes; hemispheres, pinched specimens, and others bearing either punched or different linear patterns. There are three subtypes of disks at Seh Gabi, lenticular, flat, and large, against thirty-one at Susa. The collection of disks from Susa includes lenticular, flat, and large subtypes as well but yields also high disks and twenty-one subtypes with different patterns of linear or punched markings. There are three subtypes of cones at Seh

36.4. Cylinders, Susa, Iran. Courtesy Musée du Louvre, Département des Antiquités Orientales.

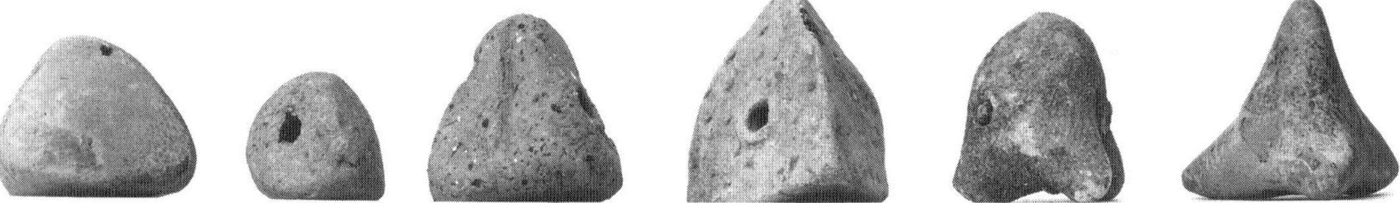

36.5. Tetrahedrons, Susa, Iran. Courtesy Musée du Louvre, Département des Antiquités Orientales.

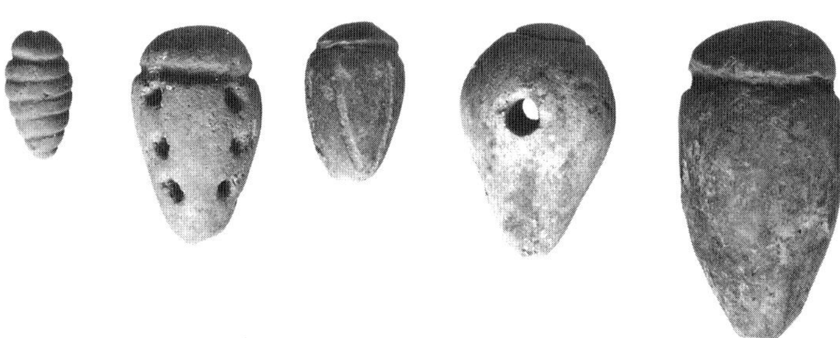

36.6. Ovoids, Susa, Iran. Courtesy Musée du Louvre, Département des Antiquités Orientales.

Gabi compared to nineteen at Susa. Seh Gabi has a single subtype of tetrahedrons and ovoids and two of cylinders, but, on the other hand, Susa has six subtypes of tetrahedrons, twelve of ovoids, and seven of cylinders.

While the collection of tokens from Susa differs from those of earlier Iranian sites, it is strikingly similar to that of Uruk in number, manufacture, types, and subtypes. First, it may not be by chance that about the same number of tokens was recovered in Eanna and on the Acropolis of Susa. Second, the objects are so alike in size, quality of clay, and color and the markings they bear are so identical that if specimens from the two sites were mixed accidentally it would be impossible to tell them apart. The resemblance between the two collections is based on both obvious and subtle details. The tokens from Susa and Uruk are specially light weight, being made of a characteristic paste, usually devoid of any inclusions. The clay tokens from both sites are characterized by a typical buff-pink color. This indicates not only a homogeneous quality of clay but also a common expertise in the technology of fir-

36.7. Rectangles, Susa, Iran. Courtesy Musée du Louvre, Département des Antiquités Orientales.

36.8. Triangles, Susa, Iran. Courtesy Musée du Louvre, Département des Antiquités Orientales.

ing. Compared to tokens of the fifth millennium B.C., which often exhibited a black core due to incomplete firing, these tokens are pink throughout. There are often examples showing black areas on the surface. This seems, however, not to derive from misfiring but rather from being mixed with ashes and charcoal, probably when they were discarded after they were no longer used. There are a few stone tokens in each assemblage; namely, nineteen at Susa and a dozen at Uruk. Susa, like Uruk, had rare specimens made of bitumen, and those were always confined to plain subtypes.[230]

Moreover, the markings on the Susa complex tokens consist of the same elements arranged according to patterns identical to those of Uruk. Lines and punctations are displayed in the same way on a single face of disks, triangles, parabolas, and other flat tokens but cover the entire surface of spheres, ovoids, cones, and other globular forms. Also, as was discussed above, Susa shares with Uruk token series among disks, cylinders, ovoids, triangles, biconoids, paraboloids, bent coils, and vessels. Finally, Susa and Uruk used the same systems of storing tokens, either by stringing them or enclosing them in clay envelopes.

36.9. Biconoids, Susa, Iran. Courtesy Musée du Louvre, Département des Antiquités Orientales.

36.10. Paraboloids, Susa, Iran. Courtesy Musée du Louvre, Département des Antiquités Orientales.

CHRONOLOGY

Susa was settled and grew to be a metropolis in the fourth millennium B.C. There is an indication that the temple built on the Acropolis enjoyed a period of splendor characterized by monumental constructions during Period I. This phase ended in a conflagration at the end of the prehistoric period, after which new structures were built on a more modest scale during Period II.[231] Many different systems of chronology have been developed to date the various phases and the material of Susa. For the sake of clarity, the results of the various teams that have worked at Susa are discussed below using their own terminology.

The stratigraphy of Chantier Acropole I, campaigns 1969 to 1978, is as follows:

Levels 17–18 (Eanna IV–VI):
plain and complex tokens
envelopes marked and unmarked
impressed tablets
Levels 19–24 (Eanna VII–XIII):
no information
Levels 25–27 (Eanna XIV–XVII):
plain tokens

36.11. Bent coils, Susa, Iran. Courtesy Musée du Louvre, Département des Antiquités Orientales.

36.12. Vessels, Susa, Iran. Courtesy Musée du Louvre, Département des Antiquités Orientales.

36.13. Tools, Susa, Iran. Courtesy Musée du Louvre, Département des Antiquités Orientales.

These data suggest that at Susa like elsewhere in Iran plain tokens were used during the prehistoric period, whereas complex and sometimes perforated tokens were present during the protoliterate period. There are, however, two shortcomings in the documentation offered by Chantier Acropole I. First, levels 19–24 did not produce meaningful assemblages.[232] It is particularly unfortunate to have a major gap in these strata, because they correspond to the critical period when complex tokens and series start occurring at Uruk. Chantier Acropole I documents therefore only the last segment in the evolution of the token system, namely, its period of florescence in Eanna VI. It fails to bring any new precision to the transition from plain to complex tokens.

The second shortcoming of Chantier Acropole I is the lack of carbon 14 dates. The material is estimated according to the relative chronology of Uruk, but as the Eanna sequence does not rely either on carbon 14 dates, the situation remains very much the case of the blind leading the blind.

The excavations of 1965 to 1968 by Steve and Gasche provide the first and only carbon 14 dates for the archaic period of Susa.[233] Accordingly, the four tokens recovered in these campaigns can be dated as follows: a painted disk from level A 2, 3420 ± 40 or 3325 ± 75 B.C.; two complex and perforated tokens with zigzag edges (type 14: 9) from A 1, 3143 ± 105 B.C.; one punched cone of the Jemdet Nasr period, ca. 2973 B.C.[234] These results are interesting because, first, they attest to the use of painted tokens in the middle of the fourth millennium B.C.; second, they indicate the use of complex and perforated tokens in A 1 in the late fourth millennium B.C. at a date comparable to tokens

36.14. Animals, type 15: 3, 5, 9, 10, 12, 24, 25, 27. Courtesy Musée du Louvre, Département des Antiquités Orientales.

of Uruk; third and lastly, the punched cone suggests that complex tokens might have lingered at Susa when they had already disappeared at Uruk. It cannot be overemphasized, however, that these statements are based on only four specimens, three of which are of unusual types having no parallel elsewhere.[235] Furthermore, none of the artifacts was recovered *in situ*. Instead, the objects were mixed in the general trash accumulated around the monumental brick terrace. The sample of tokens is therefore so poor in quantity and quality that it should probably be dismissed altogether.

A clearer picture emerges from Dyson's trenches, where both complex and plain tokens are present in the upper levels (strata 1–14 = Uruk VI–IV), whereas the lower levels produced only plain tokens (strata 15–40 = Eanna VII–XIV).[236] In fact, complex tokens occur only in the top strata 4–5, which correspond to Uruk IV, while plain tokens continue to be represented until level 38. It may be significant that the Dyson collection yields plain rectangles in levels contemporaneous with the plain rectangles of Acropole I.[237] This type of token, which is not frequent in other sites, may prove to be a regional variation.

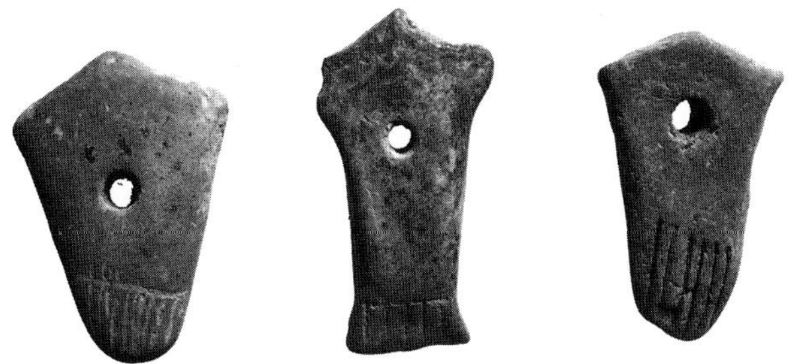

36.15. Garments (?), Susa, Iran. Courtesy Musée du Louvre, Département des Antiquités Orientales.

Le Breton included the tokens ("gaming pieces"), envelopes ("bullae"), and impressed tablets ("first tablets") excavated by Morgan and Mecquenem in his study of the chronology of Susa. On the basis of similarity with the material from Uruk, he attributed this material to his period Ca (Eanna VI–IV).[238] I propose to regard the two plain and painted cones reported by Mecquenem in layers of painted pottery as belonging to an earlier period (Ba) corresponding to Eanna VI–VIII or earlier.[239] Accordingly, the Mecquenem excavations exhibit a token assemblage characterized by plain and painted tokens in the prehistoric periods and by plain, complex, and perforated tokens in the protoliterate period.

The tokens of the *vase à la cachette* provide a further piece of information. This vessel was of Style II of Susa, irrefutably dated to the Early Dynastic period. It held not only tokens but also a collection of alabaster and metal vessels comparable to the material of the royal cemetery of Ur, which is dated to Early Dynastic III, ca. 2500 B.C.[240] It could be argued that this particular group of tokens, which were made of stone rather than clay, were not everyday artifacts but had some unknown symbolic function. Nevertheless, this may mean that tokens continued to be used in some fashion in Susa for a longer period than in Uruk, as was already suggested by the tokens of the 1965 to 1968 campaigns. In fact, tokens could have lasted as long as Proto-Elamite writing, which also ceased to exist about 2500 B.C.[241]

In sum, Period I (levels 27–23 = Eanna XIV–XI) yielded only plain or painted tokens, indicating that complex tokens appeared later at Susa than at Uruk. The first documented occurrence of complex tokens at Susa consists of five specimens, belonging to the end of Period II (levels 18–17 = Eanna VI–IV). The earliest complex tokens of Susa coincide, therefore, not with the beginning of the complex phenomenon at Eanna but rather with its period of florescence. Finally, the unique collection of tokens enclosed in the *vase à la cachette* shows that plain and stone counters remained in use at Susa, at least in certain circumstances, longer than at Uruk and as late as Period III, in the Early Dynastic period. The tokens of Susa and those of Uruk are thus synchronized only during the time corresponding to Eanna VI–IV. It is particularly noteworthy that the token system, which was in tune with the evolution of Eanna at Uruk, is out of step with the development of the Susa temple. The erection of the first high temple in Period I had seemingly no effect on the token system. As far as we know, it remained totally unchanged by the event but continued to consist of only a few subtypes of mostly plain or painted tokens. Complex tokens do not appear during the florescence of the Susa temple but rather after its destruction by fire. The innovations in accounting at Susa took place, therefore, during the period of decline of the sanctuary, when monumental architecture was being replaced by modest structures, at a time when one could expect a collapse of the economy.[242]

CONTEXT

The totality of the Susa counters originated from the Acropolis, with the exception of a group found in the adjacent Ville Royale.[243] There is no indication that any of the other tells that constitute the site of Susa yielded any tokens. Steve's excavations have revealed that the Acropolis was the seat of a major temple built upon a large mud brick terrace similar to those of Mesopotamia.[244] The presence of such a sanctuary implies, in turn, a religious precinct, including not only shrines but administrative offices, workshops, and warehouses. The extent of the precinct has never been defined, but there are some indications of its layout. For instance, Dyson noted the presence of clay cone mosaics, used in the decoration of monumental buildings, in each layer of his trench.[245] This suggests that the area he investigated east of the temple was occupied by buildings of public or religious function. According to the excavations of Mecquenem[246] and Chantier Acropole I,[247] workshops and warehouses were located in the southern part of the tell.

The tokens were not distributed evenly throughout the Acropolis but were concentrated in some particular areas and sparse in others; for example, there were only a few in the northern part. In particular, Mecquenem recovered a single envelope in the *sondage nord* (north sounding).[248] According to Steve and Dyson's trenches, there were equally few specimens in the immediate vicinity of the temple and to the east. On the other hand, almost every single trench opened in the southern half of the Acropolis has produced small or large collections of tokens loose or enclosed in envelopes. This suggests that counting and accounting took place in the vicinity of the warehouses and workshops.

It should be expected that, like Eanna at Uruk, the temple precinct of Susa was subject to constant remodeling according to the needs and vicissitudes of the temple, which may explain why at Susa, like at Eanna, the material is never found *in situ*. In Dyson's trench, tokens were part of deposits of secondary trash accumulated in or about buildings after they were abandoned.[249] The same appears to be true of the few tokens excavated in the vicinity of the monumental terrace. One of these examples was mixed, perhaps, with the ashes and remains of sacrifices performed next to the temple in the Jemdet Nasr period.[250] As will be discussed in the section devoted to the envelopes holding tokens, the material of Chantier Acropole I also does not appear *in situ*. Mecquenem found some of his material disturbed by the large necropolis of Susa and was faced with the difficulty of disentangling the funerary deposits. He seems, in some cases, to have made the wrong assumptions in attributing some of the tokens found loose, as well as clay cones used for mosaics, to funerary deposits of children's graves, interpreting the former as "gaming pieces" and the latter as "ninepins."[251]

Jordan had immediately recognized that Uruk and Susa yielded similar artifacts.[252] Since then, many scholars have emphasized that Eanna VI–IV shares with the corresponding layers of Susa, levels 18–17, a characteristic assemblage. The various reports discuss the presence of identical potteries such as beveled-rim bowls and nose-lugged jars;[253] sealings used on jars and doors, envelopes holding tokens, as well as the oblong bullae and impressed tablets, which will be discussed further in the volume;[254] cylinder seals using similar symbols and, in particular, the figure of the southern Mesopotamian priest-king, or En, with the same attire as described for those of Eanna, consisting of a net skirt and round headdress;[255] and finally, buildings decorated with the same clay cone mosaics.[256] It is well known, therefore, that the levels that produced complex tokens at Susa were of the same archaeological horizon as those of Uruk. Furthermore, Thomas W. Beale has pointed out that the material shared by Susa and Uruk was not a random assemblage but that all the items were articles belonging to a bureaucracy—headed by prestigious officials, or En's—recognizable by status symbols such as special garments and headdresses, operating in special buildings decorated by mosaics (warehouses?), and controlling real goods by the means of (1) a system of seals; (2) measuring devices such as beveled-rim bowls and other pottery containers; (3) a more precise reckoning system using complex counters; and (4) new archival techniques with clay envelopes and strings of tokens.

PARALLELS

Susa was not alone in Iran in yielding tokens in the second half of the fourth millennium B.C.; the counters endured in the other protohistoric sites. They are attested, for example, at Chogha Mish and Farukhabad in Susiana; Tepe Yahya and Shahdad in the south of the country; and at Tepe Hissar in the north.

It is remarkable, however, that most Iranian token assemblages do not give any indication of change. Instead, they maintain the usual types of counters known since the eighth millennium B.C. For example, Farukhabad,[257] Sharafabad,[258] KS 34 and KS 76 in the west,[259] Tepe Sialk on the Iranian Plateau,[260] and Tepe Yahya[261] have assemblages consisting mostly of plain cones, spheres, disks, cylinders, and tetrahedrons.

The case of Tepe Hissar is interesting. Level II, which produced tokens with a modest number of specimens bearing punctations, corresponds to a period of change in administrative and craft activities. The appearance of cylinder seals, tablet blanks, and jar stoppers coincides with an increase in copper smelting and the use of exotic materials such as gold, silver, lapis lazuli, carnelian, turquoise, and alabaster.[262]

In Iran, complex tokens are present only in the assemblages of Susa, Chogha Mish,[263] Moussian,[264] KS 54[265] and Tepe Hissar II.[266] The first four sites are all located in Susiana. Reciprocally, no complex tokens are found in sites outside of that region, except for Tepe Hissar. The phenomenon of complex tokens in Iran should be considered, therefore, as involving almost exclusively Susiana, the geographic extension of the Mesopotamian plain. Furthermore, it should be noted that not all sites of Susiana yielded complex tokens; for example, Farukhabad had none. On the other hand, Tepe Hissar II yielded administrative material, such as cylinder seals, which has parallels in Susa.[267]

The four Susiana sites feature remains of public architecture. Chogha Mish, the Iranian site which yields the greatest number of complex tokens parallel to those of Susa, was the largest center after the metropolis. Furthermore, Chogha Mish shares with Susa an assemblage including clay cone mosaics;[268] seals and sealings, some featuring the dignified, bearded En, clad in a long net kilt and wearing the headdress with a typical bun;[269] envelopes to hold tokens; and large amounts of beveled-rim bowls and nose-lugged jars.[270] Susa and Chogha Mish, therefore, shared not only complex tokens but an entire bureaucratic paraphernalia.

Moussian was an uncommonly large settlement, covering an area of about fifteen hectares, and was probably surrounded by an impressive defensive wall.[271] Lastly, the ruins of an unusually heavily constructed building were unearthed at KS 54. The site also produced copper implements and gold and lapis lazuli beads, which as assessed by Gregory A. Johnson were unlikely to have been the possessions of simple villagers.[272] The complex tokens of the four Susiana sites seem to belong to a public rather than domestic setting.

It is interesting to note that the four Susiana assemblages yielded a larger proportion of triangles than is usual elsewhere. For instance, triangles, either plain-faced or displaying one to ten lines, constitute the largest group of tokens at Susa. There are 123 specimens in the collection, amounting to 17.6 percent of the collection, compared to 72, or 9.1 percent, at Uruk. Chogha Mish has also a diversified series of triangles, including examples with a plain face and others bearing three, five, and ten lines. Furthermore, at KS 54, five of the nine tokens produced by the site were triangles, some displaying one or three lines. Finally, the only two complex specimens of the nineteen tokens of Moussian were triangles, one plain-faced and the second with two lines.

Susa is one of six Iranian sites yielding complex tokens. The fact that none of the remaining fourth-millennium sites, except Tepe Hissar II, produced complex counters demonstrates that in Iran, as in Mesopotamia, changes in the reckoning device occurred in particular places to the exclusion of others. The Iranian sites also demonstrate that changes in the token system always coincide with an increase in bureaucratic tools, such as cylinder seals and sealings. The region most involved was Susiana, contiguous to southern Mesopotamia. Susa and Chogha Mish shared the bureaucratic assemblage typical of Mesopotamia with clay cone mosaics and typical seals and sealings, but differed in having a larger proportion of triangles.

The tokens from Susa have a strong family resemblance to those of Uruk. First, the similarity of manufacture of the artifacts makes it conceivable that they came out of the same workshop. Second, the two collections include the same new complex types, subtypes, and series. Third, in both sites the counters were recovered in the vicinity of an important temple.

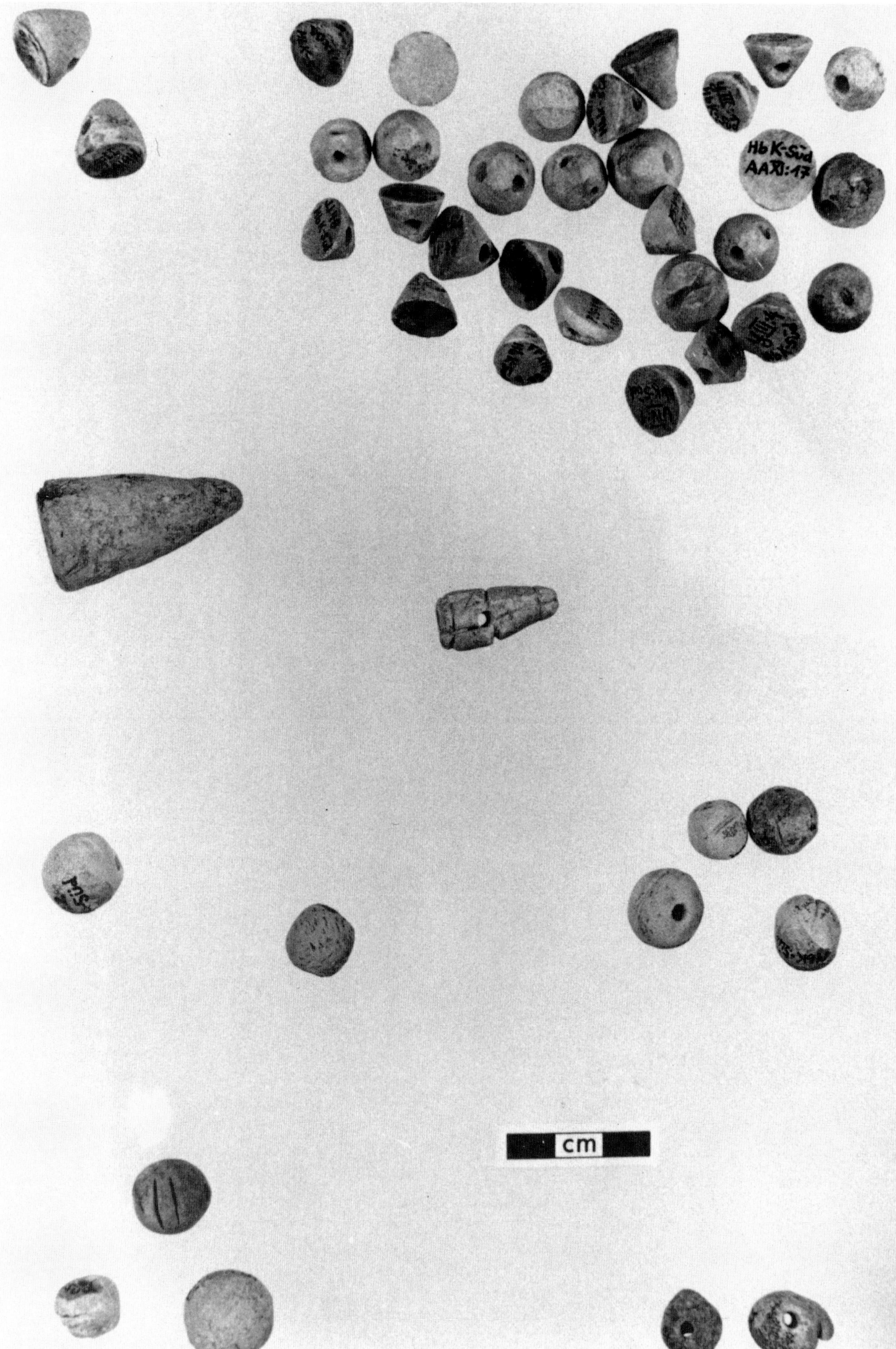
Hb K-Süd
AAXI:17
cm

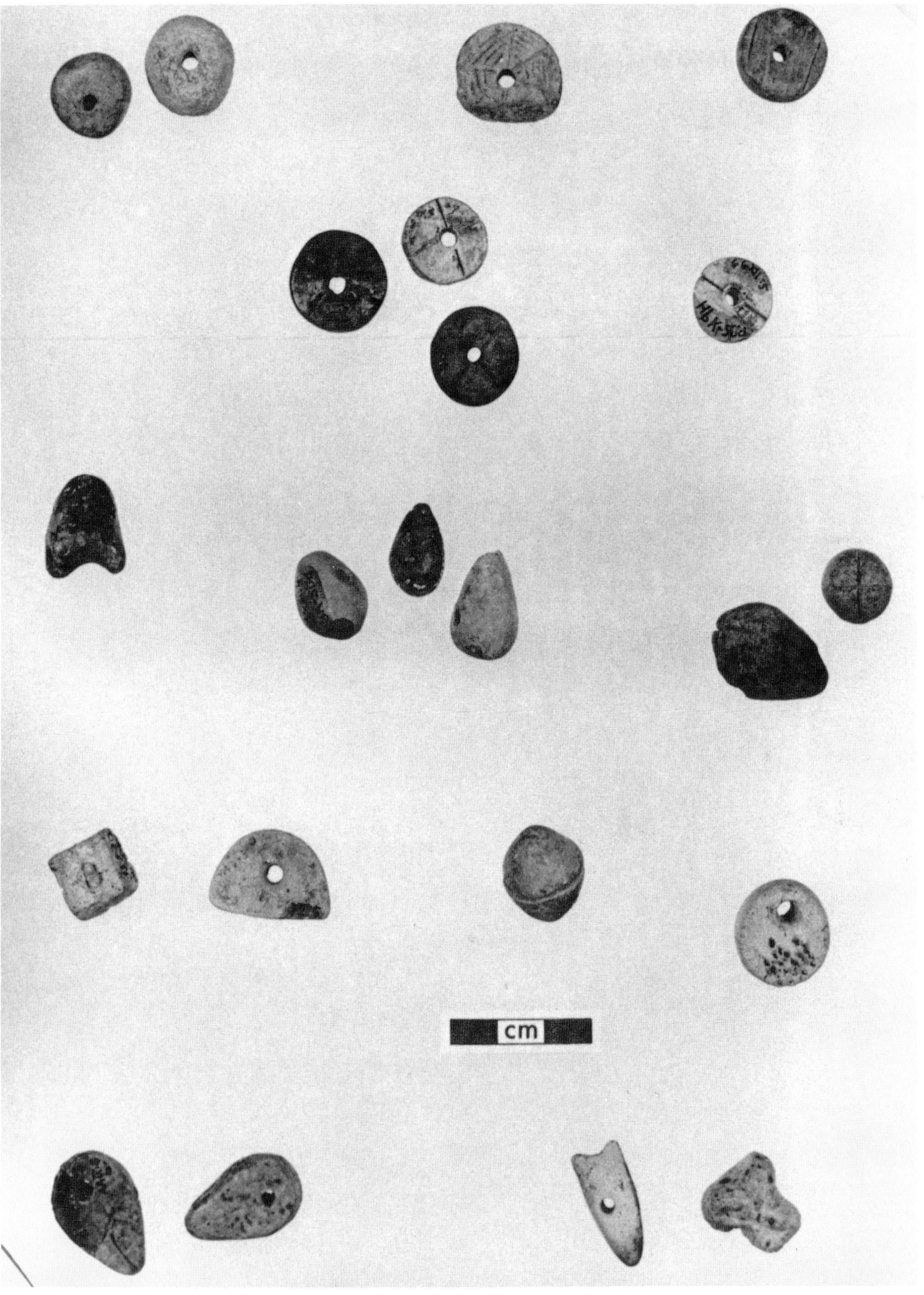

37.1. Tokens from Habuba Kabira, Syria. Photo by Klaus Anger; courtesy Museum für Vor- und Frühgeschichte, Berlin.

37.2. Tokens from Habuba Kabira, Syria. Photo by Klaus Anger; courtesy Museum für Vor- und Frühgeschichte, Berlin.

37.3. Tokens from Habuba Kabira, Syria. Photo by Klaus Anger; courtesy Museum für Vor- und Frühgeschichte, Berlin.

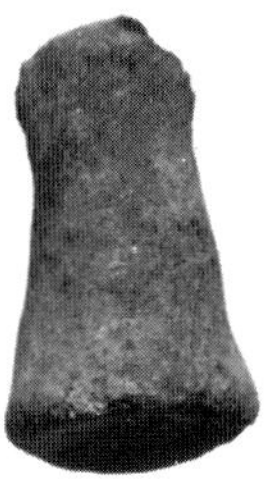

38.1. Cone, Tell Ramad I, Syria. Courtesy Henri de Contenson.

There are two major differences, however, between the two assemblages. First, the date of appearance of complex tokens at Uruk is earlier than at Susa, demonstrating that Susa followed rather than preceded Uruk. Second, the associated assemblage, consisting of monumental buildings decorated with clay cone mosaics, beveled-rim bowls, seals, and sealings, was familiar in southern Mesopotamia but foreign in Iran. As a consequence, the phenomenon of complex tokens was either inspired or brought from southern Mesopotamia to Elam.

Habuba Kabira

Habuba Kabira is located on the Euphrates River in present-day Syria.[273] It is the site of a city occupied during a short interval of about 120 years in the middle of the fourth millennium B.C.[274] The religious precinct is known under the name of Tell Kannas.[275] The excavations at Habuba Kabira have produced 141 tokens (figs. 37.1–37.3) and 2 envelopes and at Tell Kannas 58 counters. The collection is of significance, first, because many of the tokens have close parallels in Uruk and Susa while being unique in Syria. Second, sixty tokens recovered *in situ* provide new information on the distribution of the counters in a fourth-millennium city.

THE COMPLEX TOKENS AT HABUBA KABIRA AND THEIR PLACE IN SYRIA

Tokens were in use in Syria for a continuous period of five thousand years. The first counters occurred about 8000 to 7500 B.C. at Tell Mureybet III,[276] Cheikh Hassan,[277] and Tell Aswad I.[278] During the seventh to fourth millennia B.C., the token system is represented at Tell Aswad II (figs. 24.1–24.5),[279] Ghoraife,[280] and Tell Ramad;[281] Tell Halaf;[282] the Amuq,[283] Chagar Bazar,[284] Tell Brak,[285] Habuba Kabira, Tell Kannas,[286] and Jebel Aruda.[287]

As in Mesopotamia and Iran, there are two kinds of token assemblages in Syria: All the sites prior to 3500 B.C. produced plain tokens, but three assemblages after 3500 B.C., among which was Habuba Kabira–Tell Kannas, yielded complex tokens. The difference between plain and complex in Syrian assemblages is best defined by comparing the complex tokens of Habuba Kabira to the plain tokens of Tell Ramad.

The collection of 381 tokens of Tell Ramad consists merely of the six most common types of counters: cones (figs. 38.1 and 38.2), spheres, disks, cylinders, tetrahedrons, and ovoids. On the other hand, the token collection of 141 counters of Habuba Kabira has eight additional types, which never or rarely occur before 3500 B.C., such as rectangles, triangles, biconoids, paraboloids, bent coils, rhomboids, vessels, and animals.[288] Cylinders, which are absent at Habuba Kabira, are featured in the assemblage of Tell Kannas.[289] There are, therefore, twice as many types of tokens at Habuba Kabira compared to the assemblage of Tell Ramad.

Furthermore, among the 381 tokens from Tell Ramad, 379 are plain-faced and only two counters bear markings.[290] By contrast, seventy-eight (57 percent) of the counters of Habuba Kabira display markings.

38.2. Cones, Tell Ramad II, Syria. Courtesy Henri de Contenson.

Among these fifty-six (40.8 percent) feature incised lines, sixteen (11.6 percent) have notches, three (.02 percent), are punctated, and four (.03 percent) are pinched. The complex tokens of Habuba Kabira can be divided, therefore, into fifty-six subtypes[291] with the addition of six further subtypes at Tell Kannas,[292] compared to eleven subtypes at Tell Ramad.

The collection of 199 tokens and 62 subtypes of Habuba Kabira and Tell Kannas is also larger and more diversified than that of any other fourth-millennium Syrian assemblage. There are only three complex tokens at Tell Brak[293], and Jebel Aruda, located in close proximity to Habuba Kabira on the same bank of the Euphrates River, produced only a small assemblage of eleven counters with a single complex token.[294] Chagar Bazar and the Amuq yielded only plain counters. No report is available on the tokens from Qraya, a fourth-millennium site near Terqa.[295] The token assemblage of Habuba Kabira and Tell Kannas has a diversity which is, therefore, unique in Syria.

PARTICULARITIES OF MANUFACTURE

The tokens of Habuba Kabira are otherwise similar in size, material, and manufacture to those elsewhere in Syria and in the Near East. Their dimensions usually range from 1 to 3 cm with some spheres (type 2: 1) as small as 7 or 8 mm[296] and a cone (type 1: 1) as high as 39 mm.[297] The artifacts were made of clay except for a peculiar and unique series of thirty-four small equilateral stone cones (type 1: 3; fig. 37.1). Some of the counters were done with care, and among them the stone cones, several clay disks, and some ovoids, but others were sloppily modeled. The manufacture of the clay specimens consisted simply in pinching a small lump of clay between the fingers, except, perhaps, for several disks with slanting sides, and a small ridge around the upper face, which, as discussed above, may indicate the trace of a mold.[298] All the clay tokens were fired, as shown by their predominantly buff-reddish color with some greenish to blackish specimens.

In the rule, markings were traced on the tokens with a pointed tool or the fingernail when the clay was still moist. There are five instances at Habuba Kabira, however, when lines were scratched after firing either on previously plain tokens[299] or next to markings applied before firing (fig. 37.3).[300]

A square with two running incised lines and topped by a pellet (type 7: 25) seems also worthy of attention (fig. 37.3).[301] It is likely that the counter features a box secured by strings and sealed. If so, the token provides an interesting facsimile of a complete shipment showing the exact position of the sealings.

PARALLELS IN MESOPOTAMIA AND ELAM

The closest parallels to the token collection of Habuba Kabira are found in Uruk, Mesopotamia, and Susa, Elam. Habuba Kabira shares, for example, twenty-six subtypes with Uruk. In other words, 51.06 percent or seventy-two counters from Habuba Kabira have identical counterparts in Uruk,[302] with sixteen additional specimens differing only by a detail.[303] Similarly, Habuba Kabira shares twenty-three subtypes with Susa.[304] Accordingly, ninety-eight tokens or 69.5 percent of the assemblage of Habuba Kabira could just as well have originated in Susa.

The collections of about eight hundred tokens from Uruk and Susa are, of course, considerably larger than that of Habuba Kabira. They also held two additional types of counters—cylinders (present at Tell Kannas) and tools—and included 180 subtypes. On the other hand, Habuba Kabira differs from Uruk and Susa in having a greater number of stone specimens with, in particular, the unique series of stone cones discussed above.

DISTRIBUTION

Tokens were located wherever excavations took place in Habuba Kabira and, in particular, in the northern, central, and southern parts of the site. As was mentioned above, tokens were also recovered at Tell Kannas, the city's religious district. As is often the case in other sites, the counters of Habuba Kabira were occasionally recovered in courtyards or vacant spaces where they had been discarded in antiquity.[305] Sixty tokens, however, were excavated among the remains of seven buildings and in one of the city gates. The counters found *in situ* provide a unique insight into the distribution of tokens in a fourth-millennium city.

The buildings in which tokens were discovered were large structures generally laid out according to a plan familiar in southern Mesopotamia, with small rooms organized around a central courtyard. This was the case, in particular, for Buildings 2, 31, 35, 38, 40, and 43. Building 45, however, was different. Most of these structures yielded not only tokens but other administrative material. For example, Building 2 also produced two envelopes, oblong bullae, and four impressed tablets; Building 35 yielded one impressed tablet and two sealings; cylinder seals were recovered in Buildings 40 and 43; and, finally, Building 38 had a jar sealing. Otherwise, the artifacts collected in the different houses, such as flint tools, pottery, and spindle whorls, suggest domestic activities.

The number of tokens recovered in each structure varied from twenty-one in Building 40 to two in Buildings 43, 45, and 54. There were, respectively, three tokens in Buildings 31, 35, and 38, four in Building 5, and seven in Buildings 2 and 36. Also, the counters were often distributed among several rooms. For example, in the case of Building 40, which produced the largest number of tokens, the twenty-one specimens were divided into five rooms as follows: Room a, 5; b, 9; d, 1; f, 1; and h, 5. Furthermore, the small groups of tokens were usually composed of several subtypes. The twenty-one tokens of Building 40, for instance, belonged to thirteen subtypes with, among them, four disks with perpendicular lines (type 3: 51), two disks with two groups of four lines (type 3: 32), two ovoids with an incised cross (type 6: 23), and two triangles with an incised side (type 8: 38). Building 2 is unique in yielding only one type of token; namely, ovoids with an incised line (type 6: 14). Although no two buildings produced identical token assemblages, stone cones (type 1: 3) occurred in four houses; spheres with two notches (type 2: 8) and ovoids with an incised tip (type 6: 12) were recovered in two structures.

Fifteen tokens were discovered among the ruins of the southern city gate which gave access to the religious precinct of Tell Kannas. The tokens from the southern city gate consisted of four cones, six spheres, one disk, three ovoids, and one triangle. In this context also, the counters were associated with a cylinder seal and numerous oblong bullae.

The plotting of tokens at Habuba Kabira reveals three major pieces of information. First, tokens in this case did not belong to a special area of the site but to special structures, namely buildings of Sumerian plan. Second, the presence of tokens in a gateway of Habuba Kabira seems especially significant because of parallel instances elsewhere. For example, at Uruk, tokens were concentrated in the eastern and western part of Eanna, where, as discussed above, the gates to the precinct were presumably located. Also, at Godin Tepe, the largest cache of impressed tablets came from the gate room at the entrance of the compound.[306] Third, the most surprising piece of information concerns the number of tokens. They were unexpectedly few since the largest collection recovered, in Building 40, did not exceed twenty-one counters. It seems also important to realize that, except in Building 2, each cluster of tokens *in situ* consisted of multiple kinds of counters. As will be discussed later in the book, the new information on the number and kinds of tokens dealt with and the location where accounting took place is important for understanding the function of the token system.

CHRONOLOGY

Habuba Kabira was built and subsequently abandoned during an interval of some 120 years corresponding to Uruk VI and V. Consequently, the complex tokens of Habuba Kabira are dated to Eanna VI and V, corresponding to the period of floruit of the system at Uruk. At Habuba Kabira, as at Uruk, there is no evolution within the token assemblage during the interval of Eanna VI and V. For example, there is no difference between the tokens from the northern part of Habuba Kabira compared to those of the southern part of the city, estimated to have a discrepancy of about a century.

A SOUTHERN MESOPOTAMIAN ACCOUNTING SYSTEM

The complex tokens are found at Habuba Kabira, like at Susa, with artifacts typical of southern Mesopotamia but foreign to Syria and Elam.[307] First, the buildings in which tokens were recovered had a central courtyard characteristic of Sumerian structures. Second, Habuba Kabira shares with Susa a number of pottery shapes that originated in southern Mesopotamia, among which are beveled-rim bowls and nose-lugged jars with incised decorations.[308] Third, the same seals and sealings were used at the two sites, and the Mesopotamian priest-king is among the motifs which occur both at Susa and Habuba Kabira.[309] Also, the temples of Tell Kannas and Susa were faced with the same clay cone mosaics known from the Eanna precinct at Uruk.[310] On the other hand, a contemporaneous Syrian site such as Qraya, where there is no trace of architecture other than domestic, seemingly did not produce any complex tokens.[311] This information confirms that, like at Susa, the complex counters were part of a bureaucratic paraphernalia that included typical public buildings, seals and sealings, envelopes, and impressed tablets. More importantly, this administration originated in southern Mesopotamia.

Habuba Kabira provides important information on the development of the token system in Syria. First, Habuba Kabira represents the farthest extension of complex tokens toward the west. Second, the date of appearance of the complex counters in Syria coincides with that of Elam. In both cases, the first complex tokens are contemporaneous with the most developed period of the system at Eanna in level VI. Third, as at Susa, the counters of Habuba Kabira were part of a discrete assemblage, including typical buildings, potteries, and seals and sealings. This material was the hallmark of Eanna, signifying that the complex token phenomenon was of southern Mesopotamian origin and brought to Syria in the same way and at the same time as in Elam. Fourth, Habuba Kabira presents the best available information on the distribution of tokens in a fourth-millennium city, showing that the counters were used in small quantities. Fifth and finally, the fact that the complex tokens of Habuba Kabira have few parallels in Syria demonstrates that, as in Elam, complex tokens were adopted in certain centers to the exclusion of others.

The Complex Tokens Phenomenon

The three collections of Uruk, Susa, and Habuba Kabira document the composition, size, geographic extension, spacial distribution, chronology, and significance of the complex token assemblages. The Uruk collection, which yields 16 types and 241 subtypes of tokens, is the most diversified of the three collections and therefore shows best the transformation undergone by the token system in the fourth millennium B.C. In particular, the Uruk assemblage illustrates the multiplication of shapes and markings typical of complex token assemblages. The small clusters of counters located in houses of Habuba Kabira and the number of tokens recovered at each of the three sites—141 specimens at Habuba Kabira, 783 at Susa, and 812 at Uruk—suggest that complex tokens, like plain ones, were not handled in large quantities.

The complex token assemblages had a limited geographic distribution. They did not occur in Turkey or Palestine but were confined mostly to southern Mesopotamia, the adjacent Susiana plain, and the Euphrates River Valley in Syria. The complex counters from Uruk have parallels in southern Mesopotamian sites such as Tello, Ubaid, Eridu, Nippur, Jemdet Nasr, Kish, and Ur, but rarely in the north. For example, they do not exist at Tepe Gawra and are exceedingly scarce at Nineveh and Tell Billa. In Iran, Susa shared complex tokens with Chogha Mish, Moussian, and KS 54 in Susiana and Tepe Hissar in the north. Finally, Habuba Kabira was one of the three Syrian sites marking the farthest extension of the complex system westward.

In general, tokens were associated with public rather than private buildings. At Uruk the majority of the tokens was recovered in the temple of Inanna in monumental structures whose function is not known. There is indication that the counters of Susa were concentrated in an area of the temple precinct occupied by warehouses and workshops, whereas those of Habuba

Kabira belonged to special buildings of Mesopotamian character and to the gateway commanding access to the sanctuary.

Complex tokens lasted a limited period of time. At Uruk, they started in the Ubaid period, ca. 4400 B.C., reached a floruit in levels VI to IV, and declined in level IVa, about 3100 B.C. Instead, at Susa and Habuba Kabira, complex tokens were not represented before ca. 3500 B.C. Accordingly, southern Mesopotamia appears as the cradle of the complex tokens phenomenon.

The correlation between the evolution of the token system and that of the sanctuary of Eanna cannot be coincidental but points out a close relationship between the development of the southern Mesopotamian temple and complex counters. Moreover, the sites that furnish most complex token parallels with Uruk are also those which shared an entire bureaucratic paraphernalia typical of Eanna. At Tello, Susa, Chogha Mish, and Habuba Kabira–Tell Kannas the complex counters occur in levels characterized by public buildings faced with the same clay cone mosaics as those from Uruk.[312] Also, seals and sealings recovered in Susa and Habuba Kabira show identical patterns to those from Uruk. They feature, for example, the priest-king, known in Sumer as the En, wearing his characteristic attire, including a special kilt and headdress.[313] Finally, Tello, Susa, Chogha Mish, and Habuba Kabira yielded a number of pottery shapes which originated in southern Mesopotamia, such as nose-lugged jars with incised decorations and, in particular, numerous beveled-rim bowls.[314] This reveals that the reckoning device was part and parcel of the southern Mesopotamian temple bureaucracy.

4
WHERE TOKENS WERE HANDLED AND WHO USED THEM

There is one fact which can be established: the only phenomena which, always and in all parts of the world, seems to be linked with the appearance of writing . . . is the establishment of hierarchical societies, consisting of masters and slaves, and where one part of the population is made to work for the other part.

—Claude Lévi-Strauss[1]

THIS CHAPTER is devoted to a description of the contexts in which tokens have been recovered. I describe the types of settlements and structures where they were found and the artifacts with which they were associated. Finally, I focus on the rare tokens discovered in funerary contexts because these may yield important information concerning the status of the individuals with whom they were buried.

Types of Settlements

The five sites where tokens first appeared around 8000 B.C., Tepe Asiab and Ganj Dareh E in Iran and Tell Aswad, Tell Mureybet, and Cheikh Hassan in Syria, were remarkably similar. All were small open-air compounds built with characteristic round huts. Among them, the two Iranian settlements were semi-permanent, but Tell Mureybet, Cheikh Hassan, and Tell Aswad were fully sedentary, agricultural communities.

In the seventh to fourth millennia B.C., tokens spread to a great diversity of habitats. Beldibi and Belt Cave are examples of Neolithic caves and Tula'i of an encampment of nomadic herders yielding clay counters. The majority of plain tokens come, however, from sedentary villages of rectangular houses, such as Jarmo, Maghzaliyah, Tell Abada, and Yarim Tepe in Iraq; Ganj Dareh D through A, Hajji Firuz, and Seh Gabi in Iran; Tell Aswad and Tell Ramad in Syria; Ain Ghazal in Jordan; and Suberde and Can Hassan in Turkey. Complex tokens are associated, on the other hand, with the ruins of cities with monumental public architecture. This is the case, for instance, for Uruk, Tello, Ur, Jemdet Nasr, Susa, Chogha Mish, Habuba Kabira, and Tell Kannas.

Distribution within Settlements

Nothing is known about the distribution of counters in Jarmo, Arpachiyah, Hassuna, Tello, Ur, Tepe Asiab, Tepe Sarab, Anau, Mureybet, or Tell Kannas. Apparently, the grid technique of excavation experimented with at Jarmo did not allow plotting the artifacts in a coherent picture. In the other instances, the data are not published. Unfortunately, the distribution of tokens is disclosed only in a few sites, including Tell Abada, Uruk, and Tepe Gawra in Iraq; Ganj Dareh Tepe, Ali Kosh, Hajji Firuz, Tepe Gaz Tavila, Seh Gabi, Sharafabad, and Susa in Iran; and Tell Aswad and Habuba Kabira in Syria.

In most of the sites where the context of tokens was recorded, the counters were recovered partly within and partly outside buildings. At Tell Aswad, for example, a large number of spheres were located in open spaces (fig. 39).[2] The same is true at Ali Kosh,[3] Hajji Firuz,[4] or Seh Gabi,[5] where several tokens were mixed with animal bones and other debris in vacant lots in what appear to be trash deposits, where they were discarded in antiquity. At Sharafabad in the fourth millennium B.C., tokens were retrieved from an ancient

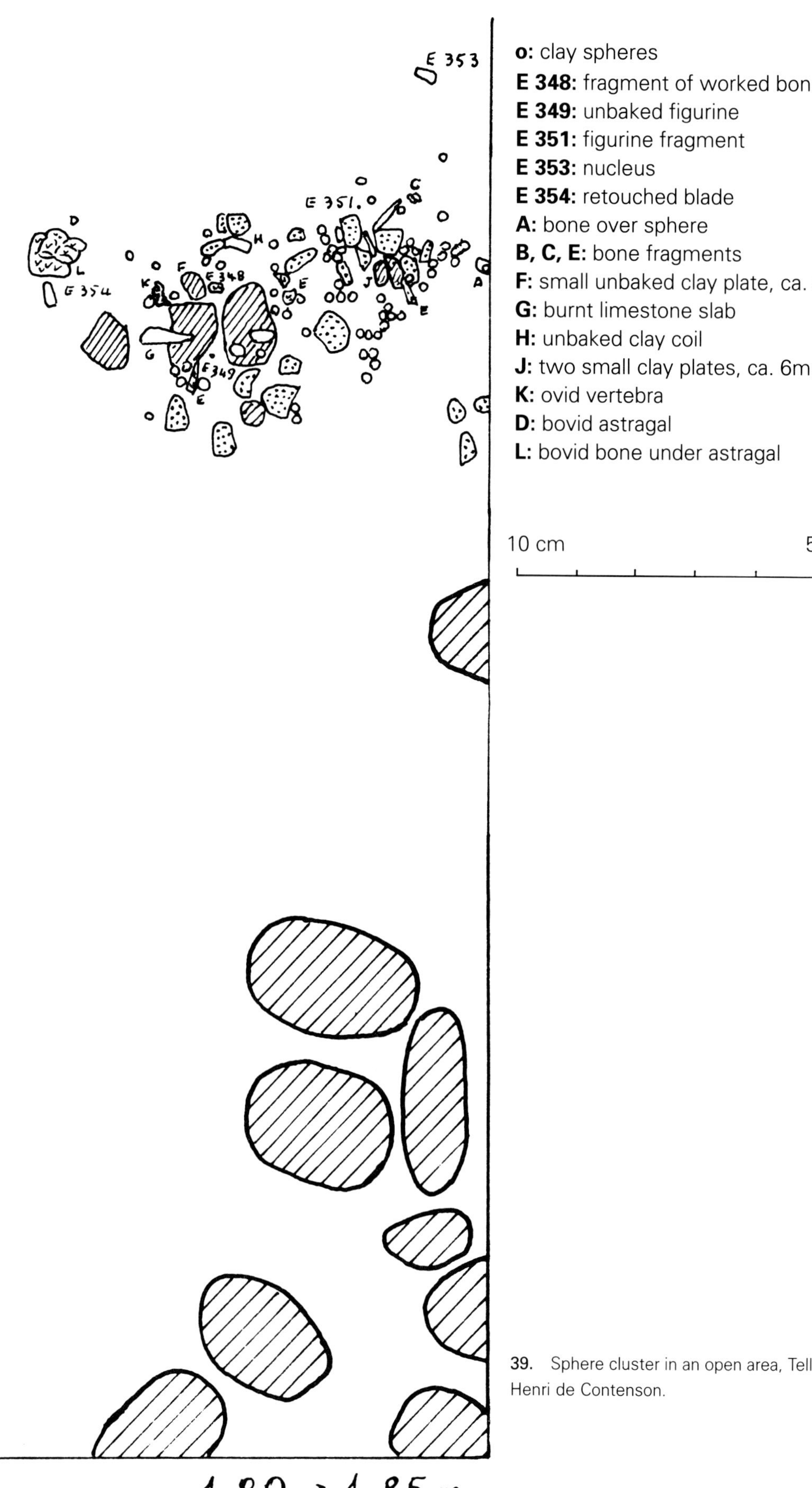

39. Sphere cluster in an open area, Tell Aswad, Syria. Courtesy Henri de Contenson.

garbage pit, where it could be determined that the counters were most often associated with early summer deposits but were rarer in layers corresponding to winter trash. Henry T. Wright noted that counters were thus discarded after the harvest in the traditional season for feasts.[6]

Both in Uruk and Susa tokens recur in close proximity to the main temples (figs. 32.1 and 32.2). In Uruk, counters were spotted all over the tell, but 719 examples, or 88.5 percent were excavated in the sacred precinct of Eanna, 43 or 5.3 percent came from the Anu Ziggurat, and 50 or 6.2 percent originated from the city's private quarters. It seems also significant that at Susa almost every single trench opened south of the main temple generated tokens, but only a few were recovered in the northern part of the same tell of the Acropolis and in the next tell de la Ville Royale. In both cities, a number of tokens originated from open spaces. For example, at Eanna tokens were scattered about on the grounds of the Stone Cone Temple[7] and of the Great Courtyard.[8] The precise excavation of R. H. Dyson, Jr., at Susa determined that most tokens occurring in his trench belonged to trash deposits.[9]

The information on the distribution of tokens within settlements, which remains scanty, suggests two important facts. First, in cities, tokens are more frequent in official rather than secular quarters. It should be kept in mind, however, that the disproportion between the number of tokens recovered in the temple precincts of Uruk and Susa compared to the private districts may reflect the amount of excavation carried out in each of these areas. Eanna, for example, was the focus of most of the work done at Uruk, whereas only sporadic trenches were dug in the city proper. In fact, at Habuba Kabira, tokens appeared in all parts of the city, including the temple area of Tell Kannas and the private quarters. The second piece of information concerning the recurrence of tokens among refuse in vacant lots is important because it suggests that the counters were discarded as soon as their function was fulfilled. In other words, this is an indication that they served primarily for record keeping rather than reckoning. This, in turn, shows a similarity with the archaic tablets of Uruk, which were also used for record keeping and are consistently found in dumps. The custom of routinely discarding economic tablets continued in historic times as alluded to in Sumerian texts.[10]

Structures

The structures which yielded tokens fall into two categories: domestic and public. At Ali Kosh, a few tokens were retrieved from a domestic setting, where they were associated with flint tools and ground stone mortars and pestles.[11] In this case, the counters give the impression of having been discarded when the house was no longer in use, rather than being *in situ*. The same is true at Seh Gabi, where some tokens were scattered among ordinary houses, here next to a jar,[12] there in a hearth.[13] In a number of sites, however, the counters were located in storage areas. At Ganj Dareh Tepe, for example, a large quantity of tokens lay among cubicles situated below the houses.[14] At Tell es-Sawwan,[15] Hajji Firuz,[16] and Gaz Tavila the objects were collected in storage rooms.[17]

The most interesting finding at Hajji Firuz consisted of a cluster of six cones located in a structure showing no trace of domestic activities such as cooking or flint chipping (fig. 40).[18] The building also differed from the remaining houses in other ways. First, it was smaller, consisting of a single room, instead of the normal two-room unit. Second, unusual features, such as a low platform and two posts, had been erected inside.[19] The structure which yielded most tokens at Hajji Firuz was apparently serving a special, yet enigmatic, function. Some of these tokens will again be discussed below, as they may also be part of a funerary setting.

At Tell Abada, the majority of the tokens, a total of forty artifacts, sometimes kept in vessels, were recovered in Building A, the largest building excavated in the settlement. The size of the building and the presence of infant burials suggested to the excavators "a religious significance."[20]

In the heavily fortified town of Tepe Gawra XIA, ca. 3700 B.C., a set of tokens was left behind in the inner citadel or "round house," but none are indicated in any of the surrounding dwellings. The six cylinders, two tetrahedrons, and two hemispheres were grouped together in one of the seventeen rooms of the building.[21]

At Uruk, tokens were related to some of the most spectacular buildings of level V, such as the Stone Cone Temple and the Limestone Temple, but the trenches laid in the city, for example in squares K–L XII, produced exceedingly few counters. Moreover, a cache of seventy-five tokens was recovered *in situ* in

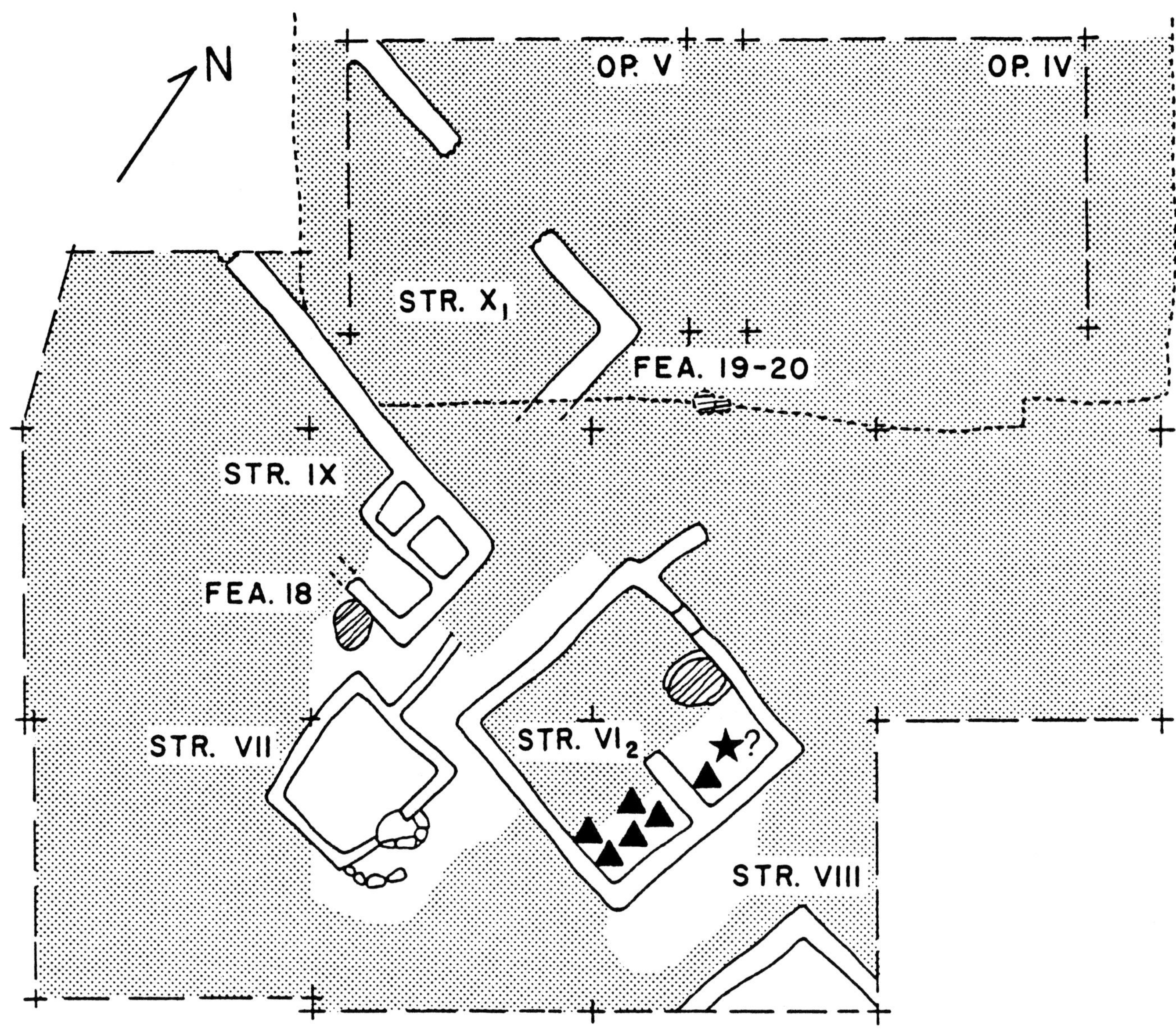

0 1 2 3 4 5M

HAJJI FIRUZ TEPE
PHASE D

▲ Cones (C-5)

★ Sealings (C-7)

Areas for which distributional data are not reliable

40. Cone distribution in Structure VI 1, Hajji Firuz, Iran. After Mary M. Voight, *Hajji Firuz Tepe, Iran: The Neolithic Settlement,* University Monograph no. 50, Hasanlu Excavations Reports, vol. I (Philadelphia: University Museum, University of Pennsylvania, 1983), p. 200, fig. 106. Courtesy University Museum, University of Pennsylvania.

the impressive complex of Buildings F, G, and H of Eanna (fig. 33). These structures, erected at right angles around a courtyard, were typical of the monumental architecture at Eanna. They were built according to the usual plan, which consisted of a large central hall flanked by smaller rooms, and their facades were decorated with niches. The sixty-one spheres, seven large spheres, three tetrahedrons, two cones, and two cylinders lay on the floor of a room extending to the north of Building H in a large circular hearth with a long appendix of the *Pfannenstiel* type.[22] It is puzzling that counters were located in fireplaces on two occasions, at Seh Gabi and Uruk. It might be hypothesized that they were intentionally placed in the hearth in order to be baked. On the other hand, it is also possible and perhaps more likely that they were brushed in the ashes with other trash in order to be discarded.

At Susa, tokens also belonged to the temple precinct, where they were clustered in a zone devoted to workshops and warehouses. For example, Mecquenem indicates that envelopes holding tokens were excavated in an area occupied by magazines.[23] The structures, made of pisé and involving decorations made with large cones, were divided into small compartments. One of these houses was still filled with long-spouted jars that held a black, powdery substance.

Eight buildings of Habuba Kabira, including one of the city gates, produced sixty clay counters, providing a unique insight into the distribution of tokens in the fourth-millennium Syrian city. It seems significant that the southern city gate, which led to the temple area, produced not only fifteen tokens but a cylinder seal and numerous oblong bullae. The remaining seven structures yielding counters were among the largest and most imposing houses of Habuba Kabira. They stood out, first, by a typical Sumerian floor plan consisting of small rooms built around a central courtyard. Second, most of these buildings produced other material of administrative significance, such as seals and sealings, oblong bullae, envelopes, and impressed tablets. Otherwise, flint tools, pottery, and spindle whorls seem to indicate domestic concerns.

The data available on the structures associated with tokens indicate that the counters were often located in storage facilities and warehouses. Even more importantly, there is evidence that as early as the sixth millennium B.C. tokens also occur in nondomestic architecture. These public buildings can take the form, over time, of a "temple" as at Uruk, a citadel as at Tepe Gawra, or a city gate as at Habuba Kabira.

Token Clusters

The clay counters are frequently found in groups varying from two to about one hundred. At Gaz Tavila, for instance, thirty-five cones and one sphere were nestled together in the corner of a storeroom (figs. 41.1 and 41.2).[24] Ganj Dareh Tepe also produced many small hoards of two to thirty-seven tokens of mixed types tightly packed together in storage cubicles. Tell Abada yielded eleven clusters of four to sixteen tokens.[25] Finally, Uruk produced the cache of seventy-five tokens composed of spheres, large spheres, cones, tetrahedrons, and cylinders described above. Moreover, there can be little doubt that some of the 155 tokens from level VI of Eanna were also clustered together.

The groups of tokens recovered in the buildings of Habuba Kabira were remarkably small. The house which yielded the largest number produced twenty-one, divided into five rooms in clusters of at most nine tokens. Furthermore, except for House 2, which only held incised ovoids, the assemblages were always composed of several types of counters. In sum, the groups of counters recovered indicate that the accounts kept with tokens dealt generally with relatively small quantities of different kinds of commodities.

Containers Holding Tokens

At Tell Abada, tokens were held in pottery bowls or jars and others were found on the floor.[26] At Gaz Tavila, Ganj Dareh Tepe, Habuba Kabira, Tepe Gawra, and Uruk the tokens were located on the floor of the buildings or storage cubicles. Because they were tightly clustered together it is likely that they were held in a container which disintegrated in time, leaving no trace.

Baskets, wooden boxes, and leather or textile pouches are among the logical choices of receptacles where the counters might have been kept. Because the quantity of counters was small, it seems unlikely that baskets or wooden boxes were involved, and it is more plausible that pouches were used. Furthermore, no impression of textiles has ever been recorded, either on tokens or on the floor where they were recovered. It is more likely, therefore, that leather was preferred to cloth for storing the clay counters. This hypothesis is supported by later texts. Marcel Sigrist has noted that tablets from the IIIrd Dynasty of Ur, ca. 2000 B.C., refer to leather bags, $^{\textbf{kuš}}$**du$_{10}$-gan**, which may be interpreted as holding counters. This is the case, for example, in a tablet referring to "1492 fat oxen in (the leather) bag," which, according to Sigrist, can be understood as "counters representing 1492 oxen kept in archive in a leather bag."[27] I want to note here that, however, because the texts do not yield a specific mention of counters, this remains an interpretation.[28]

Why the early systems for holding tokens were no longer sufficient in the fourth millennium B.C., requiring the invention of clay envelopes, is not known. Presumably, however, the envelopes and strings of tokens, which are fully discussed in the next chapter, were related to the invention of cylinder seals. Both devices provided a way to identify specific transactions by applying the necessary seals.

Associated Assemblages

IN THE EIGHTH MILLENNIUM B.C.

Several significant features coincided with the first occurrence of tokens in level III at Mureybet. First, a quantum jump in the quantity of cereal pollen implies that cultivation of fields started in that level, whereas wild grains were still gathered in the previous two strata, levels II and I, when tokens were not yet in use. Second, cereals were hoarded for the lean season in large rectangular silos, which represent the first departure from circular architecture in the Levant (fig. 102).[29]

41.1. Cone cluster in the corner of a storage area, Tepe Gaz Tavila, Iran. Courtesy Martha C. Prickett.

Third, there was an increase in obsidian trade, with the appearance of fine pieces such as an obsidian dagger.[30] Fourth, a sizable extension of the settlement reflected a rapid population growth.[31]

Subsistence also relied upon grain consumption at Ganj Dareh Tepe, Tepe Asiab, Tell Aswad, and Cheikh Hassan. On the other hand, none of the five sites, except perhaps Tepe Asiab,[32] provided any osteological evidence for domestication of animals. Herding, however, was already practiced in the region, at earlier sites such as Zawi Chemi.[33] Obsidian was generally part of the assemblages. For example, 1 percent of the stone assemblage of Tell Aswad consisted of obsidian from Ciftlik and Nemrut Dag in Anatolia.[34] There was none, however, at Ganj Dareh Tepe.

The beginning of tokens coincides with food production. The need for counting and accounting was related to agriculture or the demographic and sociopolitical changes it implies. In particular, the excavations of Mureybet indicate that reckoning coincides with the cultivation and storage of cereals. On the other hand, tokens are seemingly not related to trade and, in particular, obsidian trade for two main reasons: First, there was no obsidian at Ganj Dareh Tepe and, second, Mureybet I and II already dealt with the volcanic glass prior to the invention of counters.

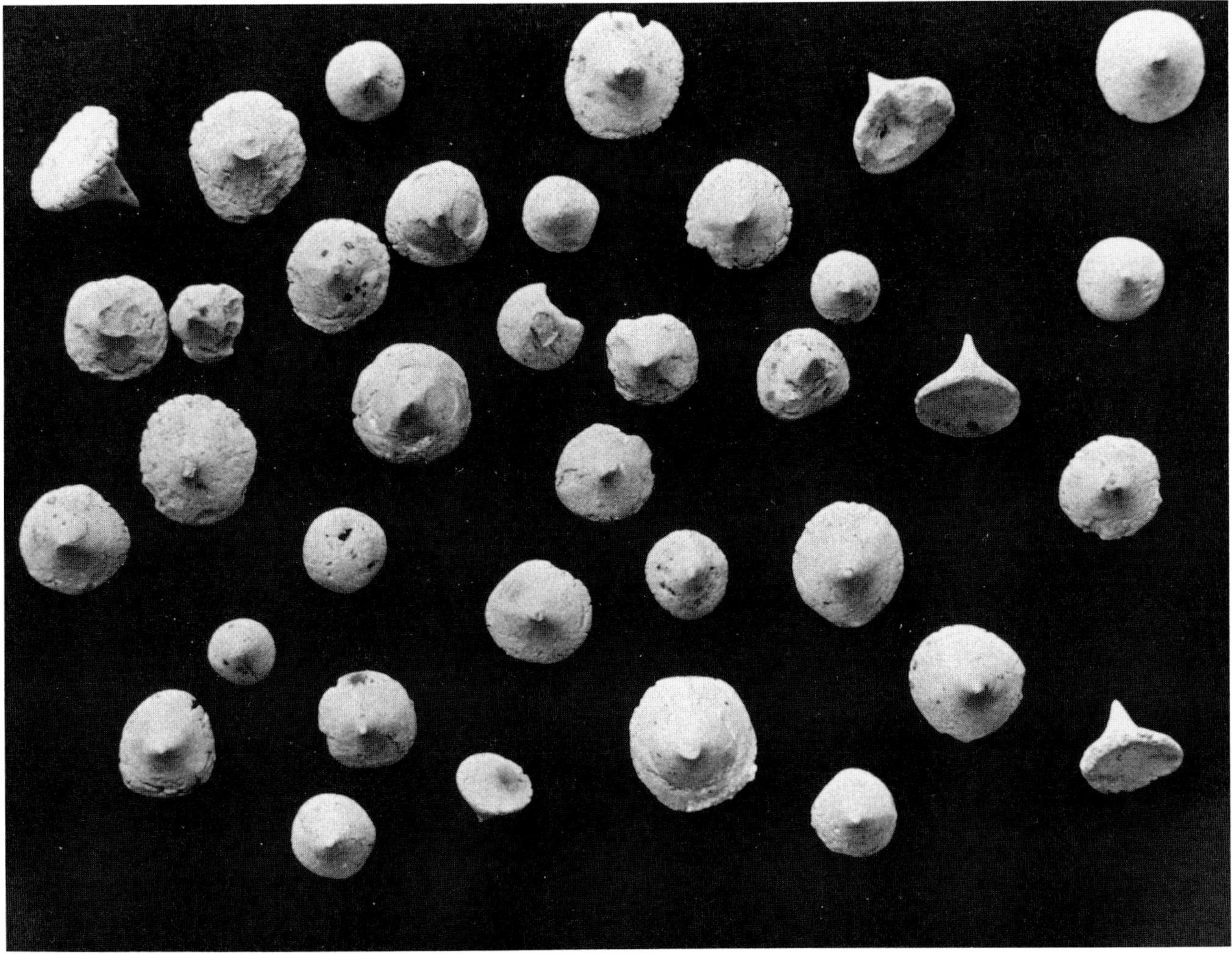

41.2. Cones, detail, Tepe Gaz Tavila, Iran. Courtesy Martha C. Prickett.

42.1. Cone mosaics, Uruk (W 3147), Iraq. Courtesy Deutsches Archaeologisches Institut, Abteilung Baghdad.

42.2. Clay cones for mosaic decoration, Habuba Kabira, Syria. Photograph by H. D. Beyer; courtesy Museum für Vor- und Frühgeschichte, Berlin.

IN THE SEVENTH–FOURTH MILLENNIUM B.C.

Tokens continued to be part of assemblages typical of agricultural communities, where they are associated with hoes, polished axes, spindle whorls, ground stone mortars and pestles, handmade pottery, and clay figurines. It is likely that tokens were closely connected to stamp seals, which were developed in the seventh millennium, but this cannot yet be demonstrated.[35] For example, no tokens are reported at Bouqras, which yielded the earliest sealing.[36] On the other hand, sites like Hassuna and Yarim Tepe held both tokens and seals in their assemblages. It is also noteworthy that Arpachiyah, which produced a large collection of sealings, among which were the first to bear sets of two different seals, had also an unusually diverse collection of tokens.[37]

IN THE LATE URUK PERIOD

The five sites that produced the largest complex tokens assemblages—Uruk and Tello in Iraq, Susa and Chogha Mish in Iran, and Habuba Kabira–Tell Kannas in Syria—have strikingly similar assemblages. Although the cities were separated by several hundred miles, they shared the same monumental architecture characterized by a central plan and a decoration of niches and clay cone mosaics (figs. 42.1 and 42.2).[38] They also yielded identical pottery vessels in the same typical shapes and decorations, such as four-lugged jars with painted and incised motifs.[39] Each of the sites held, in particular, a great number of crudely manufactured beveled-rim bowls that may have served as measures for the distribution of food rations (fig. 43).[40] Furthermore, the seals and sealings of the five cities were exactly alike, bearing analogous motifs. Among them was featured, for example, the bearded figure of the Mesopotamian priest-king, the so-called En, in his typical attire consisting of a long robe in a netlike fabric and a round headdress (figs. 44.1 and 44.2).[41] Finally, all five sites except Tello yielded envelopes holding tokens and impressed tablets. The various features which occur with consistency in the assemblages of sites yielding complex tokens—the priest-king, public monumental architecture, measures, seals, and complex tokens—represent the elements of an elaborate bureaucracy. They indicate the presence of a powerful economic institution headed by an En acting in public buildings decorated with mosaics and relying upon a control of goods involving seals, beveled-rim bowls, and complex tokens.

It is significant that the architecture decorated with cone mosaics, the beveled-rim bowls, the cylinder seals, and the motif of the En are of Mesopotamian origin but were foreign in Iran as well as Syria. In fact, they were hallmark features of the precinct of Eanna at Uruk. In this perspective, it may be particularly significant that the large collection of tokens of level VI was associated with the piles of clay cone mosaics marking the first evidence for decorated public buildings at Eanna.[42] Whereas agriculture is the major common denominator between sites yielding plain tokens, the cities which produced complex tokens shared, therefore, the same bureaucracy, which had special ties with southern Mesopotamia.

Tokens as Funerary Offerings

On rare occasions, counters were associated with funerary deposits. These burials may provide information on the individuals who were utilizing tokens.

THE SITES

Tokens were sometimes laid in burials among other funerary deposits. The earliest examples of counters used as offerings come from Tell es-Sawwan,[43] Tepe Guran,[44] and Hajji Firuz[45] in levels dating from the sixth millennium B.C. There is evidence that the custom continued in the Ubaid period at Arpachiyah[46] and Tepe Gawra XVII.[47] Finally, tokens were found in sepultures of level XI[48] and X at Tepe Gawra in the late fourth millennium B.C.[49] Tokens have also been attributed to children's burials of the protoliterate period at Susa, but the information is too scanty to be taken into consideration here.[50]

Among the five sites which furnished tokens in a funerary context, Tell es-Sawwan, Arpachiyah, and Tepe Gawra are located in northern Mesopotamia; Tepe Guran and Hajji Firuz are in Iran. The ritual was practiced, therefore, in a widespread geographic area and cannot be considered a regional development.

THE BURIALS

At each of the five sites, the number of sepultures provided with tokens is very small. Only 4 out of some 130 burials excavated in Tell es-Sawwan I yielded counters. There was a single case of tokens laid as *Beigaben* (funerary offerings) among, respectively, the fourteen interments of Hajji Firuz, the fifty Ubaid graves of Arpachiyah, the thirty graves of Tepe Gawra XVII, and the five graves of Tepe Gawra XI. Finally, only four out

43. Beveled rim bowls, Nuzi, Iraq. Courtesy Peabody Museum, Harvard University.

44.1. En. After Pierre Amiet, *La Glyptique mésopotamienne archaïque* (Paris: Editions du CNRS, 1980), pl. 46: 639.

44.2. En. After Pierre Amiet, *La Glyptique mésopotamienne archaïque* (Paris: Editions du CNRS, 1980), pl. 44: 655.

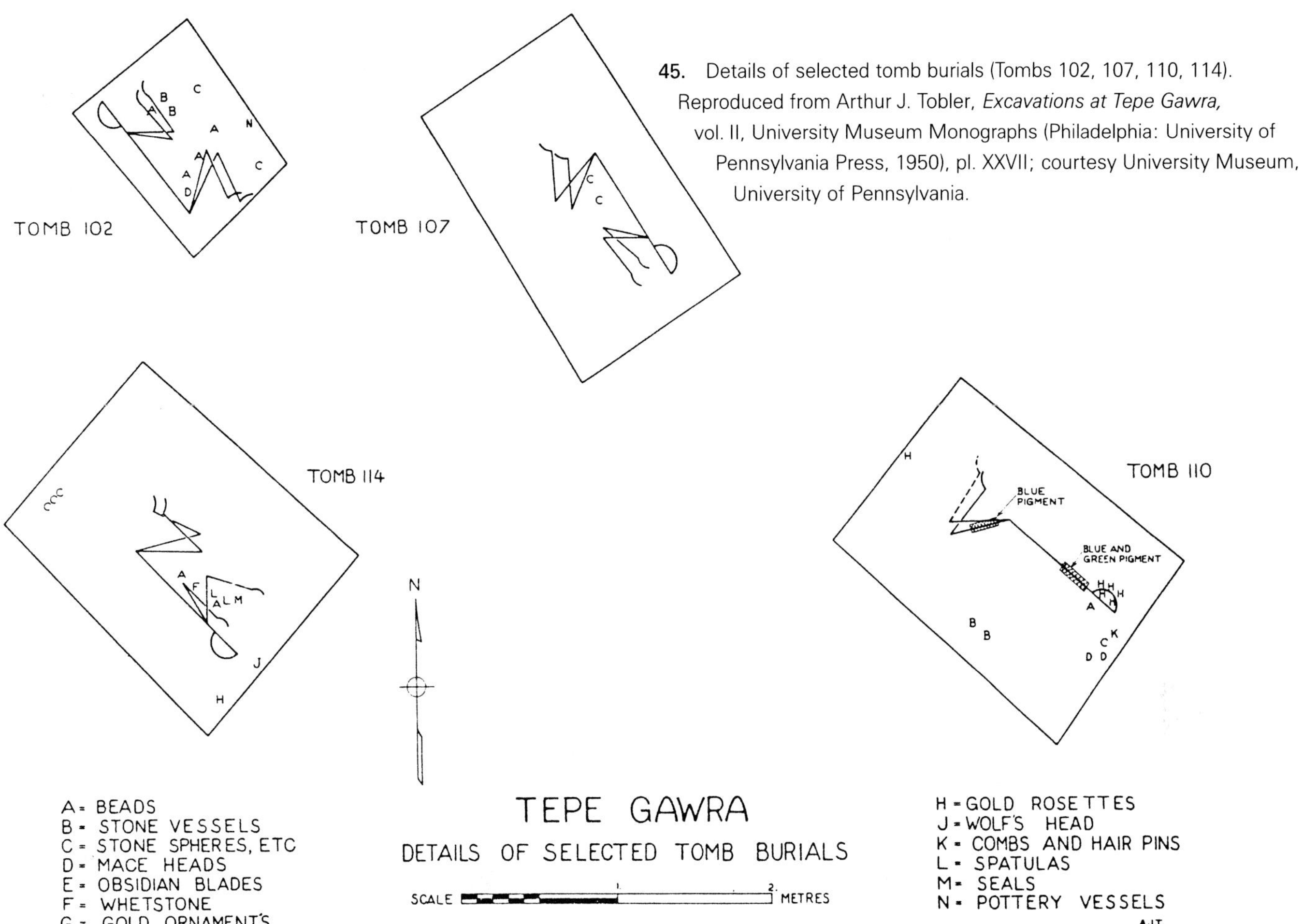

45. Details of selected tomb burials (Tombs 102, 107, 110, 114). Reproduced from Arthur J. Tobler, *Excavations at Tepe Gawra,* vol. II, University Museum Monographs (Philadelphia: University of Pennsylvania Press, 1950), pl. XXVII; courtesy University Museum, University of Pennsylvania.

of eighty tombs of Tepe Gawra X held counters. The total number of burials including tokens amounts, therefore, to no more than fourteen.

The interments provided with counters were of several types. At Hajji Firuz, tokens were mixed with the disarticulated bones of a multiple burial;[51] at Tell es-Sawwan,[52] Arpachiyah,[53] and Tepe Gawra XVII and XI,[54] tokens were part of simple graves consisting of a shallow pit dug in the earth. Finally, in Tepe Gawra X, tokens were laid in elaborate tombs involving a brick or stone enclosure (fig. 45).[55]

The various sepultures furnished with tokens belonged to adult males or children, except in the case of Hajji Firuz, where one of the four individuals of the ossuary may have been a young female.[56]

Information on the precise distribution of the counters within the sepultures is often lacking. According to the Tepe Gawra report, however, they were usually deposited in front of the dead rather than behind them.[57] Otherwise, the counters included in the Tepe Gawra burials were placed, seemingly indifferently, either near the skull, the lower chest, the hands, the pelvis, or the feet of the skeleton.[58] In the case of Tomb 102, thirty-three counters were divided into two groups with several spheres next to the elbows and the remaining spheres and cones at the feet.

It is striking that nearly all these sepultures yielding tokens show unusual features. A first group of burials is characterized by being lavishly furnished. Among them, the graves of Tell es-Sawwan had quantities of alabaster vessels and, in two cases, ornaments of either dentalia shell or carnelian.[59] At Tepe Gawra, the child grave was unique in stratum XI in holding gold ornaments (fig. 46).[60] In level X of Tepe Gawra, Tombs 102, 110, and 114 were among the richest sepultures of the site. They included obsidian (fig. 47), serpentine (fig. 48), or electrum vessels, gold ornaments in the form of studs, beads, or rosettes, stone maceheads (fig. 49), and lapis lazuli seals (fig. 50).[61]

A second group of burials was associated with uncommon architectural features. For example, at Hajji Firuz, the human bones deposited with tokens were in

46. Gold rosette from a child grave holding tokens, Tepe Gawra (level XI-A, locus 181, grave 36-6-354, G5-1419), Iraq (Tobler 1950, p. 199, pl. CLXXV and figs. 74–76); courtesy University Museum, University of Pennsylvania.

48. Serpentine beaker from Tomb 110, Tepe Gawra (35-10-315), Iraq. Courtesy University Museum, University of Pennsylvania.

47. Obsidian vessels from Tomb 102, Tepe Gawra (*left,* 35-10-287; *right,* G4-634), Iraq. Courtesy University Museum, University of Pennsylvania.

49. Hematite macehead from Tomb 114, Tepe Gawra (35-10-325), Iraq. Courtesy University Museum, University of Pennsylvania.

50. Lapis lazuli seal from Tomb 110, Tepe Gawra (G4-769), Iraq. Courtesy University Museum, University of Pennsylvania.

the small, unusual building described above.[62] The second example, Tomb 107 at Tepe Gawra, was the sepulture of an adult male who was unique in having a shrine erected upon his remains.[63] In this case, the *Beigaben* amounted to six spheres and nothing else. Finally, the most puzzling burial, the grave of Tepe Gawra XVII, belonged to an individual with both legs amputated below the knee.[64] The burial at Arpachiyah is the only one which yields tokens but has no other particularly striking features.

THE TOKENS

Among the many types and subtypes of tokens, four only were recovered in sepultures: cones, spheres, three-quarter spheres, and miniature vessels (fig. 51). Among them, spheres were, by far, most frequently used, occurring in ten of the fourteen burials with a total number of forty-nine specimens. The forty-four cones were distributed among only three sepultures, and three-quarter spheres and vessels were present in a single grave.

It seems also noteworthy that, as a rule, only one kind of counter was usually represented in each burial. For example, three graves of Tell es-Sawwan contained spheres but the fourth one had a cone;[65] Tombs 107 and 110 of Tepe Gawra held only spheres but the grave of level XVII had cones. Tomb 102 of Tepe Gawra, however, yielded both spheres and cones.[66]

Tokens laid in burials were identical in shape to those found in settlements, with the exception of the thirty-four cones included in the grave of Tepe Gawra XVII that had peculiar bent tips (fig. 52). The counters found in a funerary setting were also of the same size as the normal specimens, except for some spheres at Tell es-Sawwan that may be somewhat bigger. Otherwise, Tomb 102 of Tepe Gawra had spheres in the

51. Stone tokens Nos. 2, 3, 5, 7, 8, 9, 10, 11, 12 were located in the grave of a child yielding a gold rosette at Tepe Gawra (no. 181, stratum XI), Iraq. Courtesy University Museum, University of Pennsylvania.

usual size.[67] None of the tokens included in sepultures had either markings or perforations.

Tokens from a burial context differed from those used in daily life by often being made of stone instead of clay. Nine of the fourteen sepultures were provided with stone tokens with a total of 66 stone specimens against 41 made of clay. The stone examples were usually done with great care and show a superb skill in workmanship. The spheres, for example, are perfectly round. There is one case at Tepe Gawra, however, when spherical counters—referred to as "pebbles" in the report—were left rough. In another instance, six chips of red jasper were seemingly intended to be made into counters, but never executed.[68]

It is possible that the color of stone selected for the manufacture of tokens was meaningful since all spheres were white with the exception of two sets of red spheres[69] and a single black specimen.[70]

The number of tokens included in each sepulture varied from a minimum of one sphere at Arpachiyah to a maximum of thirty-four cones in Tepe Gawra XVII. Sets of six spheres which reoccur in three out of four tombs of Tepe Gawra X suggest that this number may have had a symbolic significance.

The ritual of depositing in burials tokens of special types, material, color, and, in particular, number is especially significant, since it lasted during three millennia in several regions of the Near East. In particular, as will be discussed in Part Three, it gives a valuable insight into the important role of the counters as status symbols. The fact that tokens occur only in rare occasions in a funerary setting and only in

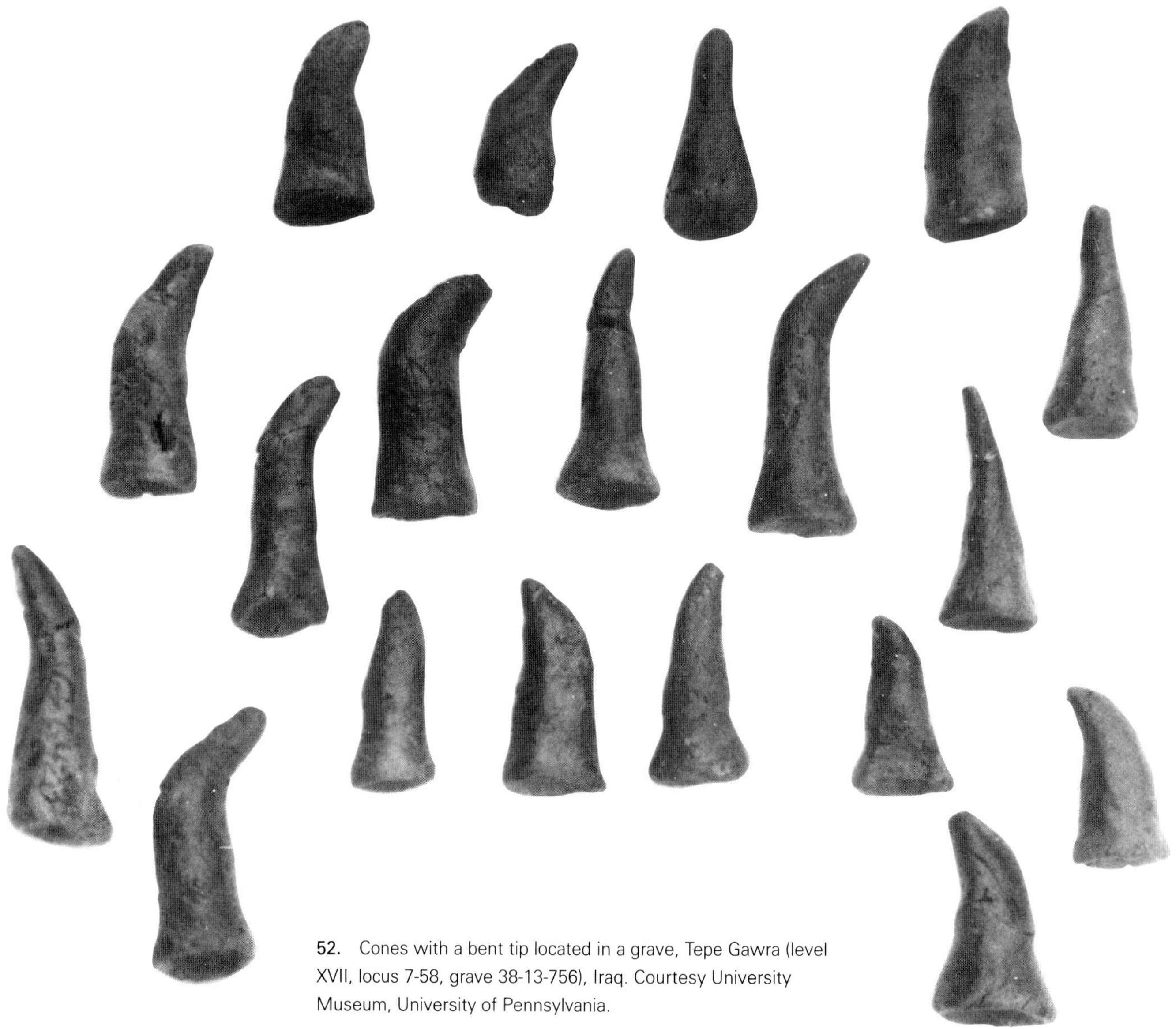

52. Cones with a bent tip located in a grave, Tepe Gawra (level XVII, locus 7-58, grave 38-13-756), Iraq. Courtesy University Museum, University of Pennsylvania.

graves of prestigious individuals points to their economic significance. It may imply that the tokens were a means of controlling goods in the hands of powerful administrators.

A FAINT SKETCH of the places and people associated with the use of counters begins to emerge. The use of tokens started in open-air compounds where subsistence was based on cultivating or, at least, hoarding cereals. On the other hand, complex tokens were the invention of the southern Mesopotamian temples. The plain specimens remained, therefore, a familiar feature in agricultural communities until the end of the system, whereas the complex ones occur in administrative centers. Starting in the fifth millennium, tokens are recurrently found in public buildings and warehouses. When they are in a domestic setting, the counters have a tendency to cluster in storage areas. The hoards of tokens found *in situ* range usually between a dozen to seventy-five artifacts, showing that in both private and public buildings the counters were never kept in large quantities. They may have been stored in leather pouches until the invention of cylinder seal ushered in the invention of clay envelopes and bullae, discussed in the following chapter. Tokens were apparently not reused but were disposed of once the transaction they represented was concluded. There is even some evidence that the counters were mostly discarded during the summer after the harvest. Tokens, together with other status symbols, are sometimes included in the burials of prestigious individuals, suggesting that they were used by members of the elite.

5
STRINGS OF TOKENS AND ENVELOPES

En secouant . . . [les boules de terre crue] près de l'oreille, on entend le bruit de petits objects s'entrechoquant dans la cavité intérieure; plusieurs d'entre elles ayant été rompues dans le dégagement, nous avons reconnu la présence de petites masses d'argile cuite aux formes variées: grains, cones, pyramides, pastilles de 0m01 de diamètre.
—R. de Mecquenem[1]

IN THE EARLY fourth millennium B.C. two methods were devised to store tokens in archives. The first consisted of tying perforated tokens with a string; the second, of enclosing the counters in clay envelopes. Both of these techniques insured that groups of tokens representing one account were securely held together and that the transaction was identified by sealings. These two devices would remain of esoteric interest but for their importance in the invention of writing. Accountants indicated the shape and number of tokens enclosed by imprinting each token on the outside surface of the envelope before enclosing it. This mutation of the three-dimensional objects to two-dimensional graphic symbols was the transition between tokens and the first system of writing.

Strings of Tokens

PERFORATED TOKENS

Some counters show a perforation throughout their thickness. The hole provided on the counters is small and is generally placed at the top of the artifact or at the center. For example, spheres are pierced in the middle, cones and ovoids generally bear the perforation at or near the maximum diameter, and triangles at the apex. There are perforated specimens among stone and clay counters; the latter were pierced while the clay was still moist.

The geographic and chronological distribution of these perforated artifacts suggests that they were not a general phenomenon but were restricted to complex token assemblages. The geographic distribution of perforated tokens is close to that of complex tokens. There are no perforated specimens in Turkey and Palestine, but some are represented in Iraq, Iran, and Syria. Occasionally, perforated tokens occur in plain token collections, for example, at the following sites: Tell Ramad in Syria; Tepe Gawra and Tell Oueili in Iraq; Tepe Sarab, Tall-i-Bakun, Jaffarabad, and Sialk in Iran. The number of perforated tokens in these assemblages is small: Tell Ramad 4, Tell Oueili 1, Tepe Gawra 2, Tall-i-Bakun 3, and Jaffarabad 3. In most cases, the perforated tokens are disks, and these disks are generally reworked sherds.

The perforated tokens are present, on the other hand, in most if not all complex token assemblages. Nineveh, Nuzi, Jebel Aruda, Moussian, and KS 54 have none, but in Syria, perforated counters occur at Habuba Kabira, Tell Kannas, and Tell Brak; in Iraq, Tell Billa, Jemdet Nasr, Kish, Nippur, Tello, Ur, and Uruk; in Iran, Chogha Mish, Hissar, and Susa. It is noteworthy that the proportion of perforated tokens varies greatly from site to site. For example, 14.7 percent of the tokens from Uruk are provided with a hole, compared to 27 percent at Susa and 84 percent at Habuba Kabira, which yielded the greatest number.

The correlation between perforated and complex tokens is also illustrated by their chronological distribution. There are no perforated tokens in the seventh millennium B.C. In the sixth and fifth millennia B.C., their number is limited to, respectively, eight[2] and six specimens.[3] Instead, perforated specimens proliferate in the fourth millennium B.C. There are, for example, 119 perforated tokens at Uruk, 189 at Susa, and 118 at Habuba Kabira. It also seems significant that perforated and complex tokens occur at the same time at Uruk; namely, among the first four tokens of Eanna XVII, two were perforated and one was complex.

In the fourth-millennium assemblages such as Uruk, Susa, and Habuba Kabira, there are perforated specimens among each of the sixteen types of tokens and among plain, incised, punched, notched, pinched, or appliqué subtypes. The greatest proportion of perforated tokens is, however, among complex types and subtypes. For example, at Habuba Kabira, 45 plain tokens are perforated compared to 73 complex; at Susa, 14 are plain and 167 complex, and 13 of the 119 Uruk perforated tokens are plain.

It is presumed that the perforations served to hold the counters with a thong or string like the beads of a necklace. If this is so, two observations can be made concerning the device. First, because the hole perforated in the counters is usually narrow, the string must have been small and consequently was not meant to be strong. Second, the perforations show no trace of wear, suggesting that the groups of tokens tied together were not transported or passed from hand to hand but were probably kept in archives.

SOLID BULLAE

It is likely that the strings of tokens fulfilled the same function as the envelopes described below, providing an alternative way of storing tokens. If this assumption is correct, presumably both ends of the string were tied together and secured by sealings identifying the account and preventing any tampering. I propose that a category of small bullae, bearing sealings, could have served this purpose (fig. 53).

The bullae are made of clay. They are solid, modeled in an oblong or biconoid shape, and measure about 7 cm in length and 5 in diameter. The artifacts show, at both ends, the trace of the strings to which they are attached and are covered with sealings (fig. 54).

The bullae have generally been viewed as tags tied on bales of merchandise.[4] The interpretation of the bullae as a device to hold tokens departs from the traditional view and is supported by the fact that the geographic distribution of the bullae also generally coincides with that of complex tokens. Tell Brak, for example, produced both kinds of artifacts,[5] and at Susa,[6] Chogha Mish,[7] and Habuba Kabira[8] complex tokens and solid bullae belong to the same horizon

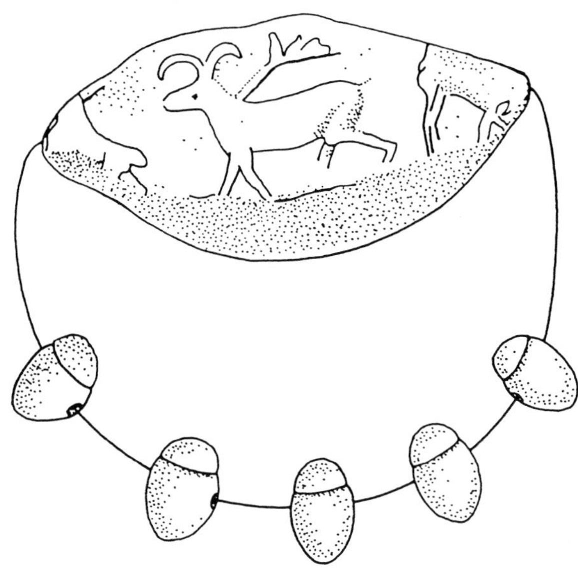

53. Proposed reconstruction of a string of tokens held by a solid bulla. Drawing by Ellen Simmons.

54. Two bullae, Susa (Sb 6298 and 9279), Iran. Courtesy Musée du Louvre, Département des Antiquités Orientales.

and in the same vicinity, although there is no reference in the reports that they were found in direct association.[9] There are, however, some exceptions. No bulla has, so far, been identified at Uruk; Nineveh[10] and Chagar Bazar produced a bulla but seemingly no perforated tokens.[11] It may be significant that the greatest number of bullae come from Habuba Kabira, the site that produced most perforated tokens, and that none have yet been recovered at Uruk, where perforated tokens were few. Furthermore, as shown by the imprints at both extremities of the bullae, the strings they held were thin and could fit adequately in the token perforations. Finally, their close resemblance to envelopes cannot be coincidental. First, the two kinds of objects have a very similar appearance: They are made of the same material, share the same size, and, sometimes, are modeled in the same oblong or biconoid shapes. Second, they bear the same sealings, showing similar motifs, including lines of peaceful animals,[12] lions in heraldic posture,[13] and humans performing tasks.[14] In fact, on some occasions the impression of the same seal appears on both types of artifacts. For example, at Susa, a particular seal impression featuring a line of peaceful animals and a line of felines was impressed on a solid bulla as well as on two envelopes.[15] The number of seals is also the same on solid bullae and envelopes: Both have mostly the impression of a single seal rolled all over their surfaces and, on occasion, two or three. Third, a few examples of solid bullae at Susa, Habuba Kabira (fig. 55), Tell Brak, and Chagar Bazar feature impressed markings such as those borne by some of the envelopes, as will be described in the following section of the chapter.[16] Fourth, as will be discussed below, some of the envelopes may also have involved a system of stringing tokens.

The two kinds of artifacts have two main differences, however. First, the envelopes were hollow and the bullae were solid. Second, the envelopes were preferred for storing plain tokens, whereas complex specimens were mostly strung. To be exact, 83.69 percent of the tokens contained in envelopes were plain and 10.57 percent were complex (5.74 percent remains undetermined). In addition, there are more perforated tokens among complex than plain specimens. It should be emphasized here, however, that there was cross-over between the two methods. Incised ovoids, which are complex tokens, were held in four envelopes, two from Habuba Kabira and two from Uruk; punched cones and tetrahedrons, triangles, rectangles, paraboloids, and animals were held in envelopes either from Susa or Uruk or both. On the other hand, thirteen plain specimens of Uruk were perforated, forty-five at Habuba Kabira, including thirty-five cones, and fourteen at Susa.

In sum, the envelopes and bullae are closely related in shape and function and it is likely that they represent two alternative ways of identifying and protecting tokens to be held in archives. For reasons that we do not know, plain tokens were most often secured by envelopes and complex tokens by solid bullae.

Envelopes

THE ARTIFACTS

The envelopes consist of spherical (fig. 56), ovoid, or oblong (fig. 57) hollow clay balls. The objects had probably a tendency to roll on the accountants' table or the archive shelf, explaining why eight envelopes from Susa are provided with a small flat surface, scratched when the clay was already hard.[17] The envelopes measure generally about 5–7 cm with some exceptions as small as 3 cm and others as large as 9 cm. The inner cavity is from 2–4 cm wide, the walls of the envelopes varying from 1.5–2.5 cm in thickness (fig. 58).

Like tokens, the envelopes are made of a paste usually devoid of inclusions, which suggests that either the clay was carefully selected or was treated by levigation, a process for removing the impurities with running water. There is no indication of tempering, except for a single envelope from Susa that shows a light pitting on the surface, which could suggest the addition of a fine vegetable matter to improve the quality of the material.[18]

55. Bulla with impressed marking, Habuba Kabira (M II: 139), Syria. Photo by Klaus Anger; courtesy Museum für Vor- und Frühgeschichte, Berlin.

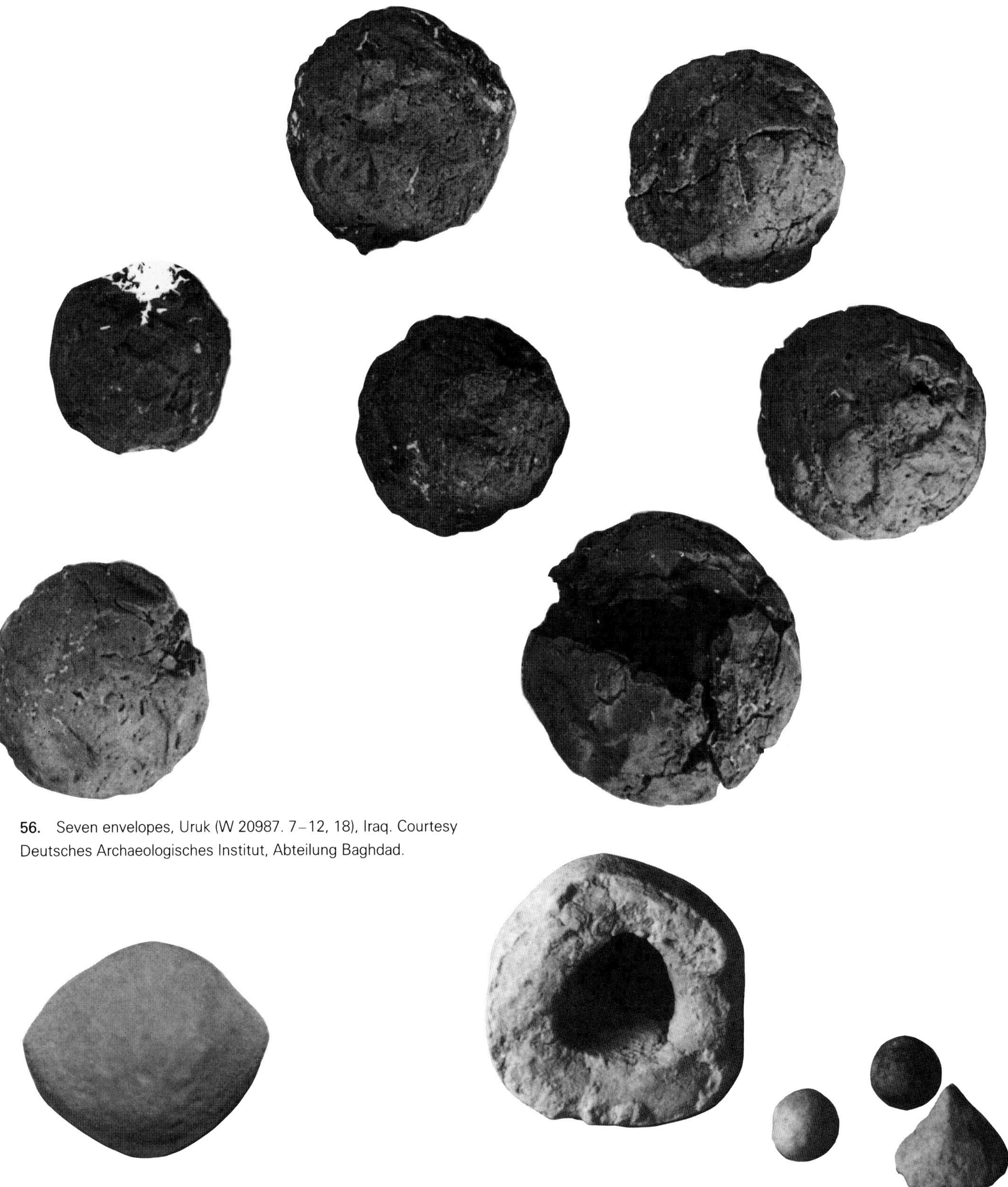

56. Seven envelopes, Uruk (W 20987. 7–12, 18), Iraq. Courtesy Deutsches Archaeologisches Institut, Abteilung Baghdad.

57. Envelope, Dumah, Israel. Courtesy Shucri Sahuri.

58. Envelope, Tepe Yahya, Iran. Courtesy Peabody Museum, Harvard University.

The composition of the clay of two samples was analyzed by neutron activation. The first, from Farukhabad[19] revealed that the variety of clay was of local origin, but in the second, from Tepe Yahya, it was not, which implies that the artifact was brought from elsewhere.[20]

The manufacture of the envelopes was simple. The cavity to hold the tokens was shaped by poking a hole into a ball of clay with the fingers, as shown by traces of fingerprints visible inside. It has been suggested that envelopes were made by fitting together two semispherical hulls, as were recovered at Sharafabad[21] and Tepe Gawra,[22] but none of the complete envelopes were prepared in this fashion. Instead, X-rays indicate that the cavity was closed by applying a patch of clay.

The red color of some of the envelopes, such as those from Dharan and Shah Dad, suggested that the artifacts were baked. The fact that envelopes were fired was confirmed by electron microscopy (fig. 59) and DTA (fig. 60) performed on a sample from Susa.[23] Like tokens, the envelopes were baked at a low temperature of about 700° C, which explains why specimens from Susa could be opened easily with a knife.

Mecquenem had hypothesized that the counters were wrapped in textile before being encased, but no trace of cloth is ever visible, either on tokens or on the cavity of the envelopes. Instead, the tokens are tightly tucked together and often even sunk into the inner wall.

DISCOVERY

The clay envelopes were first discovered at Susa. It is not clear whether they were excavated by Jacques de Morgan when he first reached the archaic layers in 1901 or by Roland de Mecquenem in 1907. At any rate, the discovery did not attract much attention and was not discussed in the reports. Leon Legrain first showed an interest in the artifacts because of the good seal impressions they bear. He presented some specimens in his volume *Empreintes de cachets élamites,* published in 1921, under the heading "bulles sphériques."[24] Legrain remarked that the artifacts showed traces of strings, which proved erroneous. Neither he nor Vincent Scheil, who also alluded to the envelopes in his publication *Textes de comptabilité protoélamite* in 1923, ever mentioned that the objects were hollow or held tokens.[25]

Roland de Mecquenem excavated further envelopes at Susa during his campaign of 1923–24. This time the "boules de terre crue" (mud balls) did not pass unnoticed, but twelve lines of the excavation report in *Revue d'Assyriologie* describe the objects as being hol-

59. Electron microscopic analysis 3,000×, envelope from Susa, Iran. Courtesy W. D. Kingery, Division of Ceramics, Massachusetts Institute of Technology.

low, rattling when shaken, and containing tokens of various shapes including "grains, cones, pyramids and pills."[26] Mecquenem also hypothesized that the envelopes served as sealings, authenticating bundles of goods, and interpreted the tokens as signatures of the individuals responsible for the shipment. Like Legrain, Pierre Amiet was led to study the Susa envelopes for his work on glyptics. He published the seal impressions of most of the specimens excavated by Morgan and Mecquenem in his *Glyptique susienne,* thus making the material for the first time available for study.[27]

GEOGRAPHIC DISTRIBUTION AND NUMBER

Five out of the ten protoliterate sites which produced envelopes are located in Iran. These sites are Shahdad, Tepe Yahya, Chogha Mish, Susa, and Farukhabad. One is in Iraq (Uruk), one in Saudi Arabia (Dharan), one in Israel (Dumah), and two in Syria (Habuba Kabira and Tell Qraya). The distribution of the envelopes is thus spread over a large region which stretches from Iran to the Levant and from Iraq to Saudi Arabia (fig. 61). None so far have been recovered in Turkey.

The total number of envelopes presently known is about 130 specimens and 70 fragments. The majority, or around one hundred complete envelopes and seventy fragments, representing 85 percent of the total assemblage, comes from Iran. Among the Iranian sites, Susa produced forty complete, fifteen fragmentary envelopes, and fifty-seven fragments.[28] The assemblage

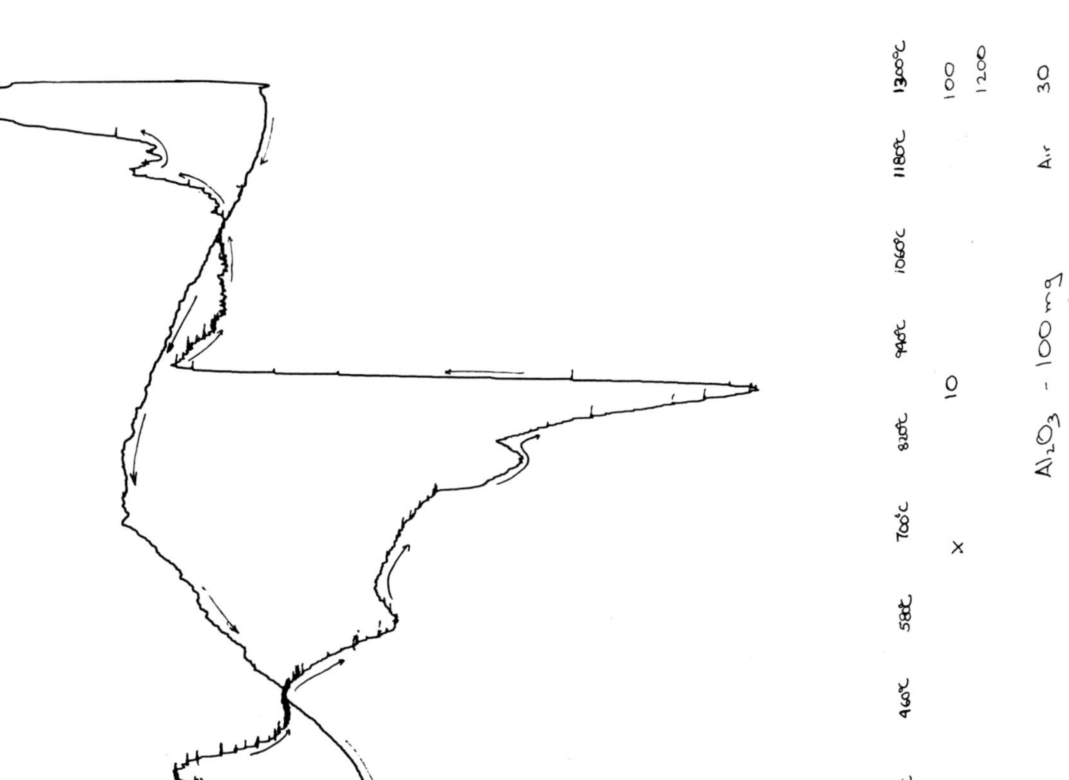

60. Differential thermal analysis graph, envelope from Susa, Iran. Courtesy W. D. Kingery, Division of Ceramics, Massachusetts Institute of Technology.

of Chogha Mish is yet unpublished, except for eight complete envelopes recovered in the second campaign, and a hoard of over twenty during the third.[29] Finally, Farukhabad,[30] Tepe Yahya,[31] and Shahdad each produced one example.[32] Iraq has a total of twenty-five envelopes, all of which come from Uruk.[33] Syria yielded two at Habuba Kabira.[34] The number of envelopes excavated at Tell Qraya is yet undisclosed.[35] The specimen from Israel, which was purchased on the antiquity market, was said to belong to a lot of two, originating from the site of Dumah, near Hebron.[36] The single envelope from Saudi Arabia is a surface find collected near the Dharan airport.[37]

CHRONOLOGY

The envelopes may be divided chronologically into two broad categories: those belonging to the protohistoric period and those dating from early historic times.

The Farukhabad envelope and those of Chogha Mish may be the earliest specimens of the first group. At Farukhabad, the envelope is attributed to layer 33, corresponding to the Middle Uruk period.[38] This coincides with the date proposed by Delougaz and Kantor for the Chogha Mish examples.[39] If this information is correct, the first envelopes can be dated to about 3700 to 3500 B.C.

Habuba Kabira was settled for a short period of about 120 years and, on the basis of pottery styles, is estimated to be contemporaneous with Eanna VI–V.[40] Consequently, these two Syrian envelopes can be placed in the Middle and Late Uruk periods, ca. 3500 B.C. and represent the earliest marked specimens. Presumably, the specimens from the Middle Uruk site of Tell Qraya are roughly contemporary.[41]

The chronology of the Uruk clay cases is only tentative since they were recovered in a disturbed context. As was discussed above, they belonged to the Stone Cone Temple area, which suggests a date as early as Eanna VI–V and is consistent with the artifacts from Habuba Kabira. On the other hand, glyptics point to a date perhaps as late as Eanna V–IVC.[42]

Louis Le Breton had assigned the fifty envelopes excavated by Morgan and Mecquenem to his period Ca, which he correlated to Eanna IV.[43] In fact, the modern excavations have identified seventeen envelopes in level 18[44] and one in level 17.[45] These two strata are now equated to Eanna VI–V.[46] Consequently, the envelopes of Susa may be considered as contemporaneous with those of Habuba Kabira. It is noteworthy that some of the envelopes of level 18 were inscribed but the example of level 17 was not.[47] This indicates that the system of markings showing the token content of envelopes was never used systematically, neither when it was introduced in level 18 nor in the following level 17.

The remaining envelopes belong probably to the historic period. It is likely that the specimen from Dumah came from one of the Early Bronze I sites around Hebron, in which case it can be dated to about 3100 to 2800 B.C. The two envelopes from Shahdad, southern Iran, and Dharan, Saudi Arabia, may be dated by the Tepe Yahya example, which belonged to the period of Tepe Yahya IV B2, about 2800 to 2600 B.C. (TF 1136, 2710 B.C.).[48]

The envelopes were in use at least several centuries. They began being used in the Middle Uruk period about 3700 to 3500 B.C. and persisted until the late Proto-Elamite period, ca. 2600 B.C. According to the present evidence, the custom of marking the artifacts started as early as Eanna VI–V, about 3500 B.C., and continued in the third millennium B.C.

CONTEXT

Envelopes, like tokens, were generally found out of context, scattered among refuse where they had been discarded in antiquity. At Uruk, Habuba Kabira, Susa, Tepe Yahya, and Nuzi, however, it is possible to identify the general setting to which the artifacts belonged.

Nothing is known of the context of the envelope from Dumah that was purchased on the antiquity market. Nothing is known either of the envelope of Dharan that was a surface find. Juris Zarins of Southwest Missouri State University, who has done archaeological work in the Dharan area, hypothesizes that the object originated from shell-midden occupations that, unfortunately, were not systematically investigated before they disappeared following the recent industrial build-up.[49]

The envelope of Shahdad was also a surface find. The site is well known for its third-millennium cemetery, furnished with bronze objects such as axes, vases, and pins. Apparently, these metal artifacts were produced locally in a large industrial area covered with slag and furnaces that has not yet been investigated. Shahdad is viewed, therefore, as a metallurgical center exploited perhaps as early as the fourth millennium B.C.[50]

The envelope from Farukhabad also provides little information on its original context since it was recovered in a pocket of ashes.[51] The site was a small center

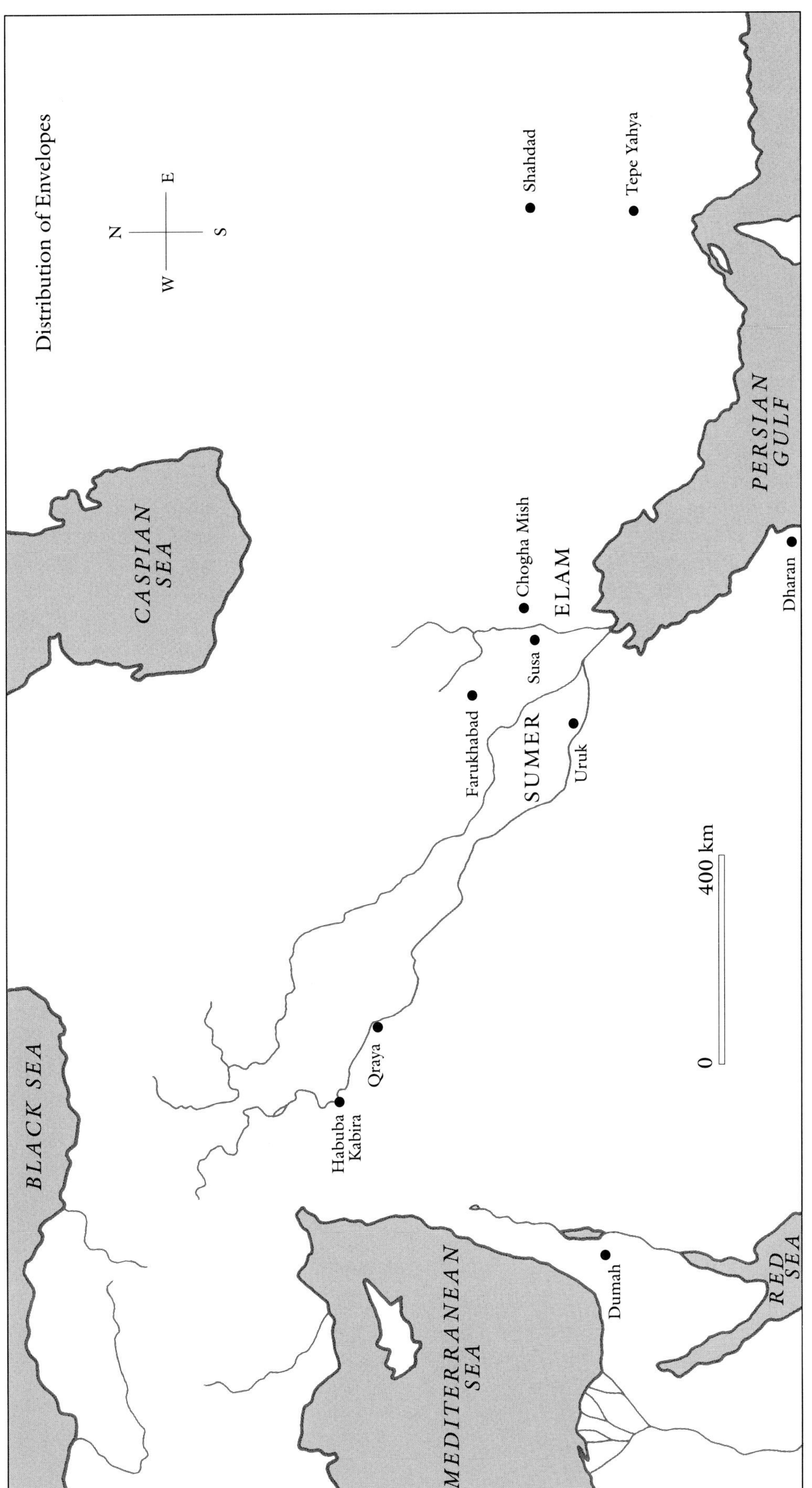

61. Distribution of envelopes.

of the Deh Luran plain in southwestern Iran which, interestingly, yielded constructions decorated with clay cone mosaics. Its assemblage also included beveled-rim bowls and sealings bearing motifs familiar in Uruk and Susa.[52] On the other hand, Farukhabad had neither complex tokens nor tablets.

Data on the location where the Chogha Mish envelopes were excavated have not yet been published. It is important to remember, however, that the site was a large center which produced complex tokens, oblong solid bullae, seals featuring the En, and clay cone mosaics.

At Uruk, the twenty-five envelopes were located in Eanna. All were on the grounds of the Stone Cone Temple, which was enclosed by a wall decorated with blue and green cone mosaics and formed a self-contained compound within the precinct.[53] The twenty-five artifacts were tucked together in a hole in a *Riemchen* wall, probably belonging to one of the most ancient construction phases of the Stone Cone Temple. Presumably, therefore, the envelopes were part of the Stone Cone Temple archives and were discarded, together with tokens, sealings, and beveled-rim bowls,[54] once the site was abandoned and became a quarry and dumping ground.

At Susa, the envelopes were excavated in the Tell of the Acropolis, where the temple was located. The some thirty envelopes from the Morgan and Mecquenem campaigns, like the bulk of the token collection, originated from the southern part of the tell, except for one found in the north.[55] The artifacts, as well as impressed tablets, were recovered at a depth of 17.5 m in a large earth lense about 30 cm deep that may have been a rubbish heap. According to Mecquenem, the area where the envelopes were found was occupied by buildings divided into small compartments that were presumably temple warehouses or workshops.[56]

In the more recent campaigns, seventeen envelopes or fragments thereof came from a building also located in the southern part of the tell. The apparent absence of any organic or vegetable material trash within or without the rooms, and in particular in the hearths, makes it unlikely that this was a domestic setting, as was proposed by the excavators.[57] Instead, the location of the structure some 30 m away from the monumental terrace of the temple makes it highly probable that it was located within the religious precinct, where it fulfilled some temple function.[58]

The envelopes, together with other administrative material including solid oblong bullae, impressed tablets, and beveled-rim bowls, were located in an L-shaped room in an otherwise nondescript structure. Although the artifacts were lying on the floor, they do not appear to be *in situ* but rather to have been dumped. This is supported by the pattern of distribution of the artifacts;[59] namely, the objects are never clustered together along a wall, as was the case of the archive excavated by Morgan, but were scattered randomly.[60] They were also grouped in odd clusters; for example, a small jar held an envelope, a spindle whorl, a flint blade, a shell, and pierced stone disks.[61] It is also obvious that the material was not abandoned in a state of emergency and sealed *in situ* by rubble but was embedded in one of the six reconstruction layers identified in levels 17–18.[62] Consequently, the envelopes and the remaining assemblage were discarded intentionally when the rooms had to be cleared for repairs or rebuilding. On the the other hand, the objects could also have been dumped from the outside during the interval when the house was in a state of disrepair. Whatever the circumstances may have been, the envelopes of Susa, like those of Uruk, came from an area close to an important temple.

Building 2 of Habuba Kabira, where the two envelopes were unearthed, was the largest and most imposing house of the northern sector of the city. It was one of several structures at the site that was laid out according to a plan familiar in southern Mesopotamia but unusual in Syria, with small rooms organized around a central courtyard. Another particularity of these typically southern Mesopotamian buildings was to yield complex tokens and various articles used in an administration, such as seals and sealings. For example, Building 2 produced not only the two envelopes and their content of incised ovoids but also a collection of oblong solid bullae and four impressed tablets. Although the function of Building 2 of Habuba Kabira cannot be fully understood, it was related in some fashion to a southern Mesopotamian administration.

The envelope of Tepe Yahya was also not *in situ* but lay in an open space near an administrative building which held plain tokens, tablets, beveled-rim bowls, nose-lugged jars, seals, and sealings.[63] The setting of Tepe Yahya thus appears similar to that of Uruk, Susa, Chogha Mish, or Habuba Kabira. It involved the same types of potteries and the same system of control. There were, however, three main differences in the Tepe Yahya assemblage: first, the tokens were plain and not complex; second, the seals and sealings were not in the southern Mesopotamian style but were typically Elamite; and third, the tablets were not impressed but bore accounts written in the Proto-Elamite script.

The envelopes appear in two settings. The majority, and in particular the specimens from Uruk, Habuba Kabira, Susa, Chogha Mish, and perhaps Farukhabad, are associated with artifacts typical of Eanna VI–IV and were connected with the southern Mesopotamian temple bureaucracy. The specimen from Tepe Yahya was Proto-Elamite.

STATE OF PRESERVATION

The envelopes have been recovered in various states of preservation. Some eighty are still intact, keeping and hiding an unknown number of tokens. Several of the pieces found whole have been subsequently opened by various methods so that their contents could be examined (table 1). Among them, four envelopes from Susa were punctured with a knife (fig. 62),[64] whereas the specimen from Tepe Yahya was carefully sawn at one extremity (fig. 58). As a result, the number of envelopes whose contents are known with absolute certainty amounts to no more than five, or less than 3 percent of the known assemblage.

Other envelopes were broken in antiquity but were still associated with their full or partial content of tokens (fig. 63; table 2). This is the case for nineteen examples from Susa, an unknown number from Chogha Mish, five in Uruk, and two in Habuba Kabira.[65] At Farukhabad, the broken envelope was separated from its token content, but the mark of a tetrahedron is visible on the inner wall.[66] Finally, five sets of tokens belonged to crushed envelopes (table 3). The first

	cones	large cones	punched cones	spheres	large spheres	flat disks	lenticular disks	high disks	cylinders	tetrahedrons	large tetrahedrons	punched tetrahedrons	ovoids	incised ovoids	rectangles	triangles	paraboloids	animals	undetermined	TOTAL	Markings
Susa Sb 1927	3	1					3													7	7
Sb 1936					1	1														2	no
Sb 1940							3		3											6	6
Sb 4338					5															5	no
Tepe Yahya	1			2																3	3
TOTAL	4	1		2	6	1	6		3											23	

Table 1. Envelopes Found Complete

62. Envelope and its content: a sphere and a disk, Susa (Sb 1936), Iran. Courtesy Musée du Louvre, Département des Antiquités Orientales.

Table 2. Envelopes Found Broken

	cones	large cones	punched cones	spheres	large spheres	flat disks	lenticular disks	high disks	cylinders	tetrahedrons	large tetrahedrons	punched tetrahedrons	ovoids	incised ovoids	rectangles	triangles	paraboloids	animals	undetermined	TOTAL	Markings
Chogha Mish	1			1	1	5														8	no
Farukhabad										1										1	?
Habuba Kabira MII:133														2						2	11
MII:134														6						6	6
Susa Sb 1930				7																7	no
Sb 1938	3			2		1		1									1			8	+
Sb 1942				2																2	no
Sb 1967				4	2					4	3	2								15	no
Sb 5340										2										2	2
Sb 6350							2		2								1	2		7	6
Sb 6946				6																6	no
No Re				1																1	no
S.ACR.I.77 1991.1							3		8											11	no
2049.1									3											3	?
2067.2	1						1													2	no
2089.1				7					3											10	no
2111.2				1					7											8	no
2111.3									6											6	6
2130.1									7											7	7
2130.4				1		1			1											3	no
2142.2									2											2	3
2142.3				3					5											8	8
2173.4			1	4					1											6	6
Uruk W 20987,3				1			1								1					3	no
W 20987,7														7						7	no
W 20987,8						2				5										7	no
W 20987, 15				4		1														5	no
W 20987,17		1		4		1	2		1											9	no
TOTAL	5	1	1	48	3	11	9	1	46	12	3	2		15	1		2	2		162	

63. Envelope found broken in antiquity, Uruk (W 20987. 20), Iraq. Courtesy Deutsches Archaeologisches Institut, Abteilung Baghdad.

64. Set of tokens belonging to crushed envelopes, Uruk (W 20987.27), Iraq. Courtesy Deutsches Archaeologisches Institut, Abteilung Baghdad.

Table 3. Groups of Tokens Separated from Envelopes

	cones	large cones	punched cones	spheres	large spheres	flat disks	lenticular disks	high disks	cylinders	tetrahedrons	large tetrahedrons	punched tetrahedrons	ovoids	incised ovoids	rectangles	triangles	paraboloids	animals	undetermined		TOTAL
Susa No. N. ber				8		1			1	3							1				14
ACR 2067.3	3								1												4
ACR 2091.2	1								6												7
Chogha Mish	12			13	2	10				11	8					1			4		61
Uruk W 20987.27				26					1	8	1		5	3		2	4	2			52
TOTAL	16			47	2	11			9	22	9		5	3		3	5	2	4		138

Table 4. Tokens Tentatively Determined by X rays

	cones	large cones	punched cones	spheres	large spheres	flat disks	lenticular disks	high disks	cylinders	tetrahedrons	large tetrahedrons	punched tetrahedrons	ovoids	incised ovoids	rectangles	triangles	paraboloids	animals	undetermined	TOTAL	Markings
Dharan																			10	10	
Dumah																			3	3	
Susa Sb 1932				7	1	1														9?	9
TOTAL				7	1	1													13	22	

group comes from Uruk and consists of fifty-two units (fig. 64),[67] the second from Chogha Mish yields sixty-one,[68] and finally, three from Susa held respectively fourteen, seven, and four tokens.[69]

The technique of tomography, which can produce X-ray pictures of predetermined plane sections inside an object, may prove to be the ideal solution for finding out the exact content of more envelopes without breaking them open. Normal X-rays have been used, with unsatisfactory results, to investigate several specimens from Chogha Mish,[70] Susa,[71] Dharan (figs. 65.1 and 65.2), and Dumah (table 4). Because the tokens are tightly clustered, they hide one another, making it difficult to take an accurate count. It is impossible to decide with certainty whether a circular shape is to be interpreted as a sphere or a disk. Furthermore, X-ray photographs do not show incised or punched markings.

TOKENS ENCLOSED IN ENVELOPES

The total number of tokens which belonged in envelopes amounts to 345. Accordingly, there is an average of 9 tokens per envelope. In reality, however, there are great discrepancies between the number of counters in each of the clay cases. For example, Sb 1936 of Susa yielded only 2, but Sb 1967 held 15 (fig. 66).

Among the 345 tokens held in envelopes, 23 came

65.1. Envelope, Dharan, Saudi Arabia. Courtesy Teresa Barger.

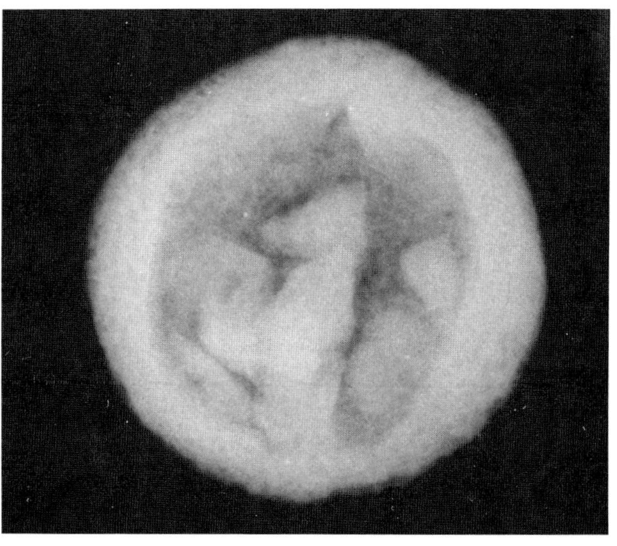

65.2. X-ray photograph, envelope, Dharan, Saudi Arabia.

66. Envelope with its content of fifteen tokens, Susa (Sb 1967), Iran. Courtesy Musée du Louvre, Département des Antiquités Orientales.

from specimens intentionally opened; 162 from envelopes accidentally broken but still associated with their contents; 138 were part of groups separated from their cases; and, finally, 22 may be tentatively identified by X-rays (table 5).

Ten types of tokens are represented among the counters found within envelopes, namely, 28 cones, 116 spheres, 40 disks, 58 cylinders, 48 tetrahedrons, 23 ovoids, 1 rectangle, 3 triangles, 7 paraboloids, 4 animals, and 17 undetermined. The composition of the assemblage is as follows: cones 8.11 percent, spheres 33.62 percent, disks 11.59 percent, cylinders 16.81 percent, tetrahedrons 13.91 percent, ovoids 6.66 percent, rectangles .29 percent, triangles .87 percent, paraboloids 2.03 percent, animals 1.16 percent, and undetermined 4.93 percent. There is yet no evidence that biconoids, bent coils, rhomboids, vessels, and tools were stored in envelopes but, of course, this may be because the sample of tokens held in envelopes is so small.

Cones, spheres, and tetrahedrons are featured in two different sizes, small and large; there are flat, lenticular, and high disks; there are examples of incised ovoids and animals and of punched cones and tetrahedrons, bringing the number of token subtypes represented in envelopes to nineteen. Among the nineteen subtypes, twelve are plain subtypes and the remaining

Table 5. Totals

	cones	large cones	punched cones	spheres	large spheres	flat disks	lenticular disks	high disks	cylinders	tetrahedrons	large tetrahedrons	punched tetrahedrons	ovoids	incised ovoids	rectangles	triangles	paraboloids	animals	undetermined		TOTAL
Envelopes Found Complete	4	1		2	6	1	6		3												23
Envelopes Found Broken	5	1	1	48	3	11	9	1	46	12	3	2		15	1		2	2			162
Separated Tokens	16			47	2	11			9	22	9		5	3		3	5	2	4		138
Tokens Determined by X rays				7?	1?	1?													13?		22?
TOTAL	25	2	1	104	12	24	15	1	58	34	12	2	5	18	1	3	7	4	17		345

67. Envelope with six incised ovoids (the full content of the envelope was seven incised ovoids), Uruk (W 20987.7), Iraq. Courtesy Deutsches Archaeologisches Institut, Abteilung Baghdad.

seven are complex. The former include cones, large cones, spheres, large spheres, flat disks, lenticular disks, high disks, cylinders, tetrahedrons, large tetrahedrons, ovoids, and rectangles. The latter consist of punched cones, punched tetrahedrons, incised ovoids (fig. 67; table 6), triangles, paraboloids (fig. 64), and two types of animal shapes. As a result, among the 345 tokens enclosed in envelopes, 287 are plain, 32 are complex, and 26 are undetermined (including the 22 tokens included in X-rayed envelopes which cannot show markings). In other words, 83.19 percent of the tokens enclosed in envelopes are plain, 9.28 percent are complex, and 7.54 percent are undetermined.

The tokens enclosed in envelopes are identical in types and subtypes to those found loose. Furthermore, the tokens contained in clay cases also occur in different sizes: There are, for example, spheres and large spheres; they bear the same kind of markings, incised or punched. The selection is smaller, probably because the assemblage is also smaller. The tokens held in envelopes, however, are often smaller in size than those found loose, measuring about 7–15 mm compared to the usual 10–30 mm. Furthermore, the counters held in cases seem more casually made than those found loose. They crumble more easily and it is likely that they were not fired.

SEALINGS

All envelopes are covered with seal impressions, except those from Tepe Yahya, Dharan, and Dumah. As a rule, a single cylinder seal was impressed all over the artifact, obviously with the intent of covering the entire surface (fig. 68). The seal seemed to be first rolled around the maximum diameter, and the empty spaces

Table 6 Tokens included in envelopes

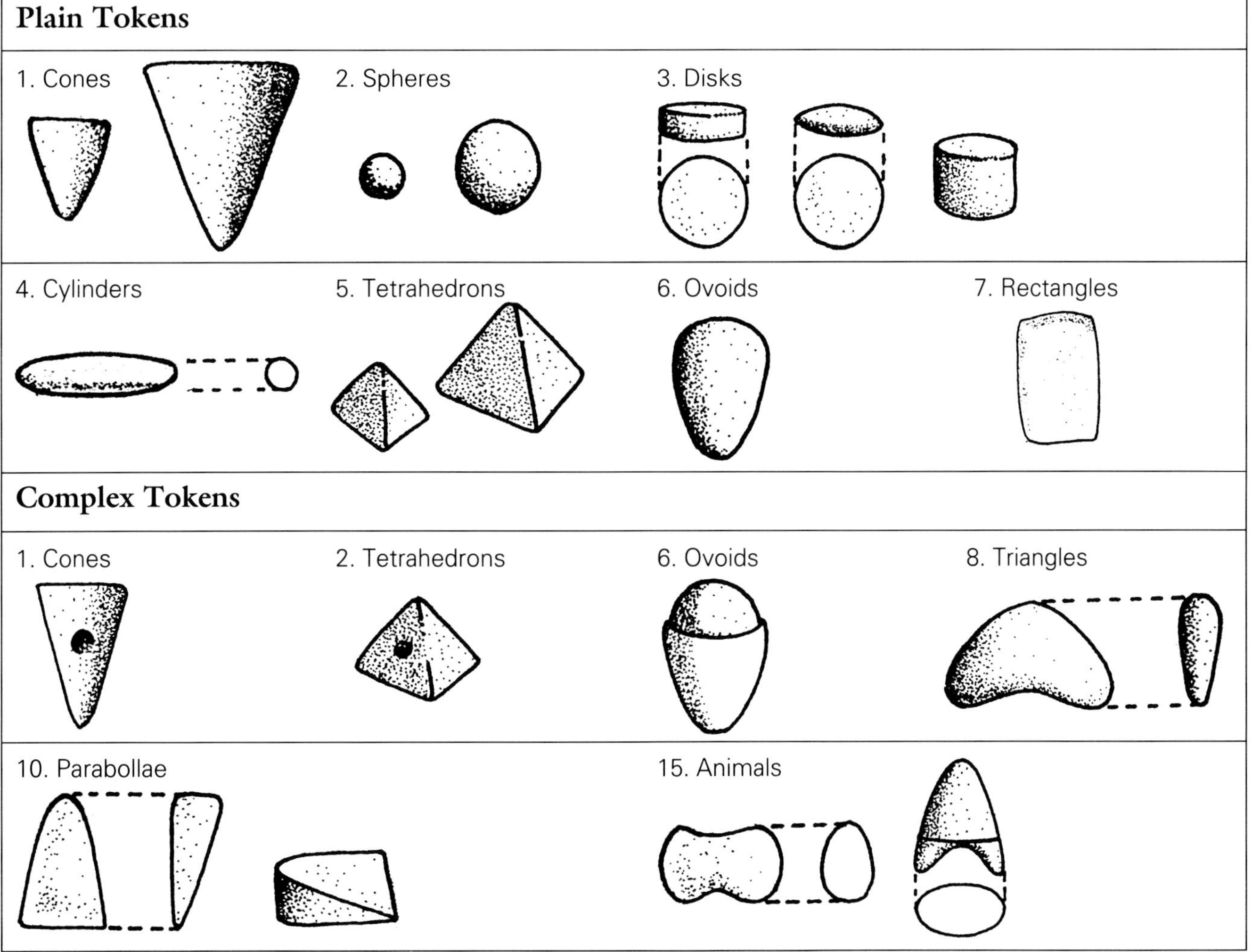

68. Envelope covered with one cylinder seal impression, Susa (Sb 1935), Iran. Courtesy Musée du Louvre, Département des Antiquités Orientales.

69. Envelope covered with two cylinder seal impressions, Susa (Sb 1937), Iran. Courtesy Musée du Louvre, Département des Antiquités Orientales.

70. Envelope covered with two cylinder seal and one stamp seal impressions, Susa (Sb 1942), Iran. Courtesy Musée du Louvre, Département des Antiquités Orientales.

71. Envelope with a set of tokens sunk into the surface, Susa (Sb 5340), Iran. Courtesy Musée du Louvre, Département des Antiquités Orientales.

were subsequently filled with a vague herringbone pattern. There are also instances when two (fig. 69)[72] and even three different seals were used (fig. 70).[73] At Shahdad, the impression of a stamp, rather than a cylinder seal, was repeated all around the envelope. Finally, there are examples when both stamp and cylinder seals were used on the same case.[74]

The patterns illustrated on seals are numerous. Among them are featured rosettes; lines of rams, goats, or cattle; and snakes and fabulous monsters in heraldic postures. The priests or kings are also represented as well as a hero mastering snakes. Individuals are shown performing various tasks in workshops or on the farm.[75] Finally, there are instances of war scenes, besieged cities with people begging for mercy,[76] and prisoners with their hands tied behind their backs.

MARKINGS

It was a great advantage to have groups of tokens secured in clay cases, often bearing seals of authority. The major drawback of the envelopes, however, was that they concealed the counters: Once the tokens were enclosed, they were no longer visible. While the string of tokens could be checked at all times, it was not possible to verify the contents of an envelope without breaking it and, therefore, without tampering with the sealings. It was probably to overcome this difficulty that systems of markings were developed. I want to note here that I use the term *marking* to refer to notations on envelopes and *sign* for notations on tablets.

Before proceeding to the description of these various markings, it should be emphasized that the total number of marked specimens amounts to only nineteen specimens, or 9 percent of the total number of artifacts. No envelope bearing markings has yet been uncovered at Uruk, Shahdad, Farukhabad,[77] Chogha Mish(?), Dharan, or Dumah. Marked envelopes are presently attested in three sites: Susa, Habuba Kabira, and Tepe Yahya. The rarity of envelopes bearing mark-

72. Envelope bearing impressed markings corresponding to the tokens held inside, Susa (Sb 1940), Iran. Courtesy Musée du Louvre, Département des Antiquités Orientales.

73. Envelope bearing impressed markings corresponding to the tokens held inside, Susa (Sb 1927), Iran. Courtesy Musée du Louvre, Département des Antiquités Orientales.

74. Envelope bearing the impression of incised ovoids, Habuba Kabira (M II: 134), Syria. Photo by Klaus Anger; courtesy Museum für Vor- und Frühgeschichte, Berlin.

75. Envelope bearing three markings scratched after the clay had dried, Tepe Yahya, Iran. Courtesy Peabody Museum, Harvard University.

76. Envelope bearing an impressed cross, Susa (Sb 1938), Iran. Courtesy Musée du Louvre, Département des Antiquités Orientales.

ings can perhaps be attributed to excavation luck, but otherwise it seems to indicate that the usage was not widespread.

The first method of showing what was inside the envelopes consisted of attaching a set of tokens, presumably identical to those enclosed, to the outer surface of the case. This was done by sinking the counters in the clay when it was still soft. This method is represented by a single fragment from Susa, displaying two plain cylinders embedded in the surface (fig. 71).[78] The fact that only one example was recovered suggests that the method was not widely used.

Fourteen envelopes, including twelve at Susa[79] and two at Habuba Kabira, bore markings impressed on their surface when the clay was still soft. In this second technique, the markings were shown in one-to-one correspondence; that is, each token enclosed was indicated by one marking on the surface of the case. For example, an envelope holding six tokens displayed six markings (fig. 72). This is supported by the fact that all the envelopes of this category, recovered intact, have a number of markings equal to the number of tokens enclosed. In other words, only broken envelopes show a discrepancy between the number of markings and the number of associated tokens. For instance, M II: 133 of Habuba Kabira, which is badly damaged, displays eleven markings but was associated with two tokens. A specimen at Susa, also broken, shows two long wedges and a circular punch but held only two cylinders.[80] Finally, an envelope from Susa, three-quarters preserved, that is stored at the Louvre with seven tokens, exhibits six signs (fig. 11).[81] Since all these specimens were opened long before excavation, presumably some of the counters were lost. In the first two cases, the missing tokens were separated from the envelopes, probably in antiquity. In the third case, it is likely that some of the tokens stored with the envelope in fact belonged to another specimen.

The markings indicated not only the number of tokens included but also the shape of each counter. For example, Sb 1940 of Susa yielded three lenticular disks and three cylinders that were shown by three circular and three long markings. Nine subtypes of tokens were represented in the thirteen envelopes bearing impressed markings. They include small, large, and punched cones, spheres, lenticular disks, cylinders, incised ovoids, and, perhaps, parabolas and animal shapes. Examination of the markings shows that little systematization was used to depict the various tokens, except for spheres and disks. These were translated by different circular markings, the former taking the shape of a deep punch, whereas the latter was a wide, shallow depression. Cones were impressed in several ways, either in profile,[82] with the tip (fig. 73),[83] or even with the base.[84] In this last instance, the token represented was a large punched cone, which was thus shown by a shallow circular marking of an even greater diameter than that of a lenticular disk. The cylinders appear as long wedges. The incised ovoids were shown by an oval impression with a small ridge left by the incision at the maximum diameter. The signs corresponding to the parabolas and animal-shaped tokens are not identified. These are the tokens associated with the fragmentary envelope Sb 6350 of Susa, to which they most probably do not belong.

There were several ways of impressing the markings in the soft clay. The most direct, illustrated by M II: 134 of Habuba Kabira, was to press the tokens against the surface of the envelope before enclosing them inside. There can be no doubt about this technique, because the incised ovoids, found associated with the Habuba Kabira envelope, fit perfectly in the oval cavities left in the clay case about fifty-five hundred years ago. It is tempting to speculate that the first method of embedding tokens on the surface of envelopes led to the second method of showing their negative imprint. The second envelope of Habuba Kabira and most examples from Susa exhibited yet another method of conveying the information. In these cases, the markings were not stamped with tokens but impressed with a stick or stylus.[85] Finally, traces of fingernails(?) on circular impressions of a Susa envelope suggest that they may have been done with the thumb.[86]

A third technique consisted of marking the envelopes when the clay was already dry (perhaps as an afterthought?). Consequently, the markings were scratched rather than impressed, making it more difficult to render the shape of the counters. In both specimens of this category the number of markings matched the tokens but their shape did not. In the first example, which comes from Tepe Yahya, there is little difference between three signs meant to represent two spheres and a cone (fig. 75). In the second specimen from Susa, no effort was made to match the shapes of six spheres, which were simply indicated by six strokes, whereas a large sphere and flat disk were shown, apparently, by a circular and a triangular punch mark.[87]

Seven specimens, again from Susa, were perforated while the clay was still moist.[88] Pairs of small holes appear either at diametrical ends of the objects or punctured through the thickness of the wall.[89] The perforations have been interpreted by some as a means of preventing the artifacts from breaking while firing.[90] It is more likely, however, that the perforations allowed the passage of a string holding a number of tokens duplicating the set inside (fig. 62). The perforated envelopes can be considered, therefore, as a possible fourth technique for indicating the content of envelopes.

A last example from Susa, marked with a cross, shows on the X-ray photograph a yield of eight tokens (fig. 76).[91] In this case, the sign apparently did not communicate the number or the shape of the tokens inside. Instead, the information concerned perhaps the nature of the transaction. Alternatively, the marking could be an accountant's colophon.

In sum, in all cases except one, the information communicated by the markings on the envelopes pertained to the number and/or types of the counters enclosed. The unique envelope of Susa, marked with a cross, perhaps had a different meaning altogether.

The various ways of indicating the tokens contained in the envelopes included (1) attaching tokens on the surface, (2) stamping the tokens in the soft clay, (3) impressing signs with a stick or stylus, (4) pressing with the thumb, (5) scratching the clay when hard, and (6) securing by a string(?). The small number of marked envelopes and the many ways used to mark them illustrate that the artifacts were in a transitional stage.

It is interesting to note that some of the techniques for showing the token contents of envelopes proved dead ends and disappeared. For example, thumb impressions were no longer used in later times. On the other hand, token impressions and markings inscribed with a blunt stylus were carried over to the first tablets. They were the beginning of writing.

The envelopes, which started as accessory to the token system, came to transform it in the most unexpected way. They triggered the mutation of the three-dimensional tokens into two-dimensional graphic symbols. This unique event was to have important consequences for communication.

THE STUDY of the token system in the fourth millennium B.C. shows an increase in complexity in several ways. First, the number of shapes of counters and of markings on their face was enlarged. Second, new systems were devised to secure tokens of particular accounts either by stringing them or enclosing them in envelopes, sometimes bearing markings. These two major transformations illustrate a new trend in communicating information by way of markings, either incised on the face of the tokens or impressed on the surface of envelopes and bullae. These important changes were the immediate steps preceding writing.

6
IMPRESSED TABLETS

And when we consider the first uses to which writing was put, it would seem quite clear that it was connected first and foremost with power: it was used for inventories, catalogues, censuses, laws and instructions; in all instances, whether the aim was to keep a check on material possessions or on human beings, it is evidence of the power exercised by some men over other men and over worldly possessions.

—Claude Lévi-Strauss[1]

THE SYSTEM of markings on envelopes ushered in a new phase of the token system. At first, the impressed notations were ancillary to the counters, but in the course of time they challenged and eventually supplanted them. This occurred when solid clay tablets bearing impressed signs replaced the hollow envelopes holding tokens (figs. 77 and 78). These impressed signs still perpetuated the shape of the tokens, but they assumed an entirely new function. Whereas the markings on envelopes repeated only the message encoded in the tokens held inside, the signs impressed on tablets were the message. The first tablets were a decisive step in the invention of writing and amounted to a revolution in communication technology. This chapter deals with the earliest tablets bearing signs in the shape of tokens. I will discuss how the tablets were discovered and identified as the most ancient documents of the Sumerian script. I will document the number of these artifacts recovered and their geographic distribution (fig. 79), context, and chronology. I will describe the tablets and the signs they bear. Most important, I will document the evolution from tokens to markings on envelopes and impressed signs on tablets. Finally, I will show that impressed signs are the immediate forerunners of the Sumerian pictographic script.

Discovery

When the first series of impressed tablets were excavated at Susa by Jacques de Morgan in 1901 to 1905, archaeology was not ready for them and the artifacts seemingly passed unnoticed.[2] Thirty years later, when impressed tablets appeared in the sondage of archaic Eanna at Uruk in the season of 1930–31, Jordan promptly identified them as the precursor of pictographic tablets: "Vorläufer von pictographischen Tontafeln."[3] This view has never been challenged and the artifacts have been recognized ever since by scholars as representing the earliest tablets of the Near East. At the time of their discovery, however, the impressed signs were interpreted as representing numerals, which explains why they have since been referred to, erroneously, as "numerical tablets." In fact, as will be discussed at the end of the chapter, the impressed signs stood for units of goods such as measures of grain and numbers of animals.

Through the years not only did further impressed tablets consistently emerge from among the material recovered at both Uruk[4] and Susa[5] but they also started appearing in other sites. As so often happens, the findings came in waves. The first ones followed shortly after the Uruk discoveries of the 1930s and were recovered at Khafaje in 1934–35[6] and Tepe Sialk in 1937.[7] The fragments of two tablets, one excavated in 1931 at Nineveh[8] and the second at Tall-i-Ghazir in 1948–49,[9] may be tentatively counted into this group of impressed tablets although they may be, in fact, two fragments of pictographic tablets. A second series started with the impressed tablet of Mari in 1964[10] and Chogha Mish in 1965–66,[11] continuing in the early seventies with those of Jebel Aruda,[12] Habuba Kabira in 1972,[13] Godin Tepe in 1973,[14] and lastly Tell Brak in 1978.[15]

The twelve places yielding impressed tablets are scattered on a radius of 1,000 km divided into three present-day countries of the Near East. Susa, Tepe Sialk, Godin Tepe, Chogha Mish, and Tall-i-Ghazir are located in Iran; Uruk, Nineveh, and Khafaje in Iraq; Mari, Habuba Kabira, Jebel Aruda, and Tell Brak in Syria.

The sites where the impressed tablets have been located share one common denominator: All were located at strategic positions along main arteries of the ancient Near East. Jebel Aruda, Habuba Kabira, and Uruk were situated on the Euphrates River, which constituted a major waterway of the ancient world. There is no doubt that the two Syrian sites upstream served as links to the Syrian hinterland, Anatolia, the Mediterranean, and the coastal road to Egypt and for the political centers situated downstream such as Uruk. Nineveh was one of the lower easy crossings of the Tigris River, in line with the ancient road leading northwest to Anatolia and west, south of Jebel Sinjar into Syria.[16] Tell Brak was on the Khabur River and controlled the ancient route from the Tigris to Ergani Madden. Mari was located on the desert road to the Levant. Susa and Chogha Mish were not only on one main access road to the Gulf, to which they were much closer than today, but also represented the southern gates to the Iranian plateau and the east. Tall-i-Ghazir was backed against the southern skirt of the Zagros Mountains in the extension of the Ram Hormuz Valley, where caravans to Mesopotamia were still assembling in A.D. 1000. The oasis site of Tepe Sialk, sandwiched between the foothills of the Zagros and the Dahst-i-Lut, commanded the unique valley connecting the northern end of the Iranian plateau with the south. Godin Tepe was in a position to control the Khorasan route and its traffic of lapis lazuli at the passage of the Gamas Ab River. The main route from the east reached Mesopotamia via the Diyala River, where Khafaje was situated.

Number

The total number of impressed tablets, complete or fragmentary, included in the present study amounts to about 240. The majority of the documents come from Iran with a total of about 150 specimens. The 90 tablets from Susa have been recovered in successive excavation campaigns by Jacques de Morgan in 1901 to 1911 and by Roland de Mecquenem in 1912 to 1946.[17] The expeditions led by Jean Perrot added 11 impressed tablets between 1969 and 1971,[18] 6 in 1972,[19] and 11 in 1977.[20] Forty-two specimens were excavated in Godin Tepe,[21] 13 from Sialk,[22] and 1 from Tall-i-Ghazir.[23] An undisclosed number of impressed tablets was discovered at Chogha Mish, of which 6 are published.[24]

The number of Iraqi examples can be estimated at about sixty-seven. A precise count cannot be provided, however, until the Uruk material is analyzed and adequately published. Presently the information available on the artifacts remains vague; for example, two of "several" impressed tablets from the area of the Anu Ziggurat were published in the season of 1930–31.[25] Green and Nissen mention that, in fact, this group consists of twenty-two specimens.[26] Two further examples are discussed in the fourth report,[27] two in the fifth,[28] five in the eighth,[29] and, finally, a single example in each

77. Impressed tablet, short wedges, Uruk (W 20650), Iraq. Courtesy Deutsches Archaeologisches Institut, Abteilung Baghdad.

78. Impressed tablet, deep circular signs, Uruk (W 21452), Iraq. Courtesy Deutsches Archaeologisches Institut, Abteilung Baghdad.

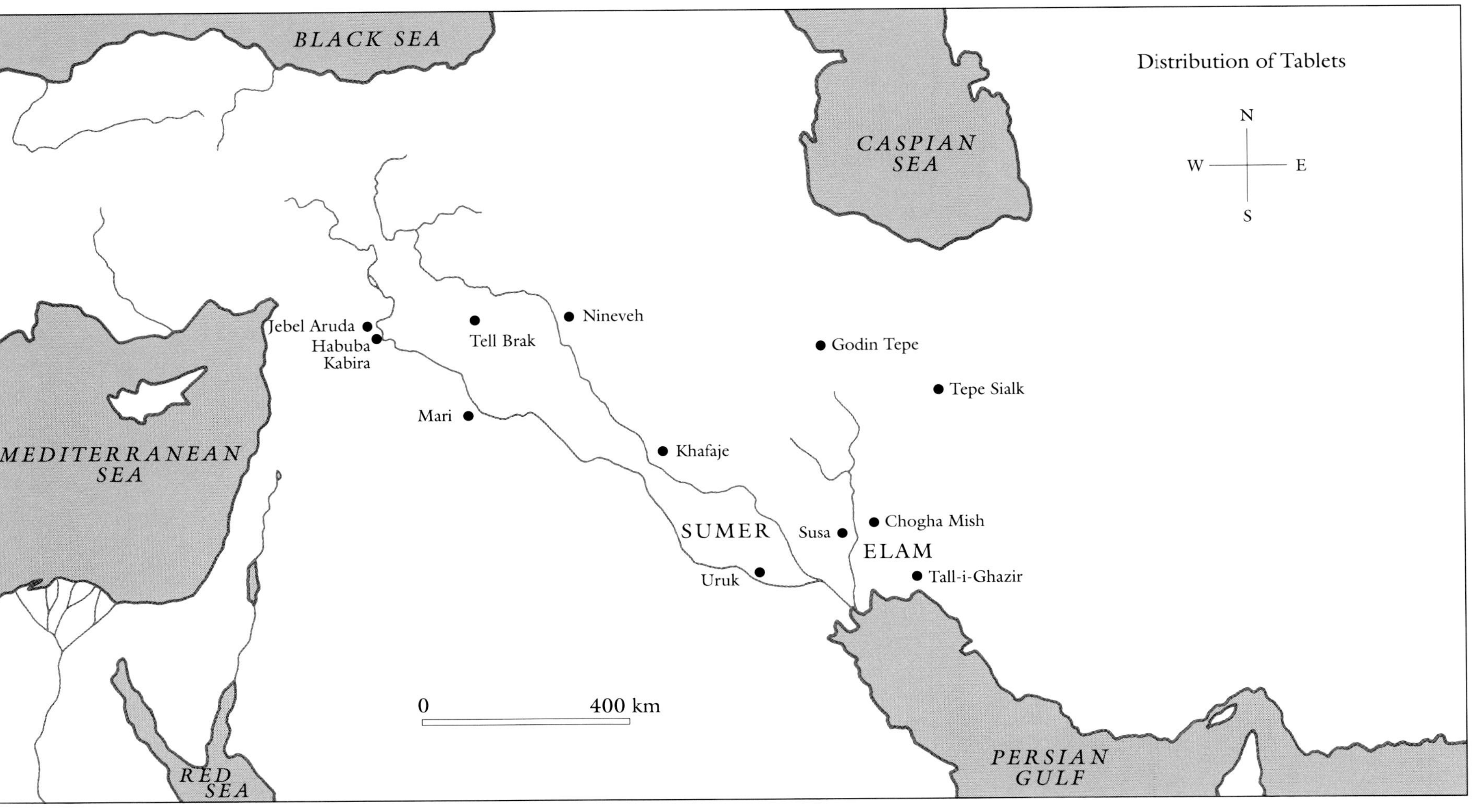

79. Distribution of tablets.

of the seventeenth, nineteenth, twentieth, twenty-second, twenty-third, twenty-fourth, and twenty-fifth seasons.[30] Twenty-nine further impressed tablets, mostly from the second season, were seemingly not reported.[31] To these sixty-five examples from Uruk can only be added the single specimen of Khafaje[32] and one fragment from Nineveh.[33] There are twenty-five tablets from Syria, with ten originating from Habuba Kabira,[34] thirteen from Jebel Aruda,[35] one from Tell Brak,[36] and one from Mari.[37]

It is interesting to note that the antiquity market, which since the late nineteenth century has supplied museum collections with a number of pictographic tablets, has not yet produced any impressed tablets and that all specimens come from controlled excavations.

Context

In the sites yielding both impressed tablets and envelopes, the two kinds of artifacts are found in the same context. At Susa, for example, tablets and envelopes were located in the same area of the Acropolis, in some cases in the same building, the same room, and, in one instance, even in the same container.[38] Building 2 of Habuba Kabira also produced both impressed tablets and envelopes,[39] and forty tablets from Uruk belonged to the sanctuary of Eanna, as did twenty-five envelopes. However, some twenty further tablets were discovered in the Anu Ziggurat, the second major sanctuary of Uruk, where so far no envelopes have been uncovered. Several of these tablets lay *in situ* on the

80. Impressed tablet with markings on obverse and two edges and cylinder seal impressions on the reverse, Godin Tepe (Gd. 73-64), Iran. Courtesy T. Cuyler Young, Jr.

floor of the White Temple, associated with an alabaster theriomorphic vessel.[40]

In the remaining sites, the impressed tablets were located, like the envelopes, in temple precincts and administrative buildings, except for those of Tepe Sialk[41] recovered in simple mud-brick houses. The tablets from Khafaje came from a deep sounding dug below the Early Dynastic complex of the Oval Temple, presumably a sacred area also in protohistoric times.[42] At Jebel Aruda, most of the thirteen tablets were located in a building adjacent to the temple, where they were associated with torn jar sealings and sherds.[43] The tablet of Tell Brak was recovered in an area adjoining the administrative precinct.[44] Finally, at Godin Tepe, the largest cache of tablets was uncovered in the gate house commanding the entrance of the compound and a second group in an imposing building probably used for official functions.[45] Unfortunately, the context of the tablets of Chogha Mish, Tall-i-Ghazir, Mari, and Nineveh is not known.

Chronology

The impressed tablets can be divided into three closely consecutive groups, ranging from about 3500 to 3000 B.C. The first group, dated to ca. 3500 B.C., includes the impressed tablets of Susa 18 and Habuba Kabira. Presumably, some of the tablets from Eanna and Chogha Mish also belong to the period of Uruk VI.

The tablets of Susa 17 date between 3300 and 3100 B.C. They are contemporaneous with the twenty-nine tablets of the Red Temple of Uruk and those of the Anu Ziggurat, estimated to Uruk IVa.[46] The forty-three tablets of Godin Tepe, including one specimen bearing an incised sign, may be included in this second group, since Godin V preceded Susa 16 and Uruk III,[47] as well as those from Jebel Aruda, whose carbon 14 dates cluster around 3200 B.C.[48]

The tablets of Sialk and Tall-i-Ghazir, associated with high beveled-rim bowls, *Blumentopf*, Proto-Elamite sealings, and lugged jars with rope appliqué bands, belong to the third group, estimated to Uruk III and Susa 16, about 3100 to 3000 B.C. The seal impression on the Nineveh tablet suggests a similar date, although it has been assigned to level V, dated to 2900 to 2500 B.C.[49]

The chronology of the impressed tablet is important because it clearly demonstrates that impressed signs preceded pictography by an interval of about two hundred years or ten generations. There are no pictographic texts contemporaneous with the earliest group of impressed tablets of Susa 18 and Uruk VI–IVc. The earliest evidence of pictography consists of a group of tablets recovered on the floor of Temple C, in Uruk Oc XVI 3, "Sur le sol, par dessous les éboulis du toit de la longue pièce en T du temple C, au niveau IVa." These seven tablets may be as early as Uruk IVb[50] or as late as IVa.[51] Consequently, it is about 3300 to 3100 B.C., during the period of the second group of impressed tablets, that the two kinds of writing started coexisting. This is well illustrated at Godin Tepe[52] and Sialk, where the two types of tablets were found together.[53]

Description

The impressed tablets constitute a homogeneous assemblage, with no noticeable difference between the groups originating from Syria, Mesopotamia, or Elam. In all cases the manufacture of the artifacts was casual rather than meticulous; for instance, no effort was made to eliminate the scribes' fingerprints. Some tablets, particularly from Susa, Uruk, and especially Jebel Aruda, are bulky and even crude.

All the impressed tablets were made of clay, except for twenty-two plaster specimens recovered in the Anu Ziggurat of Uruk.[54] No stone example is known. The clay utilized for the manufacture of the objects was usually well prepared and shows rare inclusions. To my knowledge, the traditional explanation that the tablets were dried in the sun is not based on scientific analysis. As the changes in crystal structure that take place with firing are not visible to the naked eye, this assumption may have to be revised.

The tablets are small, fitting comfortably in the palm of the hand. On average, they are about 5 cm wide, 4 cm long, and 2 cm thick. They are modeled in various shapes with the lack of standardization typical of a new craft. A number are oval, some roundish, others square or rectangular. Unlike the later cuneiform tablets, whose form is indicative of the content, there is as yet no visible link between text and format. The profile of the tablets is also highly variable, and while a majority of specimens are convex, some are flat and still others are plano-convex. The earliest tablets, such as those of Uruk, Susa, and Chogha Mish, have tapering edges, whereas the later ones, like those of Godin Tepe and Sialk, tend to have flat or slightly concave sides, providing additional space for notations (fig. 80).

81. Tablet provided with a ruled margin, Godin Tepe (Gd. 73-286), Iran. Courtesy T. Cuyler Young, Jr.

82. Tablet bearing two deep circular markings and seal impressions, Susa (Sb 2312), Iran. Courtesy Musée du Louvre, Département des Antiquités Orientales.

83. Tablet with three large wedges, one shallow circular, and four deep circular markings, Susa (Sb 2313), Iran. Courtesy Musée du Louvre, Département des Antiquités Orientales.

Some tablets have special peculiarities; for example, nine tables from Tepe Sialk are perforated, leading Ghirshman to believe that they were invoices tied to shipments of goods.[55] At Godin Tepe several examples are also unique in showing a margin or frame designed probably by pressing the shaft of a stylus along three or four of the sides (fig. 81).[56] One particular example has an additional horizontal line dividing the field into two cases.[57]

Many of these documents were authenticated by seals. The seal impressions cover the impressed signs, showing that the tablets were first inscribed and then sealed (fig. 82).

The Signs

For the sake of clarity, I call the notations on tablets *signs*, whereas those on envelopes are referred to as *markings*. Seventeen signs can be identified on the impressed tablets.

1. Short wedge
   a. small (fig. 77)
   b. large (fig. 83)
   c. punched (fig. 98)
   d. sideways
   e. apex to apex (fig. 84)
2. Deep circular
   a. small (fig. 78)
   b. large
   c. semicircular
   d. incised (fig. 85)
   e. punched
   f. appendix
3. Shallow circular
   a. lenticular
   b. flat (fig. 83)
4. Long wedge (fig. 86)
5. Oval (fig. 87)
6. Triangular
   a. plain
   b. incised (fig. 85)

THE LAYOUT

Most tablets are inscribed on the obverse only, but some bear additional notations on the reverse or along the edges (fig. 80).[58] In this case, each face presents a separate account, and in no instance does the reverse indicate a total, as is the case in later pictographic tablets. Some tablets were turned like the page of a book to read the second face,[59] but others were turned on a horizontal axis.[60] The signs are organized in horizontal lines parallel to the larger side of the tablet. Only a few tablets, among which one from Habuba Kabira (fig. 88)[61] and one from Chogha Mish, do not conform to this layout and display signs impressed along two and three perpendicular sides.[62]

Signs of different types are usually not mixed on the same line. Instead, each line consists of identical signs. For example, tablet 73–290 of Godin Tepe displays a line of four circular signs followed by a line of four wedges (fig. 89). There are only a few exceptions to this norm, such as Susa Sb 2313, which includes two different signs on the second line.

The signs are by no means randomly aligned but are organized in hierarchical order. The largest units, placed at the top of the tablets, are followed by lines of signs of decreasing value (fig. 89). For example, a line of circular signs standing for large measures of grain precedes a line of wedges, which, as will be shown later, represented smaller units of grain.

The scribes wrote parallel to the long side of a tablet, starting at the top and proceeding downward. This is illustrated by a tablet from Godin Tepe showing a complete line of signs in the upper part of the tablet with the last unit added below (fig. 90).[63]

According to symmetry, which so strongly governs Sumerian art, the signs generally occupy the center of a tablet. For example, when there are only a few signs in a line, they are placed in the middle rather than on the side. For instance, on 73-329 of Godin Tepe, the single sign fills the center (fig. 91).[64]

Because each line consisted of a series of identical signs, the tablets could be read in any direction. Several specimens indicate, however, that writing usually proceeded from right to left and perhaps continued boustrophedon. Among these examples, Sb 2313 from Susa illustrates how, on the few occasions when a line is composed of different signs, the larger units were at the right, followed by lesser units toward the left. As the scribes placed the signs in hierarchical order, starting with the largest units, it can logically be deduced that the signs on the right were written before those on the left (fig. 83). Furthermore, a tablet of Jebel Aruda displays two lines, both starting from the right,[65] but, on the other hand, tablet 73-292 of Godin Tepe has a line starting from the right and a second starting from the left, or boustrophedon (fig. 92).[66]

THE TECHNIQUE OF IMPRESSION

The techniques for impressing signs on tablets were the same as those used for envelopes. For example,

84. Tablet with five short wedges, two triangular, and one apex to apex, Godin Tepe (Gd. 73-291), Iran. Courtesy T. Cuyler Young, Jr.

85. Impressed tablet with deep circular incised and triangular incised signs, Susa (Sb 1975 bis), Iran. Courtesy Musée du Louvre, Département des Antiquités Orientales. Drawing by Ellen Simmons. (The tablet is shown upside down.)

86. Impressed tablet, long wedges, Susa (Sb 6291), Iran. Courtesy Musée du Louvre, Département des Antiquités Orientales.

87. Impressed tablet, oval sign, Habuba Kabira (M II: 128), Syria. Photo by Klaus Anger; courtesy Museum für Vor- und Frühgeschichte, Berlin.

88. Tablet with impressed signs displayed along three sides, Habuba Kabira (M II: 127), Syria. Photo by Klaus Anger; courtesy Museum für Vor- und Frühgeschichte, Berlin.

89. Tablet showing a line of four circular signs followed by a line of four short wedges, Godin Tepe (Gd. 73-19), Iran. Courtesy T. Cuyler Young, Jr.

90. Tablet with a line of eight deep circular markings and one on the second line, Godin Tepe, (Gd. 73-292), Iran. Courtesy T. Cuyler Young, Jr.

91. Impressed tablet displaying signs placed at the center of the field, Susa (Sb 4839), Iran. Courtesy Musée du Louvre, Département des Antiquités Orientales.

92. Impressed tablet, boustrophedon, Godin Tepe (Gd. 73-294), Iran. Courtesy T. Cuyler Young, Jr.

signs were still made by pressing tokens against the surface of the tablets. This is the case for Sb 2313 of Susa (fig. 83), which bears three large wedges showing distinctly the entire outline of the cone used for impressing them. Furthermore, the signs corresponding to pinched spheres, ovoids, and triangles had to be impressed with tokens since no stylus could have assumed such shapes.

It is generally assumed that circular signs and wedges were impressed with a blunt stylus or, rather, a series of three styluses measuring alternatively 3–5 mm, 7–9 mm, and 1–2 cm in diameter. Instead, I would like to propose that a particular type of stone cone, with a crisp outline, typical of the Uruk–Jemdet Nasr period, was used to inscribe both wedges and circular signs. This is illustrated by tablet Sb 2313 from Susa (fig. 83), where it seems that the shallow and deep circular signs were made by impressing alternately the base and the tip of the cone used to inscribe wedges.

Some signs can be described as representing a mixed impressed/incised technique (signs 2d and 6b). On Sb 1975 bis from Susa, a token triangle was impressed four times on the face of the tablet, and each of these triangular impressions was completed by a vertical incision performed with a pointed stylus (fig. 85), reproducing a triangle with an incised line (type 8: 11). The same tablet, Sb 1975 bis, also shows two circular impressed signs completed by incised markings, probably depicting notched spheres (type 2: 7).

THE EVOLUTION FROM TOKENS TO SIGNS

It is remarkable that each of the 17 impressed signs can be traced to a token prototype. Considering the limited sampling of 19 marked envelopes and 240 tablets, it is even more remarkable that in seven instances the development from tokens to markings on envelopes and signs on tablets can be fully documented. In documenting the evolution from token to sign, whenever possible, I note the evidence for five steps of development (A–E) and propose a translation (F).

A. A type of token found at large.
B. The same token enclosed in an unmarked envelope.
C. The corresponding marking on the surface of an envelope.
D. The matching sign impressed on a tablet.
E. The occurrence on a pictographic tablet as an impressed sign, an incised pictograph or an impressed/incised sign.
F. The proposed translation.

I will not attempt to give a complete list of all the artifacts involved but mention only diagnostic examples. When possible, I will provide a tentative interpretation of the signs according to Peter Damerow and Robert K. Englund,[67] Adam Falkenstein,[68] Jöran Friberg,[69] M. W. Green,[70] or A. A. Vaiman.[71] It should be well understood that the Sumerian standardized units which these authors are citing reflect the highly organized late fourth to early third millennium B.C. city-state society. The meaning of the signs and of their prehistoric token prototypes will be discussed in a later section of the chapter.

1a. SHORT WEDGE

A. Cone, type 1: 1.
B. Unmarked envelope: Chogha Mish,[72] Susa.[73]
C. Marking on envelope: Tepe Yahya (fig. 75),[74] Susa (fig. 11).[75]
D. Impressed sign: Chogha Mish,[76] Godin Tepe (fig. 80),[77] Jebel Aruda,[78] Khafaje,[79] Sialk,[80] Susa (fig. 91),[81] Uruk.[82]
E. ATU 892/ZATU N-1 (impressed).
F. Measure of grain (1 *ban*?).[83]

Comment: On the envelope Sb 1927 from Susa, cones were rendered by pressing the tip of the counters rather than the sides in the clay, thus resulting in mostly circular markings.[84] This same technique was perhaps perpetuated on one tablet of Susa.[85]

1b. LARGE WEDGE

A. Large cone, type 1: 2.
B. Unmarked envelope: Chogha Mish.[86]
C. Marking on envelope: Susa (fig. 73).[87]
D. Impressed sign: Jebel Aruda,[88] Susa (fig. 83).[89]
E. ATU 899/ZATU N-34 (impressed).
F. Measure of grain (180 *ban*?).[90]

1c. PUNCHED WEDGE

A. Punched cone, type 1: 19.
B. Unmarked envelope: None.
C. Marking on envelope: Susa.[91]
D. Impressed sign: None.
E. ATU 905/ZATU N-48 (impressed).
F. Measure of grain (1,800 *ban*?).[92]
Unit of land measure (1 *ese* ?).[93]

Comment: The only punched cone enclosed in an envelope was translated by the impression of its base, leaving a large circular marking rather than a punched wedge.

1d. HORIZONTAL WEDGE

A. Cone, type 1: 1.
D. Impressed sign: Godin Tepe.[94]
E. ATU 918 (impressed).
F. Fraction.[95]
Unit of land measure (1/4 *iku*?).[96]

1e. TWO WEDGES APEX TO APEX

A. Cone, type 1: 1.
D. Impressed sign: Godin Tepe (fig. 84).[97]
E. ATU 918 (impressed).
F. Measure of grain (1/10 *ban*?).[98]

2a. CIRCULAR SIGN

A. Sphere, type 2: 1.
B. Unmarked envelope: Chogha Mish.[99] Susa (fig. 66),[100] Uruk.[101]
C. Marking on envelope: Susa[102] Tepe Yahya (fig. 75).[103]
D. Impressed sign: Godin Tepe (fig. 80),[104] Jebel Aruda,[105] Habuba Kabira,[106] Khafaje,[107] Nineveh,[108] Sialk,[109] Susa (figs. 9 and 82),[110] Uruk.[111]
E. ATU 897/ZATU N-14 (impressed).
F. Unit of grain (1 *bariga*?).[112]

Comment: In one instance an envelope holding six spheres showed six strokes on the outside.[113] The markings were scratched when the clay had already hardened and when it was no longer possible to impress the tokens.

2b. LARGE CIRCULAR SIGN

A. Large sphere, type 2: 2.
B. Enclosed in unmarked envelope: Chogha Mish,[114] Susa (fig. 66).[115]
C. Marking on envelope: None.
D. Impressed sign: Susa,[116] Habuba Kabira (fig. 87),[117] Jebel Aruda.[118]
E. ATU 913/ZATU N-45 (impressed).
F. Unit of grain metrology (10 *bariga*?).[119]

Comment: Unfortunately, none of the envelopes containing large spheres featured markings. It can only be presumed that large spheres became represented by deep circular markings, larger than those standing for small spheres. This hypothesis is supported by impressed tablets, such as those of Habuba Kabira, showing the existence of deep circular markings of different sizes organized in separate lines.[120]

2c. SEMICIRCULAR

A. Half sphere, type 2: 24.
B. Unmarked envelope: None.
C. Marking on envelope: None.
D. Impressed sign: Godin Tepe (fig. 80),[121] Sialk.[122]

Comment: The half-sphere is one of the earliest token subtypes found in many assemblages, but it never occurs in large numbers. This explains, perhaps, why none were recovered in envelopes and why the corresponding sign is also unfrequently used on tablets.

2d. CIRCULAR SIGN WITH ONE INCISION

A. Notched sphere, type 2: 7.
B. Unmarked envelope: None.
C. Marking on envelope: None.
D. Impressed signs: Susa (fig. 85).[123]
E. ATU 898/ZATU N-15 (impressed).
F. Measure of wheat(?) (10 *bariga*?).[124]
Unit of land measure (1/8 *iku*?).[125]

2e. PUNCHED CIRCULAR SIGN

A. Punched sphere, type 2: 3.
B. Unmarked envelope: None.
C. Marking on envelope: None.
D. Impressed tablet: Tall-i-Ghazir.[126]
E. ZATU N-50 (impressed).
F. Unit of land measure (10 *bur*?).[127]

2f. CIRCULAR WITH AN APPENDIX

A. Pinched sphere, type 2: 15.
B. Unmarked envelope: None.
C. Marking on envelope: None.
D. Impressed signs: Susa.[128]
E. ATU 781/ZATU 240 (incised).
F. Fat-tailed sheep.

Comment: The sign ATU 781/ZATU 240 shares the same outline but bears an additional incised cross.

3a. SHALLOW CIRCULAR MARKING

A. Flat disk, type 3: 1.
B. Unmarked envelope: Chogha Mish,[129] Susa,[130] Uruk.[131]
C. Marking on envelope: None.
D. Impressed sign: Susa.[132]
E. ATU 907 (impressed).
F. Unit of grain metrology(?).[133]

Comment: Lenticular disks (type 3: 3) are represented by shallow circular markings on two envelopes from Susa.[134] However, none of the envelopes containing flat disks bear markings. It can only be hypothesized that they also were represented by large shallow circular markings showing, probably, a more defined outline than the lenticular disks. The value of the flat disk may be hypothesized from the tokens they are associated with. It is probably not fortuitous that in four instances when disks with straight edges were included in envelopes they were associated with small spheres[135] or with small and large spheres.[136] The association of spheres and flat disks in envelopes seems to correspond to the association of deep and shallow circular impressed signs on tablets.[137]

3b. CIRCULAR SIGN DERIVING FROM THE LENTICULAR DISK

A. Lenticular disk, type 3: 10.
B. Unmarked envelope: Susa.[138]
C. Marking on envelope: Susa (figs. 72 and 73).[139]
D. Impressed sign: Chogha Mish,[140] Jebel Aruda,[141] Susa,[142] Tell Brak,[143] Uruk.[144]
F. Unit of animal numeration (10 animals?).[145]

Comment: Lenticular disks held in envelopes were mostly associated with cylinders.[146] When these two kinds of tokens are translated into markings, they appear as shallow circular marking and long wedges. Accordingly, I presume that when circular signs are associated on a tablet with long wedges, they can be understood as deriving from the lenticular disk.[147]

4. LONG WEDGE

A. Cylinder, type 4: 1.
B. Unmarked envelope: Susa,[148] Uruk (fig. 64).[149]
C. Marking on envelope: Susa (fig. 72).[150]
D. Impressed sign: Godin Tepe,[151] Habuba Kabira (fig. 88),[152] Jebel Aruda,[153] Susa (fig. 86),[154] Tell Brak,[155] Uruk.[156]
F. Unit of animal numeration (1 animal?).[157]

5a. OVAL

A. Ovoid, type 6: 1.
B. Unmarked envelope: Uruk.[158]
C. Marking on envelope: None.
D. Impressed signs: Chogha Mish,[159] Habuba Kabira,[160] Jebel Aruda.[161]

5b. INCISED OVOID

A. Ovoid with an incised circular line, type 6: 14.
B. Unmarked envelope: Uruk (fig. 67).[162]
C. Marking on envelope: Habuba Kabira (fig. 74).[163]
D. Impressed sign: None.
E. ATU 733/ZATU 393.
F. Oil.

Comment: The incised ovoid is included here although it is not represented on an impressed tablet but only as a marking on an envelope. On the envelope M II: 134 of Habuba Kabira, it is clear that the markings were made by impressing the counters into the clay wall since the resulting oval impressions show a small ridge corresponding to the incision on the token. There is conflicting information concerning M II: 133. In this case, the markings may be simple wedges done with a stylus.

6a. PLAIN TRIANGULAR

A. Triangle, type 8: 2.
B. Enclosed in unmarked envelope: Uruk (fig. 64),[164] Chogha Mish.[165]
C. Marking on envelope: None.
D. Impressed sign: Godin Tepe (fig. 84).[166]
E. ATU 935/ZATU N-39a (impressed).
F. Measure of grain (1/5 *ban*?).[167]

6b. INCISED TRIANGULAR

A. Triangle with a median incised line, type 8: 11.
B. Unmarked envelope: None.
C. Marking on envelope: None.
D. Impressed sign: Susa (fig. 85).[168]
E. Impressed/incised sign: Susa.[169]
F. Unit of wheat(?) (fig. 86).[170]

Beyond the Impressed Tablets: Pictography

The documentation presented above shows that the impressed tablets represented only a transitional phase of writing leading to pictography—in this case, the graphic representation of tokens. The chart below illustrates how some of the impressed signs were supplanted by pictographs traced with a sharp stylus. For example, oval and triangular signs evolved into incised pictographs, while still other signs became impressed/incised. On the other hand, wedges and circular signs remained impressed, creating a dichotomy between two kinds of scripts: impressed and pictographic. In the following section, I will discuss how the emergence of two different scripts may be explained by the two kinds of prototypes: plain and complex tokens.

THE TOKENS AS PROTOTYPES OF IMPRESSED SIGNS

The most common types of tokens, that pervaded the entire Near East—cones, spheres, disks, and cylinders—gave rise to the most common impressed signs. These counters, including punched cones and spheres,

Sign	*Token*	*Enclosed in envelope*	*Marking on envelope*	*Sign impressed on tablet*	*Incised pictograph*

x signifies occurrence; a blank signifies no evidence

1.a	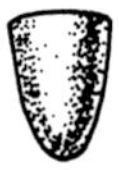	x	x		
1.b	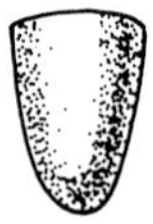	x	x		
1.c	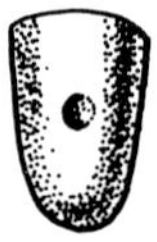	x	x		
1.d	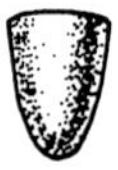				
1.e	x				
2.a		x	x		
2.b	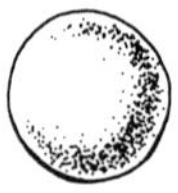	x			
2.c					
2.d	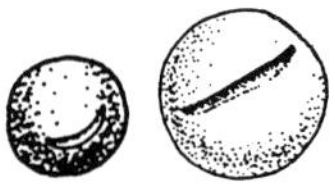				

Sign	*Token*	*Enclosed in envelope*	*Marking on envelope*	*Sign impressed on tablet*	*Incised pictograph*
x signifies occurrence; a blank signifies no evidence					
2.e					x
2.f					x
3.a	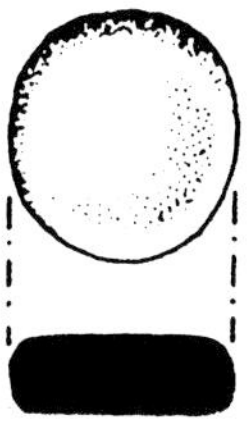	x			
3.b		x	x		
4	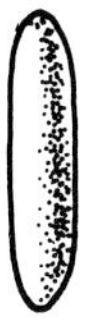	x	x		
5.a	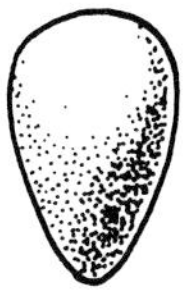	x			x
5.b	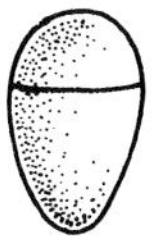	x	x		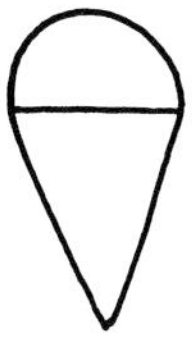
6.a	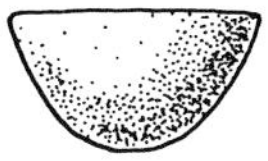	x			x
6.b	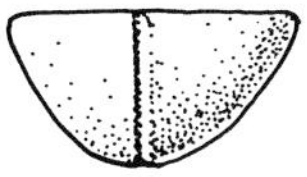	x	x		x

are also among the most ancient token shapes, that occurred among the earliest assemblages of Tepe Asiab and Ganj Dareh Tepe and persisted continuously until the fourth millennium B.C. Perhaps most significantly, cones, punched cones, spheres, disks, and cylinders are among the subtypes most frequently held in envelopes and, subsequently, most usually translated into impressed markings on the surface of envelopes. This suggests that the fashion in which tokens were kept in archives determined the resulting script.

Sign impression was the most ancient and also the most rudimentary of the two early forms of writing. The major drawback of the impressed technique was the blurring of the shapes of their token prototypes. For example, tokens of distinctive forms such as cones and cylinders or disks and spheres were transcribed, respectively, into closely related wedges or circular signs. As a result, the signs were identified by the context rather than by their shape. For example, short and long wedges representing cones and cylinders were distinguished by their position on the tablet: The long wedges were systematically placed along the edge of a tablet,[171] whereas the short wedges were traced at the center of the field.[172] The circular signs deriving from spheres and lenticular disks could be set apart by their association with other signs. Those standing for spheres were combined with short wedges[173] and those representing lenticular disks with long wedges.[174]

THE TOKENS AS PROTOTYPES OF IMPRESSED/INCISED SIGNS

Notched spheres (type 2: 7)[175] and incised triangles (type 8: 11) were the prototypes for impressed/incised signs. These signs are very important because they attest to the close relationship between impressed and incised signs. They show, beyond any doubt, that the incised pictographs came as the third and final step of the evolution from tokens to writing. The incised triangle is of particular interest since one can trace it through the following four stages of evolution: (1) complex token, (2) impressed sign, (3) impressed/incised sign, and (4) pictograph. Although the incised triangles were among the more frequent subtypes of fourth-millennium complex tokens, none so far have been found enclosed in envelopes. Impressions of incised triangles occur on the "solid clay ball" of Susa.[176] The following impressed/incised sign consisted of complementing a triangular token impression by an incised marking[177] and, finally, the pictograph ATU 900.

THE TOKENS AS PROTOTYPES OF INCISED PICTOGRAPHS

Four further impressed signs/markings evolved into incised pictographs. The technique was not new, since tokens had been marked by incised lines as early as the beginning of the system in the eighth millennium B.C., and incised markings became specially important with the complex tokens of the fourth millennium. However, the use of a stylus to trace signs on a tablet followed the impressed script, constituting a third stage in the evolution of writing in the Near East, after markings on envelopes and impressed signs. The resulting incised signs had the advantage of being far more legible than those impressed. They represented with greater accuracy the profile of the token prototypes, as well as the markings displayed on their surface. This was an important feature because the pictographs derived mostly from complex tokens characterized by bearing linear markings.

Among the impressed markings that evolved into pictographs, the incised ovoids (type 6: 14) are most important because they can be traced at each of the four steps of the evolution. First, incised ovoids were among the most common complex tokens in fourth-millennium sites; second, they were held in unmarked envelopes at Uruk;[178] third, they appear as impressed markings on an envelope of Habuba Kabira;[179] and fourth, they become the incised pictograph ATU 733/ZATU 293. There is, however, no known corresponding impressed sign.

The three remaining token subtypes perpetuated by both impressed signs and pictographs include pinched spheres (type 2: 15), plain ovoids (type 6: 1), and plain triangles (type 8: 2). These tokens can be matched to ATU 781/ZATU 240,[180] ATU 732/ZATU 280, 709, and ATU 428/ZATU 254. All these tokens are typically complex and, except for the plain ovoids, are never part of assemblages prior to the middle of the fourth millennium B.C.

The last and most important category of complex tokens that contributed to the Sumerian pictographic script have so far never been identified in envelopes. This is, perhaps, because so few envelopes are known, but more likely because, as I have discussed in the previous chapter, complex tokens were often perforated and therefore were probably usually attached by a string when they were held in archives. Their list includes the following examples:

	Token Type		*Pictograph*	*Translation*
				1. Animals
	3: 14		ATU 803 ZATU 482c	lamb
	3: 51		ATU 761 ZATU 575	sheep (fig. 93)
	3: 54		ATU 763 ZATU 571	ewe
	14: 3		ATU 45a ZATU 12	cow
	14: 8		ATU 30 ZATU 145	dog

93. Sign ATU 761/ZATU 575 "sheep," Uruk (W 21418.4), Iraq. Courtesy Deutsches Archaeologisches Institut, Abteilung Baghdad.

94. Sign ATU 750/ZATU 503 "sweet (honey?)," Uruk (W 20511.1), Iraq. Courtesy Deutsches Archaeologisches Institut, Abteilung Baghdad.

Token Type		Pictograph	Translation
			2. Foods
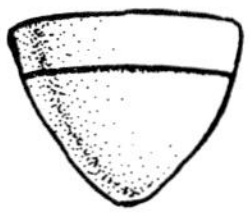 1: 29	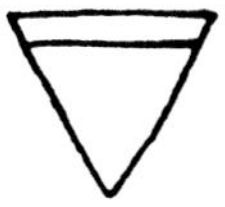	ATU 535 ZATU 196	bread
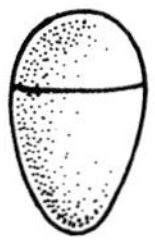 6: 14		ATU 733 ZATU 393	oil
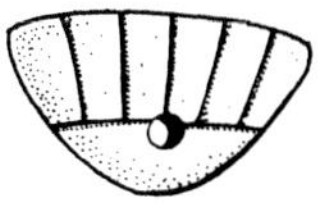 8: 29		ATU 539 ZATU 197	food
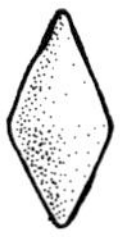 9: 1		ATU 428 ZATU 254	sweet (honey?)
 9: 15		ATU 750 ZATU 503	sweet (honey?) (fig. 94)
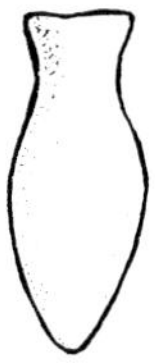 13: 3		ATU 139 ZATU 88b	beer (fig. 93)
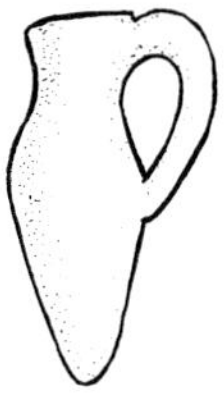 13: 7		ATU 158 ZATU 296a	sheep's milk
			3. Textiles
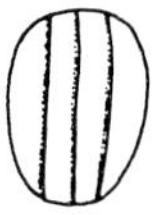 3: 20		ATU 758 ZATU 452b	textile (fig. 95)[181]
 3: 21		ATU 798 ZATU 452b	wool

Token Type	*Pictograph*	*Translation*
3: 22	ZATU 452c	type of garment or cloth
3: 24	ZATU 452b	type of garment or cloth
3: 28	ATU 755 ZATU 555	type of garment or cloth[182]
3: 30	ATU 759 ZATU 452e	type of garment or cloth[183]
3: 32	ZATU 452e	type of garment or cloth (fig. 96)

95. Sign ATU 758/ZATU 452b "textile," Uruk (W 21278), Iraq. Courtesy Deutsches Archaeologisches Institut, Abteilung Baghdad.

96. Sign ZATU 452e, "textile," Uruk (W 9657), Iraq. Courtesy Deutsches Archaeologisches Institut, Abteilung Baghdad.

Token Type		Pictograph	Translation
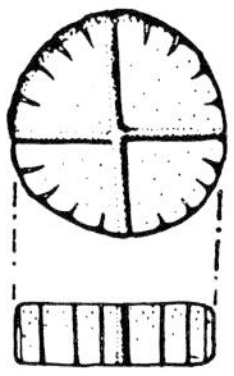 3: 52			type of garment or cloth[184]
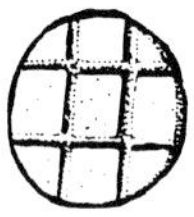 3: 55		PI 385 ZATU 452a	Wool, fleece[185]
 4: 23		ATU 508	rope
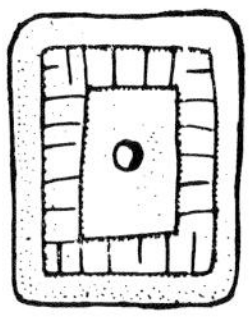 7: 18		ATU 589 ZATU 764	type of mat or rug
 10: 4		ATU 390/829 ZATU 662/663	type of garment or cloth[186]
 10: 9			type of garment or cloth[187]
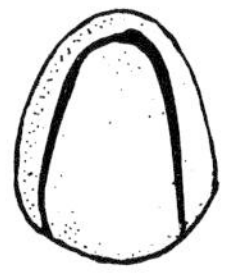 10: 12		PI 158	type of garment or cloth[188]
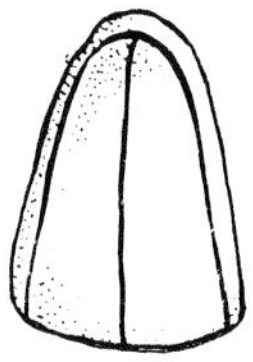 10: 13		ATU 685 ZATU 644	type of garment or cloth[189]

4. Types of Containers

Token Type		Pictograph	Translation
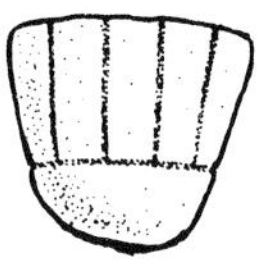 1: 34		ATU 736 ZATU 394	?

	Token Type		*Pictograph*	*Translation*
	7: 31		ATU 568 ZATU 616	granary
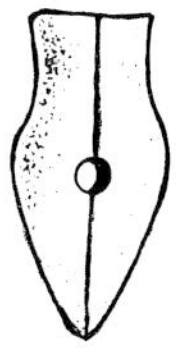	13: 6		ATU 674 ZATU 126	?

5. Commodities

	Token Type		*Pictograph*	*Translation*
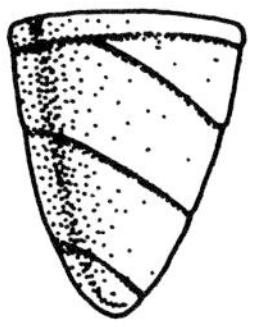	1: 38, 39		ZATU 267	perfume
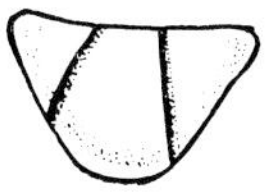	8: 14		ZATU 63	metal
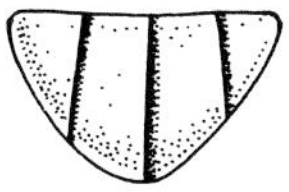	8: 15		ATU 545	metal
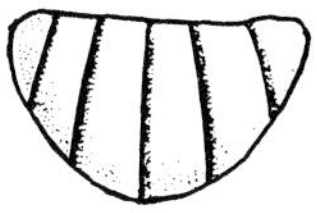	8: 17		ATU 703 ZATU 301	metal
	8: 18		ATU 545 ZATU 63	metal
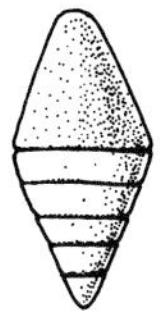	9: 13	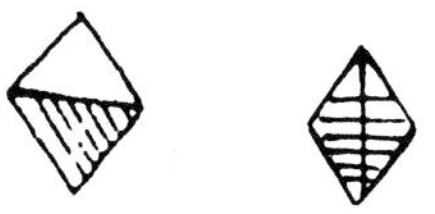	ZATU 293	bracelet, ring
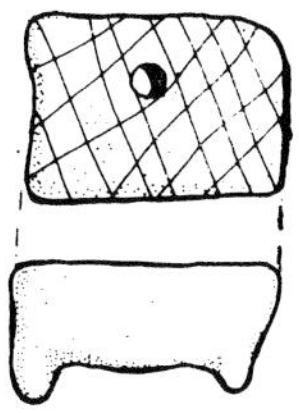	14: 10		ZATU 379	bed

	Token Type		*Pictograph*	*Translation*
				6. Service/Wo
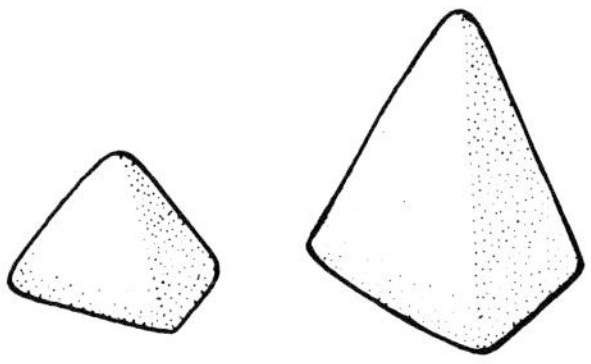	5: 1	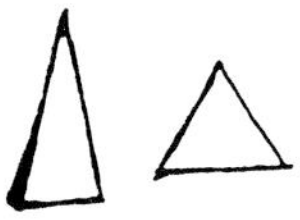	ATU 526 ZATU 280	make, build (See also figs. 97 and 98.)
				7. Miscellaneo
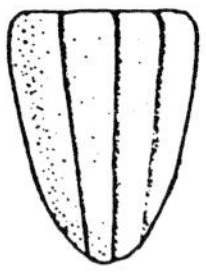	1: 33		ZATU N 38	number(?)
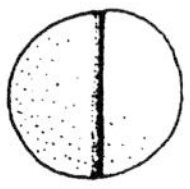	3: 19		ATU 754 ZATU 127	?
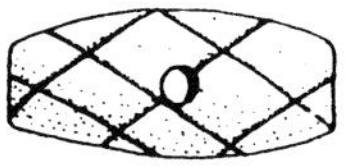	4: 20		ZATU 779	?
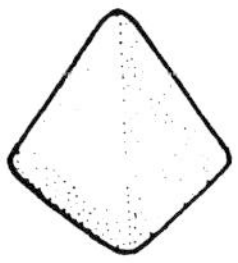	5: 1		ATU 403 ZATU 659	?
	5: 5	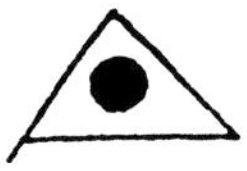	ATU 406 ZATU 661	?

97. Unlisted signs similar to tokens in the shape of a pinched sphere (type 2: 15) and a triangle, oval section, (type 8: 2), Uruk (W 21090), Iraq. Courtesy Deutsches Archaeologisches Institut, Abteilung Baghdad.

98. Unlisted sign similar to a token in the shape of a cylinder with allover strokes (type 4: 10/11), Uruk (W 20973), Iraq. Courtesy Deutsches Archaeologisches Institut, Abteilung Baghdad.

Token Type		Pictograph		Translation
	6: 1		ATU 732 ZATU 280	nail(?)
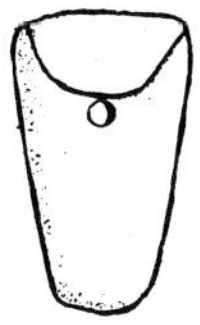	7: 12		ATU 559	?
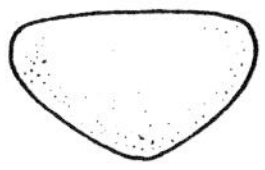	8: 1		ATU 709	?
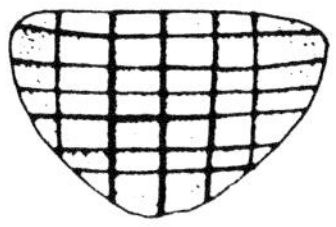	8: 37		ATU 712 ZATU 83	?
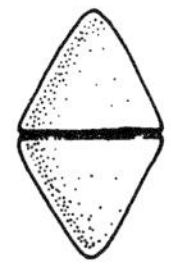	9: 6		ATU 434	?
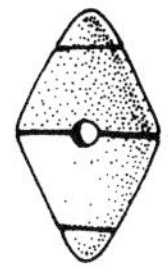	9: 7		ATU 434	?
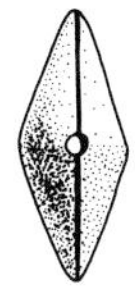	9: 10		ATU 429 ZATU 293(?)	?
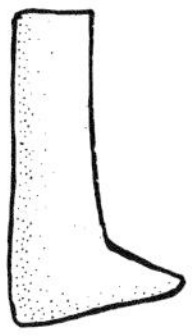	16: 6		ATU 17 ZATU 82	foot

Comment: The meaning of tetrahedrons remains enigmatic. They are among the plain tokens consistently found at large and most frequently included in envelopes. It is to be expected, therefore, that they were perpetuated in writing. However, none of the envelopes holding tetrahedrons bore impressed markings and there is yet no impressed tablet known to bear triangular impressions.

In former publications I proposed that the tetrahedron represented a unit of labor.[190] I correlated the tetrahedron to the two triangular signs ATU 403/ZATU 659, identified by Labat as *lagar,* "temple servant,"[191] or to ATU 526/ZATU 280, KAK (du3), meaning "make, build, construct." This idea was criticized by Krystyna Szarzynska and I retract it.[192]

Dockets used in the third and second millennia B.C., for example at Sippar, may provide some insight into the meaning of the tetrahedrons.[193] The dockets, representing wages earned for services and meant to be exchanged against rations of barley, were modeled in clay in the shape of tetrahedrons. It is possible, therefore, that the artifacts perpetuated both the shape and meaning of the prehistoric tokens. If it is so, my first hypothesis of the tetrahedron as a unit of work would still hold. This idea seems plausible, because manpower was an important commodity of exchange in the ancient Near East. This is attested by the numerous texts referring to workmen digging canals, constructing buildings, and harvesting fields.

If the tetrahedrons truly represent a unit of work, it would be logical to assume that the various sizes of the tokens expressed time units such as one day's work, one week, or one month, unless they referred to different salary rates according to the size of a team or the kind of labor.

IN SUM, certain tokens, mostly plain, were perpetuated by impressed signs while others, mostly complex, were transcribed into incised pictographs. It is evident that complex tokens, characterized by multiple markings, did not lend themselves to being impressed and were more conveniently translated by signs traced with a stylus. However, the reason why two different styles of script developed may lie in the way tokens were handled in various offices: Cones, punched cones, spheres, disks, and cylinders were mostly kept in envelopes, and therefore came to be translated by impressed markings. On the other hand, complex tokens were perforated and strung and thus were never transcribed into impressed markings. In turn, the different ways of keeping tokens in archives may be explained by the kinds of products each type of token represented. As is discussed below, the plain tokens represented products of the farm and the country, whereas complex tokens stood for goods manufactured in the city. It is therefore logical to assume that the two types of tokens were handled by different hands in different offices. It is noteworthy that the incised ovoids were exceptional in being sometimes kept in envelopes and sometimes perforated in order to be strung. At Uruk, for example, in the collection of thirty incised ovoids ten were held in envelopes[194] and five[195] were perforated. This may explain why the incised ovoids were transcribed into both impressed and incised signs.

The Meaning of Signs and Their Corresponding Tokens

The key to understanding the meaning of pictographs, impressed markings, and ultimately tokens lies in the cuneiform script of the third millennium B.C. Assyriologists can, in some instances, trace the evolution of cuneiform characters backwards through more and more archaic forms to their prototypes of the late fourth millennium B.C. The interpretation of pictographs and impressed signs proposed here is the outcome of such research by A. Falkenstein, M. W. Green, S. Langdon, K. Szarzynska, and A. A. Vaiman, who assumed that, logically, the original signs carried the same meaning as the derived cuneiform signs. In turn it is logical to trust that the impressed signs perpetuated the meaning of their token prototypes.

IMPRESSED SIGNS

A. Plain cones, spheres, and flat disks: Metrological units of grain(?)

Thureau Dangin in 1932 had inferred that the impressed wedges and circular signs stood for metrological units used specifically for grain.[196] This is also the outcome of more recent work by A. A. Vaiman, Jöran Friberg, and Peter Damerov and Robert K. Englund.[197] Friberg considers the short wedge as representing a unit of grain, possibly the *ban,* the most basic Sumerian cereal measure, equivalent to about 6 liters of grain. According to Friberg, a unit six times larger, the *bariga,* was represented by a circular marking.[198] I therefore propose that the shapes of the signs for grain metrology derive from tokens in the shape of cones and spheres. I consider the small cone to represent a small unit of grain of common use. Furthermore, I suggest that the sphere is to be understood as a second basic unit of grain of larger size. Large cones and spheres represent still larger units of grain metrology. According to Friberg, the large wedge, which would correspond to the large cone, was equivalent to 180 *ban* of barley. The wedges shown sideways or apex to apex were fractions of a *ban*.

Furthermore, it appears not to be fortuitous that in the four instances when flat disks were included in envelopes they were associated with small spheres[199] or with small and large spheres.[200] The association of spheres and flat disks in envelopes seems to correspond to the frequent association of deep and shallow circular impressed signs on tablets. I therefore propose the possibility that spheres, large spheres, and flat discs represent a sequence of three measures of grain corresponding respectively to such later Sumerian units as 1, 10, and (?) *bariga*. These three circular signs could correspond to ATU 897, 913, and 907.

As I will discuss at length in Chapter 9, it should be assumed, however, that during prehistory, cones, spheres, and disks represented nonstandardized measures of grain. They referred probably to containers in which the goods were traditionally handled, such as a "small basket," a "large basket," or a "granary." These units could be compared to our present informal measures a "cup of sugar" and a "pitcher of beer." As a result the prehistoric units should be assumed to be entirely nonmathematical entities. I propose that until the late fourth millennium B.C., a sphere cannot be considered as a precise multiple/fraction of a cone or disk. The measures probably became standardized metrological units not before the late Uruk period or the early historic period, when, as presented above, their ratio was as follows:

CEREALS

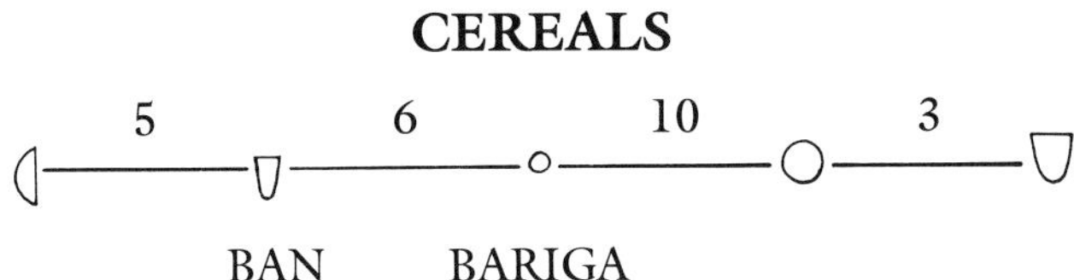

Grain measures: SĚ-system, after Jöran Friberg, *The Third Millennium Roots of Babylonian Mathematics* (Chalmers University of Technology and the University of Göteborg, 1978–79), p. 10.

B. The punched cones and spheres: Units of land measurement(?)

The Sumerian system of land measures includes units such as the *bur, eše,* and *iku* and fractions and multiples thereof represented by circular signs and wedges, some bearing a punctation or an incision.[201] The similarity in appearance of these signs with the punched cones and the notched and punched spheres suggests that these tokens may have been used to indicate units of land. The similarity of shape between counters indicating grain and land measures may, in turn, point to a common usage in early societies to calculate land measurements in term of seed ratio necessary for sowing.[202]

It is well understood that, as I discussed it above for the counters representing measures of grain, the tokens indicating units of land could not be considered as standardized measures during prehistory. It is only in the late fourth or early third millennium B.C. that they became increments of a specific ratio as follows:

LAND

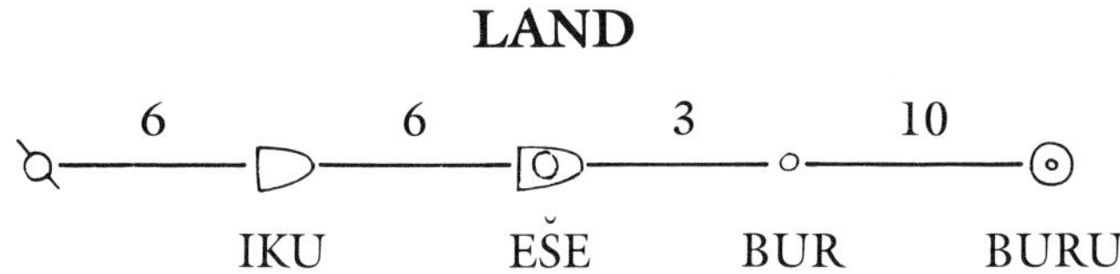

Land measures, after Jöran Friberg, *The Third Millennium Roots of Babylonian Mathematics* (Chalmers University of Technology and the University of Göteborg, 1978–79), p. 46.

C. The cylinders and lenticular disks: Units for animal counts(?)

Jöran Friberg identified a special accounting system used to keep track of animals in Elam that was also used in Uruk.[203] These signs consisted of a long wedge used to represent one animal, which I propose to view as the rendering of the cylinder (type 4: 1). This assumption is supported by envelope Sb 1940 from Susa, which bears three long wedges on its surface, corresponding to three cylinders held inside.[204] According to Friberg, the sign for ten animals was a circle, which I interpret as the graphic representation of a lenticular disk (type 3: 10). This is also supported by the envelope Sb 1940 of Susa, which held three lenticular disks translated into three circular markings on its face (fig. 95).[205] If this interpretation is correct, the lenticular disk is a unique example of a token expressing a group. As I will discuss in Chapter 9, it should be assumed that the prototype lenticular disk meant a flock. Only the late fourth- or early third-millennium impressed circular sign can be identified as standing for a precise number—ten animals.

Both cylinders and lenticular disks were used, seemingly, to count heads of animals with no specification of age and sex. Because sheep and goats were so common in Mesopotamia and Elam, it is probable that the animals meant were mostly small livestock.

ANIMALS

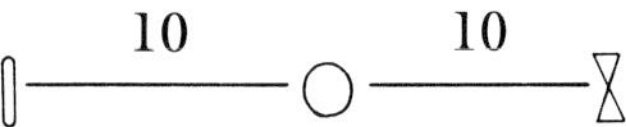

Animal units, after Jöran Friberg, *The Third Millennium Roots of Babylonian Mathematics* (Chalmers University of Technology and the University of Göteborg, 1978–79), p. 21.

The plain tokens, which were both the most common and most ancient counters, stood for quantities of staple foods—grain and livestock—and for measures of land. They gave rise to parallel sequences of impressed signs, the first representing metrological units of cereals, the second numbers of animals, and the third area measures. The tokens/signs of these three sequences are not often combined in the same envelope or on the same tablet. In one instance, however, lenticular disks were associated with cones in an envelope of Susa.[206] This particular account stood, perhaps, for quantities of fodder allotted to a number of animals.

In sum, it is my contention that the meaning of the fourth-millennium plain tokens can be extrapolated backwards from the impressed signs of the fourth to third millennium B.C. But what about the cones, spheres, disks, and cylinders extracted from the prehistoric layers of the eighth to fifth millennium B.C.? Can one assume that they held the same significance as those of the fourth millennium? Of course there is no way to know. The only clue that they might have is the fact that signs and symbols have a pervasive endurance that makes them withstand time in a unique fashion. This is exemplified, for example, by our symbols for numerals—1, 2, 3, etc.—which have remained practically unchanged since their inception in 700 B.C. After all, symbols are instituted for the purpose of communication and any deviation in their use would create miscommunication and confusion. Disjunction in symbolism, as argued by Terence Grieder, occurs only as a result of drastic social or environmental changes.[207] There is no such upheaval known to occur between the Neolithic and Chalcolithic periods in the Near East. On the contrary, the time is known as a cultural plateau characterized by great stability.

Another vexing problem concerns whether or not cones, spheres, disks, and cylinders bore the same meaning from the Mediterranean Coast to the Caspian Sea. While the question cannot be answered, several arguments support the idea that it is conceivable that they did. First, it is easier to borrow than reinvent. Second, the cones, spheres, disks, and cylinders were among the shapes easiest to make and, according to the law of least effort, represented the most common staples—grain and animals. Now, grain and animals were most common in the entire Near East, making it particularly easy to borrow the system wholesale. Third, the tokens were symbols, independent of phonetics, and they could be shared by people speaking different languages. Again, tokens can be compared to our numerals, which originated in India and stand for the same concepts for innumerable people who express them in different languages.

INCISED SIGNS

The tokens identified by pictographs stood also for units of merchandise (figs. 93–96), leading to the conclusion that during its entire existence the token system was an accounting device restricted to keeping track of goods.

Some of the complex tokens were used to keep accounts of animals and quantities of grain. They differed from the plain tokens, however, in showing greater precision. Cylinders and lenticular disks represented heads of livestock but the complex counters indicated the species, "fat-tailed sheep" (type 2: 15); the sex, "ewe" (type 3: 54); and the age, "lamb" (type 3: 14). The quantum jump in the number of token types and subtypes that occurred in large cities about 3500 B.C. seems to reflect a greater need for accuracy.

On the other hand, the majority of complex tokens familiar in the large centers of the fourth millennium B.C. stood for finished products such as bread, oil, perfume, wool, and rope and for items produced in workshops such as metal, bracelets, types of cloth, garments, mats, pieces of furniture, tools, and a variety of stone and pottery vessels. The multiplication of token shapes in the protohistoric period signals, therefore, the addition of manufactured goods among the goods accounted for in the temples.

Accordingly, plain and complex tokens varied not only in their shapes and markings and in the way they were handled and stored but also in the types of commodities they represented. The plain token stood for products of the country and the complex ones for goods manufactured in cities.

NUMERALS

The invention of numerals on pictographic tablets provided a new formula to express numbers of units of goods. The token content of envelopes demonstrates that tokens were repeated as many times as the number of items counted. "One jar of oil" was shown by one token standing for a jar of oil, "two jars of oil" by two tokens, "three jars of oil" by three tokens, and so on (fig. 67). This rudimentary system was replaced on pictographic tablets by numerals or signs used to express abstract numbers, such as 1, 2, 3, etc. As a result, the pictographs were *never repeated in a one-to-one correspondence* to indicate the number of units involved, as was still the case for impressed signs. Instead, the pictographs were preceded by a numeral. For example, the sign for "sheep" was preceded by the sign for 1, 2, 3, etc. (fig. 93).

Peter Damerow and Robert K. Englund have shown how a sequence of abstract numerals developed next to the special numerations to count grain measures, land, animals, and other commodities. In that sequence, the sign for "1" was a short wedge; 2 through 9 were indicated by 2 through 9 wedges; the sign for "10" was a circular sign; 20, 30, 40, and 50 were shown by 2, 3, 4, and 5 circular signs, the sign for 60 was a large wedge; for 600 a punched large wedge, and that for 3,600 was a large circular sign. The sign for 1 was a short wedge, identical to the sign for a small measure of grain; 2, 3, 4, 5, etc. were indicated by 2, 3, 4, or 5 wedges; the sign for 10 was a circular sign, identical to that for a larger measure of grain; the sign for 60 was a large wedge; for 600 a punched large wedge; and that for 3,600 a large circular sign.[208] It appears that the impressed signs, while retaining their primary meaning, for example as grain or land measures and as animal count, acquired a secondary meaning as numerals. This phenomenon of bifurcation is particularly explicit on tablets where, in the same text, the same signs are used alternately (but according to a different ratio) to express grain measures or numerals. Tablets recording the rations allotted to workers, for example, feature the same signs to indicate the number of workers paid and the quantities of grain they received.[209] The same is true in the Proto-Elamite system of writing.[210]

Numerals created an economy of notation, since thirty-three jars of oil could be shown by six signs: three circles and three wedges. The importance of this invention in terms of abstraction and cognitive growth will be discussed in the second part of the volume.

The Place of Impressed Tablets in the Evolution of Writing

The impressed tablets constitute the third step of the evolution from tokens to signs. They followed the stage of tokens and markings on envelopes and, in turn, were supplanted by pictography.

The link between impressed tablets and envelopes is demonstrated by the many features they share. First, the impressed tablets adopted the material of which envelopes were manufactured and, like them, were modeled in clay, with the exception of the plaster tablets from the Anu Ziggurat at Uruk. The envelopes differed, supposedly, by being fired at a low temperature, while the impressed tablets were simply dried in the sun. In fact, to my knowledge, the degree of temperature to which the archaic tablets were subjected has never been analyzed. When tests are made, they might prove that both kinds of artifacts were similarly treated by fire.

The tablets were also modeled in the same general shape and size as their immediate precursors. At Susa, a solid ball with flattened surfaces ("boule d'argile à faces aplaties") impressed with signs can be considered a transitional stage between envelopes and tablets.[211] The subsequent changes consisted in the flattening of the impressed tablets. Falkenstein noted, however, that the earliest pictographic Uruk tablets were sometimes strikingly convex, perhaps still perpetuating the roundish shape of the former envelopes.[212] Of course, envelopes and tablets had a different structure. The envelopes were hollow, since their purpose was to hold together and protect a number of tokens. Instead, the tablets were solid as tokens were eliminated.

The seal impressions covering the entire surface of most envelopes and tablets constitute another important similarity between both types of artifacts. Not only were these sealings made by the same type of seals, namely, mostly cylinders and more rarely stamp seals, but they also showed similar patterns carved in the same style. Among the many motifs which occur on both types of artifacts are featured, for example, temple representations and various types of vessels.[213] Furthermore, occasionally at Susa[214] as well as Uruk[215] a number of tablets and envelopes bore the impression of the same seal, attesting that the two ways of keeping records were handled by the same temple services or individuals.

Most importantly, the signs of the impressed tablets are comparable in form, technique, and disposition to the signs displayed on envelopes. First, the same signs reoccur on both types of artifacts. In particular, all the markings impressed on envelopes—short and long wedges, deep and shallow circles and ovals—continue unchanged in the repertory of signs on tablets.[216] The list of signs impressed on tablets is, however, longer than that of the markings on envelopes. This may be explained by the small sampling of 19 envelopes bearing markings, compared to some 240 impressed tablets. Also, by the time tablets were being used, the scribes already had exploited further the possibilities offered by two-dimensionality by creating new signs. For instance, they manipulated the wedge, turning it sideways (sign 1d) or doubling it (sign 1e).

Second, the techniques most frequently used to impress markings on envelopes prevailed on tablets. For instance, signs were still made by pressing tokens against the clay face of the tablets, as is visibly the case on Sb 2313. Otherwise, it was usual to use a blunt stylus, as illustrated.[217]

Third and finally, the signs were presented on the tablets in horizontal parallel lines, following the same hierarchical order as on the envelopes. For example, one envelope from Susa displays a line of circular signs followed by a line of wedges in exactly the same way signs were presented on a tablet.[218] In turn, it may reflect the hierarchical order and the parallel rows in which tokens were organized by prehistoric accountants.

The function of impressed signs and that of envelope markings was, however, radically different. The discrepancy lay in the role they played vis-à-vis the clay counters. The markings only repeated the information encoded in tokens for the convenience of accountants. At the stage of the tablets, however, the signs had altogether replaced the tokens.

The format inherited by the impressed tablets from the envelopes was to enjoy a long duration. Clay continued to be used to make tablets in the same cushion shape and bearing seal impressions until the Christian era.[219] Also, the same disposition and hierarchical ordering of signs persisted for centuries.[220] Even the function of the tablets remained mostly economic throughout the ages. However, the technique of writing evolved from the crudely impressed signs to more legible incised pictographs; later, writing would be done with a more functional triangular stylus.

PART TWO: THE INTERPRETATION

7
THE EVOLUTION OF SYMBOLS IN PREHISTORY

Individuals applied their minds to symbols rather than things and went beyond the world of concrete experience into the world of conceptual relations created within an enlarged time and space universe. The time world was extended beyond the range of remembered things and the space world beyond the range of known places.
—Harold A. Innis[1]

IT IS THE NATURE of archaeological research to deal with data and their interpretation. In the following three chapters I use the facts as well as the hypotheses I have presented on the token system to reflect more broadly on the significance of tokens in terms of communication, social structures, and cognitive skills. I take for granted that the reader has followed my analyses and understands that I am building on my results.

Chapter 7 deals with the place of tokens among other prehistoric symbolic systems. After reviewing the evolution of symbolism from the Paleolithic to the Neolithic periods, I will analyze what the tokens owed to their antecedents, how they revolutionized the use of symbols, and, finally, how they presaged writing.

Symbols and Signs

Symbols are things endowed with a special meaning, allowing us to conceive, express, and communicate ideas. In our society, for example, black is the symbol of death, the star-spangled banner stands for the United States of America, and the cross stands for Christianity.

Signs are a subcategory of symbols. Like symbols, signs are things which convey meaning, but they differ in carrying narrow, precise, and unambiguous information. Compare, for example, the color black, the symbol standing for death, with the sign "1." Black is a symbol loaded with a deep but diffuse significance, whereas 1 is a sign which unequivocally stands for "one." Symbols and signs are used differently; namely, symbols help us to conceive and reflect upon ideas, whereas signs are communication devices bound to action.[2]

Because the use of symbols is a characteristic human behavior it is, by definition, as old as mankind itself.[3] There can be no doubt that the first human groups used symbols, and from the beginnings of humanity, symbols have encapsulated the knowledge, experience, and beliefs of all people. Humans, from the beginning, have also communicated by signs. Symbols and signs are therefore a major key to the understanding of cultures.

Unfortunately, symbols are ephemeral and, as a rule, do not survive the societies that create them. A first reason for the impermanence of symbols is their reliance upon evanescent phenomena. We may assume, for example, that some prehistoric societies conferred a symbolic meaning on lighting, thunder, or eclipses. These symbols are obviously lost forever, since they do not leave any traces. The same is true for symbolic motions such as dance or everyday life signs of greeting or threat. Moreover, speech, which is both the most usual and most complex human symbolic system, relies on sounds that fade instantly. The only symbols from past societies that can survive the ages are items made of materials that do not disintegrate easily, such as minerals and a few organic substances like bone or antler. Furthermore, the symbolic connotation of such objects can only be perceived when suggested by a special context. Red ocher found scattered upon human skeletons, for example, is interpreted as being a symbol because it cannot be explained by a mere practical reason.

Symbols and signs are also ephemeral because the meaning they carry is arbitrary. For instance, the color black, which evokes death in our culture, may just as well stand for life in another. Or, as a second example, nodding the head, which is a sign of acquiescence in our society, means negation in others. It is a fundamental characteristic of symbols that their meaning cannot be perceived either by the senses or by logic but can only be learned from those who use them.[4] As a consequence, when a culture vanishes, the symbols left behind become enigmatic since there is no longer anyone initiated into their significance. For these reasons, the symbolic relics from prehistoric societies are not only extremely few, but those extant usually cannot be interpreted.

Lower and Middle Paleolithic Symbols

Although humans were present in Southwest Asia starting in the lower Paleolithic period as early as 600,000 years ago, no symbols have been preserved from these remote times. The first archaeological material attesting the use of symbols in the Near East belongs to the epoch of Neanderthal man, the Mousterian period, as late as 60,000 to 25,000 B.C. The data are threefold. First, fragments of ocher were recovered in the cave of Qafzeh, Israel.[5] It is certain that the material was collected intentionally and brought back to the settlement by the Neanderthal hunters, because hematite did not belong to the geological setting of the area. In turn, red pigment suggests a symbolic rather than a functional purpose. There is, of course, no way of knowing what ocher was used for in Mousterian times, but some hypothesize that it may have served for body painting.

The second set of evidence for symbolism in the Mousterian period consists of funerary paraphernalia displayed in burial sites. For example, flowers were deposited in a grave at Shanidar Cave about 60,000 B.C.[6] whereas at Qafzeh, Israel, a child's tomb was furnished with animal antlers.[7] Although there will never be a chance to know the significance that ocher, flowers, and antlers may have had for Neanderthal man, it is generally assumed that the red pigment and the funerary deposits were symbols carrying a magico-religious connotation. Accordingly, some of the earliest evidence of the use of symbols in the Near East suggests a ritual function.

The third category of artifacts bears graphic symbols—bone fragments engraved with series of notches usually arranged in a parallel fashion. One such notched bone was recovered in the cave of Kebara.[8]

The data recovered in the Near East are comparable to those of other parts of the world. It seems significant, for example, that European Paleolithic sites have produced similar evidence for symbols of ritual function. The European material is, however, earlier, more substantial, and more diversified, including, in particular, the first evidence of graphic symbols. The Abbevillian/Acheulean site of Terra Amata, France, furnished traces of the use of red ocher by *Homo erectus* as early as 300,000 B.C.[9] and deposits of red, brown, or yellow ocher or black manganese are attested in numerous European Mousterian sites.[10] Neanderthal groups of Europe also provided graves with offerings. For example, at La Chapelle aux Saints, France, a man of about fifty years of age had been buried with a few pieces of flint, several lumps of ocher, and the leg of a bison.[11] At Teshik Tash in eastern Europe, as at Qafzeh, the body of a child was buried with animal antlers.[12] The European Mousterian assemblages also yield animal teeth, small bones, oddly shaped or colorful stones, and shells,[13] sometimes grooved for suspension, that are assumed to have carried a beneficent value and to have been worn as amulets.

Europe also produced artifacts bearing markings that can be interpreted as possible graphic symbols as early as the Acheulean and Mousterian periods. François Bordes recovered at Pech de l'Azé, France, a piece of bone bearing a number of parallel engraved lines dating about 100,000 B.C.[14] At La Ferrassie, France, a slab was engraved with several shallow round markings pecked with a stone axe. The triangular stone apparently belonged to a Mousterian funerary setting, since it was found face down over the remains of a six-year-old child.[15] The incised bone and the so-called cup-marks of La Ferrassie are particularly significant because they do not represent isolated and short-lived phenomena but constitute the point of departure for a tradition of graphic symbolism that was continued by *Homo sapiens-sapiens,* our own kind, during the Upper Paleolithic period. Incised bones are also the earliest attestation of graphic symbols in the Near East, and cup-marks sculptured on stone blocks are present in several other French sites.[16]

The incised bone of Pech de l'Azé, that of Kebara

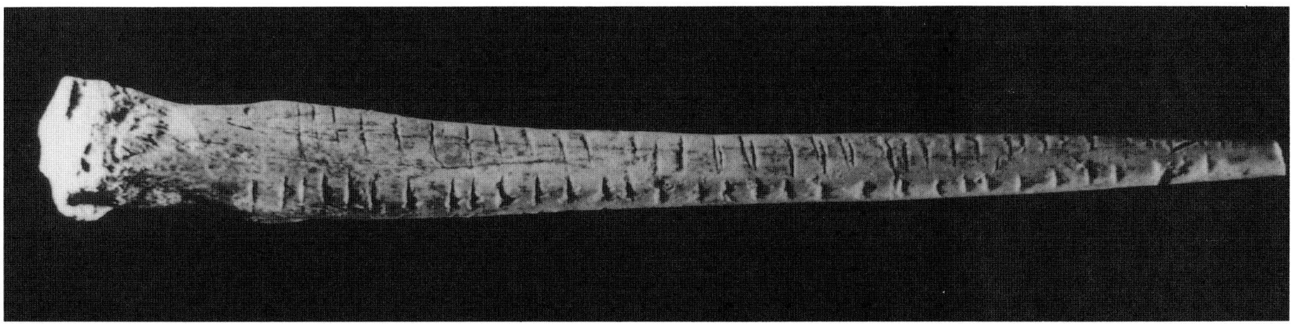

99. Notched bone, Ksar Akil, Lebanon. Courtesy Alexander Marshack, Peabody Museum, Harvard University.

100. Notched bone, Jiita, Lebanon. Courtesy Alexander Marshack, Peabody Museum, Harvard University.

Cave, and the cup-marks of La Ferrassie are important for this study because they constitute, presently, the earliest examples of manmade symbols in Europe and the Near East. While at Terra Amata and Shanidar *Homo erectus* and Neanderthal humans conferred a meaning on pigments and flowers readily available in nature, the occupants of Pech de l'Azé and Neanderthal man at Kebara and La Ferrassie started modifying materials in order to translate thought.

Upper Paleolithic and Mesolithic Symbols

Notched bones continued to be used in the Upper Paleolithic. Five deeply incised gazelle scapulae were discovered in an Aurignacian layer at Hayonim in Israel that date about 28,000 B.C.[17] The cave of Ksar Akil in Lebanon produced one bone awl about 10 cm long bearing some 170 incisions grouped along the shaft into four different columns (fig. 99).[18] The markings consist of mostly straight strokes with some instances of overlapping into V and X shapes. The rock shelter of Jiita, also in Lebanon, also yielded an incised bone used as an awl that bears three irregular rows of markings arranged in a zig-zag pattern (fig. 100).[19] The artifacts from Ksar Akil and Jiita are dated to the late Kebaran period, about 15,000 to 12,000 B.C.

Notched bones are also present in Europe during most of the Upper Paleolithic period, between 29,000 and 11,000 B.C. In western Asia the first notched bones precede the earliest occurrence of iconic symbols showing animals. In Palestine, two limestone slabs recovered at Hayonim, layer D, ca. 28,000 B.C., bear fine lines interpreted as suggesting a horse.[20] The cave of Beldibi, Turkey, dated, like Ksar Akil and Jiita, to about 15,000 to 12,000 B.C., produced further examples of graphic pictorial representations in the Near East. Two kinds of documents are involved. First, the images of two jumping animals, a bull and a deer, were traced with a flint at the entrance of the cave.[21] Second, pebbles were engraved with animal designs.[22] The evidence for the use of ocher is reported at Ksar Akil, Yabrud II, Hayonim, and Abu-Halka.[23]

There is no evidence for any major modification in the use of symbols during the Mesolithic period in the Near East. Artifacts bearing linear markings continued to be part of archaeological assemblages from the Levant to Iraq. Incised bones were recovered, for example, at the two Natufian sites of Hayonim and Ain Mallaha, Palestine, about 10,000 B.C., whereas two other Natufian settlements in the Negev, Rosh Zin and Wadi al-Hammeh in Jordan, as well as Zawi Chemi, a contemporaneous site in northern Iraq, produced pebbles and various limestone and bone implements engraved with parallel lines.[24]

Funerary paraphernalia, amulets, and animal art similar to those of the Paleolithic tradition also persisted during the Mesolithic. For instance, the Natufians of the Levant are known for burying their dead with elaborate headdresses made of dentalium shells and decorating their tools with animal motifs.[25] A new feature worthy of mention, however, consists of the earliest examples of schematic human figurines in the Near East. The objects were carved in stone and are similar to earlier European specimens and equally enigmatic.[26]

In the Near East, as in Europe, the function of the Paleolithic and Mesolithic incised bones and animal representations can only be hypothesized. Leroi-Gourhan viewed the iconic representations as symbols of magico-religious significance. According to him, the animal images referred to the numinous, each species representing one manifestation of a complex cosmology.[27] The animal figures were, therefore, symbols loaded with a deep meaning that served as instruments of thought, making it possible to grasp the abstract concepts of a cosmology. On the other hand, from the early days of archaeology, the notched bones have been interpreted as tallies, each notch representing one item.[28] According to a recent theory by Alexander Marshack, the artifacts were lunar calendars, each incised line recording one appearance of the moon. This interpretation cannot be proven or disproven nor can it be ignored.[29] Right or wrong, the linear markings are viewed as referring to discrete and concrete entities, be they successive phases of the moon or other items of importance to the Paleolithic tallier. I propose, therefore, to consider the notches as signs promoting the accumulation of knowledge for specific ends. If these hypotheses are right, the tallies constitute the evidence that signs started being used in the Near East at least by the Middle Paleolithic period, and presuming that the evidence reflects the facts, the use of signs in the Near East followed that of symbols of ritual function.

Assuming that the incised bones are tallies, the Paleolithic and Mesolithic linear markings of Kebara, Hayonim, Ksar Akil, and Jiita are of considerable interest since they represent the first attempt at storing and communicating concrete information in the Near East. This first stage in data processing signified two remarkable contributions. First, the tallies departed from the use of ritual symbols by dealing with concrete data. They translated perceptible physical phenomena, such as the successive phases of the moon, rather than evoking intangible aspects of a cosmology. Second, the notched signs abstracted data in several ways. First, they translated concrete information into abstract markings. Second, they removed the data from their context. For example, the sighting of the moon was abstracted from any simultaneous events such as atmospheric or social conditions. Finally, they separated the knowledge from the knower, presenting data, as expressed by Walter J. Ong or Marshall McLuhan, in a "cold" and static visual form, rather than the "hot" and flexible oral medium, which involves voice modulation and body gestures.[30] As a result, the graphic signs of Ksar Akil and Jiita not only brought about a new way of recording, handling, and communicating data but an unprecedented objectivity in dealing with information.

The tallies remained, however, a rudimentary device. First, the notches were nonspecific since they could have an unlimited choice of interpretations. Marshack postulates that the signs stood for phases of the moon, but others have hypothesized that they kept tally of animal kills and there is no way to verify their meaning. In fact, the notched bones were limited to storing only quantitative information concerning things known by the tallier but remaining enigmatic to anyone else. These quantities were entered according to the basic principle of one-to-one correspondence, which consisted of matching each unit of a group to be tallied with one notch. Finally, because tallies used mostly a single kind of marking, namely notches, they were confined to handling only one type of data at a time. One bone could keep track of one item, but a second one was necessary to keep track of a second set of data. Therefore, the simple method of tallies could only be adequate in communities where only a few and obvious items were being recorded, as seems to be the case in the Upper Paleolithic period.

It is certainly possible, of course, that the bone tallies were not the only devices for storing information before 10,000 B.C. It is even likely that, as in many preliterate societies, people during the Paleolithic and Mesolithic periods used pebbles, twigs, or grains for counting. If this was so, the counters shared the same inadequacies as tallies. First, pebbles, like the strokes along the shaft of a bone, lacked the capacity of indicating what item was being counted. Only the individual who traced the markings or piled up a number of pebbles knew what things were recorded. Second, because they were nonspecific, pebbles and twigs did not allow keeping track of more than a single category of item at a time. One pile of pebbles or one bone could keep track of a sequence of days, but another pile and another bone were necessary to handle quantities of animals. Third and finally, it is presumable that the loose counters were used, like tallies, in the cumbersome method of one-to-one correspondence, each pebble or each twig standing for one unit, and with no possibility of expressing abstract numbers. For example, one day was represented by one pebble; two days, by two pebbles, and so on. Presumably, the loose counters, however, facilitated data manipulation since they were easier to handle. On the other hand, the notched bones were more efficient for accumulating and preserving data since the notches were permanent and could not be easily disassembled.

Neolithic Symbols

The first agricultural communities of the Near East carried on the age-old symbolic traditions. The early farmers placed antlers in house foundations and painted their floors with pigments.[31] They performed burial rituals that sometimes also involved red ocher.[32] Colorful stones like red carnelian, black obsidian, gray steatite, white alabaster, and mother of pearl continued to be worn, and notched bones were still part of village assemblages.[33] At that time, human and animal forms were translated into clay, which is the Neolithic material *par excellence*.[34] These figurines and the other early Neolithic symbolic assemblages remain as enigmatic to us as the preceding Mesolithic and Paleolithic material and are generally assumed to bear a magico-religious significance. However, the practice of agriculture, which brought a new economy based on hoarding grains, a new way of life based on sedentariness, new settlement patterns in open air villages, new technologies such as ground and polished stone, and the use of new raw materials such as clay, also generated new symbols. These symbols were different in form and content from anything used previously. They were the clay tokens modeled in distinctive shapes, each representing a precise quantity of a product.

A NEW FORM

The primary singularity of the tokens was that they were entirely manmade. Compared to pebbles, twigs, or grains put to a secondary use for counting, and compared to tallies, which communicated meaning by slightly altering a bone, the tokens were artifacts created in specific shapes, such as cones, spheres, disks, cylinders, and tetrahedrons, from an amorphous clay mass for the unique purpose of communication and record keeping.

The tokens were an entirely new medium for conveying information. Compared to the previous tallies, the conceptual leap was to endow each token shape, such as the cone, sphere, or disk, with a specific meaning. Consequently, unlike markings on tallies, which had an infinite number of possible interpretations, each clay token was a distinct sign with a single, discrete, and unequivocal significance. While tallies were meaningless when out of context, the tokens could always be understood by anyone initiated into the system. I suggest, for example, that the cone stood for a common measure of grain and could only have this significance. The tokens presaged, therefore, pictography: Each token stood for one concept. Like the later Sumerian pictographs, the tokens were "concept symbols."[35]

The greatest novelty of the new medium, however, was to be a *system*. There was not only one type of token carrying a discrete meaning but an entire repertory of interrelated types of tokens, each with a corresponding discrete meaning. For example, besides the cone, which stood for a small measure of grain, the sphere represented a large measure of grain, the ovoid stood for a jar of oil, and so on. The system made it feasible to simultaneously manipulate information concerning different categories of items, resulting in a complexity of data processing never reached previously. It became possible to store with precision unlimited quantities of information concerning an unlimited number of goods without the risks of failure of human memory. Furthermore, the system was open, that is to say, new signs were added when necessary by creating new token shapes, and the ever increasing repertory constantly pushed the device to new frontiers of complexity.

The token system was, in fact, the first code—the earliest system of signs used for transmitting information. First, the repertory of shapes was systematized; that is to say, all the various tokens were systematically repeated in order to carry the same meaning. A sphere, for example, always signified a particular measure of grain. Second, presumably tokens were used according to a rudimentary syntax. It is likely, for example, that the counters were lined up on the accountant's table in a hierarchical order, starting on the right with tokens representing the largest units. Such was the way the Sumerians organized signs on a tablet, and it is logical to assume that the procedure was inherited from a former way of handling tokens. The fact that the tokens were systematized had also a great impact on their expansion. The counters were transmitted as a full-fledged code from community to community, ultimately spreading to the entire Near East, with each token form preserving the same meaning.

The token system owed little to the Paleolithic and Mesolithic periods. The choice of clay for manufacturing the counters was a novelty since the material had been ignored by the former hunters and gatherers. It proved particularly advantageous since clay is found abundantly in nature and is easy to work. Its remarkable plasticity when wet made it possible for villagers to create, with no tools and no particular skill, an indefinite number of forms that became permanent when dried in the sun or baked in the open fire or oven.

The format of movable units was probably one of the rare features tokens inherited from the past. It may have been inspired from a former usage of counting with pebbles, shells, twigs, or grains. It enhanced data manipulation, since the small tokens could be arranged and rearranged at will into groups of any composition and size, while notches engraved on tallies were fixed and irreversible.

The various token shapes have otherwise no known Paleolithic or Mesolithic antecedents. Instead, the counters have the merit of bringing together as a set, for the first time, all the basic geometric shapes such as the sphere, cone, cylinder, tetrahedron, triangle, quadrangle, and cube (the latter surprisingly rarely).[36] It is difficult to evaluate which of these forms was inspired by the everyday life commodities and which was fully abstract. Among the latter, the cylinders and lenticular disks, which represented, alternatively, one unit and a group of animals, are visibly arbitrary. Others such as the cone and ovoid, which stand respectively for a measure of grain and a unit of oil, were probably iconic, depicting a small cup and a pointed jar. Other tokens in the shape of animal heads were naturalistic depictions.

A NEW CONTENT

The token system was also unique in the kind of information it conveyed. Whereas Paleolithic iconic art probably evoked cosmological figures and Paleolithic or Mesolithic tallies may have counted time, the tokens dealt with economic data; namely, each token stood for one precise amount of a commodity. As mentioned above, the cone and the sphere represented measures of grain probably equivalent respectively to our liter and bushel; the cylinder and lenticular disks showed numbers of animals; the tetrahedrons were units of work, and so on.

Second, unlike tallies, which recorded only quantitative information, the tokens conveyed also qualitative information. For instance, the type of item counted was indicated by the token shape while the number of units involved was shown by the corresponding number of tokens. For example, one bushel of grain was represented by one sphere, two bushels of grain by two spheres, and so on (fig. 101). Therefore, like the previous tallies, the token system was based on the simple principle of one-to-one correspondence. This made it cumbersome, of course, to deal with large quantities of data, since humans can only identify small sets by pattern recognition. There are a few instances of tokens, however, which stood for a collection of items. Among them, the lenticular disk stood for a flock or, presumably, ten sheep; also, the large tetrahedron may have represented a week's work or the work of a gang, compared to the small tetrahedron, expressing one man-day's work.

The tokens also lacked the capacity of dissociating the numbers from the items counted. In fact, a sphere stood for one bushel of grain and three spheres for one bushel of grain, one bushel of grain, one bushel of grain, and so on. This inability to abstract numbers also contributed to the awkwardness of the system since each collection counted required an equal number of tokens of a special shape. Furthermore, the number of types and subtypes of tokens multiplied in time to satisfy the growing need for more specificity in accounting. For example, tokens to count sheep were supplemented by special tokens to count rams, ewes, and lambs. This proliferation of signs was bound to lead the system to its downfall.

The Neolithic symbolic system of clay tokens superseded the Paleolithic tallies throughout the Near East because it had the following advantages. First, the system was simple: Clay was a common material requiring no special skills or tools to be worked; the forms of the tokens were plain and easy to duplicate; the system was based on one-to-one correspondence, which is the simplest method for dealing with quantities; and the

101. Envelope holding five spheres standing for five measures of grain (?), Susa (Sb 4828), Iran. Courtesy Musée du Louvre, Département des Antiquités Orientales.

tokens stood for units of goods, were independent of phonetics, and could be meaningful in any dialect. Second, the code allowed new performances in data processing and communication: It was the first mnemonic device able to handle and store an unlimited quantity of data; it brought more flexibility in the manipulation of information by making it possible to add, substract, and rectify data at will; and it enhanced logic and rational decision making by allowing the scrutiny of complex data. Lastly, as will be discussed in the next chapter, the code was timely. It fulfilled new needs for counting and accounting brought about by agriculture. It followed or rather was an intrinsic part of the "Neolithic Revolution" spreading in the entire region of the Near East, which became involved in agriculture.

A Turning Point in Communication and Data Storage

The Neolithic token system may be considered as the second step in the evolution of communication and data processing. It followed the Paleolithic and Mesolithic mnemonic devices and preceded the invention of pictographic writing in the Urban period. The tokens are the link, therefore, between tallies and pictographs. They borrowed elements from their Paleolithic antecedents such as the tallies or pebbles used for counting. On the other hand, the counters already presaged writing in many important ways.

The main debt of the token system to Paleolithic and Mesolithic tallies consisted of the principle of abstracting data. Like tallies, tokens translated concrete information into abstract markings, removed the data from their context, separated the knowledge from the knower, and increased objectivity. The format of small movable counters was also probably inherited from a former usage of counting with pebbles, shells, or grains. Most importantly, the tokens acquired from tallies and pebbles the cumbersome way of translating quantity in one-to-one correspondence.

On the other hand, the tokens were new symbols which laid the groundwork for the invention of pictographic writing. In particular, I propose that they presaged the Sumerian writing system by the following features:[37]

1. Semanticity: Each token was meaningful and communicated information.
2. Discreteness: The information conveyed was specific. Each token shape, like each pictograph, was bestowed a unique meaning. The incised ovoid, for example, like the sign ATU 733, stood for a unit of oil.
3. Systematization: Each of the token shapes was systematically repeated in order to carry the same meaning. An incised ovoid, for example, always signified the same measure of oil.
4. Codification: The token system consisted of a multiplicity of interrelated elements. Besides the cone, which stood for a small measure of grain, the spheres represented a larger measure of grain, the ovoid meant a jar of oil, the cylinder an animal, and so on. Consequently, the token system made it feasible, for the first time, to deal simultaneously with information concerning different items.
5. Openness: The repertory of tokens could be expanded at will by creating further shapes representing new concepts. The tokens could also be combined to form any possible set. This made it feasible to store an unlimited quantity of information concerning an unlimited number of items.
6. Arbitrariness: Many of the token forms were abstract; for example, the cylinder and lenticular disks stood respectively for one and ten(?) animals. Others were arbitrary representations; for instance, the head of an animal bore a collar symbolizing the dog.
7. Discontinuity: Tokens of closely related shapes could refer to unrelated concepts. For example, the lenticular disks stood for ten(?) animals, whereas the flat disk referred to a large measure of grain.
8. Independence of phonetics: The tokens were concept signs standing for units of goods. They were independent of spoken language and phonetics and thereby could be understood by people speaking different tongues.
9. Syntax: The tokens were organized according to set rules. There is evidence, for example, that counters were arranged in lines of counters of the same kind, with the largest units placed at the right.
10. Economic contents: The tokens, like the earliest written texts, were limited to handling information concerning real goods. It is only centuries later, about 2900 B.C., that writing started being used to record historical events and religious texts.

The major drawback of the token system was its format. On the one hand, three-dimensionality gave the device the advantage of being tangible and easy to manipulate. On the other hand, the volume of the tokens constituted a major shortcoming. Although they were small, the counters were cumbersome when used in large quantities. Consequently, as is illustrated by the small number of tokens held in each envelope, the system was restricted to keeping track of small amounts of goods. The counters were also difficult to use for permanent records since a group of small objects can easily be separated and can hardly be kept in a particular order for any length of time. Finally, the system was inefficient because each commodity was expressed by a special token and thus required an ever-growing repertory of signs. In short, because the token system consisted of loose, three-dimensional counters, it was sufficient to record transactions dealing with small quantities of various goods but was ill-suited for communicating more complex messages. For example, it relied upon other means, such as seals, to identify the patron/recipient of a transaction.

In turn, the pictographic tablets inherited from tokens the system of a code based on concept symbols, a basic syntax, and their economic content. Writing did away with the greatest inadequacies of the token system by bringing four major innovations to data storage and communication. First, unlike a group of loose, three-dimensional tokens, pictographs consisted of graphic signs traced on the face of a tablet, which held information permanently. Second, the tablets accommodated more diversified information by assigning parts of the field for the recording of particular data. For example, signs representing the sponsor/recipient of the transaction were systematically placed below the symbols indicating goods. In this fashion, the scribe was able to transcribe information such as "ten sheep [received from] Kurlil," with no particular signs indicating verbs and prepositions. Third, writing put an end to the repetition in one-to-one correspondence of symbols representing commodities such as "sheep" (ATU 761/ZATU 571) or "oil" (ATU 733/ZATU 393). As will be discussed at length in Chapter 9, numerals were created. From then on, these new symbols, placed in conjunction with the signs for particular goods, indicated the quantities involved. Fourth, and finally, writing overcame the system of concept symbols by becoming phonetic and, by doing so, not only reduced the repertory of symbols but opened writing to all subjects of human endeavor.

THE FIRST TRACES of visual symbols in the prehistoric Near East date to the Mousterian period, ca. 60,000 to 25,000 B.C. These symbols, which consisted of funerary offerings and (body) paintings(?), show that Neanderthal humans had developed rituals in order to express abstract concepts.[38] The earliest evidence of signs(?), in the form of notched tallies, also date from the Middle Paleolithic. Assuming that the archaeological data reflect the facts, they suggest that symbolism was used in rituals at the same time as for the compilation of concrete information.

From its beginning about 30,000 B.C., the evolution of information processing in the prehistoric Near East proceeded in three major phases, each dealing with data of increasing specificity. First, during the Middle and late Upper Paleolithic, ca. 30,000 to 12,000 B.C., tallies referred to one unit of an unspecified item. Second, in the early Neolithic, about 8000 B.C., the tokens indicated a precise unit of a particular good. With the invention of writing, which took place in the urban period, ca. 3100 B.C., it was possible to record and communicate the name of the sponsor/recipient of the merchandise, formerly indicated by seals.

The Neolithic tokens constitute a second step, and major turning point, in information processing. They followed and inherited from Paleolithic devices the method of abstracting data. The system of counters can be credited with using signs to manipulate, for the first time, concrete commodities of daily life, whereas Paleolithic symbols dealt with ritual and tallies perhaps recorded time. The simple but brilliant invention of concepts in clay symbols provided the first means of supplementing language. It opened new avenues of tremendous importance for communication, providing the immediate background for the invention of writing.

8
TOKENS: THE SOCIOECONOMIC IMPLICATIONS

As a cultural system becomes institutionalized and achieves greater growth, there inevitably results greater abstraction.

—Raymond L. Wilder[1]

IN THE PRECEDING CHAPTER, I proposed that tallies, tokens, and pictographic tablets represent three phases in the evolution of data processing. In the present chapter, I will show how society influenced each phase of the development of prehistoric reckoning technology. I will argue that tallies and plain and complex tokens were different because they fulfilled the needs of distinct life-styles, economies, and social organizations. On the other hand, I will propose that writing was the result of yet other stimuli.

Reckoning Technology and Society

Tallies and plain and complex tokens reflected in their physical appearance the life-style of the people who created them. First, tallies belonged to and were typical of Paleolithic and Mesolithic cultures. For instance, the materials of which they were made, bone or antler, were plentiful among groups relying upon game for survival. Both substances were commonly used in those societies for manufacturing, besides tallies, daggers, harpoons, awls, needles, and tool handles. Furthermore, presumably, bone and antler had an intrinsic symbolic significance during the Paleolithic and Mesolithic periods, as is suggested by amulets consisting of small pierced bones and deposits of antlers as offerings in burials.[2] Moreover, bone and antler had the advantage of being light and shock resistant and, therefore, were well suited for transport during the perigrinations of a nomadic group. Finally, the tallies, made of antler tynes or the shaft of long bones, had an especially convenient shape, since they could be tucked in the belt, as hunters customarily carry their personal belongings.

Tokens, on the other hand, were typical of agriculturalists' assemblages. Like all major Neolithic inventions, such as brick architecture, granaries, kilns, pottery, spindle whorls, or human and animal figurines, the counters were made of clay. The Neolithic farmers exploited clay not only for practical purposes but also for expressing symbols. The heaviness, bulkiness, and fragility of ceramic, which made it unsuitable to nomadic hunters, was no longer a disadvantage in sedentary communities. The system of multiple, loose tokens, impractical to carry on an annual route, was manageable in a permanent habitat, where the counters could be stored in a pouch, box, or jar.

The fourth-millennium complex tokens brought about new sophistications characteristic of cities. The new types of counters, such as miniature jars, tools, or animals, involved far more dexterity for their manufacture than the geometric forms typical of the plain ones. Also, the token series consisting of counters bearing sets of lines or punctuations required an unprecedented accuracy of execution and new "reading skills." Moreover, whereas the Neolithic tokens had usually a black core, the complex specimens were perfectly fired throughout their thickness, showing a mastery of pyrotechnology. It is likely, therefore, that the complex counters were the product of workshops, illustrating the specialization of labor and perfection of technique typical of urban society.

In sum, plain and complex tokens occurred concurrently with major changes of life-style, suggesting that the evolution of reckoning technology was linked to cultural development. The tablets, however, belonged to and were characteristic of the same urban setting as complex tokens, and a case can be made, therefore, that writing was invented for reasons other than a mere change in the way of life.

Reckoning Technology and Economy

Life-style influenced prehistoric reckoning technologies in their form, but the economy dictated their content. As a result, tallies and plain and complex tokens kept track of vastly different items: The former may have recorded time, whereas the latter computed agricultural products and manufactured goods.

HUNTING AND GATHERING

According to Marshack's interpretation, the first item counted was time.[3] The theory is plausible because hunting depends on seasonal events, such as animal migrations, which could be anticipated by keeping track of time. Lunar notations would also make it possible for dispersed communities to gather at intervals at a particular place, at a given period, with other friendly groups, which was necessary in order to exchange women, reassert ties, and celebrate rituals. Because these early festivals would also represent opportunities for exchanging goods and raw materials, the tallies could be considered, perhaps, as indirectly related to trade.

TRADE

Contrary to a common misconception, however, the exchange of goods per se seems to play no role in the development of reckoning technology, presumably because bartering was done face to face and, therefore, did not require any bookkeeping. Archaeologists assume, for example, that during the Paleolithic period, food stuffs and raw materials were traded between kinsmen or neighboring groups on a reciprocal basis that did not call for any accounting or record keeping.[4]

Although little is known about the prehistoric long-distance trade of luxury goods such as obsidian, there is also no evidence that it involved any formal accounting. The archaeological data show no visible link, in particular, between either tallies or tokens and the traffic in volcanic glass. It is well documented that obsidian was already traded in the Mesolithic period prior to the invention of clay counters. For instance, Zarzi, Zawi Chemi, and Mureybet II are among the Mesolithic sites that produced obsidian but neither tallies nor tokens. It is likely that the obsidian trade did not necessitate accounting because the product was bartered by nomads in the course of their annual round or because it was presented as a ceremonial gift, in which cases, the transactions were carried out face to face and, like local trade, did not require any recording.[5]

Local and long-distance trade continued to have little impact on reckoning during the eighth to fifth millennium B.C. This is shown, in particular, by the striking discrepancy between the distribution of Neolithic sites yielding obsidian and those holding tokens. For example, some sites, like Ganj Dareh, had tokens, but no obsidian. On the other hand, Çatal Hüyük, which derived its prosperity from the obsidian trade, apparently did not produce any counters.[6]

The development of complex tokens cannot either, in any way, be related to trade. On the contrary, the deep sounding of Uruk shows no correspondence between the volume of imported raw materials, such as alabaster, flint, obsidian, and copper, and the frequency of tokens. Obsidian artifacts, for example, were most numerous in Uruk XIV–VII, when tokens were still rare, and, on the other hand, decrease in level VI, when tokens multiply. Although the temple was probably involved in securing these substances from distant markets, it was not reflected in the records.[7]

It is important to emphasize the consistent lack of archaeological data linking reckoning technology and trade because, erroneously, tokens, envelopes, and impressed tablets are often associated with commerce. Pierre Amiet, Eva Strommenger, and Harvey Weiss and T. Cuyler Young, Jr., are among those who have proposed that either the envelopes from Susa or those of Habuba Kabira and the impressed tablets from Godin Tepe were indicative of long-distance mercantile activity.[8] There is no indication, however, that any of the tokens included in envelopes or any signs on impressed tablets stood for imported luxury goods. Instead, they consisted mostly of plain tokens and impressed signs representing, presumably, local agricultural staples such as grain and animals. The few complex tokens such as parabolas included in the Uruk envelopes stood for typical Sumerian products such as garments. Lastly, it seems not by chance that the only two envelopes excavated at Habuba Kabira, located in a region traditionally associated with olive groves, held exclusively incised ovoids, standing for quantities of oil. Moreover, the quantities of commodities handled are typically small—the tokens included in envelopes represent probably the equivalent of some five bushels of grain, or five *sila* of oil, which could hardly sustain any sizable long-distance trade.

Finally, Pierre Amiet's hypothesis that the envelopes were bills of lading accompanying shipments of goods, which I endorsed in my first publications, does not withstand scrutiny.[9] Amiet suggested that rural producers of, say, textiles would consign a shipment of goods to an urban middleman, sending along with the shipment an envelope that contained a number of tokens descriptive of the kind and quantity of merchandise shipped. By breaking the envelope, the recipient of the shipment could verify the makeup of the load; moreover, the need to deliver an intact envelope would inhibit the carrier from tampering with the merchandise in transit. The interpretation was attractive, but it must be discarded, because it is not supported by either archaeological, textual, or even ethnographic evidence. As discussed above, the archaeological data concerning trade never jibe with the development of tokens. One should also note that until the present day there is no indication of bills of lading in the cuneiform texts before the Ur III period at the end of the third millennium B.C. I feel compelled to especially emphasize this point because, although since 1980 I have consistently made the plea that tokens, envelopes, and impressed tablets were *not* related to trade,[10] I am often misquoted as representing the contrary opinion.[11]

FARMING

The tallies of Natufian sites, such as Hayonim and Ain Mallaha, show that time(?) continued to be kept when people became sedentary.[12] Furthermore, notched bones from Yarim Tepe and Arpachiyah suggest that the artifacts were still in use, presumably for the same purpose, well into the sixth to fifth millennium B.C.[13] About 8000 B.C., however, an entirely new system of clay tokens was created to keep track of goods. The earliest specimens of these counters consisted mostly of plain spheres, cones, disks, and cylinders. Since these counters seem to stand for quantities of cereals and units of animal count, this suggests that grain and flocks played a predominant role in the first accounting.

What made accounting necessary in 8000 B.C.? Mureybet, Syria, presents convincing evidence that the invention of tokens was directly related to the cultivation of cereals. The site, occupied between 8500 and 7000 B.C., was settled in levels I and II, the two earliest layers, by a hunting and gathering Natufian community that did not use clay counters. Tokens appeared in the Neolithic village of level III about 8000 B.C., coinciding with the first sign of agriculture.[14] The synchronic occurrence of tokens and plant domestication in Mureybet III was not fortuitous but demonstrates that the new economy based on agriculture brought about the need for accounting. In fact, in each of the five sites that yielded the earliest tokens, the invention of clay counters was consistently related to evidence for harvesting or hoarding grain. For example, sickle blades, showing a sheen, were part of the tool kit of Tepe Asiab and Ganj Dareh E.[15] Tokens and tending fields also coincided at Tell Aswad I, where grain was perhaps stored in pits, whereas the villagers of Mureybet III and Cheikh Hassan built elaborate rectangular silos made of masonry (fig. 102).[16] The link between cereal consumption and keeping records of quantities of grain explains the fact that spheres, cones, and flat disks, probably standing for measures of cereals, were among the most common early Neolithic tokens.

The presence of cylinders and lenticular disks, standing for units of animal count, in the token assemblages of Cheikh Hassan, Mureybet, and Tepe Asiab suggests that animal husbandry was practiced at these sites. The archaeological evidence to prove this point is elusive, however, because it takes several generations of captivity to produce physical changes in domesticated animals. This is why, probably, none of the three sites, except perhaps Tepe Asiab, produced bones of sheep or goats showing any diagnostic proof of animal husbandry.[17] It is logical to assume, however, that accounting was also related to the domestication of animals.

INDUSTRY

Industry gave a major boost to the token system. The impact was felt in the middle of the fourth millennium B.C., evidenced by the multiplication of new types and subtypes of tokens standing for manufactured goods. The complex tokens featured finished products typical of urban workshops, such as textiles, garments, vessels, and tools; processed foods, such as oil, bread, cakes, and trussed ducks; and luxury goods, such as perfume, metal, and jewelry.

The impressed and pictographic tablets continued to deal with the same kinds of goods as the token system and in the same quantities, showing that writing was not indebted to any visible change in the economy. The Uruk tablets, for example, like the envelopes filled with counters and the strings of tokens at Habuba Ka-

102. Limestone and clay four-room rectangular structure in stratum XIV, first half of the eighth millennium B.C., Mureybet, Syria. Courtesy Mauritz N. van Loon, Oriental Institute Associate, University of Chicago.

bira, recorded small amounts of basic products such as grain, animals, oil, garments, and textiles.[18]

The economy and, in particular, farming and industry played a major role in the development of the token system. Cultivation of cereals was directly related to the invention of plain tokens, and in the fourth millennium, complex counters are linked to the beginning of industry. On the other hand, trade played, seemingly, an insignificant part in the origin of reckoning technology, being, at most, indirectly involved in the invention of tallies. There is, however, no evidence that commerce was related in any way to the creation of the token system. There is also no evidence that complex tokens or impressed and pictographic tablets had anything to do with exchanging goods. As a matter of fact, the earliest cuneiform tablets visibly dealing with commerce date no earlier than the period of Ur-Nanshe of Lagash in the third millennium B.C.[19]

Reckoning Technology and Social Organization

While the economy influenced what was being counted in a society, social organization determined the function of counting. It was the third, and most significant, factor in the development of prehistoric reckoning technology.

There are two main functions of counting: computing and accounting. Computing consists of making calculations. Accounting, on the other hand, involves keeping track of entries and withdrawals of commodities. It is my contention that computing (time) took place among egalitarian societies, but that the origin of accounting must be credited to ranked societies and the state. In other words, I propose that it was not the mere fact of hoarding grain, tending flocks, or producing manufactured goods that brought about and developed accounting. Instead, I will argue that it was the development of social structures.

EGALITARIAN SOCIETIES

There is no archaeological evidence for accounting during the Paleolithic period, which is not surprising because hunters and gatherers subsist essentially from daily catches without accumulating goods.[20] Their economy, therefore, created no need for accounting, but neither did their social organization. First, the communities were small. The transactions between members of a same group therefore took place face to face with no need for an accounting system. Second, it is assumed that Paleolithic prehistoric societies were egalitarian.[21] As in modern hunting and gathering societies, the game was divided, according to strict rules, among all members of the Paleolithic bands. Egalitarian structures required, therefore, no accounting or record keeping, since each individual received a specific share of the common resources according to his status.[22] Computing time fulfilled seemingly all the needs for counting required by the Paleolithic groups prior to the rise of a formal social organization.

RANK SOCIETIES

The system of tokens, created in order to keep track of goods, constitutes the first evidence for accounting in prehistory. I propose that the event was not a mere corollary of farming but rather of the social structures which derived from agriculture. I borrow the term *rank society,* coined by Morton Fried, to express the organizational changes which became necessary for maintaining stability in village farming communities.[23] The most important aspect of these social changes for this study consists of the creation of an elite overseeing a redistributive economy.[24] It is assumed that ranked societies had redistribution as a major element in their economy, with the headman acting as central collector and redistributor.[25] The fact that tokens were directly implemented in these events is suggested by three sets of data: first, the circumstances surrounding the first occurrence of counters at Mureybet; second, the groups of tokens laid in burials; and third, the textual and art evidence of the third and late fourth millennia B.C.

The First Tokens at Mureybet

According to Mureybet, the invention of tokens for accounting coincided not only with farming but with new social structures. As was described above, the Natufian settlements, presumably egalitarian, had no use for counters. Tokens occurred in Mureybet III at a time of considerable demographic growth. It is difficult to evaluate the size of the population which brought Mureybet III to expand from a small compound of 0.5 ha to a village of 2 or 3 ha,[26] but it is estimated that the community exceeded the maximum number of individuals manageable in an egalitarian system. Thus, the first token assemblage of Mureybet III coincided with a new social organization.[27]

Tokens as Funerary Offerings

I have described at length in Chapter 4 the various instances when tokens were recovered in a funerary setting. I noted that although the custom of depositing tokens in graves was attested in a widespread geographic area and during a period of several millennia, the burials yielding counters were exceedingly rare. In fact, the total number of graves holding tokens amounts to no more than a dozen, including one at Hajji Firuz, one at Arpachiyah, four at Tell es-Sawwan, and six at Tepe Gawra. Furthermore, the counters were visibly restricted to the richly furnished tombs of individuals of high status. For example, the interments of Tell es-Sawwan yielded a variety of alabaster vessels and ornaments of dentalia shells or carnelian. The burial of Tepe Gawra XI was unique in holding gold rosettes, and tombs 102, 110, and 114 were the richest of Tepe Gawra X, containing obsidian, serpentine, or electrum vessels and gold beads, studs, and rosettes (figs. 45–48). These particular tombs also included symbols of power, such as maceheads (fig. 49) and lapis lazuli seals (fig. 50).[28] Other burials yielding tokens were associated with special architectural features. For instance, at Hajji Firuz the tokens were located in a building showing no trace of domestic activity and featuring a platform held by posts, and a shrine had been erected above Tomb 107 at Tepe Gawra. The burial of this prestigious individual was furnished with six stone spheres as the only *Beigaben*.

The rarity of funerary tokens and their association with luxurious burial deposits, artifacts symbolizing power, and special architecture indicate that the counters did not belong to the masses but were the privilege of an elite. Tomb 107 at Tepe Gawra, which was the only interment associated with a shrine, was, obviously, that of an important individual. The fact that his funerary offerings consisted of nothing else but six white stone spheres implies that the counters were a status symbol. The use of counters as status symbols in prehistory is not surprising. Instead, it is to be expected that numeracy in prehistory played the same role as literacy in historic times. Consequently, the individuals who practiced the art of counting in prehistory enjoyed the same prestige as did the scribes in historic times. As suggested by Stephen J. Lieberman, such titles as "man of stone[s]," *lú na₄na*, or "man of clay stone[s]," *lú im na₄na*, were still listed, among other accountants, in professions lists from the city of Nippur.[29] If Lieberman's interpretation is correct, the titles could denote that in early Sumer handling tokens had been a mark of distinction of particular administrators. The association of counters and, in particular, of stone tokens with high-ranking officials is also supported by the unusual number of stone cones excavated in the ruins of the largest houses of Habuba Kabira, which, as will be discussed below, probably served as residences for a Sumerian elite.

Furthermore, the deposits of tokens in the children's graves of Tell es-Sawwan and Tepe Gawra support the common view that the youths were the progeny of members of the elite.[30] Tokens in this case perhaps signified that the children were not only destined to power but also to be trained in the art of counting. The tokens, and in particular those of white stone, may have represented symbols of knowledge and power in prehistory, compared to the more mundane clay specimens used for counting in daily life.

Of course, there are other interpretations possible for the funerary tokens, but none seems convincing. For example, Arthur J. Tobler proposed a magico-religious explanation: "The occupant of tomb 107 was . . . a man who possessed a religious standing in the Gawra community, for after his burial a shrine was erected over his tomb. Under such circumstances, a gaming function for the spheres, from this tomb at least, becomes improbable; it is more likely that they possessed a religious ritualistic significance, perhaps having been used in divination."[31] Tobler's hypothesis is interesting but is not supported by archaeological or textual evidence. There is no mention of divination using tokens in the Sumerian literature.

The tokens could be interpreted as food offerings; that is to say, spheres and cones, standing for common measures of barley, could represent quantities of grain for the dead. In particular, groups of six tokens, found in three tombs of Tepe Gawra, could be understood as a food ration for eternity. Finally, the fact that funerary tokens were made of stone rather than clay could be understood as contributions meant to last forever. The interpretation of funerary tokens as food offerings is not convincing, however, because if the counters were meant to take care of hunger for eternity, one would expect to find them frequently in burials, but it is not so. Instead, inhumations provided with tokens are very few. More importantly, symbolic food offerings are known in Egypt but not in Southwest Asia. In Mesopotamia and Iran, sepultures were furnished with real goods but not with models, as was the custom in the Nile Valley. There are only rare occasions when miniature clay facsimiles, such as sailboats, were substituted for the actual commodity.[32] The idea of tokens as food for eternity is unlikely, therefore, because it does not tally with our knowledge of funerary customs in Mesopotamia.

On the other hand, the fact that tokens are found in graves or residences of powerful individuals suggests that the counters, in particular those made of stone, served and conferred prestige on an elite. The high status of preliterate administrators is not unique to the ancient Near East but is a common phenomenon. In fact, the use of a counting device as a status symbol in a funerary setting is a tradition known in distant societies. For example, it was customary among the Incas of Peru to bury high officials with their quipus, the knotted strings they used to keep accounts.[33]

Textual and Art Evidence

The tokens laid in graves show that the counters were part of the paraphernalia of the elite, but the third- and fourth-millennium tablets and art representations explain why it was so. They suggest, in particular, that counting devices were instrumental in carrying out a redistributive economy, as was writing in the historical period.

Third Millennium B.C. It is undisputed that, during the Early Dynastic period, writing dealt with temple and palace administration. The tablets of Tello, for example, recorded with scrupulous detail the movement of goods in and out of the palace and temples.[34] Entries consisted of yields from the estates as well as offerings delivered by worshipers. Disbursements were mostly in the form of rations of barley, beer, and other commodities allotted to members of the royal family, high officials, the work force, and other dependents, but also expenditures such as animals for sacrifice, fodder for the flocks, and so on. The most obvious function of writing was, therefore, keeping account of the resources generated by the palace and the temple and their redistribution.

The second and more important function of writing was one of control. The tablets recording offerings, for instance, were official receipts of commodities delivered by individuals or guilds. They registered (1) the items received and their quantity, (2) the name of the donor, (3) the date of the delivery, such as a festival celebrated at the temple in honor of a divinity, and (4) the administrator who checked the commodities. Now, it seems well established that the so-called gifts for the gods, listed on the tablets were in fact mandatory. High officials, for example, were required to present a lamb or a kid at the monthly festival celebrated at the temple, whereas fishermen had to produce a specific quantity of fish.[35] The written records were, therefore, far more than bookkeeping. In fact, they were the backbone of the economy of redistribution that brought prosperity to Sumer. The receipts made it possible, on the one hand, to verify the contributions made by groups or individual citizens and, on the other hand, to oversee the administration of this merchandise. Writing, therefore, bestowed on the ruler the full control over the input, as well as the output, of the community properties. The leadership could regulate the amount of goods to be contributed by the community and enforce their delivery. The ruler also had total mastery over the redistribution of these commodities since the written receipts made the administration accountable for the goods received. In other words, writing endowed the third-millennium kings with full control over the communal resources.

The delivery of offerings was also one of the *leitmotivs* of Sumerian art in the third millennium B.C. as it was of the cuneiform tablets. Carvings, inlays, and figurines depict for us the ceremonies in which the "gifts" were offered to the gods. For example, relief

103. Perforated plaque, Khafaje (A. 12417), Iraq. After Pierre Amiet, *La Glyptique mesopotamienne archaïque* (Paris: Editions du CNRS, 1980), pl. 93: 1222.

carvings on perforated plaques show the king and his queen(?) attending a banquet while commoners deliver offerings including animals on the hoof and jars of goods (fig. 103).[36] The scene probably depicts the pomp of monthly festivals organized at the temple, when offerings were delivered in honor of deities of the Sumerian pantheon. The motif, in other words, illustrates how temple, king, and commoners interacted in the economy of redistribution.[37]

The theme of the banquet and offering procession is developed, in greater detail, on the famous "standard of Ur," a panel intricately inlaid with lapis lazuli and shell (fig. 104).[38] The standard is divided horizontally into several registers, the uppermost of which features a banquet scene that includes the king and six high officials. Offering bearers, led by ushers, are shown on the second register bringing cows, rams, kids, and fish. Finally, on the third register, foreigners in curious garb, carrying heavy bundles on their backs, suggest that tribute from neighboring lands also played a role in the third-millennium Sumerian economy.

The tribute delivered to Sumer may explain why the banquet scenes with their correlated procession of offering bearers is also featured in third-millennium Elamite and Syrian art (figs. 105 and 106).[39] The plaques, inlays, and figurines representing officials wearing the typical woolen Sumerian garment called a *kaunakes* and carrying a lamb or a kid excavated at Susa and Mari suggest not only that the same system of pooling communal resources was practiced in these regions but that it involved identical rituals.[40] The question remains whether the monuments depicted an indigenous Elamite and Syrian elite or a Sumerian rule abroad.

Jemdet Nasr Period. The art of the late protoliterate period leaves no doubt that the economy of redistribution was already ritualized at the end of the fourth millennium B.C. For example, the famous vase of Uruk III offers the most complete representation of a procession including nude worshipers carrying jars and baskets, following the priest-king, or En, in festive attire, wearing a long kilt and proceeding toward the gate of the Inanna temple, where accumulated goods are shown (fig. 107). It seems significant that the proliterate En himself, who was invested with a religious as well as political office, participated in the ritual, leading the congregation to the temple, instead of being segregated from the commoners, as were the third-millennium kings.

Although the late pictographic texts of Uruk III or the Jemdet Nasr period, dated 3000 to 2900 B.C., are

104. Standard, Ur, Iraq. After André Parrot, *Sumer* (Paris: Librairie Gallimard, 1960), fig. 177.

105. Two seated figures at a banquet. After André Parrot, *Mari,* Collection des Ides Photographiques 7 (Neuchatel: Editions des Ides et Calendes, 1953), fig. 65.

106. Worshipper carrying a kid, Mari, Syria. After André Parrot, *Mari,* Collection des Ides Photographiques 7 (Neuchatel: Editions des Ides et Calendes, 1953), fig. 72.

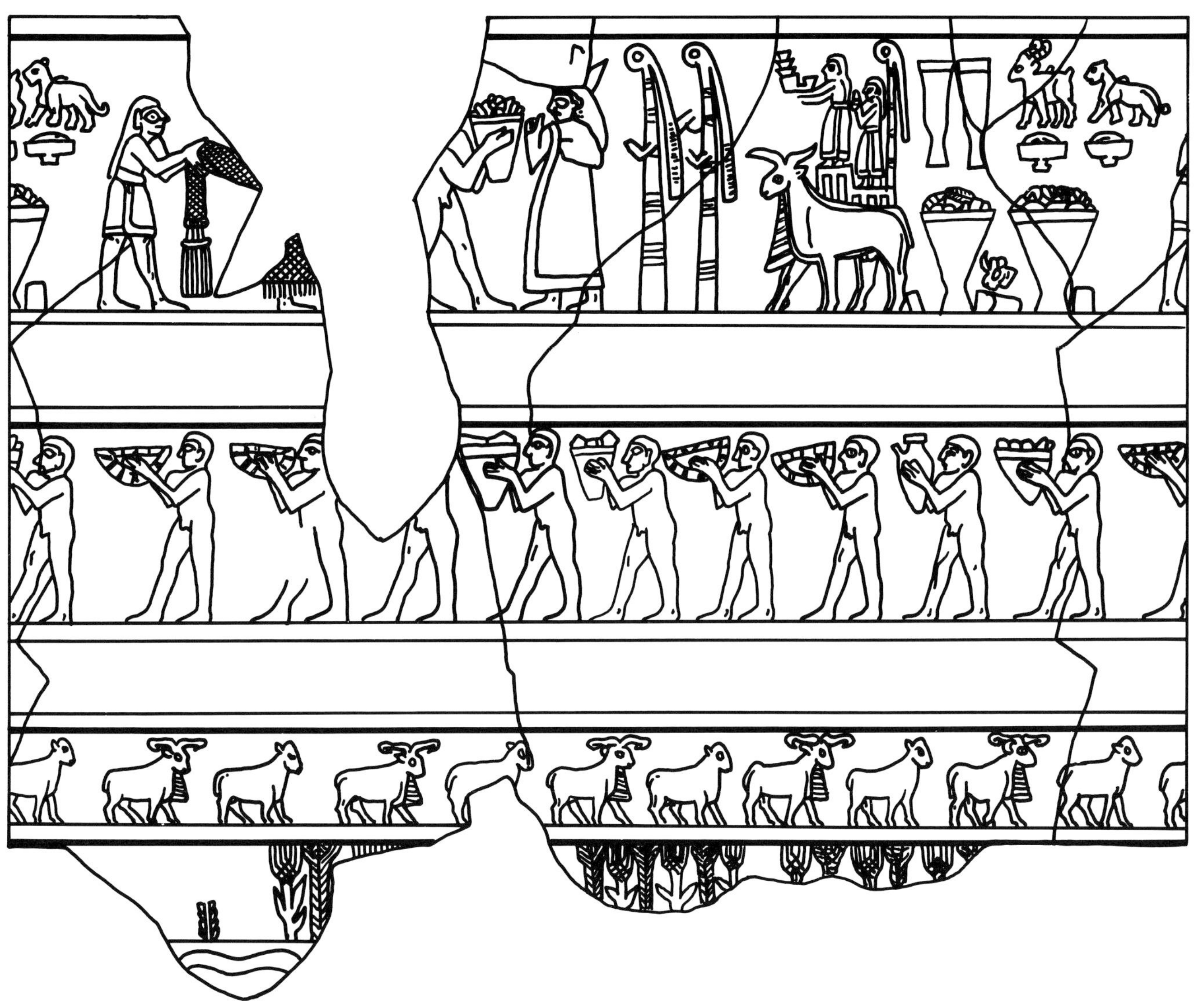

107. Sculpture on a stone vase, Uruk, Iraq. After André Parrot, *Sumer* (Paris: Librairie Gallimard, 1960), fig. 89.

still enigmatic in many ways because they are more succinct, it seems evident that, like those of the third millennium, the tablets served the bureaucracy controlling the input and output of communal goods. At Uruk, for example, the late fourth-millennium tablets belonged to the precinct of Eanna, where the temple of the goddess Inanna was located and, most probably, the site of the residence of the En. The typical Uruk texts, like those of Tello, feature small quantities of goods; the name of an individual, probably the donor; the symbol of a god, presumably at whose festival the offering was made; and, finally, an administrative service identified by a seal. The art and textual evidence of the protoliterate period concur, therefore, in showing that before kingship the main components of the Near Eastern redistributive system already consisted of (1) a religious ideology, (2) a leadership acting as the central collector and redistributor, (3) laborers generating a surplus, and (4) a reckoning technology to administer/control the goods. Like the third-millennium cuneiform tablets, the pictographic records were the key to a privileged access to community properties and the key to power.

Uruk Period. The art of the early protoliterate period further illustrates that the economy of redistribution, headed by the En, was already in place in the middle of the fourth millennium B.C. The first glyptic of Uruk VI(?)–IV and Susa 18–17, in particular, depict, time and time again, lines of worshipers bringing to the temple the products of their fields and orchards, as well as luxury goods such as bracelets and necklaces (figs. 108.1–108.5), whereas the priest-king in his long skirt contributes an animal or a vessel in that shape (figs. 109.1 and 109.2).[41] These images leave no doubt that the synthesis between temple and elite was already achieved for successfully pooling the communal goods.

In turn, it is clear that the late fifth- and fourth-millennium tokens of Uruk XVII–IVa, held by strings or enclosed in envelopes, assumed the same function of control in the redistributive economy as did the pictographic tablets. The fact that tokens and tablets dealt with identical data seems obvious, since the same symbols are used in both media. For example, the signs for grain, animals, textiles, and garments exist as three-dimensional tokens as well as impressed/incised signs. The fact that goods were handled in small quantities, similar to those of the third-millennium gifts to the gods, is illustrated by the few tokens enclosed in each envelope. For instance, the envelope W 20987.7 from Uruk yielded seven ovoids that amounted, probably,

109.1. Cylinder seal impression, the En bringing an offering. After Pierre Amiet, *La Glyptique mésopotamienne archaïque* (Paris: Editions du CNRS, 1980), pl. 44: 642.

109.2. The En bringing an offering, cylinder seal impression. After Pierre Amiet, *La Glyptique mésopotamienne archaïque* (Paris: Editions du CNRS, 1980), pl. 44: 643.

108.1. Cylinder seal impression, Tell Billa, Iraq. After Pierre Amiet, *La Glyptique mésopotamienne archaïque* (Paris: Editions du CNRS, 1980), pl. 46: 656.

108.2. Cylinder seal impression, Uruk (W 19410), Iraq. After Pierre Amiet, *La Glyptique mésopotamienne archaïque* (Paris: Editions du CNRS, 1980), pl. 13 bis, D.

108.3. Cylinder seal impression, Uruk (W 19421), Iraq. After Pierre Amiet, *La Glyptique mésopotamienne archaïque* (Paris: Editions du CNRS, 1980), pl. 13 bis, L.

108.4. Cylinder seal impression, Uruk, Iraq. After Pierre Amiet, *La Glyptique mésopotamienne archaïque* (Paris: Editions du CNRS, 1980), pl. 11, 203 B.

108.5. Cylinder seal impression, Uruk (W 21419), Iraq. Courtesy Deutsches Archaeologisches Institut, Abteilung Baghdad.

to seven measures (*sila?*) of oil. The small clusters of counters recovered *in situ* in buildings of Habuba Kabira, never exceeding some twenty tokens, further indicate that the goods dealt with never amounted to large quantities.

The fact that both pictographic tablets and tokens were used by the same temple bureaucracy is also evident, since tablets, envelopes, and strings of tokens belonged to the same Eanna precinct, where they overlapped for some time. This was the case for the group of tokens discarded with tablets in the Great Courtyard of Uruk IVa.[42] The same was true at Susa, where envelopes holding tokens, solid bullae, and impressed tablets were recovered together in an abandoned building[43] and in Building 2 of Habuba Kabira, which produced tokens, envelopes, oblong bullae, and impressed tablets. Because the tokens had the same content and belonged to the same context as the pictographic tablets that replaced them, it is logical to assume that both types of accounting devices fulfilled the same function.

In sum, starting with the better known toward the lesser known, the art and cuneiform texts of the better-known third millennium B.C. give an insight into the meaning and function of the more enigmatic protoliterate texts and the tokens that preceded them. The depictions of banquets and gift presentations in various art forms suggest that during the period of 3500 to 2500 B.C. Sumer had a redistribution economy involving three main components: First, the temple conferred meaning and pomp on the act of giving; second, an elite administered the communal property; and third, commoners produced surplus goods and surrendered them to the temple. This redistributive economy relied upon a system of record keeping and, indeed, could not have succeeded without it. This function was fulfilled in the third millennium B.C. by cuneiform writing and, going further back in time, by pictographic writing and tokens.

Plain Tokens and Redistribution Economy. The three sets of evidence presented above, namely the circumstances surrounding the first occurrence of tokens at Mureybet, the tokens laid in burials, and the textual and art evidence of the early historic period, concur in suggesting that, all along, the tokens were instrumental in a redistributive economy. The textual and art evidence of the third and fourth millennia B.C. complement the archaeological data in showing that in 3500 to 2500 B.C. writing or tokens were used by the leadership to control the delivery of goods and oversee their redistribution. Furthermore, the tokens included in special burials illustrate that the counters were continuously the prerogative of the elite throughout the Neolithic period. Finally, the data from Mureybet suggest that the first use of tokens coincides with the emergence of a new leadership. I therefore propose that during its entire duration the tokens were used by the elite to pool and redistribute communal resources.

My hypothesis agrees with commonly accepted models, which view the transition from egalitarian to ranked society as simultaneous with the beginning of an economy of redistribution. It is presumed, for instance, that the headmen of early farming communities were responsible for pooling resources and overseeing their redistribution. It is to be expected that the need for counting was boosted when subsistence came to depend on planning a harvest and storing goods. It is likely, however, that farmers did not need to invent a reckoning device to keep track either of the grain they harvested or the seeds to put aside for the next season, which they could estimate visually. Instead, record keeping was imperative when communities pooled surpluses, because it provided a way to record both the contribution and redistribution of the common property. In other words, the role of tokens was accounting rather than mere computing.

My hypothesis further agrees with the assemblages of Neolithic farming communities, which yield critical indicators of rank societies, including settlement size; population density; architecture such as, for example, large rectangular houses; and silos larger than necessary for a household. The seals ever present in Neolithic sites also point to control and administration in prehistory. It is perhaps not fortuitous that stone seals and stone tokens appear together in the Hassuna period. It is also not by chance, probably, that tokens and sealings were found together in the remains of some early farming communities.[44]

Finally, my hypothesis agrees with the idea that the Sumerian redistribution system, probably already developed full-fledged in the temple of Eanna, cannot have emerged without precedent but must draw its origin from more modest prehistoric antecedents. In sum, the plain tokens of the eighth to fifth millennium B.C. made possible the rise of rank society, preparing the background for the powerful fourth to third millennium bureaucracy. I also postulate that, vice versa, the development of political power was based on the development of reckoning technology and could not have occurred in the same way without it.[45] According to Lévi-Strauss, the first use of writing was, ultimately, a control on the production of real goods—but so were the first tokens.[46]

THE STATE

I have just argued that plain tokens were linked to the rise of rank society. I further propose that the advent of the state was responsible for the phenomenon of complex tokens. I base this hypothesis upon the fact that the complex counters appeared in conjunction with the rise of the southern Mesopotamian temple, the institution which served as the catalyst for state formation in the Near East. I will argue, in particular, that the token system played an important role in the collection of dues and tribute necessary to sustain the first city-states. I will support this conclusion by showing that the complex tokens coincided with socioeconomic changes such as monumental architecture, the monopoly of force, and bureaucracy, which point to new strategies in pooling communal resources.

Complex Tokens and the Rise of the Southern Mesopotamian Temple

The context of complex tokens shows that the changes in accounting were a temple, rather than a lay, phenomenon. For example, at Uruk, the site that yielded the largest and best-documented collection of fourth-millennium counters, 88.1 percent of the tokens was excavated in the precinct of Eanna, with an additional 5.5 percent around the Anu Ziggurat, while a mere 6.4 percent originated in the city's private quarters. The total absence of counters in the archaic village north of Uruk and their rarity in the excavations outside the religious precincts, such as squares O and K–L XII, indicate that tokens fulfilled a temple function rather than a domestic or commercial use (figs. 31.1 and 31.2). The connection between accounting and temple administration is particularly visible in level VI b2 of the deep sounding of Eanna, where a hoard of 155 tokens, the largest cluster of counters recovered at the site, was found mixed with cone mosaics, typical of temple monumental architecture. Furthermore, the only cache of tokens found *in situ* at Uruk belonged to the ruins of the impressive complex of Buildings F, G, and H in Eanna IVb. The same is true at Susa, where the token collection originated from the Acropolis, where the temple was located.

The repeated occurrence of complex tokens and impressed tablets in gate rooms and, in particular, temple gates is another clue that the counters had a formal function. At Godin Tepe, for example, the largest cache of impressed tablets came from the gate of the compound.[47] At Habuba Kabira, a group of fifteen tokens and numerous oblong bullae were recovered in the city gate, which gave access to the religious precinct of Tell Kannas. At Uruk, tokens were most numerous at the periphery of the Eanna precinct and, in particular, at the eastern and western ends, where gates to the precinct were presumably located. Gateways have traditionally been associated with administrative centers in the ancient Near East. Jean-Marie Durand has described the importance of the gate at the Palace of Mari in the time of Zimri Lim.[48] The Bible also alludes to the city gates as the location where public procedures took place and where records were kept.[49] The importance of the gateway in the administration of the fourth millennium B.C. explains why the gate of Eanna played such a prominent role in art. The two bundles of reeds symbolizing it appear time and time again in glyptics and on many fourth-millennium stone vessels.[50] In particular, it is toward the gate of Eanna, shown filled with offerings, that the En of the Uruk vase led the procession of offering bearers.[51]

The chronology of the complex tokens also suggests that the counters were linked to the development of the southern Mesopotamian temple. Specifically, the sequence of the deep sounding of Eanna shows that the first occurrence of complex and perforated tokens coincided with the establishment of the sanctuary; the beginning of public architecture decorated with cone mosaics concurred with the first token series; the floruit of the token system coincided with the era of splendor of the precinct; and, finally, the disappearance of the counters corresponded with the destruction of Eanna in level IVa. Complex tokens came and went with the rise and fall of Eanna and can be considered a hallmark of the temple administration.

In sum, the complex counters show a direct relationship to the southern Mesopotamian temple at the time of state formation. This is significant because it implies that the changes in the token system not only coincided with but also played a role in the socioeconomic changes that led to the rise of the state.

Changes in Redistribution: Taxation

I have argued in the first part of this chapter that the plain tokens were instrumental in establishing the prehistoric redistribution system. I now posit that the complex tokens played a part in the collection of taxes and tribute typical of a state economy.

In the perspective of this work, the southern Mesopotamian temple appears as the final outcome of a four-thousand-year-old economy of redistribution. It inherited from the past a tradition of pooling communal resources and still relied on the continuous outpouring of goods in kind delivered as gifts to the gods. The emergence of the city-state brought, however, a major transformation to the age-old redistributive system by establishing taxation; that is, the obligation for all individuals or guilds to deliver a fixed amount of goods in kind under penalty of sanctions. I propose that the new strategy for pooling communal resources can actually be deduced from several indices, such as monumental architecture, the monopoly of force, and the increase of bureaucracy.

Monumental Architecture. The rise of monumental architecture, which necessitated large expenditures for securing materials for construction and adornment, denotes a quantum jump in the quantity of resources available to the community. The vast temple precincts such as Eanna, therefore, imply new ways of levying goods and suggest a system of taxation. In economic terms, monuments like the Stone Cone Temple of levels VI–V of Eanna, covered with colorful stone mosaics, or the Limestone Temple of level V were extraordinary achievements since the southern Mesopotamian alluvial plain was deprived of such materials. The large-scale buildings lavishly decorated meant new ways of pooling surpluses, as well as new ways to administer them. It is not surprising, therefore, that the earliest monumental structures corresponded to the development of a more stringent bureaucracy, including a more precise accounting device. At Uruk, the first complex token series of level X, ca. 3750 B.C., follows shortly after the earliest evidence for temples with cone mosaics in level XIIb of the deep sounding of Eanna.[52]

The construction of public buildings also required a large work force of unskilled laborers as well as specialized craftsmen such as carpenters, masons, ceramicists, and painters; architects to coordinate the work; astronomers to determine the orientation of the buildings; and priests to perform the necessary rituals. The completion of building programs, such as those of Eanna, suggests new ways of controlling labor, inferring the existence of the corvée; that is, labor exacted from individuals at little or no pay or instead of taxes.

Changes in Leadership: The Monopoly of Force. The levying of taxes also presupposes a coercive system to enforce their collection. The southern Mesopotamian temple was the catalyst that produced a new type of leader who, unlike his prehistoric counterparts, had the power of sanctions.

The priest-king was the head of the complex, stratified society of the fourth millennium B.C. As such, he was differentiated from the remaining citizens by the sporting of a beard, a round headdress, and a long kilt. As depicted on several monuments of Uruk, the En's primary function was that of a religious leader: It was he, for example, who led the procession of worshipers to the gate of Eanna for the offering ceremony. The En was also the pinnacle of the complex multilevel hierarchy that administered the temple possessions, the largest accumulation of wealth of the time.[53] In fact, as the Uruk vase illustrates, both functions were intrinsically connected, since the ceremonial delivery of gifts to the gods was also the cornerstone of the redistributive economy.

Finally, sealings picturing the En overseeing corporal punishment suggest that the priest-king held the monopoly of force. The motif which shows nude men, hands tied at the back, being clubbed in the En's presence has often been viewed as representing prisoners of war (figs. 110.1, 110.2, 111.1, and 111.2).[54] The individuals, however, are not shown with the unusual hairdos denoting foreigners in Sumerian art and, therefore, the scene may also be understood as the administering of sanctions to Mesopotamian delinquents. In particular, it can be interpreted as the system of coercion necessary to enforce the delivery of dues to the temple. This sheds a new light on the significance of stone tokens among administrators' status symbols. They signified the power inherent in the administration.

The Development of Bureaucracy. Thomas W. Beale has made the case that the thousands of beveled-rim bowls that are characteristic of the Uruk period point to a major transformation in the manner of pooling communal resources (fig. 43). He argues, in particular, that the beveled-rim bowls served for the presentation of offerings. According to him, the introduction of "calibrated" vessels in the early Uruk period implies that the amounts and volume of the gifts to the gods began to be regularized, standardized, and obligatory for the general populace and can be considered taxes.[55] The general development of bureaucracy in the Uruk period reinforces Beale's view. I propose that the appearance of complex tokens, envelopes, bullae, cylinder seals, and a system of weights and measures, which represent other methods for controlling goods, shows the bureaucratic adjustments necessary for levying taxes.

Tax collection increased the need for collecting, manipulating, and storing more data with greater accuracy, which was fulfilled by complex tokens. The multiplication of counters and markings, in particular, denotes a quantum jump in the number of items accounted for. Whereas mainly staples and labor were kept track of in prehistory, the complex tokens show that in the fourth millennium B.C. bureaucracy was dealing with a large variety of commodities including processed foods such as bread, oil, or trussed ducks; manufactured products such as wool, cloth, garments, mats, rope, pieces of furniture, and tools; and precious materials such as perfume and metal. The novelty, obviously, was not the appearance of items such as bread, oil, cloth, pots, axes, and perfume, which had existed for a long time. What was new was that manufactured and finished products were being accounted for, which had not been true previously. On the one hand, the many counters representing quantities of bread, oil, trussed ducks, textile, and so on are reminiscent of or rather presage the itemization of gifts to the gods recorded as being levied in the third-millennium city-states. On the other hand, they show how the system of clay counters used in the age-old economy of redistribution adjusted to a more rigorous system of pooling communal resources. They indicate, in particular, the increased variety of goods solicited by the temple,

110.1. Corporal punishment, cylinder seal impression, Uruk, Iraq. After Pierre Amiet, *La Glyptique mésopotamienne archaïque* (Paris: Editions du CNRS, 1980), pl. 47: 661.

110.2. Corporal punishment, cylinder seal impression, Uruk, Iraq. After Pierre Amiet, *La Glyptique mésopotamienne archaïque* (Paris: Editions du CNRS, 1980), pl. 47: 660.

which included not only products of the pens, fields, and orchards but also processed foods and finished goods.

Taxation also required an increased specificity for keeping exact account of the dues delivered to the temple. This explains why the token system included new subtypes indicating with greater accuracy the species, age, and gender of animals dealt with, such as sheep, ewes, or lambs, whereas the plain cylinders simply recorded heads of unspecified domesticates. Complex tokens recording cereals also indicated whether they were, for example, wheat or barley, whereas the plain cones and spheres simply stood for quantities of grains.

Even more importantly, the levy of taxes made necessary keeping track of what had *not* been delivered and remained due to the temple. The accounting for unpaid taxes in turn increased the need for archives, perhaps explaining the invention of envelopes and bullae. Accordingly, the accounts preserved perhaps represented payments to be completed at a future date, such as, for example, the next harvest. This would account for the many sealings featured on each envelope, since differing payments would involve the authorization of several echelons in the administrative hierarchy. As Enrica Fiandra suggests, the two, three, and four seals applied on envelopes and solid bullae could correspond to the signatures of several hierarchical levels such as accountants, controllers, supervisors, or superintendents.[56]

These transformations in accounting did not occur in isolation but appeared in conjunction with other administrative devices, illustrating a general increase in bureaucracy. The changes in the token system coincided, in particular, with a major alteration in the age-old Near Eastern practice of sealing goods. Cylinder seals, which were rolled rather than impressed on spherical envelopes, oblong bullae, jar stoppers, or door sealings, replaced the former stamp seals.[57] The continuous imprint they produced was more efficient for identifying, authenticating, and controlling goods. Moreover, the depiction of entire scenes on the face of the cylinders brought new possibilities of communicating information.

Finally, the creation of a system of stone weights in the Uruk period showed a greater concern for precision in measuring goods.[58] The same was true for the beveled-rim bowls recovered by the thousands in the major fourth-millennium sites that probably served as measuring devices. Thomas W. Beale has made the case that although the vessels were not of standard sizes they could be used for measuring grain in heaped amounts with reasonable accuracy.[59]

The Uruk bureaucracy grew in volume and specific-

111.1. Corporal punishment, cylinder seal impression, Uruk (W 21660), Iraq. Courtesy Deutsches Archaeologisches Institut, Abteilung Baghdad.

111.2. Drawing of cylinder seal impression in fig. 111.1.

ity. It is credited with the development of archives, the invention of cylinder seals, and the creation of a system of weights and measures. There can be no doubt that these major administrative innovations were responses to the profound socioeconomic changes that surrounded the beginning of the state. It is logical to assume, in particular, that the increase of bureaucracy reflects the control necessary to enforce the delivery of dues to the temple.

The Levy of Tribute. Complex counters occurred not only in Mesopotamia but also in Elam and Syria. In the three regions, however, the phenomenon was restricted to sites sharing the distinctive paraphernalia of the southern Mesopotamian temple bureaucracy; that is, the monumental architecture decorated with cone mosaics,[60] cylinders seals featuring the En, beveled-rim bowls, envelopes, and bullae. I propose that the presence of complex tokens in distant countries identifies places paying tribute to the southern Mesopotamian temple.

It is undisputed that the public buildings faced with mosaics were first attested in level XIIb of Eanna; that the En was a typical southern Mesopotamian figure; that beveled-rim bowls and nose-lugged jars with incised decorations originated in Mesopotamia.[61] These elements, which, with the complex tokens, envelopes, and bullae, constitute the hallmark of the southern Mesopotamian temple, have long been recognized as intrusive in Elam and Syria.[62] Some have interpreted the Mesopotamian presence in neighboring countries as related to trade and others have raised the question of a domination.[63] The evidence provided by the chronology of tokens in Susa suggests that it was the latter.

The complex tokens appeared in Susa in circumstances different from those of Uruk. Whereas the tokens developed in full harmony with Eanna, they were consistently out of step with the temple of Susa. As far as we know, the establishment of the first high temple in Period I had no impact on the token system, which remained plain. Complex tokens, envelopes, and impressed tablets appear after the destruction of the temple, when the monumental buildings were replaced by modest structures.[64] In other words, the complex tokens coincided with the collapse of the main temple at Susa. The establishment of a southern Mesopotamian bureaucracy in Elam, immediately following the destruction of the main temple, suggests a conquest. Finally, the fact that Sumerian pictographic writing never penetrated Susa indicates a break between the two cultures in the course of Uruk IVa, shortly before the destruction of Eanna.

112. Envelope bearing the impression of a cylinder seal featuring a line of prisoners, Susa (Sb 1926), Iran. Courtesy Musée du Louvre, Département des Antiquités Orientales.

A southern Mesopotamian domination in Elam is further supported by seals picturing warfare. For example, sealings from Susa and Chogha Mish feature the En as a warrior armed with a bow, lines of prisoners, and the siege of a fortified city with people raising their hands, begging for mercy (fig. 112).[65] These images show clearly that the late Uruk period was plagued with increasing conflicts.[66] Like the third-millennium kings, the En carried out organized warfare. In this perspective, presumably the counters, used for the collection of taxes at Uruk, served to levy tribute in foreign countries.

The four Elamite sites yielding complex token assemblages may give an insight into the organization of the southern Mesopotamian bureaucracy abroad. It is interesting to note that the Elamite complex counters belonged to three types of sites, which corresponded to three types of administrative and productive units: Susa was a city, Chogha Mish a town, and Moussian and KS 54 lesser centers. The fact that Susa yielded by far the largest assemblage, consisting of 700 specimens, followed by Chogha Mish 100(?), Moussian 19, and KS 54, 7, may not be due to chance but may suggest that the southern Mesopotamian bureaucracy was organized according to three historical levels.

Habuba Kabira is regarded as a southern Mesopotamian outpost because its public and domestic architecture and its pottery, seals, and sealings had the unmistakable character of the southern Mesopotamian temple. The fact that the city was fortified also suggests that the Sumerian presence was not a peaceful trade venture but required military protection. In this light, the buildings, where complex tokens, envelopes, bullae, and impressed tablets were concentrated, were perhaps administrative services, warehouses, or the residences of Sumerian administrators. In any case, they were used by southern Mesopotamian accountants or their foreign subordinates.

The chronology of Habuba Kabira shows that the city flourished at the time when the Stone Cone and Limestone temples were at their peak. It was founded on virgin soil in the course of Uruk VI and was occupied for about a century, during Uruk V, after which it was suddenly abandoned. The southern Mesopotamian expansion to Syria took place, therefore, during the first florescence of Eanna, which marked a turning point in the use of tokens at Uruk.

The distribution of complex tokens outside southern Mesopotamia indicates Sumerian penetration abroad. When plotted on a map, the rare sites holding complex counters reveal a southern Mesopotamian administration in three main regions: first, in Iran as far east as Tepe Hissar, but with a concentration in Elam; second, in Syria, as far west as Habuba Kabira; and third, in northern Mesopotamia at Nuzi and Tell Billa. The splendors of Eanna V and VI may be explained by the influx of tribute from neighboring regions, and it could even be postulated that complex tokens, envelopes, and bullae were instrumental in that process.

IN THIS CHAPTER I have discussed how the form of tallies and tokens was determined by the life-style of the people who used them, whereas their content was dependent on the economy and their function was contingent upon the political system of the cultures involved. I showed that whereas reckoning was sufficient in hunting and gathering societies the economy of redistribution typical of the ancient Near East made accounting necessary. In other words, the pooling of communal resources was a major stimulus for the beginning of tokens. The plain counters used to implement an incipient redistributive economy were, however, no longer adequate for the early state bureaucracy. The system was perfected by the addition of more complex tokens that could handle with greater efficiency and precision the larger volume of goods generated by taxation and the levy of tribute.

Writing, which came about in the late fourth millennium B.C., cannot be explained, however, by a change of life-style, economy, or political system. I intend to demonstrate in the next chapter that its origin depended on the achievement of a higher level of abstraction.

9
COUNTING AND THE EMERGENCE OF WRITING

Mathematics is, of course, a part of culture. Every people inherits from its predecessors or contemporary neighbors, along with ways of cooking, marrying, worshiping, etc., ways of counting, calculating, and whatever else mathematics does. . . . Whether a people counts by fives, tens, twelves or twenties; whether it has no words for cardinal numbers beyond 5, or possesses the most modern and highly developed mathematical conceptions, their mathematical behavior is determined by the mathematical culture which possesses them.

—Leslie A. White[1]

IN THE PRECEDING CHAPTER I have shown that tallies and tokens reflected the culture, economy, and sociopolitical system of the people who used them. In this chapter I will argue that each reckoning device was determined by a particular mode of counting. I will interpret the archaeological evidence in the light of linguistic and anthropological data and propose that tallies, tokens, and writing reflected three major phases in the development of counting: (1) one-to-one correspondence, (2) concrete counting, and (3) abstract counting. Finally, I will postulate that writing is the outcome of abstract counting.

Before starting the discussion, I want to define some of the terms I will use. *Concrete numbers* refer to concepts like "twin" that fuse together a notion of number with that of the item counted. *Numbers* are the concept of, for example, oneness, twoness, threeness. *Numerals* are written signs such as 1, 2, 3. Finally, *number words* are the way people express these concepts in a particular language, for example, in English, "one," "two," "three" or in French "un," "deux," "trois."

Counting: The Linguistic and Anthropological Evidence

There is a common misconception that, because humans have ten fingers, they have the innate ability of counting to ten. People generally fancy that, if a child was raised by wolves, he would come to the idea of counting just by looking at his hands. Cross-cultural linguistic and anthropological studies on numbers show, however, that, in all parts of the world, many societies could thrive without having number words beyond "three." And other cultures came and went ignoring abstract numbers. Instead they counted concretely, tying the notion of number to that of the item counted. These facts show forcefully that, far from being intuitive to humans, counting is learned. It is to be assumed, therefore, that like other acquired behaviors such as language and writing, counting evolved under the influence of specific socioeconomic pressures.

ONE, TWO, MANY

Until the last century, many societies had a vocabulary limited to three number words equivalent to "one," "two," and "many." For example, in Sri Lanka, the Weddas had no specific words for numbers beyond expressions such as "a single," "a pair," "one more," and "many." The Weddas were by no means an isolated case, but a list could be compiled of cultures in Africa as well as South America and Australia who referred to groups of more than two or three objects as "many."[2]

The fact that "three" was a landmark in incipient numerations is further highlighted by the frequent recurrence of so-called two- or three-counting systems in various parts of the world such as, for instance, Australia and South America as well as South Africa. These systems consist of compounding the words for 1, 2, 3 to express 4, 5, 6, 7, etc. For example, 3 is literally "two-one," 4 = "two-two," and 5 = "two-two-one."

The linguistic and anthropological data therefore suggest that people are born with only a vague sense

Australia Gumulgal	South America Bakairi	South Africa Bushman
1 urapon	tokale	xa
2 ukasar	ahage	t'oa
3 ukasar urapon	ahage tokale (*or* ahewao)	'quo
4 ukasar-ukasar	ahage ahage	t'oa-t'oa
5 ukasar-ukasar-urapon	ahage ahage tokale	t'oa-t'oa-t'a
6 ukasar-ukasar-ukasar	ahage ahage akage	t'oa-t'oa-t'oa[3]

of numbers, perhaps limited to differentiating groups of up to three objects. Interestingly, the notion that "three" was a major hurdle in the evolution of counting, coincides with the results of studies on child number acquisition. Some developmental psychologists claim that pre-schoolers can recognize sets of one or two objects but also refer to larger groups as "many."[4] Therefore, counting "one, two, many" may be the innate capacity granted to humans for handling plurality.

It is interesting to realize that modern languages such as English have numerical expressions equivalent to "one, two, many"; for example, "monogamous," "bigamous," and "polygamous"; or "monochrome," "bichrome," and "polychrome." These show that, even today, in many instances people do not feel compelled to specify a number beyond two. Furthermore, there are a multitude of words expressing "many" such as herd, flock, crowd, heap, bunch, school, forest, orchestra, polyglot, zillions, and so on.

ONE-TO-ONE CORRESPONDENCE

Societies like that of the Weddas obviously functioned perfectly successfully without a number system. As a matter of fact, individuals from those cultures "counted" as much as necessary for coping with the necessities of everyday life: They counted in one-to-one correspondence. For instance, according to Menninger, when a Wedda wished to count coconuts, he collected a heap of sticks. To each coconut he assigned a stick: one nut = one stick. For each stick added he counted "and one more" until all the coconuts were tallied. Then, he merely pointed to his pile of sticks and said "that many."[5] The example of the Weddas is enlightening on two accounts. First, it exemplifies that counting in one-to-one correspondence is a simple and most basic way of counting which does not require a number system. Second, it demonstrates that in some groups counting did not consist of finding out how many items there were in a set but, rather, was a practical means of comparing or verifying a collection.

Here again, the Weddas were not singular; the use of sticks, pebbles, shells, grain, beans, or tallies as counters to keep track of number of things is a common phenomenon throughout the world.[6] This may suggest that, like "one, two, many," one-to-one correspondence is a universal way of manipulating collections.

CONCRETE COUNTING

Counting beyond three was achieved at a different pace and in different ways in various societies, giving rise to multiple systems of counting. I will not deal with systems that used parts of the body as metaphors to symbolize numbers, such as is still practiced in New Guinea. For example, the Paiela count to 28 by pointing to fingers, wrist, shoulder, head, nose, and so on to express particular numbers.[7] I will also not expand on counting by finger clicking as among the Ziba tribes of Africa, because, as I will show later, these various systems seem not to have been practiced in the ancient Near East.[8] Instead, I will focus on "concrete counting," which may bring new insights on the token system. Concrete counting means that, in some cultures, the number words to render "one," "two," "three," etc. were tied to concrete objects, resulting in sets of number words, or numerations, differing according to whether, for instance, men, canoes, or coconuts were being counted. Menniger cites the case of the Fiji Islanders, who call ten boats *bola* and ten coconuts *boro*.[9] Earlier, Franz Boas had reported about the Tsimshians of British Columbia, who had different sets of numbers to count men, canoes, long objects, flat objects, round objects or time, measures, and a seventh numeration for still other items (table 7).[10] The Tsimshians, for example, referred to three men as *gulal,* three canoes *galtskantk,* three trees *galtskan,* three garments *guant,* three gourds *gutle,* and three units of grain *guleont.* Gilyak, a Mongolian language, has no fewer than twenty-four classes of numbers. Gilyak speakers refer to "two eyes" as *merax;* two berries *mik,* two boots *min,* etc.[11] In this case, like that of the Tsimshians, the different sets of numerals are not totally unrelated but seem to constitute only modifications of the same root forms. The complexity of concrete counting could be compounded by the fact that each numeration could have a different base. Jack Goody relates that when he asked his LoDagaa (North-

Number	Men	Canoes	Long Objects	Flat Objects	Round Objects	Measures	Counting
1	k'al	k'amaet	k'awutskan	gak	g'erel	k'al	gyak
2	t'epqadal	g'alpeeltk	gaopskan	t'epqat	goupel	gulbel	t'epqat
3	gulal	galtskantk	galtskan	guant	gutle	guleont	guant
4	tqalpqdal	tqalpqsk	tqaapskan	tqalpq	tqalpq	tqalpqalont	tqalpq
5	kcenecal	kctoonsk	k'etoentskan	kctonc	kctonc	kctonsilont	kctonc
6	k'aldal	k'altk	k'aoltskan	k'alt	k'alt	k'aldelont	k'alt
7	t'epqaldal	t'epqaltk	t'epqaltskan	t'epqalt	t'epqalt	t'epqaldelont	t'epqalt
8	yuktleadal	yuktaltk	ek'tlaedskan	yuktalt	yuktalt	yuktaldelont	guandalt
9	kctemacal	kctemack	kctemaetskan	kctemac	kctemac	kctemasilont	kctemac
10	kpal	gy'apsk	kpeetskan	gy'ap	kpeel	kpeont	gy'ap

Seven numerations used by the Tsimshians of British Columbia, according to L. L. Conant, *The Number Concept* (New York: MacMillan, 1896). From Franz Boas, "Fifth Report on the Northwestern Tribes of Canada." *Proceedings of the British Association for the Advancement of Science,* 1889, p. 881.

ern Ghana) informant to count for him, the answer was "count what?" because, in that culture, counting cows was different from counting cowries.[12]

The examples of the Tsimshians, the Gilyaks, and the LoDagaas are not unique. In fact, the use of various numerations to count different items is widespread among Paleo-European, Paleo-Asiatic, Afrasian, and Micronesian languages.[13] Numerical classifiers determine the type of item counted in many tongues, for example, in Japanese, Aztec, and the Mayan family of languages.[14] In Tzeltal, a Mayan language of Mexico, "two men" is translated by a formula equivalent to "two [persons of the human class] men."[15]

Using different number words in specific situations is also common in Indo-European languages. English, for example, has a rich vocabulary to express "two," including expressions such as "a couple," "a brace," and "a pair" that are not interchangeable. "A brace of shoes" is incorrect, but "a brace of pheasants" and "a couple of horses" are right. English also yields concrete numbers, such as duet, trio, quartet, or twins, triplets, quadruplets. Like the special numerations of concrete counting, "trio" merges a concept of number (three) and that of the item counted (for example, musicians), with no way of separating them. Also, like the concrete numerations, those numerical expressions stop at a relatively low number, being followed by a word indicating "many." We say a quartet, a quintet, and an orchestra, dyad, triad, or myriad, triangle, quadrangle, . . . decagon, and polygon. It is well understood, however, that we do not use these terms for counting but that numerical classifiers and concrete numbers are so used.

The tendency of counting separately items of different categories corroborates studies on child number acquisition. According to developmental psychologists, when toddlers are asked to count a number of pencils, they readily report the number of blue or red pencils but must be coaxed into finding the total.[16] This leads some to conclude that children are better at counting arrays composed of homogeneous elements and that concrete counting is a common step toward grasping the concept of abstract numbers.

Unfortunately, there is little or no information on archaic reckoning devices used by societies that counted concretely. The reason may be that the artifacts were often made of perishable material, such as string, straw, or wood, and, consequently, they fell into disuse and vanished or were drastically transformed with the introduction of abstract counting. The *quipus* of Inca Peru are among the preliterate counting devices that may have originated from a tradition of concrete counting. According to the ancient chroniclers, they were made of strands of fibers of various colors meant to count different things; for example, red stood for soldiers, yellow for gold, white for silver, and green for cereals.[17] When the *quipus* were first reported in the literature, however, they were apparently already adapted to abstract counting.

Concrete counting perhaps explains why certain

cultures used altogether different implements to count different items. For instance, in Angola, special types of accounts were kept with a variety of *quipus* and in the Ryuku Islands, between Japan and Taiwan, labor, pawn shop deposits, agricultural products, woven materials, and wood were each accounted for with different types of knotted strings.[18]

ABSTRACT COUNTING

The cumbersome way of handling data with concrete counting highlights the advantages of our own system of computing. Our numbers 1, 2, 3 express the concepts of oneness, twoness, threeness as abstract entities divorced from any particular concrete entities. As a result, 1, 2, 3 are universally applicable. We can count men, canoes, and trees with the same numbers. In fact, we can count things that do not exist, such as ghosts and unicorns, which was not feasible with concrete counting. We can count for the sake of counting without any reference to any particular item.

Whereas concrete counting probably did not allow counting beyond a score of objects, there is no limit to abstract counting. We could count all the stars of the universe and all the grains of sand on the beach and, furthermore, we could add the total number of stars to that of sand particles. This was altogether impossible with concrete counting, which was confined to handling data of only one kind at a time: Triplets cannot be added to trios. Abstract counting thus marks the beginning of arithmetic and the point of departure of modern mathematics.

Historians of mathematics claim that our way of counting is the result of a long evolution. It is the view of Wilder and others that abstract counting was preceded by stages of counting of increasing levels of abstraction, including reckoning in one-to-one correspondence without a number system and concrete counting.[19] According to Bertrand Russell, "It . . . required many ages to discover that a brace of pheasants and a couple of days were both instances of the number 2."[20]

The Sumerian Philological Evidence

What do we know about counting in the ancient Near East? Is there any evidence for one-to-one correspondence or concrete counting? The question is not easy to answer because the absence of writing precludes the possibility of ever knowing the number words used in pre- and protohistory.

The earliest number words known in the Near East are those written by the Sumerians on clay tablets. Those instances are rare because there are exceedingly few tablets spelling out number words.[21] The Sumerian numerals were, as a rule, not shown phonetically but logographically (as we normally write 1, 2, 3 and not "one," "two," "three"). The main sources for identifying Sumerian number words are a school tablet from Ebla and the lexical texts, known as *Proto Ea, Aa,* and *Ea,* dated from the Old Babylonian period, 2000 to 1600 B.C. and later.[22] The Babylonian texts do not feature, systematically, complete series of numerals. Instead, the signs and their corresponding pronunciation are scattered at different points in the documents. As a result, as Marvin A. Powell puts it, the reconstruction of Sumerian numerals is "one of the thorniest problems which the Sumerologist faces."[23]

Although some Sumerian number words remain unknown, there is no possible doubt that the Sumerians of the third millennium B.C. counted abstractly just the way we do. The number words for counting from 1 to 10, held to have been most widely used in third-millennium Sumer, are reconstructed as follows:[24]

1.	aš/diš	6.	āš
2.	min	7.	imin
3.	eš	8.	ussu
4.	limmu	9.	ilimmu
5.	iā	10.	u

Igor M. Diakonoff makes a case that several other numerations are attested in various texts. Some consist in the mere modification of the numeration presented above by the addition of suffixes (-u, -a) or a copula (am).[25] Other numerations, seemingly more archaic, are based on a three-count system. Their usage is not always clear. Diakonoff remarks, however, that "be" is used in the counting of days.[26]

1.	merga	= "one"
2.	taka	= "two" (not attested)
3.	peš	= "three"
4.	pešbala	= "three-passed"
5.	pešbalage	= "three-passed-one"
6.	pešbalagege	= "three-passed-one-one"
7.	pešpešge	= "three-three-one"[27]

1.	ge	= "one"
2.	dah	= "two"
3.	PEŠ	= "three"
4.	PEŠ-ge	= "three + one"
5.	PEŠ-bala-gi$_4$	= "three-passed-one"
6.	PEŠ-bala-gi$_4$-gi$_4$	= "three-passed-one-one"
7.	PEŠ-PEŠ-gi$_4$	= "three-three-one"

1.	be	= "one"
2.	be-be	= "one-one"
3.	PEŠ	= "three"
4.	PEŠ-be	= "three-one"
5.	PEŠ-be-be	= "three-one-one"
6.	PEŠ-PEŠ	= "three-three"
7.	PEŠ-PEŠ-be	= "three-three-one"
12.	PEŠ-PEŠ-PEŠ-PEŠ	= "three-three-three-three"[28]

ABSENCE OF EVIDENCE FOR BODY COUNTING

The first important consideration concerning the Sumerian number words is the fact that they reveal no vestige of body counting. For example, the number words for the first five digits seem etymologically unrelated to the Sumerian words for "fingers" or "hand."[29] There is no indication, therefore, that body counting was the point of departure for numeration in the ancient Near East.[30]

TERNARY NUMERATION SYSTEMS

According to Diakonoff, the three-count systems point out that, as in other societies, "three" had been a major hurdle to overcome in ancient Mesopotamian numerations.[31] This is further supported by the fact that in the main Sumerian numeration, /eš/ = "three" is the same as /eš/ the plural morpheme.[32] This may suggest that Sumerian numbers still reflected a former, probably very distant, tradition of counting to a maximum of "three," which also meant "many."

MULTIPLICITY OF NUMBER WORDS

Marvin A. Powell has noted the multiplicity of expressions for rendering "one," "two," and "three." He remarks that lexical texts list seven Sumerian equivalents to the Akkadian *ištēn* = one. These numbers are as follows: "aš," "santak3," "diš," "deli," "be," "giš," and "ge".[33] There are also several forms for "2," "min" and "man," "taka," "dah," and "be-be," and two forms for "3," "eš" and "peš." Powell suggests that the different number of words attested in Sumerian texts may reflect several dialects.[34]

On the other hand, Diakonoff views the multiplicity of number words in Sumerian as possible evidence for a former tradition of concrete counting. The Russian Sumerologist compares the different forms of number words based on the addition of /-u/ and /-a/ as suffixes or the copula /-am/ to the Gilyaks' concrete numerations and proposes that concrete counting may have preceded abstract counting in Mesopotamia.[35]

Diakonoff's argument is supported by the fact that in Sumer, the earlier the texts, the more complex the numerical systems they exhibit.[36] Indeed, as A. A. Vaiman has discussed, the fourth-millennium Uruk tablets used different numeral sequences for recording area, weight, volume, or capacity measures or even quantities of wheat, barley, domesticated animals, slaves, and time.[37] Following his lead, Peter Damerow and Robert K. Englund have identified in the archaic texts of Uruk ten different systems of number signs, some using ten as a base and others using six.[38] The fact that quantities of different commodities were recorded with different signs can hardly be interpreted as denoting the pronunciations of various dialects. Furthermore, Vaiman, and after him Jöran Friberg, demonstrated that the multiplicity of signs for recording different quantities of goods was a phenomenon not unique to Sumer but was also attested in Proto-Elamite.[39] This suggests that in the Near East abstract counting may have been preceded by an archaic concrete counting system, using different numerations to count different items.

The third-millennium cuneiform texts leave no doubt of the fact that the Sumerians had developed a most elaborate sexagesimal system of counting. There is also no doubt that their arithmetic was based on abstract counting. However, the Sumerian language may demonstrate the vestiges of archaic counting systems used in former times. Some number words may point out that in a remote past some ancestors of the Sumerians counted "one, two, many." Other numerical expressions suggest that in the Near East, as in other parts of the world, concrete counting preceded the invention of abstract counting. The fact that the Sumerians used three-count systems or had relics of concrete numerations in their number systems does not imply, in any way, that they were "primitive." The preservation of ancient numerical terms in their language is comparable to the French numbers "quatre-vingt" (four-twenty), "quatre-vingt-dix" (four-twenty-ten), which are the relics of a long-forgotten base twenty.

The Near Eastern Archaeological Data

The unique sequence of reckoning devices produced by Near Eastern archaeological sites of 15,000 to 3000 B.C. provides valuable information on how counting evolved. This seems to confirm that one-to-one correspondence and concrete counting preceded the use of abstract counting in Southwest Asia.

THE PALEOLITHIC TALLIES

The Paleolithic bone tallies displaying series of notches used in the Near East about 15,000 to 10,000 B.C. (figs. 99 and 100) appear to illustrate the simplest form of counting: one-to-one correspondence, with no concept of numbers. That is to say, each mark tallied probably represented one unit of a collection. For example, according to Marshack's hypothesis, each notch may have translated to one sighting of the moon.[40] According to the ethnographic and linguistic data presented above, presumably, the Stone Age tallies were not based on our own system of abstract counting but instead consisted only of the repeated addition of one unit with no precise idea of numbers. Accordingly, the earliest artifacts interpreted as reckoning devices suggest that the Paleolithic cultures of the Near East counted in one-to-one correspondence, as was the case for numerous other preliterate societies.

The proposition that counting in one-to-one correspondence and the ability to perceive "one, two, many" is a common denominator to all humans casts a new light on counting in early societies. Neither the Paleolithic and Mesolithic humans who carved bone tallies nor the Weddas of Sri Lanka can be held as childlike or as having an incomplete logic. Instead, counting in one-to-one correspondence meant using, to the fullest extent, their given ability to deal with plurality. Because one-to-one correspondence was perfectly adequate to fulfill the modest needs for accounting of a nonredistributive economy, these cultures were not compelled to devise any new technique of accounting. Of course, counting in one-to-one correspondence did not denote a difference in brain capacity between Paleolithic and modern humans. It is well established that the human brain has not evolved since the appearance of *Homo sapiens-sapiens* about seventy thousand years ago.[41] The cave dwellers of Ksar Akil, Jiita, Ain Mallaha, and Hayonim, therefore, would have had the same aptitude as we have for grasping the idea of abstract numbers had they been confronted with it. These people had the same capability as we have to develop more sophisticated systems of counting, but their way of life, based on hunting and gathering, did not challenge them to do so.

TOKENS

Compared to the earlier tallies, the token system provided new ways of handling data that seem indicative of a second stage of counting. The innovations were twofold: cardinality and object specificity. On the other hand, however, the token system perpetuated the principle of one-to-one correspondence.

Cardinality

The most significant change that seems attested in the token system is cardinality—the ability to assign arbitrary tags, such as number words, to each item of a collection, with the final number word of the series representing the number of the set. For example, presumably, *seven* incised ovoids held in the Uruk envelope W20987.7 stood "*seven* jars of oil (fig. 67)." The hypothesis that from the beginning of the token system groups of counters were no longer the mere repetition of one unit ("and one more") but expressed a cardinal number is based on my argument that certain tokens stood for sets ($x = n$). I posit, for example, that tetrahedrons, which occur in two distinct subtypes "small" and "large" (type 5: 1 and 2), represented two different units of the same commodity (fig. 66).[42] Accordingly, if my interpretation of the tetrahedron as a unit of work (as discussed in Chapter 6) is correct, the two subtypes could indicate, respectively, different time units such as "one day" and "one week's work," unless they referred to numbers of workmen, such as "one man" and "a gang."[43]

The lenticular disk may be a second example of a token standing for a set. If, as I postulate, the cylinder and the lenticular disk (types 4: 1 and 3: 3) are the antecedents of units of the Sumerian sheep numeration, 1 cylinder = 1 animal and 1 lenticular disk = 10 animals, it is likely that these two counters represented, from their beginning in the eighth millennium, 1 cylinder = 1 animal and 1 lenticular disk = a given number of animals, a flock. The presence of these two counters among the earliest token assemblages would provide the evidence that accounting with tokens implied grasping the notion of sets. According to this premise, during the Neolithic, counting animals no longer consisted of adding "and one more," but one cylinder stood for "1 animal," two cylinders for "2 animals," three cylinders for "3 animals," and so on. It will never be possible to know when the lenticular disk took the precise value of "10 animals." Presumably, however, it was so in the late fourth millennium B.C. and, accordingly, the Susa envelope Sb 1940 containing 3 cylinders and 3 lenticular disks can be tentatively translated as "33 animals" (fig. 72). Cardinality resulted, therefore, in a considerable economy of notation since 33 sheep could be indicated by 6 tokens instead of 33.

On the other hand, I propose to view the cone, sphere, and large cone, standing for three different measures of grain, as entirely nonmathematical entities. I consider that they represented containers in which the goods were traditionally handled, comparable to our measures "a pitcher of beer" or "a carafe of wine." The vessels probably became standardized metrological units not before the late Uruk period or the early historic period, when their ratio was as shown in Chapter 6.[44] As Marvin A. Powell emphasized it, "A system of numeration is an integral part of a language. It is not a mathematical phenomenon."[45]

One-to-One Correspondence

The token system inherited from the past the archaic principle of one-to-one correspondence. The evidence that tokens were used in one-to-one correspondence during their entire duration is unambiguously presented by envelopes holding counters of a single subtype repeated several times. Among these, for example, W20987.7 from Uruk (fig. 67) and MII-134 from Habuba Kabira held, respectively, seven and five incised ovoids (fig. 74) and Sb 4328 from Susa yielded five spheres.

Other envelopes, such as Sb 1940, clearly illustrate that tokens standing for sets were also used in one-to-one correspondence (fig. 72). As stated above, the envelope yields an account of 33 animals, shown by 3 disks and 3 cylinders as follows:

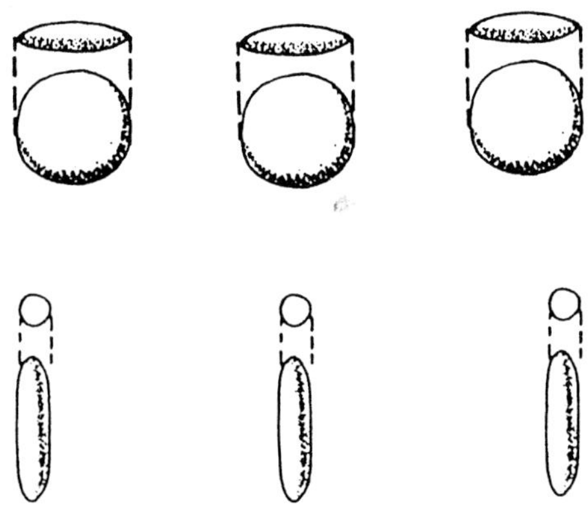

or, literally, 10 animals + 10 animals + 10 animals + 1 animal + 1 animal + 1 animal.

The content of these envelopes demonstrates that the Uruk VI accountants indicated quantities (how many) in a way radically different from ours. They did not show, as we do, "5" by a numeral. Instead, "5 jars of oil" were translated by five tokens, each standing for "1 jar of oil," as illustrated here.

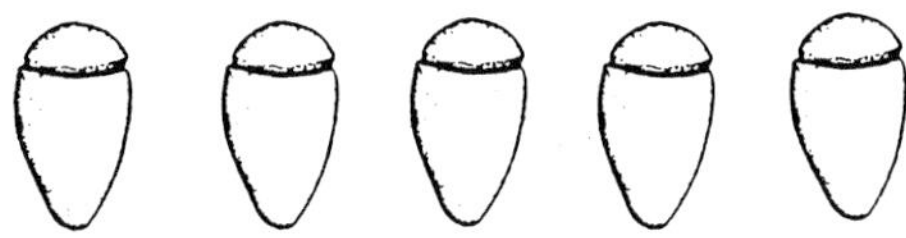

Literally, the set of tokens meant "jar of oil, jar of oil, jar of oil, jar of oil, jar of oil." The token system had no symbols for abstract numbers such as "5."

Object Specificity

Although the notion of sets was seemingly acquired, counting with tokens still differed fundamentally from abstract counting. There were no counters standing for abstract numbers such as 1, 2, 3 applicable to a wide range of goods. Instead, the token system required particular counters to deal with each type of commodity. Ovoids were used to count jars of oil and spheres to count measures of grain; vice-versa, jars of oil could only be counted with ovoids and measures of grain with spheres.

The fact that tokens varied with each commodity counted suggests that they reflected a conceptual level at which only units of the same kind could be counted together. In other words, the tokens seem to be conceived for manipulating data with a system of concrete counting. Like concrete numerations, the tokens fused together the concept of number and that of the item counted—an ovoid stood for "1" and "jar of oil" without any possible way of abstracting the two concepts. The tokens differed from concrete numbers, however, in denoting the number of units in one-to-one correspondence. As discussed above, only in some instances, tokens, like the lenticular disk, stood for a collection, "a flock" (10? animals).

The Absence of Tokens Expressing Abstract Numbers

Concrete counting provides the key to understanding the greatest peculiarity of the token system, namely, the multiplicity of counters. Put differently, if we had to imagine what kind of counters would best suit concrete counting, we would have to come up with a system similar to that of the tokens, with multiple counters to count each particular category of goods. Previous attempts at assigning numerical values to particular tokens fail to jibe with the evidence. Alain le Brun and François Vallat, who assumed that the token system relied upon our own system of abstract counting, proposed the following translations: cylinder 1; sphere 10; disk 100; cone 60, 600, or 1,000; punched cone 300; and punched sphere 36,000.[46] Their interpretation, however, leaves the remaining some four hundred subtypes of complex counters without explanation.

Following Le Brun and Vallat, Stephen J. Lieberman proposed that the plain tokens were counters, whereas the complex ones were "small clay objects of unknown use."[47] As discussed in Chapter 1, the argument that plain and complex tokens did not belong to the same reckoning device does not correspond to the evidence. Both are found together in the same sites, the same levels, and the same hoards. Envelopes such as MII-134 from Habuba Kabira (fig. 74) and W20987.7 (fig. 67) held complex tokens (incised ovoids). Why would complex tokens be enclosed in envelopes if they were not used as counters?

Pierre Amiet's views that lines and dots marked on tokens were numerical notations must also be dismissed.[48] There is no evidence that, for instance, the ovoid bearing six punctations meant "six jars of oil" (type 6: 22). Instead, the envelopes of Uruk and Habuba Kabira, which held incised ovoids, clearly demonstrate that the number of jars of oil was shown by repeating the ovoids in one-to-one correspondence and not by means of markings. Impressed signs further demonstrate the point. Consider, for instance, a tablet from Susa (Sb 1975 bis; fig. 85) that shows four impressions of the triangular token with one incised line (type 8: 11). If Amiet's interpretation was correct, the notation would consist of a triangle with four lines. The fact that the triangle was repeated four times (but not the marking) indicates that markings referred to the quality of a commodity, not the number.

The token system, which coincided with agriculture, the storage of goods, and an economy of redistribution, suggests that such innovations brought pressure for counting beyond three. Moreover, the multiplicity of counters indicates that the first farmers mastered the notion of sets or cardinality but counted concretely. In other words, they had no conception of numbers existing independently of measures of grain and animals that could be applied to either without reference to the other. The token system supports the linguistic data, therefore, that concrete counting preceded abstract counting in the prehistoric Near East.

In fact, the tokens may be the sole example of a reckoning device conceived for the unique purpose of concrete counting. As was discussed above, all other archaic devices that could conceivably have been used with a system of concrete counting, such as the Peruvian *quipus,* were modified to suit abstract counting. The token system was preserved in its integrity, first, because instead of being adjusted to abstract counting it was altogether replaced by a new form of record keeping—writing—and second, the clay counters could survive thousands of years in the Near Eastern mounds.

WRITING

The earliest impressed signs drawn on envelopes and tablets still stood for concrete units of goods, but the first pictographic tablets feature numerals. These signs expressing abstract numbers indicate a new threshold in counting. Abstract counting gave rise to a new system of data storage and communication with the development of numerals and pictography.

Impressed Markings on Envelopes and Tablets

When tokens were replaced by their images impressed on the surface of an envelope or a tablet, the resulting signs were already "more abstract" than the previous clay counters. Compared to three-dimensional clay counters, the two-dimensional markings represented commodities in greater abstraction since they could no longer be grasped in the hand and manipulated (fig. 113). The alignment of markings on the face of a tablet also contributed to decontextualizing the data.

Semantically, however, the impressed markings were identical to tokens: Each ideogram still fused together

113. Impressed tablet, Godin Tepe (Gd. 73-292), Iran. Courtesy T. Cuyler Young, Jr.

the concepts of nature/quantity (i.e., measure of oil) and the number 1. For example, the incised ovoids impressed on MII-134 of Habuba Kabira (fig. 74) or the incised triangles shown on Sb 1975 bis of Susa indicated respectively "1 measure of oil" and "1 unit of ?" in one-to-one correspondence (fig. 85). The impressed envelopes and tablets illustrate, therefore, that the Uruk VI notations still did not express abstract numbers but concrete quantities of goods.

The First Numerals

The accountants of Uruk IVa about 3100 B.C. invented the first numerals—signs encoding the concept of oneness, twoness, threeness, abstracted from any particular entity. This was not a small feat, since numerals are deemed to express some of the most abstract thoughts our minds are able to conceive. After all, "two" does not exist in nature, but only groups of two concrete items, such as two fingers, two people, two sheep, two fruits, two leaves, or even sets of heterogeneous items such as one fruit + one leaf, and so on. "Two" is the abstraction of the quality of twoness shared by such sets.

The accountants of Uruk IVa can be credited with creating numerals and by doing so revolutionizing accounting and data manipulation. In fact, the Uruk IVa accountants devised two types of signs: *numerals* (symbols encoding abstract numbers) and *pictographs* (expressing commodities). Each type of sign was traced in a different technique—pictographs were *incised*, whereas numerals were *impressed*, clearly standing out from the text. For example, a tablet from Uruk features two accounts of "5 sheep" shown by the pictograph for "sheep" (a circle with a cross) and "5" appearing as five impressed wedges (fig. 114). The notion of number was finally dissociated from that of commodity.

The numerals of the Uruk IVa tablets constitute the first evidence for the use of abstract counting and the creation of modern arithmetic. The invention of numerals is of importance equal to or greater than that of zero. Even if the notion of "nothing" was well understood by the Babylonians, the creation of a sign "0" in India about 700 B.C. changed the course of mathematics. The first numerals can also be compared to the invention of equations such as $x = (a + b)$. Like zero and the first algebraic equation, numerals were probably invented by one individual whose idea caught on because it dealt with data more efficiently. Numerals, zero, and algebraic equations represent stages of abstraction which enabled humans to manipulate and process a greater volume of information and gain a new grasp of reality. Of course, we will never know where, when, how, and by whom abstract counting was invented, but, presumably, the event coincided with the change from tokens to writing since it would seem unlikely that people would use a counting device that had become obsolete. It is also likely that the invention of abstract counting took place in Mesopotamia, rather than Syria or Iran, since pictographic writing lagged behind in the latter regions, with the only (Sumerian) pictographic tablet outside Mesopotamia being that from Godin Tepe (Gd.73.295; fig. 115).[49]

114. Tablet showing accounts of sheep, Uruk, Iraq. Courtesy Vorderasiatisches Museum, Staatliche Museen zu Berlin.

115. Incised tablet showing an account of thirty-three jars of oil (?), Godin Tepe (Gd. 73-295), Iran. Courtesy T. Cuyler Young, Jr.

The first numerals were not symbols specifically created for representing abstract numbers. Instead, they were the impressed signs, formerly indicating units of goods, such as measures of grain, endowed with a new numerical value. The wedge, which originally meant a small quantity of grain, now stood for 1; the circle, which represented a larger quantity of grain, was 10; the large wedge, punched wedge, and large circle were greater numbers.

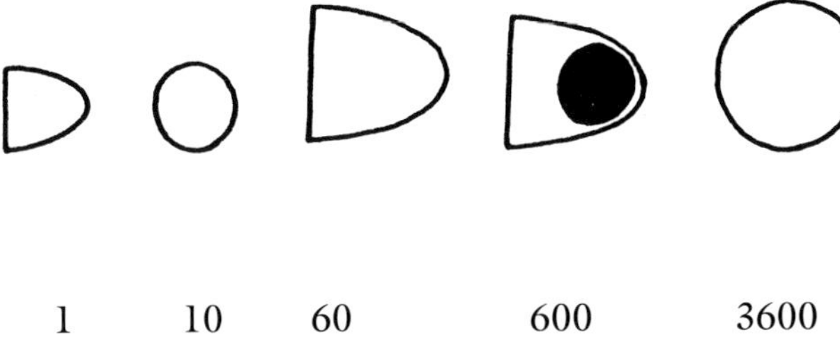

There is yet another possible alternative, as follows. The impressed units of animal numeration could also have served as numerals: the long wedge standing for 1 and the circular marking, corresponding to the former lenticular disk, for 10. In this case, the animal numeration would have produced two units of the Sumerian arithmetical system: 1 and 10. This, in turn, could explain the mixed decimal-sexagesimal Sumerian counting system, which has puzzled many. For example, Friberg notes that, on a same tablet, the circular sign may stand alternatively in the relation 1 to 6 or 1 to 10, depending upon what is being counted.[50] It could be

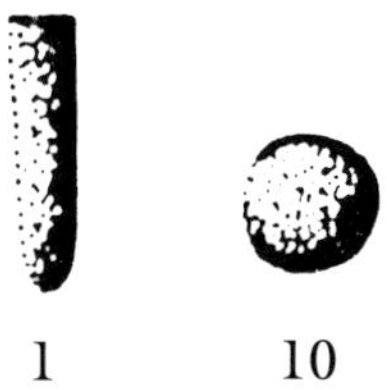

that "10" derived from the unit of animal numeration (lenticular disk) and "6" from the former unit of grain metrology (sphere). Animals would have been counted by ten, probably using the fingers. On the other hand, 60 was particularly convenient for grain metrology, having the unique property of being divisible by 1, 2, 3, 4, 5, 6, 10, 12, 15 etc. . . .[51] In either case, the preponderant role of plain tokens to count measures of grain (and domesticated animals?) in prehistory was perpetuated by the preponderant role of numerals in historic times.

In fact, the impressed signs that came to represent numerals never lost their primary meaning. Instead, according to the context, they had either an abstract or a concrete value. For example, the wedge preceding a pictograph was read "1" (figs. 114 and 115), but alone it stood for a measure of grain (fig. 113). This proved confusing to Sumerian accountants, who eventually eliminated the ambiguity by introducing a pictograph in the shape of an ear of grain (ATU 111/ZATU 511).

Abstract numbers, therefore, derived from the plain cones, spheres (cylinders and lenticular disks?) that were the most ancient tokens. The reason why these particular symbols became the first numerals can only be hypothesized. David E. Smith has remarked that in a number of societies the words for expressing numbers derived from concrete numerations of particularly frequent use. He cites languages that expressed "one, two, three" by number words that meant literally "one grain, two grains, three grains" or "one stone, two stones, three stones" or, like the Niues of the southern Pacific, "one fruit, two fruit, three fruit."[52] It may be argued, therefore, that the first Sumerian abstract numbers derived from the grain and animal numerations because they were the most commonly used in Mesopotamia. Grain, in particular, was not only the main staple but also the most usual means of exchange. Furthermore, grain metrology constituted a unique gamut of signs of increasing magnitude that could be easily converted to signify units of abstract counting such as 1, 6(?), 10, 60, 180.

The invention of numerals made a breach in but did not put an end to the age-old principle of one-to-one correspondence. It was a major break with the past that pictographs encoding commodities were no longer repeated as many times as the number of units involved. One-to-one correspondence continued governing the use of numerals, however. "Nine" was represented by nine wedges, fifty by five circles, and so on. For instance, the tablet of Godin Tepe Gd.73.295 (fig. 115) bearing the notation "33 jars of oil" displayed a single pictograph standing for "jar of oil" and expressed "33" by three impressed circles (10 + 10 + 10) and three wedges (1 + 1 + 1). This archaism, in turn, was perpetuated for centuries in the Sumero-Babylonian arithmetical system. In fact, one-to-one correspondence persisted in all numbering systems, including those of Greece and Rome, until the invention of the so-called arabic numerals in India about 700 B.C.

Pictographic and Phonetic Writing

It was not by chance that the invention of pictography and phonetic writing coincided with that of numerals; instead, both were the result of abstract counting. The abstraction of the concept of quantity (how many) from that of quality, which merged inextricably in the token prototypes, made possible the beginning of writing. Once dissociated from any notion of number, the pictographs could evolve in their own separate way. The symbols formerly used for keeping accounts of goods could expand to communicate any subjects of human endeavor. As a result, items such as "the head of a man" or "mouth" that never had a token were expressed by a picture. True pictography, that is to say, concepts represented by their images, thus was the outcome of abstract counting.

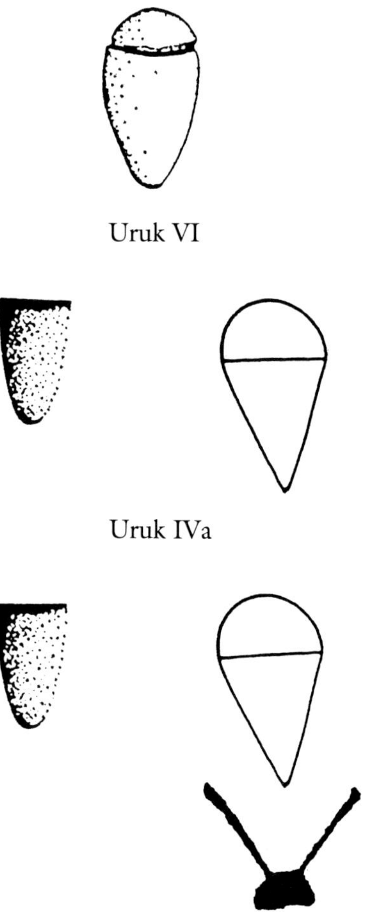

Uruk VI

Uruk IVa

Uruk III

After pictography, writing crossed several new thresholds about 3000 B.C. in the Uruk III period. The abstraction of quantity (how much) followed that of number (how many). Note, for example, that in Uruk VI it took *one* token to indicate one jar of oil, or presumably, "one *sila* of oil." In Uruk IVa, the same was written with *two* signs, namely, "1" and the pictograph "*sila* of oil." In Uruk III, however, each notion "1," "*sila*," "oil" was expressed separately, requiring a sequence of *three* signs.

Finally, symbols could function phonetically, representing not objects but, in particular cases, sounds. The incentive to resort to phonetics was seemingly prompted by new administrative requirements for recording the name of donors/recipients of goods on the tablets. Individuals' names were transcribed by symbols meant to be read phonetically as a rebus. The proper name Enlil Ti, "Enlil [Gives] Life," was rendered by two pictographs "god" (a star) and "life" (an arrow).[53] This was the point of departure for a syllabary—symbols standing not for commodities or concepts but simply for the sounds they brought to mind. Pictography led to a syllabary, which was the true takeoff of writing.

IN THE ANCIENT Near East writing emerged from a counting device. It is the main outcome of the invention of abstract counting. Tallying in one-to-one correspondence was superseded about 8000 B.C. by tokens of many shapes suited for concrete counting. Finally, writing emerged when abstract counting dissociated the concept of numbers from that of the commodity accounted. Writing resulted from a new way of handling data with an unprecedented abstraction.

Tallying in one-to-one correspondence coincided with a way of life and an economy based on hunting and gathering. Concrete counting with tokens was related to the rise of agriculture and an economy of redistribution. Complex tokens, envelopes, and impressed tablets were the consequences of urban development, the rise of industry, and the formation of the state. Pictographic and phonetic writing, about 3100 to 3000 B.C., however, seems independent of any socioeconomic event. It was the outcome of a new threshold in cognitive development: abstract counting.

CONCLUSIONS: TOKENS, THEIR ROLE IN PREHISTORY AND THEIR CONTRIBUTION TO ARCHAEOLOGY

Writing appeared in the history of humanity some three or four thousand years before the beginning of our era, at a time when humanity had already made its most essential and fundamental discoveries . . . agriculture, the domestication of animals, pottery-making, weaving—a whole range of processes which were to allow human beings to stop living from day to day as they had done in paleolithic times, when they depended on hunting or the gathering of fruit, and to accumulate. . . . We must never lose sight of the fact that certain essential forms of progress, perhaps the most essential ever achieved by humanity, were accomplished without the help of writing.

—Claude Lévi-Strauss[1]

SMALL CLAY TOKENS of multiple shapes such as cones, spheres, disks, cylinders, and tetrahedrons swept across the Near East on the coattails of agriculture, starting about 8000 B.C. They remained remarkably the same for five thousand years. Wherever they were adopted, the tokens preserved the same character: Regional variations are practically unknown. The shape, size, and manufacture of the objects varied little until the age of cities. Coinciding with the urban period, a second phase of the token system was initiated, characterized by complex tokens with a greater repertory of shapes and markings. Finally, the tokens reverted to a few plain shapes after the appearance of writing.

The tokens were mundane counters dealing with food and other basic commodities of daily life, but they played a major role in the societies that adopted them. They were used to manage goods and affected the economy; they were an instrument of power and created new social patterns; they served for data manipulation and changed the mode of thought; they were among the first ceramic objects and played a role in technology. Foremost, the tokens were a counting and record-keeping device and were the watershed of mathematics and communication.

Because they were minuscule, colorless, innocuous-looking artifacts, tokens have been mostly ignored, though they are a unique source of information on major aspects of culture during five thousand years of Near Eastern prehistory, including two critical periods: the beginnings of agriculture and cities. They were the precursor of writing and document communication in prehistory. They were the precursor of numerals and shed light on the origin of mathematics. Better than any other archaeological material, tokens illustrate vividly the dynamic interconnections between technology, cognitive skills, economy, mathematics, communication, and social structure in prehistory. They reveal how increased abstraction enhanced communication and the art of counting, resulting in a more efficient economy and a tighter control of resources, finally fostering more powerful social institutions that, in turn, in a spiral effect, promoted abstract thinking.

Technology

Tokens are among the earliest, if not the first, clay artifacts in the Near East. The choice of clay for modeling tokens had significant consequences for the evolution of communication. It also marks the beginning of a technology that became of paramount importance for the process of civilization.

The forms that emerged spontaneously when rolling a small lump of clay between the palms of the hand or pinching with the fingertips were pellets of multiple shapes: spheres, disks, cylinders, ovoids, cones, tetrahedrons, triangles, quadrangles, parabolas, and so on. These simple and striking geometric shapes were key to the creation of a code. They were ideal symbols, easy to recognize, differentiate, and remember, and they could carry specific meanings. The malleability of clay was also key to the development of a code. Clay pellets could be modeled into an infinity of distinct forms to create as many new symbols as necessary; they could be marked with lines and punctuations to convey additional information. Lastly, clay was key to the diffusion of the system because it was a cheap material, common in the Near East. It was available everywhere and required no preparation. It was easy to model with the bare hands, requiring no specialized tool.

Nothing but tokens illustrates better Cyril Smith's idea that humans discovered the properties of materials by doodling and manufacturing small trinkets.[2] Manipulating clay to manufacture the small tokens familiarized the early settlers with a raw material that had not been put to work previously. After tokens, clay was used to make figurines, pottery, and, finally, shelters and granaries, protecting people and harvest against the elements.

The clay tokens were also among the earliest if not the first artifacts of the Near East to be fired into ceramic. During their five thousand–year existence, the counters provide information on major stages in the mastery of fire. At first the tokens were baked in a campfire, later in ovens, and finally in kilns. A case can be made that experimenting with fire to harden the counters and make them more durable helped people realize the refractory properties of clay. It can be argued that baking tokens led to the invention of ovens and kilns, molds and crucibles that paved the way to metallurgy.

Mathematics

The most significant contribution of the tokens was in the realm of counting. Tokens, used to count measures of grain and animals, were the direct antecedents of the first numerals—the first landmark in the development of mathematics. The invention of mathematical symbols to express 1, 6(?), 10, 60 made possible adding, subtracting, multiplying, and all possible arithmetical operations. Numerals presaged the invention of zero.

The tokens were a primitive system of counters. One of their most awkward features consisted of indicating numbers in one-to-one correspondence: Three ovoids equaled three jars of oil. Also, each category of goods necessitated a special type of counter; for example, jars of oil were counted with ovoids and measures of grain with cones. This was the case because there were no tokens standing for 1, 2, 3 that could be applied to a variety of items. Instead, each token stood for a unit of goods, such as "one jar of oil" or "one measure of grain" or "one ingot of metal." One-to-one correspondence, object specificity, and tying together the notions of the item counted and that of number denote an archaic system of counting called "concrete counting." This way of reckoning made impossible the adding together of units of different goods.

The pictographic tablets that replaced tokens also kept track of goods, but they did so according to a new mode of counting. The tokens dealt with *concrete* counting and the pictographic tablets with *abstract* counting. The pictographic tablets had signs to express 1, 10, 60, 360, as abstract entities, unrelated to any particular goods. These first numerals consisted of *impressed signs* formerly used to indicate measures of grain which from then on carried a new abstract meaning. On the other hand, the goods counted were indicated with *incised pictographs*. The incised pictographs were no longer repeated in one-to-one correspondence since the number of units was shown by numerals.

The tokens constitute a rare source of information on the origin of mathematics. They show that counting evolved over an exceedingly long period and that abstract counting was preceded by a more archaic form of reckoning. The tokens' chronology suggests that the evolution from concrete to abstract counting proceeded as follows:

ca. 8000–3500 B.C.: Counters of multiple shapes indicate a system of concrete counting.

ca. 3500–3100 B.C.: Markings, impressed in one-to-one correspondence on envelopes and tablets and fusing together the notions of product and number, suggest that concrete counting still prevailed.

ca. 3100 B.C. (Uruk IVa): Numerals were invented. They were the first symbols expressing numbers abstractly—independently from the item counted.

ca. 3100–2500 B.C.: Archaic numerations for counting various categories of items still lingered, showing that the transition from concrete to abstract counting lasted over several centuries.

Some will want to argue that the concepts of oneness, twoness, threeness may have been grasped long before the invention of numerals. This is granted. The same was true for the invention of zero. The Babylonians of the second millennium B.C. may well have had the concept of "nothing," but it is the invention of a symbol 0 about 700 B.C. in India that changed the course of mathematics. In the same way, it was the creation of symbols for 1, 2, 3, and so on that was the origin of mathematics. There is no evidence for such numerals before Uruk IVa.

Cognitive Skills

Tokens and clay tablets functioned as an extension of the human brain to collect, manipulate, store, and retrieve data. In turn, processing an increasing volume of data with more complex tokens brought people to think in greater abstraction.

The token system dealt with data in concrete terms. First, each token represented a concrete entity: one unit of goods. Second, the tokens represented plurality as it is experienced perceptually. A set of three jars of oil was shown as it is in reality: one jar of oil plus one jar of oil plus one jar of oil. "Three" is an abstraction and there were no tokens to express such abstractions.

Pictography brought about the abstraction of numbers. The last tokens and the first pictographs of Uruk conveyed the same information, concerning the same goods, for the benefit of the same southern Mesopotamian bureaucracy. Writing did so, however, with a different degree of abstraction. The scribes recognized that three jars of oil, three animals, and three bushels of grain were all instances of "threeness." They invented symbols to express these abstract concepts. Numerals constitute the first tangible evidence for abstract counting.

The tokens are unique in prehistoric assemblages in documenting the evolution of cognitive skills in preliterate cultures. The steps from measures of grain to numerals, from tokens to writing, reflect the development of signs always further removed from real goods. Numerals represent the first mathematical symbols and the first signs expressing abstract concepts. In turn, these symbols mirror an increased capacity for abstract thinking.

Economy

The foremost function of tokens was counting goods. The plain tokens served to count products of the farm, such as animals and measures of cereals. Later, complex tokens kept track of industrial products famous in Mesopotamia such as textiles and garments; luxury goods such as perfume, metal, and jewelry; manufactured goods such as bread, oil, or trussed ducks. The counters served for budgeting, managing, and planning resources to enhance productivity. In turn, tokens can disclose to the archaeologist the resources of past communities.

Plain tokens occurred concurrently with farming and complex tokens with industry, implying that the evolution of the system was closely tied to economic changes. Vice versa, the tokens can be clues for the domestication of plants and animals and for the development of workshops. For example, cylinders, used to count flocks, can provide a proof of animal husbandry before osteological changes are noticeable, since it takes generations of domestication to alter an animal's bone structure.

Social Structure

Political power, which relied upon the control of real goods, depended upon counting and accounting. The more precise the accounting system, the more powerful institutions became.

The fact that tokens wielded power is illustrated by counters found in the tombs of prestigious individuals. These artifacts suggest that tokens were status symbols and that counting was the privilege of the elite. This suggests that the token system was tied to the development of a redistributive economy. The plain tokens served to pool resources in early farming communities; complex tokens played an essential role in the collection of the dues and tribute sustaining the first Mesopotamian city-states.

The two stages of the token system, plain and complex, correspond, therefore, to two phases in the evolution of social structures. Plain tokens imply a rank society, whereas complex tokens signal state formation in southern Mesopotamia. Furthermore, the geographic distribution of complex tokens in strategic administrative centers outlines the area controlled by the southern Mesopotamian bureaucracy and gives an insight into its organization.

Communication

The tokens were a breakthrough in communication. They processed economic information never dealt with before with geometric counters never before conceived. Their most significant achievement, however, was creating a new code.

A CODE

The conceptual leap that revolutionized communication was the creation of a set of symbols with specific shapes and endowing each shape with a unique, discrete meaning. The tokens were modeled in striking, distinct geometric shapes that were easy to recognize. The forms were simple and easy to duplicate. The counters were systematically repeated, always carrying the same meaning. The dozens of token shapes constituted a code of dozens of interrelated concept symbols concerning goods and commodities. Later, with the development of a repertory of markings, the code grew to hundreds of concept symbols. The system made it possible to deal concurrently with multiple kinds of data, thus allowing the processing and communication of a volume and complexity of information never reached previously.

THE ANTECEDENT OF WRITING

The tokens shed light on the background of Mesopotamian writing. They reveal that the first script derived from three-dimensional counters. The path that led from tokens to envelopes and tablets can be reconstructed as follows:

8000–3000 B.C.: Plain tokens were characterized by mostly geometric shapes and a plain surface.

4400–3100 B.C. (Uruk XVII–IVa): Complex tokens had a larger repertory of geometric shapes and also included more naturalistic forms. They bore a greater variety of linear and punched markings. Some specimens were perforated in order to be strung for safekeeping in archives.

3750 B.C. (Uruk X): Complex tokens formed series of counters of the same shape, with a variable number of lines or punctuations.

3500 B.C. (Uruk VI): The complex tokens reached a climax. At that time they had spread to sites of northern Mesopotamia, Susiana, and Syria, where the southern Mesopotamian bureaucracy was involved. This is indicated by artifacts typical of southern Mesopotamia such as monumental architecture with clay cone mosaics, cylinder seals, beveled-rim bowls, and nose-lugged jars.

3700–2600 B.C.: Groups of tokens representing particular transactions were enclosed in envelopes to be kept in archives.

3500–2600 B.C. (starting in Uruk VI–V): Some envelopes bore on the outside the impression of the tokens held inside. These envelopes bearing markings were the turning point between tokens and writing.

3500–3100 B.C. (starting in Uruk VI–V): Tablets displaying impressed markings in the shape of tokens superseded the envelopes.

3100–3000 B.C. (starting in Uruk IVa): Pictographic script traced with a stylus on clay tablets marked the true takeoff of writing. The tokens dwindled.

The tokens give a new perspective on the evolution of communication in prehistory. They point out that when writing began in Mesopotamia it was not a sudden, spontaneous invention, as previously thought, but the outgrowth of many thousands of years' worth of experience at manipulating signs. From tokens, the earliest script inherited fundamental aspects in form, content, and structure.

The Form

—Tokens and pictographic tablets were made of clay.

—The scribes, as well as the token accountants, used a stylus, with a pointed and a blunt end, to trace and impress signs.

—The earliest pictographs reproduced the shapes of tokens.

The Content

—Tokens and pictographic writing dealt with lists of goods.

The Structure

—Writing continued the system of concept symbols. Each pictograph was semantic in the same way a token was.

—The information conveyed was specific. Each token shape, like each pictograph, carried a unique meaning.

—Each token shape and each pictograph were systematically repeated in order to carry the same meaning.

—Tokens and pictographic writing had the ability to increase their repertory of signs by creating new ones.

—The presentation of signs on a tablet, starting with the largest units at the top or on the right and proceeding in hierarchical order, probably perpetuated the way tokens were organized.

THE LINK BETWEEN COUNTING AND WRITING

The tokens give new insights into the nature of writing. They establish that in the Near East writing emerged from a counting device and that, in fact, writing was the by-product of abstract counting. When the concepts of numbers and that of items counted were abstracted, the pictographs were no longer confined to indicating numbers of units of goods in one-to-one correspondence. With the invention of numerals, pictography was no longer restricted to accounting but could open to other fields of human endeavor. From then on, writing could become phonetic and develop into the versatile tool that it is today, able to store and convey any possible idea. The invention of abstract numerals was the beginning of mathematics, and it was also the beginning of writing.

The tokens also raise new questions concerning the essence of writing. Was the first script of the Near East unique in deriving from a counting device? Or is literacy universally tied to numeracy? Is numeracy a prerequisite for literacy?

The tokens only begin answering Thomas Astle's question:

Whence did the wond'rous
mystic art arise
Of painting speech, and
speaking to the eye?
That we by tracing magic
lines are taught
How both to colour, and
embody thought?[3]

PART THREE: THE ARTIFACTS

Drawings and Photographs

One representative example of each subtype was selected to be drawn in chart 1–16 in Volume 1. It is important to realize, however, that, because the tokens were manufactured by hand, they are not standardized. The photographic catalog in Volume II illustrates how artifacts of the same subtype show slight variations in form and style of markings (see, for example, type 6: 14 or 8: 17). Several drawings of the same subtype are provided only when major variations occur (for example, differences in profile in type 3: 51). The various painted patterns on cones (type 1: 46) or disks (type 3: 79) are not illustrated.

Perforated, rather than unperforated, artifacts have been selected for illustration in order to show the place of the perforations. When warranted, several drawings depict variations in the placement of perforations (for example, in type 3: 71, 3: 73).

Whenever possible, the drawings were based on photographs. In many instances, however, the only sources available to the artist were sketches from notes taken in museums. The scale could not be taken into account in the illustrations. The key to the drawing follows:

Perforation

Punctation

Incised line

Painted motif

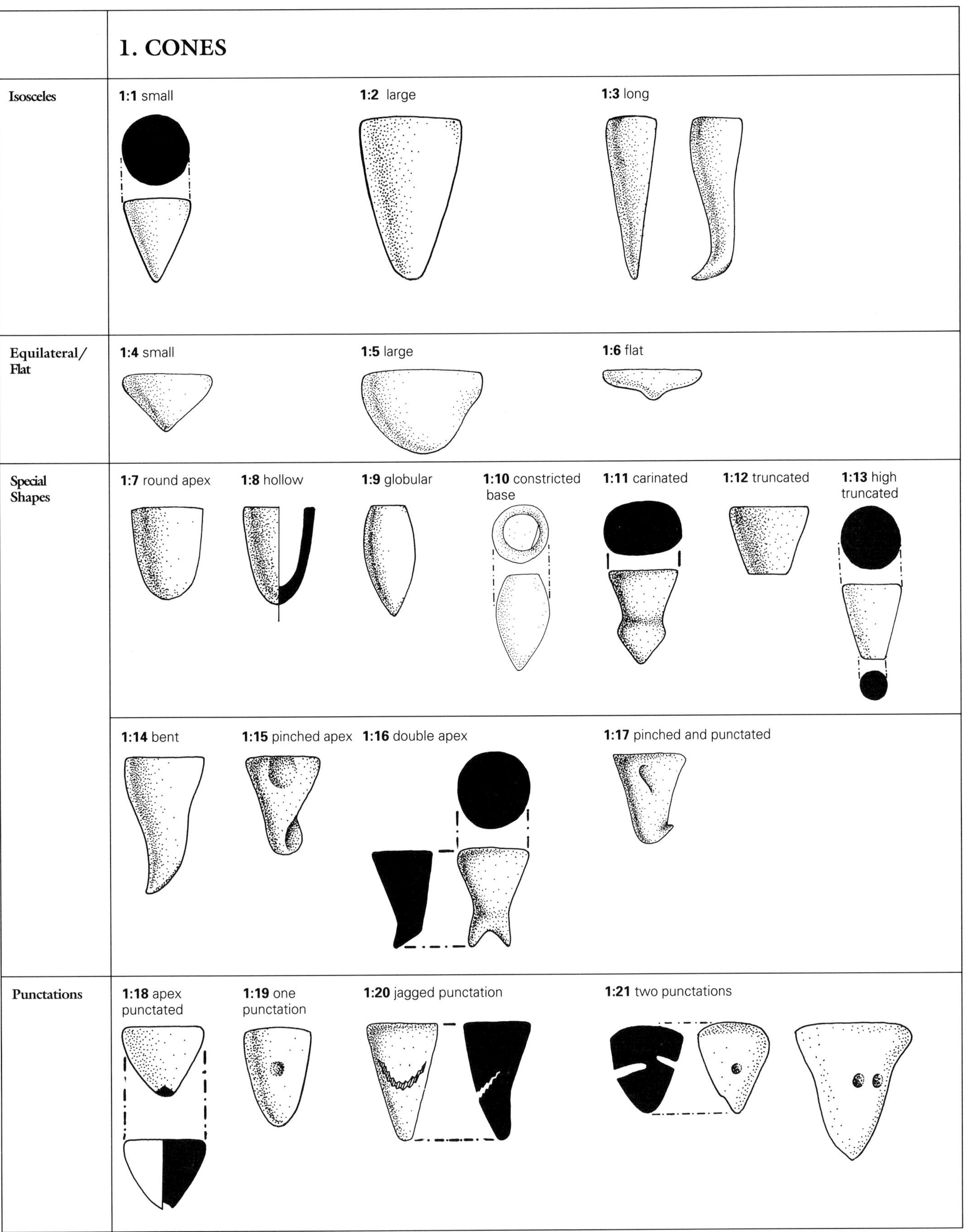
1. CONES
Isosceles
1:1 small
1:2 large
1:3 long
Equilateral/Flat
1:4 small
1:5 large
1:6 flat
Special Shapes
1:7 round apex
1:8 hollow
1:9 globular
1:10 constricted base
1:11 carinated
1:12 truncated
1:13 high truncated
1:14 bent
1:15 pinched apex
1:16 double apex
1:17 pinched and punctated
Punctations
1:18 apex punctated
1:19 one punctation
1:20 jagged punctation
1:21 two punctations

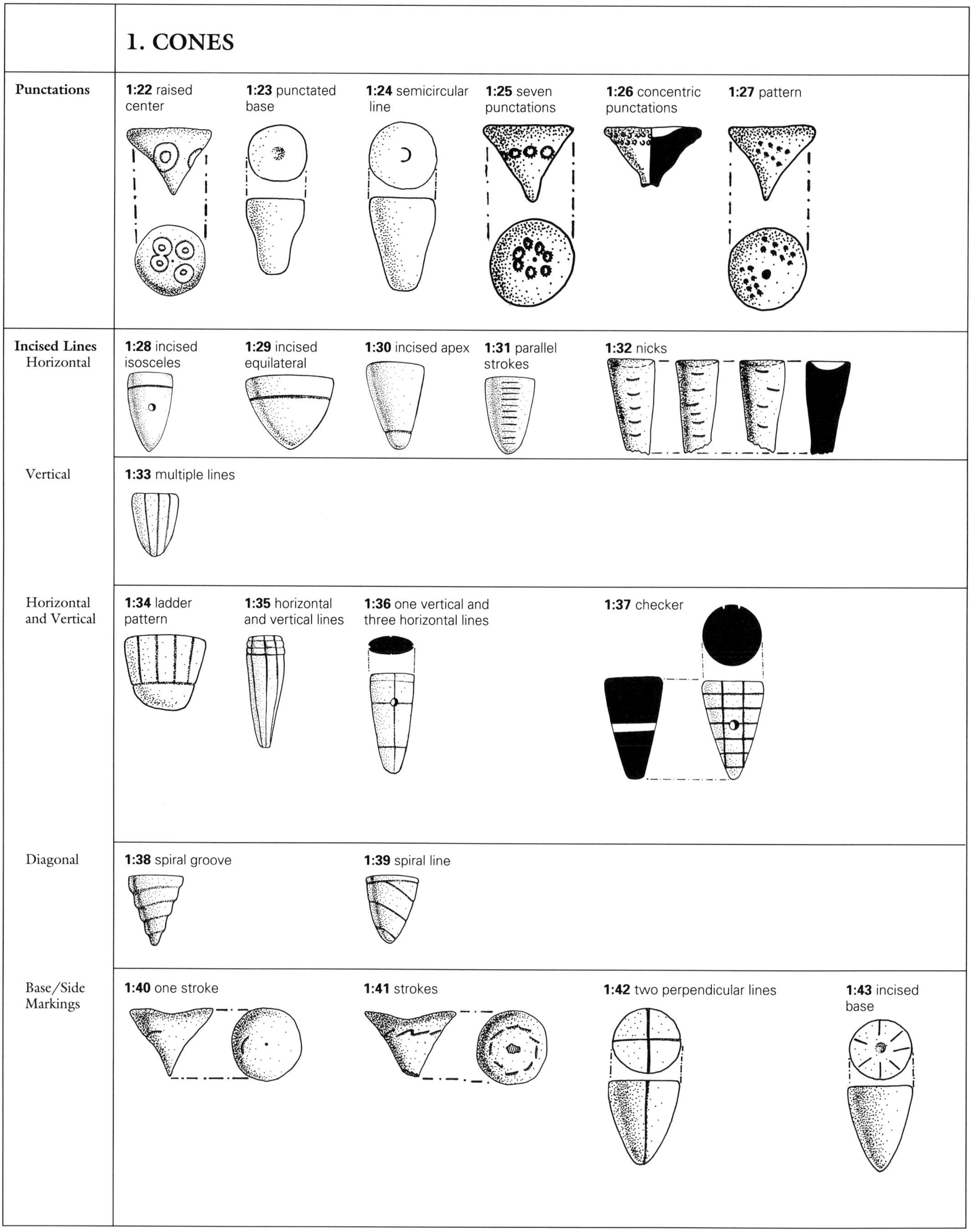

1. CONES

Punctuations

1:22 raised center

1:23 punctated base

1:24 semicircular line

1:25 seven punctations

1:26 concentric punctations

1:27 pattern

Incised Lines

Horizontal

1:28 incised isosceles

1:29 incised equilateral

1:30 incised apex

1:31 parallel strokes

1:32 nicks

Vertical

1:33 multiple lines

Horizontal and Vertical

1:34 ladder pattern

1:35 horizontal and vertical lines

1:36 one vertical and three horizontal lines

1:37 checker

Diagonal

1:38 spiral groove

1:39 spiral line

Base/Side Markings

1:40 one stroke

1:41 strokes

1:42 two perpendicular lines

1:43 incised base

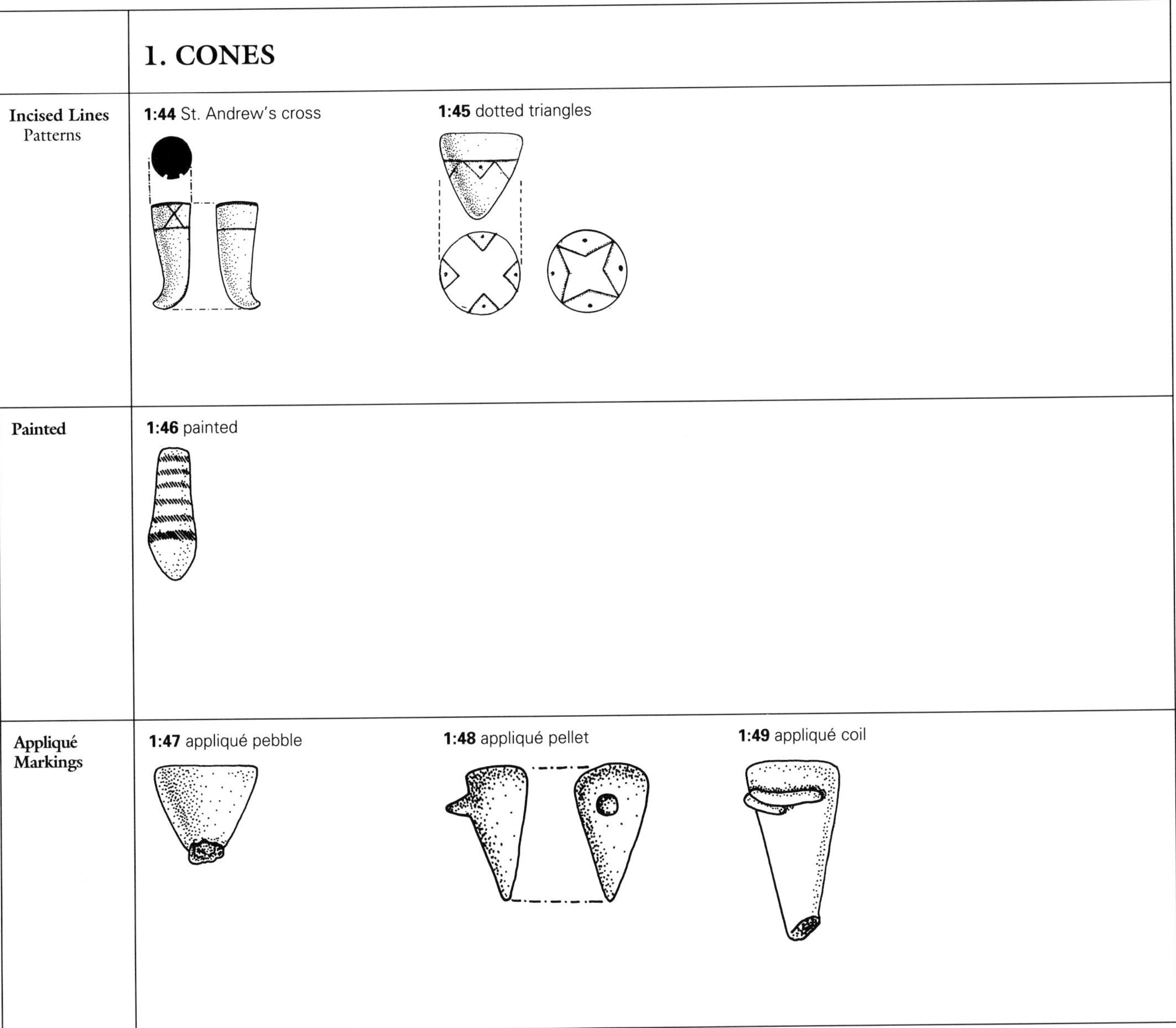
1. CONES
Incised Lines
Patterns
1:44 St. Andrew's cross
1:45 dotted triangles
Painted
1:46 painted
Appliqué
Markings
1:47 appliqué pebble
1:48 appliqué pellet
1:49 appliqué coil

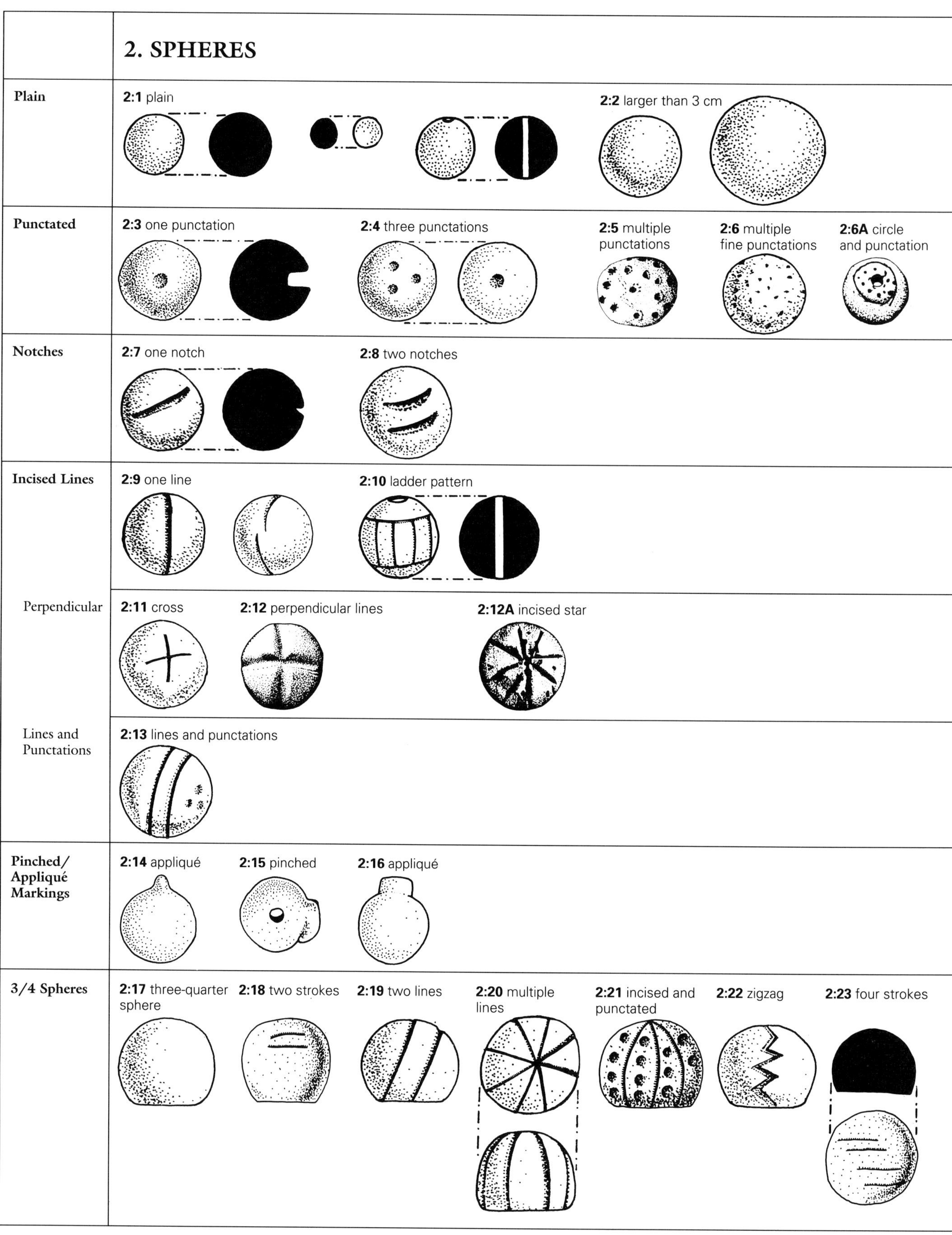
2. SPHERES
Plain
2:1 plain
2:2 larger than 3 cm
Punctated
2:3 one punctation
2:4 three punctations
2:5 multiple punctations
2:6 multiple fine punctations
2:6A circle and punctation
Notches
2:7 one notch
2:8 two notches
Incised Lines
2:9 one line
2:10 ladder pattern
Perpendicular
2:11 cross
2:12 perpendicular lines
2:12A incised star
Lines and Punctations
2:13 lines and punctations
Pinched/ Appliqué Markings
2:14 appliqué
2:15 pinched
2:16 appliqué
3/4 Spheres
2:17 three-quarter sphere
2:18 two strokes
2:19 two lines
2:20 multiple lines
2:21 incised and punctated
2:22 zigzag
2:23 four strokes

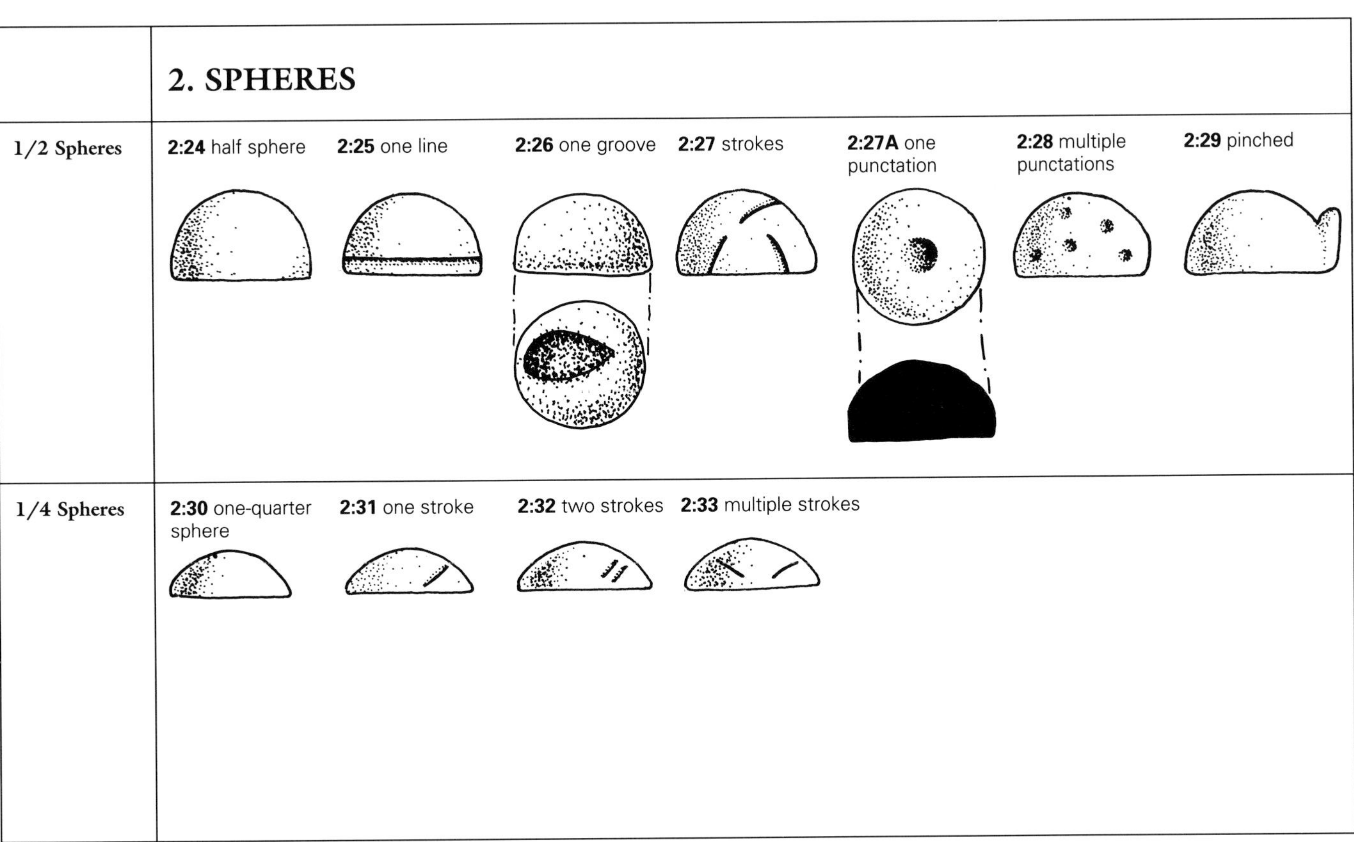
2. SPHERES
1/2 Spheres
2:24 half sphere
2:25 one line
2:26 one groove
2:27 strokes
2:27A one punctation
2:28 multiple punctations
2:29 pinched
1/4 Spheres
2:30 one-quarter sphere
2:31 one stroke
2:32 two strokes
2:33 multiple strokes

	3. DISKS
Plain	**3:1** flat; **3:2** large flat; **3:3** lenticular; **3:4** large lenticular
Special Shapes	**3:5** hollow; **3:6** concave; **3:7** concave sides
Punctations	**3:8** one punctation; **3:8A** three punctations; **3:9** six punctations; **3:10** six punctations
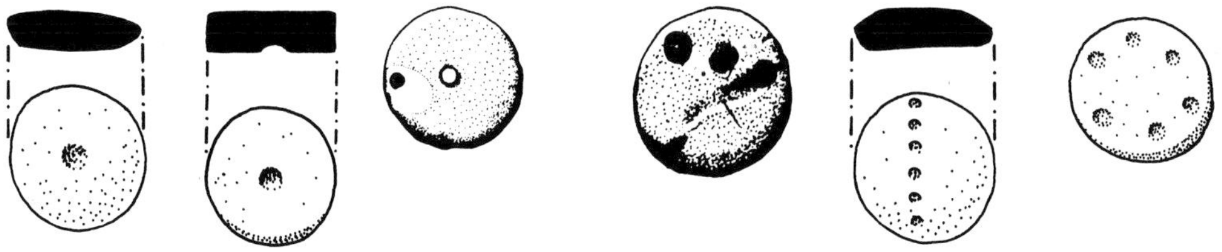	**3:11** seven punctations; **3:12** circles; **3:13** circles; **3:14** circle; **3:14A** two punctations, two concentric circles
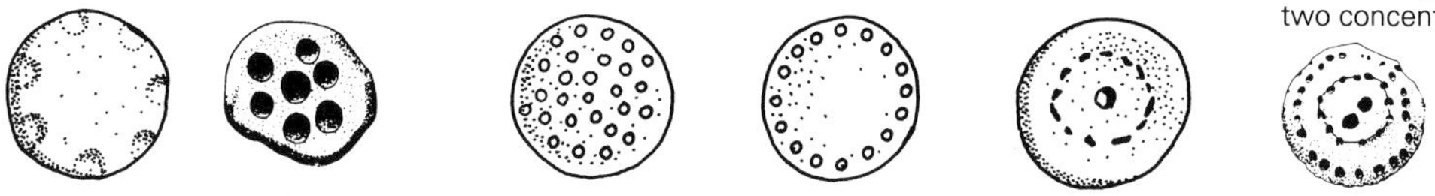	**3:14B** lines on side; **3:15** multiple punctations; **3:15A** pitted area; **3:16** nail impressions

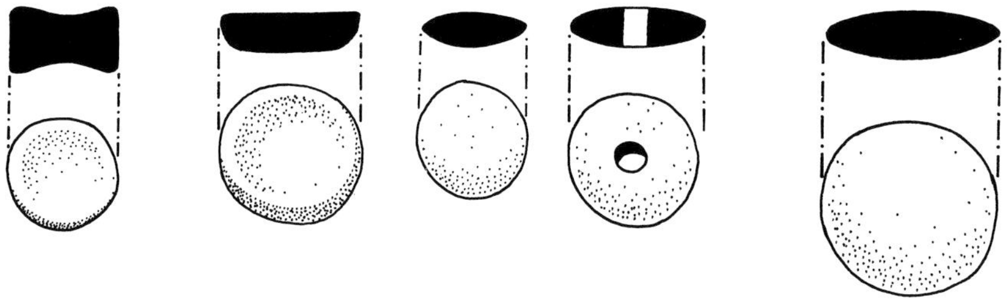

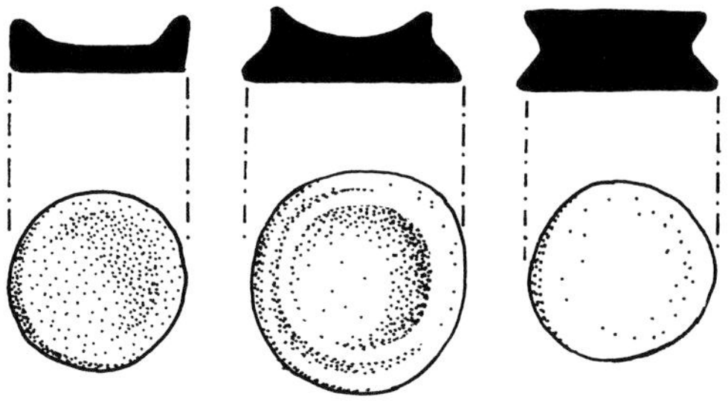

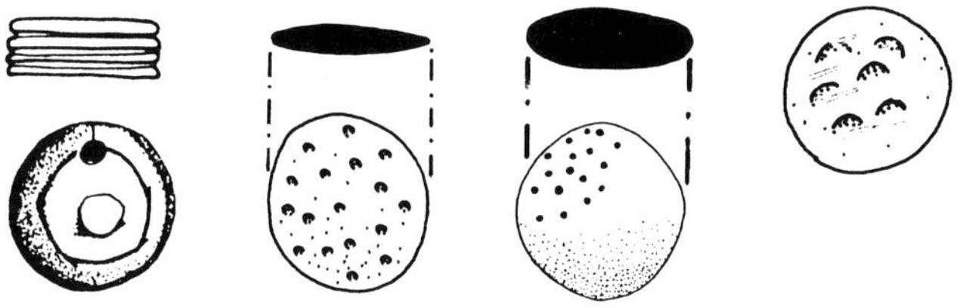

	3. DISKS				
Perforations	**3:17** two perforations	**3:18** five perforations			
Incised Lines	**3:19** median line			**3:20** three lines	**3:21** four lines
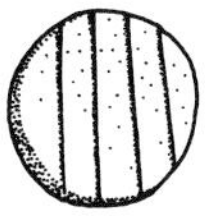	**3:22** five lines	**3:23** six lines	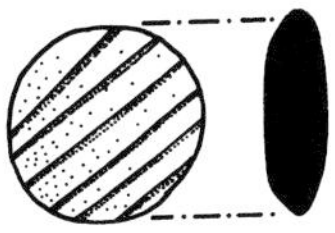	**3:24** eight lines	
	3:25 ten lines	**3:26** circle and three lines		**3:27** radiating lines	
Parallel Lines	**3:28** two lines	**3:29** two and one lines	**3:30** two and two lines	**3:31** three and three lines	
	3:32 four and four lines	**3:33** five and five lines	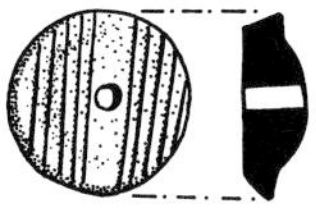	**3:34** one and one line, zigzag	**3:35** three and three lines, zigzag
Parallel Lines and Strokes	**3:36** one line, seven strokes	**3:37** two lines, one stroke	**3:37A** two lines, five strokes	**3:38** two lines, six strokes	**3:39** two lines, six strokes
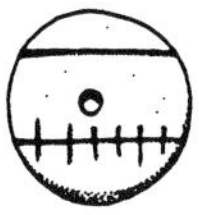	**3:40** two lines, seven strokes	**3:41** two lines, eight strokes	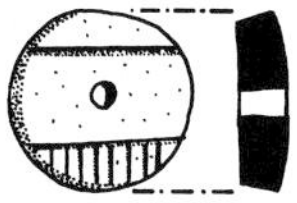	**3:42** three lines, six strokes	**3:42A** five lines, six strokes
	**3:43** five lines, seven strokes	**3:44** five lines, thirteen strokes	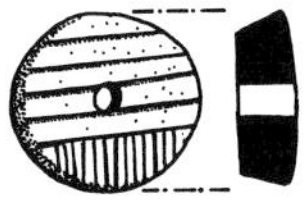	**3:45** ten lines, five strokes	**3:46** ten lines, nine strokes

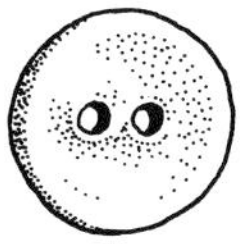

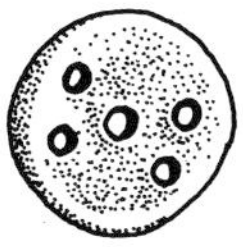

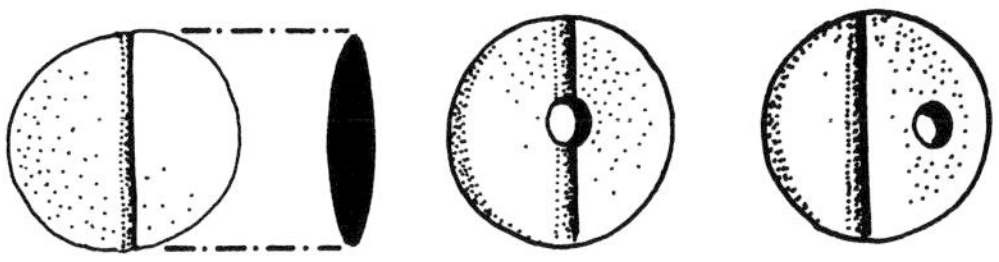

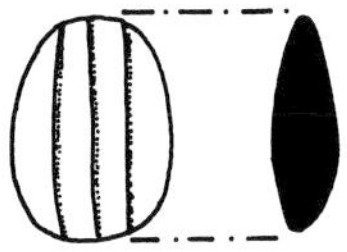

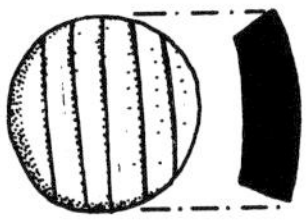

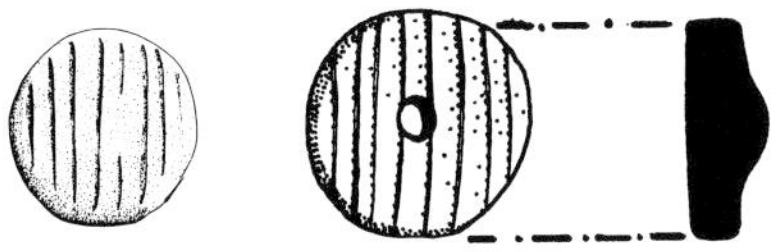

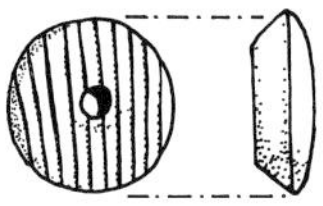

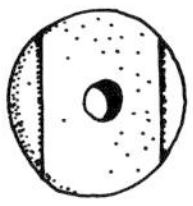

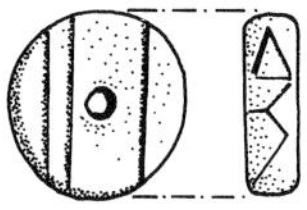

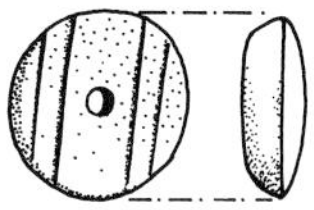

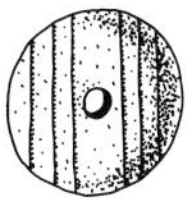

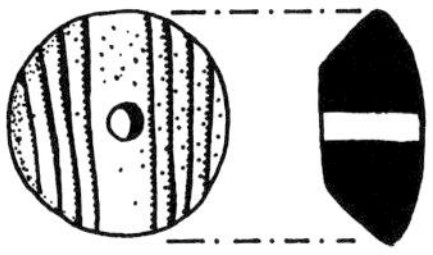

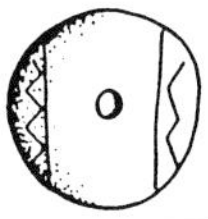

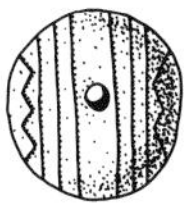

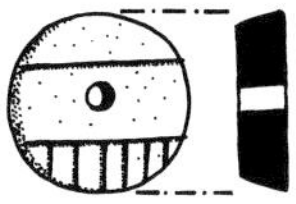

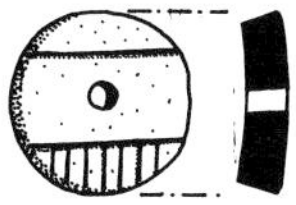

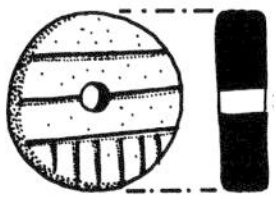

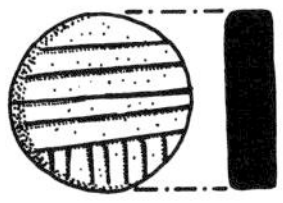

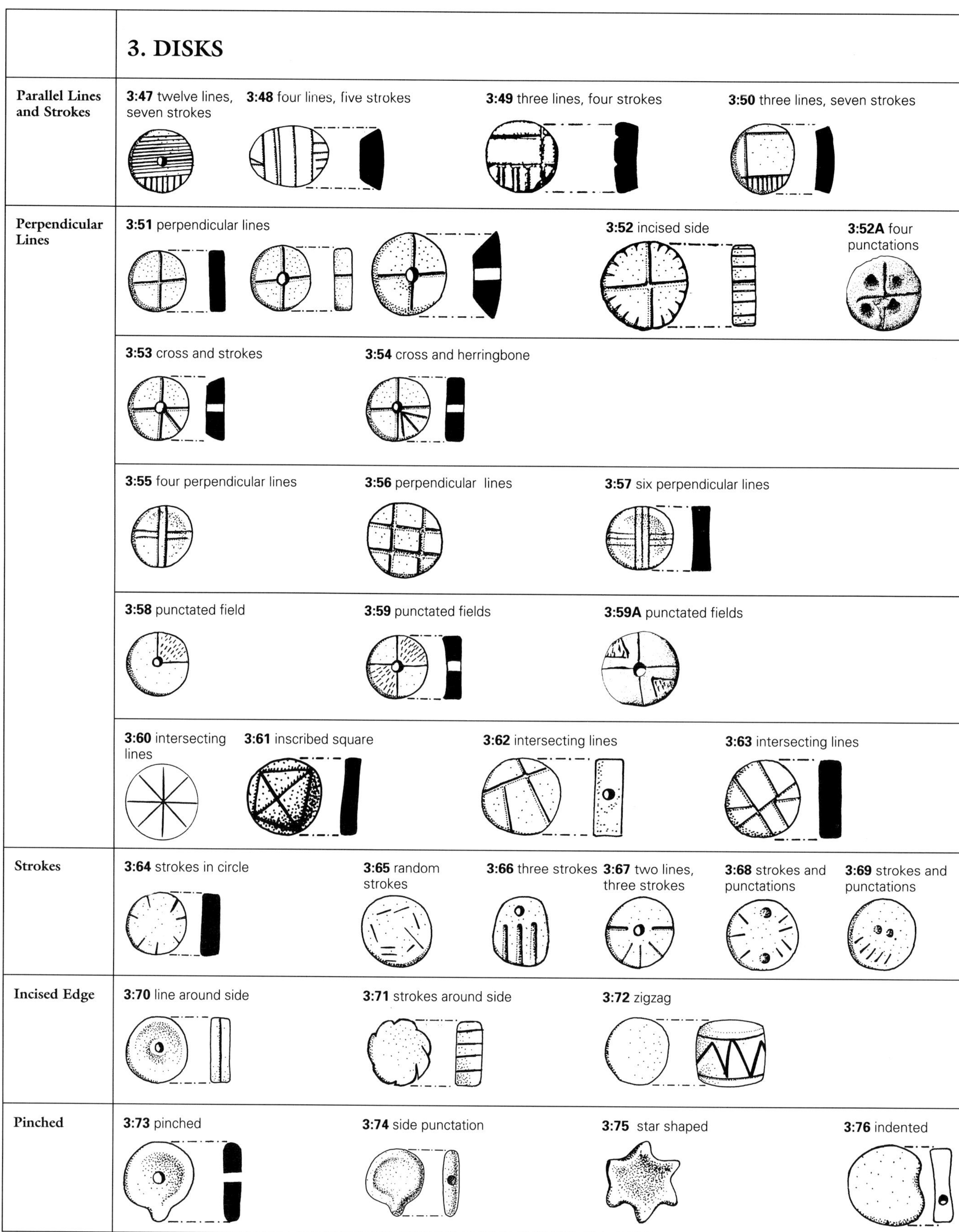
3. DISKS
Parallel Lines and Strokes
3:47 twelve lines, seven strokes
3:48 four lines, five strokes
3:49 three lines, four strokes
3:50 three lines, seven strokes
Perpendicular Lines
3:51 perpendicular lines
3:52 incised side
3:52A four punctations
3:53 cross and strokes
3:54 cross and herringbone
3:55 four perpendicular lines
3:56 perpendicular lines
3:57 six perpendicular lines
3:58 punctated field
3:59 punctated fields
3:59A punctated fields
3:60 intersecting lines
3:61 inscribed square
3:62 intersecting lines
3:63 intersecting lines
Strokes
3:64 strokes in circle
3:65 random strokes
3:66 three strokes
3:67 two lines, three strokes
3:68 strokes and punctations
3:69 strokes and punctations
Incised Edge
3:70 line around side
3:71 strokes around side
3:72 zigzag
Pinched
3:73 pinched
3:74 side punctation
3:75 star shaped
3:76 indented

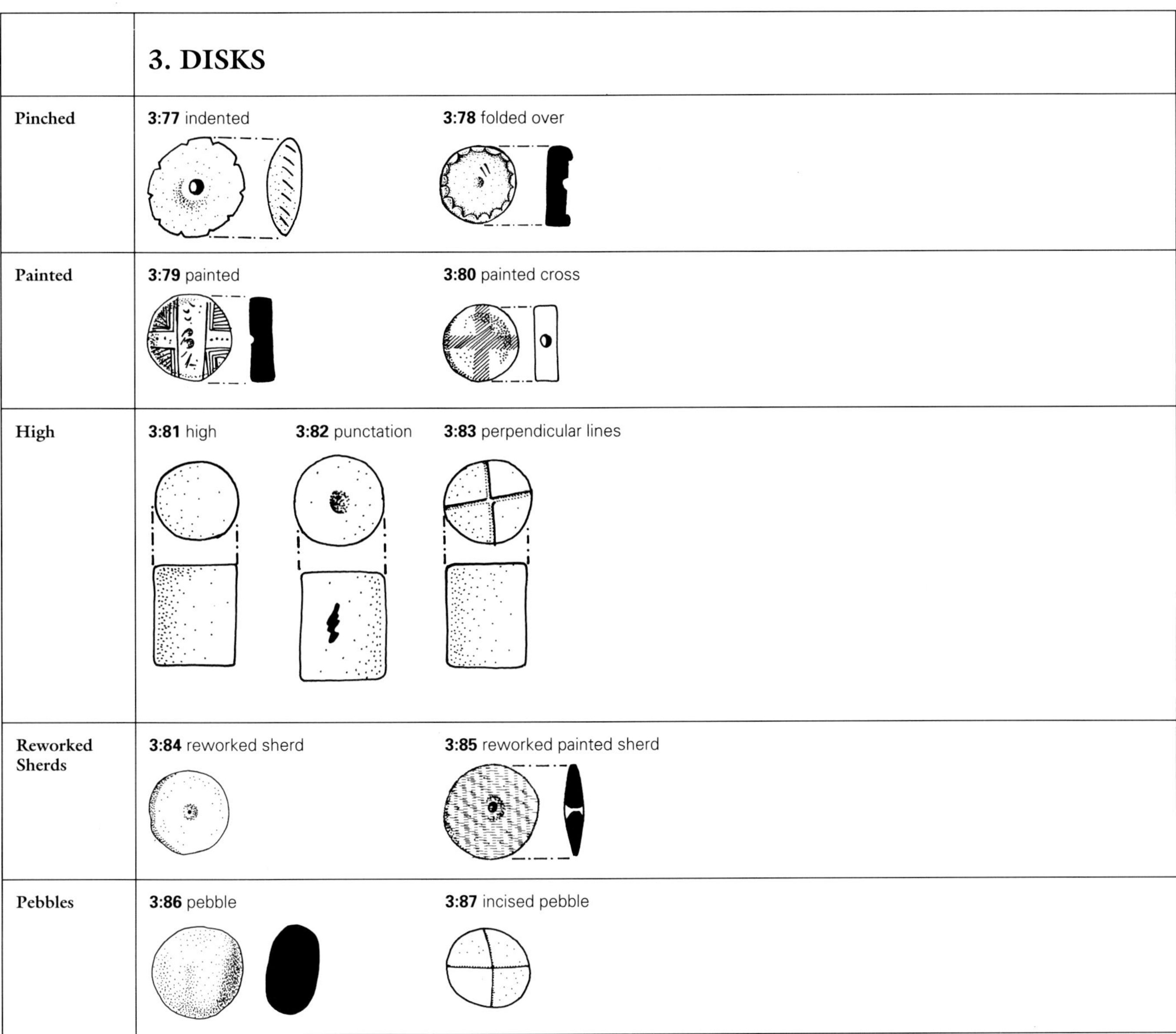
3. DISKS
Pinched
3:77 indented
3:78 folded over
Painted
3:79 painted
3:80 painted cross
High
3:81 high
3:82 punctation
3:83 perpendicular lines
Reworked Sherds
3:84 reworked sherd
3:85 reworked painted sherd
Pebbles
3:86 pebble
3:87 incised pebble

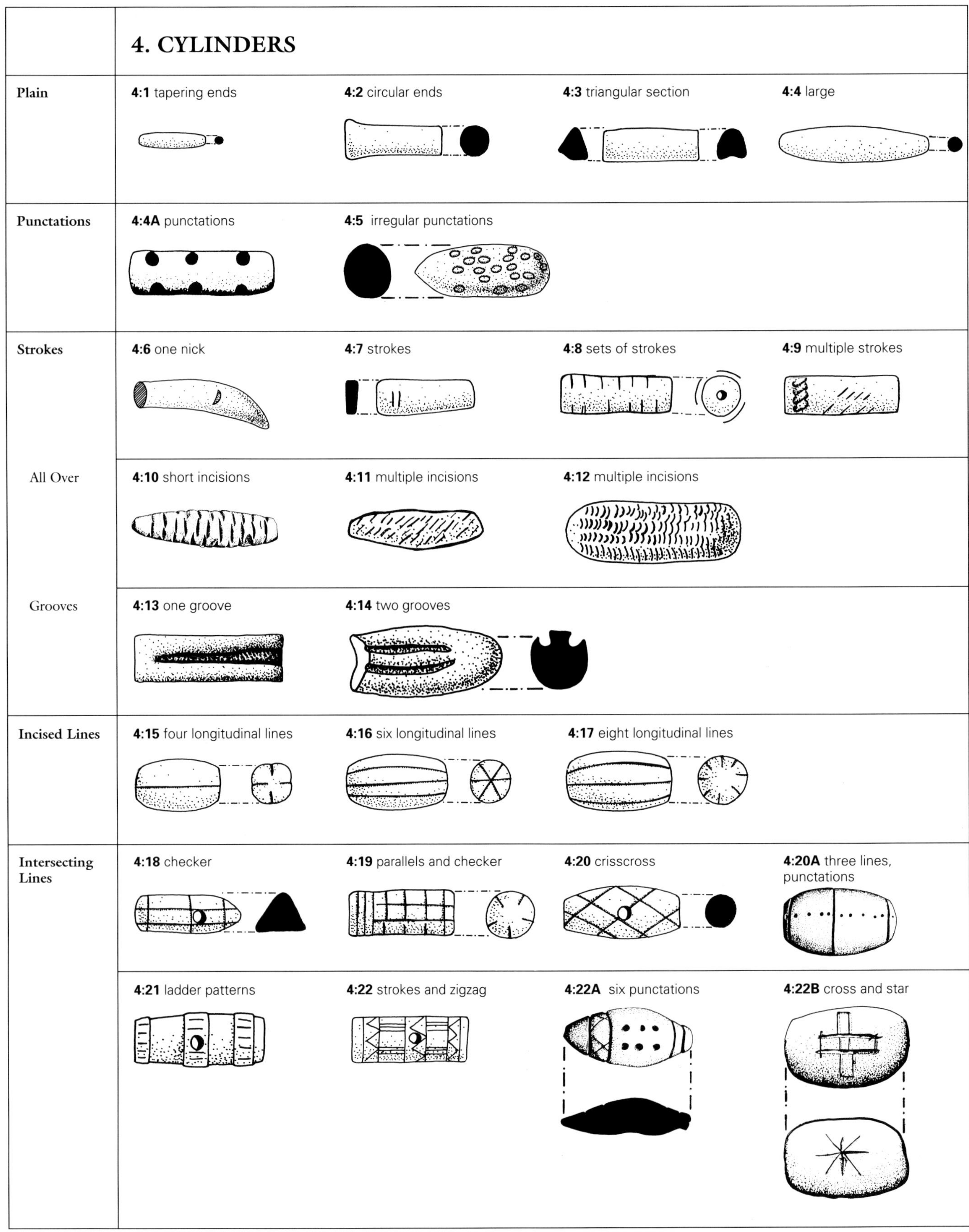
4. CYLINDERS
Plain
4:1 tapering ends
4:2 circular ends
4:3 triangular section
4:4 large
Punctations
4:4A punctations
4:5 irregular punctations
Strokes
4:6 one nick
4:7 strokes
4:8 sets of strokes
4:9 multiple strokes
All Over
4:10 short incisions
4:11 multiple incisions
4:12 multiple incisions
Grooves
4:13 one groove
4:14 two grooves
Incised Lines
4:15 four longitudinal lines
4:16 six longitudinal lines
4:17 eight longitudinal lines
Intersecting Lines
4:18 checker
4:19 parallels and checker
4:20 crisscross
4:20A three lines, punctations
4:21 ladder patterns
4:22 strokes and zigzag
4:22A six punctations
4:22B cross and star

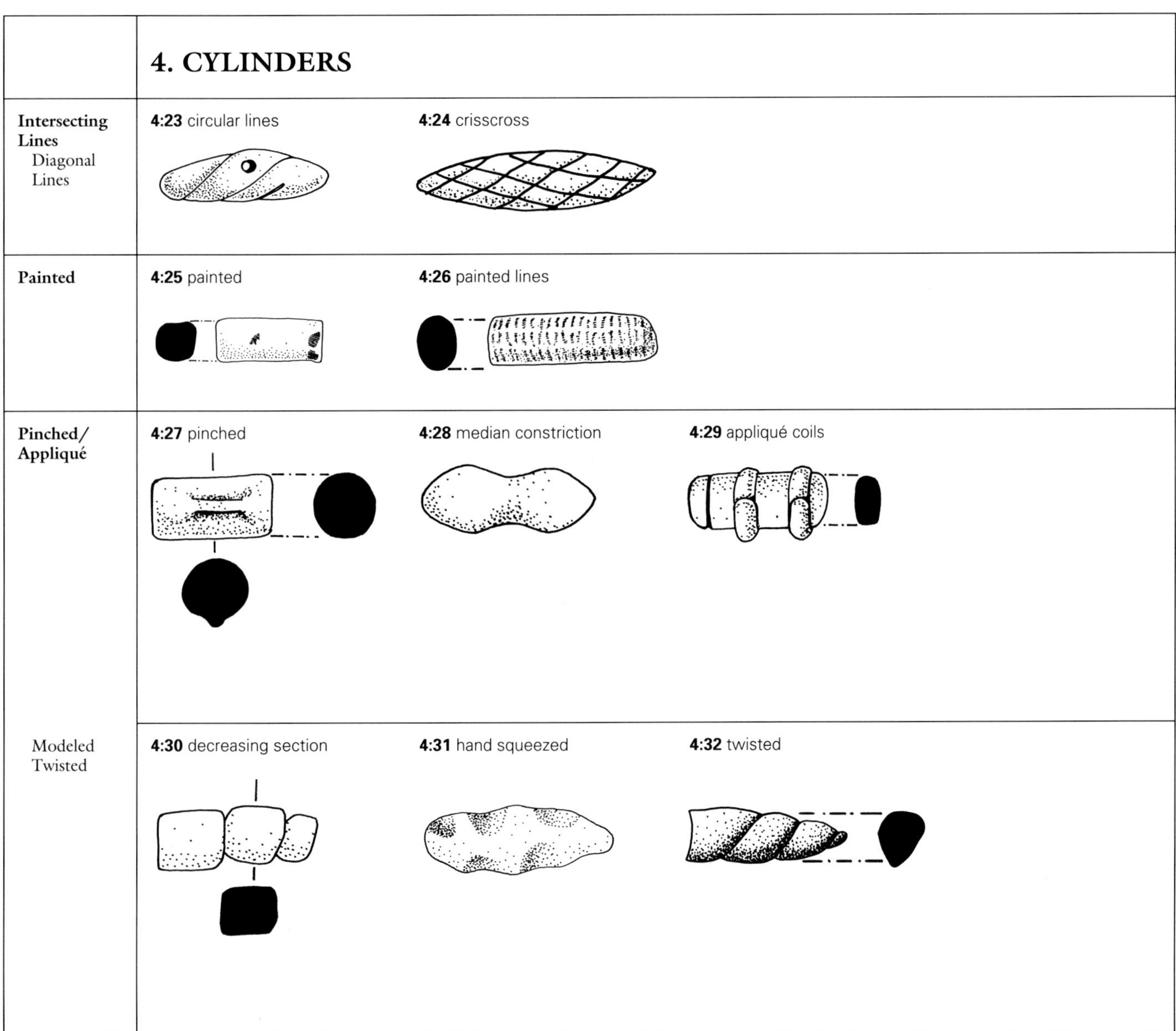
4. CYLINDERS
Intersecting Lines
Diagonal Lines
4:23 circular lines
4:24 crisscross
Painted
4:25 painted
4:26 painted lines
Pinched/ Appliqué
4:27 pinched
4:28 median constriction
4:29 appliqué coils
Modeled Twisted
4:30 decreasing section
4:31 hand squeezed
4:32 twisted

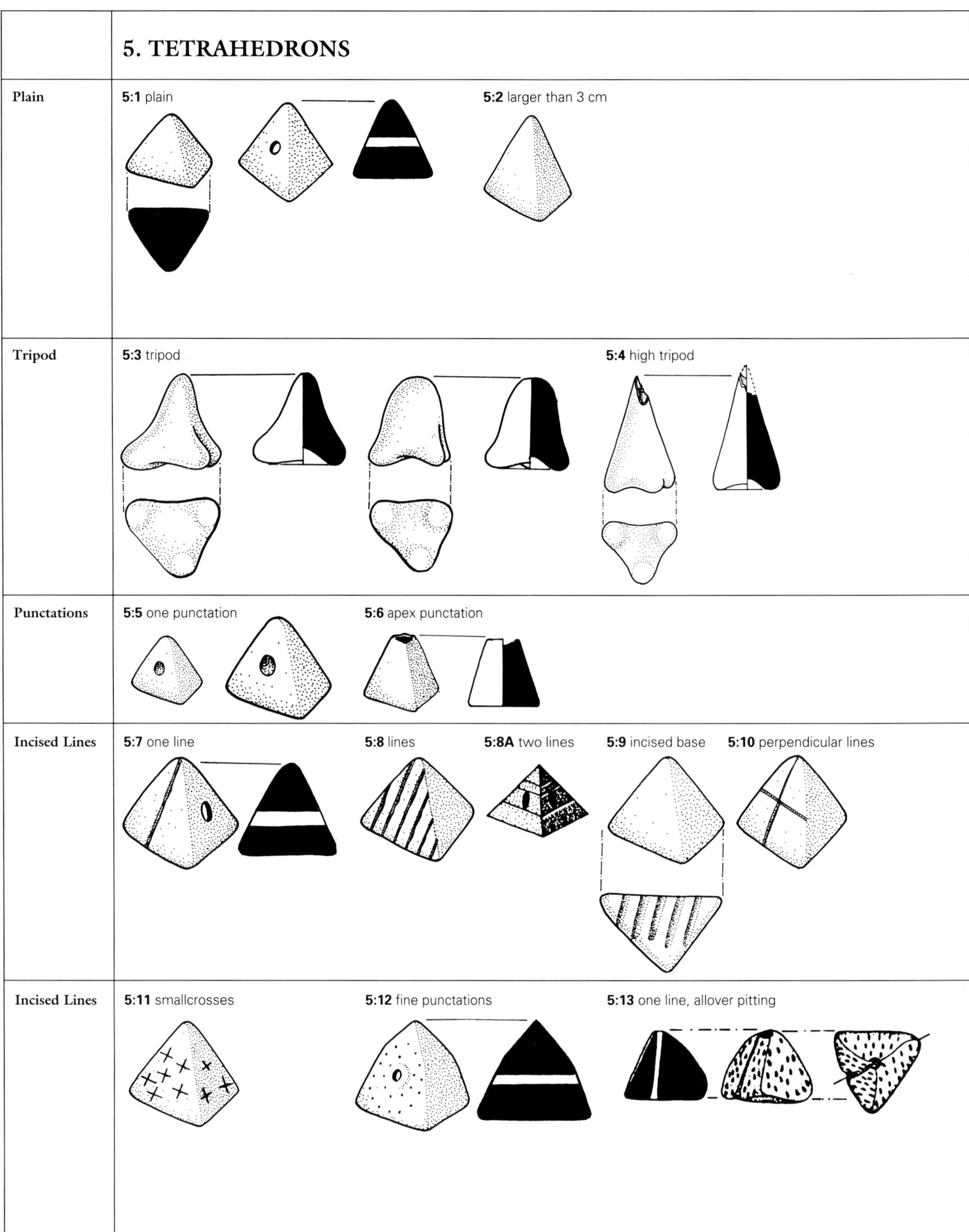
5. TETRAHEDRONS
Plain
5:1 plain
5:2 larger than 3 cm
Tripod
5:3 tripod
5:4 high tripod
Punctations
5:5 one punctation
5:6 apex punctation
Incised Lines
5:7 one line
5:8 lines
5:8A two lines
5:9 incised base
5:10 perpendicular lines
Incised Lines
5:11 smallcrosses
5:12 fine punctations
5:13 one line, allover pitting

	5. TETRAHEDRONS
Pyramids	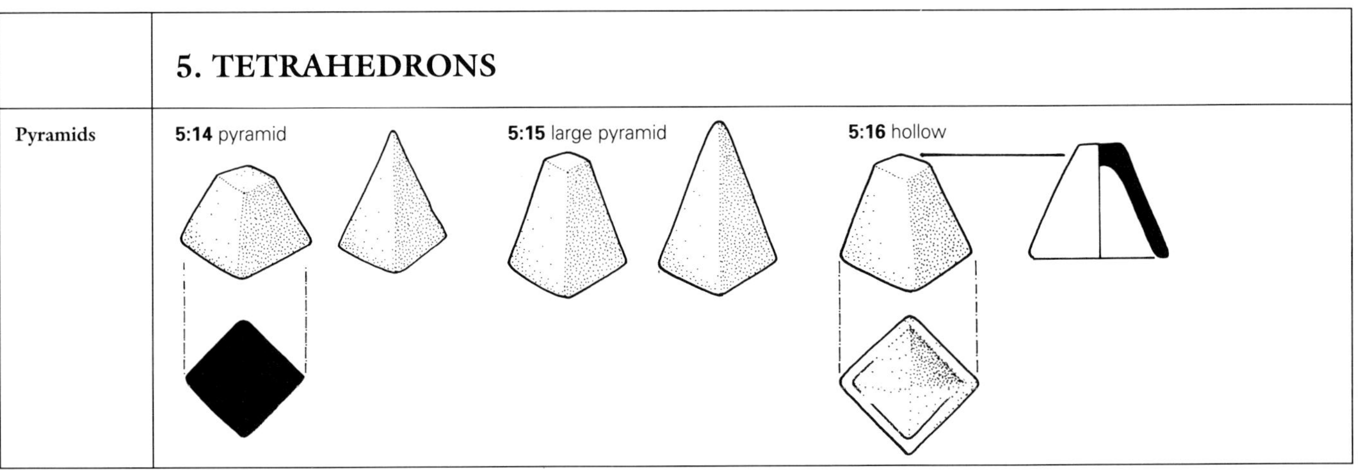

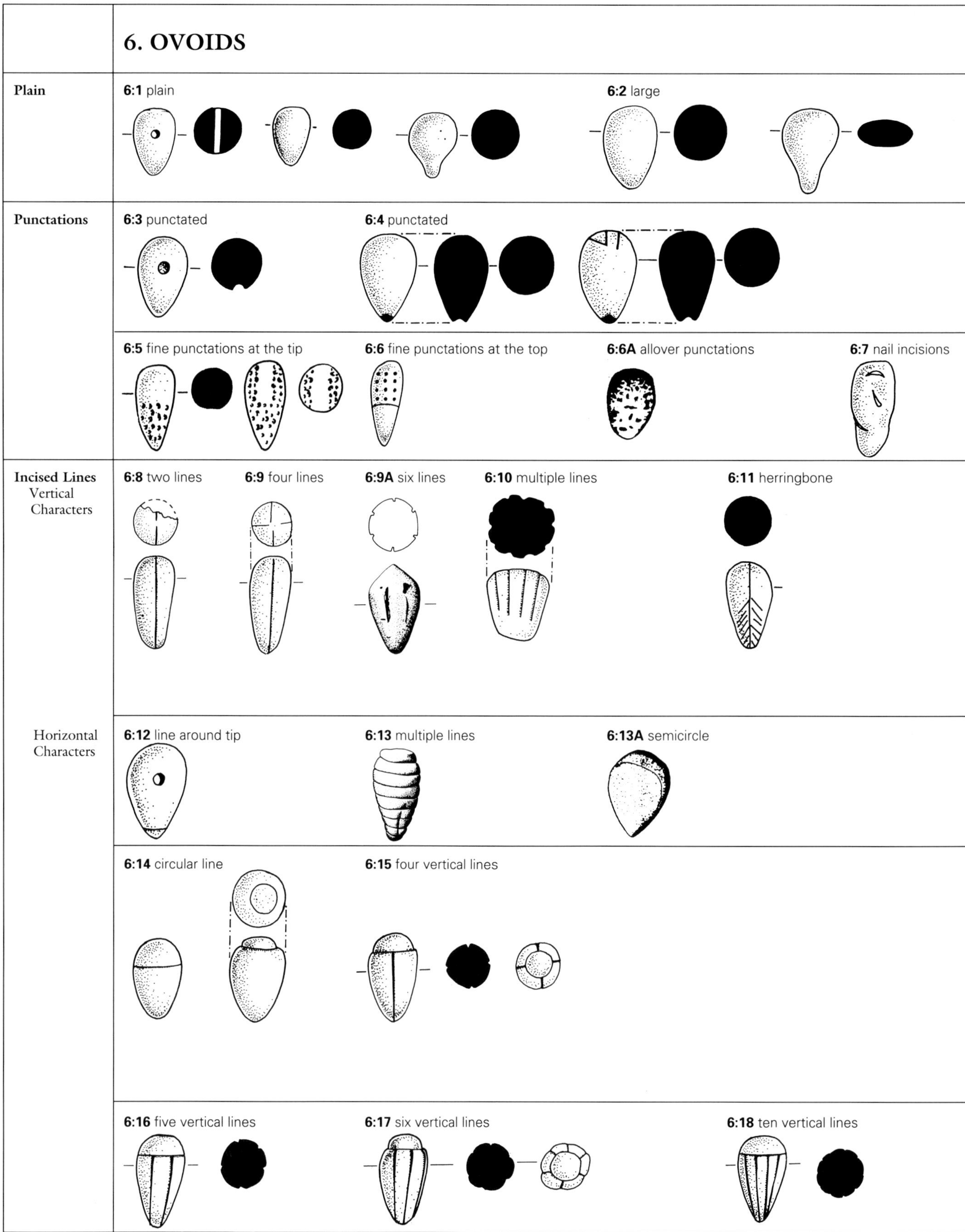
6. OVOIDS
Plain
6:1 plain
6:2 large
Punctations
6:3 punctated
6:4 punctated
6:5 fine punctations at the tip
6:6 fine punctations at the top
6:6A allover punctations
6:7 nail incisions
Incised Lines
Vertical
Characters
6:8 two lines
6:9 four lines
6:9A six lines
6:10 multiple lines
6:11 herringbone
Horizontal
Characters
6:12 line around tip
6:13 multiple lines
6:13A semicircle
6:14 circular line
6:15 four vertical lines
6:16 five vertical lines
6:17 six vertical lines
6:18 ten vertical lines

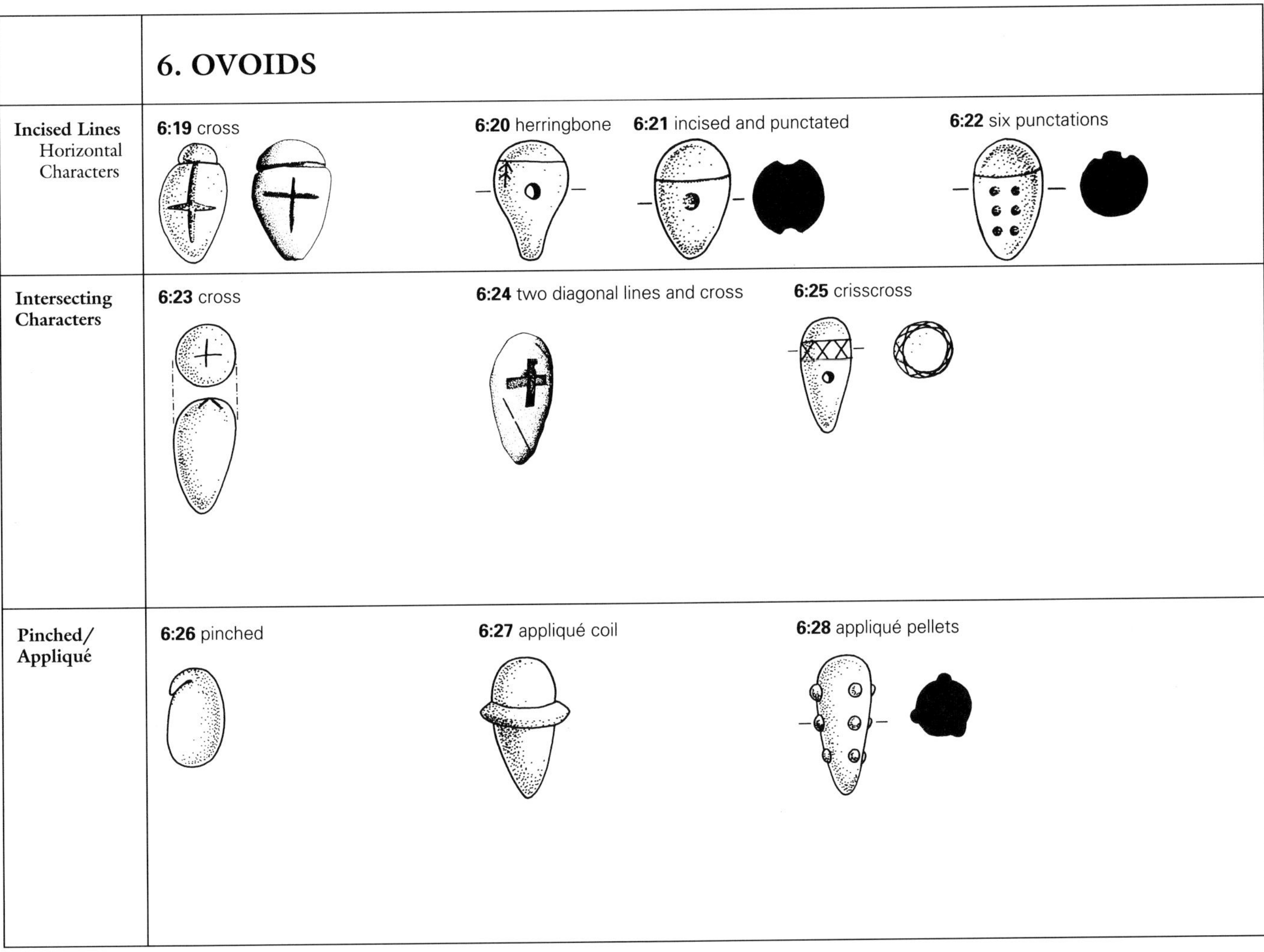
6. OVOIDS
Incised Lines
Horizontal Characters
6:19 cross
6:20 herringbone
6:21 incised and punctated
6:22 six punctations
Intersecting Characters
6:23 cross
6:24 two diagonal lines and cross
6:25 crisscross
Pinched/ Appliqué
6:26 pinched
6:27 appliqué coil
6:28 appliqué pellets

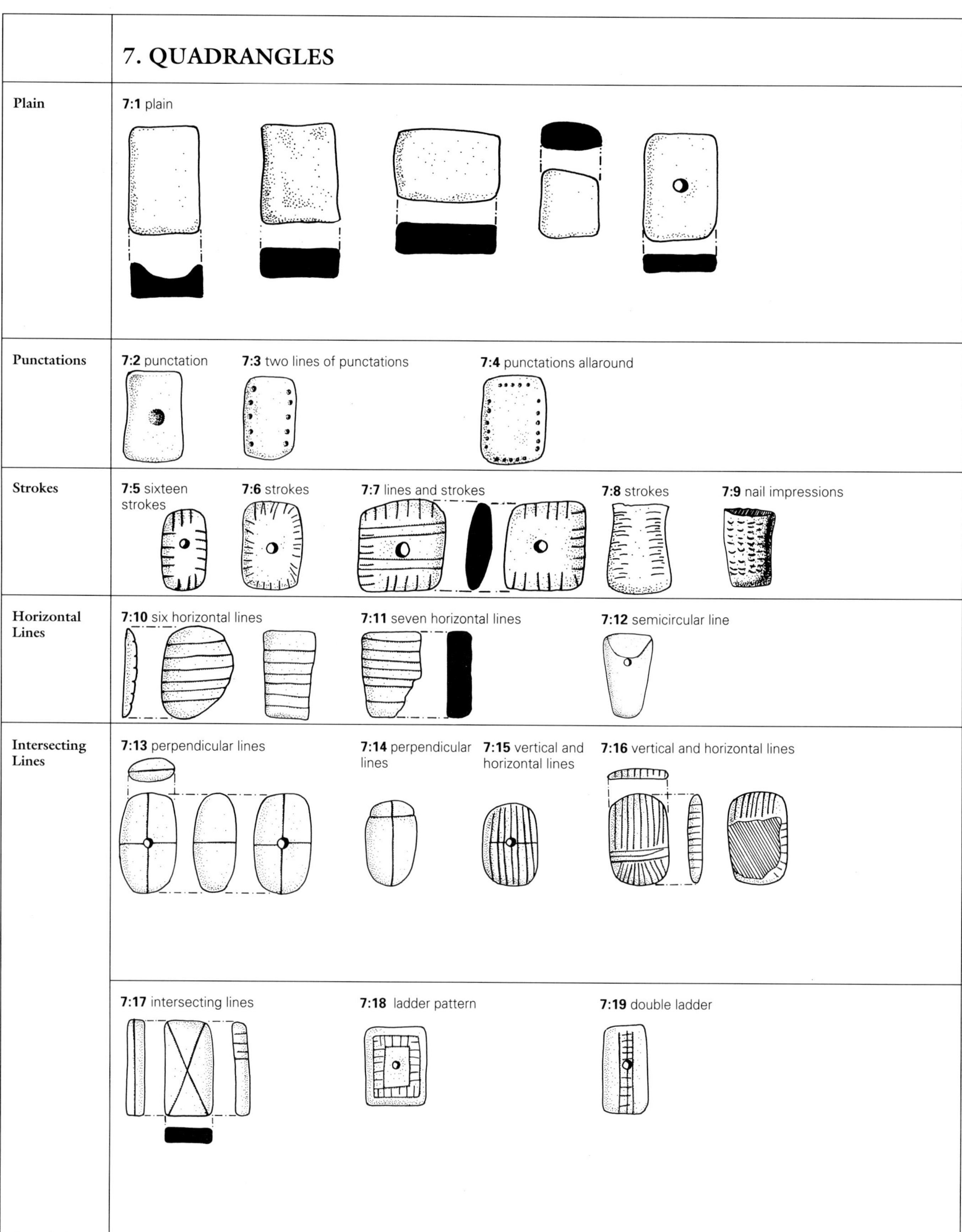
7. QUADRANGLES
Plain
7:1 plain
Punctuations
7:2 punctation
7:3 two lines of punctations
7:4 punctations allaround
Strokes
7:5 sixteen strokes
7:6 strokes
7:7 lines and strokes
7:8 strokes
7:9 nail impressions
Horizontal Lines
7:10 six horizontal lines
7:11 seven horizontal lines
7:12 semicircular line
Intersecting Lines
7:13 perpendicular lines
7:14 perpendicular lines
7:15 vertical and horizontal lines
7:16 vertical and horizontal lines
7:17 intersecting lines
7:18 ladder pattern
7:19 double ladder

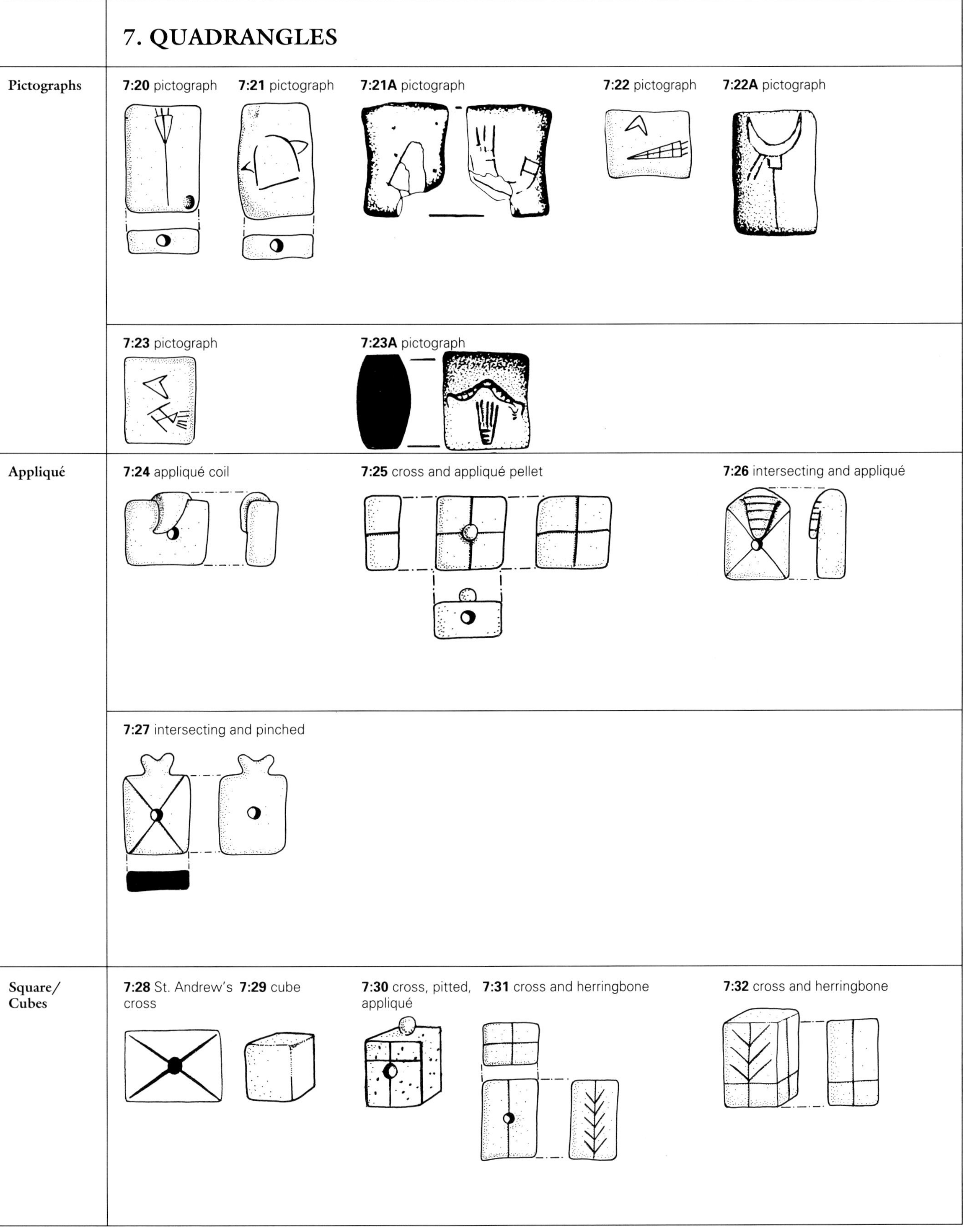
7. QUADRANGLES
Pictographs
7:20 pictograph
7:21 pictograph
7:21A pictograph
7:22 pictograph
7:22A pictograph
7:23 pictograph
7:23A pictograph
Appliqué
7:24 appliqué coil
7:25 cross and appliqué pellet
7:26 intersecting and appliqué
7:27 intersecting and pinched
Square/ Cubes
7:28 St. Andrew's cross
7:29 cube
7:30 cross, pitted, appliqué
7:31 cross and herringbone
7:32 cross and herringbone

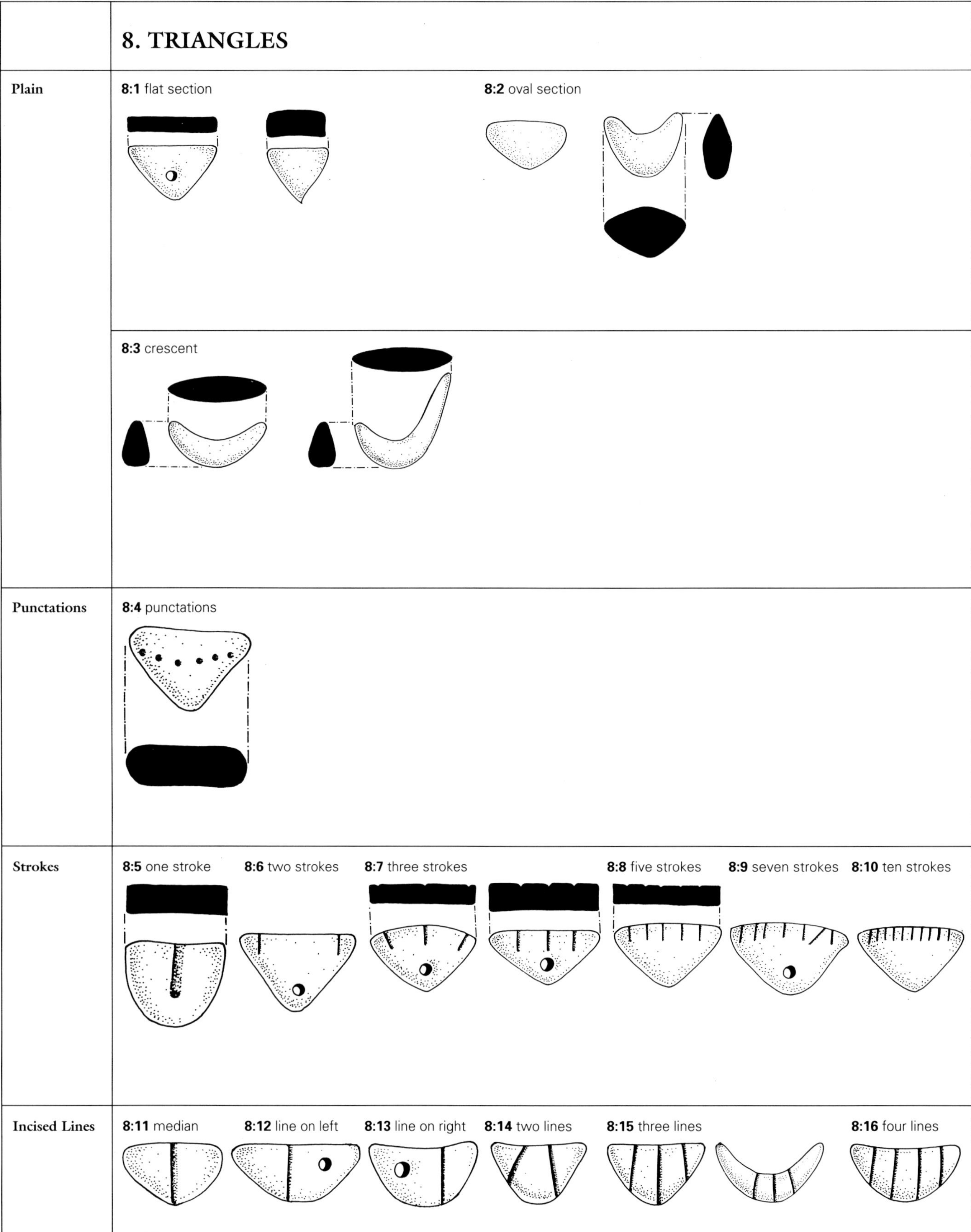
8. TRIANGLES
Plain
8:1 flat section
8:2 oval section
8:3 crescent
Punctations
8:4 punctations
Strokes
8:5 one stroke
8:6 two strokes
8:7 three strokes
8:8 five strokes
8:9 seven strokes
8:10 ten strokes
Incised Lines
8:11 median
8:12 line on left
8:13 line on right
8:14 two lines
8:15 three lines
8:16 four lines

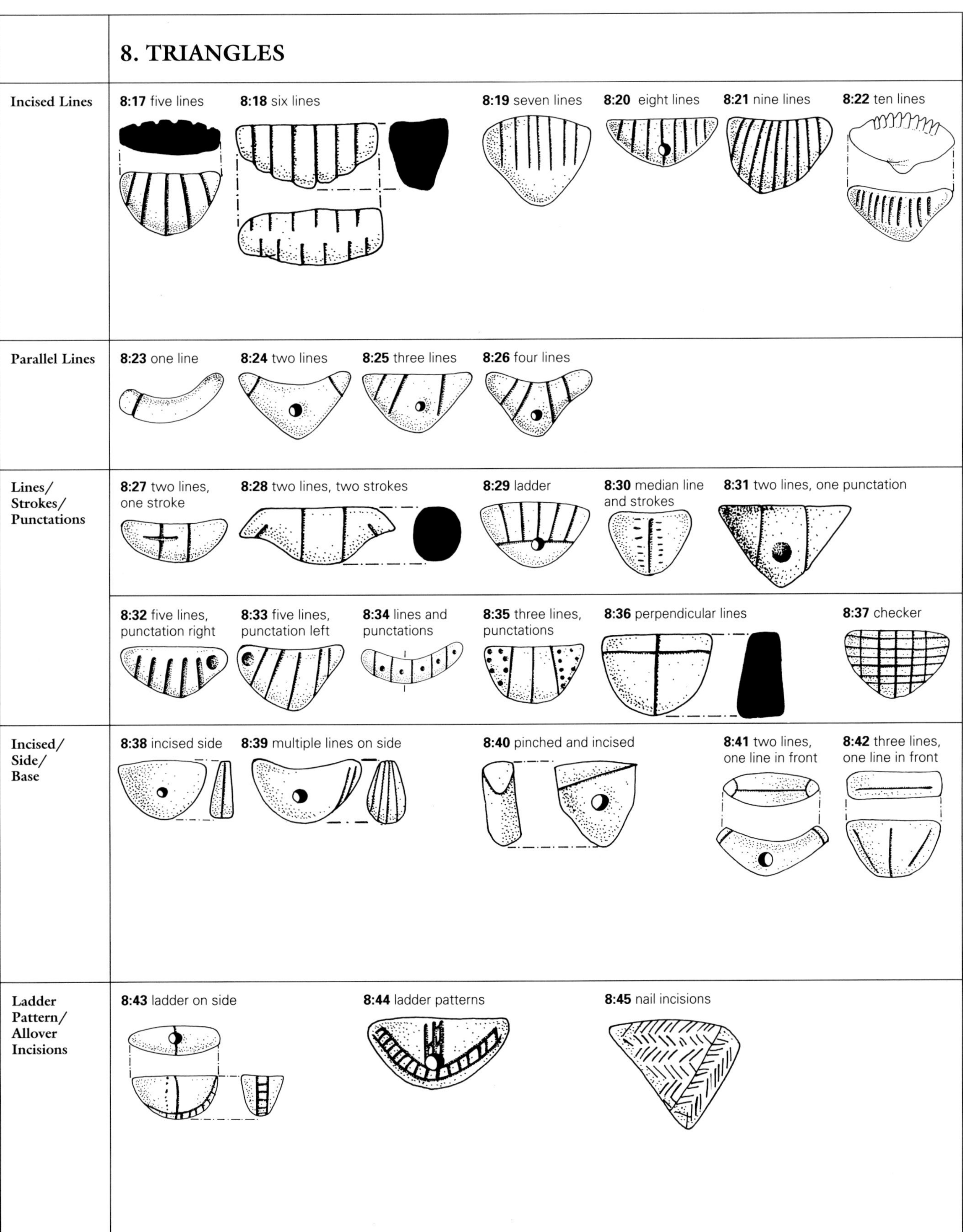
8. TRIANGLES
Incised Lines
8:17 five lines
8:18 six lines
8:19 seven lines
8:20 eight lines
8:21 nine lines
8:22 ten lines
Parallel Lines
8:23 one line
8:24 two lines
8:25 three lines
8:26 four lines
Lines/ Strokes/ Punctations
8:27 two lines, one stroke
8:28 two lines, two strokes
8:29 ladder
8:30 median line and strokes
8:31 two lines, one punctation
8:32 five lines, punctation right
8:33 five lines, punctation left
8:34 lines and punctations
8:35 three lines, punctations
8:36 perpendicular lines
8:37 checker
Incised/ Side/ Base
8:38 incised side
8:39 multiple lines on side
8:40 pinched and incised
8:41 two lines, one line in front
8:42 three lines, one line in front
Ladder Pattern/ Allover Incisions
8:43 ladder on side
8:44 ladder patterns
8:45 nail incisions

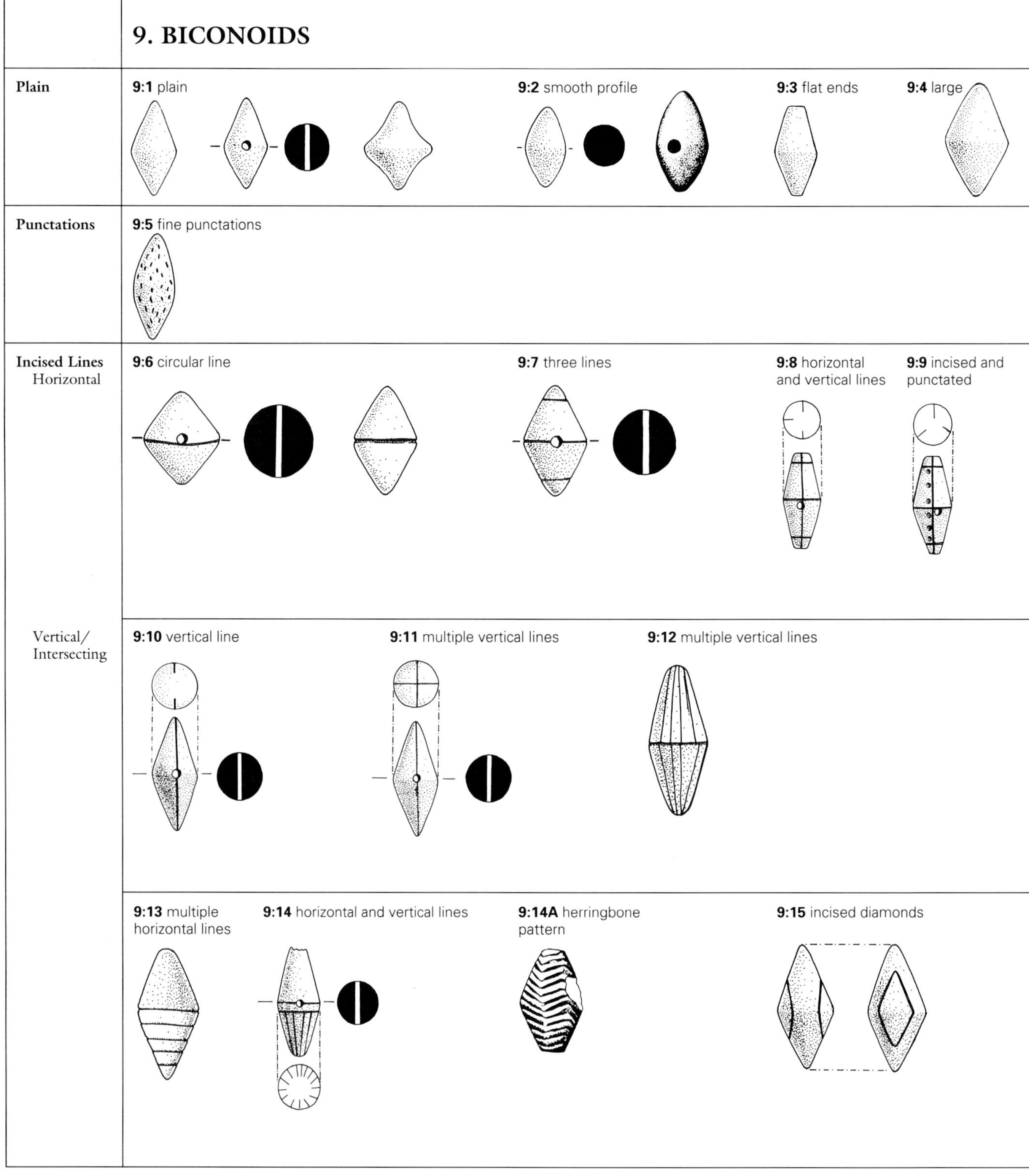
9. BICONOIDS
Plain
9:1 plain
9:2 smooth profile
9:3 flat ends
9:4 large
Punctations
9:5 fine punctations
Incised Lines
Horizontal
9:6 circular line
9:7 three lines
9:8 horizontal and vertical lines
9:9 incised and punctated
Vertical/
Intersecting
9:10 vertical line
9:11 multiple vertical lines
9:12 multiple vertical lines
9:13 multiple horizontal lines
9:14 horizontal and vertical lines
9:14A herringbone pattern
9:15 incised diamonds

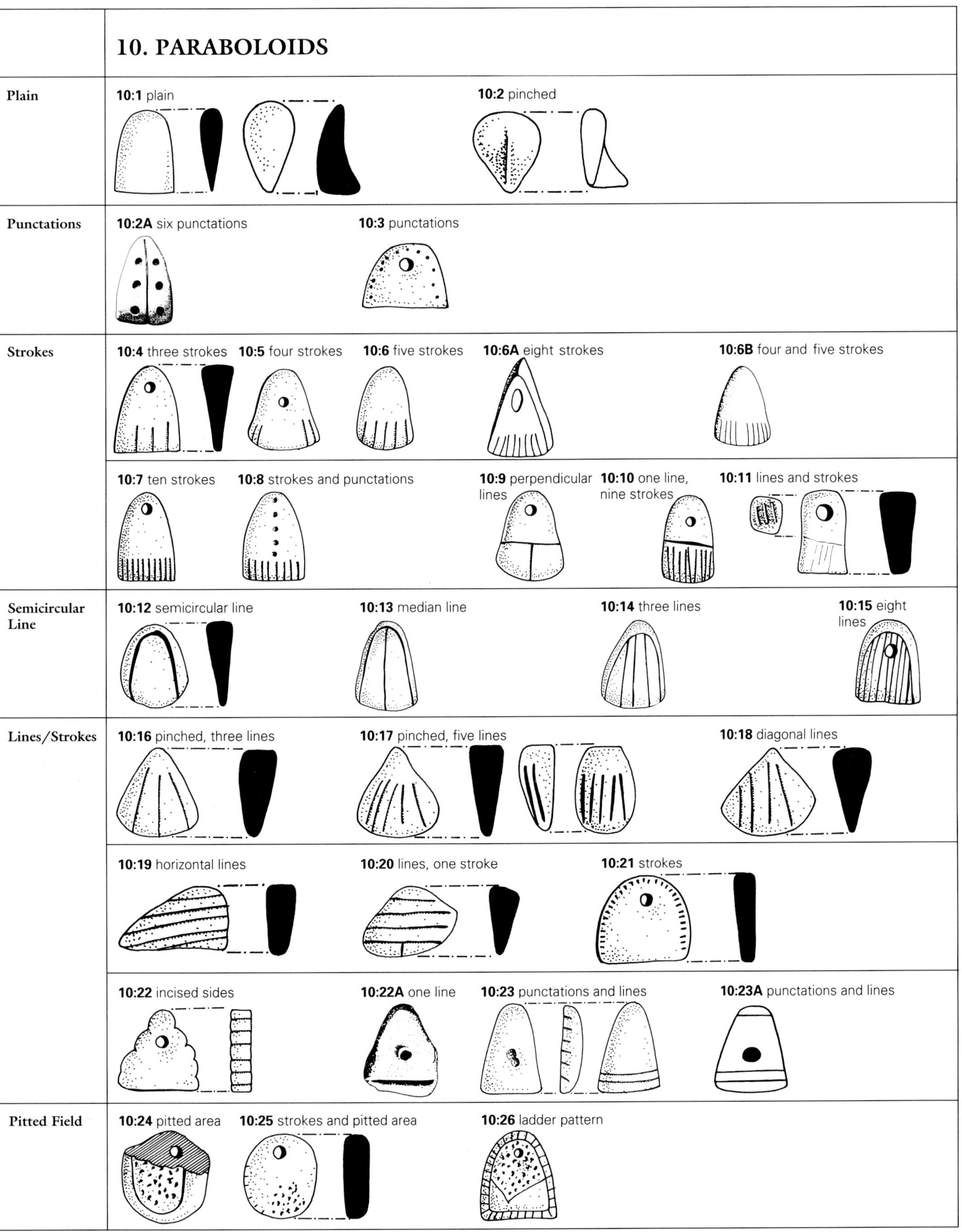
10. PARABOLOIDS
Plain
10:1 plain
10:2 pinched
Punctations
10:2A six punctations
10:3 punctations
Strokes
10:4 three strokes
10:5 four strokes
10:6 five strokes
10:6A eight strokes
10:6B four and five strokes
10:7 ten strokes
10:8 strokes and punctations
10:9 perpendicular lines
10:10 one line, nine strokes
10:11 lines and strokes
Semicircular Line
10:12 semicircular line
10:13 median line
10:14 three lines
10:15 eight lines
Lines/Strokes
10:16 pinched, three lines
10:17 pinched, five lines
10:18 diagonal lines
10:19 horizontal lines
10:20 lines, one stroke
10:21 strokes
10:22 incised sides
10:22A one line
10:23 punctations and lines
10:23A punctations and lines
Pitted Field
10:24 pitted area
10:25 strokes and pitted area
10:26 ladder pattern

	11. BENT COILS		
Convex Section	**11:1** parallel ends 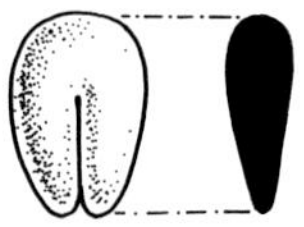	**11:2** incised side 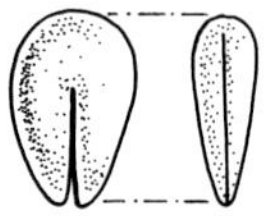	**11:3** six punctations 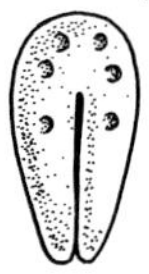
Flat Section	**11:4** incised oval 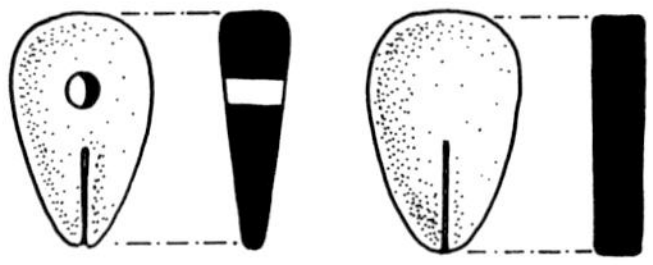	**11:5** incised side 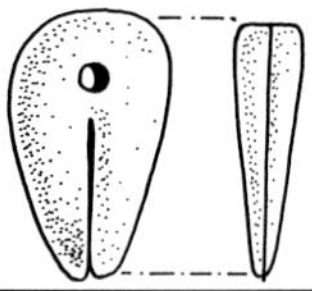	**11:6** two strokes 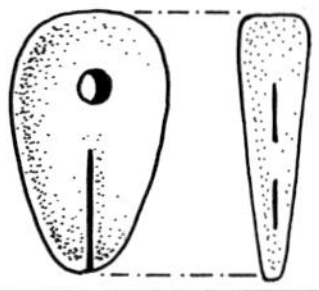
	11:7 median line 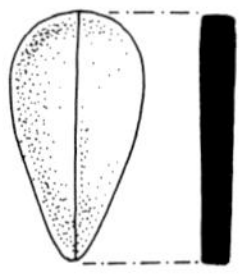	**11:8** cross 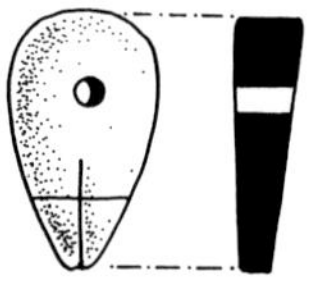	**11:9** circle and line 
Punctations	**11:10** six punctations 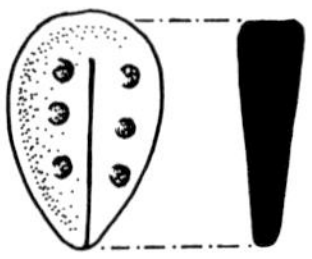	**11:11** markings on both faces 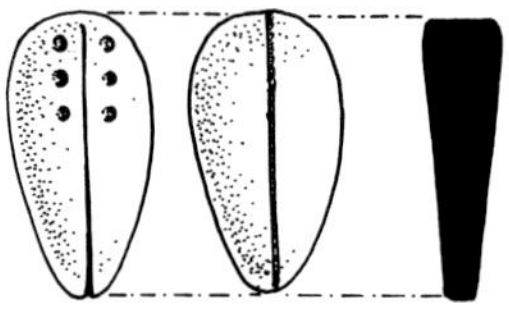	**11:12** incisions and punctations 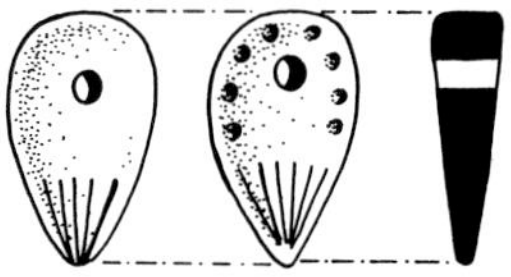

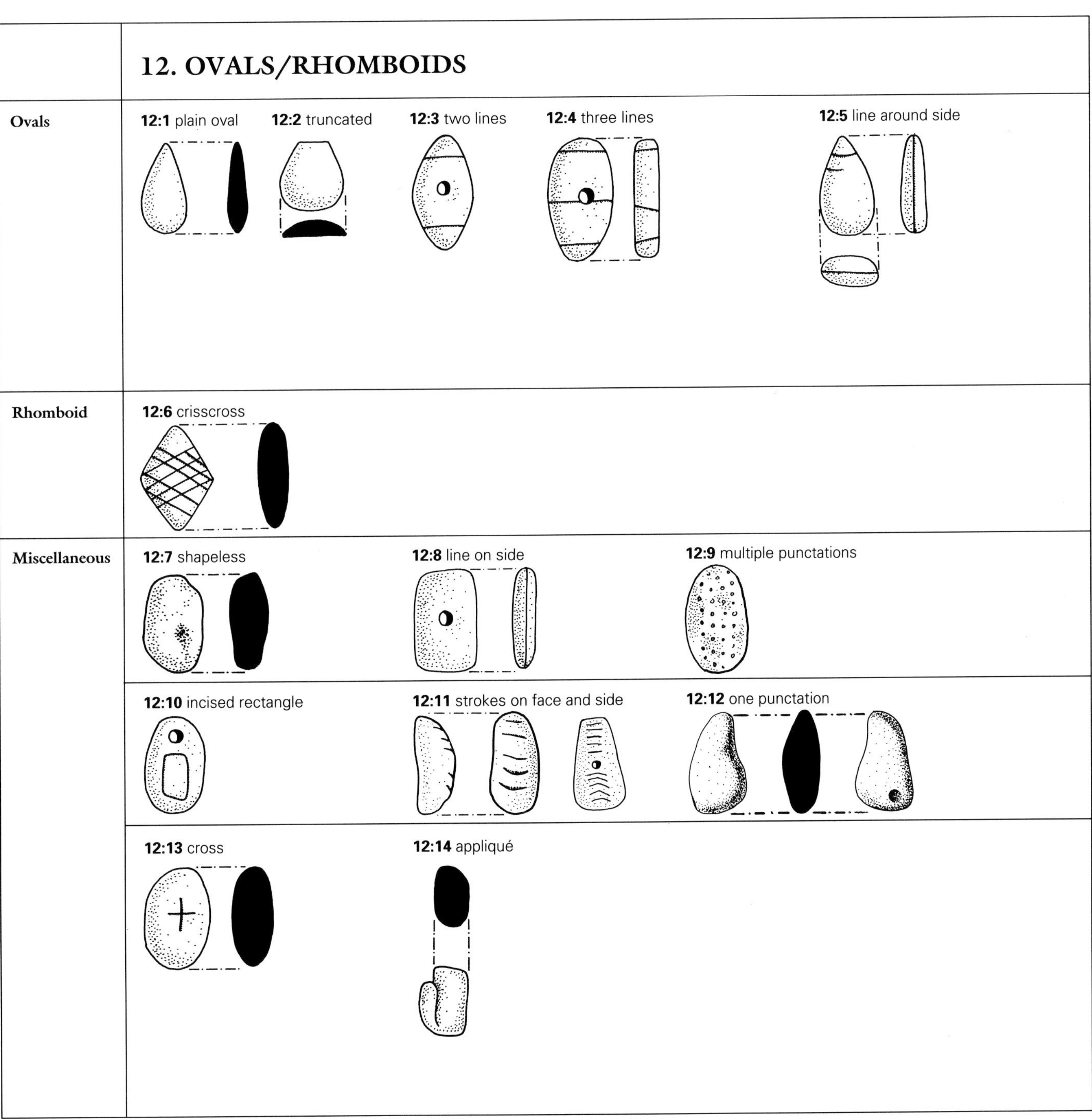
12. OVALS/RHOMBOIDS
Ovals
12:1 plain oval
12:2 truncated
12:3 two lines
12:4 three lines
12:5 line around side
Rhomboid
12:6 crisscross
Miscellaneous
12:7 shapeless
12:8 line on side
12:9 multiple punctations
12:10 incised rectangle
12:11 strokes on face and side
12:12 one punctation
12:13 cross
12:14 appliqué

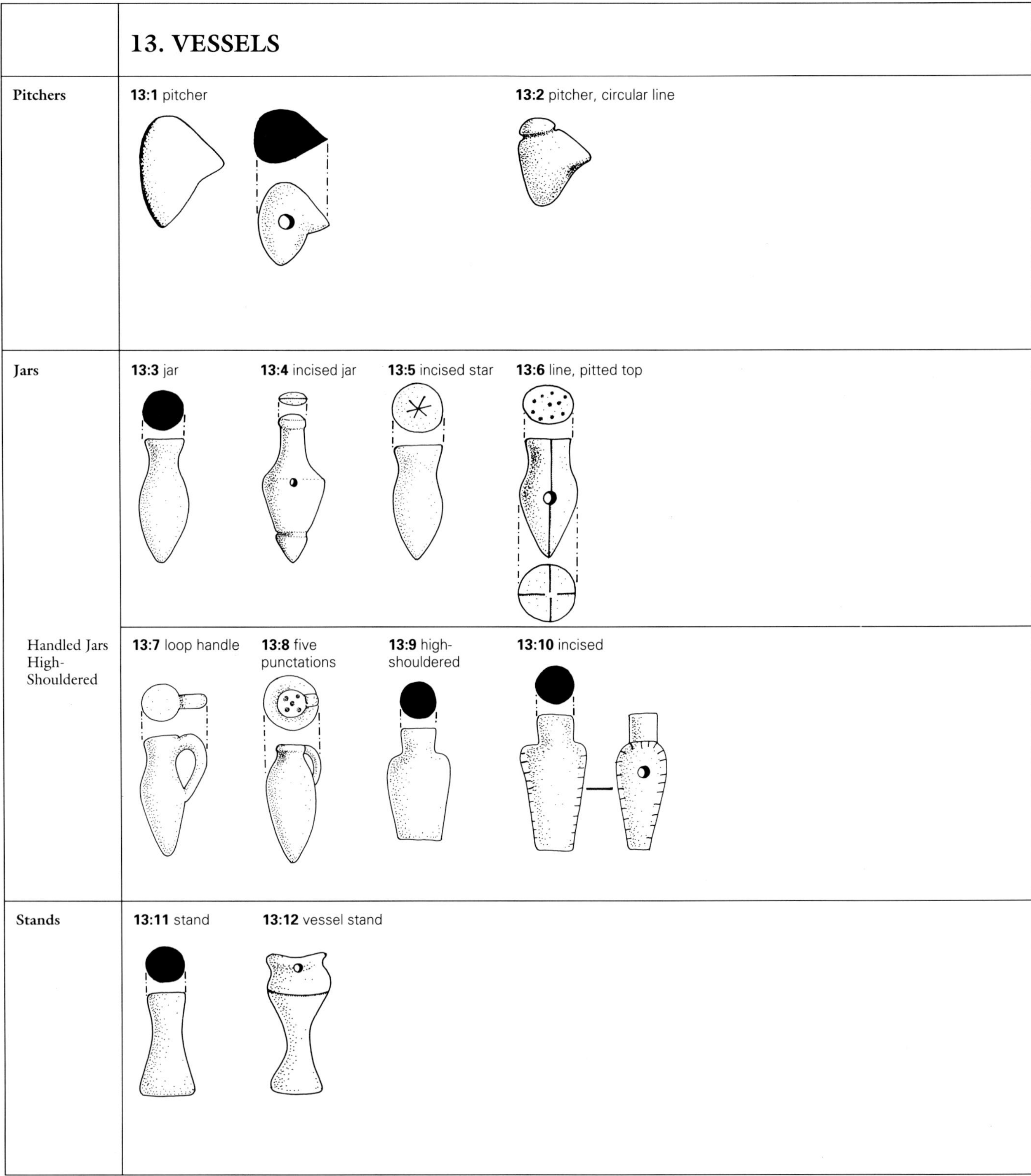
13. VESSELS
Pitchers
13:1 pitcher
13:2 pitcher, circular line
Jars
13:3 jar
13:4 incised jar
13:5 incised star
13:6 line, pitted top
Handled Jars
High-Shouldered
13:7 loop handle
13:8 five punctations
13:9 high-shouldered
13:10 incised
Stands
13:11 stand
13:12 vessel stand

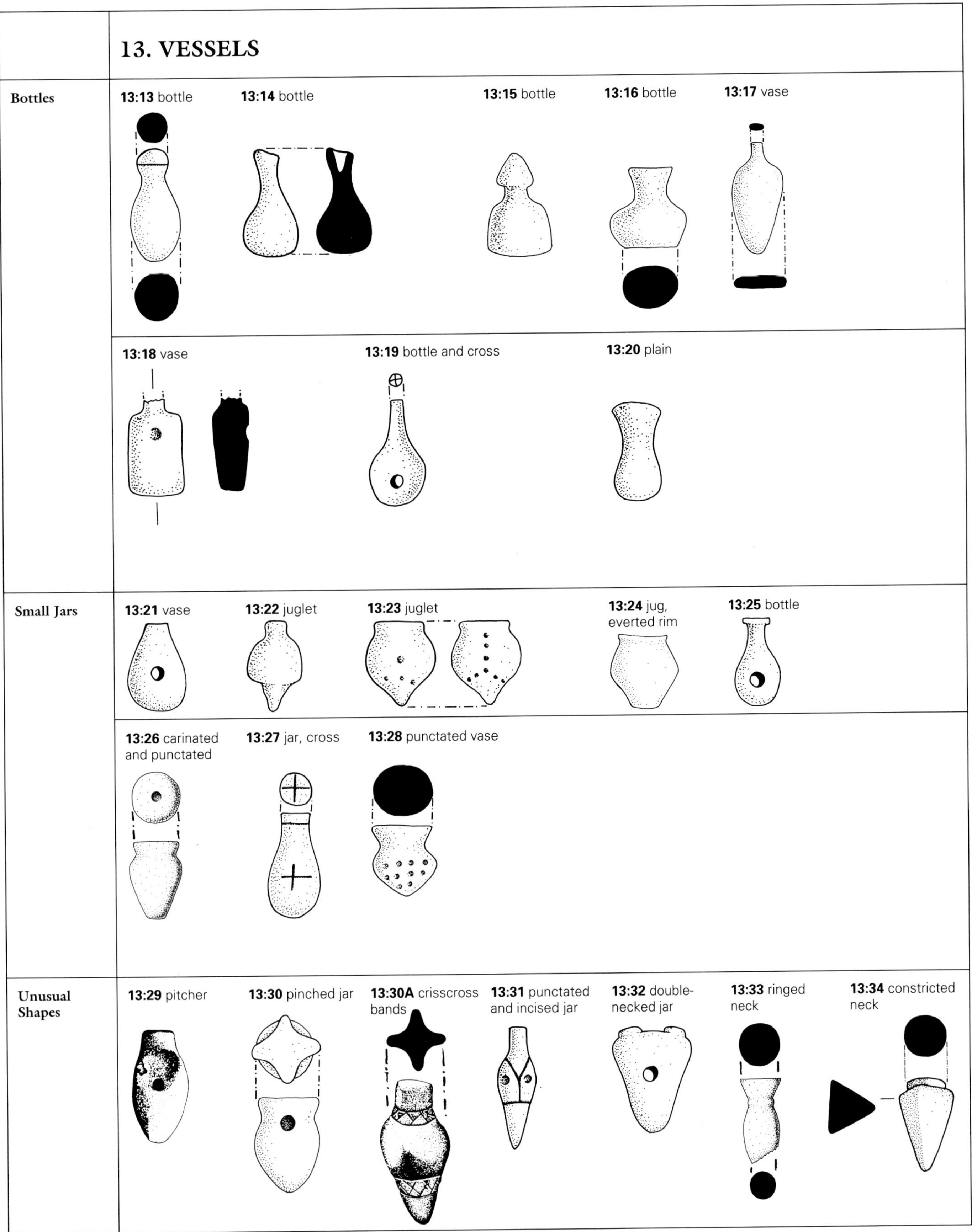
13. VESSELS
Bottles
13:13 bottle
13:14 bottle
13:15 bottle
13:16 bottle
13:17 vase
13:18 vase
13:19 bottle and cross
13:20 plain
Small Jars
13:21 vase
13:22 juglet
13:23 juglet
13:24 jug, everted rim
13:25 bottle
13:26 carinated and punctated
13:27 jar, cross
13:28 punctated vase
Unusual Shapes
13:29 pitcher
13:30 pinched jar
13:30A crisscross bands
13:31 punctated and incised jar
13:32 double-necked jar
13:33 ringed neck
13:34 constricted neck

13. VESSELS

Bowls/Cups	**13:35** round bowl; **13:36** open bowl
	**13:37** triangular juglet; **13:38** cup with ring base; **13:39** handled cup; **13:40** spout
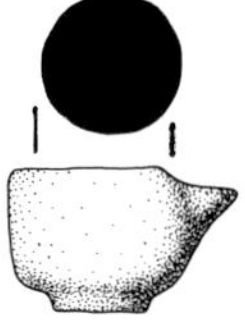	**13:41** painted goblet; **13:42** chalice; **13:43** brazier
Trays	**13:44** tray; **13:45** tray with handles; **13:46** carinated

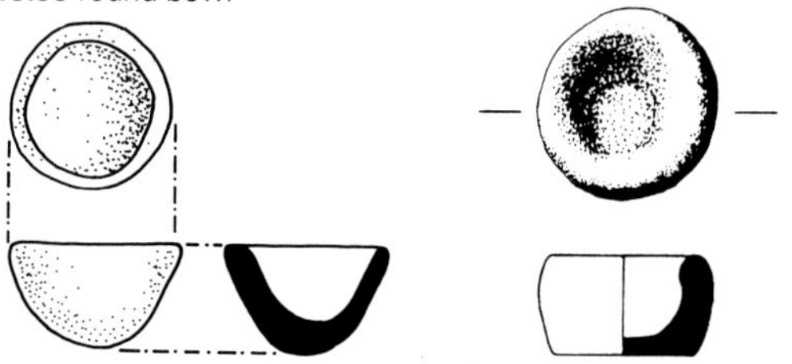

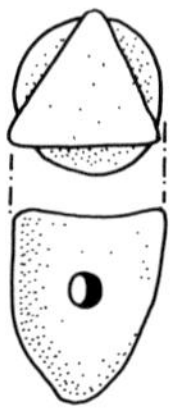

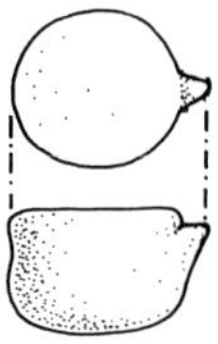

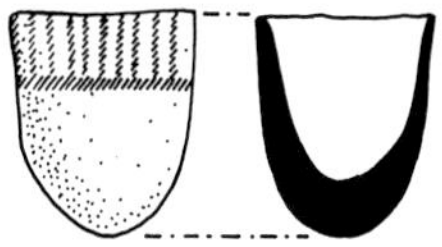

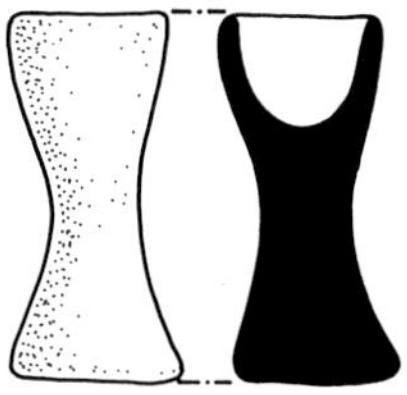

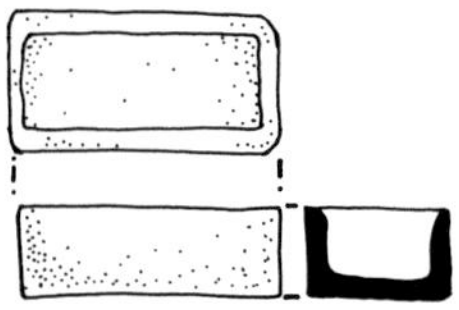

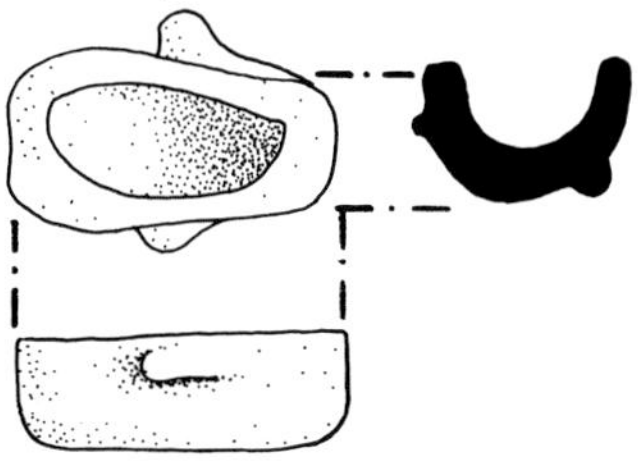

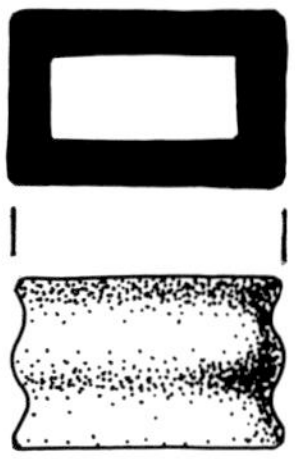

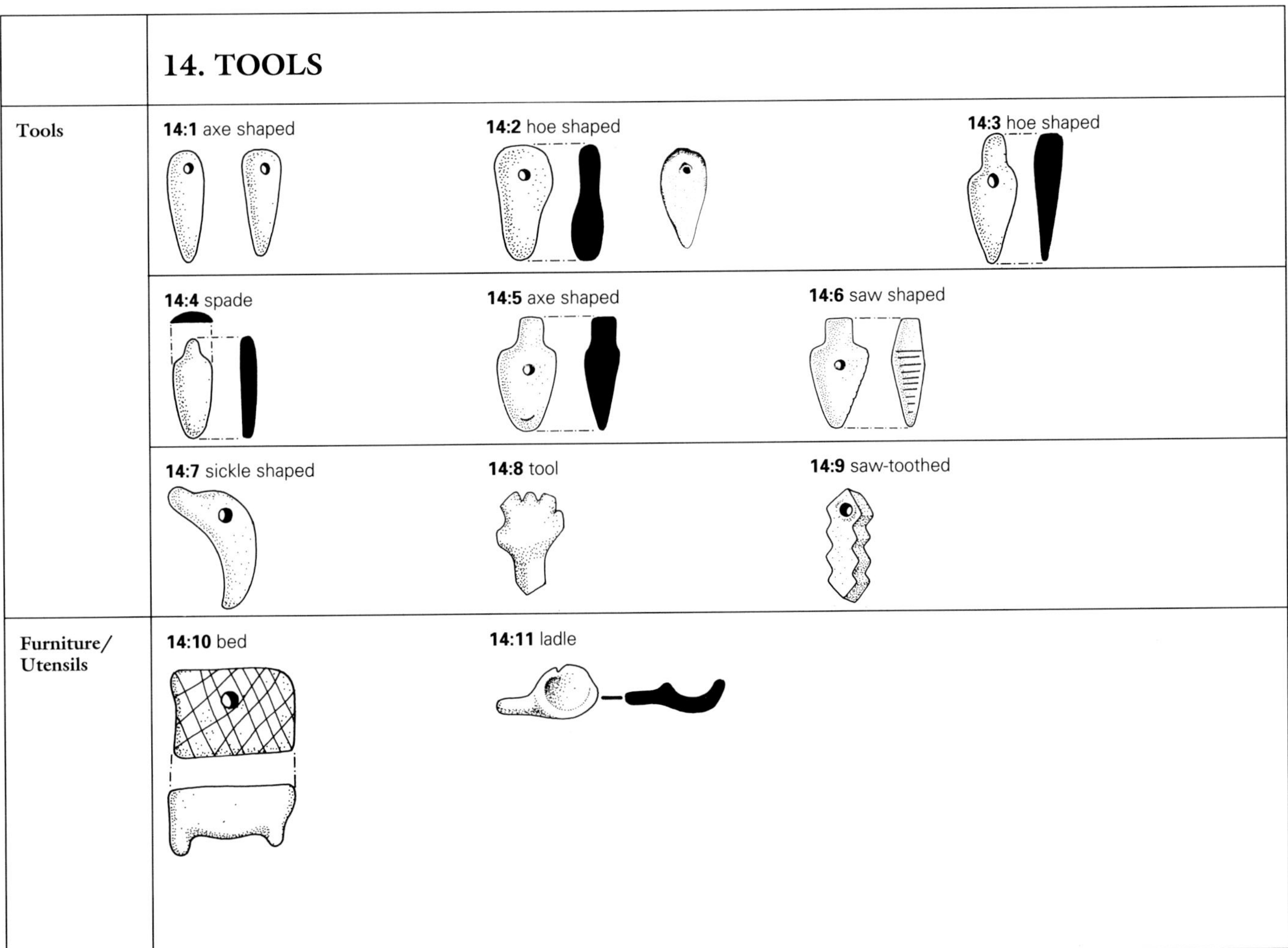
14. TOOLS
Tools
14:1 axe shaped
14:2 hoe shaped
14:3 hoe shaped
14:4 spade
14:5 axe shaped
14:6 saw shaped
14:7 sickle shaped
14:8 tool
14:9 saw-toothed
Furniture/ Utensils
14:10 bed
14:11 ladle

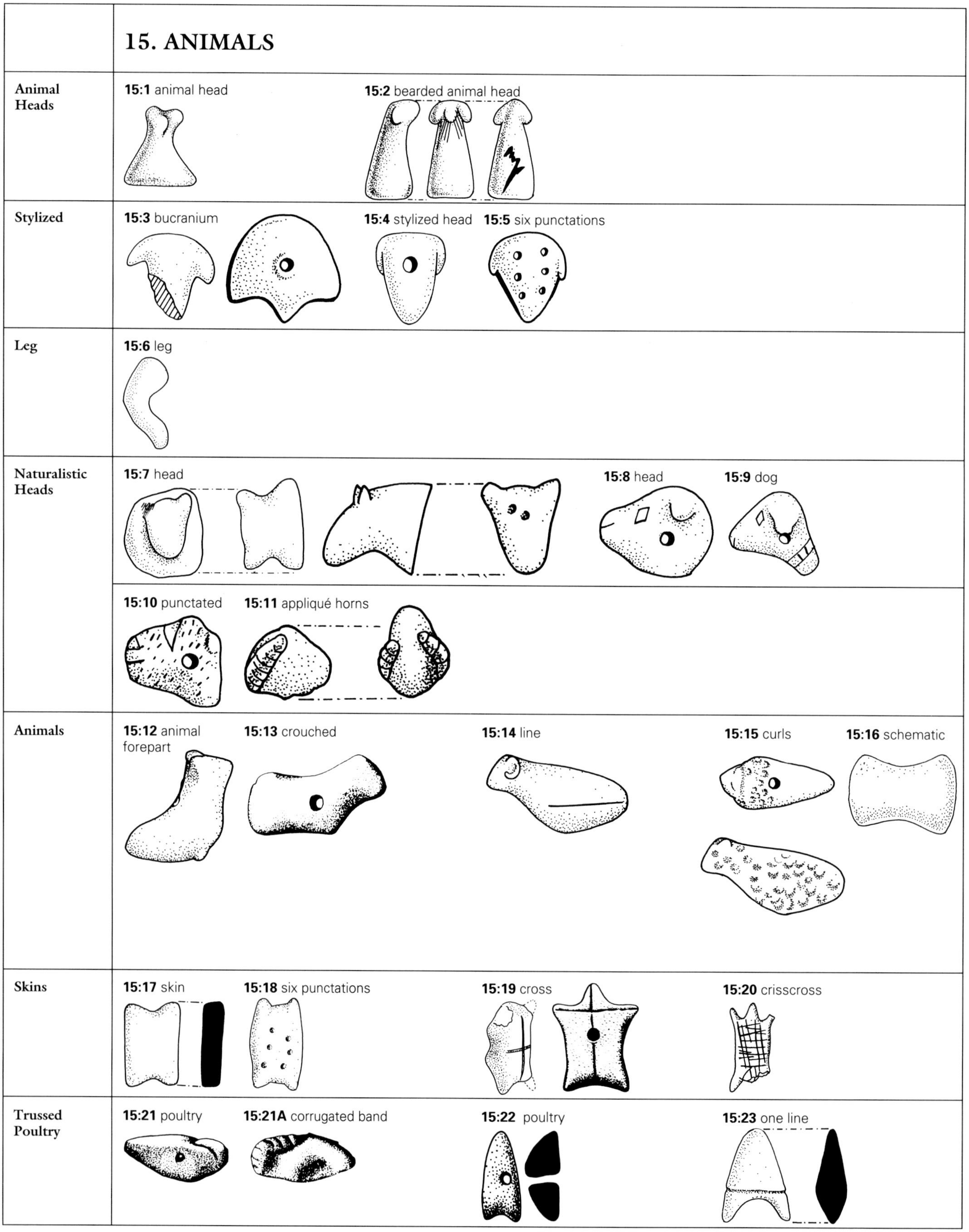

	15. ANIMALS
Animal Heads	**15:1** animal head; **15:2** bearded animal head
Stylized	**15:3** bucranium; **15:4** stylized head; **15:5** six punctations
Leg	**15:6** leg
Naturalistic Heads	**15:7** head; **15:8** head; **15:9** dog
	15:10 punctated; **15:11** appliqué horns
Animals	**15:12** animal forepart; **15:13** crouched; **15:14** line; **15:15** curls; **15:16** schematic
Skins	**15:17** skin; **15:18** six punctations; **15:19** cross; **15:20** crisscross
Trussed Poultry	**15:21** poultry; **15:21A** corrugated band; **15:22** poultry; **15:23** one line

	15. ANIMALS		
Trussed Poultry	**15:24** trussed duck	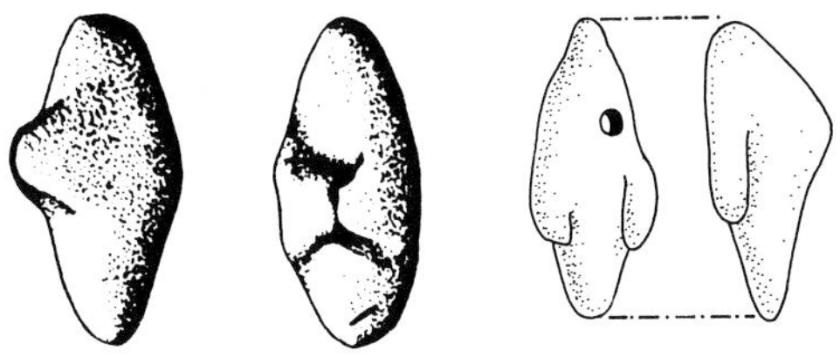	**15:25** trussed duck
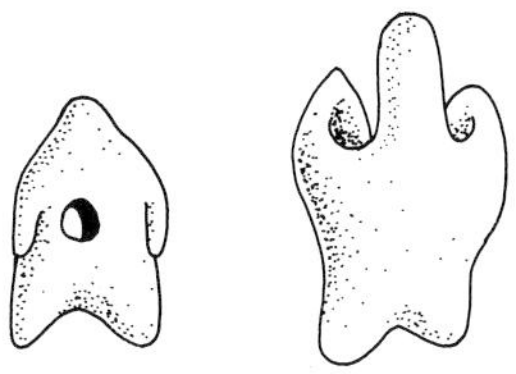	**15:26** three lines	**15:27** trussed duck	**15:28** perpendicular lines

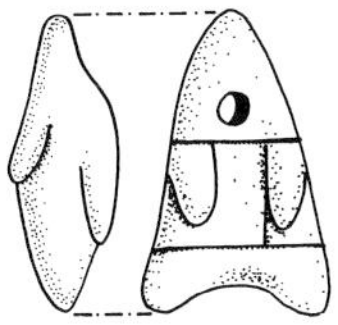

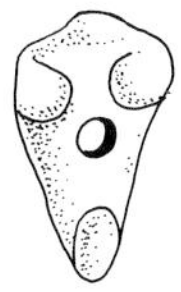

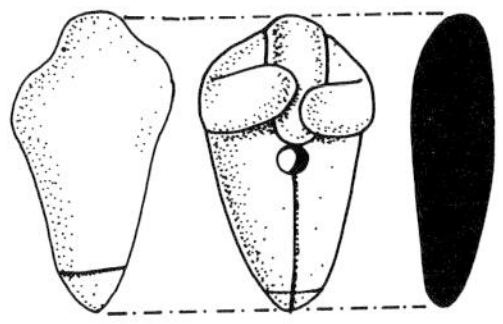

	16. MISCELLANEOUS
Human Head	**16:1** head 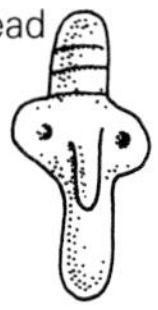
Garments (?)	**16:2** human shaped; 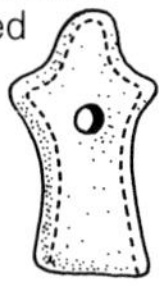 **16:3** one set of strokes; 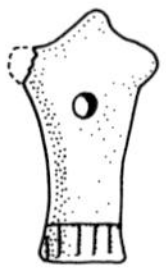 **16:4** one set of strokes; 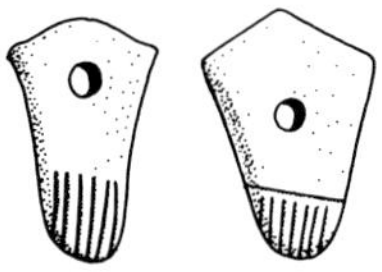 **16:5** two sets of strokes 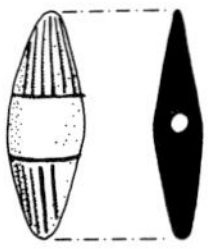
Human	**16:6** leg; 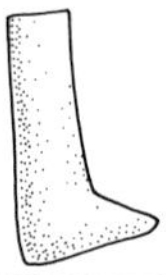 **16:7** phallus 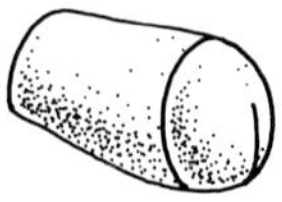
Fruit	**16:8** pomegranate 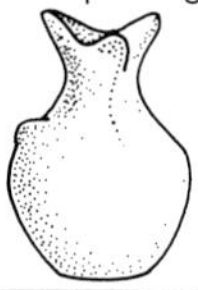
Fish	**16:9** two lines, strokes;  **16:10** crisscross 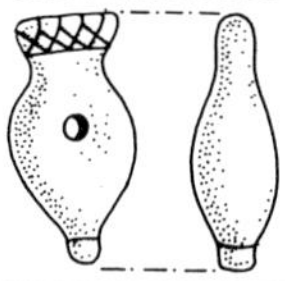
Hyperboloids/ Miscellaneous	**16:11** horned shaped; 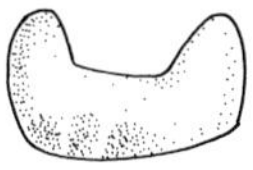 **16:12** pronged 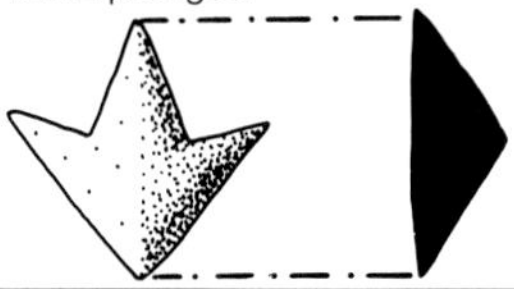
	16:13 hyperboloid; 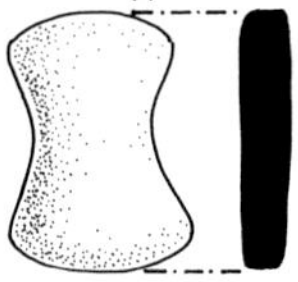 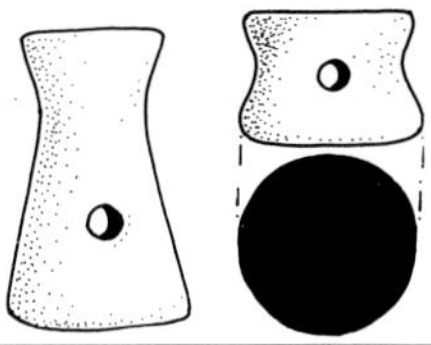 **16:14** bulging top 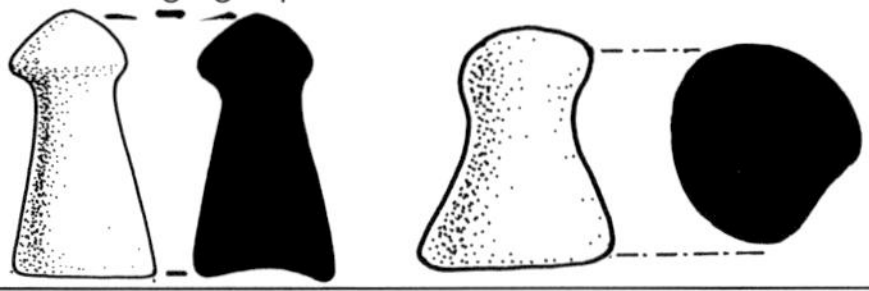
	16:15 astralagus shape; 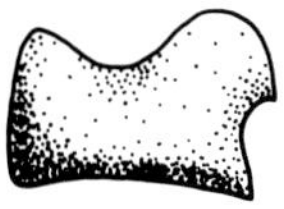 **16:16** schematic 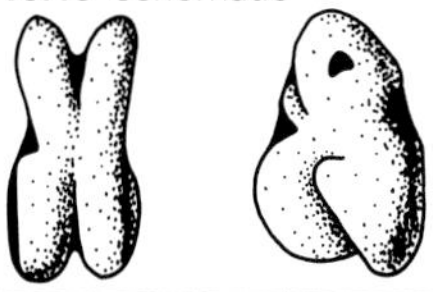
	16:17 ring;  **16:18** crisscross band 

NOTES

Abbreviations

ATU Adam Falkenstein, *Archaische Texte aus Uruk,* Ausgrabungen der deutschen Forschungsgemeinschaft in Uruk-Warka, vol. 2 (Leipzig: Kommissionsverlag Otto Harrassowitz, 1936).

BaM *Baghdader Mitteilungen* (Berlin).

BWII Denise Schmandt-Besserat, *Before Writing, Volume II: A Catalog of Near Eastern Tokens* (Austin: University of Texas Press, 1991). "Cat. no." refers to the unique number of a token at a particular site included in BWII.

Dafi 1a Geneviève Dollfus, "Les Fouilles à Djaffarabad de 1969 à 1971," *Cahiers de la Délégation Archéologique Française en Iran,* vol. 1, 1971, pp. 17–162.

Dafi 1b Alain Le Brun, "Recherches stratigraphiques à l'Acropole de Suse (1969–1971)," *Cahiers de la Délégation Archéologique Française en Iran,* vol. 1, 1971, pp. 163–216.

Dafi 1c François Vallat, "Les documents épigraphiques de l'Acropole (1969–1971)," *Cahiers de la Délégation Archéologique Française en Iran,* vol. 1, 1971, pp. 235–245.

Dafi 3 François Vallat, "Les Tablettes Proto-Elamites de l'Acropole (Campagne 1972)," *Cahiers de la Délégation Archéologique Française en Iran,* vol. 3, 1973, pp. 93–103.

Dafi 5 Geneviève Dollfus, "Les Fouilles à Djaffarabad de 1972 à 1974, Djaffarabad, périodes I et II," *Cahiers de la Délégation Archéologique Française en Iran,* vol. 5, 1975, pp. 11–219.

Dafi 8a Alain Le Brun and François Vallat, "L'Origine de l'écriture à Suse," *Cahiers de la Délégation Archéologique Française en Iran,* vol. 8, 1978, pp. 11–59.

Dafi 8b Alain Le Brun, "La Glyptique du niveau 17B de l'Acropole (Campagne 1972)," *Cahiers de la Délégation Archéologique Française en Iran,* vol. 8, 1978, pp. 61–79.

Dafi 9a Denis Canal, "La Terasse haute de l'Acropole de Suse," *Cahiers de la Délégation Archéologique Française en Iran,* vol. 9, 1978, pp. 11–55.

Dafi 9b Alain Le Brun, "Le Niveau 17B de l'Acropole de Suse (Campagne 1972)," *Cahiers de la Délégation Archéologique Française en Iran,* vol. 9, 1978, pp. 57–154.

M 7 J. de Morgan, G. Jéquier, R. de Mecquenem, B. Haussoulier, and D.-L. Graat van Roggen, *Mémoires de la Délégation en Perse,* vol. 7, *Recherches archéologiques, 2ème série* (Paris: Éditions Ernest Leroux, 1905).

M 12 M.-C. Soutzo, G. Pézard, G. Bondoux, R. de Mecquenem, M. Pézard, J.-E. Gautier, and P. Toscanne, *Mémoires de la Délégation en Perse,* vol. 12, *Recherches archéologiques, 4ème série* (Paris: Éditions Ernest Leroux, 1911).

M 13 E. Pottier, J. de Morgan, and R. de Mecquenem, *Mémoires de la Délégation en Perse,* vol. 13, *Recherches archéologiques, 5ème série. Céramique peinte de Suse et petits monuments de l'époque archaïque* (Paris: Éditions Ernest Leroux, 1912).

M 16 L. Legrain, *Mémoires de la Mission archéologique de Perse,* vol. 16, *Empreintes de cachets élamites* (Paris: Éditions Ernest Leroux, 1921).

M 17 V. Scheil, *Mémoires de la Mission archéologique de Perse,* vol. 17, *Textes de comptabilité proto-élamites (nouvelle série)* (Paris: Éditions Ernest Leroux, 1923).

M 25 Allote de la Fuye, N.-T. Belaiew, R. de Mecquenem, and J.-M. Unvala, *Mémoires de la Mission archéologique de Perse,* vol. 25, *Archéologie, métrologie et numismatique susiennes* (Paris: Éditions Ernest Leroux, 1934).

M 29 R. de Mecquenem, G. Contenau, R. Pfister, and N. Belaiew, *Mémoires de la Mission archéologique en Iran, Mission de Susiane,* vol. 29, *Archéologie susienne* (Paris: Presses Universitaires de France, 1943).

M 30 De Mecquenem, Roland, Contenau, G., Pfister, R. and Benaiew, N. *Archéologie Susienne,* Mémoires de la Mission Archéologique en Iran. Mission de Susiane, Vol. 30, Paris: Presses Universitaires, 1947.

M 43 Pierre Amiet, *Mémoires de la Délégation archéologique en Iran, Mission de Susiane,* vol. 43, *La Glyptique susienne,* vols. 1 and 2 (Paris: Librairie Orientaliste Paul Geuthner, 1972).

M 46 M. J. Steve and H. Gasche, *Mémoires de la Délégation archéologique en Iran, Mission de Susiane,* vol. 46, *L'Acropole de Suse* (Paris: E. J. Brill, Leiden and P. Geuthner, 1971).

OIP Oriental Institute Publications. Chicago: University of Chicago Press.

PI S. Langdon, *The Herbert Weld Collection in the Ashmolean Museum: Pictographic Inscriptions from Jemdet Nasr,* Oxford Editions of Cuneiform Texts 7 (Oxford, 1928).

UVB Julius Jordan, *Vorläufiger Bericht über die von der deutschen Forschungsgemeinschaft in Uruk-Warka unternommenen Ausgrabungen, Abhandlungen der preussischen Akademie der Wissenschaften, Phil.-hist. Klasse* (Berlin), vol. 2, 1931; vol. 3, 1932.

Heinrich J. Lenzen, *Vorläufiger Bericht über die von dem deutschen archäologischen Institut und der deutschen Orientgesellschaft aus Mitteln der deutschen Forschungsgemeinschaft unternommenen Ausgrabungen in Uruk-Warka* (Berlin), vol. 15, 1959; vol. 17, 1961; vol. 21, 1965; vol. 22, 1966; vol. 23, 1967; vol. 24, 1968; vol. 25, 1974.

Jürgen Schmidt, *Vorläufiger Bericht über die von dem deutschen archäologischen Institut aus Mitteln der deutschen Forschungsgemeinschaft unternommenen Ausgrabungen in Uruk-Warka* (Berlin), vols. 31 and 32, 1983.

ZATU M. W. Green and Hans J. Nissen, *Zeichenliste der archaischen Texte aus Uruk,* Ausgrabungen der deutschen Forschungsgemeinschaft in Uruk-Warka, vol. 11, *Archaische Texte aus Uruk,* vol. 2 (Berlin: Gebrüder Mann Verlag, 1987).

Introduction

1. Colin Cherry, *On Human Communication* (New York: John Wiley and Sons, 1957), p. 31.
2. Marvin A. Powell, "Three Problems in the History of Cuneiform Writing: Origins, Direction of Script, Literacy," *Visible Language* 15, no. 4 (1981): 419–420; I. J. Gelb, *A Study of Writing* (Chicago: University of Chicago Press, 1974), p. 63.
3. Geoffrey Sampson, *Writing Systems* (Stanford, Calif.: Stanford University Press, 1985), pp. 46–47.
4. Donald Jackson, *The Story of Writing* (New York: Taplinger Publishing Company, 1981), pp. 16–17.
5. Géza Komoróczy, "Zur Ätiologie der Schrift Erfindung im Enmerkar Epos," *Altorientalische Forschungen* 3 (1975): 19–24; Sol Cohen, "Enmerkar and the Lord of Aratta," Ph.D. dissertation, University of Pennsylvania, 1973, pp. 26–40; Samuel Noah Kramer, *Enmerkar and the Lord of Aratta,* Museum Monograph (Philadelphia: 1952), University Museum, University of Pennsylvania, p. 2.
6. Cohen, "Enmerkar," pp. 136–137.
7. Gertrude Farber, *Der Mythos "Inanna und Enki" unter besonderer Berücksichtigung der Liste der Me,* Studia Pohl vol. 10 (Rome: Biblical Institute Press, 1973).
8. Samuel Noah Kramer, *Sumerian Mythology,* rev. ed. (Philadelphia: University of Pennsylvania Press, 1972), pp. 65, 64.
9. Stanley Mayer Burstein, *The Babyloniaca of Berossus,* Sources from the Ancient Near East 1, No. 5 (Malibu, Calif: Undena Publications, 1978), pp. 1–14.
10. S. H. Hooke, *Babylonian and Assyrian Religion* (London: Hutchinson, 1953), p. 18.
11. Dietz O. Edzard, "Nabu," in Hans W. Haussig, *Wörterbuch der Mythologie,* vol. 1 (Stuttgart: Ernst Klett Verlag, 1965), pp. 106–107.
12. Dieter Kurth, "Thot," in Wolfgang Helck and Wolfhart Westendorf, eds., *Lexikon der Ägyptologie,* vol. 6 (Wiesbaden: Harrassowitz, 1985), col. 506.
13. B. Jowett, *The Dialogues of Plato,* vol. 1, 3d ed. (Oxford: Oxford University Press, 1924), p. 484.
14. Jacqueline de Romilly, 'Le Rôle de l'écriture dans la Grèce ancienne," *Corps Ecrit,* 1 (1982): 23.
15. Thomas Astle, *The Origin and Progress of Writing,* 2d ed. (London: J. White, 1803), p. 15.
16. Ibid., p. 31.
17. Louis Ginzberg, *The Legends of the Jews,* vol. 1, 7th impression (Philadelphia: Jewish Publication Society of America, 1913), p. 3.
18. Ibid., pp. 5–6.
19. W. M. Thackston, Jr., *The Tales of the Prophets of al-Kisa'i* (Boston: Twayne Publishers, 1978), p. 5.
20. Exodus 31:18.
21. Astle, *Origin,* p. 12, argued that writing existed prior to the Tables of the Law because Exodus 17:14 already referred to "writing in a book." According to Ernst Doblhofer, *Voices in Stone* (New York: Viking Press, 1961), p. 14, some considered the text of the Tables of the Law in Exodus 31:18 as "divine writing" compared to "human writing" noted in Isaiah 8:1. Daniel Defoe, *An Essay upon Literature* (London: Thomas Bowles, 1726), title page.
22. Alexander Top, *The Olive Leaf* (1603; reproduced by the Scholar Press Ltd., Menston, England, 1971), p. B2.
23. John Wilkins, *Essay Towards a Real Character and a Philosophical Language* (London: Gellibrand, 1668), p. 11.
24. Madeleine V.-David, *Le Débat sur les écritures et l'hiéroglyphe aux XVII et XVIIIe siècles* (Paris: Bibliothèque Générale de l'Ecole Pratique des Hautes Etudes VIe Section, SEVPEN 1965), p. 13.
25. Edmund Fry, *Pantagraphia* (London: Cooper and Wilson, 1799), pp. 28–29.
26. William Warburton, *Divine Legation of Moses* (London: Fletcher Gyles, 1738), book 4, pp. 67, 70–71, 81, 139; Abbé Etienne Mallet, "Ecriture," in Denis Diderot and Jean le Rond d'Alembert, *Encyclopédie,* vol. 5 (Paris: Briasson, David, Le Breton, Durand, 1755), pp. 358–359.
27. I. J. Gelb, *A Study of Writing* (Chicago: University of Chicago Press, 1974), p. 62.
28. Warburton, *Divine Legation,* book 4, pp. 67, 72, 71, 75, 76.
29. "Reassuring for the mind and befitting vulgarization." V.-David, *Le Débat,* p. 97.
30. Jules Oppert, *Expédition scientifique en Mésopotamie,* vol. 2 (Paris: Imprimerie Nationale, 1859), book 1, pp. 63–65; A. H. Sayce, *Elementary Grammar,* 2d ed. (London: Samuel Bagster and Sons, 1875), pp. iii, xiii; *Lectures upon the Assyrian Language and Syllabary* (London: Samuel Bagster and Sons, 1877), pp. 13–14.
31. Friedrich Delitzsch, *Die Enstehung des ältesten Schriftsystems oder der Ursprung der Keilschriftzeichen* (Leipzig:

J. C. Hinrichs'sche Buchhandlung, 1897).

32. Dietz O. Edzard, "Gunierung," in Dietz O. Edzard, ed., *Reallexikon der Assyriologie und vorderasiatischen Archäologie,* vol. 3, fascicle 9 (Berlin: Walter de Gruyter, 1971) pp. 700–701.
33. S. Langdon, *Sumerian Grammar and Chrestomathy* (Paris, 1911), pp. 21–23.
34. George A. Barton, *The Origin and Development of Babylonian Writing* (Baltimore: Johns Hopkins Press, 1913), p. xi.
35. George A. Barton, "Interpretation of the Archaic Tablet of the E. A. Hoffman Collection," *Journal of American Oriental Society* 23 (1902): 26.
36. Ellen S. Ogden, *The Origin of the gunû-Signs in Babylonian* (Leipzig: W. Drugulin, 1911).
37. Barton, *Origin,* pp. xiii, xiv.
38. William A. Mason, *A History of the Art of Writing* (New York: Macmillan Company, 1928), pp. 236–237.
39. "The Sumerian or Semitic mentality in the fourth millennium was, obviously, very different from ours." Georges Contenau, *Manuel d'archéologie orientale,* vol. 1 (Paris: Editions Auguste Picard, 1927), p. 214.
40. ATU 25, 52.
41. Edward Chiera, *They Wrote on Clay* (Chicago: University of Chicago Press, 1938), pp. 50, 58–60; Georges Roux, *Ancient Iraq* (Harmondsworth: Penguin Books, 1980), p. 80.
42. André Leroi-Gourhan, *Le Geste et la parole,* vol. 1 (Paris: Editions Albin Michel, 1964), p. 269. French text: "Les linguistes qui se sont attachés à l'étude de l'origine de l'écriture ont souvent considéré les pictographies en projetant sur elles une mentalité née de la pratique de l'écriture."
43. Ibid., p. 270. French text: "Aussi parait-il impossible de se servir de la pictographie des Esquimaux ou des Indiens comme d'un terme de comparaison pour comprendre l'idéographie des peuples antérieurs à l'écriture."
44. V. Gordon Childe, *What Happened in History,* rev. ed. (Harmondsworth: Penguin Books, 1954), p. 93.
45. Chiera, *They Wrote on Clay,* p. 51.
46. Robert Claiborne, *The Birth of Writing* (Alexandria, Va.: Time-Life Books, 1974), p. 66; Dora Jane Hamblin, *The First Cities* (New York: Time-Life Books, 1973), p. 99.
47. Childe, *What Happened,* p. 87; Samuel A. B. Mercer, *The Origin of Writing and Our Alphabet* (London: Luzac and Company, 1959), p. 1.
48. Seton Lloyd, *The Archaeology of Mesopotamia* (London: Thames and Hudson, 1978), p. 55.
49. David Diringer, *The Alphabet,* vol. 1, 3d ed. (London: Hutchinson, 1968), pp. 24, 49.
50. Carleton S. Coon, *Cave Explorations in Iran,* Museum Monographs (Philadelphia: University Museum, University of Pennsylvania, 1949), p. 75.
51. Vivian L. Broman, "Jarmo Figurines," Master's thesis, Radcliffe College, Cambridge, Mass., 1958. The work was later published as "Jarmo Figurines and Other Clay Objects," in Linda S. Braidwood, Robert J. Braidwood, et al., eds., *Prehistoric Archaeology along the Zagros Flanks,* Oriental Institute Publications 105 (Chicago: University of Chicago Press, 1983), pp. 369–423.
52. Ibid., pp. 58, 62, 63; Thorkild Jacobsen, *Human Origins,* Selected Readings, Series 2, 2d ed. (Chicago: University of Chicago Press, 1946), p. 245.
53. A. Leo Oppenheim, "On an Operational Device in Mesopotamian Bureaucracy," *Journal of Near Eastern Studies* 18 (1959): 121–128.
54. Richard F. S. Starr, *Nuzi,* vol. 1 (Cambridge, Mass.: Harvard University Press, 1939), pp. 316–317; Ernest R. Lacheman, *Excavations at Nuzi,* vol. 7, Economic and Social Documents, Harvard Semitic Series, vol. 16 (Cambridge, 1958), p. 88, no. 311.
55. It is likely that the tablet was meant for Puhisenni's archive and the envelope was intended for Ziqarru, who was probably illiterate; Starr, *Nuzi,* pp. 316–317; Lacheman, *Excavations at Nuzi,* p. v. Tzvi Abusch explains why both texts were found in the same archive in "Notes on a Pair of Matching Texts: A Shepherd's Bulla and an Owner's Receipt," in Martha A. Morrison and David I. Owen, eds., *Studies on the Civilization and Culture of Nuzi and the Hurrians* (Winona Lake, Ind.: Eisenbrauns, 1981), pp. 1–9.
56. Abusch, "Notes," pp. 2–3.
57. Starr, *Nuzi,* p. 316.
58. Oppenheim, "On an Operational Device," pp. 125–126.
59. The Sumerian form is borrowed into Akkadian as *tuk(k)annu* (personal communication from Marcel Sigrist). The text is published in G. Pettinato, S. A. Picchioni, and F. Reshid, *Testi Economici Dell'Iraq Museum-Baghdad,* Materiali per il Vocabulario Neosumerico vol. 8 (Rome: Multigrafica Editrice, 1979), pl. XLVIII, no. 148; P. Dhorme, "Tablettes de Drehem à Jérusalem," *Revue d'Assyriologie et d'Archéologie Orientale* 9 (1912): pl. I: SA 19.
60. Starr, *Nuzi,* p. 316.
61. Pierre Amiet, "Il y a 5000 ans les Elamites inventaient l'écriture," *Archeologia* 12 (1966): 20–22.
62. Ibid., p. 22.
63. Amiet assumed that Nineveh also yielded an envelope, but the artifact he had in mind is a solid oval bulla. Pierre Amiet, *Elam,* (Auvers-sur-Oise: Archée Editeur, 1966), p. 70.
64. "A series of round or long notches, similar to the ciphers featured on tablets and corresponding to the number of calculi enclosed inside. The shape of the notches, however, is not as varied as that of the calculi." M43, p. 69.
65. "I was thus wondering whether this script was not related to some of the calculi enclosed in the bullae." Pierre Amiet, *L'Age des échanges inter-iraniens* (Paris: Editions de la Réunion des Musées Nationaux, 1986), p. 76.
66. "Writing, here as elsewhere, imitated true things." Maurice Lambert, "Pourquoi l'écriture est née en Mésopotamie," *Archeologia* 12 (1966): 30.
67. Denise Schmandt-Besserat, "The Use of Clay before Pottery in the Zagros," *Expedition* 16, no. 2 (1974): 10–17; "An Archaic Recording System and the Origin

of Writing," *Syro-Mesopotamian Studies* 1, no. 2 (1977): 1–32; "The Earliest Precursor of Writing," *Scientific American* 238, no. 6 (1978): 50–58; "Tokens and Counting," *Biblical Archaeologist* 46 (1983): 117–120; "Before Numerals," *Visible Language* 18, no. 1 (1986): 48–60.

1. What Are Tokens?

1. "The manufacture of small objects modelled in clay and hardened with fire was a particularly important activity at Tell Aswad, especially in level II, in the first half of the seventh millennium . . . These were . . . artifacts of geometric shapes, such as balls, disks, and small cups." Henri de Contenson, "Recherches sur le Néolithique de Syrie (1967–76)," *Comptes Rendus, Académie des Inscriptions et Belles-Lettres* (1978): 821–22.
2. Cyril S. Smith, "A Matter of Form," *Isis* 76, no. 4 (1985): 586.
3. The following tokens bear incised lines on the sides: disks (type 3: 29, 52, 70–72), rectangles (type 7: 13, 17, 25), triangles (type 8: 38–39, 41–42, 43–44), paraboloids (type 10: 22, 23), and bent coils (type 11: 5–6).
4. One rectangle and one bent coil are among the exceptions (types 7: 7 and 11: 11).
5. Type 1: 28 has a simple arrangement.
6. ATU 781, "fat tail sheep"; ZATU 240.
7. Cat. no. 43, TG 5679; Cat. no. 40, IM 18864, in Denise Schmandt-Besserat, *Before Writing, Volume II: A Catalog of Tokens* (Austin: University of Texas Press, 1991); hereafter, BWII.
8. Cat. no. 57, IM 14937; Cat. no. 7, 1359.1, ibid.
9. Cat. nos. 266–268, ibid.
10. ATU 111/ZATU 511, ATU 568/ZATU 616.
11. ATU 234/ZATU 355; ATU 192/ZATU 31; ZATU 290.
12. Krystyna Szarzynska, "Sumerian Labels," unpublished ms., Oriental Institute, University of Warsaw, 1989.
13. Jean Bottero, UVB 22, p. 45; ZATU 749.
14. I am grateful to Robert K. Englund for this information.
15. ATU 305/ZATU 19.
16. Krystyna Szarzynska, "Z Badan Nad Najshtarszymi Zapisami Sumeryjskimi Z Miasta Uruk," [Some of the cult elements in the oldest Sumerian texts], Ph.D. dissertation, Oriental Institute, University of Warsaw, 1986.
17. Denise Schmandt-Besserat, "The Use of Clay before Pottery in the Zagros," *Expedition* 16, no. 2 (1974): 11–13.
18. Tepe Gawra yielded ninety-five stone tokens and Tell es Sawwan fifty-four.
19. E. Bostanci, "Beldibi ve Mağracikta Yapilan 1967 Yaz Mevsimi Kazilari ve Yeni Buluntular," *Türk Arkeoloji Dergisi* 16, no. 1 (1967): 58, fig. 3.
20. Denise Schmandt-Besserat, "Tokens at Uruk," *BaM* 19 (1988): cat. nos. 23, 104, and 107; Susa, Cat. nos. 170, 658, and 659, BWII.
21. Jacques Bordaz, "The Suberde Excavations in Southwest Turkey, an Interim Report," *Türk Arkeoloji Dergisi* 17, no. 2 (1969): 51.
22. M 46, pl. 37: 12. Agnès Spycket has shown that molds for figurines did not occur before the later part of the third millennium B.C. in "Transposition du modelage ou moulage à Suse à la fin du IIIé millenaire av. J.C." *Mélanges offerts à M. J. Steve*, Fragmenta Historiae Emamicae (Paris: Editions Recherche sur les Civilisations, 1986), pp. 79–82.
23. M. 29, pp. 13–14, fig. 8: 3–5.
24. FF XII 1C; CC X 84; and EE XII 21 .
25. DD XI 50 was originally of subtype 28 and changed to subtype 30 by the addition of two lines; a median line was added on GG XII 5.
26. Schmandt-Besserat, "The Use of Clay," p. 13.
27. W. D. Kingery, B. François, and C. DuPont, "Micrographic Examination of Some Archaeological Sherds," unpublished ms., 1971. I am grateful to W. David Kingery, director of the Division of Ceramics, Massachusetts Institute of Technology for his time and interest in supervising the analysis. The samples of Tepe Asiab and Tepe Sarab were kindly provided by Robert J. Braidwood, director, Prehistoric Project, Oriental Institute, University of Chicago. Those from Susa were loaned by Pierre Amiet, conservateur en chef, Département des Antiquités Orientales, Musée du Louvre, Paris.
28. W. D. Kingery, R. J. Brooks, R. L. Anderson, et al., "Progress Report on a Cursory Technical Examination of Some Near Eastern Ceramic Sherds," unpublished ms., 1971.
29. The final report by Judith Pullar, *Tepe Abdul Hosein*, Oxford: BAR International Series 563, 1990, includes 44 tokens: 20 cones, 10 spheres, 2 discs, 12 cylinders. Permission to include the tokens from Chogha Mish and Ganj Dareh Tepe was not granted pending their publication elsewhere. The information concerning the tokens from Shar-i Sokhta was received too late to be included in the catalog.
30. I am grateful to Stefan Karol Koslowski for communicating to me the information on Nemrik. Unfortunately it came too late to be included in the catalog.
31. Sabah Aboud Jasim, *The Ubaid Period in Iraq*, part 1, International Series =S267 (Oxford: BAR 1985), pp. 69–73.
32. Robert J. Braidwood and Bruce Howe, *Prehistoric Investigations in Iraqi Kurdistan,* Studies in Ancient Civilization, vol. 31 (Chicago: Oriental Institute, University of Chicago, 1960), p. 30.
33. Seton Lloyd and Fuad Safar, "Tell Hassuna: Excavations by the Iraq Government Directorate General of Antiquities in 1943 and 1944," *Journal of Near Eastern Studies* 4 (1945): 258.
34. Ernest Mackay, *Report on Excavations at Jemdet Nasr, Iraq,* Anthropology Memoirs vol. 1, no. 3 (Chicago: Field Museum of Natural History, 1931), p. 278.
35. M. E. L. Mallowan and J. Cruikshank Rose, "Excavations at Tall Arpachiyah, 1933," *Iraq* 2, part 1 (1935): 88.
36. Lloyd and Safar, "Tell Hassuna," pl. X, 1: 22–23.
37. Arthur J. Tobler, *Excavations at Tepe Gawra,* vol. 2, University Museum Monograph (Philadelphia: Uni-

versity of Pennsylvania Press, 1950), pp. 170–171, 205.

38. H. R. Hall, *Ur Excavations,* vol. 1, *Al Ubaid* (Oxford: Oxford University Press, 1927), p. 41, fig. 4.

39. Vivian L. Broman, "Jarmo Figurines," Master's thesis, Radcliffe College, 1958. The work was later published as "Jarmo Figurines and Other Clay Objects," in Linda S. Braidwood, Robert J. Braidwood, et al., eds., *Prehistoric Archaeology along the Zagros Flanks,* Oriental Institute Publications 105 (Chicago: University of Chicago Press, 1983), pp. 369–423.

2. *Plain Tokens*

1. Ernest Mackay, *Report on Excavations at Jemdet Nasr, Iraq,* Anthropology Memoirs vol. 1, no. 3 (Chicago: Field Museum of Natural History, 1931), p. 278.
2. Abu Hureyra, Amuq, Chagar Bazar, Cheikh Hassan, Ghoraife, Habuba Kabira, Hadidi, Hama, Jebel Aruda, Mureybet, Ras Shamra, Tell Aswad, Tell Brak, Tell Halaf, Tell Kannas, and Tell Ramad.
3. Ain Ghazal, Beidha, Beisamoun, Jericho, Ktar Tell Kazarei, Megiddo, Munhata, and Tell Ephek.
4. A. J. Arkell, *Early Khartoum* (Oxford: Oxford University Press, 1949), pp. 79ff.
5. The list of Iraqi sites is as follows: Arpachiyah, Billa, Choga Mami, Eridu, Fara, Gird Ali Agha, Gird Banahilk, Hassuna, Ischali, Jarmo, Jemdet Nasr, Khafaje, Kish, Larsa, Maghzaliyah, Matarrah, M'lefaat, Nemrik, Nineveh, Nippur, Nuzi, Ras al Amiya, Sippar, Tell Abada, Tell Agrab, Tell Asmar, Tell es-Sawwan, Tell Oueili, Tell Raschid, Tell Songor, Tello, Tell Yelkhi, Telul eth Thalathat, Tepe Gawra, Ubaid, Umm Dabaghiyah, Umm Hafriyat, Uqair, Ur, Uruk, and Yarim Tepe.
6. The information on the sixty-nine tokens from Nemrik communicated by Stefan Karol Koslowski came too late to be included in the catalog.
7. Shinji Fukai, Kiyoharu Horiuchi, and Toshio Matsutani, *Marv-Dasht III, the Excavation at Tall-i-Mushki, 1965,* Tokyo University Iraq-Iran Archaeological Expedition Report 14 (Tokyo: Institute of Oriental Culture, University of Tokyo, 1973), pls. XXXVIII, XXXIX, LIV, and LV. The tokens are not included in the catalog.
8. The fifty-three tokens from Shahr-i Sokhta could not be included in the catalog.
9. Anau, Bampur, Belt Cave, Chagha Sefid, Chogha Bonut, Chogha Mish, Dalma Tepe, Deh Luran, Ganj Dareh, Geoy Tepe, Hajji Firuz, Jaffarabad, Jeitun, KS 34., KS 54., KS 76., Malyan, Moussian, Sharafabad, Seh Gabi, Sialk, Sorkh-i-Dom, Susa, Tall-i-Bakun, Tal-i-Iblis, Tepe Abdul Hosein, Tepe Asiab, Tepe Bouhallan, Tepe Farukhabad, Tepe Gaz Tavila, Tepe Giyan, Tepe Guran, Tepe Hissar, Tepe Muradabad, Tepe Sarab, Tepe Siahbid, Tepe Yahya, Tula'i, and Zagheh. (Permission to include the tokens from Chogha Mish and Ganj Dareh Tepe was not granted pending their publication elsewhere.)
10. Personal communication, Thomas C. Barger, La Jolla, California.
11. Personal communication, Jean-François Jarrige.
12. I have based my general chronology on Robert W. Ehrich, *Chronologies in Old World Archaeology,* 3d ed. (Chicago: University of Chicago Press, forthcoming). The carbon 14 dates quoted are those indicated in Olivier Aurenche, Jacques Evin, and Francis Hours, eds., *Chronologies du Proche Orient,* BAR International Series =S379 (Oxford, 1987), pp. 691–736; James Mellaart, *The Neolithic of the Near East* (New York: Charles Scribner's Sons, 1975), pp. 283–288. When not otherwise indicated, they are conventional, uncalibrated radiocarbon dates, calculated with Libby half-life of 5,568 years.
13. Jacques Cauvin, *Les Premiers Villages de Syrie-Palestine du IXème au VIIème millénaire avant J. C.,* Collection de la Maison de L'Orient Mediterranéen Ancien, no. 4, Série Archéologique 3 (Lyon, France: Maison de l'Orient, 1978), pp. 144–145.
14. Ibid., p. 41.
15. Henri de Contenson, "Chronologie absolue de Tell Aswad (Damascène, Syrie)," *Bulletin de la Société Préhistorique Française* 70 (1973): 253; "Tell Aswad (Damascène)," *Paléorient* 5 (1979): 155; "La Région de Damas au Néolithique," *Annales Archéologiques Arabes Syriennes* 35 (1985): 9.
16. Philip E. L. Smith, "An Interim Report on Ganj Dareh Tepe Iran," *American Journal of Archaeology* (1982): 178–180.
17. Contenson, "La Région de Damas," p. 12.
18. Ibid., p. 18.
19. Ibid., p. 20.
20. Julius Jordan, UVB 3, pp. 18, 29–31; UVB 4, p. 6, pl. 2. The *Tiefschnitt* has been re-evaluated in Dietrich Sürenhagen, "Archaische Keramik aus Uruk-Warka. Erster Teil: Die Keramik der Schichten XVI–VI aus der Sondagen 'Tiefschnitt' und 'Sägegraben' in Eanna," *BaM* (1986): 7–95.
21. Robert H. Dyson, Jr., "The Relative and Absolute Chronology of Hissar II and the Proto-Elamite Horizon of Northern Iran," in Aurenche, Evin, and Hours, eds., *Chronologies,* p. 675.
22. Denise Schmandt-Besserat, "The Use of Clay before Pottery in the Zagros," *Expedition* 16, no. 2 (1974): 12.
23. Mary Voigt, "Relative and Absolute Chronologies for Iran between 6500 and 3500 Cal BC," in Aurenche, Evin, and Hours, eds., *Chronologies,* p. 624.
24. Philip E. L. Smith, "An Interim Report on Ganj Dareh Tepe, Iran," *American Journal of Archaeology* 82, no. 4 (1978): 538.
25. Robert J. Braidwood, Bruce Howe, and Charles A. Reed, "The Iranian Prehistoric Project," *Science* 133, no. 3469 (1961): 2008.
26. Philip E. L. Smith, "Ganj Dareh Tepe," *Paléorient* 2, no. 1 (1974): 207.
27. Reiner Protsch and Rainer Berger, "Earliest Radiocarbon Dates for Domesticated Animals," *Science* 179, no. 4070 (1973): 238; Sandor Bökönyi, Robert J. Braid-

wood, and Charles A. Reed, "Earliest Animal Domestication Dated?" *Science* 182 (1973): 1161.

28. Robert J. Braidwood, "Seeking the World's First Farmers in Persian Kurdistan: A Full Scale Investigation of Prehistoric Sites near Kermanshah," *Illustrated London News*, October 22, 1960, p. 695.
29. Smith, "Ganj Dareh Tepe," p. 207.
30. Mellaart, *Neolithic of the Near East*, p. 77.
31. Smith, "Ganj Dareh Tepe," p. 208.
32. Schmandt-Besserat, "The Use of Clay," p. 12.
33. Hole, Flannery, and Neely, *Prehistory and Human Ecology of the Deh Luran Plain*, p. 230.
34. Smith, "An Interim Report," p. 539.
35. Philip E. L. Smith, "Ganj Dareh Tepe," *Iran* 10 (1972): 166.
36. Coon, *Cave Explorations*, p. 75.
37. Frank Hole, "Tepe Tula'i: An Early Campsite in Khuzistan, Iran," *Paléorient* 2 (1974): fig. 15 h, o–t.
38. Braidwood, "Seeking the World's First Farmers," p. 696. In a recent study on Tepe Sarab, Vivian Broman Morales reports 79 spheres, 123 disks, 76 cones, 40 tetrahedrons, and 70 objects of varied shapes among which are 18 cylinders. The publication came too late to be included in this volume. Vivian Broman Morales, *Figurines and Other Clay Objects from Sarab and Cayönü*, Oriental Institute Communications, no. 25 (Chicago: Oriental Institute of the University of Chicago, 1990).
39. Shahmirzadi, *Tepe Zagheh*, pp. 368–372; Masson and Sarianidi, *Central Asia*, p. 35.
40. Shahmirzadi, *Tepe Zagheh*, p. 372, pl. XIX: 7–8.
41. Mellaart, *The Neolithic*, p. 215, fig. 133: m.
42. Braidwood, Howe, and Reed, "The Iranian Prehistoric Project," pp. 2008–2009.
43. Hole, Flannery, and Neely, *Prehistory and Human Ecology*, p. 230; Hole, *Studies in the Archaeological History*, p. 237, table 74; Judith Pullar, "Tepe Abdul Hosein," *Iran* 17 (1979): 153–155, and personal communications, Anne Hastings (in her final report on Tepe Abdul Hosein [1991], Judith Pullar includes 44 tokens: 20 cones, 10 spheres, 2 discs, 12 cylinders). Peder Mortensen, "Additional Remarks on the Chronology of Early Village-Farming Communities in the Zagros Area," *Sumer* 20 (1964): 28–36.
44. Personal communication, Frank Hole, letter of May 24, 1984.
45. Hans J. Nissen, "The Archaic Texts from Uruk," *World Archaeology* 17, no. 3 (1986): 319.
46. GI-1219 was associated with tomb 13: GI-1236 with tomb 9–11. The information was available in the excavation files.
47. GI-D 446, stored at the National Museum, Copenhagen; Hole, "Tepe Tula'i," fig. 15: p–r.
48. Pumpelly, *Explorations in Turkestan*. The tokens are not mentioned in the report.
49. Mary M. Voigt, *Hajji Firuz Tepe, Iran: The Neolithic Settlement*, Hasanlu Excavations Reports, vol. 1, University Museum Monograph no. 50 (Philadelphia: University Museum, University of Pennsylvania, 1983), pp. 181–184.
50. Ibid., pp. 184–185.
51. H.F. 68–104, personal communication, M. M. Voigt.
52. H.F. 68–122, 170, 171, 189, and 195; Voigt, *Hajji Firuz Tepe*, p. 87.
53. Hole, Flannery, and Neely, *Prehistory and Human Ecology*, p. 230; Hole, *Studies in Archaeological History*, p. 237.
54. Frank Hole, "Archaeology of the Village Period," in Frank Hole, ed., *The Archaeology of Western Iran* (Washington, D.C.: Smithsonian Institution Press, 1987), p. 34.
55. Hole, *Studies in Archaeological History*, pp. 15–19, 34–36.
56. Dafi 5, p. 34.
57. Helene Kantor, "Chogha Bonut," *Oriental Institute Annual Report* (1977/78): 16.
58. T. Cuyler Young, Jr., and Louis Levine, *Excavations of the Godin Project: Second Progress Report*, Occasional Paper 26 (Toronto: Royal Ontario Museum, 1974), p. 10 and fig. 15: 4, 6, 18, and 19.
59. Personal communication, C. C. Lamberg-Karlovsky.
60. Daniel Evett, "Artifacts and Architecture of the Iblis I Period: Areas D, F, and G," in *Investigations at Tal-i-Iblis*, Illinois State Museum Preliminary Reports no. 9, ed. Joseph R. Caldwell (Springfield: Illinois State Museum Society, 1967), p. 217, fig. 8: 3, 5, and 9.
61. Alexander Langsdorf and Donald E. McCown, *Tall-i-Bakun A*, OIP no. LIX (Chicago: University of Chicago Press, 1942). The 56 tokens are not included in the report. They are stored at the Peabody Museum, Harvard University, and at the Oriental Institute, University of Chicago.
62. Erich F. Schmidt, *Excavations at Tepe Hissar Damghan* (Philadelphia: University of Pennsylvania Press, 1937), pp. 53–54.
63. Dafi 1a, p. 55; fig. 21: 18, 19, 24; fig. 22: 15, 16; fig. 27: 4, 8; Dafi 5, pp. 57–58.
64. M 29, fig. 3: 15, 16; M 46, pl. 41: 8; Dafi 1b, figs. 35: 4 and 41: 15; Robert H. Dyson, Jr., "Excavations on the Acropolis at Susa and Problems of Susa A, B, and C," Ph.D. dissertation, Harvard University, 1966, p. 285 and pl. LXII: 108, 330.
65. Personal communication, Frederick R. Matson.
66. Carol Hamlin, "Dalma Tepe," *Iran* 13 (1975): 117, pl. Ib.
67. Georges Contenau and Roman Ghirshman, *Fouilles du Tépé-Giyan*, Série Archéologique 3 (Paris: Librairie Orientaliste Paul Geuthner, 1935), pl. 37: 20.
68. Henry T. Wright, *An Early Town on the Deh Luran Plain, Excavations at Tepe Farukhabad*, Memoirs of the Museum of Anthropology 13 (Ann Arbor: University of Michigan, 1981), pp. 66–68, 53.
69. Abbas Alizadeh, "Socio-Economic Complexity in Southwestern Iran during the Fifth and Fourth Millennia B.C.: The Evidence from Tall-i Bakun A," *Iran* 24 (1988): 26.
70. Contenau and Ghirshman, *Tépé-Giyan*, p. 66; Schmidt, *Tepe Hissar*, pp. 54–56; C. C. Lamberg-Karlovsky, "The Proto-Elamite Settlement at Tepe Yahya," *Iran* 9 (1971): 88; Wright, *An Early Town*, p. 67.
71. Dafi 1a, fig. 27: 8; M 29, fig. 112: 11; Hole, Flannery, and Neely, *Prehistory and Human Ecology*, pl. 36 e.
72. Red-painted disk (61-27-34), stored at the University Museum, University of Pennsylvania, Philadelphia;

M 29, fig. 3: 15, and M 46, pl. 41: 8; Dafi 1a, figs. 21: 18 and 24; 22: 15.

73. Martha C. Prickett, "Man, Land and Water: Settlement Distribution and the Development of Irrigation Agriculture in the Upper Rud-i Gushk Drainage, Southeastern Iran," Ph.D. dissertation, Harvard University, 1985, pp. 676–679.
74. I am thankful to Elizabeth F. Hendrickson for communicating to me the information on the context of tokens at Seh Gabi. 71–144; 71–143 and 71–144; F. 46–20.
75. The information for sites such as Tal-i-Mushki that yield tokens is not included in the catalog. See Shinji Fukai, Kiyoharu Horiuchi, and Toshio Matsutani, *Marv-Dasht III, Excavations at Tall-i-Mushki 1965* (Tokyo: Institute of Oriental Culture, University of Tokyo, 1973), pls. XXXVIII–XXXIX.
76. Robert J. Braidwood and Bruce Howe, *Prehistoric Investigations in Iraqi Kurdistan,* Studies in Ancient Oriental Civilization 31 (Chicago: Oriental Institute, University of Chicago, 1960), p. 51.
77. Robert J. Braidwood, *Prehistoric Men,* 7th ed. (Glenview, Ill.: Scott, Foreman and Company, 1967), p. 101; James Mellaart, *The Neolithic of the Near East* (New York: Charles Scribner's Sons, 1975), p. 16.
78. Personal communication, Stefan Karol Koslowski, August 1989.
79. R. M. Munchaev and N. J. Merpert, *Earliest Agricultural Settlements of Northern Mesopotamia* (Moscow: Publishing House "Nauka," 1981), p. 270.
80. Vivian Broman Morales, "Jarmo Figurines and Other Clay Objects," in *Prehistoric Archaeology along the Zagros Flanks,* ed. Linda S. Braidwood et al., Oriental Institute Publications 105 (Chicago: Oriental Institute, University of Chicago, 1983), pp. 387–388, 389, 391, fig. 169: 11.
81. Braidwood and Howe, *Prehistoric Investigations,* p. 44.
82. Braidwood, *Prehistoric Men,* p. 101.
83. Broman Morales, "Jarmo Figurines," p. 388.
84. Diana Kirkbride, "Umm Dabaghiyah 1971: A Preliminary Report," *Iraq* 34, no. 1 (1972): 8; "Umm Dabaghiyah 1973: A Third Preliminary Report," *Iraq* 35, no. 1 (1973): 209.
85. Seton Lloyd and Fuad Safar, "Tell Hassuna: Excavations by the Iraq Government Directorate General of Antiquities in 1943 and 1944," *Journal of Near Eastern Studies* 4 (1945): 258 and pl. X, 1: 22–23.
86. Nicolai Merpert and Rauf Munchajev, "Excavations at Yarim Tepe 1970," *Sumer* 27, nos. 1–2 (1971): 17; S. Fukai and T. Matsutani, "Excavations at Telul eth-Thalathat," *Sumer* 33, no. 1 (1977): 54.
87. R. Campbell Thompson and M. E. L. Mallowan, "The British Excavation at Nineveh, 1931–32," *University of Liverpool, Annals of Archeology and Anthropology* 20 (1933): 135, pl. 65: 4 (MM-75).
88. Braidwood and Howe, *Prehistoric Investigations,* pp. 38, 30.
89. Faisal El-Wailly and Behnam Abu es-Soof, "The Excavations at Tell Es-Sawwan, First Preliminary Report (1964)," *Sumer* 21 (1965): 26, 28, 31.
90. Cat. no. 60, BWII, a sphere with one punch, displayed at the Iraq National Museum in Baghdad, is labeled with a grave provenience.
91. Ghanim Wahida, "The Excavations of the Third Season at Tell as-Sawwan, 1966," *Sumer* 23, nos. 1–2 (1967): 169; El-Wailly and Abu es-Soof, "First Preliminary Report," 31, fig. 70, rooms 2 and 8.
92. Joan Oates, "Choga Mami, 1967–68: A Preliminary Report," *Iraq* 31, no. 2 (1969): 131, 130.
93. M. E. L. Mallowan and J. Cruikshank Rose, "Excavations at Tall Arpachiyah, 1933," *Iraq* 2, no. 1 (1935): 88, fig. 49, 13–14 and p. xi.
94. Ismail Hijara et al., "Arpachiyah 1976," *Iraq* 42, no. 2 (1980): 144; Mellaart, *The Neolithic,* p. 168.
95. Braidwood and Howe, *Prehistoric Investigations,* p. 34.
96. Alwo von Wickede, "Die Entwicklung der Stempel Glyptick in der Frühzeit vorderasiens," Ph.D. dissertation, Munich, 1987.
97. Arthur J. Tobler, *Excavations at Tepe Gawra,* vol. 2, University Museum Monograph (Philadelphia: University of Pennsylvania Press, 1950), pp. 170, 205, fig. 51.
98. Sabah Aboud Jasim, "Tell 'abada," *Sumer* 32, nos. 1–2 (1979): 529, and Sabah Aboud Jasim, *The Ubaid Period in Iraq,* pt. 1, International Series =S267 (Oxford: BAR, 1985), pp. 69–73.
99. Four disks, not included in the catalog, are reported in Catherine Breniquet, "Les Petits Objects de la Fouille de Tell ell 'Oueili, 1983," in Jean-Louis Huot, *Larsa (10e campagne, 1983) et 'Oueili (4e campagne, 1983), Rapport Préliminaire,* Mémoire no. 73, Editions Recherche sur les Civilisations (Paris, 1987), p. 142 and pl. I: 5 and II: 1.
100. Mallowan and Cruikshank Rose, "Tall Arpachiyah," p. 40; Tobler, *Tepe Gawra,* p. 116.
101. David Stronach, "Excavations at Ras Al 'Amiya," *Iraq* 23, no. 2 (1961): 106–107.
102. Fuad Safar, Mohammad Ali Mustafa and Seton Lloyd, *Eridu* (Baghdad: Republic of Iraq, Ministry of Culture and Information, State Organization of Antiquities and Heritage, 1981).
103. Tobler, *Tepe Gawra,* pp. 170–171, 205.
104. Ibid. Level XII: 2 stone spheres and 1 stone disk; level XIA: 6 spheres, 3 hemispheres, 3 disks, 2 ovoids, 2 vessels, and 1 hyperboloid made of stone and 2 hemispheres, 2 tetrahedrons, and 6 cylinders made of clay; level XI: 12 spheres, 7 disks, 7 ovoids of stone against 7 clay spheres. Tobler also states that levels XA, X, and IX each produced 2 or 3 stone spheres and disks. The 57 additional stone tokens are itemized in the following note.
105. Ibid., p. 118 and pl. XCVI: 2, 3, 5, 7–12, grave 181: 4 spheres, 3 hemispheres, and 2 vessels; p. 94, tomb 102: 3 cones, 23 spheres, and 4 "pebbles" (spheres or ovoids?); p. 94, tomb 107: 6 spheres; p. 95, tomb 110: 6 spheres; p. 96, tomb 114: 6 "pebbles."
106. Namio Egami, *Telul eth Thalathat, the Excavation of Tell II, 1956–57,* Tokyo University Iraq-Iran Expedition Report I (Tokyo: Yamakawa Publishing Company, 1959), pp. 17, pl. 78: 14; 20, pl. 68: 11.

107. Tell Billa, type 3: 8 and 55; Tepe Gawra, type 1: 19; type 6: 14.

3. *Complex Tokens*

1. "Finally, curious small clay artifacts should be mentioned as part of our level IV . . . I consider them to be representations of various daily life objects . . . They may have served in the temple cult, of which we still have little understanding." UVB 2, p. 48.
2. W. K. Loftus, *Travels and Researches in Chaldea and Susiana* (New York, 1857).
3. W 601–4944. Twelve tokens bearing numbers from 1 to 600 have not been entered in the catalog because the corresponding register cannot be located. These tokens are W 28, 30, 277, 306, 308, 497c, 509, 530, and 541 (three specimens).
4. UVB 2, pp. 47–48, fig. 41. Field numbers W 4945–7596.
5. December 4, 1930, "In the deep sounding, at about 1.95 m, under the stone foundations of level V, is a layer of clay cone mosaics;" December 5, "Many small clay objects representing, for example, date stones, loaves of bread, tetrahedrons, cones, small spheres are mixed in this layer of clay cone mosaics;" December 6, "In the deep sounding, the layer of clay cone mosaics is very large. Thick and thin small mosaic cones . . . mixed with them are further small clay artifacts." Excavation register, vol. 3, p. 367.
6. "Clay objects featuring spheres, pyramids, cones, date stones, and other things." UVB 3, p. 19. Field numbers W 7597–10584.
7. W 10585–12276.
8. Level V: W 12277–14447; Level VI: W 14448–15290; Level VII: W 15291–16042; Level VIII: W 16043–16730; Level IX: W 16731–17106; Level X: W 17107–17717; Level XI: W 17718–17982; Level XII: W 17983–18163; Level XIII: W 18164–18384; Level XIV: W 18385–18707.
9. UVB 15, p. 21, pl. 18c: W 18708–19022.
10. W 19023–19464.
11. UVB 17, pp. 36–37, pl. 24g, h, m–v: W 19465–19811.
12. Level XVIII: W 19812–20052; Level XIX: W 20053–20535; Level XX: W 20536–20808.
13. UVB 21, pp. 31–32, pls. 17–19b, c; p. 25, pl. 14g. Mark A. Brandes, *Siegelabrollungen aus den archaischen Bauschichten in Uruk-Warka,* Freiburger Altorientalische Studien, vol. 3 (Wiesbaden, 1979), pp. 36–40; "Modelage et imprimerie aux débuts de l'écriture en Mésopotamie," *Akkadica* 18 (1980): 1–30: W 20809–21178.
14. UVB 22, p. 40, pl. 19b, c; p. 45: W 21179–21419.
15. UVB 23, pp. 45–46, pl. 23d, e: W 21179–21419.
16. UVB 24, p. 28, pl. 22n; p. 36, pl. 17i: W 21623–21811.
17. UVB 25, p. 29, pl. 20e, f; pp. 32–33, pl. 22 1, o–q; p. 40: W 21812–21973.
18. Level XXVII: W 21974–22211; Level XXVII: W 22212–22418; Level XXX: W 22789–23323; Level XXXI: 23324–23477; Level XXXII: W 23478– 23889; Level XXXIII: 23890–24057; Level XXXIV: W 24058–24248.
19. W 24247A–24311.
20. *BaM* 15 (1984): 129, pl. 5; pp. 132–133, pl. 6: 33–36. *BaM* 16 (1985): 146–148, pl. 23: 146–152. Level XXXVI: W 24312–24455; Level XXXVII: W 24486– 24725.
21. Cat. nos. 1–25, 43–218, 235–244, 248–296, 376–377, 378–431, 446–477, BWII.
22. Cat. nos. 312–319 and 774, type 2: 19, 22, 24, 25, ibid.
23. Cat. nos. 322–335, type 2: 28–30, 32, 34–35, ibid.
24. Cat. nos. 336–349, type 2: 39–43, 46, 48–50, ibid.
25. Cat. nos. 350–355, type 2: 51, ibid.
26. Cat. nos. 356–367, type 2: 52–52A, 54–59, ibid.
27. Cat. nos. 507–509, type 6: 8–9, ibid.
28. Cat. nos. 514–538, type 6: 14–21, ibid.
29. Cat. nos. 578–582, type 8: 7–8, 10, ibid.
30. Cat. nos. 583–624, type 8: 11–22, ibid.
31. Cat. nos. 639–643, type 9: 6, 8–9, ibid.
32. Cat. nos. 656–665, type 10: 4, 6–7, ibid.
33. Cat. nos. 668–681, type 10: 13–15, ibid.
34. The number of perforated specimens in each type is as follows: cones: 5, 11.5 percent; spheres: 14, 6.8 percent; disks: 27, 20.4 percent; cylinders: 2, 3 percent; tetrahedrons: 3, 7.7 percent; ovoids: 8, 13.8 percent; rectangles: 6, 33.3 percent; triangles: 16, 22.2 percent; biconoids: 5, 31.2 percent; Paraboloids: 3, 7.1 percent; bent coils: 8, 33.3 percent; ovals-rhomboids: 5, 33.3 percent; vessels: 2, 11.1 percent; tools: 8, 61.5 percent; animals: 5, 35.7 percent; miscellaneous, 2, 50 percent.
35. Cat. nos. 26, 28, 35?, 98?, 368, 474, 487, 505, 528, 564, 736?, 738?, BWII.
36. Cat. nos. 23, 104, 107, 521, ibid.
37. UVB 21, pp. 31–32, pls. 17–19b.
38. The information on the contents of the envelopes stored at Heidelberg was kindly provided by Nadja Wrede.
39. UVB 21, p. 32, pl. 19b.
40. I am thankful to Dietrich Sürenhagen for providing this information based on his work, "Archaische Keramik aus Uruk-Warka. Erster Teil: Die Keramik der Schichten XVI–VI aus der Sondagen 'Tiefschnitt' und 'Sägegraben' in Eanna," *BaM* 17 (1986): 7–95.
41. I am following the chronology proposed in Ernst Heinrich, *Die Tempel und Heiligtümer im Alten Mesopotamien* (Berlin, 1982), pl. 112, except for the date of Building H, which has been re-evaluated by Jürgen Schmidt to IVd in UVB 31–32, pp. 23–24. The dates are generally earlier than those in Heinrich J. Lenzen, "Die Architektur in Eanna in der Uruk IV Periode," *Iraq* 34 (1974): 111–128.
42. Heinrich J. Lenzen, "Die Tempel der Schicht archaish IV in Uruk," *Zeitschrift fur Assyriologie* 15 (1950): 5.
43. Ibid., p. 5.
44. Hans J. Nissen, *Grundzüge einer Geschichte der Frühzeit des vorderen Orients* (Darmstadt, 1983), p. 112.
45. Heinrich J. Lenzen, "New Discoveries at Warka in Southern Iraq," *Archaeology* 17, no. 2 (1972): 128; Hans J. Nissen, "The City Wall of Uruk," in P. J. Ucko, R. Tringham, and G. W. Dimbleby, eds., *Man, Settlement and Urbanism* (Cambridge, Mass., 1972), p. 000. 794; Peter Charvat has discussed the evidence for a wide-

spread crisis occurring in Mesopotamia at the end of the fourth millennium B.C. in "The Kish Evidence and the Emergence of States in Mesopotamia," *Current Anthropology* 22, no. 6 (1981): 686.
46. Heinrich, *Die Tempel*, p. 90.
47. One disk, cat. no. 270, W 19334, BWII, is reported from the site of Frehat an Nufegi, outside the city walls, toward the north.
48. ZATU, p. 21.
49. UVB 3, p. 19.
50. UVB 2, p. 13.
51. UVB 3, p. 18; UVB 4, p. 6 and pl. 2.
52. UVB 3, pp. 29–31. The *Tiefschnitt* has been re-evaluated in Sürenhagen, "Archaische Keramik," pp. 7–95.
53. UVB 3, pls. 10 and 13.
54. Nissen, "The City Wall," pp. 794, 797: 8.
55. Julius Jordan, UVB 3, pls. 10 and 13.
56. Nissen, *Grundzüge einer Geschichte*, p. 93.
57. The distribution of tokens in P XVI is as follows: Pa 2: 1; Pa 3: 2; Pa 4: 3; Pb 1: 2; Pb 2: 2; Pb 3: 5; Pb 4: 13; Pb 5: 2; Pc 1: 1; Pc 2: 5; Pc 3: 3; Pc 4 (*Tiefschnitt*): 170; Pc 5: 3; Pd 2: 2; Pd 3: 21; Pd/Pe 3: 6; Pd 4: 2; Pd 5: 7; Pe 1: 2; Pe 2: 10; Pe 3: 5; Pe 4: 3; Pe 5: 4.
58. Cat. nos. 109, W 9939; 430, W 5381; 501, W 8659; 640, W 5325; 644, W 5450; 702, W 9241, BWII.
59. Among these are Cat. nos. 301, W 2960; 593, W 3328; 594, W 3490; 223, W 3862; 583, W 3979; 543, W 4416; 1, W 4020; 548, W 4067; 511, W 4073; 637, W 4143; 366, W 4215; 2, W 4656; 694, W 6145; 732, W 15727; and on the north side of the Ziggurat in P XV: Cat. nos. 632, W 4301; 581 and 769, W 4523a–b; and 304, W 4537, ibid.
60. Cat. no. 520, W 11026, ibid.
61. Cat. no. 241, W 6255; No. 508, W 7935; No. 701, W 9116, ibid.
62. Lenzen, "Die Architektur," p. 123.
63. UVB 2, pp. 31–48.
64. Lenzen, "Die Tempel," p. 8, fig. 22; p. 7; p. 6, figs. 9, 10, and 11.
65. Cat. no. 598, W 6785, BWII; see location in UVB 3, pl. 7.
66. Cat. no. 440, W 8230, BWII, is identified as close to a niche of the Red Temple. UVB 2, pp. 47–48, fig. 41.
67. Cat. nos. 224, W 6938; 25, W 7094; and 549, W 8068, BWII.
68. In the fill estimated of level III: Cat. nos. 5, W 6037; 29, W 7020; and 43, W 7026b; over level II: Cat. no. 711, W 5993, ibid.
69. Cat. nos. 229, W 13864; 267, W 11087; and 432, W 13876, ibid.
70. The distribution of tokens in Q XVI is as follows: Qa 1: 5; Qa 2; 5; Qa 3: 3; Qb 1: 1; Qb 3: 1; Qe 1: 1.
71. Among the envelopes with a known content are W 20987, 3: 1 sphere (type 2: 1), 1 flat disk (type 3: 1) and 1 rectangle (type 7: 1); W 20987, 7: 7 incised ovoids (type 6: 14); W 20987, 8: 2 flat disks (type 3: 1) and 5 tetrahedrons (type 5: 1); W 20987, 17: 3 spheres (type 2: 1), 1 flat disk (type 3: 1), 2 lenticular disks (type 3: 3), 1 cylinder (type 4: 1), 1 small tetrahedron (type 5: 1), 1 large tetrahedron (type 5: 2). A group of 52 tokens, W 20987, 27, originating from broken envelopes is reported in UVB 21, p. 32, pl. 19b.
72. The distribution is as follows: Mc XV 4: 1; Md XV 4: 2; Md XV 5: 25 envelopes, 78 tokens contained in envelopes, 2 tokens found loose; Me XV 4: 13; Me XV 5: 1; Me XVI 1: 1; Me XVI 2: 2; Me XV 5/Na XV 5: 3; Na XV 5: 1; N c–d XV 1: 1; N c–d XV 4: 2; Ne XV 5: 2; Na XVI 1: 2; Na XVI 2: 7; Nb XVI 2: 3.
73. Lenzen, "Die Architektur," pp. 112–116. The building formerly identified by Lenzen as belonging to V–IVa is now dated by Heinrich to VI(?)–IVc or b and by Jürgen Schmidt to V–IVC–a: Heinrich, *Die Tempel*, pp. 70, 72; UVB 31–32, p. 30.
74. UVB 21, pp. 31–32. pls. 17–19b; Brandes, *Siegelabrollungen*, pp. 36–40.
75. Mc XV 4: 1; Md XV 4: 2; Me XV 4: 13; Me XV 5: 1; UVB 17, p. 37, pl. 24 g–h, m–n, p–t, and v.
76. Me XVI 1: 1; Me XVI 2: 2; Na XVI 1: 2; Na XVI 2: 7, UVB 17, p. 37, pl. 24: o; and Nb XVI 3: 3, UVB 17, p. 37, pl. 24: u.
77. UVB 15, p. 21, W 18987.
78. UVB 15, p. 21, pl. 18.
79. Cat. nos. 617, W 21041; 663, W 18986, BWII.
80. The *Riemchen* building was dated to IVa by Lenzen: UVB 15, pp. 18–19. It is now estimated to IV b–a; Heinrich, *Die Tempel*, pp. 72–73.
81. Cat. nos. 526, W 18666; No. 680, W 18725 o, BWII; UVB 15, p. 21, pl. 18: c.
82. Cat. nos. 668, W 18700.14; no. 330, W 18700.25, BWII.
83. UVB 15, pp. 10–11.
84. Buildings F, G, and H are dated to level IVc in Heinrich, *Die Tempel*, p. 74 and fig. 116; Jürgen Schmidt proposes a date of IVb in UVB 31–32, pp. 23–25, pl. 54.
85. UVB 31–32, p. 27.
86. Ibid., pp. 24–25, fig. 4.
87. UVB 25, p. 40 (Da XV 4/5 is to be read Oa XV 4/5).
88. UVB 31–32, p. 25.
89. The distribution in O XV is as follows: Oa 3: 6; Oa 4: 1; Oa 4/5: 75; Oa 5: 2; Ob 3: 1; Ob 4: 6; Oc 3: 5; Oc 4: 1; Oe 4: 1.
90. The distribution is as follows: Ne XV 5: 2; Oa XVI 1: 1; Ob XVI 1: 3; W 21454, 21483, 21501, 21510, 21523, UVB 23, pp. 45–46, pl. 23e; W 21672, UVB 24, p. 28, pl. 22n.
91. UVB 23, pp. 45–46.
92. The distribution in P XV is as follows: Pa 3: 4; Pa 4: 3; Pa 5: 3; Pb 1: 2; Pd 4: 1.
93. Cat. no. 98, W 8417, 3.25 m below "Urnammu Lehmziegel"; Cat. no. 323, W 8336, 3.80 m below the surface, BWII.
94. Cat. nos. 515, W 2566; 218, W 2653, ibid.
95. The distribution in N XVI, outside the Stone Cone Temple complex discussed above, is as follows: Nb 3: 4, UVB 17, p. 37, pl. 24u; Nb 4: 9; Nc 1: 1; Nc 3: 1; Nc 4: 1; Nc 4/5: 2; Nc 5: 2, UVB 21, p. 32, pl. 19c; Nd 1: 1; Nd 2: 2, UVB 22, p. 40; Nd 3: 3: Nd 4: 1; Nd 5: 3; Ne 3: 2; Ne 4: 2. Some of these tokens are discussed/illustrated in UVB 21, p. 32, pl. 19c; UVB 22, p. 40; UVB 24, p. 36.

96. UVB 17, p. 10; ZATU, pp. 23, 41–44.
97. Cat. no. 625, W 20963, BWII; UVB 21, p. 32, pl. 19c; Cat. no. 554, W 21854, BWII; UVB 25, p. 33, pl. 22p; UVB 31–32, p. 30.
98. UVB 25, pp. 15–18.
99. Brandes, *Siegelabrollungen,* p. 33.
100. Cat. no. 760, W 21173, BWII; UVB 21, p. 25, pl. 14g; Cat. no. 554, W 21183, BWII; UVB 22, p. 40, pl. 19b.
101. The distribution in the area of Temple D is as follows: Od XVI 4: 2, No. 552, W 20883, UVB 21, p. 32, pl. 39c; Od XVI 5: 4; Oe XVI 4: 1; Oe XVI 5: 1; Oc XVII 2: 1; Od XVII 1: 1; Oe XVII 2: 1, No. 763, W 21266, UVB 22, p. 40, pl. 19c; Oc/d XVII 2: 1; Oe–d XVII 1: No. 362, W 21830, UVB 25, p. 33, pl. 22 o.
102. Cat. no. 746, W 16543, BWII. For a description of the building, see UVB 8, p. 56 ff., pl. 24.
103. Cat. nos. 295–296, 354–355, W 21939.1–4, BWII.
104. Cat. no. 107, W 9682, ibid.
105. Cat. nos. 569, W 12432 and 762, W 17392, ibid., and UVB 25, p. 29, pl. 20 e, f.
106. For example, Cat. nos. 325, W 12048, and 601, W 12312, BWII.
107. Cat. nos. 499, W 21448; 723, W 21567; 470, W 21579, BWII. UVB 23, pp. 45–46, pl. 23d. Cat. nos. 263, W 8661; 751, W 16576; 14, W 16630; 737, W 23379, BWII.
108. Cat. no. 15, W 16823, BWII.
109. Cat. no. 28, W 23401, ibid.
110. I: Cat. no. 700, W 8149; II: Cat. no. 260, W 8159; Cat. no. 10, W 8680; IV: Cat. no. 97, W 8271; V: Cat. no. 728, W 8301; VIII: Cat. no. 24, W 9495. Also Cat. no. 347, W 21901, ibid.; UVB 25, p. 33, pl. 22q.
111. Cat. no. 706, W 22406, BWII.
112. UVB 26/27, p. 18, pls. 3–12.
113. Cat. nos. 497–498, W 16972a–b, BWII.
114. *BaM* 15 (1984): 129, 132–133, pl. 6; *BaM* 16 (1985): 146–148, pl. 23: 146–152.
115. The distribution is as follows: 1 in O/P VIII, V VIII, Q X, P XI, R XII, U XII, E XIII, E XV, G XV, T XV, L XVI, H XVII, U XVIII, V XVIII, G XX, O XX; 2 in O XI/XII, L XII, R XIII, P XXI; 3 in Q XVI; and 4 in O XII.
116. Cat. no. 361, W 20840, BWII.
117. Uwe Finkbeiner, "Uruk-Warka XXXV: Survey des Stadtgebietes von Uruk," *BaM* 14 (1983): 21, fig. 3.
118. Hans J. Nissen, "Grabung in den Quadraten K/L XII in Uruk-Warka," *BaM* 5 (1970): 101–191.
119. In O XI/XII: Cat. no. 521, W 14344; O XII: Cat. nos. 309, W 15827, 310, W 15832b, 337, W 15846, 495, W 15847; K XII: none; L XII: Cat. nos. 626, W 17428, 735, W 17429, BWII.
120. Eva Strommenger, "Archaische Siedlung," in UVB 19, pp. 45–46.
121. Hans J. Nissen, "The Development of Writing and Glyptic Art," in Uwe Finkbeiner and Wolfgang Rollig, *Gamdat Nasr Period or Regional Style?* (Wiesbaden: Ernst Heinrich Verlag, 1986), pp. 318–331; Barthel Hrouda, "Zur Datierung frühsumerischer Bildwerke aus Uruk-Warka," *BaM* 5 (1970): 33–44.
122. UVB 3, pp. 29–31, pls. 12–13.
123. Ibid., pl. 11.
124. Cat. nos. 117, W 10284; 120, W 10353; W 11087 not included in catalog; 418, W 10394, BWII.
125. W 9951, W 9816, W 9641, and W 9467 not included in BWII. *BaM,* Uruk catalog Nos. 12, 108, 106, and 577.
126. W 9155 not included in BWII. *BaM,* Uruk catalog No. 576.
127. Cat. no. 86, W 8514, BWII.
128. Julius Jordan, UVB 3, p. 19.
129. Plain: I, 1; II, 1; III, 1, 3; IV, 1; V, 1; IX, 1. Complex: I, 33; II, 7; VI, 9, 14, 26; VIII, 1, 2, 3, 15, 17, 19, 21, 34; X, 2, 20; XII, 7, 14; XIII, 19; XV, 3.
130. Perforated specimens: Cat. nos. 225, 245, 490, 659, and 660, BWII.
131. Cat. no. 528, W 8172 aq, ibid.; W 8277 not included in catalog, *BaM,* Uruk catalog No. 568; No. 538, W 8001 ah.
132. Three lines: Cat. nos. 561, W 8001c, 562, 8136h, BWII; W 8277 not included in catalog, *BaM,* Uruk catalog No. 606; five lines: W 7847, not included in catalog, *BaM,* Uruk catalog No. 615; Cat. no. 569, W 8136g, BWII; seven lines: Cat. no. 574, W 8404 1, BWII; nine lines: Cat. no. 575, W 8172a, BWII.
133. Cat. no. 585, W 8001 b, BWII.
134. Cat. nos. 486, W 8066; 490, W 8206, ibid.
135. Cat. nos. 110–112, W 10284 and 10353; 12, W 9951; 266, W 10258b, ibid. Denise Schmandt-Besserat, "Decipherment of the Earliest Tablets," *Science* 211 (1981): 283–285.
136. Cat. no. 517, W 8206, BWII. Denise Schmandt-Besserat, "From Tokens to Tablets: A Re-evaluation of the So-called 'Numerical Tablets,'" *Visible Language* 15, no. 4 (1981): 330–340.
137. Cat. nos. 615–616, W 7847, 8136g, BWII.
138. Cat. no. 225, W 8162, ibid.
139. Stephen J. Lieberman, "Of Clay Pebbles, Hollow Clay Balls, and Writing: A Sumerian View," *American Journal of Archaeology* 84, no. 3 (1980): 358; Sabah Aboud Jasim and Joan Oates, "Early Tokens and Tablets in Mesopotamia: New Information from Tell Abada and Tell Brak," *World Archaeology* 17, no. 3 (1986): 349.
140. Cat. no. 267, W 11087, type 3: 1 (−1, +16); the remaining tokens from the *Sägegraben* are as follows: cat. nos. 229, W 13864 (+18.9), and 432, W 13876 (+19), BWII. Sürenhagen, "Archaische Keramik," pp. 63–87.
141. Cat. nos. 25, W 7094 (1: 7); 224, W 6938 (2: 7); 587, W 8068 (8: 11), BWII.
142. UVB 21, pp. 31–32, pls. 17–19b.
143. Ibid., p. 32, pl. 19b.
144. Heinrich, *Die Tempel,* p. 70, pls. 104, 106, 108, and 112.
145. UVB 31–32, p. 30.
146. UVB 17, p. 26.
147. Brandes, *Siegelabrollungen,* p. 38.
148. Ibid., p. 39.
149. Ibid., p. 38; Lenzen, "Die Tempel," pp. 8–13.
150. UVB 21, p. 32, pl. 19a.
151. Brandes, *Siegelabrollungen,* pp. 37, 189.
152. Dietrich Sürenhagen and E. Töpperwein, "Kleine Funde," Vierter vorläufiger Bericht über die von der deutschen Orientgesellschaft mit Mitteln der Stiftung Volkswagenwerk in Habuba Kabira und in Mumbaqat

unternommenen archäologischen Untersuchungen, *Mitteilungen des deutschen Orientgesellschaft* 105 (1973): 21, 26; Denise Schmandt-Besserat, "Tokens, Envelopes and Impressed Tablets at Habuba Kabira," in Eva Strommenger and Kay Kohlmeyer, eds., *Habuba Kabira Süd—Die Kleine Funde,* Wissenschaftliche Veröffentlichung des deutschen Orient Gesellschaft (forthcoming).

153. Dafi 8a, pp. 15–17; Reinhard Dittmann, *Betrachtungen zur Frühzeit des Südwest-Iran,* part 1 (Berlin: Dietrich Reimer Verlag, 1986), p. 102.
154. Henry T. Wright, *An Early Town on the Deh Luran Plain,* Memoirs of the Museum of Anthropology no. 13 (Lansing: University of Michigan, 1981), p. 156, fig. 75d, pl. 16e.
155. Heinrich, *Die Tempel,* p. 74, pls. 112, 116.
156. UVB 31–32, p. 23.
157. Cat. no. 589, W 19711 (8: 11), BWII; UVB 17, p. 37, pl. 24u; Cat. no. 356, W 21204 (3: 52), BWII; UVB 22, p. 40.
158. Lenzen, "Die Architektur," p. 127.
159. Cat. nos. 553, W 20419; 551, W 20420 (7: 22A, 21A), BWII.
160. Jean Bottero, UVB 22, p. 45.
161. Cat. no. 553, W 20419, BWII. The information was kindly provided by Robert K. Englund.
162. Cat. no. 551, W 20420, BWII; ZATU 749 (−c). The information was kindly provided by Robert K. Englund.
163. Cat. no. 554, W 21183 (7: 23), BWII; UVB 22, pp. 40, 45, pl. 19b; Cat. no. 552, W 20883 (7: 22), BWII; UVB 21, pl. 19c.
164. ATU.
165. I am grateful to M. W. Green for this information.
166. Cat. no. 555, W 19372, BWII; ZATU 758. The information was kindly provided by Robert K. Englund.
167. Cat. no. 760, W 21173, BWII; UVB 21, p. 25, pl. 14g.
168. Ibid., pp. 14–15.
169. Cat. no. 29, W 7020, BWII. The entry in the register reads: "Pd XVI 4, 2m no. des ersten Sarkophages in gleicher Höhe, SCH III."
170. Cat. no. 589, W 19711 (8: 11), BWII; UVB 17, p. 37, pl. 24u; Cat. no. 356, W 21204 (3: 52), BWII; UVB 22, p. 40.
171. Type 3: 55, University Museum, University of Pennsylvania (no accession number).
172. Type 3: 19, Oriental Institute, University of Chicago, A32206.
173. Type 3: 13, R. F. S. Starr, *Nuzi* (Cambridge, Mass.: Harvard University Press, 1939), p. 30, pl. 117v.
174. Type 8: 2, Musée du Louvre (no museum number).
175. Type 8: 11 and 17, personal communication, Gregory A. Johnson.
176. Type 6: 14, C. Leonard Woolley, *Ur Excavations,* vol. 4: *The Early Periods* (Philadelphia: University Museum, London British Museum, 1955), p. 179, pl. 16.
177. Types 1: 1, 2, 4, 7, 12, 33, 42; 2: 1, 7, 12, 24; 3: 1, 3, 4, 14, 21, 25, 28, 32, 40, 51, 52, 73, 81; 4: 1, 20; 5: 1, 2, 3; 6: 1, 2, 13, 14, 15, 19, 21, 26; 7: 1, 10; 8: 1, 2, 11, 14, 15, 17, 36, 41; 9: 6; 10: 1, 2, 12, 13, 14, 15, 18; 11: 1, 4; 13: 1, 2, 35; 14: 2, 4, 6; 15: 3, and 8. The tokens are stored at the Musée du Louvre.
178. Pinhas P. Delougaz and Helene J. Kantor, *Choghba Mish: An Interim Report on the First Five Seasons of Excavations, 1961–1971,* Oriental Institute Publications (forthcoming), pl. 118. The collection is unpublished and is kept at the Oriental Institute, University of Chicago, and at the Iran Bastan Museum, Tehran, Iran.
179. Types 1: 1, 2, 3, 4, 12; 2: 1, 7; 3: 1, 3, 19, 51, 75, 84; 5: 1, 3; 6: 1, 2, 14; 7: 1; 8: 3, 11, 14, 17; 10: 1, 14, 15; 11: 10; and 14: 2. Henri de Genouillac, *Fouilles de Telloh,* Vol. 1, *Epoques présargoniques* (Paris: Paul Geuthner, 1934), pp. 8, 47, 57–59, 63, pls. 37 and 43; Denise Schmandt-Besserat, "The Tokens from Tello Revisited," unpublished manuscript. The tokens from Tello are stored at the Louvre.
180. Types 1: 1, 2, 4, 29; 2: 1, 7; 3: 1, 25, 28, 30, 32, 51; 5: 3; 6: 1, 12, 14, 25; 7: 1; 8: 1, 2, 7, 8, 39; 9: 1, 6; 10: 4, 6; 11: 4; 15: 28. Schmandt-Besserat, "Tokens, Envelopes and Impressed Tablets at Habuba Kabira." The tokens from Habuba Kabira are stored in the Museum für Vor- und Frühgeschichte, Schloss Charlottenburg, West Berlin and at the Aleppo Museum, Syria.
181. The assemblage of Chogha Mish cannot be discussed in detail because the collection is unpublished.
182. Uruk: subtypes 19, 21, 22, 23, 24; Susa: 19, 21, 24, 25; Tello: 19; Habuba Kabira: 25.
183. Uruk: subtypes 26, 28, 29, 30, 32, 34, 35; Susa: 28, 31, 32, 33; Habuba Kabira: 28, 30, 32.
184. The distribution is as follows, Uruk: subtypes 37, 37A, 38, 39, 40, 41, 43, 46, 48; Susa: 36, 40, 42; Habuba Kabira: 44, 45.
185. Uruk: subtypes 7, 8, 10, 11, 14, 15, 17, 18, 19, 21, 22, 27; Susa: 5, 6, 9, 11, 12, 13, 14, 15, 16, 17, 20, 24, 25, 26; Habuba Kabira: 7, 8, 23; Tello: 11, 14, 17.
186. Uruk: subtypes 4, 6, 6A, 6B, 7, 8, 12, 13, 14, 15; Susa: 5, 9, 10, 12, 13, 14, 15; Tello: 13, 14, 15; Habuba Kabira: 4, 6.
187. Arthur J. Tobler, *Excavations at Tepe Gawra,* vol. 2, University Museum Monograph (Philadelphia: University of Pennsylania Press, 1950), pp. 170–171, 205.
188. Roland de Mecquenem, "Les Fouilleurs de Suse," *Iranica Antiqua,* 15 (1980): 2.
189. M 7, p. 40, figs. 48 53.
190. M 12, p. 225; M 13, pp. 24, 144 and pl. XXIV; M 25, pp. 189–190 and fig. 21.
191. M 12, p. 163, fig. 234.
192. M 16, p. 7, and pl. XIX: 298.
193. M 17, p. 3.
194. Roland de Mecquenem, "Fouilles de Suse (Campagnes 1923–1924)," *Revue d'Assyriologie et d'Archéologie Orientale* 21, no. 3 (1924): 106–107.
195. M 25, pp. 192–193 and fig. 28.
196. Ibid., p. 196.
197. M 29, p. 9, fig. 3: 15–16.
198. Ibid., p. 45.
199. Ibid., p. 43, fig. 38: 4, 5, 6, 9, 10.
200. Ibid., p. 13.
201. Ibid., p. 27.
202. Ibid., pp. 18–19.
203. Ibid., pp. 41, 43–44, fig. 38: 4–6, 9–10.
204. Ibid., p. 18.
205. Ibid., p. 17.
206. Ibid., pp. 13, 27, and fig. 23.

207. Ibid., p. 25.
208. Ibid., p. 27.
209. Ibid., p. 9, fig. 3: 15–16.
210. Ibid., p. 5.
211. Robert H. Dyson, Jr., "Excavations on the Acropolis at Susa and Problems of Susa A, B, and C.," Ph.D. dissertation, Harvard University, 1966, pp. 281–288, pls. LXI: 19, 210, 213, 214; LXII: 330, 108, 5, 40.
212. M 46, pp. 25–41.
213. M 12, p. 65.
214. M 46, pl. 41: 8; 37: 13, 14; 28: 24.
215. Ibid., pl. 37: 13, 14.
216. Ibid., p. 133.
217. Dafi 1b, pp. 206–210.
218. Ibid., figs. 35: 4 and 41: 15.
219. Ibid., fig. 57: 7.
220. Ibid., fig. 56: 3.
221. M 43, vol. 1, pp. 69–70.
222. Pierre Amiet, *Elam* (Auvers-sur-Oise: Archée Editeur, 1966), p. 70.
223. Denise Schmandt-Besserat, "The Envelopes that Bear the First Writing," *Technology and Culture* 21, no. 3 (1980): 380, 381; Piotr Steinkeller, "Observations on the Function and Use of the Uruk Clay Bullae," 194th Annual Meeting of the American Oriental Society, Seattle, March 25, 1984.
224. Dafi 8b, pp. 62–63.
225. Dafi 9b, p. 72, fig. 40: 3.
226. Ibid., fig. 40: 9, fig. 41: 16.
227. Dafi 8a, pp. 13–21.
228. Ibid., p. 21 and 23, pl. VI, 7b, and fig. 6: 2.
229. Personal communication, T. Cuyler Young, Jr., and Louis D. Levine. I am also indebted to Elisabeth F. Hendrickson, who has worked with the material of Seh Gabi and shared information with me on various aspects of the assemblage.
230. Dyson, "Excavations on the Acropolis," p. 283; Dafi 1c, fig. 41: 15.
231. Dafi 9a, p. 44.
232. Alain Le Brun, "Suse, Chantier," Acropole I, *Paléorient* 4 (1978): 183.
233. M 46, p. 38.
234. Ibid., pl. 28: 24 and p. 136.
235. The tokens with serrated edges have parallels in Susa: M 46, pl. 37: 13, 14; M 7, p. 40, Fig. 48.
236. Dyson, "Excavations on the Acropolis," pp. 281–288; "Problems in the Relative Chronology of Iran, 6000–2000 B.C.," in Robert W. Ehrich, ed., *Chronologies in Old World Archaeology,* (Chicago: University of Chicago Press, 1965), pp. 222–224.
237. Dafi 1b, p. 206, figs. 35: 4 and 41: 15.
238. Louis Le Breton, "The Early Periods at Susa, Mesopotamian Relations," *Iraq* 19, no. 2 (1957): 97, 104, 112, fig. 33.
239. M 29, p. 9, fig. 3: 15–16.
240. Le Breton, "The Early Periods," pp. 118–119, fig. 40.
241. Ibid., p. 120.
242. Dafi 9a, p. 44.
243. M 29, pp. 43–44, fig. 38: 4–6, 9–10.
244. M 46, p. 41; Dafi 9a, pp. 11–50.
245. Dyson, "Excavations on the Acropolis," p. 269.
246. M 29, p. 18.
247. Dafi 9b, pp. 64, 67.
248. M 43, vol. 1, p. 92: 549, Sb 1926, excavations of 1924.
249. Dyson, "Excavations on the Acropolis," pp. 260, 262–266.
250. M 46, p. 133, pl. 28: 24.
251. M 29, p. 13.
252. Julius Jordan, UVB 2, p. 48.
253. Mecquenem, "Fouilles de Suse," pp. 106–107 and fig. 1; Le Breton, "Early Periods at Susa," 98–100, fig. 11: 20–21; Le Brun, Dafi 9b, pp. 73–74, 76, and fig. 24: 4.
254. Dyson, "Excavations on the Acropolis," p. 285; Dafi 9b, p. 83.
255. M 43, pl. 18: 695; Le Breton, "Early Periods at Susa," fig. 20.
256. Dyson, "Excavations on the Acropolis," p. 281, 283, 285, 288; M 29, p. 13.
257. Henry T. Wright, ed., *An Early Town on the Deh Luran Plain, Excavations at Farukhabad,* Memoirs of the Museum of Anthropology, University of Michigan, no. 13 (Ann Arbor, 1981), p. 156.
258. Henry T. Wright, Naomi Miller, and Richard Redding, "Time and Process in an Uruk Rural Center," in Marie-Thérèse Barrelet, ed., *L'Archéologie de l'Iraq du début de l'époque néolithique à 333 avant notre ère,* Colloques Internationaux du Centre National de la Recherche Scientifique, no. 580 (Paris, 1978), p. 277.
259. Gregory A. Johnson, *Local Exchange and Early State Development in Southwestern Iran,* Memoirs of the Museum of Anthropology, University of Michigan, no. 51 (Ann Arbor, 1973), p. 92; "Uruk Villages on the Susiana Plain," *Iran* 14 (1976): 171–172; and personal communication.
260. Roman Ghirshman, *Fouilles de Sialk,* vol. 1, Librairie Orientaliste Paul Geuthner (Paris, 1938), pp. 21, 24, pl. LII: 26–31 and 37–39; the collection is stored at the Louvre, Département des Antiquités Orientales.
261. C. C. Lamberg-Karlovsky, *Excavations at Tepe Yahya, Iran, 1967–69: Progress Report 1,* American School of Prehistoric Research, Bulletin no. 27, Peabody Museum (Cambridge, Mass.: Harvard University, 1971); and personal communication.
262. Robert H. Dyson, Jr., "The Relative and Absolute Chronology of Hissar II and the Proto-Elamite Horizon of Northern Iran," in Olivier Aurenche, Jacques Evin, and Francis Hours, eds. *Chronologies in the Near East,* BAR International Series =S379 (Oxford, 1987), pp. 655–657.
263. Pinhas P. Delougaz and Helene J. Kantor, "New Evidence for the Prehistoric and Protoliterate Culture Development of Khuzestan," *Vth International Congress of Iranian Art and Archaeology,* vol. 1 (Tehran: Offset Press, 1972), p. 27; and personal communication from Helene J. Kantor.
264. Collections stored at the Louvre, Département des Antiquités Orientales.
265. Johnson, *Local Exchange,* p. 92; "Uruk Villages," pp.

171–172; and personal communication.

266. Erich F. Schmidt, *Excavations at Tepe Hissar, Damghan 1931–33* (Philadelphia: University of Pennsylvania Press, 1937), p. 117; Dyson, "Relative and Absolute Chronology," pp. 658–659. The collections are stored at the University Museum, University of Pennsylvania, Philadelphia.
267. Dyson, "Relative and Absolute Chronology," p. 657.
268. Delougaz and Kantor, "New Evidence," p. 27.
269. Ibid., p. 32, pl. Xc.
270. Ibid., pp. 26–27, pl. VII.
271. Henry T. Wright, "Susiana Hinterlands—Era of Primary State Formation," in Frank Hole, ed., *The Archaeology of Western Iran* (Washington, D.C.: Smithsonian Institution Press, 1987), p. 148.
272. Gregory A. Johnson, "Changing Organization of Uruk Administration," in Hole, ed., *Archaeology of Western Iran,* p. 127.
273. The first report on the assemblage was prepared for a contribution in Strommenger and Kohlmeyer, eds., *Habuba Kabira Süd—Die Kleine Funde.*
274. Habuba Kabira was an excavation of the Deutschen Orient Gesellschaft, directed by Eva Strommenger. Eva Strommenger, *Habuba Kabira* (Mainz am Rhein: Verlag Philipp von Zabern, 1980).
275. Tell Kannas was excavated by the Comité Belge de Recherches historiques, épigraphiques et archéologiques en Mésopotamie under the direction of André Finet. André Finet, "Les Temples sumériens du Tell Kannas," *Syria* 52 (1975): 157–174.
276. Jacques Cauvin, *Les Premiers Villages de Syrie-Palestine du IXème au VIIème millénaire avant J.C.,* Collection de la Maison de l'Orient Méditerraneen Ancien, no. 4, Série Archéologique 3 (Lyon: Maison de l'Orient, 1978), p. 136.
277. Ibid.
278. Henri de Contenson, "Tell Aswad. Fouilles de 1971," *Annales Archéologiques Arabes Syriennes* 22 (1972): 78.
279. Henri de Contenson, "Tell Aswad (Damascène)," *Paléorient* 5 (1979): 156.
280. Henri de Contenson, "Nouvelles données sur le Néolithique précéramique dans la région de Damas (Syrie) d'après les Fouilles à Ghoraife en 1974," *Bulletin de la Société Préhistorique Française* 73 (1976): 80; and personal communication.
281. Henri de Contenson, "Septième Campagne de Fouilles à Tell Ramad en 1970. Rapport Préliminaire," *Annales Archéologiques Arabes Syriennes* 20 (1970): 78; and personal communication.
282. Tokens stored at the British Museum.
283. Robert J. Braidwood and Linda S. Braidwood, *Excavations in the Plain of Antioch,* Oriental Institute Publications, vol. 61 (Chicago: University of Chicago Press, 1960), p. 118, figs. 92: 8–9; 160: 18.
284. Tokens from Mallowan's excavations stored at the British Museum.
285. Tokens stored at the British Museum.
286. Personal communication, André Finet.
287. G. van Driel and C. van Driel-Murray, "Jebel Aruda 1977–1978," *Akkadica* 12 (1979): 26; personal communication, S. E. van der Leeuw.
288. The composition of the Habuba Kabira token assemblage is as follows: 42 cones, 24 spheres, 19 disks, 1 tetrahedron, 22 ovoids, 6 rectangles, 9 triangles, 2 biconoids, 3 paraboloids, 4 bent coils, 1 rhomboid, 4 vessels, and 4 animals.
289. The composition of the Tell Kannas token assemblage is as follows: 18 cones, 2 spheres, 24 disks, 3 cylinders, 7 ovoids, 3 paraboloids, and 1 animal.
290. A cone with a punctuation at the apex and a cone with an added coil around the base.
291. The breakdown of subtypes is as follows: cones, 5; spheres, 5; disks, 11; tetrahedrons, 1; ovoids, 6; rectangles, 6; triangles, 7; biconoids, 2; paraboloids, 3; bent coils, 3; rhomboids, 1; vessels, 2; and animals, 4.
292. Additional subtypes of tokens: truncated cone; disk with two perforations; punctuated ovoid; paraboloid with (*a*) punctations, (*b*) four strokes, and (*c*) incised sides.
293. Two incised cones, 1939-2-8-157 and 170.
294. A bent coil.
295. Kay Simpson, "Qraya Modular Reports, No. 1: Early Soundings," *Syro-Mesopotamian Studies* 4, no. 4 (1988).
296. Oberfl. and AA XI: 21.
297. M. IV: 15.
298. CC X: 2, 40, 52a, 52b; JJ: 37; and Oberfl. 18.
299. CC X: 84; EE XII: 21; and FF XII: 1c.
300. DD XI: 50 originally of type 3: 28 was changed to type 3: 30 by the addition of two lines; the median line was added on GG XII: 5.
301. JJ: 30.
302. Among the specimens present in both sites, are 10 cones (type 1: 1, 2, 29); 16 spheres (type 2: 1, 7, 15); 11 disks (type 3: 1, 28, 32, 51); 1 tetrahedron (type 5: 3); 18 ovoids (type 6: 1, 12, 14, 25); 1 rectangle (type 7: 1); 6 triangles (type 8: 1, 2, 7, 8, 39); 2 biconoids (type 9: 1, 6); 2 paraboloids (type 10: 4, 6); 2 bent coils (type 11: 4); 1 oval-rhomboid (type 12: 11); 1 vessel (type 13: 2); and 1 animal (type 15: 22).
303. 1 cone (type 1: 36); 7 spheres (type 2: 8); 4 disks (type 3: 25, 44, 45, 53); 1 rectangle (type 7: 31); 1 vessel (type 13: 6); and 2 animals (type 14: 27, 28).
304. 48 cones (type 1: 1, 2, 4); 16 spheres (type 2: 1, 7, 15); 12 discs (type 3: 1, 25, 28, 32, 51); 1 tetrahedron (type 5: 3); 11 ovoids (type 6: 1, 14); 1 rectangle (type 7: 1): 3 triangles (type 8: 1, 2, 39); 1 biconoid (type 9: 6); 2 bent coils (type 11: 4); 1 vessel (type 13: 2); 2 animals (type 15: 12, 27).
305. Locus 36, 54, and 55
306. Harvey Weiss and T. Cuyler Young, Jr., "The Merchants of Susa; Godin V and Plateau-Lowland Relations in the Late Fourth Millennium B.C.," *Iran* 13 (1975): 8.
307. Pierre Amiet, "Alternance et dualité, essai d'interprétation de l'histoire élamite," *Akkadica* 15 (1979): 19.
308. Eva Strommenger, "The Chronological Division of the Archaic Levels of Uruk-Eanna VI–III/II: Past and Present," *American Journal of Archaeology* 84, no. 4

(1980): 485–486.

309. The En is featured on an oblong bulla, 72 Hb 102.

310. André Finet, "Bilan provisoire des fouilles belges du Tell Kannas," *Annual of the American Schools of Oriental Research* 44 (1979): 93.

311. Simpson, "Qraya Modular Reports," p. 26.

312. UVB 2, figs. 16–17; de Genouillac, *Fouilles de Telloh I,* p. 64; p. 151 and pl. 89; Delougaz and Kantor, "New Evidence," p. 27; Finet, "Bilan provisoire," p. 93.

313. The En is represented on an oblong bulla from Habuba Kabira (72 Hb 102). I am grateful to Eva Strommenger for this communication. M 43, vol. 2, pl. 18: 695.

314. Strommenger, "Chronological Division," pp. 485–486; Louis le Breton, "The Early Periods at Susa, Mesopotamian Relations," *Iraq* 19, no. 2 (1957): p. 97–113; Dittmann, *Betrachtungen,* pp. 98–121; Delougaz and Kantor, "New Evidence," pp. 26–33.

4. *Where Tokens Were Handled and Who Used Them*

1. Georges Charbonnier, *Conversations with Claude Lévi-Strauss* (London: Jonathan Cape, 1961), pp. 29–30.
2. Personal communication, Henri de Contenson.
3. Personal communication, Frank Hole.
4. Mary M. Voigt, *Hajji Firuz Tepe, Iran: The Neolithic Settlement,* Hasanlu Excavations Reports, vol. 1, University Museum Monograph no. 50 (Philadelphia: University Museum, University of Pennsylvania, 1983), p. 182, HF 68–107, 68–114, 68–190, 68–216; p. 199, HF 68–158.
5. I am thankful to Elizabeth F. Hendrickson for communicating to me the information on the context of tokens at Seh Gabi.
6. Henry T. Wright, Naomi Miller, and Richard Redding. "Time and Process in an Uruk Rural Center," in *L'Archéologie de L'Iraq du début de l'époque néolithique à 333 avant notre ère* (Paris: Colloques Internationaux du Centre National de la Recherche Scientifique, 1980), p. 277.
7. Heinrich J. Lenzen, UVB 17, pp. 36–37, pl. 24 g–h, m–n, p–t, v.
8. Ibid., p. 37 and UVB 22, p. 40.
9. Dyson, "Excavations on the Acropolis," pp. 281–288.
10. Yvonne Rosengarten, *Le Concept sumérien de consommation dans la vie économique et religieuse* (Paris: Editions E. de Boccard, 1960), p. 32.
11. Personal communication, Frank Hole.
12. Cat. no. 43, 71–129, BWII; T. Cuyler Young, Jr., and Louis D. Levine, *Excavations of the Godin Project: Second Progress Report,* Royal Ontario Museum Art and Archaeology Occasional Paper 26 (Toronto, 1974), p. 61, fig. 6: G 20.
13. Cat. nos. 21: 71–144 and 51: 71–143, BWII: ibid., p. 59, fig. 4.
14. Philip E. L. Smith, "Prehistoric Excavations at Ganj Dareh Tepe in 1967," *Fifth International Congress of Iranian Art and Archaeology,* Teheran 1968, Vol. 1, p. 188.
15. Ghanim Wahida, "The Excavations of the Third Season at Tell as-Sawwan, 1966," *Sumer* 23, nos. 1–2 (1967): 169.
16. Voigt, *Hajji Firuz Tepe,* p. 182, HF 68–81.
17. Martha Prickett, "Man, Land and Water: Settlement Distribution and the Development of Irrigation Agriculture in the Upper Rud-i Gushk Drainage, Southeastern Iran," Ph.D. dissertation, Harvard University, 1985, p. 539.
18. Voigt, *Hajji Firuz Tepe,* pp. 87, 181–184, HF 68–122, 68–170–172, 68–189, 68–195.
19. Ibid., pp. 47–49.
20. Sabah Aboud Jasim and Joan Oates, "Early Tokens and Tablets in Mesopotamia: New Information from Tell Abada and Tell Brak," *World Archaeology* 17, no. 3 (1986): 352–355.
21. Arthur J. Tobler, *Excavations at Tepe Gawra,* vol. 2, University Museum Monographs (Philadelphia: University of Pennsylvania Press, 1950), p. 170 and pl. LXXXIV a.
22. Heinrich J. Lenzen, UVB 25, p. 40.
23. M 29, pp. 13, 17–18, 25, 27, and fig. 23.
24. Prickett, "Man, Land and Water," p. 539.
25. Jasim and Oates, "Early Tokens," pp. 352, 355.
26. Ibid., p. 355.
27. I am thankful to Marcel Sigrist for communicating to me the two references: D. Calvot, *Textes économiques de Ṣelluš-Dagan du Musée du Louvre et du Collège de France,* Materiali per il Vocabulario Neosumerico vol. 8 (Rome: Multigrafica Editrice, 1979), pl. XLVIII, MVN 8, 147; and P. Dhorme, "Tablettes de Drehem à Jérusalem," *Revue d'Assyriologie et d'Archéologie Orientale* 9 (1912): pl. I: SA 19.
28. I am thankful to Marvin A. Powell for providing translations for the texts quoted above: Calvot, *Textes économiques,* pl. XLVIII, MVN 8, 147. [!] indicates partly restored from context; / indicates end of line: "37[!] fattened oxen / 116 [!] oxen / positive-balance (of) accounting / (of the) year Sasru was destroyed [= Sulgi 42] / 1492[!] oxen / in (? the leather bag / total: 1645[!] oxen / (this is the) capital (literally perhaps: head of what has been heaped up) / out of it: / 1626 oxen / expended / 13 oxen / are (in the process of being?) [expe]nded (?) / total: 1639[!] oxen / expended. / [positive balan]ce 6 oxen. / Accounting of Enlila / from (the) month of eating gazelle (= month 1) / to (the) month of cutting grain (= month 12) / (of the) year: (the) en (-priestess) of Nanna was chosen by omen [= Sulgi 43]." According to Marvin A. Powell, the text may be understood as follows: "Balanced account of Enlila for months 1–12 of the 43rd year of King Sulgi: 153 oxen were brought forward as a positive balance from the 42nd year of King Sulgi. 1492 oxen came into Enlila's account and are represented by documents in/of (the leather) bag(s) containing the receipts from income. This makes the total capital assets 1645 oxen. From this 1639 oxen have been expended, leaving a positive balance of 6 oxen."

Dhorme, "Tablettes," pl. I: SA 19. This is what is usually called an "archive label." These labels were made by modelling a piece of clay around a cord, which was then attached to the basket containing the records (i.e., tablets) of a particular individual or of a particular bureau: "basket of tablet[s] / income [literally: it has been brought in] / and [what has been] expended / [leather] bag / seal[s] / tablet[s] [of] Naram-ili / from Nasa / from [the] month Akiti [= 6th month] / to [and including the] month Feast of Ninazu [= 5th month] / it is [the] 12th month [i.e., it includes twelve months] / year: Urbilum was destroyed [= Sulgi 45]."

29. Jacques Cauvin, *Les Premiers Villages de Syrie-Palestine du IXème au VIIème millénaire avant J.C.*, Collection de la Maison de L'Orient Méditerranéen Ancien, no. 4, Série Archéologique 3 (Lyons, France: Maison de l'Orient, 1978), pp. 74, 73, 43.
30. Jacques Cauvin, "Nouvelles fouilles à Mureybet (Syrie), 1971–72 rapport préliminaire," *Annales Archéologiques Arabes Syriennes* 22 (1972): p. 110.
31. Olivier Aurenche, Jacques Cauvin, et al., "Chronologie et organisation de l'espace dans le Proche Orient," in *Préhistoire du Levant,* Colloque CNRS no. 598 (Lyons, 1980), pp. 7–8.
32. Reiner Protsch and Rainer Berger, "Earliest Radiocarbon Dates for Domesticated Animals," *Science* 179, no. 4070 (1973): 237; Sandor Bökönyi, Robert J. Braidwood, and Charles A. Reed, "Earliest Animal Domestication Dated?" *Science* 182 (1973): 1161.
33. Dexter Perkins, Jr., "Prehistoric Fauna from Shanidar, Iraq," *Science* 144, no. 3626 (1964): 1565.
34. Henri de Contenson, "Tell Aswad (Damascène)," *Paléorient* 5 (1979): 155.
35. Alwo von Wickede, "Die Entwicklung der Stempel Glyptick in der Frühzeit Vorderasiens," Ph.D. dissertation, University of Munich, 1987.
36. P. A. Akkermans, M. N. van Loon, J. J. Roodenberg, and H. T. Waterbolk, "The 1976–1977 Excavations at Tell Bouqras," *Annales Archéologiques Arabes Syriennes* 32 (1982): 56, fig. 11: 11–12.
37. Wickede, "Die Entwicklung."
38. Henri de Genouillac, *Fouilles de Telloh I,* p. 64; M 46, p. 151, pl. 89; Delougaz and Kantor, "New Evidence," p. 27; André Finet, "Bilan provisoire des fouilles belges du Tell Kannas," *Annual of the American Schools of Oriental Research,* Vol. 44 (1979), p. 93.
39. Eva Strommenger, "The Chronological Division of the Archaic Levels of Uruk-Eanna VI to III/II: Past and Present," *American Journal of Archaeology* 84, no. 4 (1980): 485–486; Louis le Breton, "The Early Periods at Susa, Mesopotamian Relations," *Iraq* 19, no. 2 (1957): 97–113; Delougaz and Kantor, "New Evidence," pp. 26–33.
40. Hans J. Nissen, *Grundzüge einer Geschichte der Frühzeit des vorderen Orients* (Darmstadt: Wissenschaftliche Buchgesellschaft, 1983), pp. 92–93.
41. M 43, vol. 2, pl. 18: 695; Delougaz and Kantor, "New Evidence," p. 32, pl. Xc. The En is represented on an oblong bulla from Habuba Kabira (72 Hb 102), personal communication, Eva Strommenger.
42. Julius Jordan, UVB 3, pls. 10 and 13.
43. Faisal El-Wailly and Behnam Abu Es-Soof, "Excavations at Tell es-Sawwan, First Preliminary Report (1964)," *Sumer* 21, nos. 1–2 (1965): 26, 28.
44. Peder Mortensen, "Additional Remarks on the Chronology of Early Village-Farming Communities in the Zagros Area," *Sumer* 20 (1964): 28–36. GI-1219 was associated with Tomb 13 and GI-1236 with Tombs 9–11. I thank Peder Mortensen for making available to me the excavation files of Tepe Guran stored at the National Museum, Copenhagen, Denmark.
45. Voigt, *Hajji Firuz Tepe,* p. 87, HF 68–122, 170, 171, 189, 195.
46. M. E. L. Mallowan and J. Cruikshank Rose, "Excavations at Tall Arpachiyah, 1933," *Iraq* 2, part 1 (1935): 40.
47. Tobler, *Excavations,* Locus 7–58, pp. 116, 120, 170 and pl. LXXXIV.c.
48. Ibid., grave 181, pp. 117–118, 205, pl. XCVI.a: 2, 3, 5, 7–12 and CLXXIX: 53.
49. Ibid., Tombs 102, 107, 110, and 114, pp. 84–85, 94–96, pls. XXII, XXVII, and XLVI.a.
50. M 25, pp. 192–193.
51. Voigt, *Hajji Firuz Tepe,* pp. 86–87, H12 B3.
52. El-Wailly and Abu Es-Soof, "Excavations," p. 23.
53. Mallowan and Cruikshank Rose, "Excavations," p. 35.
54. Tobler, *Excavations,* pp. 106–107.
55. Ibid., pp. 70–75, pls. XXIV and XLVI.a.
56. Voigt, *Hajji Firuz Tepe,* p. 86.
57. Tobler, *Excavations,* pp. 84–85, 116, 205 and pl. XXVII.
58. Ibid., pp. 84–85.
59. El-Wailly and Abu Es-Soof, "Excavations," pp. 26, 28.
60. Tobler, *Excavations,* p. 199, pl. CLXXV, and figs. 74–76.
61. Ibid., pp. 94–96, pls. LIII.b, c, e; LV.a: 1 and 4; LVIII.a; 1 and b: 3; LIX.a: 6–8; CIII: 7–8; CIV: 13–14, 20–21; CVI: 37–38; CVII: 55–56; CVIII: 58, 60, and 65.
62. Voigt, *Hajji Firuz Tepe,* pp. 47–49, Structure VI.
63. Tobler, *Excavations,* pp. 110–111.
64. Ibid.
65. El-Wailly and Abu Es-Soof, "Excavations," pp. 28, 26.
66. Tobler, *Excavations,* pp. 84–85, 116.
67. Ibid., pp. 170, 85 and pl. LXXXIV c.
68. Ibid., pp. 94, 84, 96.
69. Ibid., pp. 84–85.
70. El-Wailly and Abu Es-Soof, "Excavations," p. 28.

5. Strings of Tokens and Envelopes

1. "The sound of small objects knocking against one another in the inner cavity can be heard when . . . [the mud balls are] shaken at ear level. Since several of these mud balls were broken in the course of the excavations, we could identify that they held small terra cotta objects in various shapes: grains, cones, pyramids, pills measuring 1 cm in diameter." R. de Mecquenem, "Fouilles de Suse," *Revue d'Assyriologie et d'Archéologie Orientale* 21, no. 3 (1924): 106.
2. Two spheres, one lenticular disk, and one cylinder at Tell Ramad II and four disks at Tepe Sarab.

3. One disk, one cylinder, and one miniature vessel at Jaffarabad and three disks at Tall-i-Bakun.
4. M 43, vol. 1, p. 70.
5. David Oates, "Tell Brak," in John Curtis, ed., *Fifty Years of Mesopotamian Discovery* (London: British School of Archaeology in Iraq, 1982), p. 66, fig. 52.
6. M 43, vols. 1 and 2, 510, 540, 541, 544, 547, 567, 585, 599, 644, 649, 665; Dafi 8a, pp. 20–21, pl. V; Dafi 9b, p. 72.
7. Delougaz and Kantor, "New Evidence," p. 27.
8. Eva Strommenger, *Habuba Kabira* (Mainz am Rhein: Verlag Philipp von Zabern, 1980), p. 63 and fig. 57.
9. At Susa, a perforated token and a bulla were located in the same square, J-4, room 830, Dafi 9b, p. 142, fig. 40: 9 and p. 64.
10. Donald J. Wiseman, *Catalogue of the Western Asiatic Seals in the British Museum, Cylinder Seals,* vol. 1, *Uruk-Early Dynastic Periods* (London, 1962), pl. 32.
11. John Curtis, "Chagar Bazar," in John Curtis, ed., *Fifty Years of Mesopotamian Discovery* (London: British School of Archaeology in Iraq, 1982), p. 81, fig. 61.
12. M 43, vols. 1 and 2, 540, 541, 544, 547; Dafi 8a, pp. 20–21, nos. 35 and 37; Strommenger, *Habuba Kabira,* p. 64, fig. 56.
13. M 43, vols. 1 and 2, 510 and 465, Dafi 8a, pp. 20–21, no. 36.
14. M 43, vols. 1 and 2, 644, 649, and 655; Dafi 8a, pp. 20–21, nos. 32 and 34.
15. Dafi 8a, p. 35.
16. In Susa: Sb 1945 bis and 4850; in Habuba Kabira, Eva Strommenger, "Habuba Kabira am syrischen Euphrat," *Antike Welt* 8, no. 1 (1977): 19, fig. 13b.
17. Sb 1928, 1929, 1930, 1933, 4838, 5310, 6312, and 6947.
18. Sb 1950.
19. Henry T. Wright, *An Early Town in the Deh Luran Plain,* Memoirs of the Museum of Anthropology, no. 13 (Ann Arbor: University of Michigan, 1981), p. 156.
20. Personal communication, C. C. Lamberg-Karlovsky.
21. Henry T. Wright and Gregory A. Johnson, "Population, Exchange and Early State Formation in Southwestern Iran," *American Anthropologist* 77, no. 2 (1975): 271.
22. A 31 52 92 and A 31 52 93, unpublished, University Museum, University of Pennsylvania, Philadelphia.
23. I am thankful to W. David Kingery, head of the Ceramics Department, MIT, for the analyses.
24. M 16, pp. 7–8, fig. 298.
25. M 17, p. 1.
26. Roland de Mecquenem, "Fouilles de Suse (campagnes 1923–24)," *Revue d'Assyriologie et d'Archéologie Orientale* 21, no. 3 (1924): 106–107.
27. M 43, vol. 1, pp. 69–70.
28. Ibid., pp. 69–70; Dafi 8a, pp. 15–18.
29. Delougaz and Kantor, "New Evidence," vol. 1, p. 27.
30. Wright, *An Early Town,* p. 156.
31. Denise Schmandt-Besserat and S. M. Alexander, *The First Civilization: The Legacy of Sumer* (Austin, Texas, 1975), pp. 51, 53.
32. Ali Hakemi, *Catalogue de l'exposition: Lut (Shahdad) xabis* (Tehran, 1972), p. 20, item 54 and pl. 22A.
33. Heinrich J. Lenzen, UVB 21, pp. 30–32 and pls. 17–19.
34. Dietrich Sürenhagen and E. Töpperwein, "Kleine Funde," Vierter Vorläufiger Bericht über die von der deutschen Orientgesellschaft mit Mitteln der Stiftung Volkswagenwerk in Habuba Kabira und Mumbaqat unternommenen archäologischen Untersuchungen, *Mitteilungen der deutschen Orientgesellschaft,* vol. 105 (1973), pp. 21, 26; Denise Schmandt-Besserat, "Tokens, Envelopes and Impressed Tablets at Habuba Kabira," in Eva Strommenger and Kay Kohlmeyer, eds., *Habuba Kabira Süd—Die kleinen Funde,* Wissenschaftliche Veröffentlichung der deutschen Orient Gesellschaft (forthcoming).
35. Stephen Reimer, "Tell Qraya," *Syrian Archaeology Bulletin* 1 (1988): 6.
36. Collection of Shucri Sahuri, Amman, Jordan.
37. Collection of Thomas C. Barger, La Jolla, California.
38. Wright, *An Early Town,* p. 156.
39. Delougaz and Kantor, "New Evidence," p. 27; Helene J. Kantor and Pinhas P. Delougaz, "New Light on the Emergence of Civilization in the Near East," *Unesco Courier* (November 1969): 23.
40. Strommenger, "Chronological Division," pp. 485–486; Dietrich Sürenhagen, "Archaische Keramik aus Uruk-Warka. Erster Teil: Die Keramik der Schichten XVI–VI aus den Sondagen 'Tiefschnitt' und 'Sägegraben' in Eanna," BaM 17 (1986): 7–95.
41. Stephen Reimer, "Tell Qraya," *Syrian Archaeology Bulletin* 1 (1988): 6.
42. Mark A. Brandes, *Siegelabrollungen aus den Archaischen Bauschichten in Uruk-Warka,* Freiburger Altorientalische Studien, vol. 3 (Wiesbaden: Franz Steiner Verlag GMBH, 1979), pp. 37, 189.
43. Louis Le Breton, "The Early Periods at Susa, Mesopotamian Relations," *Iraq* 19, no. 2 (1957): 104–105.
44. Dafi 8a, p. 31.
45. Ibid., pp. 62, 78.
46. Reinhard Dittmann, *Betrachtungen zur Frühzeit des Südwest-Iran,* part 1 (Berlin: Dietrich Reimer Verlag, 1986), p. 102.
47. Dafi 8b, pp. 76, 62.
48. Personal communication, C. C. Lamberg-Karlovsky.
49. Personal communication, Juris Zarins, letter of October 14, 1983.
50. S. Salvatori and M. Vidale, "A Brief Surface Survey of the Protohistoric Site of Shahdad (Kerman, Iran): Preliminary Report," *Rivista di Archeologia* 6 (1982): 5–10.
51. Wright, *An Early Town,* p. 156.
52. Ibid., p. 155, fig. 76: C, pp. 369, 156.
53. Heinrich J. Lenzen, "Die Architektur in Eanna in der Uruk IV Periode," *Iraq* 34 (1974): 112–116.
54. Heinrich J. Lenzen, UVB 15, p. 21, W 18987; UVB 17, p. 26.
55. M 43, vol. 1, p. 92, no. 549, Sb 1926.
56. M 29, pp. 17, 18.
57. Dafi 8a, p. 36.
58. Dafi 9a, p. 14, fig. 1.
59. Dafi 8a, figs. 1 and 2.
60. M 17, p. 1.

61. Dafi 8a, p. 15.
62. Dafi 1c, pp. 235–237 (levels 17 A and B); Dafi 8a, p. 12, (level 18, four phases).
63. Personal communication, C. C. Lamberg-Karlovsky.
64. Sb 1927, 1936, 1940, and 4338.
65. Susa: Sb 1930, 1938, 1942, 1967, 5340, 6350, 6946, no reference, S. ACR I.77: 1999.1, 2049.1, 2067.2, 2089.1, 2111.2, 2111.3, 2130.1, 2130.4, 2142.2, 2142.3, 2173.4; Chogha Mish: Delougaz and Kantor, "New Evidence," p. 27, pl. IXa; Uruk: W 20987, 3; W 20987, 7; W 20987, 15; W 20987, 8; W 20987, 17; Habuba Kabira: MII 133, MII 134.
66. Wright, *An Early Town,* p. 156.
67. Heinrich J. Lenzen, UVB 21, p. 32 and pl. 19b, W 20987, 27.
68. Delougaz and Kantor, "New Evidence," p. 30, pl. IX,b.
69. The first group is stored at the Louvre; Dafi 8a, p. 18, S.ACR.I.77 2091.2 and S.ACR.I.77 2067.3.
70. Delougaz and Kantor, "New Evidence," p. 27.
71. Sb 1932, Pierre Amiet, *L'Age des échanges inter-iraniens,* Notes et Documents des Musées de France, vol. 11 (Paris: Ministère de la Culture et de la Communication, Editions de la Réunion des Musées Nationaux, 1986), p. 85 and pls. 29, 31: 7, 8.
72. Uruk: W 20987, 8, 13–14, 16, 18, 21; Susa: The seal impressions are published in M 43, Sb 1926: 549 and 683; Sb 1931: 550 and 552; Sb 1932: 465 and 574; Sb 1934: 470 and 596; Sb 1936: 467 and 594; Sb 1937: 465 and 574; Sb 1941: 566 and 579; Sb 1967: 488 and 668; Sb 4838: 565 and 595; S. ACR I.77.2111.3; 2119.1.
73. Uruk: Susa: Sb 6294, Gs 548, 586, and 697; Habuba Kabira: MII 134.
74. Uruk: W 20 987, 17 and 26; Susa: Sb 1948, GS 456 and 655; Sb 1942, GS 460, 557, and 577.
75. M 43, pp. 72–83; Mark A. Brandes, *Siegelabrollungen aus den archaischen Bauschichten in Uruk-Warka,* part 1, Freiburger Altorientalische Studien, Vol. 3 (Wiesbaden: Franz Steiner Verlag GMBH, 1979), p. 39.
76. Delougaz and Kantor, "New Evidence," p. 32, pl. Xd.
77. Henry T. Wright views the Farukhabad envelope as bearing markings. Because the scratches are different from the usual markings, I consider them as unintentional.
78. Sb 5340.
79. Sb 1927, 1940, 2286, 6350; S ACR I.77.2089.1, 2111.3, 2130.1, 2130.2, 2142.2, 2142.3, 2162.1, 2173.4.
80. Dafi 1, p. 17, no. 11; S.ACR.I.77 2142.2.
81. Sb 6350.
82. Sb 1927.
83. Sb 1927.
84. Dafi 8a, fig. 3: 3.
85. Habuba Kabira: M II: 133.
86. Sb 1940.
87. Sb 1932.
88. Sb 1928, 1929, 1936, 1944, 1950, 1974, and 1978.
89. Sb 1950.
90. Mona Spangler Phillips, "The Manufacture of Ancient Middle Eastern Clay Envelopes," *Technology and Culture* 24, no. 2 (1983): 256–257.
91. Sb 1938.

6. *Impressed Tablets*

1. Georges Charbonnier, *Conversations with Claude Lévi-Strauss,* (London: Cape Editions, 1973), p. 30.
2. For example, in M 43, vol. 1, Sb 4839, 100: 629; Sb 4851, 87: 501 and 97: 600; Sb 4854, 85: 479; Sb 6289, 90: 534; Sb 6291, 89: 520; Sb 6293, 93: 559; Sb 6299, 104: 666; Sb 6959, 101: 642.
3. "Forerunners of pictographic tablets." UVB 3, p. 29.
4. Ibid., pl. 19b (W 10133 a, b); UVB 4, p. 28, pl. 14c–h (W 9656 h, ea; W 9656 eb); UVB 8, p. 51, pl. 51c (W 16184); UVB 17, p. 56 (W 19727); Adam Falkenstein, "Zu den Inschriften der Grabung in Uruk-Warka, 1960–61," *BaM* 2 (1963): 2 (W 20239); UVB 20, p. 23, pl. 26g, 28c (W 20777); UVB 22, pp. 59–60, Nos. 134–140 (W 21300–1–7); UVB 23, pp. 37–38 (W 21452); p. 40 (W 21654,1); UVB 25, p. 38 and pl. 27k, n (W 21859).
5. M 17, p. 10; Dafi 1c, p. 236; Dafi 3, pp. 93–103; Dafi 8a, pp. 18–20.
6. Henri Frankfort, "Progress of the Work of the Oriental Institute in Iraq, 1934–35, Fifth Preliminary Report of the Iraq Expedition," *OIC* N20 (1936): 25, fig. 19; Pinhas P. Delougaz, Harold D. Hill, and Seton Lloyd, *Private Houses and Graves in the Diyala Region,* OIP 37 (Chicago: University of Chicago Press, 1967), p. 2.
7. Roman Ghirshman, *Fouilles de Sialk,* vol. 1 (Paris: Geuthner, 1938), pp. 65–68.
8. Dominique Collon and Julian Reade, "Archaic Nineveh," *BaM* 14 (1983): 13–14.
9. Joseph Caldwell, "Tall-i Ghazir," *Reallexikon der Assyriologie und Vorderasiatischen Archaeologie* 3 (1968): 348–355; Donald S. Whitcomb, "The Proto-Elamite Period at Tall-i Ghazir, Iran," Master's thesis, University of Georgia, Athens, 1971, p. 31, pl. XIA.
10. André Parrot, "Les Fouilles de Mari, quatorzième campagne (printemps 1964)," *Syria* 42 (1965): 12.
11. Pinhas P. Delougaz and Helene J. Kantor, "The Iranian Expedition: Chogha Mish Excavations," in *The Oriental Institute, Report for 1967–68* (Chicago: University of Chicago Press), p. 11.
12. G. van Driel, "Tablets from Jebel Aruda," in G. van Driel, Th. J. H. Krispijn, M. Stol, and K. R. Veenhof, eds., *Zikir Šumin,* Assyriological Studies Presented to F. R. Kraus on the Occasion of his Seventieth Birthday (Leiden: E. J. Brill, 1982), pp. 12–25.
13. Dietrich Sürenhagen and E. Töpperwein, "Kleinfunde," Vierter vorläufiger Bericht über die von der deutschen Orientgesellschaft mit Mitteln der Stiftung Volkswagenwerk in Habuba Kabira (Habuba Kabira, Herbstkampagne 1971 und 1972 sowie Testgrabung Frühyahr 1973) und in Mumbaqat (Tall Mumbaqat, Herbstkampagne 1971) unternommenen archaeologischen Untersuchungen, *Mitteilungen der deutschen Orientgesellschaft* 105 (1973): 20–33.
14. Harvey Weiss and T. Cuyler Young, Jr., "The Merchants of Susa; Godin V and Plateau Lowlands Relations in the Late Fourth Millennium B.C.," *Iran* 13 (1975): 8–11.
15. John Curtis, ed., *Fifty Years of Mesopotamian Discovery*

(London: British School of Archaeology in Iraq, 1982), pp. 64–65, fig. 51.
16. David Stronach, "Nineveh and Early Urbanism in Northern Mesopotamia," unpublished ms., 1987.
17. M 17, p. I; M 43, vol. 1, pp. 68–69.
18. François Vallat, "Les Documents épigraphiques de l'Acropole," Dafi 1c (1971): 236, fig. 43.
19. François Vallat, "Les Tablettes Proto-Elamite de l'Acropole," Dafi 3 (1973): 93–94, fig. 14.
20. Dafi 8a, pp. 18–20, pl. IV, fig. 4.
21. Weiss and Young, "Merchants of Susa," pp. 8–11.
22. Ghirshman, *Fouilles de Sialk,* pp. 65–68, pls. XCII–XCIII.
23. Whitcomb, "Proto-Elamite Period," p. 31, pl. XIA.
24. Delougaz and Kantor, "Iranian Expedition," p. 11; Helene J. Kantor, "Excavations at Chogha Mish," *Report for 1974–75* (Chicago: Oriental Institute of the University of Chicago, 1975), p. 22; "Excavations at Chogha Mish: 1974–75," *Second Annual Report* (Los Angeles: Institute of Archaeology, University of California, 1974–75), pp. 10, 17: 6–7.
25. UVB 3, p. 29, pl. 19b.
26. ZATU, p. 34.
27. UVB 4, p. 28, pl. 14 c–h (W 9656 h, ea; W 9656 eb).
28. UVB 5, p. 14, pl. 14 b, d (W 14148, 14210).
29. UVB 8, p. 51, pl. 51 c (W 16184).
30. UVB 17, p. 56 (W 19727); Falkenstein, "Zu den Inschriften," p. 2 (W 20239); UVB 20, p. 23, pl. 26 g, 28 c (W 20777); UVB 22, pp. 59–60, Nos. 134–140 (W 21300–1–7); UVB 23, pp. 37–38 (W 21452); p. 40 (W 21654,1); UVB 25, p. 38, pl. 27 k, n (W 21859).
31. ZATU, p. 34.
32. Frankfort, "Progress," p. 25, fig. 19.
33. Dominique Collon and Julian Reade, "Archaic Nineveh," p. 33.
34. Sürenhagen and Töpperwein, "Kleinfunde," pp. 20–21, fig. 4; Eva Strommenger, "Ausgrabungen in Habuba Kabira und Mumbaqat," *Archiv für Orientforschung* 24 (1973): 170–171, fig. 17; "Habuba Kabira am syrischen Euphrat," *Antike Welt* 8, no. 1 (1977): 18, fig. 11; "Ausgrabungen der deutschen Orient-Gesellschaft in Habuba Kabira," in David Noel Freedman, ed., *Archaeological Reports from the Tabqa Dam Project—Euphrates Valley, Syria* (Cambridge, Mass.: American Schools of Oriental Research, 1979), p. 68, fig. 14.
35. Driel, "Tablets," p. 12.
36. Curtis, *Fifty Years,* pp. 64–65, fig. 51.
37. Parrot, *Syria.* 42, p. 12.
38. Dafi 8a, p. 19.
39. Denise Schmandt-Besserat, "Tokens, Envelopes and Impressed Tablets," in Eva Strommenger and Kay Kohlmeyer, eds., *Habuba Kabira Süd—Die kleine Funde, wissenschaftliche Veröffentlichung der deutschen Orient Gesellschaft* (forthcoming).
40. UVB 3, p. 29.
41. Ghirshman, *Fouilles de Sialk,* p. 67.
42. Frankfort, "Progress," p. 25.
43. Driel, "Tablets," p. 12.
44. Curtis, *Fifty Years,* p. 64.
45. Weiss and Young, "Merchants of Susa," p. 3.
46. ZATU, pp. 48–49.
47. Weiss and Young, "Merchants of Susa," p. 8.
48. G. van Driel and C. van Driel-Murray, "Jebel Aruda 1977–1978," *Akkadica* 12 (1979): 24.
49. Collon and Reade, "Archaic Nineveh," p. 33.
50. "On the floor, under the collapsed roof of Temple C's T-shaped hall, in level IVa." UVB 22, pp. 59–60, nos. W 21300, 1–7.
51. ZATU, pp. 39–40.
52. Weiss and Young, "Merchants of Susa," p. 9, fig. 4: 2.
53. Ghirshman, *Fouilles de Sialk,* pls. XCII–XCIII.
54. UVB 3, p. 29; ZATU, p. 48.
55. Ghirshman, *Fouilles de Sialk,* p. 67.
56. Gd 73–61, unpublished; Gd 73–286, Weiss and Young, "Merchants of Susa," fig. 4: 6.
57. Gd 73–286, Weiss and Young, "Merchants of Susa," fig. 4: 6.
58. Gd 73–64 and 286, ibid., p. 9, fig. 4: 5 and 6.
59. Ibid., fig. 4: 6.
60. Ibid., fig. 4: 5.
61. M II: 127.
62. Delougaz and Kantor, "Iranian Expedition," p. 11.
63. Gd 73–292, Weiss and Young, "Merchants of Susa," p. 10, fig. 5: 1.
64. Ibid., p. 9, fig. 4: 6.
65. Driel, "Tablets," p. 14: 4.
66. Weiss and Young, "Merchants of Susa," p. 10, fig. 5: 1.
67. Peter Damerow and Robert K. Englund, "Die Zahlzeichensysteme der archaischen Texte aus Uruk," in ZATU, pp. 117–166.
68. Adam Falkenstein, *Archaische Texte aus Uruk,* Ausgrabungen der deutschen Forschungsgemeinschaft in Uruk-Warka, vol. 2 (Berlin: Kommissions-Verlag Harrassowitz, 1936).
69. Jöran Friberg, *The Third Millennium Roots of Babylonian Mathematics. 1. A Method for the Decipherment, through Mathematical and Metrological Analysis, of Proto-Sumerian and Proto-Elamite Semi-pictographic Inscriptions* (Chalmers University of Technology and the University of Göteborg, 1978–79).
70. ZATU.
71. A. A. Vaiman, "Über die Protosumerische Schrift," *Acta Antiqua Academiae Scientiarum Hungaricae* 22 (1974): 17–22; "Protosumerische Mass- und Zahlsysteme," *BaM* 20 (1989): 114–120.
72. Delougaz and Kantor, "New Evidence," p. 30, pl. IX b.
73. Sb 1938, M 43, p. 95: 582, pl. 72.
74. Denise Schmandt-Besserat and S. M. Alexander, *The First Civilization: The Legacy of Sumer* (Austin, Texas, 1975), pp. 51, 53.
75. Sb 6350, M 43, vols. 1 and 2, p. 66, pl. 61: 460 bis; Sb 1927, M 43, vols. 1 and 2, p. 91, pl. 68: 539.
76. Kantor, "Excavations: 1974–75," p. 17, fig. 6.
77. Gd. 73–64, obverse, Weiss and Young, "Merchants of Susa," p. 9, fig. 4: 5.
78. Driel, "Tablets," p. 14: 1, 2, 4.
79. Frankfort, "Progress," p. 25.
80. Ghirshman, *Fouilles de Sialk,* p. 67, pl. XCIII: S 539.

81. Sb 4839, M 43, vol. 1, p. 100: 629.
82. W 9656 eb, UVB 4, p. 28, pl. 14.
83. Damerow and Englund, "Die Zahlzeichensysteme," p. 136; Friberg, *Third Millennium Roots,* p. 10; Vaiman, "Protosumerische Schrift," p. 19.
84. Sb 1927, M 43, vols. 1 and 2, p. 91: 539, pl. 68.
85. Sb 6959, M 43, vols. 1 and 2, p. 101: 642, pl. 79.
86. Delougaz and Kantor, "New Evidence," p. 30, pl. IXb.
87. Sb 1927, M 43, vols. 1 and 2, p. 91: 539, pl. 68.
88. Driel, "Tablets," p. 14: 1 and 6.
89. Sb 2313, M 43, vols. 1 and 2, p. 128: 622; MT, M 43, vols. 1 and 2, p. 91: 545, pl. 68.
90. Damerow and Englund, "Die Zahlzeichensysteme," p. 136; Friberg, *Third Millennium Roots,* p. 10.
91. Susa, S. ACR. I. 77. 2173.4, Dafi 8a, p. 15, no. 2; pl. I: 3; fig. 3: 3.
92. Damerow and Englund, "Die Zahlzeichensysteme," p. 136; Vaiman, "Protosumerische Schrift," p. 19.
93. Damerow and Englund, "Die Zahlzeichensysteme," p. 141; Friberg, *Third Millennium Roots,* p. 46.
94. Gd 73–299, unpublished.
95. Falkenstein, *Archaische Texte,* p. 918.
96. Friberg, *Third Millennium Roots,* p. 46.
97. Gd 73–291, unpublished.
98. Vaiman, "Protosumerische Schrift," p. 19; Friberg, *Third Millennium Roots,* p. 25.
99. Delougaz and Kantor, "New Evidence," p. 30, pl. IX b.
100. Sb 1967, M 43, Vols. 1 and 2, p. 86, pl. 64: 488.
101. W 20987, 15, unpublished.
102. S. ACR. I. 77. 2173.4, Dafi 8a, p. 15, no. 2; pl. I: 3; fig. 3: 3.
103. Schmandt-Besserat and Alexander, *First Civilization,* pp. 51, 53.
104. Weiss and Young, "Merchants of Susa," p. 9, fig. 4: 1–6, fig. 5: 1.
105. Driel, "Tablets," p. 14: 1–4 and pp. 15, 7, and 13.
106. MII 128, unpublished.
107. Frankfort, "Progress," p. 25.
108. Collon and Reade, "Archaic Nineveh," p. 34, fig. 1a.
109. Ghirshman, *Fouilles de Sialk,* pl. XCIII, S 539.
110. Sb 2312, M 43, vols. 1 and 2, p. 87, pl. 65; 491; Sb 2316, M 43, vols. 1 and 2, p. 85, pl. 63: 475; Sb 6289, M 43, Vols. 1 and 2, p. 102, pl. 67: 650.
111. W 10133 a and b, UVB 3, p. 29, pl. 19b.
112. Damerow and Englund, "Die Zahlzeichensysteme," p. 136; Friberg, *Third Millennium Roots,* p. 10; Vaiman, "Protosumerische Schrift," p. 19.
113. Sb 1932, Pierre Amiet, *L'Age des échanges inter-iraniens* (Paris: Ministère de la Culture et de la Communication, 1986), p. 85, fig. 29.
114. Delougaz and Kantor, "New Evidence," p. 30, pl. IX b.
115. Sb 1967, M 43, vols. 1 and 2, p. 86, pl. 64: 488.
116. Sb 2315, M 43, vols. 1 and 2, p. 89: 521, pl. 66.
117. MII 128 and 130, unpublished.
118. Driel, "Tablets," p. 14, fig. 3.
119. Damerow and Englund, "Die Zahlzeichensysteme," p. 136; Friberg, *Third Millennium Roots,* p. 10; Vaiman, "Protosumerische Schrift," p. 19.
120. MII 130, unpublished; MII 128, Eva Strommenger, "Ausgrabungen in Habuba Kabira und Mumbaqat," *Archiv für Orientforschung* 24 (1973): 171, fig. 17.
121. Weiss and Young, "Merchants of Susa," p. 9, fig. 4: 5, Gd 73–64.
122. Ghirshman, *Fouilles de Sialk,* pl. XCIII, S 1627.
123. Sb 1966 bis, M 43, vols. 1 and 2, p. 104: 671, pl. 82; Sb 1975 bis, M 43, vols. 1 and 2, p. 101: 641, pl. 79.
124. Damerow and Englund, "Die Zahlzeichensysteme," p. 130; Vaiman, "Protosumerische Schrift," p. 21.
125. Friberg, *Third Millennium Roots,* p. 46.
126. Whitcomb, "Proto-Elamite Period," p. 31, pl. XI.
127. Damerow and Englund, "Die Zahlzeichensysteme," p. 141; Friberg, *Third Millennium Roots,* p. 46; Vaiman, "Protosumerische Schrift," fig. 4.
128. Susa ACR. I. 77. 2128.2 and 3, Dafi 8a, p. 19, nos. 20 and 23, pl. IV: 7 and 6, fig. 4: 2 and 5.
129. Delougaz and Kantor, "New Evidence," p. 30, pl. IX a and b.
130. Sb 1938, M 43, p. 95, pl. 72: 582.
131. W 20987, 8, 15, and 17, unpublished.
132. Sb 6959, M 43, Vols. 1 and 2, p. 101: 642, pl. 79; Sb 2313, M 43, vols. 1 and 2, p. 128: 922, pl. 99.
133. Friberg, *Third Millennium Roots,* p. 10.
134. Sb 1927 and 1940, M 43, vols. 1 and 2, p. 91; 539 and p. 92: 555, pl. 68.
135. Susa, Sb 1938, M 43, vols. 1 and 2, p. 95 and pl. 72: 582; and 1946, M 43, vol. 1, p. 93: 563; S. ACR. I.77 2130.4, Dafi 8a, p. 16.
136. Chogha Mish, envelope on exhibition at the Oriental Institute, University of Chicago.
137. Sb 2313, M 43, p. 128: 922, pl. 99.
138. S. ACR.I.77 1999.1, Dafi 8a, 1978, p. 17.
139. Sb 1927, M 43, vols. 1 and 2, p. 91, pl. 68: 539; Sb 1940, M 43, vols. 1 and 2, p. 92, pl. 69: 555.
140. Delougaz and Kantor, "Iranian Expedition," p. 11.
141. Driel, "Tablets," p. 15, fig. 1b: 10.
142. Susa, Sb 6299, M 43, vols. 1 and 2, p. 104: 666, pl. 81.
143. Curtis, *Fifty Years,* p. 65, fig. 51.
144. W 21859, UVB 25, p. 38, pl. 27, k.
145. Friberg, *Third Millennium Roots,* p. 21.
146. Sb 1940, M 43, vol. 1, p. 92: 555.
147. Sb 6299, M 43, vols. 1 and 2, p. 104: 666, pl. 81.
148. S. ACR.I.77 1999.1, Dafi 8a, p. 17; S. ACR.I.77 2089.1, Dafi 8a, p. 17; S. ACR.I.77 2111.2, Dafi 8a, p. 17.
149. W 20987.27, UVB 21, pl. 19b.
150. Sb 1940, M 43, vols. 1 and 2, p. 92, pl. 69: 555; S. ACR.I.77 2049.1, Dafi 8a, p. 16.
151. Gd 73–293.
152. M II: 127, Eva Strommenger, "Habuba Kabira am syrischen Euphrates," *Antike Welt* 8 (1977): 18, fig. 11.
153. Driel, "Tablets," p. 15, fig. 1b: 9 and 10.
154. Sb 4854, M 43, vols. 1 and 2, p. 85: 479, pl. 63; Sb 6291, M 43, vols. 1 and 2, p. 89: 520, pl. 66; Sb 6299, M 43, vols. 1 and 2, p. 104: 666, pl. 81.
155. Curtis, *Fifty Years,* p. 65, fig. 51.
156. W 21859, UVB 25, p. 38, pl. 27, k.
157. Friberg, *Third Millennium Roots,* p. 21. The long wedge standing for one animal is present in the Uruk archaic tablets; for example, on W 28 859, UVB 25, pl. 27k. This

has not been recognized by Damerow and Englund, who have not differentiated between the short and long wedge.

158. UVB 21, pl. 19b.
159. Kantor, "Excavations: 1974–75," pl. 17: 7.
160. Strommenger, "Ausgrabungen," p. 171, fig. 17.
161. Driel, "Tablets," p. 14, fig. 1a: 4.
162. W 20987.27, UVB 21, pl. 19b; W 20987.7.
163. M II: 133 and 134; Sürenhagen and Töpperwein, "Kleinfunde," pp. 21, 26; Denise Schmandt-Besserat, "Tokens, Envelopes and Impressed Tablets at Habuba Kabira," in Eva Strommenger and Kay Kohlmeyer, eds., *Habuba Kabira Süd—Die kleinen Funde,* Wissenschaftliche Veröffentlichung der deutschen Orient Gesellschaft (forthcoming).
164. UVB 21, pl. 19b.
165. Delougaz and Kantor, "New Evidence," p. 30, pl. IXb.
166. Gd 73–291, obverse and reverse, unpublished.
167. Damerow and Englund, "Die Zahlzeichensysteme," p. 136; Friberg, *Third Millennium Roots,* p. 25; Vaiman, "Protosumerische Schrift," p. 19.
168. Susa, Dafi 8a, S. ACR. I.77.2089.1, p. 21, pl. II: 5; fig. 6: 2.
169. Susa, Sb 1975 bis, M 43, vols. 1 and 2, p. 101, pl. 79: 641.
170. Vaiman, "Protosumerische Schrift," pp. 20–21, fig. 3.
171. Sb 6291, M 43, vols. 1 and 2, p. 89: 520, pl. 66.
172. Sb 6289, M 43, vols. 1 and 2, p. 90: 534, pl. 67.
173. For example, Sb 4829, M 43, vols. 1 and 2, p. 100, pl. 78: 629.
174. For example, Sb 6299, M 43, vols. 1 and 2, p. 104, pl. 81: 666.
175. Sb 1966 bis, M 43, vols. 1 and 2, p. 104, pl. 82: 671; Sb 1975 bis, M 43, vols. 1 and 2, p. 101, pl. 79: 641.
176. Dafi 8a, p. 21, S.ACR.I.77.2073.4.
177. Susa, Sb 1975 bis, M 43, vols. 1 and 2, p. 101, pl. 79: 641.
178. UVB 21, pl. 19b; W 20987.7.
179. M II: 134; Schmandt-Besserat, "Tokens, Envelopes and Impressed Tablets."
180. ATU 781 bears an additional incised cross.
181. Krystyna Szarzynska, "Records of Cloths and Garments in Archaic Uruk/Warka," *Altorientalische Forschungen,* 15, no. 2 (1988): 228: T-20.
182. Ibid., T-18.
183. Ibid., T-20.
184. Ibid., T-29.
185. Ibid., T-38.
186. Ibid., T-6.
187. Ibid., T-12.
188. Ibid., T-10.
189. Ibid., T-11.
190. Denise Schmandt-Besserat, "The Envelopes that Bear the First Writing," *Technology and Culture* 21, no. 3 (1980): 375.
191. René Labat, *Manuel d'épigraphie akkadienne* (Paris, 1948), pp. 204–205.
192. Krystyna Szarzynska, "Records of Garments and Cloths in Archaic Uruk," unpublished ms.
193. Mogens Weitemeyer, *Some Aspects of the Hiring of Workers in the Sippar Region at the Time of Hammurabi* (Copenhagen, 1962), p. 12.
194. W 20987.7: 7 and 20987.27: 3.
195. W 2566, 7176, 8206, 8945, 16235.
196. François Thureau-Dangin, "Notes assyriologiques," *Revue d'Assyriologie et d'Archéologie Orientale* 29, no. 1 (1932): 23.
197. Vaiman, "Protosumerische Schrift," pp. 17–22; Friberg, *Third Millennium Roots,* pp. 10, 20. Friberg refers to the signs as "cups" and "discs." Damerow and Englund, "Die Zahlzeichensysteme," pp. 165–166.
198. Jöran Friberg, "Numbers and Measures in the Earliest Written Records," *Scientific American* 250, no. 2 (1984): 116.
199. Susa, Sb 1938, M 43, vols. 1 and 2, p. 95, pl. 72: 582; Sb 1946, M 43, vol. 1, p. 93: 563; S. ACR.I.2130.4; Dafi 8a, p. 16.
200. Chogha Mish, envelope on exhibition at the Oriental Institute, University of Chicago.
201. Friberg, *Third Millennium Roots,* p. 46.
202. Marvin A. Powell, Jr., "Sumerian Area Measures and the Alleged Decimal Substratum," *Zeitschrift für Assyriologie* 62, no. 3 (1973): 201; John Chadwick, *The Mycenaean World* (Cambridge, 1976), p. 110.
203. Friberg, *Third Millennium Roots,* p. 21; W 21859, UVB 25, pl. 27k.
204. Sb 1940, M 43, p. 92: 555.
205. Sb 1940, M 43, vol. 1, p. 92: 555.
206. Sb 1927, M 43, vols. 1 and 2, p. 91, pl. 68: 539.
207. Terence Grieder, "The Interpretation of Ancient Symbols," *American Anthropologist* 77, no. 4 (1975): 849–855.
208. Damerow and Englund, "Die Zahlzeichensysteme," pp. 165–166.
209. Friberg, "Numbers and Measures," p. 111.
210. Ibid., p. 118.
211. Dafi 8a, p. 21, no. 38, pl. VI: 7 a–b.
212. ATU, p. 7.
213. M 43, vol. 2, pl. 15: 692, 629, and 633.
214. Dafi 8a, pp. 52–53, fig. 7: 2 and 8.
215. Mark A. Brandes, *Siegelabrollungen aus den archaischen Bauschichten in Uruk-Warka,* Freiburger altorientalische Studien, vol. 3 (Wiesbaden: Franz Steiner Verlag GMBH, 1979), p. 39.
216. The same way of impressing cones by the tip practiced on envelope Sb 1927, M 43, vol. 2, pl. 68: 539 seems repeated on tablet Sb 6959, M 43, vol. 2, pl. 79: 620.
217. Sb 6289, M 43, vol. 1, p. 102: 650.
218. Sb 1940, M 43, vol. 1, p. 92: 555.
219. Interestingly, starting in the Ur III period in the late third millennium B.C., some tablets were protected by clay envelopes.
220. A. A. Vaiman, "Formal'nye osobennosti protosumerkish tekstov," *Vestnik Drevnej Istorii* 119, no. 1 (1972): 124–131 (I am thankful to Robert K. Englund for lending me the German translation by Ingrid Damerow); M. W. Green, "The Construction and Implementation of the Cuneiform Writing System," *Visible Language* 15, no. 4 (1981): 345–372; D. Silvestri, L. Tonelli, and V. Valeri, *Testi e Segni di Uruk IV* (Naples: Istituto Universitario Orientale, Dipartimento di Studi del Mondo

Classico e del Mediterraneo Antico, 1985), pp. 34–42.

7. *The Evolution of Symbols in Prehistory*

1. Harold A. Innis, *Empire and Communications* (Oxford: Clarendon Press, 1950), p. 11.
2. Suzanne K. Langer, *Philosophy in a New Key* (Cambridge, Mass.: Harvard University Press, 1960), pp. 41–43.
3. Jerome S. Bruner, "On Cognitive Growth II," in Jerome S. Bruner, Rose R. Olver, Patricia M. Greenfield, et al., *Studies in Cognitive Growth* (New York: John Wiley and Sons, 1966), p. 47.
4. Ibid., p. 31.
5. B. Vandermeersch, "Ce que révèlent les sépultures Moustériennes de Qafzeh en Israël," *Archeologia* 45 (1972): 12.
6. Ralph S. Solecki, *Shanidar* (London: Allen Lane, Penguin Press, 1972), pp. 174–178.
7. Vandermeersch, "Ce que révèlent les sépultures," p. 5.
8. Simon Davis, "Incised Bones from the Mousterian of Kebara Cave (Mount Carmel) and the Aurignacian of Ha-Yonim Cave (Western Galilee), Israel," *Paléorient* 2, no. 1 (1974): 181–182.
9. Henri de Lumley, "A Paleolithic Camp at Nice," *Scientific American* 220 (May 1969): 49.
10. François Bordes, *A Tale of Two Caves* (New York: Harper and Row, 1972), p. 93; André Leroi-Gourhan, "Les Fouilles d'Arcy-sur-Cure," *Gallia Préhistoire* 4 (1961): 5, and 15; Richard G. Klein, "The Mousterian of Upper Russia," Ph.D. dissertation, University of Chicago, 1966, p. 187.
11. A. Bouyssonie, J. Bouyssonie, and L. Bardon, "Découverte d'un Squelette Humain Moustérien à la Bouffia de la Chapelle aux Saints (Corrèze)," *L'Anthropologie* 19 (1908): 517.
12. Halam L. Movius, "Teshik-Tash, a Mousterian Cave Site in Central Asia," in *Mélanges en hommage au Professeur Hamal-Nandrin* (Brussels: Société Royale Belge d'Anthropologie et de Préhistoire, Imprimerie Administrative, 1953), p. 75.
13. André Leroi-Gourhan, *Les Hommes de la Préhistoire* (Paris: Editions Bourrelier, 1955), p. 83.
14. Bordes, *A Tale of Two Caves,* p. 62 and fig. 17; Alexander Marshack, "The Meander as a System: The Analysis and Recognition of Iconographic Units in Upper Palaeolithic Compositions," in Peter J. Ucko, ed., *Form in Indigenous Art* (Canberra: Australian Institute of Aboriginal Studies, 1977), pp. 290–292.
15. Denis Peyrony, "La Ferrassie," *Préhistoire* 3 (1934): 34, fig. 33.
16. André Leroi-Gourhan, *Préhistoire de l'Art Occidental* (Paris: Editions Lucien Mazenod, 1971), p. 148.
17. Davis, "Incised Bones," pp. 181–182.
18. Jacques Tixier, "Poinçon décoré du Paléolithique Supérieur à Ksar'Aqil (Liban)," *Paléorient* 2, no. 1 (1974): 187–192.
19. Loraine Copeland and Francis Hours, "Engraved and Plain Bone Tools from Jiita (Lebanon) and Their Early Kebaran Context," *Proceedings of the Prehistoric Society* 43 (1977): 295–301.
20. Anna Belfer-Cohen and Ofer Bar-Yosef, "The Aurignacian at Hayonim Cave," *Paléorient* 7, no. 2 (1981): fig. 8.
21. Enver Y. Bostanci, "Researches on the Mediterranean Coast of Anatolia, a New Paleolithic Site at Beldibi near Antalya," *Anatolia* 4 (1959): 140, pl. 11.
22. Enver Y. Bostanci, "Important Artistic Objects from the Beldibi Excavations," *Antropoloji* 1, no. 2 (1964): 25–31.
23. Ofer Bar-Yosef and Anna Belfer-Cohen, "The Early Upper Paleolithic in Levantine Caves," in J. F. Hoffecker and C. A. Wolf, eds., *The Early Upper Paleolithic, Evidence from Europe and the Near East,* BAR International Series =S437, (Oxford, 1988), p. 29.
24. Ofer Bar-Yosef and N. Goren, "Natufian Remains in Hayonim Cave," *Paléorient* 1 (1973): fig. 8: 16–17. Jean Perrot, "Le Gisement Natufien de Mallaha (Eynan), Israel," *L'Anthropologie* 70, nos. 5–6 (1966): fig. 22: 26. An incised bone radius from Kharaneh IV, Phase D, may also date from the same period. See Mujahed Muheisen, "The Epipalaeolithic Phases of Kharaneh IV," *Colloque International CNRS, Préhistoire du Levant 2* (Lyon, 1988), p. 11, fig. 7. Donald O. Henry, "Preagricultural Sedentism: The Natufian Example," in T. Douglas Price and James A. Brown, eds., *Prehistoric Hunter-Gatherers* (New York: Academic Press, 1985), p. 376. Phillip C. Edwards, "Late Pleistocene Occupation in Wadi al-Hammeh, Jordan Valley," Ph.D. dissertation, Department of Archaeology, University of Sydney, 1987, fig. 4.29: 3–8. Rose L. Solecki, *An Early Village Site at Zawi Chemi Shanidar,* Bibliotheca Mesopotamica, vol. 13 (Malibu, Calif.: Undena Publications, 1981), pp. 43, 48, 50, pl. 8r, fig. 15p.
25. François R. Vallat, *Le Natoufien,* Cahiers de la Revue Biblique no. 15 (Gabalda, 1975), pp. 109–111, 104.
26. Ibid., pp. 104–106, fig. 22: 1–3; Leroi-Gourhan, *Préhistoire,* pp. 64–66.
27. Leroi-Gourhan, *Préhistoire,* pp. 119–121.
28. Denis Peyrony, *Eléments de préhistoire* (Ussel: G. Eyboulet et Fils, 1927), p. 54.
29. Alexander Marshack, *The Roots of Civilization* (New York: McGraw Hill, 1972). For opposers of Marshack's theory, see Randall White, "The Manipulation of Burins in Incision and Notation," *Canadian Journal of Anthropology* 2, no. 2 (1982): 134, and Francesco d'Errico, "Paleolithic Lunar Calendars: A Case of Wishful Thinking?" *Current Anthropology* 30 (1989): 117. See also Marshack's answer: "The Tai Plaque and Calendrical Notation in the Upper Paleolithic," *Cambridge Archaeological Journal* 1, no. 1 (1991). A supporting viewpoint is presented by Claude Couraud, "Numérations et Rythmes Préhistoriques," *La Recherche* 11, no. 109 (1980): 356–358.
30. Walter J. Ong, *Orality and Literacy* (New York: Methuen, 1982), p. 46; Marshall McLuhan, *Understanding Media* (New York: New American Library, 1964), pp. 81–90.

31. Jacques Cauvin, *Les Premiers Villages de Syrie-Palestine du IXème au VIIème millénaire avant J.C.*, Collection de la Maison de l'Orient Méditerranéen Ancien no. 4, Série Archéologique 3 (Lyons, 1978), p. 111; Jacques Cauvin, "Nouvelles fouilles à Mureybet (Syrie) 1971–72, rapport préliminaire," *Annales Archéologiques Arabes Syriennes* (1972): 110.
32. Robert J. Braidwood, Bruce Howe, and Charles A. Reed, "The Iranian Prehistoric Project," *Science* 133, no. 3469 (1961): 2008.
33. Henri de Contenson, "Tell Aswad. Fouilles de 1971," *Annales Archéologiques Arabes Syriennes* (1972): 77; Charles L. Redman, *The Rise of Civilization* (San Francisco: W. H. Freeman and Company, 1978), p. 163, fig. 5–18: A.
34. Denise Schmandt-Besserat, "The Use of Clay before Pottery in the Zagros," *Expedition* 16, no. 2 (1974): 11–12; "The Earliest Uses of Clay in Syria," *Expedition* 19, no. 3 (1977): 30–31.
35. I. J. Gelb, *A Study of Writing* (Chicago: University of Chicago Press, 1974), p. 65.
36. Cyril S. Smith, "A Matter of Form," *Isis* 76, no. 4 (1985): 586.
37. C. F. Hockett, "The Origin of Speech," *Scientific American* 203 (1960): 90–91.
38. M. Shackley, *Neanderthal Man* (Hamden, Conn.: Archon Books, 1980), p. 113.

8. *Tokens: The Socioeconomic Implications*

1. Raymond L. Wilder, *Mathematics as a Cultural System* (New York: Pergamon Press, 1981), p. 30.
2. François R. Vallat, *Le Natoufien,* Cahiers de la Revue Biblique no. 15 (1975), pp. 109–111, fig. 23: 10; B. Vandermeersch, "Ce que revèlent les sépultures Moustériennes de Qafzeh en Israël," *Archeologia* 45 (1972): 12.
3. Alexander Marshack, *The Roots of Civilization* (New York: McGraw Hill, 1972).
4. Timothy K. Earle and Jonathon E. Ericson, *Exchange Systems in Prehistory* (New York: Academic Press, 1977), p. 227; Gary A. Wright, *Obsidian Analyses and Prehistoric Near Eastern Trade: 7500 to 3500 B.C.*, Anthropological Papers no. 57, Museum of Anthropology (Ann Arbor: University of Michigan, 1969), p. 3.
5. Harriet Crawford, "The Mechanics of the Obsidian Trade: A Suggestion," *Antiquity* 2 (1979): 130; Fredrik Barth, *Nomads of South Persia* (Oslo, Norway: Oslo University Press, 1961), p. 99; Jack Goody, *The Domestication of the Savage Mind* (Cambridge: Cambridge University Press, 1978), p. 15.
6. Philip E. L. Smith, "Prehistoric Excavations at Ganj Dareh Tepe in 1967," *Vth International Congress of Iranian Art and Archaeology* (Tehran, 1968), p. 186; James Mellaart, *Çatal Hüyük* (New York: McGraw Hill, 1967).
7. Dietrich Sürenhagen, in Denise Schmandt-Besserat, "Tokens at Uruk," *BaM* 19 (1988): 38; Morris Silver, *Economic Structures of the Ancient Near East* (London: Croom Helm, 1985).
8. Pierre Amiet, "Alternance et dualité, Essai d'interprétation de l'histoire élamite," *Akkadica* 15 (1979): 16; Eva Strommenger, "Habuba Kabira am Syrischen Euphrat," *Antike Welt* 8, no. 1 (1977): 19; Harvey Weiss and T. Cuyler Young, Jr., "The Merchants of Susa; Godin Tepe V and Plateau-Lowland Relations in the late Fourth Millennium B.C.," *Iran* 13 (1975): 14–16.
9. Pierre Amiet, *L'Age des échanges inter-iraniens* (Paris: Editions de la Réunion des Musées Nationaux, 1986), p. 88.
10. For example, Denise Schmandt-Besserat, "The Envelopes that Bear the First Writing," *Technology and Culture* 21, no. 3 (1980): 380–381; "From Tokens to Tablets: A Re-evaluation of the So-called Numerical Tablets," *Visible Language* 15, no. 4 (1981): 340; "The Emergence of Recording," *American Anthropologist* 84, no. 4 (1982): 873–874.
11. For example, Brian Fagan, *New Treasures of the Past* (London: Quarto Publishing, 1987), pp. 75–77; Roy Harris, *The Origin of Writing* (London: Gerald Duckworth and Company, 1986), p. 72; Geoffrey Sampson, *Writing Systems* (Stanford: Stanford University Press, 1985), p. 58; Paul Heyer, *Communications and History* (New York: Greenwood Press, 1988), p. 159.
12. Ofer Bar-Yosef and N. Goren, "Natufian Remains in Hayonim Cave," *Paléorient* 1 (1973): 64, fig. 8: 15–17; Jean Perrot, "Le Gisement Natufian de Mallaha (Eynan), Israël," *L'Anthropologie* 70, nos. 5–6 (1966): fig. 22: 26.
13. Nicolai Merpert and Rauf Munchajev, "Excavations at Yarim Tepe 1970," *Sumer* 27, nos. 1–2 (1971): pl. VI, fig. 6c; M. E. L. Mallowan and J. Cruikshank Rose, "Excavations at Tall Arpachiyah," *Iraq* 2 pt. 1 (1933): 103 and pl. XIIa.
14. Jacques Cauvin, *Les Premiers Villages de Syrie-Palestine du IXème au VIIème millénaire avant J.C.*, Collection de la Maison de l'Orient Méditerranéen Ancien, no. 4, Série Archéologique, vol. 3 (Lyons: Maison de l'Orient, 1978), p. 74.
15. Robert J. Braidwood, "Seeking the World's First Farmers in Persian Kurdistan," *Illustrated London News,* October 22, 1960, p. 695; Smith, "Prehistoric Excavations," p. 187.
16. Henri de Contenson, "La Région de Damas au Néolithique," *Annales Archéologiques Arabes Syriennes* 35 (1985): 9–10; "Tell Aswad (Damascène)," *Paléorient* 5 (1979): 153–154; Cauvin, *Les Premiers Villages,* pp. 40, 41–42.
17. Reiner Protsch and Rainer Berger, "Earliest Radiocarbon Dates for Domesticated Animals," *Science* 179, no. 4070 (1973): 238; Sandor Bökönyi, Robert J. Braidwood, and Charles A. Reed, "Earliest Animal Domestication Dated?" *Science* 182 (1973): 1161.
18. Hans J. Nissen, "The Archaic Texts from Uruk," *World Archaeology* 17, no. 3 (1986): 326.
19. Wolfgang Heimpel, "Das Untere Meer," *Zeitschrift für Assyriologie* 77, no. 1 (1987): 40.
20. Claude Meillassoux, "On the Mode of Production of the Hunting Band," in Pierre Alexandre, ed., *French*

Perspectives in African Studies (London: Oxford University Press, 1973), pp. 189, 194.

21. Mark Nathan Cohen, "Prehistoric Hunter-Gatherers: The Meaning of Social Complexity," in T. Douglas Price and James A. Brown, eds., *Prehistoric Hunter-Gatherers* (New York: Academic Press, 1985), p. 99.
22. Meillassoux, "On the Mode of Production," p. 194.
23. Morton H. Fried, *The Evolution of Political Society: An Essay in Political Anthropology* (New York: Random House: 1967), p. 109.
24. Cohen, "Prehistoric Hunter-Gatherers," p. 105.
25. Charles L. Redman, *The Rise of Civilization* (San Francisco: W. H. Freeman and Company, 1978), p. 203.
26. Cauvin, *Les Premiers Villages,* p. 43.
27. Olivier Aurenche, "Chronologie et organisation de l'espace dans le Proche Orient," *Préhistoire du Levant,* Colloque CNRS no. 598 (Lyons, 1980), pp. 1–11.
28. Arthur J. Tobler, *Excavations at Tepe Gawra,* Vol. II, University Museum Monographs (Philadelphia: University of Pennsylvania Press, 1950).
29. Stephen J. Lieberman, letter to the editor, *Scientific American* (November 1978): 15.
30. Redman, *Rise of Civilization,* p. 197.
31. Tobler, *Excavations at Tepe Gawra,* p. 85.
32. Fuad Safar, Mohammad Ali Mustafa, and Seton Lloyd, *Eridu* (Baghdad: Ministry of Culture and Information, State Organization of Antiquities and Heritage, 1981), p. 230, fig. 111.
33. Marcia Ascher and Robert Ascher, *Code of the Quipu* (Ann Arbor: University of Michigan Press, 1981), p. 63.
34. Yvonne Rosengarten, *Le Concept sumérien de consommation dans la vie économique et religieuse* (Paris: Editions E. de Boccard, 1960).
35. Tohru Maeda, "On the Agricultural Festivals in Sumer," *Acta Sumerologica* 5, no. 1 (1979): 24–25; Rosengarten, *Le Concept sumérien,* p. 255.
36. Anton Moortgat, *The Art of Ancient Mesopotamia* (London: Phaidon Publishers, 1969), fig. 42.
37. Albert A. Trouwborst, "From Tribute to Taxation: On the Dynamics of the Early State," in Henri J. M. Claessen and Pieter van de Velde, eds., *Early State Dynamics* (Leiden: E. J. Brill, 1987), p. 133.
38. Pierre Amiet, *L'Art antique du Proche-Orient* (Paris: Editions d'Art Lucien Mazenod, 1977), p. 366, fig. 314.
39. Pierre Amiet, *Elam* (Auvers-sur-Oise: Archée Editeur, 1966), pp. 178–179, figs. 130–131; André Parrot, *Mari* (Neuchatel: Editions Ides et Calendes, 1953), figs. 65 and 72.
40. Amiet, *Elam,* pp. 190–192, figs. 140–142; Parrot, *Mari,* fig. 76.
41. Pierre Amiet, *La Glyptique mésopotamienne archaïque* (Paris: editions du CNRS, 1980), p. 434, pl. 46: 656; p. 499, pl. 120: 1606–1607, 1609; Briggs Buchanan, *Early Near Eastern Seals* (New Haven: Yale University Press, 1981), pp. 44–45: 135.
42. UVB 17, p. 10.
43. Dafi 8a, figs. 1 and 2.
44. For example, at Hajji Firuz: Voigt, *Hajji Firuz Tepe,* pp. 184–185.
45. Donald O. Henry views the Natufian social and political structures as those of a chiefdom. This would represent a major alternative to the redistribution economy which developed in other Near Eastern cultures. *From Foraging to Agriculture* (Philadelphia: University of Pennsylvania Press, 1989), pp. 209–211.
46. Georges Charbonnier, "Entretiens avec Claude Lévi-Strauss," *Lettres Nouvelles* 10 (1961): 32–33.
47. Harvey Weiss and T. Cuyler Young, Jr., "The Merchants of Susa; Godin V and Plateau-Lowland Relations in the Late Fourth Millennium B.C.," *Iran* 13 (1975): 8.
48. Jean-Marie Durand, "L'Organisation de l'espace dans le Palais de Mari: Le Témoignage des textes," in E. Levy, ed., *Le Système palatial en Orient, en Grèce et à Rome,* Actes du Colloque de Strasbourg 19–22 juin 1985, Travaux du Centre de Recherche sur le Proche-Orient et la Grèce Antique, vol. 9 (Strasbourg: Université des Sciences Humaines de Strasbourg, 1987), pp. 44–48.
49. J. Andrew Dearman, "On Record Keeping and the Preservation of Documents in Ancient Israel (1000 to 587 BCE)," *Libraries and Culture* 24, no. 3 (1989): 346.
50. Anton Moortgat, *Vorderasiatische Rollsiegel* (Berlin: Gebrüder Man Verlag, 1988), p. 7, pl. 2: 9; 5: 29b; 6: 30, 31; Pierre Amiet, *L'Art antique du Proche Orient* (Paris: Edition d'Art Lucien Mazenod, 1977), pp. 354–355, figs. 231, 236.
51. Ibid., fig. 27.
52. Dietrich Sürenhagen, in Schmandt-Besserat, "Tokens at Uruk," p. 38, Table 3.
53. Gregory A. Johnson, *Local Exchange and Early State Development in Southwestern Iran,* University of Michigan Museum of Anthropology, Anthropological Papers, no. 51 (Ann Arbor, 1973), p. 2.
54. Mark A. Brandes, *Siegelabrollungen aus den archaischen Bauschichten in Uruk-Warka,* Freiburger Altorientalische Studien, vol. 3 (Wiesbaden: Franz Steiner Verlag GMBH, 1979), pt. 2, pls. 1–11.
55. Thomas W. Beale, "Beveled Rim Bowls and Their Implications for Change and Economic Organization in the Later Fourth Millennium B.C.," *Journal of Near Eastern Studies* 37, no. 4 (1978): 310.
56. Enrica Fiandra, "The Connection between Clay Sealings and Tablets in Administration," *South Asian Archaeology* (1979): 36–38.
57. Dominique Collon, *First Impressions: Cylinder Seals in the Ancient Near East* (London: British Museum Publications, 1987), p. 13.
58. Marvin A. Powell, Jr., "Sumerian Numeration and Metrology," Ph.D. dissertation, University of Minnesota, 1971, p. 208.
59. Beale, "Beveled Rim Bowls," pp. 291–292.
60. UVB 2, figs. 16–17; Genouillac, *Fouilles de Telloh I,* p. 64; M 46, p. 151 and pl. 89; Delougaz and Kantor, "New Evidence," p. 27; André Finet, "Bilan Provisoire des Fouilles Belges du Tell Kannas," *Annual of the American Schools of Oriental Research* 44 (1979): 93.
61. Dietrich Sürenhagen, in Schmandt-Besserat, "Tokens

at Uruk," p. 38, Table 3. The En is represented on an oblong bulla from Habuba Kabira (72 Hb 102). I am grateful to Eva Strommenger for communicating to me the information. M 43, vol. 2, pl. 18: 695. For the origin of beveled-rim bowls and nose-lugged jars in Mesopotamia, see Eva Strommenger, "The Chronological Division of the Archaic Levels of Uruk-Eanna VI–III/II: Past and Present," *American Journal of Archaeology* 84, no. 4 (1980): 485–486; Louis le Breton, "The Early Periods at Susa, Mesopotamian Relations," *Iraq* 19, no. 2 (1957): 97–113; Reinhard Dittmann, *Betrachtungen zur Frühzeit des Südwest-Iran,* Part 1 (Berlin: Dietrich Reimer Verlag 1986), pp. 98–121; Delougaz and Kantor, "New Evidence," pp. 26–33.

62. Louis le Breton, "The Early Periods at Susa, Mesopotamian Relations," *Iraq* 19, no. 2 (1957): 94.

63. Amiet, "Alternance," p. 19 and Strommenger, "Habuba Kabira," p. 19; S. E. van der Leeuw, "Sondages à Ta'as, Hadidi et Jebel 'Aruda," in *Antiquités de L'Euphrate* (Aleppo: Aleppo Museum, 1974), p. 80.

64. Dafi 9a, p. 44.

65. M 43, vol. 2, pl. 18: 695; Brandes, *Siegelabrollungen,* pl. 12 and M 43, vol. 2, pl. 18: 682–683; Delougaz and Delougaz, "New Evidence," p. 32, pl. X,d.

66. Henry T. Wright, "Susiana Hinterlands—Era of Primary State Formation," in Frank Hole, ed., *The Archaeology of Western Iran* (Washington, D.C.: Smithsonian Institution Press, 1987), p. 146.

9. *Counting and the Emergence of Writing*

1. Leslie A. White, *The Science of Culture* (New York: Grove Press, 1949), p. 286.
2. Levi Leonard Conant, *The Number Concept* (London: Macmillan, 1896), p. 28; Arthur Chervin, *Anthropologie Bolivienne* (Paris: Librairie H. le Soudier, 1908), p. 229; Georges Ifrah, *From One to Zero* (New York: Viking Penguin, 1985), p. 7; David Eugene Smith, *History of Mathematics,* vol. 1 (Boston: Ginn and Company, 1951), p. 6.
3. A. Seidenberg, *The Diffusion of Counting Practices* (Berkeley and Los Angeles: University of California Press, 1960), p. 216.
4. A. Descoeudres, *Le Développement de l'enfant de deux à sept ans* (Paris: Editions Delachaux et Niestle S.A., 1930), p. 265.
5. Karl Menninger, *Number Words and Number Symbols,* rev. ed. (Cambridge, Mass.: MIT Press, 1977), p. 33.
6. Melville J. Herkovits, *Dahomey,* vol. 1, (New York: J. J. Augustin Publisher, 1938), p. 114.
7. Aletta Biersack, "The Logic of Misplaced Concreteness: Paiela Body Counting and the Nature of the Primitive Mind," *American Anthropologist* 84, no. 4 (1982): 813.
8. Claudia Zaslavsky, *Africa Counts* (Westport, Conn.: Lawrence Hill and Company, 1973), p. 241.
9. Menninger, *Number Words,* p. 11.
10. Franz Boas, "Fifth Report on the Northwestern Tribes of Canada," *Proceedings of the British Association for the Advancement of Science* (1889): 881.
11. Igor M. Diakonoff, "Some Reflections on Numerals in Sumerian towards a History of Mathematical Speculations," *Journal of the American Oriental Society* 103, no. 1 (1983): 88.
12. Jack Goody, *The Domestication of the Savage Mind* (Cambridge: Cambridge University Press, 1977), p. 13.
13. Menninger, *Number Words,* pp. 11, 21; Diakonoff, "Some Reflections," pp. 87, 88, and 93; Martin G. Silverman, "Numeral Classifiers in the Gilbertese Language," *Anthropology Tomorrow* 8 (1962): 41–56.
14. J. H. Greenberg, "Numeral Classifiers and Substantival Number: Problems in the Genesis of a Linguistic Type," in A. Makkai et al., eds. *Linguistics at the Crossroads* (Lake Bluff, Ill.: Jupiter Press, 1977), pp. 276–300; Pamela Downing, "The Anaphoric Use of Classifiers in Japanese," in Colette Craig, ed., *Noun Classes and Categorization* (Amsterdam: John Benjamins Publishing Co., 1986), pp. 345–375; Mary Sanches, "Language Acquisition and Language Change: Japanese Numeral Classifiers," in Ben Blount and Mary Sanches, eds., *Sociocultural Dimensions of Language Change* (New York: Academic Press, 1977), p. 51; Colette Grinevald Craig, "Jacaltec Noun Classifiers, a Study in Language and Culture," in Colette Craig, ed., *Noun Classes and Categorization* (Amsterdam: John Benjamins Publishing Co., 1986), pp. 263–293; J. Eric S. Thompson, *Maya Hieroglyphic Writing,* 6th printing (Norman, Okla.: University of Oklahoma Press, 1978), pp. 54–57; Alfred M. Tozzer, *A Maya Grammar,* Papers of the Peabody Museum of American Archaeology and Ethnology, Harvard University, vol. 9 (1921), pp. 290–292.
15. Brent Berlin, *Tzeltal Numeral Classifiers* (Paris: Mouton, 1968), p. 23.
16. H. Beckman, "Die Entwicklung der Zahlleistung bei 2–6 jährigen Kindern," *Zeitschrift für angewandte Psychologie* 22 (1924): 1–72.
17. Richard Andree, *Ethnographische Parallelen und Vergleiche* (Stuttgart: Julius Maier Verlag, 1878), p. 195.
18. Ibid., p. 185; Lyle Jacobsen, "Early Accounting Data Bases of the Pacific: Knotted Cords in the Ryuku Islands," in A. T. Craswell, ed., *Collected Papers of the Fifth World Congress of Accounting Historians* (Sydney: Accounting and Finance Foundation, University of Sydney, Australia, 1988), paper no. 213, figs. 1–8.
19. Raymond L. Wilder, *Evolution of Mathematical Concepts* (New York: John Wiley and Sons, 1968), p. 180; Tobias Danzig, *Number: The Language of Science,* 4th ed. (New York: Macmillan, 1959), p. 6; Graham Flegg, *Numbers, Their History and Meaning* (New York: Schocken Books, 1983), pp. 8–14; Edna E. Kramer, *The Nature and Growth of Modern Mathematics* (New York: Hawthorn Books, 1970), pp. 4–5; David E. Smith, *History of Mathematics,* vol. 1 (Boston: Ginn and Company, 1951), pp. 6–8.
20. Bertrand Russell, *Introduction to Mathematical Philosophy,* 10th impression (London: George Allen and Unwin, 1960), p. 3.

21. Jöran Friberg, "The Early Roots of Babylonian Mathematics, III. Three Remarkable Texts from Ancient Ebla," *Vicino Oriente* 6 (1986): 3–25.
22. Dietz O. Edzard, "Sumerisch 1 bis 10 in Ebla," *Studi Eblaiti* 3 (1980): 121–127.
23. Marvin A. Powell, Jr., "Sumerian Numeration and Metrology." Ph.D. dissertation, University of Minnesota, 1971, p. 2.
24. The numerations are transcribed as they appear in the texts quoted. This accounts for slight differences in style. Marvin A. Powell, Jr., *Sumerian Numeration,* p. 47.
25. Diakonoff, "Some Reflections," p. 85.

    1. aš
    2. man, min
    3. êš
    4. lim
    5. i (not attested)
    6. i-aš > âš
    7. i-min > u-mun
    8. ûš (not attested)
    9. i-lim (not attested)
    10. haw (not attested)

1.	aš-u	aš-a
2.	min-u	min-a
3.	êš-u	êš-e < eš-a
4.	lim-u	lim-a > lim-u
5.	i-u	i-a
6.	i-aš-u	i-aš-a (not attested)
7.	i-mi-nu	i-min-a
8.	û-(s)u	us-(s)a
9.	i-lim-u	i-lim-(m)u < i-lim-a
10.	hû	ha (not attested)

    1. aš-am
    2. min-am
    3. ê-îš-(š)am
    4. lim-mu (<lim-um<lim-am)
    5. i-am
    6. i-aš-am
    7. i-min-am
    8. us-(s)am
    9. i-lim-(m)u(m)

26. Ibid., p. 90.
27. Powell, "Sumerian Numeration," p. 30.
28. Diakonoff, "Some Reflections," p. 90.
29. Ibid., p. 91.
30. Ibid. suggests that "niš" = 20 may have its origin in the word for "a whole human," "man," in which case it might be argued that "20" referred to ten fingers and ten toes.
31. François Thureau-Dangin, "Le Système ternaire dans la numération sumérienne," *Revue d'Assyriologie et d'Archéologie Orientale* 25, no. 2 (1928): 119–121; Diakonoff, "Some Reflections," p. 92.
32. Powell, "Sumerian Numeration," pp. 27–28.
33. Powell notes that "diš" is attested for counting plots of lands. Ibid., pp. 18, 13.
34. Ibid., pp. 23, 28–29, 14.
35. Diakonoff, "Some Reflections," pp. 84–87.
36. Ibid., p. 88.
37. A. A. Vaiman, "Die Bezeichnung von Sklaven und Sklavinnen in der protosumerischen Schrift," *BaM* 20 (1989): 126–127; Vaiman, "Protosumerische Schrift," pp. 20–23.
38. Damerow and Englund, "Die Zahlzeichensysteme," p. 165.
39. Friberg, *Third Millennium Roots,* pp. 10, 15, 21, and 46.
40. Alexander Marshack, *The Roots of Civilization* (New York: McGraw Hill, 1972).
41. Dean Falk, "Implications of the Evolution of Writing for the Origin of Language: Can a Paleoneurologist Find Happiness in the Neolithic?" in Bruno Chiarelli, ed., *Anthropological Approach to the Origin of Human Language,* vol. 1, Proceedings of the NATO Advanced Study Institute, Cortona, Italy (forthcoming).
42. There can be no doubt about the distinction between these two subtypes since both large and small tetrahedrons are included in a same envelope from Susa, Sb 1967.
43. In fact, Sb 1967 from Susa yields tetrahedrons of three subtypes: small, large, and punctated.
44. Friberg, *Third Millennium Roots,* p. 10.
45. Marvin A. Powell, Jr., "Sumerian Area Measures and the Alleged Decimal Substratum," *Zeitschrift für Assyriologie* 62 (1972): 171.
46. Dafi 8a, pp. 32–34.
47. Stephen J. Lieberman, "Of Clay Pebbles, Hollow Clay Balls and Writing: A Sumerian View," *American Journal of Archaeology* 184, no. 3 (1980): 339–358.
48. Pierre Amiet, *L'Age des échanges inter-iraniens* (Paris: Editions de la Réunion des Musées Nationaux, 1986), p. 87.
49. Weiss and Young, "Merchants of Susa," p. 9, fig. 4: 2.
50. Jöran Friberg, "Numbers and Measures in the Earliest Written Records," *Scientific American* 250, no. 2 (1984): 116.
51. François Thureau-Dangin, *Esquisse d'une histoire du système sexagesimal* (Paris: Librairie Orientaliste Paul Geuthner, 1932), pp. 6–7.
52. David E. Smith, *Number and Numerals* (New York: Bureau of Publications, Teachers College, Columbia University, 1937), p. 8.
53. I. J. Gelb, *A Study of Writing,* rev. ed. (Chicago: University of Chicago Press, 1974), p. 67.

Conclusions

1. Georges Charbonnier, *Conversations with Claude Lévi-Strauss* (London: Cape Editions, 1973), pp. 27–28.
2. Cyril S. Smith, "Cyril Stanley Smith, on Art, Invention and Technology," *Technological Review* 78 (1976): 40.
3. Thomas Astle, *The Origin and Progress of Writing* (London: T. Bentley, Bolt Court, 1803), p. ii.

INDEX

Page numbers in italics refer to figures.

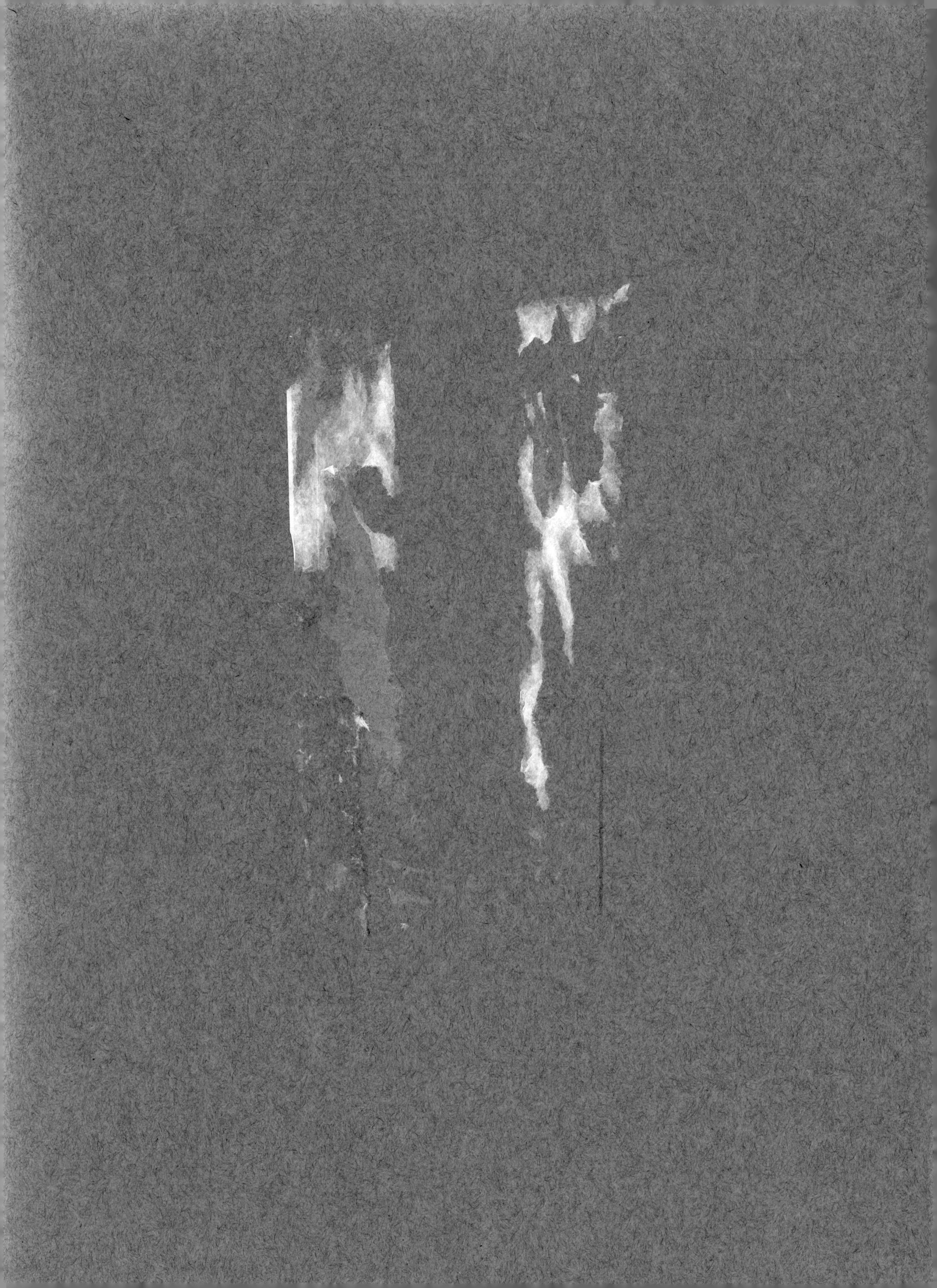